CCDA® CISCO® CERTIFIED DESIGN ASSOCIATE EXAM OBJECTIVES (EXAM 640-441)

Overall Exam Objectives

1) Design a network that meets a customer's requirements for performance, security, capacity, and scalability.
2) Assemble Cisco product lines into an end-to-end networking solution.

Small- to Medium-Sized Business Solutions Framework

CHAPTER 1-5

3) Describe a framework you can use to simplify the complexities associated with analyzing customer network problems and creating Cisco scalable solutions.

Identify Customer Needs - Characterize the Existing Network

CHAPTER 6

4) Identify all the data you should gather to characterize the customer's existing network.
5) Document the customer's current applications, protocols, topology, and number of users.

CHAPTER 7, 8

6) Document the customer's business issues that are relevant to a network design project.

CHAPTER 8

7) Assess the health of the customer's existing network and make conclusions about the network's ability to support growth.
8) Determine the customer's requirements for new applications, protocols, number of users, peak usage hours, security, and network management.
9) Diagram the flow of information for new applications.
10) Isolate the customer's criteria for accepting the performance of a network.
11) List some tools that will help you characterize new network traffic.
12) Predict the amount of traffic and the type of traffic caused by the applications, given charts that characterize typical network traffic.

Design the Network Structure

CHAPTER 9

13) Describe the advantages, disadvantages, scalability issues, and applicability of standard internetwork topologies.
14) Draw a topology map that meets the customer's needs and includes a high-level view of internetworking devices and interconnecting media.

CHAPTER 10

15) Recognize scalability constraints and issues for standard LAN technologies.
16) Recommend Cisco products and LAN technologies that will meet a customer's requirements for performance, capacity, and scalability in small-to-medium-sized networks.

CHAPTER 11

17) Update the network topology drawing you created in the previous section to include hardware and media.
18) Recognize scalability constraints and issues for standard WAN technologies.
19) Recognize scalability constraints and performance budgets for major Cisco products.
20) Recommend Cisco products and WAN technologies that will meet the customer's requirements for performance, capacity, and scalability in an enterprise network.

CHAPTER 12

21) Propose an addressing model for the customer's areas, networks, subnetworks, and end stations that meet scalability requirements.
22) Propose a plan for configuring addresses.
23) Propose a naming scheme for servers, routers, and user stations.

CHAPTER 12, 13

24) Identify scalability constraints and issues for IGRP, Enhanced IGRP, IP RIP, IPX RIP/SAP, NLSP, AppleTalk RTMP and AURP, static routing, and bridging protocols.

CHAPTER 13

25) Recommend routing and bridging protocols that meet a customer's requirements for performance, security, and capacity.

CHAPTER 14

26) Recognize scalability issues for various Cisco IOS software features such as access lists, proxy services, encryption, compression, and queuing.
27) Recommend Cisco IOS software features that meet a customer's requirements for performance, security, capacity, and scalability.

Build a Prototype or Pilot for the Network Structure

CHAPTER 15

28) Determine how much of the network structure must be built to prove that the network design meets the customer's needs.
29) List the tasks required to build a prototype or pilot that demonstrates the functionality of the network design.
30) List the Cisco IOS software commands you should use to determine if a network structure meets the customer's performance and scalability goals.
31) Describe how to demonstrate the prototype or pilot to the customer so that the customer understands that the proposed design meets requirements for performance, security, capacity, and scalability, and that the costs and risks are acceptable.

These objectives may be revised at any time subject to Cisco's sole discretion. Visit Cisco's web site, www.cisco.com, for the most current information on exam objectives.

CCDA Cisco Certified Design Associate Study Guide

(Exam 640-441)

CCDA Cisco Certified Design Associate Study Guide

(Exam 640-441)

Syngress Media, Inc.

Osborne/McGraw-Hill

Berkeley New York St. Louis San Francisco Auckland Bogotá Hamburg London Madrid Mexico City
Milan Montreal New Delhi Panama City Paris São Paulo Singapore Sydney Tokyo Toronto

Osborne/**McGraw-Hill**
2600 Tenth Street
Berkeley, California 94710
U.S.A.

For information on translations or book distributors outside the U.S.A., or to arrange bulk purchase discounts for sales promotions, premiums, or fund-raisers, please contact Osborne/**McGraw-Hill** at the above address.

CCDA Cisco Certified Design Associate Study Guide

1234567890 DOC DOC 019876543210

Book P/N 0-07-212157-2   and   CD P/N 0-07-212158-0
parts of
ISBN 0-07-212159-9

Publisher Brandon A. Nordin	**Acquisitions Coordinator** Tara Davis	**Computer Designers** Jani Beckwith Elizabeth Jang
Associate Publisher and Editor-in-Chief Scott Rogers	**Series Editor** Mark Buchmann	Jim Kussow
Editorial Director Gareth Hancock	**Technical Editor** Ryan Neil Sokolowski	**Illustrators** Bob Hansen Michael Mueller
Associate Acquisitions Editor Timothy Green	**Copy Editors** Linda Devine Adaya Henis	Beth Young
Editorial Management Syngress Media, Inc.	**Proofreader** Linda Medoff	**Series Design** Roberta Steele
Project Editors Eva Banaszek Emily Rader	**Indexer** Valerie Robbins	

This book was composed with Corel VENTURA™ Publisher.

About Syngress Media

Syngress Media creates books and software for Information Technology professionals seeking skill enhancement and career advancement. Its products are designed to comply with vendor and industry-standard course curricula, and are optimized for certification exam preparation. Visit the Syngress Web site at http://www.syngress.com.

Contributors

Damon Merchant (CCDP, CCNP, CCNA, CCDA, MCSE, MCP, CNE, CAN) is the President of Corbus Systems, Inc., an information technology firm in Detroit, Michigan. He has about ten years of experience in networking. Not only is he a network-engineering guru, he is also a seasoned software developer. His most recent application, Touch-Tone Administrator for NT, allows network administrators to manage their Windows NT networks from a telephone. Damon also provides training and technical workshops for IT professionals. In his spare time, Damon enjoys playing basketball, ping pong, and video games, and weight lifting.

More information about Damon Merchant and his software products can be found at his company's Web site, at http://www.corbus-systems.com. Damon can be e-mailed at damon@corbus-systems.com.

Mark Edwards (CCNP, CCDP, MCSE, CNE) is a Systems Engineer based in South Wales, UK. He has been working as a freelance consultant since qualifying from the University of Glamorgan with a BSc(Hons) in Computer Science in 1994. He is currently working on achieving CCIE status and is set to take the lab in the summer of 2000. Mark has worked for many large international organizations and has held a wide variety of roles in various major projects. These have included network design,

v

management and upgrading, software and hardware rollouts, training, and testing.

At the time of writing for this book, Mark is working for Reader's Digest UK assisting it in the redesign of its large ATM LANE network and global WAN. Mark lives near Cardiff, Wales, with his wife Sarah.

Eric L. McMasters (CCNA, CCDA) works as a Senior Network Engineer for Sprint PCS in the Kansas City Metro Area.

Eric has just recently left the U.S. Air Force, having worked for nine years with various telecommunications technologies, specializing in the last four years in network design and implementation, with a focus on Cisco devices. Eric has extensive experience in designing and implementing simple and complex networks, utilizing a variety of technologies as well as a broad range of Cisco products.

Eric holds an Associate Degree in Electronic Technologies from the Community College of the Air Force. His certifications include Cisco Certified Network Associate (CCNA) and Cisco Certified Design Associate (CCDA), and he is currently pursuing his Cisco Certified Network Professional (CCNP) and Cisco Certified Design Professional (CCDA) certifications.

Eric, his wife Sally, and a newborn son, Shane, presently reside in Overland Park, Kansas.

Don Taylor (CCNA, CCDA, CVE) has been involved in wide area networking since 1997, focusing on ISDN, Frame Relay, ATM, and DSL technologies. At Pacific Bell Network Integration, Don was one of the primary provisioners for two large, remote-access VPN projects, in which his duties included verifying circuit availability and custom configuration of several brands of routers and access devices. In 1999, he joined KPMG as a consultant. Currently, Don is engaged in documenting the infrastructure of a large application service provider and in recommending solutions for both remote access and extranet VPNs for customers. He holds his Certified Videoconferencing Engineer degree and expects to obtain his CCNP and CCDP within a year.

Don may be reached by e-mail at don_t_2@earthling.net.

Jack Coates (CCNA, CCDA, MCSE) is a Systems Engineer at Rainfinity. He also has experience with Linux and NetWare. Previously,

Jack worked for Pacific Bell Network Integration and studied English at the University of California at Berkeley. Jack can be contacted by e-mail at jack@monkeynoodle.org.

Brad Lucas (CCNA, CCDA) is a LAN/WAN Administrator for CHRISTUS St. Frances Cabrini Hospital in Alexandria, Louisiana. In addition to the CCNA and CCDA certifications, Brad is pursuing CCNP and CCDP certifications, and expects to attain them by the end of April, 2000. He also has earned a B.S. degree from Louisiana Tech University in 1997. Brad's responsibilities at CHRISTUS St. Frances Cabrini Hospital include maintenance of the hospital's existing infrastructure, as well as providing design services for new installations and upgrades. His hobbies include duck hunting; fishing; and training his yellow Labrador, Ben.

Brad dedicates his work on this book to his parents Betty and Cliff and to his grandparents in deep appreciation of all the support they have given him throughout the year. He also extends his warmest thanks to Christy Goynes and family.

Yuri Gordienko (CCNA, CCDA, MCSE, MCP+Internet) is a senior network engineer for the Government of Ontario, Canada. He has a wide range of experience in the communications industry, including designing and installing high-speed LAN switching solutions and diagnosing advanced LAN and WAN access problems.

About the Series Editor

Mark Buchmann (CCIE #3556, CCSI #95062) is a Cisco Certified Internetworking Expert and has been a Certified Cisco Systems Instructor since 1995. He is the owner of MAB Enterprises, Inc., a company providing consulting, network support, training, and various other services. Mark is also co-owner of http://www.CertaNet.com, a company providing online certification assistance for a variety of network career paths including all the various Cisco certifications. In his free time he enjoys spending time with his family and boating. He currently lives in Raleigh, North Carolina. Mark is Series Editor for Syngress Cisco books.

About the Technical Editor

Ryan Neil Sokolowski (MCSE, CCNA, CCDA, CNE, CNA, VCE) currently works as a Senior Technical Analyst in the Design and Engineering group at a Fortune 100 company in Minneapolis, MN. He also operates Onyx Consulting, an independent consulting company. He participates in the Internet Engineering Task Force and is a member of several organizations, including the Institute of Electrical and Electronics Engineers, the SANS Institute, the Association of Windows NT Systems Professionals, and NetWare Users International. With a true love of technology and a strong background in design, implementation, engineering, and consulting services, Ryan specializes in network operating systems, directory services, and Cisco environments. In addition to the technical review and editing, Ryan also authored a number of chapters for this text. He dedicates this book to his parents, who taught him everything they knew and how to learn more by himself.

ACKNOWLEDGMENTS

W would like to thank the following people:

- Richard Kristof of Global Knowledge for championing the series and providing access to some great people and information.

- All the incredibly hard-working folks at Osborne/McGraw-Hill: Brandon Nordin, Scott Rogers, Gareth Hancock, and Tim Green for their help in launching a great series and being solid team players. In addition, Emily Rader and Tara Davis, for their help in fine-tuning the book.

CONTENTS AT A GLANCE

CONTENTS

This book's primary objective is to help you prepare for and pass the required Cisco Design Associate Certification exam so you can begin to reap the career benefits of certification. We believe that the only way to do this is to help you increase your knowledge and build your skills. After completing this book, you should feel confident that you have thoroughly reviewed all of the objectives that Cisco has established for the exam.

In This Book

This book is organized around the actual structure of the CCDA exam administered at Sylvan Testing Centers. Cisco has let us know all the topics we need to cover for the exam. We've followed their list carefully, so you can be assured you're not missing anything.

In Every Chapter

We've created a set of chapter components that call your attention to important items, reinforce important points, and provide helpful exam-taking hints. Take a look at what you'll find in every chapter:

- Every chapter begins with the **Certification Objectives**—what you need to know in order to pass the section on the exam dealing with the chapter topic. The Certification Objectives headings identify the objectives within the chapter, so you'll always know an objective when you see it!

- **Exam Watch** notes call attention to information about, and potential pitfalls in, the exam. These helpful hints are written by CCDAs who have taken the exams and received their certification—who better to tell you what to worry about? They know what you're about to experience!

- **On the Job** notes point out procedures and techniques important for coding actual applications for employers or contract jobs.

EXERCISE

- **Certification Exercises** are interspersed throughout the chapters. These are step-by-step exercises that mirror vendor-recommended labs. They help you master skills that are likely to be an area of focus on the exam. Don't just read through the exercises; they are hands-on practice that you should be comfortable completing. Learning by doing is an effective way to increase your competency with a product.

- **From the Field** sidebars describe key issues that come up most frequently in the field. You've studied, taken the classes, and now you're out in the real world—these sidebars give you a valuable hands-on perspective that goes beyond certification to the actual application of certification objectives. As certification exams become increasingly difficult, your success will hinge on your ability to demonstrate real-world expertise.

- **Q & A** sections lay out problems and solutions in a quick-read format. For example,

QUESTIONS AND ANSWERS

A user wishes to save a file to a pre-existing filename.	Inform the user that the file exists and prompt as to whether he or she wishes to overwrite the file.
A CFile object throws an exception during construction.	Ensure that the program cannot go on to attempt to use that object.

- The **Certification Summary** is a succinct review of the chapter and a restatement of salient points regarding the exam.

- The **Two-Minute Drill** at the end of every chapter is a checklist of the main points of the chapter. It can be used for last-minute review.

- The **Self Test** offers questions similar to those found on the certification exams, including multiple choice and fill-in-the-blank. The answers to these questions, as well as explanations of the answers, can be found at the end of each chapter. By taking the

Self Test after completing each chapter, you'll reinforce what you've learned from that chapter, while becoming familiar with the structure of the exam questions.

Some Pointers

Once you've finished reading this book, set aside some time to do a thorough review. You might want to return to the book several times and make use of all the methods it offers for reviewing the material:

1. *Reread all the Two-Minute Drills*, or have someone quiz you. You also can use the drills as a way to do a quick cram before the exam.

2. *Reread all the Exam Watch notes.* Remember that these are written by people who have taken the exam and passed. They know what you should expect—and what you should be careful about.

3. *Review all the Q & A scenarios* for quick problem solving.

4. *Retake the Self Tests.* Taking the tests right after you've read the chapter is a good idea, because it helps reinforce what you've just learned. However, it's an even better idea to go back later and do all the questions in the book in one sitting. Pretend you're taking the exam. (For this reason, you should mark your answers on a separate piece of paper when you answer the questions the first time.)

5. *Complete the exercises.* Did you do the exercises when you read through each chapter? If not, do them! These exercises are designed to cover exam topics, and there's no better way to get to know this material than by practicing.

How to Take a Cisco Certification Examination

This introduction covers the importance of your CCDA certification and prepares you for taking the actual examination. It gives you a few pointers on methods of preparing for the exam, including how to study and register, what to expect, and what to do on exam day.

Catch the Wave!

Congratulations on your pursuit of Cisco certification! In this fast-paced world of networking, few certification programs are as valuable as the one offered by Cisco.

The networking industry has virtually exploded in recent years, accelerated by nonstop innovation and the Internet's popularity. Cisco has stayed at the forefront of this tidal wave, maintaining a dominant role in the industry.

The networking industry is highly competitive, and evolving technology only increases in its complexity, so the rapid growth of the networking industry has created a vacuum of qualified people. There simply aren't enough skilled networking people to meet the demand. Even the most experienced professionals must keep current with the latest technology in order to provide the skills that the industry demands. That's where Cisco certification programs can help networking professionals succeed as they pursue their careers.

Cisco started its certification program many years ago, offering only the designation Cisco Certified Internetwork Expert (CCIE). Through the CCIE program, Cisco provided a means to meet the growing demand for experts in the field of networking. However, the CCIE tests are brutal, with a failure rate of over 80 percent. (Fewer than 5 percent of candidates pass on their first attempt.) As you might imagine, very few people ever attain CCIE status.

In early 1998, Cisco recognized the need for intermediate certifications, and several new programs were created. Four intermediate certifications were added: CCNA (Cisco Certified Network Associate), CCNP (Cisco Certified Network Professional), CCDA (Cisco Certified Design Associate), and CCDP (Cisco Certified Design Professional). Two specialties were also created for the CCIE program: WAN Switching and ISP Dial-up.

CCDA
@dvice

I would encourage you to take beta tests when they are available. Not only are the beta exams less expensive than the final exams (some are even free!), but also, if you pass the beta, you will receive credit for passing the exam. If you don't pass the beta, you will have seen every question in the pool of available questions, and can use this information when you prepare to take the exam for the second time. Remember to jot down important information immediately after the exam, if you didn't pass. You will have to do this after leaving the exam area, since materials written during the exam are retained by the testing center. This information can be helpful when you need to determine which areas of the exam were most challenging for you as you study for the subsequent test.

Why Vendor Certification?

Over the years, vendors have created their own certification programs because of industry demand. This demand arises when the marketplace needs skilled professionals and an easy way to identify them. Vendors benefit because it promotes people skilled in their product. Professionals benefit because it boosts their careers. Employers benefit because it helps them identify qualified people.

In the networking industry, technology changes too often and too quickly to rely on traditional means of certification, such as universities and trade associations. Because of the investment and effort required to keep network certification programs current, vendors are the only organizations suited to keep pace with the changes. In general, such vendor certification programs are excellent, with most of them requiring a solid foundation in the essentials, as well as their particular product line.

Corporate America has come to appreciate these vendor certification programs and the value they provide. Employers recognize that certifications, like university degrees, do not guarantee a level of knowledge, experience, or performance; rather, they establish a baseline for comparison. By seeking to hire vendor-certified employees, a company can assure itself that not only has it found a person skilled in networking, but also it has hired a person skilled in the specific products the company uses.

Technical professionals have also begun to recognize the value of certification and the impact it can have on their careers. By completing a certification program, professionals gain an endorsement of their skills from a major industry source. This endorsement can boost their current position, and it makes finding the next job even easier. Often a certification determines whether a first interview is even granted.

Today a certification may place you ahead of the pack. Tomorrow it will be a necessity to keep from being left in the dust.

CCDA
@dvice

Signing up for an exam has become easier with the new Web-based test registration system. To sign up for the CCDA exam, access http://www.2test.com, and register for the Cisco Career Certification path. You will need to get an Internet account and password, if you do not already have one for 2test.com. Just select the option for first-time registration, and the Web site will walk you through that process. The registration wizard even provides maps to the testing centers, something that is not available when you call Sylvan Prometric on the telephone.

Cisco's Certification Program

Cisco now has six certifications for the Routing and Switching career track, and four certifications for the WAN Switching career track. While Cisco recommends a series of courses for each of these certifications, they are not required. Ultimately, certification is dependent upon a candidate's passing a series of exams. With the right experience and study materials, you can pass each of these exams without taking the associated class. The following table shows the various Cisco certifications and tracks.

Track	Certification	Acronym
Routing and Switching: Network Support	Cisco Certified Network Associate	CCNA
Routing and Switching: Network Support	Cisco Certified Network Professional	CCNP
Routing and Switching: Network Support	Cisco Certified Internetwork Expert (Routing and Switching)	CCIE-R/S
Routing and Switching: Network Support	Cisco Certified Internetwork Expert (ISP Dial Technology)	CCIE-ISP Dial
Routing and Switching: Network Design	Cisco Certified Design Associate	CCDA
Routing and Switching: Network Design	Cisco Certified Design Professional	CCDP
WAN Switching: Network Support	Cisco Certified Network Associate—WAN Switching	CCNA-WAN Switching
WAN Switching: Network Support	Cisco Certified Network Professional—WAN Switching	CCNP-WAN Switching
WAN Switching: Network Support	Cisco Certified Internetwork Expert—WAN Switching	CCIE-WAN Switching
WAN Switching: Network Design	Cisco Certified Design Professional—WAN Switching	CCDP-WAN Switching

The following illustration shows Cisco's Routing and Switching track, with both the Network Design and Network Support paths. The CCNA is the foundation of the Routing and Switching track, after which candidates can pursue either the Network Design path to CCDA and CCDP, or the Network Support path to CCNP and CCIE.

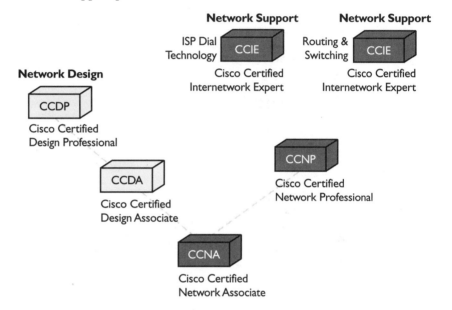

In addition to the technical objectives that are being tested for in each exam, you will find much more useful information on Cisco's Web site at http://www.cisco.com/warp/public/10/wwtraining/certprog. You will find information on becoming certified, exam-specific information, sample test questions, and the latest news on Cisco certification. This is the most important site you will find on your journey to becoming Cisco certified.

Note that candidates have the choice of taking either the single Foundation R/S exam, or the set of three ACRC, CLSC, and CMTD exams—all four exams are not required. The following table shows a matrix of the exams required for each Cisco certification.

Exam Name	Exam #	CCNA	CCDA	CCNP	CCDP	CCIE
CCNA 1.0	640-407	x	x	x	x	
CCDA 1.0	641-441		x		x	
Foundation Routing and Switching	640-409			x	x	
ACRC	640-403			x	x	
CLSC	640-404			x	x	
CMTD	640-405			x	x	
CIT 3.0	640-406 (or exam 640-440)			x		
CIT 4.0	640-440			x		
CID	640-025				x	
CCIE R/S Qualifying						x
CCIE Lab						x

You may hear veterans refer to this CCIE R/S Qualifying Exam as the "Cisco Drake test." This is a carryover from the early days, when Sylvan Prometric's name was Drake Testing Centers, and Cisco had only the one exam.

Recently, Cisco has added the CCNA 2.0, CCDA 2.0, CCNP 2.0, and CCDP 2.0 paths. Any new test takers planning to achieve Cisco certification are encouraged to follow the guidelines of the 2.0 path. The following table is a guideline to follow when pursuing the CCNP 2.0 path. Any candidate who is currently pursuing CCNP status and has taken tests under the 1.0 path may continue to take the courses under 1.0 to achieve the CCNP.

CCNP 1.0		CCNP 2.0	
CCNA 1.0 or 2.0 Certification		**CCNA 1.0 or 2.0 Certification**	
Single Exam Path	**Foundation Exam Path**	**Single Exam Path**	**Foundation Exam Path**
ACRC 640-403	Foundation R/S 640-409	Routing 640-503	Foundation 2.0 640-509
CLSC 640-404	CIT 640-440	Switching 640-504	Support 640-506
CMTD 640-405		Remote Access 640-505	
CIT 640-440		Support 640-506	

CCDA
@dvice

When I find myself stumped answering multiple-choice questions, I use my scratch paper to write down the two or three answers I consider the strongest, and then underline the answer I feel is most likely correct. Here is an example of what my scratch paper looks like when I've gone through the test once:

21. B or __C__
33. __A__ or C

It is extremely helpful to you to mark the question and then continue. You can return to the question and immediately pick up your thought process where you left off. Use this technique to avoid having to reread and rethink questions.

You will also need to use your scratch paper during complex, text-based scenario questions to create visual images to help you understand the question. For example, during the CCDA exam you will need to draw multiple networks and the connections between them. By drawing the layout while you are interpreting the question, you may find a hint that you would not have found without your own visual aid. This technique is especially helpful if you are a visual learner.

Computer-Based Testing

In a perfect world, you would be assessed for your true knowledge of a subject, not simply how you respond to a series of test questions. But life isn't perfect, and it just isn't practical to evaluate everyone's knowledge on a one-to-one basis. (Cisco actually does have a one-to-one evaluation, but it's reserved for the CCIE Laboratory exam, and the waiting list is quite long.)

For the majority of its certifications, Cisco evaluates candidates using a computer-based testing service operated by Sylvan Prometric. This service is quite popular in the industry, and it is used for a number of vendor certification programs, including Novell's CNE and Microsoft's MCSE. Thanks to Sylvan Prometric's large number of facilities, exams can be administered worldwide, generally in the same town as a prospective candidate lives.

For the most part, Sylvan Prometric exams work similarly from vendor to vendor. However, there is an important fact to know about Cisco's exams: they use the traditional Sylvan Prometric test format, not the newer adaptive format. This gives the candidate an advantage, since the traditional format allows answers to be reviewed and revised during the test. (The adaptive format does not.)

CCDA advice

Many experienced test takers do not go back and change answers unless they have a good reason to do so. You should change an answer only when you feel you may have misread or misinterpreted the question the first time. Nervousness may make you second-guess every answer and talk yourself out of a correct one.

To discourage simple memorization, Cisco exams present a different set of questions every time the exam is administered. In the development of the exam, hundreds of questions are compiled and refined, using beta testers. From this large collection, a random sampling is drawn for each test.

Each Cisco exam has a specific number of questions and test duration. Testing time is typically generous, and the time remaining is always displayed in the corner of the testing screen, along with the number of remaining questions. If time expires during an exam, the test terminates, and incomplete answers are counted as incorrect.

CCDA Advice

I have found it extremely helpful to put a check mark next to each objective as I find it is satisfied by the proposed solution. If the proposed solution does not satisfy an objective, you do not need to continue with the rest of the objectives. Once you have determined which objectives are fulfilled, you can count your check marks and answer the question appropriately. This is a very effective testing technique!

At the end of the exam, your test is immediately graded, and the results are displayed on the screen. Scores for each subject area are also provided, but the system will not indicate which specific questions were missed. A report is automatically printed at the proctor's desk for your files. The test score is electronically transmitted back to Cisco.

In the end, this computer-based system of evaluation is reasonably fair. You might feel that one or two questions were poorly worded; this can certainly happen, but you shouldn't worry too much. Ultimately, it's all factored into the required passing score.

Question Types

Cisco exams pose questions in a variety of formats, most of which are discussed here. As candidates progress toward the more advanced certifications, the difficulty of the exams is intensified, through both the subject matter and the question formats.

CCDA Online

In order to pass these challenging exams, you may want to talk with other test takers to determine what is being tested, and what to expect in terms of difficulty. The most helpful way to communicate with other CCDA hopefuls is the Cisco mailing list. With this mailing list, you will receive e-mail every day from other members, discussing everything imaginable concerning Cisco networking equipment and certification. Access http://www.cisco.com/warp/public/84/1.html to learn how to subscribe to this source of a wealth of information.

True/False

The classic true/false question format is not used in the Cisco exams, for the obvious reason that a simple guess has a 50 percent chance of being correct. Instead, true/false questions are posed in multiple-choice format, requiring the candidate to identify the true or false statement from a group of selections.

Multiple Choice

Multiple choice is the primary format for questions in Cisco exams. These questions may be posed in a variety of ways.

Choose the Correct Answer   This is the classic multiple-choice question, in which the candidate selects a single answer from a list of about four choices. In addition to the question's wording, the choices are presented in a Windows radio button format, in which only one answer can be selected at a time.

Choose the Three Correct Answers   The multiple-answer version is similar to the single-choice version, but multiple answers must be provided. This is an all-or-nothing format; all the correct answers must be selected, or the entire question is incorrect. In this format, the question specifies exactly how many answers must be selected. Choices are presented in a check box format, allowing more than one answer to be selected. In addition, the testing software prevents too many answers from being selected.

Choose All That Apply   The open-ended version is the most difficult multiple-choice format, since the candidate does not know how many answers should be selected. As with the multiple-answer version, all the correct answers must be selected to gain credit for the question. If too many answers are selected, no credit is given. This format presents choices in check box format, but the testing software does not advise the candidates whether they've selected the correct number of answers.

CCDA Online

Make it easy on yourself and find some "braindumps." These are notes about the exam from test takers, which indicate the most difficult concepts tested, what to look out for, and sometimes even what not to bother studying. Several of these can be found at http://www.dejanews.com. Simply do a search for CCDA and browse the recent postings. Another good resource is at http://www.groupstudy.com.

Freeform Response

Freeform responses are prevalent in Cisco's advanced exams, particularly where the subject focuses on router configuration and commands. In the freeform format, no choices are provided. Instead, the test prompts for user input, and the candidate must type the correct answer. This format is similar to an essay question, except the response must be specific, allowing the computer to evaluate the answer.

For example, the question

Type the command for viewing routes learned via the EIGRP protocol.

requires the answer

show ip route eigrp

For safety's sake, you should completely spell out router commands, rather than using abbreviations. In this example, the abbreviated command sh ip rou ei works on a real router, but might be counted as wrong by the testing software. The freeform response questions almost always are answered by commands used in the Cisco IOS.

Fill in the Blank

Fill-in-the-blank questions are less common in Cisco exams. They may be presented in multiple-choice or freeform response format.

Exhibits

Exhibits, usually showing a network diagram or a router configuration, accompany many exam questions. These exhibits are displayed in a separate window, which is opened by clicking the Exhibit button at the bottom of the screen. In some cases, the testing center may provide exhibits in printed format at the start of the exam.

Scenarios

While the normal line of questioning tests a candidate's "book knowledge," scenarios add a level of complexity. Rather than asking only technical questions, they apply the candidate's knowledge to real-world situations.

Scenarios generally consist of one or two paragraphs and an exhibit that describes a company's needs or network configuration. This description is followed by a series of questions and problems that challenge the candidate's ability to address the situation. Scenario-based questions are commonly found in exams relating to network design, but they appear to some degree in each of the Cisco exams.

You will know when you are coming to a series of scenario questions, because they are preceded by a blue screen, indicating that the following questions will have the same scenario, but different solutions. You must remember that the scenario will be the same during the series of questions, which means that you do not have to spend time reading the scenario again.

Exam Objectives for CCDA

Cisco has a clear set of objectives for the CCDA exam, upon which the exam questions are based. The following list gives a good summary, by topic, of the things a candidate must know how to do for this exam:

DCN 1.0 (Designing Cisco Networks)—Exam Objectives (641-441)

Overall Course Objectives

1. Design a network that meets a customer's requirements for performance, security, capacity, and scalability.

2. Assemble Cisco product lines into an end-to-end networking solution.

Small- to Medium-Sized Business Solutions Framework

3. Upon completion of this introduction, you will be able to describe a framework you can use to simplify the complexities associated with analyzing customer network problems and creating Cisco scalable solutions.

Identify Customer Needs—Characterize the Existing Network

4. Identify all the data you should gather to characterize the customer's existing network.

5. Document the customer's current applications, protocols, topology, and number of users.

6. Document the customer's business issues that are relevant to a network design project.

7. Assess the health of the customer's existing network and draw conclusions about the network's ability to support growth.

8. Determine the customer's requirements for new applications, protocols, number of users, peak usage hours, security, and network management.

9. Diagram the flow of information for new applications.

10. Isolate the customer's criteria for accepting the performance of a network.

11. List some tools that will help you characterize new network traffic.

12. Predict the amount of traffic and the type of traffic caused by the applications, given charts that characterize typical network traffic.

Design the Network Structure

13. Describe the advantages, disadvantages, scalability issues, and applicability of standard internetwork topologies.

14. Draw a topology map that meets the customer's needs and includes a high-level view of internetworking devices and interconnecting media.

15. Recognize scalability constraints and issues for standard LAN technologies.

16. Recommend Cisco products and LAN technologies that will meet a customer's requirements for performance, capacity, and scalability in small- to medium-sized networks.

17. Update the network topology drawing you created in the previous section to include hardware and media.

18. Recognize scalability constraints and issues for standard WAN technologies.

19. Recognize scalability constraints and performance budgets for major Cisco products.

20. Recommend Cisco products and WAN technologies that will meet the customer's requirements for performance, capacity, and scalability in an enterprise network.

21. Propose an addressing model for the customer's areas, networks, subnetworks, and end stations that meet scalability requirements.

22. Propose a plan for configuring addresses.

23. Propose a naming scheme for servers, routers, and user stations.

24. Identify scalability constraints and issues for IGRP, Enhanced IGRP, IP RIP, IPX RIP/SAP, NLSP, AppleTalk RTMP, and AURP static routings and bridging protocols.

25. Recommend routing and bridging protocols that meet a customer's requirements for performance, security, and capacity.

26. Recognize scalability issues for various Cisco IOS software features such as access lists, proxy services, encryption, compression, and queuing.

27. Recommend Cisco IOS software features that meet a customer's requirements for performance, security, capacity, and scalability.

Studying Techniques

First and foremost, give yourself plenty of time to study. Networking is a complex field, and you can't expect to cram what you need to know into a single study session. It is a field best learned over time, by studying a subject and then applying your knowledge. Build yourself a study schedule and stick to it, but be reasonable about the pressure you put on yourself, especially if you're studying in addition to your regular duties at work.

CCDA
advice

One easy technique to use in studying for certification exams is the 30-minutes-per-day effort. Simply study for a minimum of 30 minutes every day. It is a small but significant commitment. On a day when you just can't focus, then give up at 30 minutes. On a day when it flows completely for you, study longer. As long as you have more of the flow days, your chances of succeeding are extremely high.

Second, practice and experiment. In networking, you need more than knowledge; you need understanding, too. You can't just memorize facts to be effective; you need to understand why events happen, how things work, and (most important) how they break.

The best way to gain deep understanding is to take your book knowledge to the lab. Try it out. Make it work. Change it a little. Break it. Fix it. Snoop around "under the hood." If you have access to a network analyzer, like Network Associate Sniffer, put it to use. You can gain amazing insight to the inner workings of a network by watching devices communicate with each other.

Unless you have a very understanding boss, don't experiment with router commands on a production router. A seemingly innocuous command can have a nasty side effect. If you don't have a lab, your local Cisco office or Cisco users' group may be able to help. Many training centers also allow students access to their lab equipment during off-hours.

Another excellent way to study is through case studies. Case studies are articles or interactive discussions that offer real-world examples of how technology is applied to meet a need. These examples can serve to cement your understanding of a technique or technology by seeing it put to use. Interactive discussions offer added value because you can also pose questions of your own. User groups are an excellent source of examples, since the purpose of these groups is to share information and learn from each other's experiences.

The Cisco Networkers conference is not to be missed. Although renowned for its wild party and crazy antics, this conference offers a wealth of information. Held every year in cities around the world, it includes three days of technical seminars and presentations on a variety of subjects. As you might imagine, it's very popular. You have to register early to get the classes you want.

Then, of course, there is the Cisco Web site. This little gem is loaded with collections of technical documents and white papers. As you progress to more advanced subjects, you will find great value in the large number of examples and reference materials available. But be warned: You need to do a lot of digging to find the really good stuff. Often your only option is to browse every document returned by the search engine to find exactly the one you need. This effort pays off. Most CCIEs I know have compiled six to ten binders of reference material from Cisco's site alone.

Scheduling Your Exam

The Cisco exams are scheduled by calling Sylvan Prometric directly at (800) 204-3926. For locations outside the United States, your local number can be found on Sylvan's Web site at http://www.prometric.com. Sylvan representatives can schedule your exam, but they don't have information about the certification programs. Questions about certifications should be directed to Cisco's training department.

This Sylvan telephone number is specific to Cisco exams, and it goes directly to the Cisco representatives inside Sylvan. These representatives are familiar enough with the exams to find them by name, but it's best if you have the specific exam number handy when you call. After all, you wouldn't want to be scheduled and charged for the wrong exam (for example, the instructor's version, which is significantly harder).

Exams can be scheduled up to a year in advance, although it's really not necessary. Generally, scheduling a week or two ahead is sufficient to reserve the day and time you prefer. When you call to schedule, operators will search for testing centers in your area. For convenience, they can also tell which testing centers you've used before.

Sylvan accepts a variety of payment methods, with credit cards being the most convenient. When you pay by credit card, you can even take tests the same day you call—provided, of course, that the testing center has room. (Quick scheduling can be handy, especially if you want to retake an exam immediately.) Sylvan will mail you a receipt and confirmation of your testing date, although this generally arrives after the test has been taken. If you need to cancel or reschedule an exam, remember to call at least one day before your exam, or you'll lose your test fee.

When you register for the exam, you will be asked for your ID number. This number is used to track your exam results back to Cisco. It's important that you use the same ID number each time you register, so that Cisco can follow your progress. Address information provided when you first register is also used by Cisco to ship certificates and other related material. In the United States, your Social Security number is commonly used as your ID number. However, Sylvan can assign you a unique ID number if you prefer not to use your Social Security number.

The following table shows the available Cisco exams and the number of questions and duration of each. This information is subject to change as Cisco revises the exams, so it's a good idea to verify the details when you register for an exam.

Exam Title	Exam Number	Number of Questions	Duration (minutes)	Exam Fee (U.S. $)
Cisco Certified Design Associate (CCDA)	641-441	80	180	$100

Exam Title	Exam Number	Number of Questions	Duration (minutes)	Exam Fee (U.S. $)
Cisco Internetwork Design (CID)	640-025	100	120	$100
Advanced Cisco Router Configuration (ACRC)	640-403	72	90	$100
Cisco LAN Switch Configuration (CLSC)	640-404	70	60	$100
Configuring, Monitoring, and Troubleshooting Dialup Services (CMTD)	640-405	64	90	$100
Cisco Internetwork Troubleshooting (CIT)*	640-440	77	105	$100
Cisco Certified Network Associate (CCNA)	640-407	70	90	$100
Foundation Routing & Switching	640-409	132	165	$200
CCIE Routing & Switching Qualification	350-001	100	120	$200
CCIE Certification Laboratory	N/A	N/A	2 days	$1,000

*As of this writing, Cisco is still offering the CIT, exam 640-406, which has 69 questions and runs 60 minutes. The exam will likely retire once the new exam is established.

In addition to the regular Sylvan Prometric testing sites, Cisco also offers facilities for taking exams free of charge at each Networkers conference in the United States. As you might imagine, this option is quite popular, so reserve your exam time as soon as you arrive at the conference.

Arriving at the Exam

As with any test, you'll be tempted to cram the night before. Resist that temptation. You should know the material by this point; and if you're too groggy in the morning, you won't remember what you studied anyway. Instead, get a good night's sleep.

Arrive early for your exam; it gives you time to relax and review key facts. Take the opportunity to review your notes. If you get burned out on studying, you can usually start your exam a few minutes early. On the other hand, I don't recommend arriving late. Your test could be canceled, or you might be left without enough time to complete the exam.

When you arrive at the testing center, you'll need to sign in with the exam administrator. In order to sign in, you need to provide two forms of identification. Acceptable forms include government-issued IDs (for example, passport or driver's license), credit cards, and company ID badge. One form of ID must include a photograph.

Aside from a brain full of facts, you don't need to bring anything else to the exam. In fact, your brain is about all you're allowed to take into the exam. All the tests are closed book, meaning that you don't get to bring any reference materials with you. You're also not allowed to take any notes out of the exam room. The test administrator will provide you with paper and a pencil. Some testing centers may provide a small marker board instead.

Calculators are not allowed, so be prepared to do any necessary math (such as hex-binary-decimal conversions or subnet masks) in your head or on paper. Additional paper is available if you need it.

Leave your pager and telephone in the car, or turn them off. They only add stress to the situation, since they are not allowed in the exam room, and can sometimes still be heard if they ring outside the room. Purses, books, and other materials must be left with the administrator before you enter. While you're in the exam room, it's important that you don't disturb other candidates; talking is not allowed during the exam.

In the exam room, the exam administrator logs onto your exam, and you have to verify that your ID number and the exam number are correct. If this is the first time you've taken a Cisco test, you can select a brief tutorial for the exam software. Before the test begins, you will be provided with facts about the exam, including the duration, the number of questions, and the score required for passing. Then the clock starts ticking, and the fun begins.

The testing software is Windows based, but you won't have access to the main desktop or to any of the accessories. The exam is presented in full screen, with a single question per screen. Navigation buttons allow you to move forward and backward between questions. In the upper-right corner of the screen, counters show the number of questions and time remaining. Most important, there is a Mark check box in the upper-left corner of the screen—this will prove to be a critical tool in your testing technique.

Test-Taking Techniques

One of the most frequent excuses I hear for failing a Cisco exam is "poor time management." Without a plan of attack, candidates are overwhelmed by the exam or become sidetracked and run out of time. For the most part, if you are comfortable with the material, the allotted time is more than enough to complete the exam. The trick is to keep the time from slipping away when you work on any one particular problem.

Your obvious goal in taking an exam is to answer the questions effectively, although other aspects of the exam can distract from this goal. After taking a fair number of computer-based exams, I've developed a technique for tackling the problem, which I share with you here. Of course, you still need to learn the material. These steps just help you take the exam more efficiently.

Size Up the Challenge

First take a quick pass through all the questions in the exam. "Cherry-pick" the easy questions, answering them on the spot. Briefly read each question, noticing the type of question and the subject. As a guideline, try to spend less than 25 percent of your testing time in this pass.

This step lets you assess the scope and complexity of the exam, and it helps you determine how to pace your time. It also gives you an idea of where to find potential answers to some of the questions. Often the answer to one question is shown in the exhibit of another. Sometimes the wording of one question might lend clues or jog your thoughts for another question.

Imagine that the following questions are posed in this order:

Question 1: Review the router configurations and network diagram in exhibit XYZ (not shown here). Which devices should be able to ping each other?

Question 2: If RIP routing were added to exhibit XYZ, which devices would be able to ping each other?

The first question seems straightforward. Exhibit XYZ probably includes a diagram and a couple of router configurations. Everything looks normal, so you decide that all devices can ping each other.

Now consider the hint left by Question 2. When you answered Question 1, did you notice that the configurations were missing the routing protocol? Oops! Being alert to such clues can help you catch your own mistakes.

If you're not entirely confident with your answer to a question, answer it anyway, but check the Mark check box to flag it for later review. If you run out of time, at least you've provided a first-guess answer, rather than leaving it blank.

Take on the Scenario Questions

Second, go back through the entire test, using the insight you gained from the first go-through. For example, if the entire test looks difficult, you'll know better than to spend more than a minute or so on each question. Break down the pacing into small milestones; for example, "I need to answer 10 questions every 15 minutes."

At this stage, it's probably a good idea to skip past the time-consuming questions, marking them for the next pass. Try to finish this phase before you're 50 to 60 percent through the testing time.

By now, you probably have a good idea where the scenario questions are found. A single scenario tends to have several questions associated with it, but they aren't necessarily grouped together in the exam. Rather than rereading the scenario every time you encounter a related question, save some time by answering the questions as a group.

Tackle the Complex Problems

Third, go back through all the questions you marked for review, using the Review Marked button in the question review screen. This step includes taking a second look at all the questions you were unsure of in previous passes, as well as tackling the time-consuming ones you postponed until now. Chisel away at this group of questions until you've answered them all.

If you're more comfortable with a previously marked question, unmark it now. Otherwise, leave it marked. Work your way now through the time-consuming questions, especially those requiring manual calculations. Unmark them when you're satisfied with the answer.

By the end of this step, you've answered every question in the test, despite your reservations about some of your answers. If you run out of time in the next step, at least you won't lose points for lack of an answer. You're in great shape if you still have 10 to 20 percent of your time remaining.

Review Your Answers

Now you're cruising! You've answered all the questions, and you're ready to do a quality check. Take yet another pass (yes, one more) through the entire test, briefly rereading each question and your answer. Be cautious about revising answers at this point unless you're sure a change is warranted. If there's a doubt about changing the answer, I always trust my first instinct and leave the original answer intact.

Trick questions are rarely asked, so don't read too much into the questions. Again, if the wording of the question confuses you, leave the answer intact. Your first impression was probably right.

Be alert for last-minute clues. You're pretty familiar with nearly every question at this point, and you may find a few clues that you missed before.

The Grand Finale

When you're confident with all your answers, finish the exam by submitting it for grading. After what will seem like the longest ten seconds of your life, the testing software will respond with your score. This is usually displayed as a bar graph, showing the minimum passing score, your score, and a PASS/FAIL indicator.

If you're curious, you can review the statistics of your score at this time. Answers to specific questions are not presented; rather, questions are lumped into categories, and results are tallied for each category. This detail is also given on a report that has been automatically printed at the exam administrator's desk.

As you leave the exam, you'll need to leave your scratch paper behind or return it to the administrator. (Some testing centers track the number of sheets you've been given, so be sure to return them all.) In exchange, you'll receive a copy of the test report.

This report will be embossed with the testing center's seal, and you should keep it in a safe place. Normally, the results are automatically transmitted to Cisco, but occasionally you might need the paper report to prove that you passed the exam. Your personnel file is probably a good place to keep this report; the file tends to follow you everywhere, and it doesn't hurt to have favorable exam results turn up during a performance review.

Retesting

If you don't pass the exam, don't be discouraged—networking is complex stuff. Try to have a good attitude about the experience, and get ready to try again. Consider yourself a little more educated. You know the format of the test a little better, and the report shows which areas you need to strengthen.

If you bounce back quickly, you'll probably remember several of the questions you might have missed. This will help you focus your study efforts in the right area. Serious go-getters will reschedule the exam for a couple of days after the previous attempt, while the study material is still fresh in their minds.

Ultimately, remember that Cisco certifications are valuable because they're hard to get. After all, if anyone could get one, what value would it have? In the end, it takes a good attitude and a lot of studying, but you can do it!

1

Basic Networking and Design Issues

T he intent of this book is to help you acquire the skills necessary to take and pass the Sylvan Prometric exam to earn Cisco's associate-level certification in network design, the Cisco Certified Design Associate (CCDA). After learning the material in this book, you should feel confident in your ability to design and implement network systems for small- to medium-sized businesses.

The skills particularly required by the CCDA exam include an understanding of the basic networking concepts and terminology that we cover in this chapter.

The OSI Model

The Open Systems Interconnection (OSI) model for internetworking is a seven-layer model. Although nothing in the real world maps exactly to the OSI model, it provides networkers with a common frame of reference to aid them in design and troubleshooting.

The preferred approach to network design is from the top down. In other words, first determine what you want to accomplish with the network, and then take steps to achieve that goal by selecting the applications you wish to run, determining how objects will be distributed, and so on down to selecting hardware and media. We also cover the OSI model in reverse order, from layer 7 to layer 1. We use a Web browser as an underlying example as we run through the layers.

Layer 7, the top layer, is the application layer. It consists of the actual applications running on the workstations and servers. Application selection needs to be taken into consideration in network design because some applications are sensitive to delay in transfer. Voice- and videoconferencing applications are two examples in which delay is immediately noticeable. In our Web browser example, the application layer is the actual browser program.

Layer 6, the presentation layer, has to do with formatting the data to be sent across the network. Because data is useful to a computer only if it can be understood, a common formatting must be agreed upon. The presentation layer, in our example, covers the common media formats available on the Web: HTML, Java, JPEG, and GIF graphics and various types of streaming audio and video.

Layer 5, the session layer, keeps track of multiple data streams as users access the Internet. If a company has a single T1 circuit but 30 users all vying for use of the Internet at the same time, there must be some way to make sure all users receive their data. In our browser example, the session layer allows you to view two Web pages, send an e-mail, and download a file simultaneously. Your e-mail will not be confused with the HTML you're viewing, and your file download doesn't have to complete before you can look at another Web page.

Layer 4, the transport layer, takes care of keeping track of the frames that are sent across the network. If a frame arrives at its destination with errors, the transport layer drops it and requests a retransmission. If frames arrive out of sequence (very common with asynchronous transfer mode [ATM], in which each cell may take a different path), the transport layer puts them back in order. Transport Control Protocol (TCP) is usually considered to be a layer-4 protocol. When TCP receives an error-free packet, it sends an acknowledgment (ACK) to the source, and thus guarantees delivery. If the source never receives the ACK, it will retransmit the packet. In our example, the status bar you may have on your browser that shows you how much of a Web page or file has been downloaded can be considered your view of the transport layer. When the transport layer has accepted a frame as error free and in order, it will pass the frame on to the higher protocols, which results in updating your status bar.

Layer 3, the network layer, is concerned with routing. The purpose of routing is to get a packet from its source to a remote destination for which it knows the address but not how to get there. As an example, when I'm at my workstation in California and want to view a Web page that is hosted on a computer in New York, I can type in the address, www.nypage.com, and it will be resolved to an IP address. Now my computer knows the IP address of the Web page, but the packet requesting the data still needs to go from my computer to the host computer in New York. My computer sends the packet to my modem (they're directly connected, so no routing takes place yet). My modem passes it on to my Internet service provider (ISP), where a router makes a decision on how to forward my packet. From here, another router makes another forwarding decision, and so on, until my packet arrives at the host computer in New York. Every router along the way reads the address my packet is trying to get to and determines the best way to get it there based on the router's knowledge of the networks it is directly connected to and information gathered from neighboring routers. In order for traffic to be routed, we must first address the various nodes on a network. The Internet Protocol (IP) is a layer-3 protocol, as are IPX, AppleTalk, and others. The network-layer addressing is assigned by the network administrator. This method is in contrast to that for the media access control (MAC) address, discussed shortly, which is assigned by the manufacturer. In order to participate on the Internet, your computer must be identified with an IP address. If you use a dial-up service, whenever you connect to your ISP, you are loaned an IP address for that session. If you have a permanent connection, such as a cable modem or digital subscriber line (DSL), you may have a permanent IP address. The IP address allows your computer to talk to your ISP's router, via modem. In some cases, such as on a private local area network (LAN), you may be assigned a "nonroutable" IP address. A nonroutable IP address is one of several blocks of IP addresses that have been set aside by the Internet Assigned Numbers Authority (IANA) to be available for private use only. These blocks include the network 10.*x.x.x*, 172.16.*x.x* through 172.31.*x.x*, and 192.168.*x.x*. When such addressing is used on a LAN that intends to have Internet access, network address translation (NAT) allows dynamic translation between the private address and a public (routable) address. This is automatic and transparent to the end user.

Layer 2, the data-link layer, concerns the framing of data and MAC addressing, in which two end nodes agree on how they will signify the beginning and end of a frame. Just after your modem dials out to connect to your ISP, but before your browser fills up with a Web page, those horrible screeching sounds you hear from your modem are your modem and your ISP's modem discussing specifications like data rate, parity, and stop bits. Cable modems and DSL users' devices also do this (minus the screeching) whenever they are turned off and on again. Network interface cards (NICs) operate at this layer. Every device that interfaces with a network has a MAC address, including NICs, bridges, switches, and each router interface. Every MAC address is unique and is assigned by the manufacturer of each networking device. Devices advertise their MAC addresses periodically so that other devices on the same segment will know of their existence. Bridges and switches use these addresses to make forwarding decisions. At this layer, for a packet to get from source to destination, the source must have immediate knowledge of the destination's location. It is at this layer that the 1's and 0's are first organized into logical units.

Layer 1, the physical layer, covers the actual, physical, and electrical components on a network. In our Web browser example, it may be your phone line, your cable antenna, your computer, or your ISP's computer. In a LAN or wide area network (WAN), it refers to the cabling, routers, switches, workstations, and so on, that make up the internetwork. Layer 1 also covers wireless media, such as microwave towers and microwaves, infrared, and satellites. At this level, all data is seen as 1's and 0's.

CERTIFICATION OBJECTIVE 1.02

Local Area Networking Technology Terms

As networkers, we may rightly feel proud of enriching the English language with our plethora of specialized terminology and acronyms. Occasionally, though, our zeal can backfire, and we end up becoming the ones confused by the different terms. Following is an overview of some of the more common terms you'll encounter in networking.

Ethernet

When the LAN was born, a few vendors offered their solutions for communication standards. *Ethernet* is a broadcast medium invented by

Xerox in the 1970s. It operates at 10 megabits per second (Mbps) using CSMA/CD, which stands for carrier sense multiple access with collision detection.

When a node on an Ethernet network wants to transmit, it first listens to see if there is traffic on the network (carrier sense). If no other devices are actively using the LAN, the device will transmit the data (multiple access). All nodes on the segment receive the transmitted data, but only the intended recipient accepts the data; this is based on addressing. All other nodes, those not addressed, discard the data. It is possible for two nodes to transmit at the same time, which would result in a collision. Collisions occur when two or more devices think that no other devices are using the LAN, so they start to transmit data. Because both are talking at the same time, a collision occurs. When this happens, both devices will stop sending data, start sending a "jam" signal to inform all other devices that a collision has occurred, temporarily go into a random hold-down period, and then start the whole sequence over by listening to see if any other device is transmitting. Ethernet resides on a physical bus topology.

The Institute of Electrical and Electronics Engineers (IEEE) redefined the original Xerox specification and classified it as 802.3 in 1983. Ethernet version 2.0, which is most widely used today, was jointly developed by Digital Equipment Corporation, IBM, and Xerox, and it is sometimes referred to as DIX Ethernet.

There are also new flavors of Ethernet coloring the landscape, including 100-Mbps (100BaseT Fast Ethernet) and 1,000-Mbps (Gigabit Ethernet) speeds, which are quickly gaining popularity.

Token Ring

Token Ring is a LAN specification that was developed by IBM in the 1980s for PC-based networks and classified by the IEEE as 802.5. It specifies a star topology physically and a ring topology logically. It runs at either 4 Mbps or 16 Mbps, but all nodes on the ring must run at the same speed. In the original specification, all the end nodes (workstations) were connected to a multistation access unit (MSAU, also referred to as a MAU). The MSAU controls network resiliency by closing the circuit in case of a node failure. The MSAU also controls the passing of the "token" around the network. The token is a special data unit that, when possessed by an end node, allows transmission on the network. Because devices can transmit only when they possess the token, no collisions are possible.

Token Ring is so named because the token is passed from node to node, each one in turn, as on a carousel. Although the original specification defined a physical star with a logical ring, with the addition of multiple MSAUs, a physical ring topology may also be used. Take note of how many nodes are on a Token Ring network. Because the token must stop at each node to provide it a chance to transmit, as nodes are added, the token must make more stops, thereby increasing latency. However, the token goes to each device on the ring, so it does guarantee that each device will be able to transmit sooner or later.

Token Bus

Token Bus can be thought of as "Token Ring over Ethernet." This is a physical bus topology and broadcast medium, like Ethernet, with a single controller that broadcasts a token, specifying a recipient. When a node is designated as the recipient of the token, it may transmit on the network.

FDDI

Fiber Distributed Data Interface (FDDI) is a 100-Mbps fiber-optic (not copper wire) network, also characterized by its counter-rotating, ring-style topology, which works as built-in redundancy in case of a break in the main ring. FDDI is often used as a backbone network because of its speed and reliability. It generally connects file servers and other high-traffic nodes.

A sister of FDDI is Copper Distributed Data Interface (CDDI). Functionally, it is the same as FDDI. Its primary difference is that it runs over copper and not fiber. CDDI is not very popular; however, it has been used by companies that did not want to replace the copper wiring with fiber but still wanted to gain the speed that CDDI gave them.

Exercise 1-1 will help reinforce your understanding of LAN terminology.

Local Area Networking Technology Terms

Match the LAN technology terms on the left with the explanations on the right.

LAN Term	Explanation
1) Ethernet	a) Broadcast medium that specifies a recipient; only one node may transmit at a time.
2) Token Ring	b) The most widely used LAN medium; multiple stations may broadcast simultaneously, which causes collisions.
3) Token Bus	c) May be a physical star or ring, depending on the number of MSAUs; all end stations must directly connect to an MSAU.
4) FDDI	d) A high-speed network, often used as a backbone and characterized by a counter-rotating, ring-style topology.

Answers to Exercise 1-1

1-b; 2-c; 3-a; 4-d. Ethernet is the most widely used LAN medium today and is characterized by CSMA/CD, which specifies that multiple stations may occasionally transmit at the same time and will cause a collision. Token Ring requires all end stations to connect to an MSAU, and it was originally specified as a physical star topology; but with the addition of multiple MSAUs, it may become a physical ring. Token Bus is a broadcast medium, like Ethernet, but it is not characterized by CSMA/CD; rather, like Token Ring, it allows only one station to transmit at a time. FDDI is a 100-Mbps dual-ring network, often used to connect file servers and other high-traffic devices on the network backbone. Its counter-rotating rings allow for redundancy in case of a fault in the main ring.

CERTIFICATION OBJECTIVE 1.03

Wide Area Networking Technology Terms

The local area network was well received by businesses, but it did not address the issue of linking two or more offices that were geographically distant, whether that meant across town from one another or on the other side of the globe. WAN technologies address these issues in several ways.

Point to Point

A *point-to-point connection* is one in which point A connects to point B with no side trips. A *point-to-point circuit* is a private circuit with only two endpoints. There is also a *Point-to-Point Protocol (PPP)*, which is a serial communication protocol most commonly used to connect a personal computer to an ISP. PPP is the successor to *Serial Line Internet Protocol (SLIP)* and may be used over both synchronous and asynchronous circuits.

Point-to-point connections are established when the transmitting node sends a Link Control Protocol (LCP) frame to the destination to configure the link. Once the two nodes have established basic communication, LCP may optionally test the link to determine if it is of high enough quality to establish network-layer communication.

The originating node continues by transmitting Network Control Protocol (NCP) frames to determine what network-layer protocols will be accepted. Once the network-layer protocols are configured, traffic may begin to flow.

Cisco's default synchronous serial link protocol is *High-Level Data Link Control (HDLC)*. Many vendors support HDLC, but there is not yet an established standard for it. Cisco's HDLC is proprietary and will not work with other vendors' versions of HDLC.

Cisco's default asynchronous serial link protocol is Serial Line Internet Protocol (SLIP) because SLIP was the de facto standard when Cisco first came out with asynchronous interfaces for the routers. Today, most users will change this encapsulation to PPP because it has replaced SLIP as the de facto standard.

on the Job

One of the most aggravating things I encountered when I was new to wide area networking was a WAN circuit that crossed multiple carriers. I was working in a network operations center (NOC) that monitored many customers all across the country. I saw the circuit go down on the network monitor and immediately called the carrier to have it run a test. In an hour, I was called back and informed that the circuit was fine, yet it still showed down on my monitor. After several minutes of explaining to the tester that the circuit was not fine, to my chagrin, I was informed that the carrier's portion of the circuit was fine, but it crossed two other carriers. If I wanted those portions tested, I'd have to call the other carriers. The hour lost testing the wrong piece of the circuit was bad enough, but now I needed to call another carrier and ask it to test a circuit for which I had no information other than my customer's name. This would not have been a problem if I'd had a circuit ID to work with, but my documentation said nothing about multiple carriers. Documentation is extremely important in designing and building a network. This particular issue was eventually resolved when the first carrier referenced the network-to-network interface where it handed off to the second carrier, which allowed the second carrier to identify the correct circuit. But the time lost in tracking down this information was very costly.

exam Watch

Remember that CCDA will test your knowledge of design rather than all the nuances of a particular transport or protocol. Also remember that because it's a Cisco test, you would be well advised to acquaint yourself with the Cisco product line. For example, learn the basic differences between the 7000 series routers, the 5000 series switches, and the 2500 and 1600 series routers.

X.25

X.25 is an International Telecommunication Union – Telecommunication (ITU-T) Standardization Sector standard and is one of the first successful attempts at a standard for data communication across a WAN. Various telephone companies put it into use across multiple vendors' equipment as a solution for data transport.

X.25 is similar to Frame Relay in that it takes an original piece of data and then segments it for easier transmission through a packet assembler/ disassembler (PAD). Each segment is packet switched through the cloud; but unlike Frame Relay, which passes along each packet it receives, X.25 will compute a checksum value that is appended to each packet. As each packet is received by the switches in the cloud, the checksum is recomputed. If there are no errors, an ACK is sent to the preceding switch or PAD, indicating that the packet arrived intact. Otherwise, a negative acknowledgement (NAK) is sent, indicating a request for retransmission. Once all the packets are received at the destination, the PAD strips off the X.25 headers, reassembles the original data unit, and forwards it.

X.25 is slow by modern standards. However, since each switch in the cloud checks the data for reliability, reliable data flow is guaranteed. And with advances in line-encoding techniques, error-checking algorithms, and faster system processors, it was possible to streamline the original X.25 specification; thus evolved Frame Relay.

Frame Relay

Frame Relay was originally designed to run over ISDN interfaces and is considered the successor to X.25.

Frame is a generic term used to specify a single unit of data, which is most often a fragment of a larger unit. Much like a picture frame that defines the edges of the picture, a Frame Relay frame defines the beginning and end of a single unit of data, wherein the payload may be up to 4,096 bytes (4,096 × 8 bits per byte = 32,768 bits).

The idea of relaying these frames is in how they are transported across the network. Frames are packet switched, or relayed, from device to device within the network until they reach their destinations.

Devices in a Frame Relay network are either *data terminal equipment (DTE)* or *data circuit-terminating equipment (DCE)*. Both of these are logical descriptions of physical equipment. Typically, the term DTE is used to describe a router, bridge, computer, or terminal at the customer end. DTE devices communicate with DCE devices, which are usually housed at the carrier's premises. DCE devices are usually packet switches, although routers and other devices may also be configured as DCE. There may be multiple DCE devices that a Frame Relay frame must traverse before reaching its destination DTE. Modern Frame Relay networks use ATM within the cloud and run Frame Relay only to the end devices at the customer's location.

One of the nicest things about Frame Relay is that it is protocol independent. In other words, *any* protocol may be transported over Frame Relay, with no attempt made to convert the data. That task, along with packet reassembly, lost packet detection, and error detection, is left up to higher protocols. This is in contrast to X.25, which takes responsibility for ensuring data is transported intact. The beauty of Frame Relay is that, less these CPU-intensive encumbrances, the transport is now streamlined for speed.

Frame Relay uses a common error-checking algorithm known as *cyclical redundancy check (CRC)* to ensure data integrity. When a frame is being assembled, a checksum is calculated and appended to the frame. This frame then passes through the network with no further error control until it reaches its destination. At the destination, the checksum is recalculated and compared with what is contained in the header. If they match, the frame is accepted; if not, a retransmission is requested.

Frame Relay is a connection-oriented, packet-switched technology that can run from 16 Kbps to over 2 Mbps, with the most common instances being multiples of 64 Kbps. *Connection oriented* means that there is a specific pathway through the network that all traffic must follow and that network resources are reserved for that traffic. In Frame Relay, one of the most important network resources is the *committed information rate (CIR)*.

CIR and More

The CIR is basically the maximum guaranteed throughput for a Frame Relay line. In other words, if you pay for a 128KB line, you'll get 128KB throughput. There are, however, some exceptions. First, because the same circuit within the cloud may service more than one customer's Frame Relay circuit, there will be times when everyone tries to transmit at the same time, and the physical bandwidth of the medium is exceeded and congestion occurs. Conversely, there will be times when only one customer is trying to transmit. At these times, the customer transmitting may be able to "burst" over guaranteed capacity.

The *committed burst size, Bc* (pronounced "bee sub see"), is related to the CIR in that it determines the maximum number of bits on a virtual circuit that are guaranteed to be transmitted over a certain time period (*committed rate measurement interval,* or *Tc*), assuming they are received contiguously by the Frame Relay switch. The sum of the individual Bc values for all virtual circuits on the stream should be less than or equal to the physical link speed. Bc is a configurable parameter and is usually computed as Bc = *average number of bits per frame* multiplied by *average number of frames per transmission.*

Whereas Bc determines the maximum number of bits on a virtual circuit that are guaranteed to be transmitted, *burst excess size* (*Be,* pronounced "bee sub e") allows an additional number of bits to be received if bandwidth is available (for example, if other virtual circuits are currently not using their allotted bandwidth).

Frame transmission that is greater than Bc, but within Be, is marked as discard eligible (DE) by the cloud. This marking notifies downstream network devices that, if they experience congestion, these frames should be discarded, as indicated in Figure 1-1. Some frames may also be preferentially marked DE when congestion is high, allowing mission-critical data to pass through the network and dropping less important data. Traffic shaping filters often use this

FIGURE 1-1

Committed information
rate, committed burst, and
excess burst

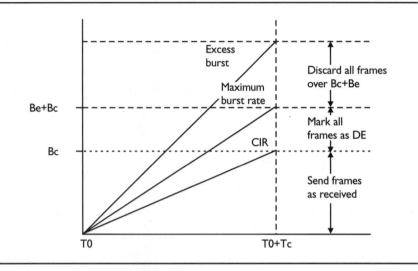

marking when voice (or video) and data are carried over the same medium. Since voice is delay sensitive and data is not, the data frames may be marked DE during periods of congestion to ensure the voice frames pass through with as little delay as possible.

In addition to DE, Frame Relay utilizes other flags to indicate problems. The forward explicit congestion notification (FECN) and backward explicit congestion notification (BECN) are indicated by a single bit in the Frame Relay header. This bit indicates congestion on the segment. Because Frame Relay does not explicitly provide for flow control, this information is passed up the OSI chain to upper protocols that can make a decision to either ignore the congestion or throttle back the rate of throughput.

SVC

A *switched virtual circuit (SVC)* is the wide area networking equivalent of a telephone call. That is, a connection is established when it's required and torn down when it isn't. SVCs are used extensively in X.25 networks and also in Frame Relay, though not to as great an extent. In some cases, SVCs are used as load balancers or congestion relievers; that is, a second pathway is created during periods of heavy traffic.

PVC

A *permanent virtual circuit (PVC)* is very common in Frame Relay. It is a predefined pathway through the public telephone network that is set up during the provisioning period and never torn down. Multiple PVCs may reside on a single physical circuit, which allows a company to purchase a single T1 at its headquarters and split it into, for example, one 384-Kbps circuit to remote location A, one 256-Kbps circuit to location B, and one 128-Kbps circuit to location C, with 768-Kbps access to the Internet. The division of the physical circuit is managed through the use of *data-link connection identifiers* (*DLCIs*, pronounced "DELsees"). These are the addresses used by Frame Relay, in combination with time division multiplexing (TDM), to keep different data separate, regardless of its simultaneous transmission.

The cloud (public telecommunications network) knows that any packet coming into this DLCI will travel a predetermined path (the PVC) to another DLCI at the other end of the cloud, and from there it will travel to its ultimate destination (the remote router). DLCIs are logical entities, existing within a multiplexer to properly divide the bandwidth of a single physical circuit so that it can service several virtual circuits. Also, DLCIs are significant only locally. That means that a packet entering DLCI 16 at the source end may come out a completely different DLCI at its destination. So once the physical circuit reaches the service provider's network, it may be split onto separate physical circuits along with data from other customers to carry it through the network to its final destination.

Standard addressing for a DLCI will take 10 bits, with a range from 0 to 1023. However, several addresses are reserved. For example, 0 and 1023 are reserved for the local management interface (LMI).

FROM THE FIELD

After visiting several sites that were undergoing new network changes, several network engineers have had problems understanding what it means to be "locally significant." To understand this term, we must first understand how the Frame Relay cloud works.

Most frame clouds are run by ATM at the core. This means that all the Frame Relay packets are turned into ATM cells and forwarded through an ATM backbone. No DLCI is required as that is taking place; that's related to ATM.

To see where the DLCI addressing works, let's look at the original Frame Relay network. This network was a mass of switches that made forwarding decisions based on DLCI addressing and a built-in matrix. Remember that the range for the DLCI is only 10 bits in length and that several addresses are reserved.

In fact, the range that we can use is from 16 to 1022 or so (it changes by provider). If all edge devices required a unique address within a Frame Relay cloud, there could only be about 1,000 devices per cloud. Obviously, that would not work for the major providers.

So, each switch within the cloud is given a matrix. The matrix is broken down by interface and assigned DLCIs per interface. This allows serial 0 of a switch to have the same DLCI number assigned to it as serial 7 of the same switch. The DLCI number and the interface the packet is received on will determine the new DLCI and interface that the packet will be sent out of. Doing the math will tell you that each switch interface within the cloud could support about 1,000 DLCI destinations simultaneously. It's a new application of an old method.

LMI

Because a carrier switch also handles Frame Relay traffic for other customers, how can a customer router keep track of the status of its own PVCs? The answer lies in the LMI.

The *LMI* isn't really an interface at all. It's actually a protocol that periodically (usually about every 10 seconds) requests status information from the cloud. There are three flavors of LMI: One is referred to as "the gang of four," or Cisco LMI; another is ANSI Annex D; and the third is ITU Q933a. All do basically the same thing, just in different ways. Being aware of the existence of the different types of LMI will become important in troubleshooting a newly installed network. If, as an example, a router requests ANSI updates from a switch that provides Cisco type, the result will be a lost connection. Most public switched telephone network (PSTN) switches are configured to auto-detect the LMI type from the customer equipment, and most often this works without incident. Occasionally, the auto-detect doesn't work as expected, and it's necessary to have the carrier network manually change the LMI type at the switch.

The information that LMI gets from the cloud includes link status (up or down) and congestion information. Also, the very act of querying the switch works to inform it that the router is still up and active. This is known as a *keepalive*. If a router is not transmitting data, there is no way for the router at the other end to know whether it is still functioning except through the keepalive packets.

ISDN

In *Integrated Services Digital Network (ISDN)*, "Integrated Services" indicates that the provider offers voice *and* data services over the same medium. "Digital Network" is a reminder that ISDN was born out of the digital nature of the inter- and intracarrier networks. Analog circuits are prone to noise interference from electromagnetic interference (EMI) and other causes. Analog signals also attenuate (lose strength) after a certain distance. Amplifiers attached to the analog circuit make the signal louder but also amplify the noise. After too much noise has mixed in with the desired signal, there is no way to differentiate the two.

The digital standard was devised to remedy the noise problem. Once a discrete signal in place of analog was instituted, signals could be carried further. EMI noise still affects a digital circuit the same way it does analog, but a repeater placed on the digital circuit reads the signal before the noise causes too much interference. The repeater then regenerates the signal from scratch, rather than amplifying it, so that it can be carried further.

ISDN runs across the same copper wiring that carries regular telephone service. The maximum distance an ISDN circuit can run before attenuation and noise cause the signal to be unintelligible is 18,000 feet. A repeater doubles this distance to 36,000 feet.

Components of ISDN fall into one of three categories:

- **Terminal equipment**   There are two basic terminal types in the ISDN specification:

  - **Terminal equipment Type 1 (TE1)**   A TE1 is a specialized ISDN terminal used to connect to ISDN through a four-wire, twisted-pair digital link.

  - **Terminal equipment Type 2 (TE2)**   A TE2 is a non-ISDN terminal that predates the ISDN standards. It connects to an ISDN link through a *terminal adapter (TA)*, which may be either a standalone device or a board inside the TE2.

- **Termination devices**   ISDN specifies a type of intermediate equipment called a *network termination (NT)* device. NTs connect the four-wire subscriber wiring to two-wire local loops. There are three supported NT types:

  - **NT Type 1 (NT1)**   An NT1 is treated as customer premises equipment (CPE) in North America, but it is the carrier's responsibility elsewhere.

  - **NT Type 2 (NT2)**   An NT2 is typically found in digital private branch exchange (PBX) equipment. An NT2 performs OSI layer-2 (data link) and layer-3 (network) protocol functions and concentration services.

  - **NT Type 1/2 (NT1/2)**   An NT1/2 provides combined functions of separate NT1 and NT2 devices. An NT1/2 is compatible with NT1 and NT2 devices and is used to replace separate NT1 and NT2 devices.

- **Reference points**   ISDN reference points define logical interfaces. Four reference points are defined in ISDN:

  - **R reference point**   The R reference point defines the reference point between non-ISDN equipment and a TA.

  - **S reference point**   The S reference point defines the reference point between user terminals and an NT2.

- **T reference point**   The T reference point defines the reference point between NT1 and NT2 devices.

- **U reference point**   The U reference point defines the reference point between NT1 devices and line-termination equipment in a carrier network. (This is only in North America, where the NT1 function is not provided by the carrier network.)

Note that in many cases, these reference points no longer refer to separate pieces of equipment. Figure 1-2 helps to clarify how these reference points fit into an ISDN network.

Speed is another benefit of ISDN. In contrast to the time it takes for a modem to dial and negotiate transmission parameters, ISDN can set up a call almost instantaneously. And the communication speed after call setup is much faster than that for the fastest modems. ISDN is sold in both basic rate interface (BRI) and primary rate interface (PRI).

ISDN is regulated by several families of standards. The most important of these is the "I" family of standards, which explains what ISDN is about; the "Q" standards, which cover control and signaling; and the "H" standards, which cover videoconferencing.

FIGURE 1-2

ISDN reference points

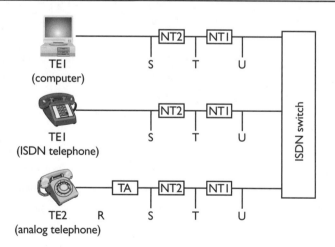

Basic Rate Interface

Basic Rate Interface (BRI) format is made up of two 64-Kbps B channels, used for data or voice, and one 16-Kbps D channel, used by the carrier for control and signaling. Other configurations are possible, but this is the most common. Each B channel can be used to make a second connection, or the channels can be used together. This allows for the user to make a data connection to the Internet or to a corporate LAN and use the other channel for voice. When the second channel is not needed for voice, it may be used to double the amount of bandwidth available for data. It is also possible to configure both B channels to connect at all times or only when bandwidth requirements dictate.

BRIs are often used as dial-on-demand solutions—that is, as WAN links that exist only when there is traffic to transmit. They are also seen as "nailed-up" links that never go down, though with point-to-point and Frame Relay as alternatives, this use is becoming less prevalent because of cost.

BRIs are very popular as links for telecommuters to a corporate LAN. Typically, the company will pay for the installation of the ISDN line and for the ISDN terminal adapter or router at the user's home, and for the access charges incurred for using them. This is a budgetary concern to be aware of when you include ISDN in your network design.

ISDN lines are assigned numbers, just as analog phone lines are. These are the directory numbers. These numbers are advertised to the public ISDN network so that a connection may be established when one ISDN device calls another device. In addition to the directory numbers, service profile identifiers (SPIDs) may or may not be assigned to your ISDN lines and can be used to configure your ISDN equipment to communicate with the telephone company switch. You must also know the type of switch you will communicate with and configure your ISDN equipment with this information. In the United States, you will most likely run into the Northern Telecom DMS-100 type: AT&T's 5ESS or 4ESS, or the NI1 or NI2 national standards (you can get this information from your ISDN provider).

Primary Rate Interface

Primary Rate Interface (PRI) is made up of up to 23 64-Kbps B channels (30 B channels in Europe) and one 64-Kbps D channel for a total bandwidth of 1.544 Mbps (2.048 Mbps in Europe), with all but 64 Kbps (the D channel) available for data. Just as with the BRI, every channel may make a separate call, multiple channels may be combined for greater bandwidth, or all channels may be used at once as a single link. These alternatives provide for great flexibility in designing remote access solutions.

Videoconferencing equipment often uses ISDN as its transport protocol. 384 Kbps seems to be the magic number to allow for smooth video and clear audio, so both PRI and tri-BRI solutions are in place.

on the Job

Be aware that, although most telephone company switches have undergone upgrading, there are still legacy switches in use (switches that don't conform to the Switching System #7 [SS7] standard), particularly in more remote locations, that do not support out-of-band signaling. That means that the D channel, which is used for control and signaling, doesn't exist, and signaling information must be taken from the B channels. In a BRI, 8 Kbps is taken from each of the B channels to form the 16 Kbps necessary for signaling. If ISDN is to be a part of your network design, be sure to verify whether the switches your circuit will pass through conform to the SS7 standard to provide "clear-channel" throughput. Also, be sure to determine how many ISDN connections you'll actually need. In some cases, buying multiple BRIs instead of a single PRI can be cost-effective.

Dial-Up

Dial-up solutions are characterized by the use of modems connected to PCs or routers. Typically, a user on a PC will use a modem to dial into a bank of modems to connect to an ISP or to gain access to a corporate LAN. Modems are also used as both primary and backup devices for WANs. If you've ever made a purchase with a credit card, you may have seen the cashier swipe your card through a card reader. You then had to wait as the device contacted the local modem, caused it to dial out to that company's bank, and authorized your purchase. That is an example of using a modem as a primary WAN link.

In a chain store or multiple campus environment, you are more likely to run into permanent connections to a central hub site via a reliable Frame Relay or point-to-point circuits. However, accidents do happen, and a reasonable and very inexpensive backup solution to the possibility of those permanent links going down is to attach a modem to the routers at the hub site and the remote site.

Wide Area Networking Technology Terms

Match the WAN technology terms on the left with the explanations on the right.

WAN Term	Explanation
1) Point-to-point	a) A digital connection that comes in both primary and basic rates.
2) Frame Relay	b) An extremely reliable protocol designed to run over multivendor networks and characterized by virtual circuits; performs checksum analysis.
3) X.25	c) A pathway through the public phone network that is established when needed and that is part of a larger physical circuit.
4) SVC	d) Characterized by the use of a modem and a serial protocol.
5) PVC	e) A streamlined version of its predecessor that can handle multiple payload sizes and is characterized by virtual circuits; does not perform checksum analysis.
6) ISDN	f) A serial protocol used to connect PCs to ISPs; also, a circuit characterized by only two endpoints.
7) Dial-up	g) A predefined pathway through the public phone network that is part of a larger physical circuit.

Answers to Exercise 1-2

1-f; 2-e; 3-b; 4-c; 5-g; 6-a; 7-d. Point-to-point circuits are circuits that have only two endpoints; also, PPP is used to connect PCs to ISPs. Frame Relay is a streamlined version of X.25, but does not perform checksum analysis—instead, leaving it up to higher layers of the OSI model—and it utilizes virtual circuits. X.25, is the predecessor to Frame Relay, and it includes the use of virtual circuits, but it also provides error control in the form of checksum analysis. A switched virtual circuit is set up when required, and there may be multiple SVCs on the same physical circuit. A permanent virtual circuit is similar to an SVC except that the pathway is predefined and the circuit is always up. ISDN is an all-digital signal that comes in basic (BRI) and primary (PRI) rates. Dial-up involves using a modem and either PPP or SLIP to connect to a remote device.

Bridge

When LANs get too big, especially in a bus topology like Ethernet, collisions become more prevalent. Two or more nodes on the same bus may try to transmit, sensing that the line is open only because the packet that was sent first has not had time to traverse to the far end of the wire, as shown in Figure 1-3.

A *bridge* physically divides a larger logical network, as shown in Figure 1-4. Bridges operate on layer 2 of the OSI model, which is the data-link layer. When a bridge first activates and receives a frame, it floods it out all its physical interfaces except the interface the frame came through. In addition, the bridge will take note of the transmitting node; and from that point on, whenever a frame comes through the bridge, it will know which interface to send it out to reach its destination.

One way to remember what bridges do is to remember F-F-F: filter, forward, flood. When a bridge receives a frame, if it recognizes the destination MAC or hardware address, it will *filter* the frame from exiting all interfaces except the one the destination node is connected to. It will then *forward* the frame to the correct interface. If the bridge doesn't yet recognize the destination MAC address, it will *flood* the frame out all its physical interfaces (except the one through which the frame was received).

FIGURE 1-3

When multiple nodes transmit simultaneously, collisions occur

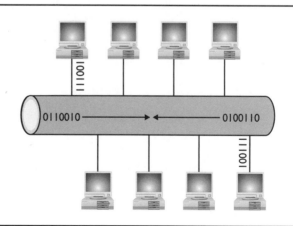

FIGURE 1-4

Bridges both logically
connect and physically
separate larger networks

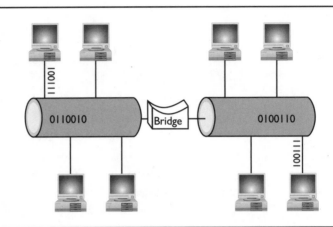

*Older bridges worked at layer 1 of the OSI model (the physical layer).
That is, they served only as physical connectors between LAN segments
and as signal regenerators. Obviously, the amount of traffic traversing
your network is of great concern and can mean the difference between
success and failure for your network design.*

*If your design is destined to replace an older network, you will first
want to establish a baseline of the existing network to compare its
current capabilities with the requirements of your customer. This
baseline will also be of use once your network design is in place. You
will be able to show your client documented evidence that your design
is more efficient than that of the original network. Replacing a layer-1
bridge, which causes undue traffic over multiple segments, with a layer-2
bridge, which filters frames and floods only when it doesn't recognize a
destination MAC address, can only serve to improve network availability.*

Transparent Bridging

Transparent bridging is used primarily in Ethernet networks, but it may also
be found in Token Ring and FDDI. It is so named because the bridge's
existence is transparent to the rest of the network. Remember that bridges
learn MAC addresses as nodes transmit through the bridge, and then they
forward, filter, or flood, depending on whether they know where the
destination node lies.

With multiple bridges, though, is the possibility of introducing an endless loop; so to be fully transparent to the network, a transparent bridge is required to ensure a loop-free topology. A loop occurs in a network when multiple paths exist between two segments. Multiple paths can be very useful in designing for redundancy, but they may become harmful if two or more bridges retransmit the same frame. What is even worse is if the frame the bridges receive is a broadcast. Consider Figure 1-5.

In the network in Figure 1-5, suppose a workstation on Segment A transmitted a broadcast onto the network. Both bridges would receive the broadcast frame on their e0 interfaces and forward it through their e1 interfaces. At this point, both bridges would receive a new broadcast through their e1 interfaces—the one the other bridge just forwarded—and they would both forward the "new" broadcast through their e0 interfaces. The process would continue until the network became so bogged down with broadcasts that it would effectively shut down. Such an occurrence is called a *broadcast storm.*

The remedy to bridging loops and broadcast storms is in the *Spanning Tree Protocol (STP).* STP allows for redundant pathways, but it allows only one to be active at a time. In case of a network failure, the secondary pathway is allowed to open. STP was developed by Digital Equipment Corporation and revised by the IEEE. Today we have two standards, DEC and IEEE 802.1d. It is important to use only one or the other within a network because they do not communicate with each other.

FIGURE 1-5

Multiple bridges offer redundancy, but watch out for loops

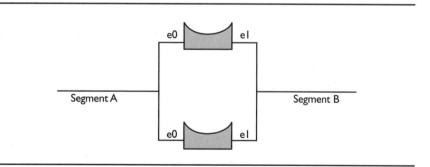

Source Route Bridging

Source route bridging (SRB) was invented by IBM and is applicable only to Token Ring networks. Token Ring provides for an optional field in the frame header called the *routing information field (RIF)*. The RIF is made up of 12 bits for the ring identifier and 4 bits for the bridge identifier.

When a node on a Token Ring network wants to transmit to a destination for which it doesn't know the path, it first transmits a discovery frame. This frame is either broadcast as an "all rings, all routes" or based on IBM's spanning tree algorithm. As each bridge on the LAN receives the discovery frame, it inserts its own bridge number and the ring number that the frame arrived on into the RIF. The first frame to arrive at the destination node is transmitted back to the sender, with the RIF thereafter functioning to identify the pathway through the LAN.

Because source route bridges read the RIF to make forwarding decisions, source route bridges can be used to create physical loops in a network without fear of infinite loops. Also, a Token Ring LAN will remove a frame that has circulated a ring more than once.

The use of source route bridging requires the network administrator to configure ring numbers and bridge numbers for each port connection.

Figure 1-6 shows how SRB information stored in the RIF aids in frame forwarding. If Source A doesn't know the route to Destination B, it will send out an explorer frame. This will be broadcast across all rings and eventually will arrive at Destination B. Each bridge adds its own bridge number and ring number as the explorer frame passes through. Because the path across Bridge 1 and Bridge 2 is shorter than the path across Bridges 5, 4, and 3, the former route will transmit the explorer frame faster than the latter. Destination B will reply to all the explorer frames it receives and reverse the path information so that the reply takes the same route as the initial explorer frame. When the first reply has been received back at Source A, that pathway will be used for further transmission to Destination B.

Mixed-Media Bridging

Mixed-media bridging (also called *encapsulated bridging*) involves transporting frames between one media type (Ethernet) and another (Token Ring or

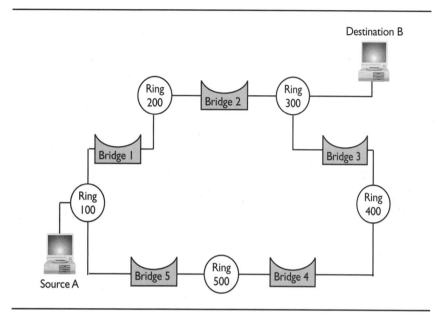

FIGURE 1-6

Source route bridging
leaves path selection up
to the source node

FDDI). Because of the differences in framing among these protocols, certain issues must be resolved before they can be successfully bridged. In particular, Ethernet does not allow for the inclusion of the RIF that SRB requires, nor does Token Ring allow for a variable payload size.

Source route/translational bridging (SR/TLB) was introduced to allow SRB and transparent bridging domains to communicate. SR/TLB employs an intermediate bridge that translates between the two bridging protocols. There is no set standard for how this is accomplished.

Source route/transparent bridging (SR/T) was introduced by IBM to address some of the weaknesses of SR/TLB. SR/T devices include both SRB and transparent bridging protocols and don't translate between the two. Instead, to accomplish SR/T bridging, any node that wants to transmit out of its own domain must include a new field in the frame header. That new field is 1 bit long and known as the *Routing Information Indicator (RII)*. When an SR/T bridge receives a frame, it first checks to see whether the RII bit is set. If the RII is set, the bridge performs SRB. If the RII is not set, the bridge performs transparent bridging.

exam

ⓦatch

The CCDA exam will expect you to know the Open Systems Interconnection model very well, to the point of being able to identify which layer is represented by a given protocol or transport mechanism. For example, you should know that bridging takes place at layer 2 (data link), and routing takes place at layer 3 (network).

Switch

For a basic understanding of switches, you can use the previous definition of a bridge. Switches are basically bridges with higher throughput capability. There are differences, of course. One important difference is the ability of a switch to support full-duplex operation. That is, a switch can receive and transmit at full bandwidth at the same time, whereas a bridge can do only one or the other. Switches determine the route to a destination based on the MAC address contained in the frame.

Some switches also include layer-3 functionality, such as making switching decisions based on more than just the MAC address. This can lead to access control or blocking (or at least management) of multicast or broadcast traffic.

There are also multilayer switches, which can make the decision whether to switch or route traffic, depending on the destination.

Unless otherwise indicated in the question, you should assume a layer-2–only switch when taking the CCDA exam.

Router

A *router* is an interface between two networks and operates on layer 3 of the OSI model, the network layer. Routers are the usual method for connecting different media, such as Ethernet to Token Ring or Frame Relay to ATM.

Routers are concerned with reading the network (IP, IPX, or AppleTalk) address of an incoming packet. Routers keep track of all the networks they hear about through the use of a *routing table*. They also advertise their own existence and their entire routing table with their neighbors. In this way, routers learn enough of the topology of the network to determine the optimal route for packet forwarding.

Routers are often used as gateways to the Internet. A typical design might include a Frame Relay T1 circuit coming into the router's serial interface to allow data to flow from the Internet to the Ethernet or Token Ring interface that connects with the client's LAN. In larger networks, routers may be employed to route two separate subnets (for example, the sales department and accounting) to the same server.

Purpose and Operation of Routing Protocols

Routing protocols make routers work together. Routers keep track of the networks they're directly connected to, as well as other routers on those networks, in order to forward packets to foreign networks. A router maintains this information in its routing table and periodically shares information from that table to other routers on the network. This sharing is called a *routing update*. This information is used by the router to determine the best route for an incoming packet to take to reach its destination.

There are two main types of routing protocols: *Interior Gateway Protocols (IGPs)* and *Exterior Gateway Protocols (EGPs)*. EGPs are used primarily on the Internet and in larger campus networks where autonomous systems need to communicate. IGPs are used within autonomous systems.

An *autonomous system (AS)* is a logical or physical network community that is self-sufficient. Most routers within the AS don't need to know about the existence of any other AS. Within an AS there are special routers that connect to another AS. These are called *border* or *edge routers*. Within the AS, routers communicate using an IGP, such as RIP, IPX RIP, IGRP (Cisco proprietary), EIGRP (Cisco proprietary), OSPF, IS-IS, and others. The edge router communicates with the edge router of another AS using an EGP, such as the aptly named EGP or BGP.

The purpose behind using EGPs is to reduce the number of entries in the networks' routers' routing tables. If every router had to know about the existence of every other router, routing tables could quickly become unmanageable. Instead, the division of EGP and IGP allows for routers within an AS to know about only the routers within that AS and for the edge routers to know about routers between multiple ASs. The IGPs are further divided into distance vector and link-state protocols.

Distance Vector Protocols   *Distance vector protocols*, of which *Routing Information Protocol (RIP)* is the most common, simply count the number of hops (how many routers the packet must cross) to make routing decisions. RIP comes in two varieties, version 1 and version 2. The primary difference between RIP version 1 and RIP version 2 is that version 2 allows for the passing of subnet mask information in routing updates. RIP version 1 was the original IGP. It was designed for small internetworks and has the built-in limitation of allowing for up to 15 hops (other IGPs, such as Cisco's IGRP, allow for much larger networks). As the first IGP, it saw widespread usage and was included in some distributions of UNIX. By default, RIP will send a routing update every 30 seconds. This update includes the address of the destination host or network, the IP address of the gateway sending the update, and a metric (hop count) that indicates the distance to the destination.

When a router receives a routing update, it compares the new information with what is contained in the routing table. If there is a new destination network, that network is added to the routing table. Also, if an update contains a smaller metric to an existing network, that entry is replaced with the new information. If a specific route or gateway isn't heard from in 180 seconds (six routing updates), it is considered unavailable and a special message is sent to the router's neighbors indicating the route is invalid. After 270 seconds (nine routing updates), if the route still hasn't been heard from, the entry is removed from the routing table.

Loops present a problem in a routed network, just as they do in a bridged or switched network. One way that some routing protocols, including RIP, prevent loops is *split horizon.* Split horizon causes the router to send updates out every interface except the one from which it first heard about a given network. This solution is similar to the operation of a layer-2 bridge. A small modification to split horizon exists in the *poison reverse* update. Poison reverse, instead of sending an update out the interface from which a route was originally learned, sends the update with a metric of infinity (in the case of RIP, infinity is 16) so that the route will never be used.

Interior Gateway Routing Protocol (IGRP) is a Cisco proprietary distance vector routing protocol. Like RIP version 1, IGRP does not allow for the passing of subnet mask information in routing updates. Cisco later improved on IGRP by releasing *Enhanced Interior Gateway Routing Protocol (EIGRP)*, which employs both distance vector and link-state properties to determine the best path and does allow for the passing of subnet mask information. Both IGRP and EIGRP will work on only Cisco equipment. Any heterogeneous network implementation requires another routing protocol choice.

Link-State Protocols   *Link-state protocols* take into account the entire cost of the route, which includes the speed of the link as well as the distance, by learning the entire topology of the network. A link-state router sends out *link-state advertisements (LSAs)* to its neighbors to advertise a given link's cost. This advertisement is forwarded to all routers on the network, so all routers on the network receive first-hand updates. Compare this to distance vector protocols in which the update is received only by a neighbor, then put into that neighbor's routing table. That neighbor's routing table is then passed on. This allows convergence (synchronization of all routers on the network) to occur more quickly through the use of link-state protocols.

The most popular link-state protocol is *Open Shortest Path First (OSPF)*. This protocol is based on Dijkstra's algorithm, which it uses to compute the cost of different routes to the same destination. It then selects the route with the lowest cost and enters that one into the routing table. The larger the network, the more route possibilities there are, which means more CPU cycles required to calculate the best one.

OSPF is an open standard, developed by the Internet Engineering Task Force (IETF) and supports only IP routing. It is a good solution choice for larger heterogeneous networks because most router vendors support it.

Intermediate System to Intermediate System (IS-IS) is another link-state protocol, designed by the International Organization for Standardization (ISO). It is based on DECnet Phase V routing but was later modified to include support for other protocols, including TCP/IP.

	Distance Vector	**Link State**
Periodic updates	Router sends its entire routing table to its neighbors	Router sends updates to the entire network but only for those links that are directly connected
Routing table	Built on second-hand information	Built on first-hand information
Size of updates	Large	Small
Overhead	Uses more bandwidth to distribute entire routing table	Less bandwidth usage but CPU intensive
Convergence	Slow	Fast
Routing loops	Uses split-horizon, poison reverse, and timers to avoid loops	A consistent network map makes loops less likely
Routing metric	Hops	Cost

Table 1-1 provides a convenient reference of the main differences between distance vector and link-state routing protocols.

What Is a Protocol?

I had a beginning French teacher in college who taught nearly the entire course in French. She began the first class by instructing the students, "Levez-vous!" ("Stand up!") and motioning for us to stand. She then asked in English the meaning of what she had just said, and we couldn't answer because none of us yet knew French, although we had obeyed! Terms like "protocol" always make me think of that story because it's a term we use—perhaps even overuse—yet actually defining it can present a challenge.

A *protocol* is simply a set of rules governing a level of communication. Two computers cannot communicate unless they first agree on *how* to communicate. My brother-in-law once told me he thinks of everything (in networking, at least) as a protocol. The first agreement two devices must make is over what medium they will communicate: copper wire, optical cable, radio waves, and so on. That is one protocol. From there, they agree on how to frame their messages, meaning where they begin and end. This is yet another protocol.

We cover more specific protocols later on in this book. Just don't let the terminology confuse you. Basically, every piece of any communication puzzle is governed by a protocol.

Network Management

Network management is a combination of software, hardware, and operational procedures designed specifically to keep a network operational and at maximum efficiency.

Network management falls into five general areas:

- **Configuration management** This deals with installing, modifying, and tracking the various configuration parameters of network hardware and software. It also includes boot loading utilizing Boot Protocol (BOOTP) or dynamic host configuration protocol (DHCP).

- **Fault management** When a network grows beyond just a few nodes, fault management software becomes invaluable in the troubleshooting and timely repairing of faults. This is used to isolate areas where the trouble lies and generally sounds an audible alarm to alert administrative personnel to the existence of a fault. In the case of a wide area network circuit, it may alert both client-side and carrier-side personnel to the fault.

- **Security management** This type allows administrative personnel to restrict access to certain areas of the network. Security may include a hardware or software firewall system, password authentication, and levels of access.

- **Performance management** Its tools allow network administrators to monitor the number of packets, frames, or bytes passing through a given segment within the network. This data may also include the number of collisions, retransmissions, and errors incurred. On WAN segments, this helps management know whether carriers are adhering to negotiated service-level agreements (SLAs). It also defines which servers are being accessed the most and how many users are logged on at a given time.

- **Accounting management** This helps define the costs of running various parts and services of the network. It is used to measure the amount of resources consumed and may be used for billing purposes.

Network management is achieved through the placement of one or more monitors (computers running monitoring software) on the network. These monitors send out probes (packets) onto the network at specified intervals to measure various parameters, including latency and error frequency. When the packets return to the monitor, the statistics they've captured are included in a database. The most popular network monitoring protocols are *Simple Network Management Protocol (SNMP)* versions 1 and 2, and *Remote Monitoring (RMON)* specification.

CERTIFICATION OBJECTIVE 1.04

Operation and Implementation

This section deals with the steps involved in actually designing a network. There are three overall points of concern:

- Identify your network requirements.
- Design the new network structure.
- Build and test a prototype.

Identifying Your Network Requirements

Putting a network together first requires that you decide what it should do. These requirements should come from your customers, outlining exactly what work they expect to perform on the network. When deciding what the network should do, don't forget to ask your clients to take the future into consideration. A network solution that won't scale is not likely to bring you future business.

When considering future needs, include the possible phasing out of older technologies and applications, increases in the number of users, telecommuting requirements, and additional remote offices. Also, ask your clients to explain the corporate hierarchy so that you can identify major user clusters. Where will the information servers be located within the company? These are likely to be your heaviest traffic areas. Does your client's company intend to access the Internet? What is their expected usage?

You may be tasked with designing a replacement or partial replacement for an already existing network. In this case, you first need to determine what type of traffic exists on the network and how much of each type there is. For example, a particular network may employ Systems Network Architecture (SNA) for an IBM mainframe, Novell NetWare for printer and file sharing, and IP for an Internet connection.

Interviews with the users on the network can help you identify the type of applications being used and learn the perceived response time of the network. On segments for which there are complaints about slow response, a packet analyzer can offer you a peek inside the network to check for contention (too many nodes fighting for the same resources). Be sure to sample the traffic patterns over a period of a few days for an accurate assessment. Sampling the traffic during the lunch hour will not give an accurate traffic report, nor will sampling in the morning when all the computers are booting or close to quitting time when the users are rushing to finish their work.

This information will provide you with a baseline to design a solution that addresses the problems you encounter. You will also want to draw a map of the existing internetwork, including traffic flow. This will help you identify bottlenecks.

Pre-identifying faulty segments and the average time those segments stay operational (*mean time between failures*, or *MTBF*) and determining how long it generally takes to correct the fault (*mean time to repair*, or *MTTR*) will also aid you in assessing your own design once it's in place. If you increase the MTBF and decrease the MTTR, your clients will be pleased, provided your design also addresses their other needs.

Designing the New Network Structure

When all the design requirements are outlined and any existing traffic has been characterized, you are ready to begin your design. Cisco provides a three-layer model for network design. The three layers are core, distribution, and access.

The *core layer* is the backbone of the network. This is crucial to the stability of the network and should provide for redundancy and fault tolerance. Because the core is where all the corporate data transfer occurs, the equipment you select should have low latency and good manageability. Access lists and other filters should be avoided in this layer.

The *distribution layer* separates the access layer from the core layer. This layer has the job of implementing policy, security, defining areas, and workgroups; and routing between them and media translation (for example, Ethernet to Token Ring). This is where most access lists and quality of service implementations should be made.

The *access layer* provides a way for users to come into contact with the network. LAN switches at this layer segment the LAN to avoid too many collisions on Ethernet or to reduce the number of nodes requiring the token on Token Ring. This layer may also include banks of modems or ISDN equipment for remote users to dial into.

Determine the hardware requirements for your design, including the infrastructure cabling, and routing, switching, and bridging equipment. Table 1-2 provides a convenient reminder of where a router instead of a bridge or switch may be useful. It offers a guideline to help avoid contention problems in the flat (switched or bridged) segments of your network.

When your hardware has been selected, you'll need to design a network-layer addressing scheme (maybe more than one scheme, depending on how many routed protocols you include). Take into account how many, if any, users on your network will require Internet access. Will you assign

TABLE 1-2	Protocol	Maximum Number of Workstations
	IP	500
Scalability Constraints for Flat Networks	IPX	300
	AppleTalk	200
	NetBIOS	200
	Mixed	200

routable addresses or use private addressing with NAT? Will you assign addresses manually or use an automated method, such as DHCP?

You will need to decide one or more routing protocols and bridging protocols to allow the different components on the network to know of each other's existence and to determine the flow of traffic. You will also want to implement a network management strategy here, possibly by using SNMP or RMON software to collect network statistics and report faults. Network management includes the human factor. Document how you want users to report problems.

Building and Testing a Prototype

When your design is complete, you may opt to build a prototype (a smaller representation of your network design) or start a pilot program (build the network to scale with basic functionality and begin using it, without removing the old network). In the case of a large-scale design, a prototype is probably more feasible.

In a prototyping situation, be sure to build those segments of the network that had the worst MTBF record to test how your design improves it. Also be sure to test those portions of the network that are most critical to your customer's business.

QUESTIONS AND ANSWERS

Your customer is planning to incorporate Internet access in all workstations in the business. They currently run Novell NetWare.	Novell NetWare 5 includes a TCP/IP stack, which can run concurrently with Novell's IPX/SPX protocol or alone. You may also recommend a complete paradigm shift to the TCP/IP standard.
Your customer is currently on a totally flat (bridged) network. During periods of high usage, the network is unbearably slow.	Determine whether there is a lot of broadcast traffic. If there is, a router will help to break up the traffic. If not, further breaking up the segments with bridges should help.
Your company, which runs AppleTalk on Macintosh computers, has just been bought by another company that has standardized on the PC, running TCP/IP. You will continue to use Macintosh but need to be able to share files with the new owner via a wide area connection.	Installing a TCP/IP stack on the Macintosh computers will allow communication across the WAN.

CERTIFICATION SUMMARY

The CCDA exam will present you with questions challenging your ability to design around customer requirements, which may include technological and monetary constraints. Therefore, you will be expected to have some underlying familiarity with the media types and protocols you're presented with. In this chapter, you've read an overview of LAN and WAN terms, concepts, and technologies.

The Sylvan exam will ask you to apply your knowledge of the Cisco design model, recommend particular lines of equipment to accomplish particular jobs, and suggest routing and routed protocols. A thorough understanding of what's presented in this chapter will prepare you to fully respond to the scenarios the exam challenges you with.

✓ TWO-MINUTE DRILL

- ❑ The OSI model is a seven-layer model.
- ❑ The OSI model aids in design and troubleshooting.
- ❑ Layer 7, the application layer, consists of the programs running on the network.
- ❑ Layer 6, the presentation layer, is the formatting of data.
- ❑ Layer 5, the session layer, keeps track of multiple data streams.
- ❑ Layer 4, the transport layer, keeps frames in order and handles error checking.
- ❑ Layer 3, the network layer, allows for node addressing.
- ❑ Layer 2, the data-link layer, defines framing of data.
- ❑ Layer 1, the physical layer, covers the physical network components.
- ❑ The Internet Assigned Numbers Authority (IANA) has defined blocks of address space that are only for private use: 10.*x.x.x*; 172.16.*x.x*–172.31.*x.x*; 192.168.*x.x*.
- ❑ NAT allows for privately addressed networks to access the Internet.
- ❑ Design networks use a top-down approach.
- ❑ Voice and video are delay sensitive.
- ❑ Ethernet is a broadcast medium on a bus topology. It uses CSMA/CD and runs at 10 Mbps. Fast Ethernet runs at 100 Mbps. Gigabit Ethernet runs at 1,000 Mbps.
- ❑ Every new node on Ethernet increases the chance of collision.
- ❑ Token Ring is an IBM standard. It runs at either 4 Mbps or 16 Mbps.
- ❑ Token Ring passes a "token" to each node to allow transmission on the network.
- ❑ Every new node on a Token Ring network increases latency.

❑   Token bus is a broadcast medium that uses token passing.

❑   FDDI runs at 100 Mbps and uses counter-rotating, fiber-optic rings for redundancy.

❑   Point-to-point circuits connect to endpoints.

❑   PPP is used over synchronous and asynchronous connections.

❑   LCP frames are used to establish a PPP link between nodes, and then NCP frames determine what network protocols will be used.

❑   Cisco's default serial link protocol is HDLC.

❑   X.25 was one of the first successful WAN protocols.

❑   X.25 is the predecessor of Frame Relay.

❑   X.25 provides error checking.

❑   Frame Relay devices are either DTE or DCE.

❑   DTE devices are usually equipment at the customer's premises.

❑   DCE devices are usually carrier packet switches.

❑   Frame Relay is protocol independent.

❑   Frame Relay does not perform error or flow control.

❑   Frame Relay uses CRC to ensure data integrity.

❑   Frame Relay is a connection-oriented, packet-switched technology.

❑   CIR is the maximum guaranteed throughput for a WAN link.

❑   In Frame Relay, you may occasionally "burst" over CIR.

❑   If you burst over CIR and congestion occurs, your packets may be marked "discard eligible."

❑   FECN and BECN are two congestion notification mechanisms.

❑   Frame Relay and X.25 both use SVCs and PVCs.

❑   An SVC requires setup and tear-down every time it is used.

❑   SVCs are often used to create a second pathway to relieve congestion.

❑   PVCs are permanent connections through the cloud and do not require setup or tear-down.

❑   DLCIs keep track of PVCs and are only locally significant.

❏ PVCs are used to break up a single physical circuit into multiple connections.

❏ LMI allows a customer's router to request updates on its PVCs.

❏ There are three types of LMI: Cisco, ANSI Annex D, and Q933a.

❏ An LMI mismatch can cause a loss of communication.

❏ ISDN offers voice and data over the same medium.

❏ EMI causes problems on analog circuits. Digital circuits are less susceptible.

❏ ISDN lines can be up to 18,000 feet long or up to 36,000 feet long with a repeater.

❏ ISDN can be either a BRI or PRI. BRIs have two B channels and one D channel. PRIs have 23 B channels (30 in Europe) and one D channel.

❏ Three requirements for configuring ISDN are directory numbers, SPIDs, and switch type.

❏ Modems can provide for an inexpensive, low-bandwidth WAN solution.

❏ Bridges are layer-2 devices that break up collision domains.

❏ Bridges may filter, forward, or flood frames.

❏ Transparent bridging is used in broadcast media, such as Ethernet.

❏ Multiple paths may cause loops. Loops can be avoided by use of the Spanning Tree Protocol.

❏ Source route bridging uses the RIF to make forwarding decisions.

❏ SR/TLB allows one media type to be translated to another, but there is no approved standard for such translation.

❏ SR/T uses the RII bit to determine whether to source route bridge or transparent bridge.

❏ Routers make forwarding decisions based on network-layer information and are required between different media types.

❏ Routers advertise their own existence and share routing table information with other routers via routing protocols.

❏ Routing protocols may be either Interior Gateway Protocols or Exterior Gateway Protocols.

❑ EGPs communicate information between edge routers of autonomous systems.

❑ IGPs communicate information within autonomous systems.

❑ Distance vector IGPs count hops to make routing decisions and periodically share their entire routing table with their neighbors.

❑ Link-state IGPs make decisions based on the cost of the route and pass on updates, as required, to the entire network.

❑ A protocol is a set of rules that governs communication.

❑ Network management involves providing for the configuration of network devices, repair of faults, security, performance analysis, and accounting.

❑ SNMP and RMON are the two most popular remote management protocols.

❑ The three steps in implementing a network are identify customer requirements, design the network, and build and test a prototype.

❑ Determine a baseline for performance to compare your design with the one being replaced.

❑ Cisco's three-layer network design model consists of the core, distribution, and access layers.

SELF TEST

The following Self Test questions will help you measure your understanding of the material presented in this chapter. Read all the choices carefully because there may be more than one correct answer. Choose all correct answers for each question.

1. How does the OSI model aid networkers?

    A. It provides an exact map to follow.

    B. It provides a reference map to aid in troubleshooting.

    C. Following the steps of the OSI will result in a workable model.

    D. The OSI model is useless.

2. You're designing a network for a company that intends to use it for videoconferencing. What should be of primary concern in this regard?

    A. High bandwidth should take precedence over all other concerns.

    B. Videoconferencing automatically means the company will need an ATM backbone.

    C. Videoconferencing should be attempted only with a dedicated point-to-point circuit and videoconferencing equipment.

    D. Too much packet latency will cause a degradation in quality.

3. Your client has a LAN already in place using private address space and doesn't want to readdress the entire network but still wants to add Internet access. What solution will you suggest?

    A. Multiple address on each node will allow Internet access and keep the current addressing.

    B. Private addressing space is administered by the IANA.

    C. The private address scheme can be used in conjunction with NAT.

    D. A new addressing scheme will have to be put in place.

4. How does an Ethernet network pass frames from node to node?

    A. The token carries the frame across the network.

    B. A segmentwide broadcast carries the frame to every node.

    C. The frame is addressed and sent to its destination.

    D. Frames are bridged across a network.

5. When designing for a Token Ring network you should be concerned about what? (Choose all that apply.)

   A. Excess traffic and collisions as multiple stations attempt to transmit

   B. How and whether the Spanning Tree Protocol is implemented

   C. The number of workstations on the network

   D. The speed of each node's network interface

6. Your customer has a multivendor network, including routers from Cisco and Nortel Networks. How might this setup affect your choice of WAN protocols between the two?

   A. You'll have to use something other than the default serial link protocol.

   B. OSPF makes sense as a nonproprietary protocol.

   C. There shouldn't be any problem with using the default protocols.

   D. It won't work unless both ends have routers from the same manufacturer.

7. Your client has an existing WAN that uses X.25 with PVCs. The company would like to upgrade to a new technology that will offer the same or better performance than its existing WAN but with similar features. What will you recommend?

   A. Frame Relay offers PVCs and other significant improvements over X.25.

   B. Switching to SVCs instead of PVCs will improve performance.

   C. An ISDN PRI will provide greater bandwidth.

   D. FDDI will provide the best performance.

8. Your customers have a Frame Relay WAN that they use for data as well as voice. They're unhappy with the delayed performance of the voice and would like you to suggest a solution.

   A. A second T1 strictly for voice is the best solution.

   B. They should use the Frame Relay for data and use phones for voice.

   C. A traffic filter that assigns highest priority to voice packets is a good start.

   D. ISDN would provide a better voice signal.

9. Your company has three remote offices that all connect to a single headquarters. The only WAN traffic consists of intracompany e-mail and daily receipts at the close of business. The current WAN solutions include T1 point-to-point circuits to each office. How might you suggest an improvement in cost-effectiveness?

A. Get rid of the T1s and install ISDN BRIs at all the remotes to have them dial into the host only when there is data to be transmitted.

B. The use of multiple T1 circuits is exactly the right design for this scenario.

C. A single Frame Relay circuit from the host could be divided into three PVCs to reach each remote.

D. With such minimal traffic, a modem solution will suffice.

10. When a segment of a broadcast medium becomes overtaxed with traffic, how can you effect relief?

A. Physically divide the network with a transparent bridge.

B. Remove the nodes causing the excess traffic.

C. Subnet the nodes on the segment to logically divide them.

D. Reconfigure the bridge with access lists.

11. What special issues should a designer consider when including redundant paths in a bridged network on a broadcast bus?

A. Redundant paths allow for load balancing.

B. Redundant paths will cause broadcast storms.

C. Redundant paths are indicative of a bad design.

D. Redundant paths can cause endless loops.

12. What special issues should a designer consider when including redundant paths in a bridged Token Ring network?

A. Redundant paths are indicative of a bad design.

B. Redundant paths are automatically supported by Token Ring bridges.

C. Redundant paths can cause endless loops.

D. Redundant paths will cause broadcast storms.

13. Your client's current network design is one large autonomous system. The routers are nearing routing table capacity limits. What would you recommend as a remedy?

A. Divide the current design into multiple autonomous systems to allow for smaller routing tables within each system.

B. Add RAM to each router.

C. Reduce the number of protocols running on the network.

D. Use higher-capacity routers.

14. Your customers have an existing LAN that uses a non-Cisco brand of router. They've just bought a company that uses Cisco routers and want to fully integrate the two LANs. What points should you keep in mind when developing your design? (Choose two.)

    A. The two LANs should have at least one network-layer protocol in common.

    B. One company may have to change its network-layer protocol to match that of the other.

    C. ISDN would be a good WAN choice.

    D. The routing protocol should be supported by both router brands.

15. Your customer wants a solution to monitor and analyze the network utilization. What can you suggest? (Choose all that apply.)

    A. SNMP

    B. RMON

    C. A dedicated monitoring station

    D. TCP/IP

16. Your client wants you to completely redesign its current network solution to make it perform better. How should you begin this task? (Choose two.)

    A. Buy all Cisco routers.

    B. Include a fiber-optic backbone.

    C. Record a baseline for the current network.

    D. Identify high-traffic areas.

17. You want to use the Cisco model in your next network design. What are the layers? (Choose all that apply.)

    A. Distribution

    B. Presentation

    C. Core

    D. Access

18. You've just completed a design for a very large network and need to test before implementation. How do you recommend testing?

    A. Pilot the new network.

    B. Implement the new network and make a list of all issues that arise.

    C. Build a prototype.

    D. Simulate the new network using software.

19. When you are building a prototype, are there certain segments you should focus on?

    A. Plug all the routers back to back to make sure they operate correctly.

    B. Build and test all the segments that are critical to your customer's business.

    C. Test everything.

    D. No testing is necessary.

SELF TEST ANSWERS

1. ☑ **B.** The OSI model allows networkers to eliminate various parts of the communication process during troubleshooting to further locate the problem.
   ☒ **A** is incorrect because the OSI model is not a cookbook with a recipe for a perfect network. **C** is incorrect because OSI is a seven-layer model, not a seven-step program. **D** is incorrect because networkers often use the OSI model as a common reference.

2. ☑ **D.** Latency can severely disrupt video and voice transmission because they are both time sensitive. Care should be taken to design around this constraint.
   ☒ **A** is incorrect because bandwidth cannot always compensate for a bad design and can easily use up your budget. **B** is incorrect because videoconferencing can take place over any medium, including dial-up, although there may be quality tradeoffs. **C** is incorrect because there already exist many successful implementations of LAN videoconferencing.

3. ☑ **C.** NAT was designed to provide exactly this type of solution.
   ☒ **A** is incorrect because multiple addresses also require more hardware. **B** is incorrect because, although the IANA does administer private address space, this does not provide a solution to the problem. **D** is incorrect because NAT will allow the private addressing to stay in place yet still allow Internet access.

4. ☑ **B.** Ethernet is a broadcast medium. When a node transmits, all nodes on the segment receive the same information, but all but the intended recipient discard it.
   ☒ **A** is incorrect because tokens exist only in Token Ring and token bus networks. **C** is incorrect because, although the statement is true, it does not address the question of *how* the information is carried. **D** is incorrect because an Ethernet segment may or may not have a bridge.

5. ☑ **C and D.** Because a node may transmit only when it possesses the token, as more nodes are added to the network, the token must make more stops, and all nodes on the ring must be of the same speed.
   ☒ **A** is incorrect because only one node may transmit at a time in Token Ring. **B** is incorrect because the Spanning Tree Protocol is implemented only on bridges.

6. ☑ **A.** HDLC is Cisco's default protocol, but there is no established standard, so it may not work with Nortel equipment.
   ☒ **B** is incorrect because OSPF is a routing protocol, not a WAN protocol. **C** is incorrect because Cisco's default protocol is not standardized. **D** is incorrect because multivendor networks do indeed work.

7. ☑ **A.** Frame Relay is a streamlined and faster technology than X.25 and also offers PVCs.
☒ **B** is incorrect because SVCs do not provide a performance advantage over PVCs. **C** is incorrect because a PRI offers the same speed as Frame Relay but without PVCs. **D** is incorrect because FDDI is not a WAN protocol.

8. ☑ **C.** A traffic filter to assign high priority to voice packets is the best solution because it allows them to keep their existing technology with no further investment.
☒ **A** is incorrect because a second T1 would likely destroy any economic benefit they're trying to achieve by using their WAN connection for long distance. **B** is incorrect because it's likely the whole reason for them to use their WAN for voice is to reduce long distance costs. **D** is incorrect because, although it is true, Frame Relay can provide quite acceptable voice quality and will not cause any further expense.

9. ☑ **C.** Frame Relay allows a single circuit at the host to be subdivided into smaller circuits to service multiple sites. Full T1 bandwidth is not necessary for this amount of traffic.
☒ **A** is incorrect because of the periodic e-mail. This would constantly bring the ISDN up, which could easily cost as much as the T1s. **B** is incorrect because the amount of traffic over the WAN is too small to justify the amount of bandwidth. **D** is also incorrect because of the periodic nature of e-mail. Although such a design would work, long distance charges could offset any savings from the Frame Relay solution, and modems are usually too slow to trust to mission-critical transmissions.

10. ☑ **A.** Adding a bridge will physically divide the segment and prevent traffic from traversing the entire segment unless it is actually destined for the side beyond the bridge.
☒ **B** could work, but it is rarely a reasonable choice because more traffic usually means more network usage, which indicates a need to grow the network. **C** is incorrect because layer-3 addressing has nothing to do with the amount of traffic on the wire. **D** is incorrect because a bridge cannot be configured with access lists.

11. ☑ **D.** On a broadcast bus, multiple paths can cause endless loops as each bridge receives frames from other bridges in the network. Implementing the Spanning Tree Protocol can prevent these loops while still providing redundancy.
☒ **A** is incorrect because bridges do not load balance. **B** is incorrect because, although broadcast storms are most definitely a problem, the real issue is the creation of an endless loop, of which a broadcast storm is the worst. **C** is incorrect because redundancy is very often a desired quality in a network.

12. ☑ **B.** On a Token Ring network, multiple paths are automatically supported by the inclusion of the RIF in source route bridging frames.

    ☒ **A** is incorrect because redundancy is very often a desired quality in a network. **C** is incorrect because redundant paths never cause endless loops on Token Ring networks. **D** is incorrect because broadcast storms do not happen on Token Ring networks.

13. ☑ **A.** Dividing the current network into multiple autonomous systems will reduce the number of entries in each routing table.

    ☒ **B** may work for a while but is really a "bandage" solution to a deeper problem. **C** is incorrect because, although each running protocol must be stored in its own table, the problem does not indicate that more than one protocol is currently running. **D** also might work, but again, this does not solve the real problem of a bad design.

14. ☑ **A and D.** The two LANs will not be able to share information if they don't have at least one network-layer protocol in common. The Internet, for example, works only because all nodes that use the Internet route TCP/IP. Also, in order for the two networks to know about each other, they must have a routing protocol in common, and it must be supported by both router brands. OSPF would be a good choice.

    ☒ **B** is incorrect because both LANs can keep their current network-layer protocols, although one or both may have to adopt a second protocol to intercommunicate. **C** is incorrect because there is no information about the bandwidth requirements or distance between the two sites.

15. ☑ **A, B, and C.** SNMP and RMON are the two most popular network monitoring protocols, and a dedicated monitoring station is required to store the statistics.

    ☒ **D** is incorrect because TCP/IP doesn't offer a network monitoring solution.

16. ☑ **C and D.** You must record a baseline for the current network in order to be able to compare your design later. Identifying high traffic areas will allow you to intelligently choose components to handle the traffic.

    ☒ **A** is incorrect because it assumes new equipment will be necessary, which is not necessarily the case. **B** is incorrect because it also assumes that a fiber-optic backbone isn't already in place.

17. ☑ **A, C, and D.** The core, distribution, and access layers are the three layers, in order, of the Cisco design model.

    ☒ **B** is incorrect because the presentation layer is part of the OSI model.

18. ☑ C. For large network designs, the best test choice is usually a prototype because the cost of a full-scale implementation or pilot program could be prohibitive.

    ☒ A is incorrect because a pilot program for a large network is usually cost prohibitive. B is incorrect because implementing a network that hasn't been tested is asking for trouble. D is incorrect because, although a software simulation is a good design tool, it cannot fully test real-world situations.

19. ☑ B. When you can't build the entire network to scale for test purposes, you should at least focus on those segments that are critical to your customer's business.

    ☒ A is incorrect because testing whether the routers work doesn't test the network design. C is incorrect because testing the entire network negates the cost-effectiveness of building a prototype. D is incorrect because testing is a very important aspect of network design.

2

Overview of Routed Protocols

The importance of data sharing is evident in the world around us. Businesses would not be as efficient without the ability to provide multiple users access to the same files or to facilitate interpersonal communication via e-mail or voice- and videoconferencing. But simply wiring computers together cannot make them communicate, just as two people who speak different languages would not be able to communicate via telephone. In order for these two people to communicate, they must agree on and learn a common language.

For two devices to be linked and communicate, they also must speak the same language. Just as in human language, protocols that allow this communication are abundant and rely heavily on both parties' following certain rules. This chapter covers several of the more important communications protocols, with an emphasis on the Internet Protocol (IP).

CERTIFICATION OBJECTIVE 2.01

TCP/IP

Transmission Control Protocol/Internet Protocol (TCP/IP) is the standard protocol suite of the Internet and is the most widely used protocol in the world today. Currently, TCP/IP is mostly thought of in terms of version 4, which is the version in use on the Internet. Version 6 is in development and expected to replace version 4 in the near future. Figure 2-1 compares the TCP/IP suite with the Open Systems Interconnection (OSI) model.

Brief History of IP

In the 1960s, Defense Advanced Research Projects Agency (DARPA) in the United States noted that the multiple computers that existed in the military were from different vendors. At that time, interoperability between multiple vendors didn't exist. Expansion of a certain computer system meant purchasing more equipment from the same vendor that sold the computer in the first place. Because allowing these different computers to share information

| FIGURE 2-1 | The TCP/IP suite compared with the OSI model |

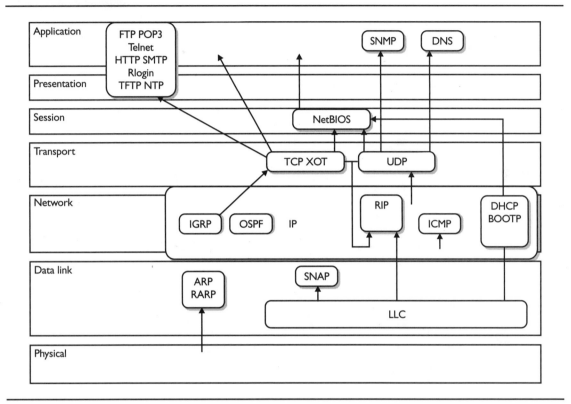

would allow less duplication of effort and faster information processing time, the Department of Defense (DoD) required DARPA to define a common communication system to allow the heterogeneous equipment to work together.

DARPA's original experiment was to interconnect the University of California at Los Angeles, the University of California at Santa Barbara, the University of Utah, and SRI International. When this experiment proved successful, more sites were added to the network, which was named ARPAnet. By 1972, there were 50 nodes and 20 hosts on the ARPAnet. The developers staged a successful demonstration of their communications protocol suite, Network Control Protocol (NCP).

In 1978, the OSI Reference Model was developed by the International Organization for Standardization (ISO). Its goal was to define a standard that could be used for the development of open systems and as a comparative platform between proposed systems.

Here is a recap of the layers of the OSI model:

- Physical layer, 1
- Data-link layer, 2
- Network layer, 3
- Transport layer, 4
- Session layer, 5
- Presentation layer, 6
- Application layer, 7

The principles applied when it was decided how the layers should be divided were these:

- A layer should be created only when a new level of abstraction is needed.
- Each layer should provide a well-defined function.
- The function of each layer should be chosen so that it defines internationally standardized protocols.
- The layer boundaries should be chosen to minimize the information flow across layer interfaces.
- Distinct functions should be defined in separate layers, but the number of layers should be small enough that the architecture does not become unwieldy.

Part of TCP/IP's popularity results because it was included in the BSD release of UNIX. UNIX itself owes a good deal of its popularity to its price—it is free. Most universities adopted BSD UNIX and, therefore, had access to the TCP/IP suite. In addition, vendors grew tired of waiting for the development and maturing of OSI protocols. And considering that there was already a mature TCP/IP protocol suite, several vendors started developing flavors of this suite to run on microcomputers, as well as applications that made use of networking ability.

In 1983, ARPAnet itself converted to the use of TCP/IP. ARPAnet continued to grow, including more university and military networks; and by 1986, all major universities, the military network (MILNET), some research facilities, and a few international sites were included. ARPAnet eventually gave way to the Internet, which now carries more commercial than scientific traffic.

How Does TCP/IP Work?

TCP/IP works by assigning a unique number, via software, to every addressable node on the network. The current version of IP (version 4) is made up of 32-bit addresses. Although computers view the 32 bits as a series of ones and zeros, humans find it easier to refer to them in decimal format. The most usual way of depicting an IP address is in dotted decimal format, as in the example address 192.168.10.1. To a computer, this address would look like 11000000101010000000101000000001, which isn't very decipherable to most humans. Rather, we divide the 32 bits into groups of 8 bits each, called *octets*, and divide them with decimal points.

In the preceding example, 11000000101010000000101000000001 would become 11000000.10101000.00001010.00000001. Then, each octet is converted to binary for ease of reading. The pattern 11000000 becomes 192; 10101000 becomes 168; 00001010 becomes 10; and 00000001 becomes 1.

This section continues after a recap of how the binary and decimal numbering systems relate to each other.

Binary-to-Decimal Conversion

If you are already comfortable with converting from binary to decimal and back, you may skip this section. You should expect a few questions on this topic on the CCDA exam, however, so it is presented here as a review.

We grew up with the decimal numbering system. The word *decimal* means powers of 10. That is, we have 10 digits in our numbering system: 0, 1, 2, 3, 4, 5, 6, 7, 8, and 9. In order to count any higher than 9, we must begin combining digits. Hence, 9 plus 1 equals 10. Note that the numeral 10 is made up of two digits, one and zero, instead of a single symbol to denote "ten."

Binary, which means powers of two, is simply a numbering system that includes two digits: 0 and 1. When we run out of digits, we must start to combine, so in binary, 1 plus 1 equals 10. Now we see that the symbol "10" may mean "ten" or "two," depending on the numbering system in use. To further clarify what system is in use, for the rest of this section we refer to decimal numbers with a base-ten notation, as in 10_{10} (ten) and to binary numbers with a base-two notation, as in 10_2 (two).

Remember back in elementary school when we learned about the base-ten numbering system for a moment. We were instructed that the first place to the left of the decimal point was the ones place, next was the tens place, then the hundreds place, and so on. We didn't know it then, but that rule was based on a mathematical principle. Remember that decimal means powers of ten. Ten to the zero power equals one ($10^0 = 1$), ten to the one power equals ten ($10^1 = 10$), and ten to the two power equals one hundred ($10^2 = 100$). The same holds true in binary, but the values of each place have changed.

In binary, two to the zero power equals one ($2^0 = 1$), two to the one power equals two ($2^1 = 2$), and two to the two power equals four ($2^2 = 4$). Because IP addresses are broken into octets, we generally only have to compute out to eight places, beginning at 0 and ending at 7; therefore, the largest value will be two to the seven power ($2^7 = 128$). Table 2-1 can help illustrate this.

TABLE 2-1 Powers of Two and How They Relate to IP Addresses

Power of two	2^7	2^6	2^5	2^4	2^3	2^2	2^1	2^0
Value	128	64	32	16	8	4	2	1
Bit placement	10000000	01000000	00100000	00010000	00001000	00000100	00000010	00000001

e x a m

ⓌatCh *If you're like me, you haven't been doing decimal-to-binary conversion since kindergarten, so it's not exactly second nature. But understanding how IP addresses and masks relate to bits is absolutely necessary when you are working with TCP/IP, and this will show up several times on the CCDA exam. Converting numbers is time consuming, and because the CCDA exam is timed, you don't want to put yourself in jeopardy by spending all your time converting. You can give yourself a hand by writing out a table like the one in Table 2-2.*

Another table that would be useful to write out ahead of time is that of the common classless interdomain routing (CIDR) values and their corresponding masks. A sample is shown in Table 2-2. CIDR is covered in the subsection "The Role of the Mask."

TABLE 2-2	CIDR	Mask
	/8	255.0.0.0
Handy Table of CIDR and Masks	/9	255.128.0.0
	/10	255.192.0.0
	/11	255.224.0.0
	/12	255.240.0.0
	/13	255.248.0.0
	/14	255.252.0.0
	/15	255.255.254.0
	/16	255.255.0.0
	/17	255.255.128.0
	/18	255.255.192.0
	/19	255.255.224.0
	/20	255.255.240.0
	/21	255.255.248.0
	/22	255.255.252.0
	/23	255.255.254.0

CIDR	Mask
/24	255.255.255.0
/25	255.255.255.128
/26	255.255.255.192
/27	255.255.255.224
/28	255.255.255.240
/29	255.255.255.248
/30	255.255.255.252
/31	N/A

Based on this table, we can see that, whenever the bit in a given place is set (turned to 1), the value of that place is added to the value of the total octet. For example, in the bit pattern 01100011, the leftmost bit is 0, so we *won't* add 128 (2^7) to the final value. The next bit *is* set, so we'll add the value of that place (64) to the final sum (0+64). The next bit is also set, and its value is 32, so we'll add 32 to the sum of the octet (0+64+32). Continuing on, the next three bits are all 0, so we won't add 16, 8, or 4 to our octet (0+64+32+0+0+0). The last two bits are set, with values of 2 and 1, respectively. Adding those to our octet (0+64+32+0+0+0+2+1), we see that the value for the entire eight bits is 99.

Converting binary back to decimal is just as easy. Begin with any value up to 255. It takes all eight bits set to 1 to equal 255, so any value over 255 would have to be represented by more than eight bits and, therefore, more than one octet. For this exercise, let's use 215. Again, start with the value of the leftmost bit, 128. Can it be subtracted from our beginning number, 215? Yes, it can: 215 minus 128 is 87 (215 – 128 = 87). Continuing to the right, can the next bit place value (64) be subtracted from 87? Again, it can: 87 minus 64 is 23 (215 – 128 – 64 = 23). If we continue this to the end of the octet, we see that 32 *cannot* be subtracted from 23 (215 – 128 – 64 – 0 = 23); 16 can be subtracted, which leaves us 7 (215 – 128 – 64 – 0 – 16 = 7). Eight cannot be subtracted from 7 (215–128–64–0–16–0 = 7), but 4 can be, leaving us 3 (215 – 128 – 64 – 0 – 16 – 0 – 4 = 3). Two can be subtracted from 3, leaving us 1 (215 – 128 – 64 – 0 – 16 – 0 – 4 – 2 = 1); and 1 can be subtracted from 1, leaving 0 (215 − 128 − 64 − 0 − 16 − 4 − 2 − 1 = 0). In total, we had to subtract 128, 64, 16, 4, 2, and 1. Using Table 2-1, if you were to place a 1 in the fields that corresponded to the values we subtracted, you would end up with the bit pattern 11010111_2, which equals 215_{10}.

Since practice makes perfect, some practice exercises follow.

EXERCISE 2-1

TCP/IP

Convert the following binary numbers to decimal. The answers are in the right column.

Binary	Decimal
00000001	1
01011001	89
10000011	131
10101010	170
11111111	255

Convert the following decimal numbers to binary.

Decimal	Binary
3	00000011
127	01111111
42	00101010
197	11000101
254	11111110

In some cases, the network administrator may choose not to assign IP addresses to nodes statically, but rather to let a server assign them as required. In such a case, when a workstation boots, it transmits a DHCDISCOVER packet to locate a Dynamic Host Configuration Protocol (DHCP) server. This is a broadcast packet that advertises the workstation's MAC address. When the

DHCP or Boot Protocol (BOOTP) server is located, an IP address is selected from a pool and sent back to the workstation.

Every IP address is divided into two parts, network and node. Before the advent of subnetting, the network portion of an address could be recognized based on the class of the IP address. In *classful addressing*, all addresses that begin with a 0 in the leftmost bit place of the most significant octet are Class A addresses. All addresses that start with 10 are Class B, and all addresses that start with 110 are Class C. Likewise, Class D and Class E addresses begin with 1110 and 11110, respectively. Converting the preceding binary values to decimal, we can see that Class A addresses run from 1.0.0.0 to 126.255.255.255; Class B addresses begin at 128.0.0.0 and run through 191.255.255.255; Class C begins at 192.0.0.0 and runs through 223.255.255.255; Class D ranges from 224.0.0.0 through 239.255.255.255; and Class E is from 240.0.0.0 through 254.255.255.255. The 127.0.0.0 network is reserved.

Note that the addressing of Class A networks does *not* start at 0.0.0.0, nor does Class E end at 255.255.255.255. One of the rules of TCP/IP is that all zeros and all ones may not be used in addressing. These *are* valid addresses, but they have special meanings and so are not allowed.

Classful addressing is mostly obsolete since the introduction of subnetting, but the terminology has stayed with us.

The Role of the Mask

Historically, each class had a mask that was used by a router or computer to separate the network portion from the node portion of the address. The natural mask of a Class A network is 255.0.0.0, which means that the first eight bits of the address are regarded as the network portion, and everything else is the node. Class A networks were reserved for very large networks because they allow up to 16,777,214 nodes. Because most networks don't have anywhere near that many addressable nodes and because there are only 126 Class A networks in existence, these were given out very rarely.

Class B networks' natural mask is 255.255.0.0, so the first 16 bits are used for the network address. Class B networks are the next size down from Class A, with up to 65,534 nodes supported.

Class C networks are the smallest of the assignable classes, although subnetting now allows assigning of even smaller network addresses. Their natural mask is 255.255.255.0, which regards the first 24 bits as the network portion. Class C addressing supports up to 254 nodes.

Class D addressing is reserved for multicasting, such as when routing protocols advertise network information; and Class E is reserved for testing. Table 2-3 provides a convenient reference.

When interest in the Internet began to skyrocket, the Internet Assigned Number Authority (IANA) realized that without some relief, the Internet would run out of numbers to assign. TCP/IP was popular in the use of LANs, metropolitan area networks (MANs), and private WANs; but if any of these networks ever wanted to access the Internet, there was a risk of two networks using the same numbering system. To allow for the continued use of TCP/IP on private networks as well as remove the threat of introducing identical addressing schemes to the Internet, the IANA set aside several blocks of IP addresses that are for private use only. These addresses are not allowed to traverse the public Internet.

The Class A reserved range is from 10.0.0.0 through 10.255.255.255. For Class B networks, the range from 172.16.0.0 through 172.31.255.255 is allowed. And for Class C networks, the range from 192.168.0.0 through 192.168.255.255 is reserved for private use only. Note that Classes B and C also allow for more addressable nodes than would be allowed if these were public addresses. For example, the natural mask of a Class C

TABLE 2-3		Classful Addressing Ranges		
Class	**Range**	**Natural Mask**	**Number of Networks**	**Number of Hosts**
A	1.0.0.0– 127.255.255.255	255.0.0.0	126	16,777,214
B	128.0.0.0– 191.255.255.255	255.255.0.0	49,151	65,534
C	192.0.0.0– 223.255.255.255	255.255.255.0	14,680,063	254

is 255.255.255.0. If that were applied to the address 192.168.10.0, only the range 192.168.10.1 through 192.168.10.254 could be used. But because the reserved address space opens up the last two octets instead of just the last one, we can have 254 *networks* with up to 254 nodes *each!*

Besides this reserved address space, another tool was developed to maximize the efficiency of the addresses that were assigned: subnetting. There are many companies that desire Internet access but don't have enough addressable nodes to qualify for an entire Class C network address. Suppose a company has only five computers and wants each of them to have Internet access. It would be a great waste to assign an entire Class C. *Subnetting* allows us to use bits that would normally be reserved for node addressing as part of the network address.

To continue our example of the company with only five computers, let's assume it has petitioned for Internet access and has been assigned the address space 215.60.31.0 with a mask of 255.255.255.248. That's a different looking mask from the natural masks we covered earlier. If we were to convert it to bits, it would be 11111111.11111111.11111111.11111000.

The term *mask* refers to what it does with the network address. There are a few logical binary operations that can be done in electronics. Masking uses the logical "and" function. When you compare two bits, if they are both 1, the result is 1. If either or both of them is 0, the result is 0. If we logically "and" the binary version of our address 215.60.31.0 to the binary version of our mask 255.255.255.248, we'll see how the router or computer sees the node address.

11010111.00111100.00011111.00000000 (215.60.31.0)
11111111.11111111.11111111.11111000 (255.255.255.248)
11010111.00111100.00011111.00000000 (215.60.31.0)

We ended up with the same result as when we started. So what have we proved? We'll find out. Note that the last three bits of the mask are zeros. Suppose, then, that the last three bits of the address were *not* zeros and we assigned the node address 215.60.31.1 to one computer, 215.60.31.2 to another computer, and so on through 215.6.31.5. Also, one address in our space must go to our Internet service provider (ISP); otherwise, we won't be able to access it. So our ISP is assigned 215.60.31.6.

The next address is 215.60.31.7, but let's see what that looks like in binary:

11010111.00111100.00011111.00000111 (215.60.31.7, address)
11111111.11111111.11111111.11111000 (255.255.255.248, mask)
11010111.00111100.00011111.00000000 (215.60.31.0, still the same network)

Note that the last three bits are all set to one, and recall that our mask is all ones *except* the last three bits. This means that we are free to use any of the last three bits for our addressing. However, the all-zeros and all-ones combinations are reserved. The all-zeros address (215.60.31.0) is our network address. You may find it useful to think of this as the address of the actual wire. The all-ones address is the broadcast address. This is used to communicate with all nodes on the network.

We can't use 215.60.31.7 because it's our broadcast address, so suppose we add another computer to our network and give it the address 215.60.31.8. What would that look like in binary?

11010111.00111100.00011111.00001000 (215.60.31.8, address)
11111111.11111111.11111111.11111000 (255.255.255.248, mask)
11010111.00111100.00011111.00001000 (215.60.31.8, *new* subnet!)

In the previous example, where we joined with "and" 215.60.31.7 and 255.255.255.248, we ended up with 215.60.31.0, which showed that we were still on our own subnetwork. In this example, joining 215.60.31.8 and 255.255.255.248 with "and" resulted in a new subnetwork. This method may be used to determine whether the address you intend to use is actually a part of your network.

This shows how our ISP can assign us a block of eight total addresses. Two of them, the all-ones and all-zeros addresses, are reserved, and one address must remain with the ISP so that we can access it. That leaves us five addresses for our own use. Assuming another company, also with only five computers or fewer, petitions our ISP for address space, it may be assigned this new network, 215.60.31.8 with a mask of 255.255.255.248. Its available address space, then, will be from 215.60.31.8 (network address, all zeros) to 215.60.31.15 (broadcast, all ones).

In some cases, you may want to further subnet the subnet. For example, if your company has 100 employees in sales and only 50 in accounting and 50 in MIS, and you have a single Class C address, you might want to subdivide it to allow for three networks, with one that is twice as large as the other two. This can be accomplished via *variable-length subnet masking (VLSM)*. Taking again our example IP of 215.60.31.0, let's first divide the range in half by applying a mask of 255.255.255.128. In binary, it looks like this:

11010111.00111100.00011111.00000000 (215.60.31.0)
<u>11111111.11111111.11111111.10000000</u> (255.255.255.128)
11010111.00111100.00011111.00000000 (215.60.31.0)

This allows us to assign node addresses from 215.60.31.1 through 215.60.31.126 (215.60.31.127 will be all one and, therefore, the reserved broadcast address). The dividing point is 215.60.31.128, which is the network address of the next logical segment. We can further subdivide this half of the Class C by applying a mask of 255.255.255.192 to the net network address, 215.60.31.128. Let's see how that looks.

11010111.00111100.00011111.10000000 (215.60.31.128)
<u>11111111.11111111.11111111.11000000</u> (255.255.255.192)
11010111.00111100.00011111.10000000 (215.60.31.128)

We can now address the new segment with the range 215.60.31.129 (the first usable node address) through 215.60.31.190 (11010111.00111100.00011111.10111110). The next address will be 215.60.31.191, which will consist of all ones for this subnet and, therefore, is the broadcast address. The next address will be 215.60.31.192, the new network. Let's look again at the binary representation.

11010111.00111100.00011111.11000000 (215.60.31.192)
<u>11111111.11111111.11111111.11000000</u> (255.255.255.192)
11010111.00111100.00011111.11000000 (215.60.31.192)

The range for this new segment is from 215.60.31.193 through 215.60.31.254. Note that the first segment (215.60.31.0 masked with 255.255.255.128) allows for 126 addressable nodes, but the next two segments allow for only 61 nodes each. This works out very well for our example company. It accommodates all current personnel, segments the network for manageability, and provides room for future growth.

It is also possible to assign multiple IP addresses to a single network and, by use of *supernetting,* meld the multiple ranges into a single network range. Let's look at an example of a company that needs more than 254 host addresses. If this company qualifies for two full Class C addresses, say 215.60.30.0 and 215.60.31.0, it may choose to merge the two by applying a mask of 255.255.254.0. Contrary to subnetting, in which bits are borrowed from the node portion of the address, in supernetting, bits are borrowed from the network portion. Looking at this in binary, we can see that when we apply the 255.255.254.0 mask to our Class C networks, 215.60.30.0 and 215.60.31.0, both of them are actually on the *same* logical network.

> 11010111.00111100.00011110.00000000 (215.60.30.0)
> <u>11111111.11111111.11111110</u>.00000000 (255.255.254.0)
> 11010111.00111100.00011110.00000000 (215.60.30.0, resulting
> network)

> 11010111.00111100.00011111.00000000 (215.60.31.0)
> <u>11111111.11111111.11111110</u>.00000000 (255.255.254.0)
> 11010111.00111100.00011110.00000000 (215.60.30.0, *same* network
> as above)

All that writing the mask out in full binary or dotted decimal format gets tedious. Fortunately, there's a shortcut. Because all the bits in a mask are contiguous, it's easy to simply count them and write that number next to the IP address. For example, in the mask 255.255.255.248, the binary representation would be 11111111.11111111.11111111.11111000. There are 29 contiguous ones in that mask, so a short way of writing it next to an IP address (for example, 192.168.1.1) would be 192.168.1.1/29. This method of notation is called *classless interdomain routing.* There is more to CIDR than simplifying the writing of masks, but this is the most common usage.

exam
ⓦatch

At times, a mask may be made up of discontiguous ones, as in
11111111.11111111.11111110.01110000 = 255.255.254.112;
but this is difficult to manage and not recommended.

ICMP

Although IP leaves reliable delivery up to other protocols, it does provide
for alert and diagnostic messages. These messages comprise the *Internet
Control Message Protocol (ICMP)* module. Some of the services ICMP offers
are listed here:

- **Echo**   Used as a diagnostic to determine reachability.

- **Destination unreachable**   Used to indicate that a node is
  not reachable.

- **Source quench**   Informs the source of network congestion.

- **Redirect**   Used by routers to inform of alternate routes.

- **Time exceeded**   Indicates that a packet has exceeded its time to
  live (TTL) and been discarded.

- **Timestamp**   Useful for measuring latency on a network.

- **Address mask**   Provides subnet mask information for the network.

There is no standard for ICMP implementation other than the
requirement that it be included in any implementation of IP. As far as
how it's implemented, that is left to the software developer. In addition
to ICMP, most TCP/IP implementations include the packet internetwork
groper (ping) utility. Ping is very useful in diagnostics, but as with ICMP,
its implementation is mostly left up to the software developer. This
utility is most often used to determine whether a node on the network
is reachable via IP.

On an MS-DOS-based computer that used ping on its Ethernet
interface, the following resulted:

```
Pinging 192.168.1.1 with 32 bytes of data:
Reply from 192.168.1.1: bytes=32 time<10ms TTL=128
Reply from 192.168.1.1: bytes=32 time<10ms TTL=128
```

```
Reply from 192.168.1.1: bytes=32 time<10ms TTL=128
Reply from 192.168.1.1: bytes=32 time<10ms TTL=128
Ping statistics for 192.168.1.1:
    Packets: Sent = 4, Received = 4, Lost = 0 (0% loss),
Approximate round trip times in milli-seconds:
    Minimum = 0ms, Maximum =  0ms, Average =  0ms
```

These results indicate that the computer sent out 32 bytes of data to node 192.168.1.1 and received a response for each datagram. Each reply took under 10ms, the datagram's TTL is 128 (it can pass through up to 128 routers before being discarded), and 0% packet loss was encountered.

When the ping utility was initiated, it was through ICMP Echo (message 8). The responses that were received used Echo Reply (message 0). The time it took for the packets to make the round trip via ICMP Timestamp and Timestamp Reply (messages 13 and 14) was reported.

The default parameters for this instance of ping were used, but the size of the packet and the number of iterations could have been adjusted.

Cisco routers provide output similar to the above, as well as similar control over the ping utility. One useful parameter worth noting is the ability to change the source address of a ping packet to test connectivity on a segment. By default, a Cisco router will use the outbound interface as its source address when initiating a ping. Suppose, though, you were to Telnet into a router and wanted to test connectivity from the Ethernet interface to the Ethernet interface of a remote router, across a WAN link. The ping packet would go out over the WAN interface, and by default, the router would use that interface's address as the source. Fortunately, Cisco provides a way for us to specify the Ethernet interface as the source.

TCP Versus UDP

Now that we've focused on the IP portion of TCP/IP, let's take a look at the Transport Control Protocol. TCP is used to guarantee delivery of datagrams over an IP network. Applications speak to TCP by sending it bytes of information. TCP keeps track of these bytes and the order in which it receives them. Because TCP sees all data as a series of bytes rather than a fixed-length data unit, TCP can make the decision to transport the data any way it wants to. For example, an application may send a 1,500-byte data unit to TCP, and TCP may have to deliver it to another application that requires smaller data units. TCP can make the decision to break up the 1,500 bytes into two sets of 750 bytes, four sets of 375 bytes, or some other combination.

The guarantee that TCP makes is that data will be received by the destination in the same order that TCP received it from the source. This is accomplished via the positive acknowledgement retransmission (PAR) scheme. In PAR, data is sent from the source to the destination while TCP keeps track of the sequence of data. The TCP module in the destination node acknowledges receipt of that data by sending an acknowledgement (ACK) back to the TCP module in the source. If the source does not receive an ACK within a certain amount of time, the data is retransmitted. As the data is received by the destination, TCP puts the data in order and eliminates any duplicates.

The TCP header includes a checksum field that is used to detect errors in transmission. Errored data segments are discarded and not acknowledged.

Because TCP is used in environments where nodes may have widely varying communication speeds, it is possible that a sender may be able to offer data much faster than a receiver can accept it. To combat this discrepancy, TCP uses the concept of a *sliding window.* The destination sends to the source permission to transmit a specified range of sequence numbers (the window) *before* it receives an ACK for the previous range. For example, if the source has already sent sequence numbers 1 through 5, the destination can give permission to send the next 10 sequence numbers before receiving ACKs for the first five. As ACKs are passed to the source, the acceptable sequence number range is updated.

If congestion occurs or if bandwidth is freed up, the destination may make the range smaller or larger (sliding) in an attempt to keep the link saturated with data. It is possible that the window may be downsized to zero, indicating that the destination's buffers are full. As they free up, the window will be resized.

The previous chapter used an example of a Web browser that can download two Web pages at the same time. This is part of the session layer, which is partly covered by TCP (TCP maps approximately to the transport layer but has elements of other layers as well). TCP keeps track of separate data streams via port numbers. When your computer at IP address 192.168.100.2 requests data from two different sources on the Internet, both of those sources will begin sending data to 192.168.100.2. TCP keeps your e-mail separate from your HTML by appending port numbers to your address to identify the application or process that is making the data request.

There are several port numbers that are predefined on the Internet. Table 2-4 provides a convenient look-up tool for some of the more common ones.

On some occasions, the vim and vigor of TCP are not required. If an application needs only a simple datagram protocol with rudimentary error checking, *User Datagram Protocol (UDP)* fits the bill quite nicely. UDP is also sometimes called Unreliable Datagram Protocol, as a reference to its function. Unlike TCP, UDP does not send ACKs or any other sort of acknowledgement of receipt once the datagram has been sent from the source, nor does it notify the source of any transmission failure.

UDP is connectionless. That means that instead of taking the time to set up a connection from one point to another, UDP simply passes a datagram to the IP layer where it is passed on to the network for delivery.

TABLE 2-4	Port Name	Port Number
Common Port Numbers	FTP	21
	Telnet	23
	SMTP	25
	HTTP (WWW)	80
	POP3 (post office)	110
	NNTP (news)	119
	SNMP	161
	SNMP Traps	162

UDP is useful on LAN segments where a reliable transport medium exists and datagrams are not likely to be dropped or received out of order. One example of such usage that you will encounter in your study of Cisco equipment is in the Trivial File Transfer Protocol (TFTP) application. TFTP is a less robust version of FTP and is very often used in the networking world for upgrading images on routing and switching equipment. More and more, UDP is found on WAN links also in multicast applications. At one job, I worked in a building that was somewhat shielded from radio waves and fairly distant from my favorite station. But I happened to know that the station encoded its broadcast and passed it on to the Internet. By using an application that was able to read those multicast UDP packets, I was still able to listen to the radio at work through my computer. The station could have used TCP, but that would have required opening a connection to my application and acknowledging the receipt of every datagram. That might be acceptable if I were the only one listening, but if we multiply this overhead by 1,000 or more, the overhead that comes with TCP isn't acceptable.

The Domain Name Server (DNS) also uses UDP. Whenever you try to surf to www.cisco.com, a UDP datagram is sent to the Internet authority, where a hierarchical search takes place to resolve the name to an IP address. Sometimes the datagram may be dropped and you'll receive an error in your browser stating that the name could not be resolved. Yet, if you were to at that moment type in 192.31.7.130 (Cisco's Web server address), you would still wind up at www.cisco.com. This indicates that the link to Cisco's site was actually up, but the DNS query didn't make it through.

SNMP is another UDP customer. SNMP is a protocol that watches for certain occurrences on a network, called *traps*, and then sends a notification of the occurrence to a server. This is often used to alert a network operation center (NOC) of the change in status of a link; for instance, when the link to the Internet goes down.

Routing Information Protocol (RIP), the original routing protocol, also uses UDP datagrams to update its neighbors on the contents of its routing table.

FROM THE FIELD

I once got a call from a customer who had been assigned an IP range for his Ethernet network with a mask of 255.255.255.252, which will allow only two valid addresses, and one of them had to go to the router for his wide area link. This customer had much more than a single node he wanted to connect to the Internet and wanted me to change his router's configuration to include a mask of 255.255.255.0, which would allow him up to 254 valid addresses. Unfortunately, I was unable to comply because the address space he was asking for was not mine to give. These addresses are assigned by an ISP, which, in turn, has to request them from InterNIC, the Internet authority. If I had changed this customer's mask to allow him more addresses and happened to cross over into address space that had already been assigned to one of his ISP's other customers, I would have created a routing problem for the Internet because there would have been two destinations with the same address.

CERTIFICATION OBJECTIVE 2.02

Brief Overview of IPX and Its Subprotocols

IPX is Novell NetWare's *Internetwork Packet Exchange*, which only recently gave way to TCP/IP as the preferred LAN communication protocol. IPX was based on the Xerox Network Systems (XNS) protocols, which are covered later in this chapter in the section "XNS."

The IPX protocol stack includes a few other protocols:

■ **RIP** This is similar to the RIP mentioned in Chapter 1. RIP is a routing protocol that advertises its routing table to the rest of the IPX routers on the network every 30 seconds. It is also used by IPX clients to find paths to other networks and to measure the distance to other routers. In addition to hop count, IPX RIP utilizes tick count. One tick equals 1/18 second.

- **SPX** Sequenced Packet Exchange maps to layer 4 of the OSI model, the transport layer. SPX is used to add reliability to the connectionless nature of the IPX datagram. It adds fields to the IPX header, allowing for guaranteed packet delivery.

- **NCP** NetWare Core Protocol is used by clients in a NetWare network to access NetWare servers' services and to manage those connections as well as to access shared files and printers.

- **SAP** The Service Advertising Protocol is used by NetWare servers and routers to advertise their available services. Other routers and servers on the network keep track of the services being provided and the servers that are providing them in an internal database, much like keeping a routing table. NetWare clients send SAP get nearest server (GNS) requests to locate the nearest server that provides a given service.

- **NetBIOS emulation** NetBIOS is an IBM protocol originally used in the company's own PC LAN offering. NetBIOS emulation is included in NetWare to allow NetBIOS applications to run over an IPX network.

Figure 2-2 shows how NetWare protocols relate to the seven-layer OSI model.

An IPX address is also made up of the network and node portions but is much larger than a TCP/IP address. An IPX network address is 32 bits long and may be any unique number. It is generally written in hexadecimal (base 16) with leading zeros omitted. Valid addressing includes networks from 1_{16} to $ffffffff_{16}$. The node portion of the address is generally copied from the MAC address of the node attached to the network. This makes addressing easier for the administrator because only network numbers need to be assigned manually. The node address is also generally written in hexadecimal form, with a dot inserted every four characters to improve readability.

FIGURE 2-2   How the IPX protocol suite relates to the OSI model

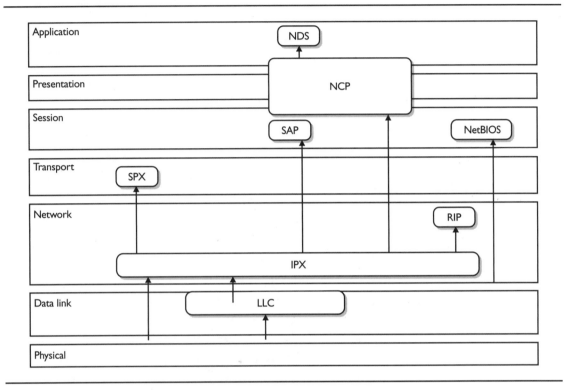

As in TCP/IP, there are some restrictions on numbering in IPX. The network address 0 is reserved and refers to the local network, which is the same network that the transmitting node is on. Also, the node address ffff.ffff.ffff is the hexadecimal equivalent of all ones in binary and is the broadcast address for a given network. An IPX packet addressed to 1a2b.ffff.ffff.ffff will be received by all nodes on network 1a2b. The node address 0000.0000.0001 is also reserved. This address refers to the internal virtual IPX network within every NetWare file server. This network is used in all internal communication. If a server has two interfaces, each with its own node address and possibly each on a different network, the internal network address is used to route between the two interfaces.

IPX uses 16-bit socket numbers to identify individual processes running over the network. A given node may have multiple processes running over IPX simultaneously. Some socket numbers are reserved, while others are available for use by clients. With the network, node, and socket specified, a single process can be identified on a network.

When an IPX node wants to send a packet to a remote network, it first needs to locate a router that knows a path to the remote network. It does this by using SAP GNS. The client queries the network for a routing service to the specified network, and a router that knows of a path to that network will respond. The client then passes the packet to the router, which forwards it through the network, possibly including hops through other IPX routers, to its final destination.

IPX supports four different encapsulation types. These are Ethernet II ("arpa" in Cisco-speak), Ethernet 802.2 ("SAP," though not the same as Service Advertising Protocol), Ethernet 802.3 ("Novell-ether"), and Ethernet SNAP ("SNAP") types. Note that these encapsulation types are referred to as some flavor of Ethernet, which is a data-link layer protocol. Therefore, before any IPX packets may be transmitted onto a network, they must first be placed inside a MAC frame. The format of the MAC frame depends on the media type in use.

Once the IPX packet is encapsulated in a MAC frame and placed on the network, it is transported to the next hop. The receiving router will remove the MAC frame to read the IPX header and re-encapsulate it for transmission to the next hop.

In order for two devices to communicate, they must be using the same frame type. As mentioned earlier, Novell supports four different MAC encapsulation types in order to facilitate communication between two networks with different frame types. It is possible to configure a NetWare server, which is actually a router, to support multiple frame types on the same interface. It's also possible to include multiple network interfaces on a single NetWare server, with each one supporting one or more frame types. However, only one encapsulation type may be supported per logical network. See Figure 2-3 for an illustration of this concept.

Note how, in Figure 2-3, Node A supports four different encapsulation types, though it has only one physical interface. In order to support this, Node A must be a part of four different logical networks: 100, 200, 300, and 400. Physically, all five devices are connected, but four of them are running incompatible encapsulations and must be routed through Node A to communicate with each other.

The default encapsulation for NetWare versions through 3.11 is Ethernet 802.3. For NetWare versions 3.12 and later, the default encapsulation is Ethernet 802.2. This is an important point to keep in mind when you are

FIGURE 2-3   Multiple encapsulations on the same physical interface result in multiple logical networks

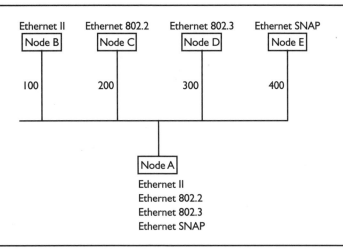

integrating two NetWare networks. They will not be able to communicate unless one encapsulation is agreed upon or a router is placed between the two to make the conversion.

For a brief description of the differences between encapsulation types, please refer to Table 2-5.

TABLE 2-5   Novell and Cisco Use Different Encapsulation Terminology

Novell Encapsulation	Cisco Terminology	Characteristics
Ethernet II	Arpa	Includes 6 bytes for the destination MAC address; 6 bytes for the source MAC address; 2 bytes for the protocol type (IPX, SPX, etc.); 46–1,500 bytes for the payload; and 4 bytes for the frame check sequence (FCS).
Ethernet 802.2	SAP	Default encapsulation for NetWare 3.12–4.x. Includes 6 bytes for the destination MAC address; 6 bytes for the source MAC address; 2 bytes to indicate the number of bytes in the payload; 1 byte for the Destination Service Access Point (DSAP), which specifies the protocol being carried; 1 byte for the Source Service Access Point (SSAP), which specifies the protocol being carried; 1 byte for Control, which identifies the type of frame; 43–1,497 bytes for payload data; and 4 bytes for FCS.
Ethernet 802.3	Novell-ether	Default encapsulation for NetWare version through 3.11. Includes 6 bytes for the destination MAC address; 6 bytes for the source MAC address; 2 bytes to indicate the length of the payload data; 46–1,500 bytes for the payload; and 4 bytes for the FCS.
Ethernet SNAP	SNAP	Includes 6 bytes for the destination MAC address; 6 bytes for the source MAC address; 2 bytes to indicate the length of the payload data; 1 byte for the DSAP; 1 byte for the SSAP; 1 Control byte; 3 bytes for the Organization Code; 2 bytes to indicate the Ethernet type; and 38–1,492 bytes for payload data.

FROM THE FIELD

Some months ago, I had occasion to troubleshoot over the phone with a network administrator who had just taken over his position from his predecessor. He had three separate NetWare LANs that he wanted to integrate, via Cisco routers, over a Frame Relay connection. My only view of his network was through the routers, to which I had dial-up access. I checked and double-checked all the network numbers, and the Cisco configurations looked good, but the administrator still complained of not being able to see anything but his local servers and those from one remote. From within his local router, I was able to ping the other Cisco routers on the network, and even Telnet to them, so I knew the WAN was working fine. Finally, I asked him if all the LANs were using the same encapsulation type. After taking a road trip out to the misbehaving site, he determined that two sites were running Ethernet 802.2, and the third was running Ethernet 802.3. A quick change to the Cisco router's configuration allowed him to see all his servers from any site.

on the **job**

Whereas in TCP/IP, an address by itself is meaningless without a corresponding mask to show how many bits to use for the network portion, in NetWare, it is always the number to the left of the first dot. And one of the nice things about NetWare is the flexibility of naming networks. The network administrator can use up to eight digits in hexadecimal, which means that every network can have a unique name. Some administrators like to make words out of the hexadecimal characters, such as BEEF, DEAD, F00, and ABBA. Another trick of the trade is to use one of the characters to indicate the encapsulation type running on a particular network. A common practice is to use 1 or A to indicate Ethernet II; 2 or B for Ethernet 802.2; 3 or C for Ethernet 802.3; and 4 or D for Ethernet SNAP. With networks like 1111A or ABBA3, it's easy to see at a glance that the first one is running Ethernet II and the second is running Ethernet 802.3.

As mentioned earlier, multiple encapsulations are supported on the same physical interface, but a logical network must be created for each encapsulation. Remember that each of these logical networks must deal with broadcasts and routing updates. As you take the CCDA exam, keep in mind the bandwidth of a given link and how much overhead traffic will have to traverse it. A 64-Kbps WAN link, for example, probably will not be sufficient to connect two LANs running four encapsulations each.

Where Is IPX Used Today?

IPX remains a popular LAN solution, though it has recently given way to TCP/IP as the preferred choice. You will encounter IPX in many legacy networks and need to understand the basics of its operation in order to upgrade existing networks or to make a recommendation to change. IPX implementations exist in public utility and industrial networks. Because of the size of these implementations, clients are often looking for not an entirely new solution, but rather an upgrade to their existing network.

IPX still has an influence on the networking community, so you should expect to see scenarios that include NetWare on the CCDA exam.

CERTIFICATION OBJECTIVE 2.03

AppleTalk and Its Basic Operation

The AppleTalk protocol suite was developed by Apple Computer for use in its Macintosh line of personal computers. Macintosh computers are very popular in the education and art industries, so familiarity with the way they communicate using their native protocol is very useful. Cisco itself made regular use of Macintosh through the early 1990s, and its support for this protocol is evident in Cisco Internetwork Operating System (IOS).

AppleTalk includes several subprotocols, listed next.

- **AFP**   AppleTalk Filing Protocol is used to find and manipulate files on hosts using the AppleShare file sharing software.

- **ZIP**   Zone Information Protocol keeps track of AppleTalk workgroups, known as *zones,* and restricts queries for network services to the local workgroup rather than propagating them across the entire network.

- **ADSP**   AppleTalk Data Stream Protocol is used for application-to-application data transfer. It provides a reliable bi-directional transport over DDP.

- **RTMP**   Routing Table Maintenance Protocol is Apple's distance vector routing protocol, which, by default, broadcasts its routing table to its neighbors every 10 seconds.

- **AURP**   Apple Update-based Routing Protocol, as the name implies, is a routing protocol that only passes along updates to the routing table.

- **ATP**   AppleTalk Transaction Protocol is similar to ADSP but not used as often.

- **NBP**   Name Binding Protocol keeps track of the names associated with resources' addresses in AppleTalk that are assigned for ease of recognition by the end user. NBP's function is similar to that of DNS in the TCP/IP world.

- **DDP**   Datagram Delivery Protocol provides a connectionless datagram service for AppleTalk networks. DDP allows AppleTalk to be routed rather than bridged.

- **EtherTalk, TokenTalk, FDDITalk, and LocalTalk**   These are Apple's implementations of Ethernet, Token Ring, FDDI, and LocalTalk, which is a proprietary 230-Kbps protocol that comes standard on all Macintosh computers.

Figure 2-4 shows the relationship of AppleTalk to the OSI model.

FIGURE 2-4   The relationship of AppleTalk to OSI

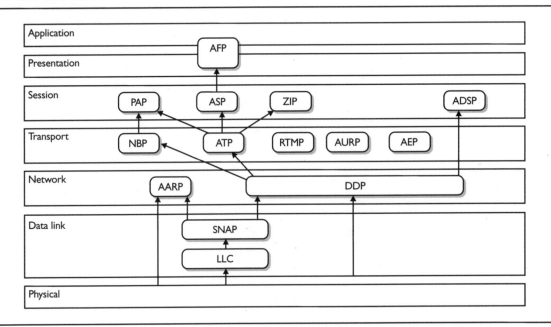

AppleTalk addresses are 24 bits long, with 16 bits reserved for the network address and 8 bits for the node, which allows for only up to 254 hosts per network (0 and 255 are reserved addresses). In the original AppleTalk specification, AppleTalk Phase 1, networks were restricted to a single number. The current version, AppleTalk Phase 2, which is supported by Cisco IOS, supports a range of network numbers for the network address. This range is known as the *cable range,* and it allows for networks with more than 254 nodes per segment. Figure 2-5 illustrates the difference between the two.

The popularity of AppleTalk is due in part to its ease of administration. To attach a new Macintosh to a network, the administrator must simply plug it in. The computer dynamically assigns itself an address in the correct cable range. Adding a Cisco router to a network is almost as easy. The administrator must tell the router to which cable range it belongs, and the router will find its own address.

FIGURE 2-5   AppleTalk Phase 1 uses a single network address; AppleTalk Phase 2 allows for a range of addresses

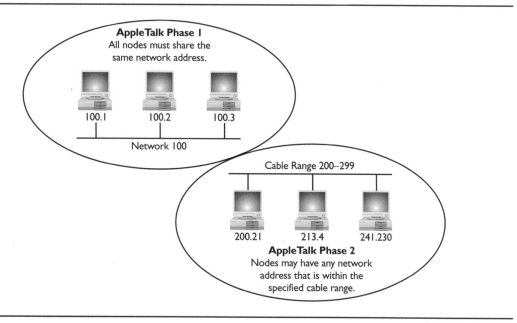

One of the main things to remember in designing an AppleTalk network is that cable ranges cannot overlap. The range 100 through 200, for example, would overlap the range 200 through 300 and is an illegal assignment. A better, legal design would be to assign the ranges 100 through 199 and 200 through 299. Another important factor is the routing protocol used. RTMP, which is the default, will broadcast its routing table every 10 seconds. Other protocols, like ZIP, also rely on broadcasts to keep lists of services up to date within zones (workgroups). This amount of traffic can work on a LAN but can spell disaster across slower WAN links. Generally, AURP is the routing protocol of choice for WAN links and works to reduce the amount of unnecessary traffic. Also, for further filtering, Cisco IOS supports AppleTalk access lists, which, among other things, allow you to specify specific cable ranges that RTMP should advertise.

Quick Overview of SNA

Systems Network Architecture (SNA) was developed by IBM in the mainframe computer era (1974, to be precise) as a way of getting its various products to communicate with each other for distributed processing. SNA is a line of products designed to make other products cooperate. In your career of designing network solutions, you should expect to run into SNA from time to time because many of the bigger companies (i.e., banks, healthcare institutions, and government offices) bought IBM equipment and will be reluctant to part with their investment.

SNA was one of the first protocols to use a layered model and was also influential in the design of the OSI model.

SNA information may be transmitted within various protocols. Two protocols that are often used to carry SNA information are Synchronous (or Serial) Data Link Control (SDLC) and Qualified Logical Link Control (QLLC), which carries SNA information over X.25. Figure 2-6 shows SNA in relation to the OSI model.

SNA is a proprietary protocol that runs over SDLC exclusively, although it may be transported within other protocols, such as X.25 and Token Ring. It is designed as a hierarchy and consists of a collection of machines called *nodes*. There are four main types of nodes:

- **Type 1**   Terminals
- **Type 2**   Controllers and machines that manage terminals
    - **Type 2.1**   Enhanced cluster controller that can independently initiate communication with other cluster controllers
- **Type 4**   Front-end processors (FEPs) and machines that take some load off the main CPU
- **Type 5**   The main host

Type 3 has never been defined by IBM.

The main host communicates with its FEPs and controllers, and the controllers, in turn, communicate with the terminals.

FIGURE 2-6   SNA compared with the OSI model

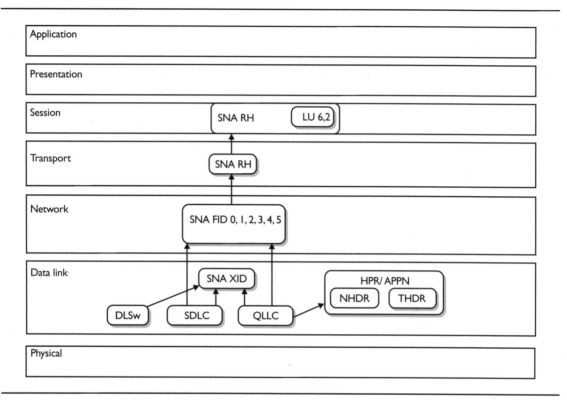

Each node has at least one *network addressable unit (NAU)*. The NAU enables a process to use the network by giving it an address it can then use to reach other NAUs. A NAU can be one of three types: *logical unit (LU)*, *physical unit (PU)*, or *system services control point (SSCP)*. There is usually one SSCP for each Type 5 node and none in the other nodes.

SNA distinguishes five different kinds of sessions: SSCP-SSCP, SSCP-PU, SSCP-LU, LU-LU, and PU-PU.

The SSCP is usually implemented in IBM mainframes that use channels to connect to control devices such as disks, tapes, and communication controllers. The communication controller (the FEP) is used to connect SDLC lines. Together, the SSCPs, FEPs, channels, and SDLC lines connecting them make up the backbone. Using SDLC, the FEPs also connect Token Ring or X.25 links and other types of SNA devices such as cluster controllers, which, in turn, manage the endpoints of the network, such as the display terminal (the 3270 family).

How Does DECnet Work?

Digital Equipment Corporation (DEC) developed the *DECnet protocol* as part of its Digital Network Architecture (DNA) protocol stack to allow communication between DEC minicomputers across local and wide area networks. Digital was a primary competitor of IBM in the 1970s, and DNA was introduced shortly after IBM's introduction of SNA.

The DECnet suite includes

- **RP** Routing Protocol distributes routing information among DECnet hosts. It divides routing classes into two levels: level 1, which handles intra-area routing; and level 2, which handles interarea routing.

- **MOP** Maintenance Operation Protocol is used for utility services such as the uploading and downloading of system software, remote testing, and diagnostics.

- **NSP** Network Service Protocol provides reliable virtual connection services with flow control to the network-layer Routing Protocol.

- **SCP** Session Control Protocol manages logical links for DECnet connections.

- **DAP** Data Access Protocol provides remote file access to systems supporting DNA.

- **CTERM** Command Terminal is the terminal emulation protocol of DNA. CTERM uses DECnet to provide a command terminal connection between DEC terminals and DEC operating systems such as VMS and RSTS/E.

- **LAT** Local Area Transport is designed to handle multiplexed terminal traffic to and from time-sharing hosts.

- ■ **STP**   Spanning Tree Protocol prevents the formation of logical looping in the network.
- ■ **LAVC**   Local Area VAX Cluster communicates between VAX computers in a cluster.

The relationship to the OSI model is represented in Figure 2-7.

DECnet possesses many of the characteristics of the routing protocol OSPF, including the concept of areas and adjacencies. Also, in studying DECnet, you will hear references to DECnet Phase IV and DECnet Phase V. DECnet Phase V uses the IS-IS protocol, which will be covered next and is a radical departure from Phase IV. DECnet Phase IV was introduced in the early 1980s and is still in use; it will be the focus for this section.

FIGURE 2-7   DECnet's relationship to OSI

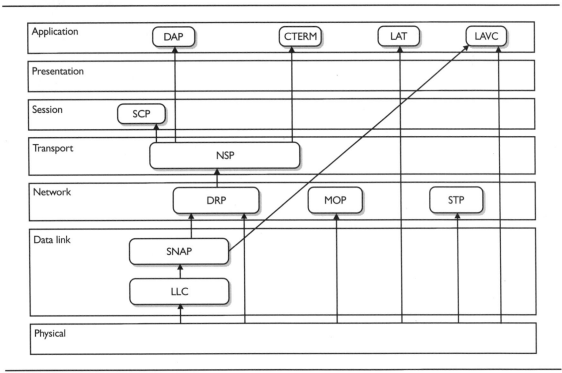

Although DECnet and OSPF have similarities, DECnet is not a link-state routing protocol. It also has characteristics found in distance vector protocols, such as its use of split horizon to avoiding routing loops (remember that split horizon will not allow a routing update to go out the same interface through which it entered the router).

The key parts of DECnet routing are these:

- **End-node**   A device that cannot route
- **Node**   A device that can route (including minicomputers that are equipped to route)
- **Area**   A group of nodes and end-nodes
- **Router-types**   Either level 1, which handles intra-area (within one area) routing, or level 2, which handles interarea (between multiple areas) routing

DECnet has some interesting characteristics. For instance, unlike with other protocols, each interface on a router does *not* receive a unique address. Instead, the entire router is assigned a single address. Also, routing tables in DECnet include entries for every node and end-node within an area, unlike with other protocols that keep entries only for networks. Planning your network to wisely divide routing domains into separate areas can keep routing tables small.

DECnet routes are based on the *router identifier (RID)*, which is the DECnet address of the router. Because each interface doesn't get its own address, in order to make a particular interface the preferred route, you must assign it a lower cost than any other route. DECnet also supports the designated router concept. Routers learn about each other by sending hello packets, as in OSPF. On an Ethernet network, if there are multiple routers, one is elected the designated router based upon which one has the lowest router priority number (this is user configurable).

Modification of the MAC Address for the Area and Node

DECnet addressing is made up of 16 bits, which are divided into 6 bits for the area designation and 10 bits for the node address. This division limits a single DECnet implementation to only 63 areas with up to 1,023 nodes in each.

DECnet does not use the network interface's MAC address, but assigns its own using an algorithm. When DECnet is enabled on an interface, it takes the user-defined area address and multiplies it by 1,024. It then adds the node address and switches the two low-order bytes of the hexadecimal result, which it appends to the DEC registered prefix AA00.0400.

Let's use the area.node address 1.10 as an example. First, the area is multiplied by 1,024: $1024 \times 1 = 1024$. Then it adds the node address, 10 in our case: $1,024 + 10 = 1,034$; $1,034_{10} = 040A_{16}$. Switching the low-order bytes results in 0A04. Now appending this to the DEC registered prefix, we end up with AA00.0400.0A04, which allows us to use our third-party hardware (a Cisco router, for example) in a DECnet implementation. Note that this manipulation of MAC addresses, although required, can cause problems with protocols that use the native MAC address (such as IPX). It is generally best to configure DECnet first when you are configuring a multiprotocol network.

CERTIFICATION OBJECTIVE 2.06

IS-IS

Intermediate System to Intermediate System (IS-IS) was developed by the International Organization for Standardization (ISO), the same people who brought us the seven-layer model. Routers using this protocol share intradomain routing information based on a single metric to determine network topology. IS-IS is designed to work in conjunction with *End System to Intermediate System (ES-IS)* and *Connectionless Network Service (CLNS)*, also developed by ISO. IS-IS is based on work originally done at Digital Equipment Corporation for Phase V DECnet. Although IS-IS was created to route in *Connectionless Network Protocol (CLNP)* networks, a version has since been created to support both CLNP and IP networks. This variety of IS-IS is usually referred to as *integrated IS-IS* and has also been called *dual IS-IS*. Figure 2-8 compares the OSI model with the ISO suite.

Terminology in the IS-IS world is similar to that of DECnet, from which it was derived:

- **Area** A group of contiguous networks and attached hosts that are specified to be an area by a network administrator or manager

- **Domain** A collection of connected areas (Routing domains provide full connectivity to all end systems within them.)

- **Level-1 routing** Routing within an area

- **Level-2 routing** Routing between areas

FIGURE 2-8 The ISO protocol suite compared with the OSI model

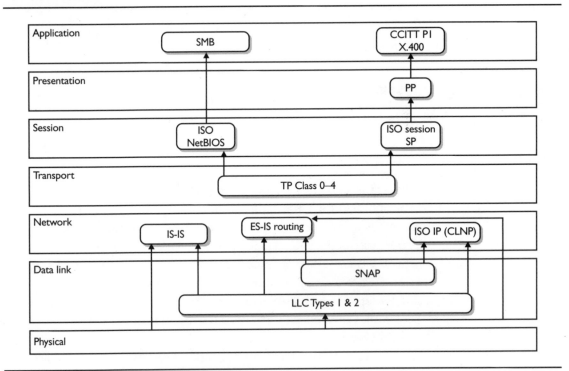

ES-ISs communicate with one another through *hello* messages. These hello messages are intended primarily to convey the subnetwork and network-layer addresses of the systems that generate them. ES-IS attempts to send configuration information to many systems simultaneously. On broadcast subnetworks, ES-IS hello messages are sent to all ISs through a special multicast address. ISs send hello messages to a special multicast address designating all end systems.

Addresses in the ISO protocols are referred to as *network service access point (NSAP)* addresses, the interface between layer 3 and layer 4, and *network entity titles (NETs)*, the network-layer entity in an intermediate system. Each node in an OSI network has one or more NETs. OSI subnetwork addresses, or *subnetwork points of attachment (SNPAs)*, are the points at which an ES or IS is physically attached to a subnetwork. The SNPA address uniquely identifies each system attached to the subnetwork. In an Ethernet network, the SNPA is the 48-bit MAC address. Part of the information transmitted by ES-IS is the NSAP-to-SNPA or NET-to-SNPA mapping. In addition, each node has many NSAP addresses. Each NSAP address differs from one of the NETs for that node in only the last byte. This byte is called the *n-selector*, and it is similar to the port number in other protocols.

Cisco's implementation supports all NSAP address formats that are defined by ISO document 8348/Ad2. However, dynamic routing (ISO-IGRP or IS-IS routing) is provided only for NSAP addresses that conform to the address constraints defined in the ISO standard for IS-IS (ISO 10589).

IS-IS is a link-state routing protocol. It floods the network with link-state information in order to build a complete, consistent picture of network topology. To simplify router design and operation, IS-IS distinguishes between level-1 and level-2 ISs. Level-1 ISs communicate with other Level-1 ISs in the same area. Level-2 ISs communicate with ISs in other areas. Simply put, level-1 ISs *form* level-1 areas, whereas level-2 ISs *route* between level-1 areas.

Level-2 ISs can get to other level-2 ISs by traversing only level-2 ISs, thus creating a backbone. This backbone simplifies design because level-1 ISs need only a route to the nearest level-2 IS. The backbone routing protocol can also change without impacting the intra-area routing protocol.

How Does Banyan VINES Work and Where Is It Used?

Banyan VINES (virtual networking system) is based on the UNIX operating system. It uses the characteristic UNIX multiuser and multitasking characteristics to internetwork LANs and WANs. The Banyan suite includes the following protocols:

- **VARP** VINES Address Resolution Protocol. VARP is used to find node Data Link Control (DLC) addresses from the node IP address.

- **VIP** VINES Internet Protocol moves datagrams throughout the network.

- **ICP** Internet Control Protocol is used to notify the user of an error and to advertise changes in network topology.

- **RTP** Routing Update Protocol is used to distribute network topology.

- **IPC** Interprocess Communications Protocol provides both datagram and reliable message delivery service.

- **SPP** Sequenced Packet Protocol provides a reliable virtual connection service for private connections.

- **NetRPC** NetRemote Procedure Call is used to access VINES applications such as StreetTalk and VINES Mail. A program number and version identify all VINES applications. Calls to VINES applications must specify the program number, program version, and specific procedure within the program.

■ **StreetTalk** StreetTalk maintains a distributed directory of the names of network resources. In VINES, names are global across the Internet and independent of the network topology.

The relationship of VINES to the OSI model is illustrated in Figure 2-9. The number of new VINES implementations is in decline, but current VINES users are very happy with their choice of network operating system and will likely want to keep it. VINES's popularity among its users is due to its rating as one of the easiest networks to manage. This is in large part due to its StreetTalk naming system.

FIGURE 2-9   A comparison of the Banyan VINES protocol suite and the OSI model

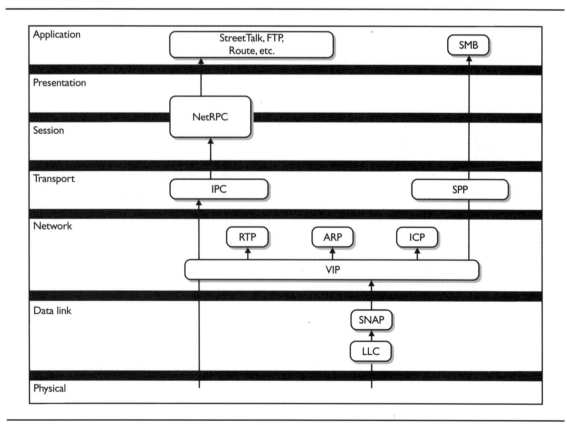

StreetTalk supports a number of features for associating a variety of data with users, all based on their network names. This data can be textual in nature or graphical. StreetTalk revolves around a naming process seen as Item@Group@Organization. This is reminiscent of the format of e-mail addresses.

The item can be a user, a file server, a printer, or other entity. The group is the logical association in which the item can be found. The organization is the logical association in which the group can be found. As an example, take the company ACME. If ACME is running StreetTalk over VINES, you might expect to find a breakdown of groups such as administration, secretarial, and sales. And each entity within the group would also have a unique item name, such as

Joe Smith@Sales@ACME
LaserPrinter2@Secretarial@ACME
Payroll Data@Administration@ACME

To connect a pure VINES network to the Internet, you'll need to implement routing on your network. VINES can perform several types of routing, including TCP/IP routing, which allows TCP/IP traffic to pass through a VINES network. It is also a licensing requirement for those using PC/TCP from Banyan.

IBANYAN is FTP's PC/TCP software for Banyan. It works with all Banyan clients, including Ethernet, Token Ring, and PC-Dialin (Banyan's dial-up solution). When using IBANYAN, the client PC encapsulates its TCP/IP traffic in VINES packets. The VINES IP packet passes through the VINES network, and then the VINES information is stripped off, turning the packet back into pure TCP/IP that is sent to a TCP/IP host. The client always transmits VINES IP, which means that the routing is controlled at the server.

EBANYAN is almost identical to the PC/TCP from FTP, except it uses Banyan's network interface card (NIC) drivers instead of packet drivers or drivers specific to FTP cards. EBANYAN works only with Ethernet clients, not with VINES PC-Dialin or Token Ring.

VINES network-layer addresses are 48-bit addresses that consist of a network number. In Cisco documentation, VINES addresses are expressed in the format *network:host*. We'll use that convention for consistency.

The network number identifies a VINES logical network, which consists of a *single* server and a group of client nodes. The network number consists of 32 bits and is the serial number of the server. The subnetwork number consists of 16 bits. For servers, the subnetwork number is always 1. For client nodes, it can have a value from 0×8001 through 0×FFFE, or 32,766 possibilities.

Here is an example of a VINES network address: 2010671B:0001. In this address, the serial number of the service node is 2010671B, and the host number is 0001, indicating that this is a server.

On networks without any servers, the router provides special processing for certain broadcast packets and certain packets directed at the router. This allows clients on the serverless network to find the services that are provided by a server on another network. This special processing is especially important when two networks, one with a server and one without a server, are connected to the same router.

Client systems on VINES networks are assigned network addresses dynamically. When a VINES client boots, it sends a broadcast request asking a server to provide it with a network-layer address. A router will respond to this broadcast request if there are no VINES servers on the physical network segment. The router then assigns an address to the client and acts as a network communication service provider for that client. The router generates a unique network number for the client based on its own VINES address. A VINES file server must still be present somewhere on the network in order for the client to connect to all other network services.

CERTIFICATION OBJECTIVE 2.08

XNS

The *Xerox Network System (XNS)* is a distributed-file system LAN architecture that Xerox developed in the 1970s. XNS is similar to the TCP/IP suite, but it is a five-layer model and was the basis for the OSI seven-layer model. XNS was adopted in part by Novell. Its subprotocols include the following:

- **IDP**   Internet Datagram Protocol is a connectionless datagram protocol that forms the basis for XNS addressing. IDP packets are limited to a maximum size of 576 bytes, excluding the data-link header.

- **RIP**   Routing Information Protocol is used by XNS to maintain a database of network hosts and exchange information about the topology of the network.

- **PEP**   Packet Exchange Protocol provides a more reliable datagram delivery service than IDP. A unique number is used to identify responses as belonging to a particular request. The sending host sets the packet ID field to a fixed value, and then looks for PEP responses containing the same packet ID value.

- **SPP**   Sequenced Packet Protocol provides reliable transport delivery with flow control. SPP establishes connection IDs at the time of connection to distinguish between multiple transport connections. Each packet transmitted is assigned a sequence number, and the destination host acknowledges receipt.

- **Error**   The Error protocol, which reports errors, is used as a diagnostic tool, as well as a means of improving performance, and is not normally accessed by users.

- **Echo**   The Echo protocol causes a host to echo the packet it receives and is often used to test the accessibility of another site on the Internet. If no user application is attached to the echo port, the kernel automatically responds to the echo request from another host.

Figure 2-10 illustrates the relationship of the XNS protocol suite to the OSI model.

XNS is designed to run over Ethernet networks. The host ID in the XNS address uses the Ethernet MAC address. Multiple Ethernet hardware

FIGURE 2-10   Comparison of the XNS protocol suite with the OSI model

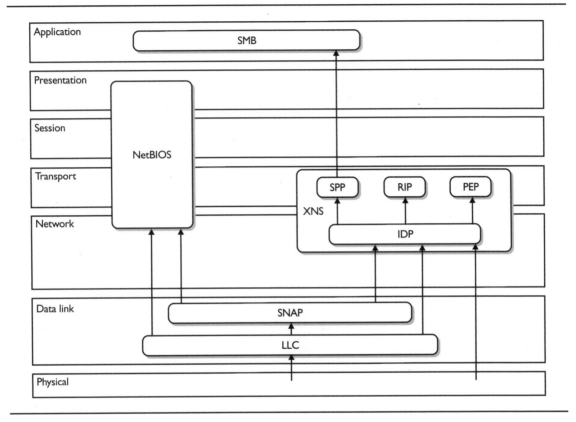

interfaces are supported within the same host, and one host ID for each Ethernet interface is used, so packets destined for a specific host ID are received and processed accordingly.

If routing is required on an XNS network, you'll need to set up a routing table to properly route packets. The current implementation of XNS automatically forwards all incoming XNS Internet packets to the appropriate router or network, as long as the packet is not destined for the local host and the destination network information is maintained in the routing table. Indirectly, the local host can be used as a router.

An XNS address takes up 12 bytes and consists of three parts:

- A 32-bit network identifier
- A 48-bit host identifier
- A 16-bit port number

The host identifier is an absolute number that must be unique to all XNS Internets. The Ethernet MAC address is generally used as the host identifier. With unique host identifiers, the network identifier is redundant but is required for routing purposes.

XNS addresses can be represented by several means. For the sake of consistency, we use a format reminiscent of Novell NetWare: a 32-bit network identifier in hexadecimal, followed by a dot, followed by the 48-bit Ethernet MAC address in dotted hexadecimal format. This similarity between XNS and NetWare means that knowing one will allow you to begin working with the other with very little difficulty.

QUESTIONS AND ANSWERS

Your customer has a Macintosh network and wants to expand by opening a branch office across town. How can he connect his networks with a WAN link?	Apple's default network protocol is RTMP, which sends updates every 10 seconds. That amount of traffic can kill the efficiency of a WAN link. Using AURP on the WAN link will cause less traffic yet still keep the routing tables up to date.
Your customer has had a network with the numbering scheme of 10.x.x.x for years and now wants to connect to the Internet. He doesn't want to renumber his existing network. What will you suggest?	Network address translation was created for exactly this problem. It will allow your customer to use his existing network scheme and translate his private address space dynamically when his employees access the Internet.
Your customer's two NetWare networks run different encapsulations. How can you connect them?	You have two options. You can change the encapsulation of one network to match the other network, or you can put a router that supports both encapsulations between the two.

CERTIFICATION SUMMARY

This chapter provides an overview of many of the protocols in the world of networking, including the ways they handle addressing, the types of routing protocols they employ, and the characteristics that make them unique. The information presented will allow you to speak comfortably about the various protocol suites you may encounter as a network designer, as well as provide you with a basis for increasing your knowledge.

The focus is particularly on TCP/IPv4 because that is the standard for the largest network in the world—the Internet. Most new design scenarios will include some sort of IP integration as businesses connect to the Internet for e-mail, research, virtual private networking (VPN), and other reasons.

 # TWO-MINUTE DRILL

- ❑ Protocols are standards that are agreed upon by computer systems to facilitate information sharing.
- ❑ TCP/IP is the standard used on the Internet.
- ❑ TCP/IP version 4 is the current version, and version 6 is in development.
- ❑ TCP/IP was included in the UNIX operating system, which increased its popularity.
- ❑ OSI protocols were slow to mature, whereas TCP/IP was already very mature.
- ❑ IPv4 uses 32 bits to assign a unique number to every addressable node on a network.
- ❑ The dotted decimal form is used to facilitate readability by humans, but the dots don't indicate any breakdown of the binary representation of the same address.
- ❑ The IP address is divided into network and node portions.
- ❑ The binary numbering system is made up of ones and zeros and is based on powers of 2.

❑ DHCP and BOOTP servers assign IP addresses to workstations that request them.

❑ Class A addresses are in the range 1.0.0.0 to 126.255.255.255.

❑ Class B addresses are in the range 128.0.0.0 to 191.255.255.255.

❑ Class C addresses are in the range 192.0.0.0 to 223.255.255.255.

❑ Class D addresses are in the range 224.0.0.0 to 239.255.255.255 and are used for multicasting.

❑ Class E addresses are in the range 240.0.0.0 to 254.255.255.255 and are reserved for testing.

❑ The 127.0.0.0 network is reserved.

❑ Addresses with all zeros or all ones cannot be assigned.

❑ The natural mask of a Class A address is 255.0.0.0.

❑ The natural mask of a Class B address is 255.255.0.0.

❑ The natural mask of a Class C address is 255.255.255.0.

❑ The IANA reserved some address space in each class for use by private networks.

❑ The reserved Class A space is 10.0.0.0–10.255.255.255.

❑ The reserved Class B space is 172.16.0.0–172.31.255.255.

❑ The reserved Class C space is 192.168.0.0–192.168.255.255.

❑ Reserved addresses are not allowed on the Internet.

❑ Network address translation allows reserved addresses to be translated into unique addresses that are allowed on the Internet.

❑ Subnetting allows a network administrator to break up a large network into smaller, manageable networks.

❑ Supernetting allows multiple, contiguous network address ranges to be aggregated and made into a larger network.

❑ A shorter way of writing the subnet mask is by using CIDR to indicate the number of bits being masked.

❑ A subnet mask should be made up of contiguous bits.

❑ ICMP messages are provided with every implementation of IP.

❑ ICMP messages are useful in diagnostics.

❑ The ping utility uses ICMP Echo and Echo Reply and may use other ICMP messages.

❑ TCP provides a reliable transport by guaranteeing delivery of datagrams.

❑ TCP keeps track of the order in which it receives data and passes that data to its destination in the same order.

❑ TCP can break data units into smaller units.

❑ The positive acknowledgement retransmission scheme provides an acknowledgement for every TCP datagram received by the destination.

❑ If an ACK is not received, the source will retransmit.

❑ TCP includes a checksum field that is used to detect errors.

❑ TCP uses the sliding window concept to keep the bandwidth saturated with data.

❑ If congestion occurs, TCP can resize the window to restrict traffic flow.

❑ TCP maps approximately to layer 4 of the OSI model but has elements of other layers.

❑ Port numbers are used to keep data streams separate.

❑ UDP is an unreliable datagram protocol.

❑ UDP does not send ACKs and does not set up a connection.

❑ UDP should be used over a reliable transport medium.

❑ TFTP, DNS, SNMP, and RIP all use UDP datagrams.

❑ Novell IPX is the second most popular LAN protocol suite, after TCP/IP.

❑ SPX is the tool NetWare uses to guarantee packet delivery.

❑ SAP is used by NetWare to advertise services. SAP GNSs are used by workstations to find servers that offer specific services.

❑ An IPX address is made up of a 32-bit network address and the 48-bit MAC address plus a 16-bit socket number.

❑ All ones in an IPX network is the broadcast address of that network.

❑ A node address of 0000.0000.0001 refers to the internal network of the server.

❑ IPX supports four Ethernet encapsulations: Ethernet II, 802.2 and 802.3, and SNAP.

❑ Every encapsulation running on a single interface requires another logical network.

❑ AppleTalk is made up of 24 bits: 16 bits for the network address and 8 bits for the node.

❑ AppleTalk exists in two phases.

❑ Phase 1 supports only up to 254 nodes per segment. Phase 2 supports a range of network addresses called the cable range, with up to 254 nodes each.

❑ AppleTalk ranges cannot overlap.

❑ AppleTalk relies on broadcast traffic to keep the list of network services and routing tables up to date.

❑ SNA runs over SDLC, though it may be transported within other protocols.

❑ IBM hosts (Type 5) talk to FEPs (Type 4), which talk to cluster controllers (Type 2), which talk to terminals (Type 1).

❑ DECnet has many characteristics in common with OSPF.

❑ DECnet Phase IV is its own routing protocol; DECnet Phase V uses IS-IS.

❑ DECnet is a distance vector protocol with some link-state properties.

❑ Level-1 routers communicate within a single area. Level-2 routers communicate between areas.

❑ The entire router, rather than each interface, in a DECnet network is assigned an address,.

❑ DECnet routing tables include entries for every node within an area.

❑ DECnet routers communicate with each other through hello packets.

❑ DECnet addresses are made up of 16 bits: 6 bits for the network and 10 bits for the node.

❏ DECnet modifies the Ethernet MAC address to make it conform to DECnet standards.

❏ IS-IS was designed to be used in conjunction with ES-IS and CLNS. It can also support IP networks.

❏ ISP protocol addresses are NSAPs and NETs. Subnetwork addresses are called SNPAs and are the MAC addresses of the interfaces attaching the device to the network.

❏ IS-IS is a link-state routing protocol.

❏ Banyan VINES is based on the UNIX OS, employing its multiuser and multitasking characteristics.

❏ Support for VINES is strong, in part due to its StreetTalk naming system.

❏ VINES supports TCP/IP.

❏ VINES addresses are made up of 48 bits that include 32 bits for the network (the serial number of the server) and 16 bits for the node.

❏ XNS is similar to the TCP/IP suite.

❏ XNS is designed to run over Ethernet networks.

❏ An XNS address is made up of 12 bytes: 32 bits for the network identifier, 48 bits for the host identifier (generally the MAC address), and 16 bits for the port number.

SELF TEST

The following Self Test questions will help you measure your understanding of the material presented in this chapter. Read all the choices carefully because there may be more than one correct answer. Choose all correct answers for each question.

1. What is required to make two computers communicate?

   A. TCP/IP

   B. A common protocol

   C. The correct encapsulation

   D. Being on the same segment

2. Your customer runs UNIX mainframes and workstations and wants to know your recommendation for a routed protocol for his proposed network.

   A. Novell NetWare

   B. AppleTalk

   C. Banyan VINES

   D. TCP/IP

3. Your customer is curious about the significance of the dot in his IP address. What can you tell him?

   A. There is no significance.

   B. It divides the network from the node.

   C. It makes addresses easier for humans to read.

   D. It is used by the computer to count bytes.

4. Is it true that you can determine the class of address, and therefore its associated subnet mask, from the first octet of the IP address?

   A. You can determine both.

   B. You can't determine either.

   C. You can determine the class but not the mask.

   D. You can determine the mask but not the class.

5. Your customer wants to know why he wasn't assigned a full Class B network address for his 1,000-node network. What will you say?

   A. His network isn't important enough to assign a full Class B.

   B. The Internet has run out of addresses.

   C. He'll need to double the number of nodes for a full Class B.

   D. His network is more suited to multiple Class C addresses or a subset of a Class B.

6. You have a sniffer on your network and see traffic from network 224.0.0.0, which you don't recognize. Where could this traffic be coming from?

   A. There is probably a multicast routing protocol on the network.

   B. It must be coming from a remote network.

   C. It's evidence of a hacker on my network.

   D. It must be a glitch in the sniffer.

7. Your company has been assigned a full Class C address to access the Internet, but your boss wants to keep the company's different departments managed separately. How can you accomplish this?

   A. Use IPv6.

   B. Physically separate the departments.

   C. Run NAT.

   D. Subnet the Class C.

8. Your boss just got his range of IP addresses from his ISP. He was assigned the range 215.60.31.0/28. He's happy because this allows him to address up to 16 nodes—doesn't it?

   A. Yes it does.

   B. No, it provides 28 addresses.

   C. No, it provides 14 addresses.

   D. No, it provides 254 addresses.

9. Subnetting sounds like a great idea to your boss, but his network would benefit from subnets of differing sizes. Is this possible?

   A. Yes, VLSM allows subnets of differing sizes.

   B. Differing sizes are possible, but not with IPv4.

   C. Differing sizes are possible only in a hub-and-spoke environment.

   D. No, it isn't possible.

10. Your users are complaining of an inability to reach the Internet. You know that if they can reach the gateway to the ISP, it's the ISP's problem; if not, it may be yours. What can you do to determine whether they can reach the ISP?

   A. Call the ISP and ask.

   B. Use the ping utility to try to reach the ISP gateway.

   C. Wait until connectivity is restored. If the problem goes away without any action on your part, it was never your problem to begin with.

   D. Put a sniffer on the network.

11. How does TCP guarantee packet delivery?

   A. It doesn't; UDP is the guaranteed service.

   B. It uses the checksum field in the TCP header.

   C. The destination sends ACKs to the source after every good packet delivery.

   D. TCP doesn't guarantee packet delivery; that is left to higher protocols.

12. How can TCP control packet flow?

   A. TCP uses the concept of the sliding window.

   B. FECNs and BECNs are used to notify end-nodes of congestion.

   C. IP, not TCP, controls flow control.

   D. Flow control is left up to the hardware.

13. UDP is a connectionless protocol. What does that mean?

   A. It's used in wireless data transfer.

   B. It's used only by servers.

   C. It's best left to applications such as e-mail.

   D. UDP passes datagrams to IP where it is passed on to the network for delivery with no acknowledgement mechanism.

14. How do workstations in a NetWare environment find routers?

    A. They send out hello packets.

    B. They look for the gateway of last resort.

    C. They look up the list of routers in a table.

    D. They broadcast a SAP GNS.

15. You have two networks running NetWare with different encapsulations. How can you interconnect them?

    A. A router placed between them running both encapsulations will do it.

    B. Run RIP on all the servers.

    C. Create a new subnet to handle the encapsulations.

    D. A complete redesign is in order.

16. In designing a new AppleTalk network, you assign one cable range as 1–100 and the second as 100–200. What are the issues to consider here? (Choose two.)

    A. Cable ranges must start at 100, not at 1.

    B. Cable ranges cannot overlap.

    C. You can't have more than one cable range in AppleTalk.

    D. Cable ranges are not compatible with the Internet.

17. Your customer wants to tie two AppleTalk networks together over a WAN link. What is the best way to do this?

    A. Run RIP between the two.

    B. Run AURP between the two.

    C. Run RTMP between the two.

    D. Run OSPF between the two.

18. You wish to integrate two existing DECnet Phase IV networks. What must be done to route between the two?

    A. A bridge will connect the two networks physically, and they will dynamically learn each other's topology.

    B. A level-1 router must be added to route between areas.

    C. A level-2 router must be added to route between areas.

    D. RIP must be run on both networks.

19. The StreetTalk naming system in Banyan VINES makes network administration very easy. You can see at a glance that Printer@Accounting@QMart is the address of

    A. The accounting workgroup

    B. The routing domain QMart

    C. The printer in the accounting workgroup within the domain QMart

    D. Unable to tell

SELF TEST ANSWERS

1. ☑ **B.** A common protocol is required to make any two systems communicate.
   ☒ A is incorrect because TCP/IP may not run on all platforms. C is incorrect because, although using the correct encapsulation may be an involved element, the overall issue is that two systems agree on a common protocol. D is incorrect because merely adding a router eliminates the need for a common segment.

2. ☑ **D.** TCP/IP is the best answer because it is included with many releases of UNIX already and is available free for most platforms. It is also the standard protocol of the Internet, so future connectivity to the Internet will be very easy.
   ☒ A is incorrect because, although such an implementation could work, it would require purchasing the license to run NetWare, so it would be a more costly solution. B is incorrect because AppleTalk is designed for Macintosh computers. C is incorrect for the same reason that choice A is; such an implementation could work, but is more costly than choice **D**.

3. ☑ **C.** The dots in an IP address are useful only to humans for the sake of readability.
   ☒ A is incorrect because, although there is no significance to the computer, the dots make it easier for the network administrator to read the address. B is incorrect because if this were true, there would be only one dot per address. D is incorrect because the computer never sees the dot.

4. ☑ **C.** The rules for class addressing are based on the first bits of the first octet. However, since subnetting and supernetting were invented, it is impossible to determine the mask associated with an IP address.
   ☒ A is incorrect because the subnet cannot be assumed based on the class. B is incorrect because you can determine the class of the address from the first bits in the first octet. D is exactly the opposite of the correct answer; you can determine the class, but not the mask.

5. ☑ **D.** A full Class B is for networks of over 65,000 nodes. His 1,000-node network can fit into four Class C addresses or into a smaller subnet of a Class B.
   ☒ A is incorrect because address assignment is based not on importance, but on number of nodes. B is incorrect because the Internet has *not* run out of addresses. C is incorrect because even a network of 2,000 nodes is not enough to qualify for a full Class B.

6. ☑ **A.** Routing protocols such as Cisco's EIGRP and others use multicast addressing to propagate routing table information.

☒   **B** is incorrect because the 224.0.0.0 network is part of the D class of addressing, which is not used except for multicasting. **C** is incorrect because this is an illegal address for anyone to have assigned. **D** is incorrect because multicast addresses are very likely to be found on a network running certain routing protocols.

7. ☑ **D.** Subnetting the Class C to form multiple logical networks is the best solution.
    ☒ **A** is incorrect because the Internet currently uses IPv4, and merely changing protocols doesn't inherently divide the departments. **B** is incorrect because this will only allow one of the departments to access the Internet. **C** is incorrect because NAT is designed to translate private addressing to public but not to divide networks.

8. ☑ **C.** The range 215.60.31.0/28 is from 215.60.31.0 through 215.60.31.15. The first address is the network address and is unassignable; the last address is the broadcast address and is also unassignable. Zero through 15 is 16 total addresses, minus the two unassignable ones, equals 14.
    ☒ **A** is incorrect because this range provides 16 addresses, but your boss can't use them all. **B** is incorrect because the /28 is a way of indicating the mask, not the number of addresses. **D** is incorrect because the mask /28 (255.255.255.240) does not use a full Class C block.

9. ☑ **A.** VLSM, or variable-length subnet masking, allows you to subnet the subnet to provide subnets of differing sizes.
    ☒ **B** is incorrect because IPv4 is the protocol for which subnetting was invented. **C** is incorrect because the topology has nothing to do with subnetting. **D** is incorrect because differently sized subnets are possible.

10. ☑ **B.** Ping was designed to test for reachability. If you can reach your ISP from your network, there is a problem beyond your connection to your ISP.
    ☒ **A** is incorrect because the ISP will run the same ping test you will. The downtime spent in contacting a representative who can perform the test is costly to your company. Choice **B** is better because it more quickly isolates the problem to either your network or your ISP's and, therefore, costs your company less money. **C** is incorrect because if the problem is on your end, it will never be fixed; if the problem is on the ISP's side, it may not have noticed it yet, and your downtime will be increased. **D** is incorrect because a sniffer will show you only what traffic is on the network. Your users have already told you they can't reach the Internet, so you won't see any traffic from the Internet with the sniffer.

11. ☑ **C.** Every packet received that passes the checksum is acknowledged. Packets that are never received or that do not pass the checksum are not acknowledged and are retransmitted by the source.

⊠ **A** is incorrect because TCP does guarantee packet delivery. **B** is incorrect because the checksum field has nothing to do with guarantee of delivery. **D** is incorrect because TCP is the highest protocol in the TCP/IP suite and does indeed guarantee delivery.

12. ☑ **A.** The sliding window concept is used to control flow. When there is no congestion, the window is widened. When congestion occurs, the window may be made smaller or closed completely.
    ⊠ **B** is incorrect because FECNs and BECNs are Frame Relay congestion notification mechanisms. **C** is incorrect because TCP, not IP, controls flow. **D** is incorrect because hardware responds to input from software, including flow control information from TCP.

13. ☑ **D.** Unlike TCP, UDP provides only best-effort datagram delivery. It does not acknowledge packet delivery.
    ⊠ **A** is incorrect because "connectionless" with regard to UDP says nothing about the medium over which datagrams are transmitted. **B** is incorrect because workstations also use UDP, particularly in DNS queries. **C** is incorrect because e-mail requires TCP, and this does not address the issue of "connectionless."

14. ☑ **D.** The SAP GNS (get nearest server) broadcast is designed to find servers offering specific services, including that of routing.
    ⊠ **A** is incorrect because NetWare clients do not send out hello packets. **B** is incorrect because this is how routers make routing decisions but not how the routers are found in the first place. **C** is incorrect because before any table can exist, the router must first be known.

15. ☑ **A.** Routers were designed partly to interconnect incompatible transport systems. Different Ethernet encapsulations are not a problem.
    ⊠ **B** is incorrect because RIP is a routing protocol, not a media solution. **C** is incorrect because, although it would be possible to route all traffic to a new subnet that handles both encapsulations, this is an inelegant solution that uses up bandwidth. **D** is incorrect because a router placed between the networks will solve the problem without redesigning anything (though a quick look at the network numbers to guarantee uniqueness is certainly in order).

16. ☑ **B and D.** The ranges 1–100 and 100–200 overlap. A better design might be 1–100 and 101–200. The fact that AppleTalk cable ranges are not compatible with the Internet may or may not be an issue. The question doesn't state whether Internet connectivity is required; however, it is still worth bringing to your employer's attention, just in case Internet connectivity may be desired.

☒ **A** is incorrect because cable ranges can start at 1. **C** is incorrect because multiple cable ranges are supported.

17. ☑ **B.** AURP is an update-based link-state routing protocol that is native to AppleTalk and best for slower WAN links.

☒ **A** is incorrect because RIP is not native to AppleTalk. **C** is incorrect because RTMP is very "chatty," sending updates every 10 seconds. This protocol could easily bog down the WAN link. **D** is incorrect because OSPF is not native to AppleTalk.

18. ☑ **C.** A router will physically connect the two networks, but only a level-2 router will route between the two areas.

☒ **A** is incorrect because routing is not possible with a bridge. **B** is incorrect because a level-1 router routes only within an area, not between areas. **D** is incorrect because running a routing protocol will not accomplish anything unless the two networks are first physically connected by a level-2 router.

19. ☑ **C.** StreetTalk follows the Item@Group@Organization format, so this address identifies the routing domain, the workgroup, and the node.

☒ **A** is incorrect because more than just the workgroup can be identified. **B** is incorrect because more than just the routing domain can be identified. **D** is incorrect because the given address makes it easy to see the node, workgroup, and domain.

CISCO CERTIFIED DESIGN ASSOCIATE

3

Routing Protocol Basics

Choosing the correct routing protocol when designing a network can be the most important step in the success of the network design. There is a multitude of routing protocols to choose from, and understanding each type will be valuable in making your final decision. This chapter covers the most commonly used protocols in networking today and offers specific information about each. With this information, you should be able to make informed decisions regarding each routing protocol and the ways it can be used in different situations.

In the following sections, we cover specific information about each routing protocol already identified. After reviewing each of the routing protocols, we compare and contrast them so that you can fully understand all of their benefits and features. This chapter also contains several diagrams and questions to assess your comprehension on the presented information.

CERTIFICATION OBJECTIVE 3.01

How Does RIP Work?

Routing Information Protocol (RIP) was one of the first routing protocol standards for TCP/IP that was widely implemented around the world. RIP is still a very widely used routing protocol today because of its easy configuration and troubleshooting. RIP is still supported across all routing platforms and vendors, which is also an attractive feature for interoperability.

Request for Comments (RFCs) 1058 defines RIP and its operation; some of the major characteristics of RIP are these:

- Uses hop count as the only metric for determining route paths.

- Provides load balancing across multiple paths by default.

- Advertises its entire routing table every 30 seconds by default.

- Allows for a hop count of only 15; anything over 16 is considered unreachable.

- Does not support *variable-length subnet masks (VLSMs).*

RIP will allow load balancing across multiple paths as long as the hop count is the same across each link to reach the destination. In Figure 3-1, Host A is sending a packet across a WAN network to Host B. As you can see, with the meshed network, once the packet arrives at Router 1, it has three paths to reach Router 5. The connections that link Routers 2, 3, and 4 represent only one hop each, so they all have the same route metric in the routing table of Routers 1 and 5. Therefore, Hosts A and B can load balance across the WAN and utilize available bandwidth between the various routers in the network.

e x a m
Ⓦatch

RIP is categorized as a distance vector routing protocol, which means that it calculates distance to other networks via metrics like hop count.

| FIGURE 3-1 | How RIP will load balance across multiple networks |

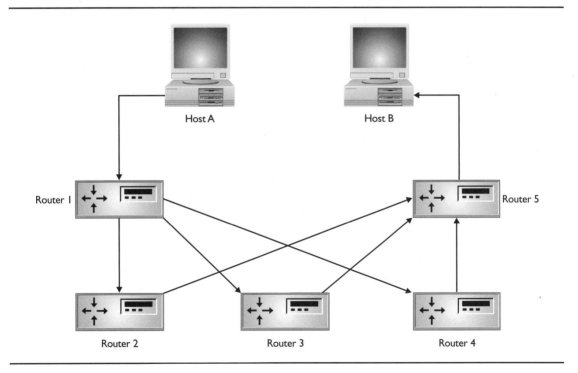

How to Configure RIP

One of the reasons that RIP has been around for so long and is still a very popular protocol is that it is so easy to configure. Ease of configuration should be a consideration in designing a network in any instance. The administrators who will be maintaining the network may have only a basic understanding of routing protocols. So, in some cases, the lower the learning curve, the better.

There are really only two commands that you need to know when configuring RIP: the *router rip* and *network* commands. The router rip command specifies that you are using the RIP routing process. The network command associates an IP address with a network that is connected to the router. Once these commands are implemented, the routing process will associate IP addresses with router interfaces, and the router will start processing traffic. The following example displays the syntax in which the two commands are used.

```
Router-1(config)#router   rip
Router-1(config-router)#network network-number
```

With these two commands, you can set up a simple network that is easy to configure and understand. They will come in handy when you are training the administrators who will maintain the network that you are designing.

Viewing RIP Routing Information

There are several commands that can be used to view pertinent RIP information on a network, but here we cover only the ones that are used on a day-to-day basis. The output of these commands can provide essential information for troubleshooting many of the network problems that may arise. The following are the commands and explanations of them:

■ **Show ip route rip**   Shows the routes known to the router through the RIP process. This is one of the best ways to determine if there is connectivity between the local router and the rest of the network. The following is a display of the output of this command.

```
Router-1#sh ip route rip
     10.0.0.0/8 is variably subnetted, 3 subnets
R       10.1.6.0/32[120/1] via 10.1.6.1, 00:00:28, Ethernet0
R       10.2.6.0/32[120/1] via 10.2.6.1, 00:00:11, Ethernet1
R       10.3.6.0/32[120/1] via 10.3.6.1, 00:00:28, Serial0
```

■ **Show ip protocol** Shows the routing timers and information about the entire router itself. This can be used to see if a router is delivering routing updates and to determine how often they are being broadcast. The following example is the output of this command.

```
Router-1#sh ip protocol
Routing Protocol is "rip"
  Sending updates every 30 seconds, next due in 6 seconds
  Invalid after 180 seconds, hold down 1, flushed after 240
  Outgoing update filter list for all interfaces is not set
  Incoming update filter list for all interfaces is not set
Redistributing: rip
Routing for Networks:
  10.0.0.0
Routing Information Sources:
  Gateway      Distance      Last Update
  10.1.6.1     120      00:00:08
  10.2.6.1     120      00:00:17
  10.3.6.1     120      00:00:00
Distance: (default is 120)
```

■ **Debug ip rip** A handy command in troubleshooting RIP problems in a network. The output of this command shows information such as routing updates sent and received through the interfaces through which the information is processed. It even shows the metric and hop count associated with networks that are being learned and distributed. The following example shows the output of a debug ip rip session.

```
Router-1#debug ip rip
RIP protocol debugging is on
Router-1#
RIP: received update from 10/1//1 on Ethernet0
  10.1.1.1 in 1 hops
  10.0.0.1 in 5 hops
RIP: received update from 10.3.6.1 on Serial0
    10.10.10.1 in 15 hops
RIP: sending update to 255.255.255.255 via Ethernet1 (10.2.6.1)
  subnet 10.1.1.1. metric 4
  subnet 10.0.0.1. metric 10
  subnet 10.10.10.1. metric 2
```

What Is Novell RIP?

We have been discussing IP RIP and its configuration, functionality, and ways to troubleshoot in an IP environment. This section briefly covers Novell RIP and the ways it works in a Novell environment. *Novell RIP*, also known as *IPX RIP*, is a distance vector routing protocol like IP RIP, but with a major difference. IPX RIP uses two metrics in making routing decisions on a network: ticks to measure time and hop count. RIP will first check the tick metric for alternative paths, and if two or more paths are equal, it moves on to hop count. It makes the decision based on the age of the entry and the most recent entry wins.

Each IPX router on a network will periodically (every 60 seconds) broadcast its routing table to its directly connected networks. The neighboring IPX routers will then add the distance vectors that are required before broadcasting their copies of the routing table to their neighbors. An information-aging function handles conditions when an IPX router becomes unreachable without sending any explicit messages to its neighbors. Any periodic updates can reset the aging timers.

CERTIFICATION OBJECTIVE 3.02

How Does IGRP Work?

Interior Gateway Routing Protocol (IGRP) was developed by Cisco Systems in the mid-1980s in response to the demand for a more versatile routing protocol. Many customers migrated from RIP to IGRP because IGRP improved on many of the downfalls inherent with RIP. These improvements are as follows:

- ■ **Scalability** IGRP is able to handle large internetworks.
- ■ **Faster response to network changes** IGRP sends updates when route topology changes.
- ■ **Multiple paths** IGRP can load balance among up to four nonequal paths.

- **Composite metric**   IGRP uses a metric of bandwidth, load, reliability, and delay. IGRP also overcomes the 15-hop-count limitation of RIP.

As just described, IGRP uses a composite metric of bandwidth, load, reliability, and delay to determine through which paths to route. A brief description of each of the metrics mentioned is as follows:

- **Bandwidth**   IGRP uses the minimum path bandwidth to determine a routing metric. This command does not adjust the actual bandwidth of an interface.
- **Delay**   A sum of all delays, for interfaces in a path, is inversely proportional to the bandwidth of the interface. Delay is not dynamically calculated.
- **Reliability**   Reliability is used only when the *metric weights* command is configured. When it is configured, reliability is dynamically calculated based on the ability to send and receive keepalive packets.
- **Load**   Load, like reliability, is used only when the *metric weights* command is configured. When it is necessary, configured load is dynamically calculated to determine the heaviest load on any link.

exam
☼atch   *IGRP is used in IP networks that require a simple, robust, and scalable routing protocol.*

Like RIP, IGRP is a distance vector routing protocol. IGRP has updated features that improve its performance and reliability. These features, along with a brief description of each, are as follows:

- **Hold-down timers**   Hold-down timers are used to prevent routing loops during network convergence. They neither advertise nor accept advertisements about a route for a specific length of time. This time is three times the update interval (90 seconds) plus 10 seconds, or 280 seconds by default.

- **Split horizon** This is a routing technique in which route information is prevented from exiting the router interface through the information that was received.

- **Poison reverse** This is another form of split horizon. Instead of marking a network as unreachable, poison reverse does not include it in routing updates as split horizon does. Poison reverse sends out *poison reverse updates,* which state whether or not a network is unreachable.

- **Flash updates** A *flash update* is sent asynchronously when a network topology change has been detected. It works in correlation with IGRP's periodic routing updates.

How to Configure IGRP

IGRP is similar to RIP in that it, too, is easy to configure and troubleshoot, even though IGRP allows for only one autonomous system per IGRP routing process. Hence, if you wanted to establish more than one autonomous system, you would need to configure another routing process. This is a handy option to have if you are maintaining a network that is merging with another company or if you want to isolate traffic from certain areas of your network.

There are really only two commands that you need to know when configuring IGRP: the *router igrp* and *network* commands. The router igrp command specifies that you are using the IGRP routing process. The network command associates an IP address with a network that is connected to the router. Once these commands are implemented, the routing process will associate IP addresses with router interfaces, and the router will start processing traffic. The following example displays the syntax in which the previous commands are used.

```
Router-1 (config)#router igrp autonomous system number
Router-1 (config-router)#network network-number
```

The only difference, in the initial configuration, between IGRP and RIP is that IGRP uses an autonomous system number to separate routing processes. This routing protocol also provides a simple network that is easy to configure and understand. You will find this handy when you train the administrators who will maintain the network you are designing.

Displaying IGRP Information

You will need to learn a couple of additional commands for viewing IGRP information. The output of these commands can provide information that is essential in troubleshooting many of the network problems that may arise. The following are the commands and explanations of them:

- **Show ip route igrp**   Shows the routes known to the router through the IGRP process. This is one of the best ways to determine if there is connectivity between the local router and the rest of the network.

- **Show ip protocols**   Shows the routing timers and information about the entire router itself. This can be used to see if a router is delivering routing updates and to determine how often they are being broadcast.

- **Debug ip igrp transactions**   Shows information on IGRP routing transactions that take place in the router. An IP address of a neighbor router can be specified, resulting in output messages describing updates to and from that router. The following example shows the output of this command.

```
Router-1#debug ip igrp transactions

IGRP: received update from 10.1.6.1 on Ethernet0
subnet 10.1.1.0, metric 1200 [neighbor 1100]
subnet 10.1.2.0, metric 6867 [neighbor 6767]
subnet 10.1.3.0, metric 1300 [neighbor 1200]
network 10.10.10.0, metric 158500 [neighbor 158400]
network 10.10.1.0, metric 1111550 [neighbor 1110550]
```

- **Debug ip igrp events**   Shows a summary of the IGRP routing information instead of individual routes. It indicates the source and destination of each update, as well as the number of routes in each update. This keeps your console from being flooded with route information and possibly making your router unstable. The following shows the output of this command.

```
Router-1#debug ip igrp events

IGRP: Sending update to 255.255.255.255 via Ethernet0 (10.1.1.1)
IGRP: Update contains 26 interior, 40 system, and 3 exterior routes.
IGRP: Total routes in update: 69
IGRP: Received update from 10.1.2.1 on Ethernet1
IGRP: Update contains 15 interior, 2 system, and 0 exterior routes.
IGRP: Total routes in update: 17
```


CERTIFICATION OBJECTIVE 3.03

How Does EIGRP Work?

Enhanced IGRP (EIGRP) is another Cisco proprietary protocol that combines the advantages of a distant vector routing protocol with those of a link-state routing protocol. The combination of these two types of protocols is called a *hybrid protocol*, and it gives users the flexibility of both types all rolled up into one package. This new type of protocol brings along with it several new features, as follows:

- **Reduced bandwidth usage** EIGRP sends partial updates about a route when either the topology or the metric changes. When the changes are detected, an update about the link only is sent, and it is sent only to the routers that need this updated information.

- **Multiple network–layer support** EIGRP supports the use of multiple protocols like AppleTalk, IP, and Novell NetWare through the use of *protocol-dependent modules (PDMs)*. These PDMs are responsible for network layer–specific protocol information.

- **Rapid convergence** EIGRP uses an algorithm called *diffusing update algorithm (DUAL)* to achieve rapid convergence across a network. A router running EIGRP stores backup or alternate routes. If there is no alternate route in the route table, EIGRP will query its neighbors to discover the alternate route. These queries will propagate the network until a feasible alternate route is found. DUAL also guarantees loop-free operation during route computation and allows all routers involved in a route change to synchronize at the same time. All other routers that are not affected by the route change are not involved in recomputations.

The operation of EIGRP is different from that of all the other routing protocols we have discussed because it is a hybrid protocol. It does utilize the advantages of both the distance vector and link-state routing protocols, so we cover the following related to EIGRP:

- **Neighbor table** The purpose of the *neighbor table* is to ensure communication between the directly connected neighbors. EIGRP multicasts hello packets to discover neighbor routers and exchange route updates. Each router builds a neighbor table from the hello packets that it receives from neighbor EIGRP routers running the same network-layer protocol.

- **Route discover** When a new router comes up on a link, the first thing it does is send out a hello packet through all of its interfaces. Any router receiving this hello packet will reply with update packets that contain all the routes they currently have in their routing table. The new router then replies to each neighbor with an acknowledgment (ACK) packet indicating that it has received the updates. It then puts all the update routes into its topology table, which organizes each route destination and shows how each neighbor can get to the destination. The new router then exchanges update packets with its neighbors, and they reply with an ACK packet.

- **Route selection** Route selection has several characteristics that set it apart from most other routing protocols. EIGRP selects its primary and secondary routes, which are kept in the topology table. The primaries are then put into the routing table. EIGRP supports many different types of routes, such as internal, external (non-EIGRP), and summary routes. DUAL is run on the topology table to determine the primary and backup loop-free routes to each destination. The next hop router on the primary route is called the *successor,* and the backup next hop router is the *feasible successor.* The successors and feasible successors are kept in the topology table with all other routes and referred to as *possible successors.* The only routes that are removed are those with a metric of infinity or unreachable.

EIGRP uses the same composite metric as IGRP to determine the best path.

How to Configure EIGRP

EIGRP can be easy to configure, but the multitude of associated commands can make it very complex. EIGRP, like IGRP, allows for only one autonomous system per EIGRP routing process. Hence, if you wanted to establish more than one autonomous system, you would need to configure another routing process. This is a handy option to have if you are maintaining a network that is merging with that of another company or if you want to isolate traffic from certain areas of your network. You just need to make sure that all the routers in your internetwork have the same autonomous system number.

Once again, the commands for basic configuration are the same as for IGRP: the *router eigrp* and *network* commands. The router eigrp command specifies that you are using the EIGRP routing process. The network command associates an IP address with a network that is connected to the router. Once these commands are implemented, the routing process will associate IP addresses with router interfaces, and the router will start processing traffic. The following example displays the syntax in which the previous commands are used.

```
Router-1 (config)#router eigrp 1
Router-1 (config-router)#network 10.1.6.0
```

The *autonomous-system-number* identifies routers that belong within an internetwork. This number must be the same on all routers across the internetwork in order for the systems to communicate and share routing information.

Displaying EIGRP Information

You will need to learn a couple of additional commands to view EIGRP information. The output of these commands can provide essential information for troubleshooting many of the network problems that may arise. The following are the commands and an explanation of them:

- **Show ip eigrp neighbors**   Displays neighbor routers that have been discovered through the EIGRP routing process.

- **Show ip route eigrp**   Displays EIGRP routes that are entered into the routing table as shown here:

```
Router-1#show ip route eigrp
     10.0.0.0/8 is variably subnetted, 3 subnets
D       10.1.6.0/32 [120/1] via 10.1.6.1, 00:00:28, Ethernet0
D       10.2.6.0/32 [120/1] via 10.2.6.1, 00:00:10, Ethernet1
D       10.3.6.0/32 [120/1] via 10.3.6.1, 00:00:45, Ethernet2
```

- **Show ip eigrp traffic**   Displays the number of packets sent and received through EIGRP. This also displays statistics on hello, queries, acknowledgments, updates, and replies.

- **Debug ip eigrp**   Displays packet information that can help you analyze packets that are sent and received on an interface. Because this command generates a large amount of traffic, you need to use it with extreme caution.

- **Debug eigrp packet**   Displays the transmission and receipt of EIGRP packets. They may be hello, update, query, reply, or request packets. This also displays the sequence and acknowledgment numbers used by the EIGRP algorithm. The following example shows the output of this command.

```
Router-1#debug eigrp packet
EIGRP: Sending HELLO on Ethernet0
   AS 1, Flags 0x0, Seq 0, Ack 0
EIGRP: Received UPDATE on Ethernet0 from 10.1.1.1,
   AS 1, Flags 0x0, Seq 0, Ack 0
EIGRP: Sending HELLO/ACK on Ethernet0 to 10.1.1.1,
   AS 1, Flags 0x0, Seq 0, Ack 0
```

- **Debug eigrp fsm**   Displays debugging information about the EIGRP feasible successor metrics (FSMs). This command helps you observe EIGRP FSM activity to determine where route updates are being installed and deleted by the routing process.

How Does OSPF Work?

This section covers the basic operation, configuration, and verification of the *Open Shortest Path First (OSPF)* routing algorithm. OSPF is the first true link-state routing protocol we talk about, as opposed to the distance vector and hybrid routing protocols already covered. This routing protocol was written for large and rapidly growing networks because it allows you to break down a large network into smaller more manageable areas.

Link-state routers maintain an overall picture of the network and exchange route information upon changes within the network. Routers that use a link-state routing protocol do not broadcast their routing tables as distance vector routing protocols do. Instead, when a change is detected, routing changes are flooded immediately to all routers in the network, which are affected by the change. The changes are computed across the network at the same time.

OSPF improved on the traditional distance vector routing protocols by incorporating new options and improving on some existing technologies. OSPF was developed in 1988 by the Internet Engineering Task Force (IETF), which used the Dijkstra algorithm, and the most recent version, OSPF version 2, is described in RFC 2178. OSPF was developed to address the needs for a routing protocol that can be used in large, scalable internetworks. The areas of improvement that OSPF addressed were as follows:

- **Path selection** OSPF uses a *cost* variable, which is based on the speed of the link.

- **Bandwidth usage** OSPF multicasts link-state updates and then send these updates only when the topology of the network changes.

- **Network reachability** OSPF has virtually no limitations on reachability.

- **Variable-length subnet masks (VLSMs)** OSPF supports subnet masking and VLSMs.

■ **Convergence speed**   OSPF converges quickly because updates are sent not periodically, but only when changes occur. The routing changes are flooded, and computing is accomplished in parallel.

Along with these improvements are various terms associated with OSPF and link-state routing protocols in general, as follows:

■ **Cost**   Rather than assigning hops to a link, link-state protocols assign a cost, which is based on the speed of the medium connecting an interface.

■ **Link**   This is a router interface.

■ **Link-state**   This is the relationship between a router interface and its neighbors.

■ **Area**   An area is an internetwork that has the same area identification on all routers. All routers within the same area share the same link-state information.

■ **Designated router (DR) and backup designated router (BDR)** Each network has a DR and a BDR. The DR is the elected router that represents all the routers on the network. The BDR accomplishes the same thing if the DR fails.

■ **Adjacencies database**   This is a list of all the neighbors with which a router has bi-directional communication.

■ **Link-state database**   This is also called the *topological database*. It shows the internetwork topology information about all routers in the network.

■ **Routing table**   This is also called the *forwarding database*. The routing table is generated when an algorithm is run on the database. Each router has a unique routing table.

exam
ⓦatch   *The benefits of OSPF include no hop count limitation, the capability to multicast routing updates, faster convergence, and better path selection.*

How to Configure OSPF

OSPF is probably the most difficult of the routing protocols covered to configure because of the number of commands and functionality that OSPF presents. The whole point of OSPF is to configure *areas* in the internetwork to minimize routing tables. This is a convenient option to have if you have a large network that can be divided into areas. Each router in an area will display routes to only routers in the same area, allowing for summarization of networks across the internetwork backbone area.

The commands for OSPF basic configurations are fairly simple but can get complex quickly depending on the size of your network. We cover just the basic configuration commands for getting OSPF working on a router. The commands needed are *router ospf process-id* and the *network/area* commands. The router ospf *process-id* command specifies that you are using the OSPF routing process. The network command associates an IP address, address mask, area, and area-id with a network that is connected to the router. Once these commands are implemented, the routing process will associate IP addresses and areas with router interfaces, and the router will start processing traffic. The following example displays the syntax in which these commands are used.

```
Router-1 (config)#router ospf 123
Router-1 (config-router)#network 10.0.0.0.0.255.255.255 area 0
```

You must identify the area to which the network belongs. The value of the network can be either the network address supported by the router or the interface addresses that are configured. The router can interpret the address by comparing it with the address mask in the configuration.

Displaying OSPF Information

There are several common commands you should become very familiar with to verify correct configuration and operation of an OSPF network. Since OSPF is more complex than other routing protocols, more can go wrong. Therefore, more commands to display information are necessary:

- **Show ip route ospf**   Displays the routes known to the router through the OSPF process. This is one of the best ways to determine connectivity between OSPF routers in a network.

- **Show ip ospf interface**   Verifies that interfaces have been configured in the areas that they were intended to be configured in. It also gives the intervals for hello timers and neighbor adjacencies.

- **Show ip ospf**   Displays the number of times that the shortest path first (SPF) algorithm has been executed on a router. It also shows the link-state update interval.

- **Show ip ospf neighbor detail**   Displays a detailed list of neighbor routers, their states, and their priorities. This is shown in the following example.

```
Router-1#show ip ospf neigh detail
Neighbor Router-2, interface address 10.2.6.1
  In the area 0 via interface FastEthernet0/0
  Neighbor priority is 1, State is FULL
  Options 2
  Dead timer due in 00:00:35
  Link State retransmission due in 00:00:03
    LSA in retransmission queue 2
Neighbor Router-3, interface address 10.3.6.1
  In the area 0 via interface ATM4/0
  Neighbor priority is 1, State is FULL
  Options 2
  Dead timer due in 00:00:38
```

- **Show ip ospf database**   Displays the contents of the topological database in a router. It also displays the router ID and process ID.

- **Debug ip ospf events**   Displays information on OSPF-related events, such as adjacencies, flooding information, DR selection, and the SPF calculation. The following example displays the output of this command.

```
Router-1#debug ip ospf events
OSPF events debugging is on
Router-1#
*Dec 7 03:11:12: OSPF: service_maxage: Trying to delete MAXAGE LSA
*Dec 7 03:11:42: OSPF: service_maxage: Trying to delete MAXAGE LSA
*Dec 7 03:12:12: OSPF: service_maxage: Trying to delete MAXAGE LSA
```

- **Debug ip ospf packet** Displays the output of each OSPF packet received on a given router. This command provides a separate output for each OSPF packet received on a router. This can be a CPU-intensive command, so use caution when implementing it.

Several debug commands are associated with OSPF, so be sure that you research or test the different commands. Doing so will allow you to have a broad knowledge of commands' specific information, which can be very important when you are troubleshooting a complex OSPF issue.

CERTIFICATION OBJECTIVE 3.05

Use and Basic Operation of BGP

Border Gateway Protocol (BGP) is the primary routing protocol used throughout the Internet by Internet service providers (ISPs) to connect enterprise networks. BGP is known as an interdomain routing protocol that guarantees loop-free operation and exchange of routing information among different autonomous systems. BGP is defined in detail in RFCs 1163, 1267, 1654, 1772, and 1930. The routing protocols discussed earlier were Interior Gateway Protocols (IGPs). BGP is different from IGP protocols in the following ways:

- BGP does not use technical metrics to make its routing decisions. Instead, it is a policy-based routing protocol, meaning that routing decisions are made based on policies established in the router.

- BGP uses Transmission Control Protocol (TCP) connections to exchange routing updates with other BGP routers. This means that TCP transactions must be completed prior to an exchange of updates.

This complex routing protocol has other differences, which make it very complicated to configure and maintain. This is why you pay ISPs to take care of the majority of the BGP configuration when you connect to the Internet.

There is a saying that sums up a person's need for BGP: "If you think you need BGP, you probably don't." This means that there are only a few circumstances in which BGP is actually the right solution. BGP technology and implementation are more complex than any IGP protocol like OSPF or EIGPR. The best way to determine if you really need BGP is to refer to RFC 1930, *Guidelines for Creation, Selection, and Registration of an Autonomous System,* or RFC 1772, *Application of the Border Gateway Protocol in the Internet.* These two documents should answer any questions you have concerning BGP and its appropriateness as a solution for you.

exam
ⓦatch

It is necessary to use BGP to connect to an ISP only when you and the ISP have different policy requirements.

For those connecting to two or more ISPs, it is frequently necessary to use BGP as the routing protocol to make the connection. Redundancy, load sharing, and lower tariffs are the main factors driving some administrators to connect to more than one ISP. You can usually get by with a combination of static and default routes instead of BGP; but any time your policy requirements differ from those of your ISP, BGP is required.

BGP sessions are carried via TCP, as discussed earlier. There are two types of sessions associated with BGP exchanges between a router and its neighbors. These two types are described as follows:

- **External BGP (EBGP) session**   This allows routers from two different autonomous systems to exchange information. These routers are usually adjacent to each other and share the same medium and subnet.

- **Internal BGP (IBGP) session**   This allows routers in the same autonomous system to exchange information. It is used to synchronize and coordinate routing policy throughout the autonomous system. These routers can be located anywhere within the autonomous system.

How to Configure BGP

BGP command syntax is similar to that for other routing protocols, but there are also significant differences in the way that it functions. The autonomous system (AS) number will be assigned to you by the InterNIC because this number is different from the AS number for IGRP or OSPF in which any number can be assigned. We will also be adding the routers' neighbors into the router configuration so that there will be an exchange of information between routers of different autonomous systems.

When you are configuring BGP on a router, there are steps you need to follow to ensure proper operation. The following steps will make configuration of BGP on a router a little simpler:

■ Configure the BGP routing process using the *router bgp* command.

■ Configure the networks internal to the AS that will be advertised using the *network* command.

■ Configure the relationship that this router will have with other routers using the *neighbor* command.

■ Configure administrative weights to paths to control path selection.

Following these steps, you can configure a router for basic BGP operation. If you feel you need to take full advantage of BGP's features, talk to a Cisco Systems engineer who can help you customize BGP on your internetwork. The following example displays the configuration commands for BGP operation.

```
Router-1 (config)#router bgp 1
Router-1 (config-router)#network 10.1.1.0
Router-1 (config-router)#neighbor 10.1.2.1.remote-as 1
Router-1 (config-router)#neighbor 10.1.3.1.remote-as 2
```

Displaying BGP Information

There are several common commands you should become very familiar with to verify correct configuration and operation of a BGP network. Because BGP is more complex than other routing protocols, more can go wrong, and more commands are available to help you troubleshoot. BGP operation can be verified through the following commands:

- **Show ip bgp neighbors**   Displays the status of all BGP connected neighbors.

- **Show ip bgp paths**   Displays all possible paths that BGP has in its database.

- **Show ip bgp summary**   Displays the status of all BGP connections.

- **Show ip bgp**   Displays all entries in the BGP routing table. You can also either use the *subnets* keyword to find specific information on a network or add the network number at the end of the command.

- **Debug ip bgp**   Displays debug messages about BGP events, including inbound updates.

- **Debug ip-bgp-events**   Displays debug messages about BGP events, including BGP state machine changes and outbound updates.

- **Debug ip-bgp-updates**   Displays debug messages about BGP events, including per-update messages.

Knowing what information each of these commands can provide and knowing what the information means will benefit you when you are troubleshooting or configuring BGP on a router. More information can be found in user documentation or via the Cisco Web site.

on the Job   *Use the clear command with the asterisk (*) option whenever you make changes to a configuration so that those changes take immediate effect. By doing this, you force propagation of this change across the network, thus alleviating problems when a configuration change does not occur on the network.*

CERTIFICATION OBJECTIVE 3.06

What Is IP Multicast, and When Is It Used?

Traditional IP allows a single host to send packets to another host in what is referred to as a *unicast transmission*. When a host sends packets to all hosts on a network, that is referred to as a *broadcast transmission*. *IP multicast* provides a third scheme, which allows a host to send packets to a subset of all hosts, also known as a *group transmission*. Packets delivered to group members are identified by a single multicast group address. These multicast packets are delivered to a group with best-effort reliability, much as for IP unicast packets.

The multicast environment consists of senders and receivers. Every host is capable of sending to a group, regardless of whether it is a member, but only the members of a group receive the message. A multicast address is chosen for the receivers in a multicast group, and the senders use that address as the destination address of a datagram to reach all members of the group. Membership in a multicast group is dynamic, allowing hosts to join or leave at any time. This means that there is no restriction on location or number of members in a multicast group. Routers running a multicast routing protocol, such as Protocol-Independent Multicast (PIM), maintain forwarding tables so that multicast datagrams can be routed. Routers use the Internet Group Management Protocol (IGMP) to learn whether members of a group are present on their directly attached subnets. Hosts join a multicast group by sending IGMP report messages.

How to Configure IP Multicasting

IP multicast routing tasks are divided into basic and advanced tasks. The first two basic tasks discussed here are required to configure IP multicast routing. We also cover a couple of optional commands that are not required, but may be used:

- **IP multicast-routing**   This command enables IP multicast routing on the router.

- **IP pim dense-mode**   This command must be applied to an interface on the router. Dense mode interfaces are always added to the multicast routing table.

- **IP pim sparse-mode**   This command must be applied to an interface on the router. Sparse mode interfaces are added to the multicast routing table only when changes occur in the network topology.

Note: You must select either dense mode or sparse mode because this command enables IGMP operation on that particular interface.

- **IP pim rp-address** This command configures the address of a PIM rendezvous point.

Many commands are associated with configuring IP multicast routing, so if you intend to implement IP multicast routing, consult a Cisco Engineer. Doing so will allow you to grasp the full functionality of IP multicasting, and it will allow you to implement this functionality with a knowledgeable Cisco Engineer who should be able to answer any of your questions or concerns. The following are examples of configuring PIM dense mode and sparse mode interfaces.

```
Router-1 (config)#ip multicast-routing
Router-1 (config)#interface ethernet 0
Router-1 (config-int)#ip pim dense-mode

Router-1 (config)#ip multicast-routing
Router-1 (config)#ip pim rp-address 10.8.0.20 1
Router-1 (config)#interface ethernet 1
Router-1 (config-int)#ip pim sparse-mode
```

How to Display IP Multicast Routing Information

You can display specific statistical information such as the contents of IP routing tables, caches, and databases. The information provided can be used to determine resource utilization and solve network problems. These commands will also display information about node reachability and discover the routing path that your device is taking through the network. The following commands can help you get this information:

- **Mrinfo** *[hostname or address] [source address or interface]* This command will query a multicast router about which neighboring multicast routers are peering with it.

- **Mstat** *source [destination] [group]* This command displays IP multicast packet rate and loss information.

- **Show ip igmp interface**   This command displays multicast-related information about a particular interface.

- **Show ip mroute**   This command displays the contents of the IP multicast routing table.

- **Debug ip mpacket**   This command displays IP multicast packets received and transmitted. You can use the *detail* option to display IP header information, as well as MAC address information.

- **Debug ip mrouting**   This command displays changes to the IP multicast routing table. The following example shows the output of this command.

```
Router-1#debug ip mrouting

IP multicast routing debugging is on
MRT: Delete (10.0.0.0/8, 224.2.0.1) MRT: Delete (10.3.0.0/16, 224.2.0.1)
MRT: Delete (10.2.0.0/16, 224.2.0.1) MRT: Delete (10.5.0.0/16, 224.2.0.1)
MRT: Delete (10.4.0.0/16, 224.2.0.1) MRT: Create (*, 224.2.0.1), if_input
NULL
MRT: Create (10.10.10.0/24, 225.2.2.4), if_input Ethernet0, RPF nbr
10.10.10.1
MRT: Create (10.10.0.0/24, 225.2.2.4), if_input Ethernet1. RPF nbr 0.0.0.0
MRT: Create (10.0.0.0/8, 224.2.0.1), if_input Ehternet1, RPF nbr 0.0.0.0
MRT: Create (10.6.0.0/16, 224.2.0.1), if_input Ethernet 1, RPF nbr 0.0.0.0
MRT: Create (10.8.0.0/16, 224.2.0.1), if_input Ethernet1, RPF nbr 0.0.0.0
MRT: Create (10.12.0.016, 224.2.0.1), if_input Ethernet1, RPF nbr 0.0.0.0
MRT: Create (10.14.0.0/16, 224.2.0.1), if_input Ethernet1, RPF nbr 0.0.0.0
```

CERTIFICATION OBJECTIVE 3.07

What Is NLSP and When Is It Used?

Novell's *NetWare Link Services Protocol (NLSP)* is a link-state routing protocol that provides fast convergence and reduced routing and service update traffic in an IPX environment. NLSP is based on the International Organization for Standardization (ISO) Intermediate System–to–Intermediate System (IS-IS) protocol. NLSP was created to improve scalability, reduce overhead, manage demands more effectively, and increase efficiency and effectiveness of routing in an IPX network.

By using NLSP, you can take advantage of several improvements and features that NSLP has over the other IPX routing protocol IPX RIP, which is a distance vector protocol. The following are the features and improvements NLSP provides:

- NSLP is backward compatible with RIP and SAP.

- NLSP virtually alleviates routing loops because the routers receive information firsthand.

- NLSP uses a cost metric, similar to that for OSPF.

- NLSP has a greater hop count enable, so you are not limited to 15 hops as you would be with RIP.

- NSLP only updates sends when the network topology or the default setting of every two hours changes.

- NLSP has a faster convergence than RIP because NLSP takes the information from a routing update and copies the information from each packet and then forwards it. RIP must update its routing table before it can forward it.

- NLSP supports multiple areas and route aggregation. This allows for route summarization and definition of logical areas.

Before an NLSP router can exchange information, it must complete a process that includes learning about other routers on the network and learning the network topology. The routes will exchange hello packets with neighbors to establish adjacencies and determine the designated router for the network. Each router then sends a link-state packet (LSP) that will include the information from its routing database. This LSP will include service and route information for each connection that the router is aware of. The LSP is flooded to all routers across the network.

The router then takes the LSP that it receives and copies the information from it into its database so that it has a current view of the network topology. To ensure that all router LSP databases are synchronized, the DR will periodically flood a summary of its database in a complete sequence number packet (CSNP) to all routers on the network. The non-DR routers compare this CSNP packet with that on their database, and if it is the same, the packet is discarded. If there is a difference, one of two things will occur:

■ If the non-DR router is missing information, it will multicast a partial sequence number packet (PSNP), requesting the complete database. The DR will then multicast the complete database to all routers on the network.

■ If the non-DR router has a more up-to-date database, it will flood the LSP across the network. Using the database and using cost as a metric, each router will determine the best path to each network. The routers will independently calculate the shortest path to each network by using the SPF algorithm. These results are then placed in a forwarding database, and the router forwards packets based on the information listed in the forwarding database.

How to Configure NLSP

Configuration of NLSP is a bit different from that for other protocols because a number of global and interface configuration commands must be executed. Global IPX routing must already be enabled before NSLP commands will be accepted. NLSP LAN interfaces must already have a hexadecimal IPX network number entry in the configuration. The following commands are needed for configuration:

■ **IPX internal-network** *network-number*   This number is set as a primary network number that is associated with the router. It must be hexadecimal in value and up to four bytes long.

■ **IPX router nlsp**   This enables the NLSP routing process on the router.

■ **Area address** *address-mask*   This mandatory command sets the area for link-state networking. If the area address and mask are both set to 0, then all networks are included in the area.

■ **IPX nslp enable**   This is an interface command that starts the NLSP process on each interface that you want to use NLSP on.

Displaying NLSP Information

Problems with displaying NLSP information and troubleshooting NLSP problems can be greatly reduced if you know a couple of commands that list this information. As stated earlier, the more you understand about a command and the information it displays, the easier your life will be when problems crop up, and they will. The following is a list of several commands that can be used to display NLSP information:

- **Show ipx route**   Displays a summarized routing table for a router.

- **Show ipx nlsp neighbor detail**   Displays the network address of connected nodes on each interface.

- **Show ipx nlsp database**   Displays the link-state database on each router to include adjacencies, link-state, and forwarding databases.

- **Debug ipx routing**   Displays information on IPX routing packets that the router sends and receives. The following example shows the output of this command.

```
Router-1# debug ipx routingNovellNLSP: update from
9999.0260.8c6a.1733
     110801 in 1 hops, delay 2
NovellRIP: sending update to 12FF02:ffff.ffff.ffff via Ethernet 1
     network 555, metric 2, delay 3
     network 1234, metric 3, delay 4
```

CERTIFICATION OBJECTIVE 3.08

How Does AppleTalk Routing Work?

This section briefly covers AppleTalk routing protocols and where they are used in a network environment. *AppleTalk* is a local area networking system that was developed by Apple Computer, Inc. AppleTalk networks can run over a variety of networks that include Ethernet, FDDI, and Token Ring, as well as Apple's proprietary media system LocalTalk. Along with developing its own protocols and media system, Apple decided it would need a routing protocol that could move the information across the network and came up with the *Routing Table Maintenance Protocol (RTMP)*.

RTMP is responsible for establishing and maintaining the routing table in all routers that are running AppleTalk. RTMP falls into the category of distance vector routing protocols such as RIP and IGRP. It is similar to RIP in that it has only one routing metric, which is hop count, and it sends out its routing table in periodic updates every 10 seconds.

When a failure in the network is detected, a router will send its update to all its neighbors. The router continues to send out its updates at the specified interval even if there is no response from a neighbor. After there has been no response from a particular router within the update interval, that route is marked as *suspect*. A route will be marked as *bad* if there is no response within 20 seconds and then finally removed from the routing table completely if there is no response within 60 seconds.

RTMP was designed primarily for use on LANs, but it can be used on WAN interfaces. This is not recommended, though, because routing updates are broadcast every 10 seconds and could cause a severe degradation of service across the WAN. Apple realized that with a growing network, RTMP was not the best solution for a routing protocol for use over WAN interfaces, which led to the development of *AppleTalk Update Routing Protocol (AURP)*.

AURP is also a distance vector protocol, but it broadcasts changes only to a routing table, reducing the amount of traffic being processed across the WAN link and thus increasing performance. AURP does not, however, replace RTMP as the routing protocol of choice in a LAN environment because AURP can be implemented only on "tunnel" interfaces that run across an IP network. The AURP protocol takes all traffic and encapsulates it into an IP packet for transmission across the tunnel. Once it reaches the other end, it is unencapsulated back into its original form.

CERTIFICATION OBJECTIVE 3.09

How Does IBM Routing Work?

IBM technologies have been a mainstay in the networking arena for many years now. Cisco routers are usually integrated into an IBM network to connect mainframes or to replace front-end processors (FEPs). With the advent of personal computers, client/server operations, and multiprotocol networks, there was a need to change IBM platforms to a less hierarchical architecture. With this in mind, IBM evolved its Systems Network Architecture (SNA) protocol into a more robust protocol with the creation of Advanced Peer-to-Peer Networking (APPN) and Advanced Program-to-Program Computing (APPC), with all three being used in networks to this day. Because IBM applications will be around for quite awhile, it made more sense to be able to integrate them into a multiprotocol network than to create a separate network just for IBM traffic. There are many ways to implement IBM applications into a multiprotocol environment, ranging from direct channel attachments to a mainframe to encapsulation of SNA in IP packets via serial tunnel (STUN) or data-link switching (DLSw).

The biggest problem with migrating into a multiprotocol environment is that those responsible for delivery of application support lose the ability to guarantee response times. IBM traffic typically required low bandwidth, and TCP/IP applications are prone to bursty traffic that has high-bandwidth requirements. With this in mind, you can implement *priority output queuing* that will enable you to prioritize traffic based on protocol, size, physical interface, or SNA device.

How to Configure STUN

STUN was designed to allow IBM FEPs to communicate with each other over an IP network. FEPs use Synchronous Data Link Control (SDLC) frames to communicate, and STUN takes the SDLC frames and encapsulates them in an IP packet for transmission across the network. STUN enables routers to communicate on a peer-to-peer basis, which leaves us needing a way to identify a router to its peer or peers. We can accomplish this by configuring a peer name for each router. The name is an IP address on the router, and more so, the IP address on a loopback interface because the loopback interface is up as long as the router is up. When configuring STUN, you need to be aware of some specialized commands that are described as follows.

- **STUN protocol-group** Defines the type of STUN operation for the link.

- **STUN peer name** Defines the STUN ID of the local router.

- **STUN route address** Associates the SDLC address number with the serial interface through which you wish to direct STUN frames.

- **SDLC address** Interface configuration command to assign a set of secondary stations attached to the serial link.

Because we have covered the commands that are required, it would be helpful for you to see how this configuration would look. The following example shows the configuration of two routers that will be using STUN to communicate across an IP-based network.

```
Router-1#                                Router-2#
STUN PEER-NAME 10.10.10.1                STUN PEER-NAME 10.11.11.1
STUN PROTOCOL-GROUP 1 SDLC               STUN PROTOCOL-GROUP 1 SDLC
!                                        !
INTERFACE SERIAL0                        INTERFACE SERIAL0
NO IP ADDRESS                            NO IP ADDRESS
ENCAPSULATION STUN                       ENCAPSULATION STUN
SDLC ADDRESS01                           SDLC ADDRESS01
STUN ROUTE ADDRESS 01 INT SERIAL1        STUN ROUTE ADDRESS 01 INT SERIAL1
STUN ROUTE ADDRESS FF INT SERIAL1        STUN ROUTE ADDRESS 01 INT SERIAL1
CLOCKRATE 56000                          CLOCKRATE 56000
!                                        !
INTERFACE SERIAL1                        INTERFACE SERIAL1
10.10.1.1.255.255.255.252                10.10.1.1.255.255.255.252
!                                        !
INTERFACE LOOPBACK0                      INTERFACE LOOPBACK0
IP ADDRESS 10.1.1.1 255.255.255.         10.1.1.1 255.255.255.0
!                                        !
ROUTER IGRP                              ROUTER IGRP
NETWORK 10.0.0.0                         NETWORK 10.0.0.0
```

Displaying STUN Information

Once you have STUN configured on your router, how will you troubleshoot any problems that arise? The following commands can assist you in troubleshooting problems associated with STUN interfaces on your network:

- **Show STUN** This displays the current status of STUN connections.

■ **Debug STUN packet** This command shows packet information that is traveling through STUN interfaces. You can also use the *group* or *address* options with this command. This command is CPU intensive, so be careful when applying it to a router. The following example shows the output of this command.

```
Router-1#debug stun packet

STUN sdlc: 0:00:04 Serial0    NDI: (OC2/008) U:SNRM    PF:I
STUN sdlc: 0:00:01 Serial0    SDI: (OC2/008) U:UA      PF:I
STUN sdlc: 0:00:00 Serial0    SDI: (OC2/008) S:RR      PF:I NR:000
STUN sdlc: 0:00:00 Serial0    NDI: (OC2/008) I:        PF:I NS:000
```

■ **SDLC test** This command is used to determine the status of end stations. There are several options to this command, so learn their effects before implementing them.

How to Configure DLSw

After seeing how to interface IBM equipment with an IP network through a STUN interface, we learn how to do the same with DLSw. DLSw was designed to allow SNA and NetBIOS traffic to travel across an IP network. DLSw was implemented to overcome some of the problems inherent in source route bridging in large networks. Keep in mind that DLSw is not a layer-3 protocol. When implemented, it becomes layer 2 between the routers that are configured. The commands that are required to configure DLSw are described as follows:

■ **DLSw local-peer peer-id** This command enables DLSw on the router and specifies its DLSw ID.

■ **DLSw remote-peer** This command uses TCP to identify a remote peer with which to exchange DLSw information.

■ **SDLC VMAC** This command sets a MAC address for the serial port connecting to the SDLC controller. This enables complete source-to-destination addressing with link-level addresses.

■ **SDLC role primary** This command sets the end of the link specified as the primary.

- **SDLC xid**   Exchange identifier (XID) requests and responses are exchanged before the link between the router and the controller, reaching an "up" status. XID is derived from virtual telecommunications access method (VTAM) parameters that are established by the IBM administrators.

- **SDLC partner**   This defines the MAC address of the interface on the remote router that will be communicated with. It also contains the SDLC ID of the two DLSw routers that are connected.

- **SDLC DLSw**   This command associates the SDLC process with the DLSw process so that DLSw will switch SDLC traffic.

- **Source-bridge**   This command enables source route bridging on the router.

- **Source-bridge spanning**   This identifies the ports that will participate in defining the spanning tree on the network.

As you can see from the list of commands, configuring DLSw on a network is not a minor undertaking. It requires a thorough understanding of the situation and assistance from the IBM administrators who are involved in the project. The following example shows a basic configuration for two routers utilizing DLSw across an IP WAN to a Token Ring network at the distant end.

```
Router-1#                                   Router-2#
SOURCE-BRIDGE RING-GROUP 1000               SOURCE-BRIDGE RING-GROUP 1000
DLSW LOCAL-PEER PEER-ID 10.1.1.1            DLSW LOCAL-PEER PEER-ID 10.1.1.1
DLSW REMOTE-PEER 1000 TCP 10.1.1.           DLSW REMOTE-PEER 1000 TCP 10.1.1.2
!                                           !
INTERFACE LOOPBACK0                         INTERFACE LOOPBACK0
IP ADDRESS 10.1.1.1 255.255.255.0           IP ADDRESS 10.1.1.1 255.255.255.0
!                                           !
INTERFACE SERIAL0                           INTERFACE TOKEN RING0
NO IP ADDRESS                               IP ADDRESS 10.10.10.1 255.255.255.0
SDLC VMAC 1234.1234.1234.                   RING-SPEED 16
ENCAPSULATION SDLC                          SOURCE-BRIDGE 12 1000
CLOCKRATE 56000                             SOURCE-BRIDGE SPANNING 5
SDLC ROLE PRIMARY                           !
SDLC ADDRESS 04                             INTERFACE SERIAL1
SDLC XID 06 12345                           IP ADDRESS 10.10.1.2.255.255.255.252
SDLC PARTNER 1234.1234.ABCD 06
SDLC DLSW 1
!
INTERFACE SERIAL1
IP ADDRESS 10.10.1.1 255.255.255.252
```

Displaying DLSw Information

With DLSw fully configured on your router, how will you troubleshoot any problems that arise? The following commands can help you troubleshoot problems associated with DLSw interfaces that may show up on your network:

- **Show DLSW peers** This command allows you to show the status of remote peers. If the peer is not in *connect* status, no data traffic will be able to flow between end stations.

- **Show DLSW reachability** This command is used to determine which SNA or NetBIOS DLSw end stations a router has in its cache.

- **Debug DLSW** This enables the debugging of data-link switching. Several options can be used with this command, but be aware that using this command with no options enables all options.

- **Debug SDLC** This displays information on SDLC frames received and sent by any router serial interface involved in supporting SDLC end-station functions.

- **Debug SDLC packet** This displays packet information on SDLC frames sent and received by any router serial interface involved in supporting SDLC end-station functions. The following example shows the output of this command.

```
Router-1#debug sdlc packet 20
 Serial0 SDLC Output
00000 C3842C00 02010010 019000C5 C5C5C5C% Cd...........EEEEE
00010 C5C5C5C5                   EEEE
 Serial0 SDLC Output
00000 C3952C00 02010011 039020F2     Co...........2
 Serial0 SDLC Output
00000 V4962C00 0201000C 039020F2     Do...........2
 Serial0 SDLC input
00000   C491
```

CERTIFICATION OBJECTIVE 3.10

What Does DECnet Do for Routing?

Digital Equipment Corporation designed the DECnet protocol as part of its Digital Network Architecture (DNA). DECnet supports both connectionless and connection-oriented network layers implemented by the Open Systems Interconnection (OSI) protocols. DECnet's most recent product release is called Phase V, which is equivalent to ISO Connectionless Network Service (CLNS). Phase V is fully compatible with DECnet's earlier version, Phase IV, as well as all OSI protocols.

DECnet supports two types of nodes: end nodes and routing nodes. Although both can send and receive network information, only routing nodes can provide routing services. DECnet addresses are not associated with the physical networks to which the nodes are connected. DECnet locates hosts using area and node address pairs. Areas can span many nodes, and one cable can support many areas.

How to Configure DECnet

DECnet routing nodes are either level-1 or level-2 routers. A level-1 router communicates with end nodes and with other level-1 routers in a particular area. Level-2 routers communicate with level-1 routers in the same area and with level-2 routers in different areas. The following commands are used to configure DECnet on a router:

- **DECnet** *network-number* **routing** *decnet-address*   This enables the DECnet routing protocol on a global basis.

- **DECnet** *network-number* **node-type area**   This command specifies an interarea node type of router.

- **DECnet** *network-number* **node-type routing-iv**   This command specifies an intra-area node type of router.

- **DECnet cost**   This assigns a cost to an interface on the router.

  Following is the command syntax for implementing DECnet on a router.

  ```
  Router-1 (config)#decnet routing 4.27
  Router-1 (config-router)#decnet node area
  Router-1 (config)#interface ethernet 0
  Router-1 (config-int)#decnet cost 4
  Router-1 (config)#interface serial 1
  Router-1 (config-int)#decnet cost 10
  ```

How to Display DECnet Information

Configuring DECnet on your router was the easy part, but now how will you be able to verify correct operation? The following commands can help you troubleshoot network problems associated with the DECnet routing process:

- **Show decnet route**   Use this command to display the DECnet routing table.

- **Show decnet traffic**   This command shows the DECnet traffic statistics, including datagrams sent, received, and forwarded.

- **Show decnet interface**   This command displays the global DECnet status and configuration for all interfaces or the status and configuration for a specified interface.

- **Debug decnet events**   This displays debugging information on DECnet events.

- **Debug decnet packets**   This displays debugging information on DECnet packet events.

- **Debug decnet routing**   This displays all DECnet routing-related events occurring at the router. The following example shows the output of this command.

```
Router-1#debug decnet routing

DNET-RT: Received level-1 routing from 1.3 onEthernet0 at 1:16:34
DNET-RT: Sending routes
DNET-RT: Sending normal routing updates on Ethernet0
DNET-RT: level 1 routes from 1.5 on Ethernet0: entry for node 5 created
DNET-RT: route update triggered by after split route pointers in dn_rt_input
DNET-RT: Received level-1 routing from 1.5 on Ethernet 0 at 1:18:35
DNET-RT: Sending L1 triggered routes
DNET-RT: Sending L1 triggered routing updates on Ethernet0
DNET-RT: removing route to node 5
```

CERTIFICATION OBJECTIVE 3.11

What Are the Basics of IS-IS and Why Run It?

Intermediate System to Intermediate System (IS-IS) is an ISO dynamic routing specification. A link-state routing protocol, IS-IS is utilized in Digital

Equipment Corporation's DECnet Phase V. The protocol was made an "integrated" protocol so that it would carry information for protocols other than OSI protocols.

The technology incorporated into this protocol is similar to OSPF. IS-IS uses LSAs sent to communicate with all routers in a given area and hello packets to detect if a router is functioning properly. We cover some of the basic commands to configure IS-IS, but if you would like to know more, IS-IS is described in complete detail in ISO 10589.

How to Configure IS-IS

Enabling IS-IS requires that you create an IS-IS routing process and assign it to specific interfaces rather than to networks. Only one IS-IS process may be configured per router, whether you run integrated mode, ISO CLNS, or IP-only. Network entity titles (NETs) define the area addresses for the IS-IS area and the system ID of the router. The following commands are needed to configure IS-IS:

- **Router isis** This enables the IS-IS routing process and allows you to specify an IS-IS process for IP.

- **Net** *network-entity-title* This configures NETs for the routing process. You are allowed to specify a name as well as an address for the NET.

- **IP router isis** This command specifies the interface that should be actively routing IS-IS. This command must be applied under the **interface** *interface-type*.

Here is the command syntax for implementing IS-IS on a router:

```
Router-1 (config)#router isis
Router-1 (config-router)#net 49.0001.0000.0000.000a.00
Router-1 (config)#interface ethernet 0
Router-1 (config-int)#ip router isis
Router-1 (config)#interface serial 0
Router-1 (config-int)#ip router isis
```

How to Display IS-IS Information

The following commands can help you troubleshoot problems associated with the IS-IS routing process and verify proper configuration and operation of your router and IS-IS routing process:

- **Show isis database** Displays the IS-IS link-state database. There are several options to this command that yield more specific information.

- **Show isis spf-log** Displays how often and why the router has run a full SPF calculation.

- **Debug isis adj packets** Displays information on all adjacency-related activities such as hello packets sent and received, and IS-IS adjacencies going up and down.

- **Debug isis spf statistics** Displays statistical information about building routes between intermediate systems.

- **Debug isis update-packets** Displays various sequence number protocol data units and link-state packets that are detected by a router. The following example shows the output of this command.

```
Router# debug isis update-packets

ISIS-Update:Sending L1 CSNP on Ethernet0
ISIS-Update:Sending L2 CSNP on Ethernet0
ISIS-Update:Updating L2 LSP
ISIS-Update:Delete link 888.8800.0181.00 from/
 L2 LSP 1600.8906.4022.00-00, seq E
ISIS-Update:Updating L1 LSP
ISIS-Update:Sending L1 CSNP on Ethernet0
ISIS-Update:Sending L2 CSNP on Ethernet0
ISIS-Update:Add link 888.8800.0181.00 from L2/
 LSP 1600.8906.4022.00-00, new seq 10, len 91
ISIS-Update:Sending L2 LSP 1600.8906.4022.00-00, seq 10,ht 1198 on Tunnel0
ISIS-Update:Sending L2 CSNP on Tunnel0
ISIS-Update:Updating L2 LSP
ISIS-Update:Rate limiting L2 LSP 1600.8906.4022.00-00, seq 11 (Tunnel0)
ISIS-Update:Updating L1 LSP
ISIS-Update: Rec L2 LSP 888.8800.0181.00.00-00 (Tunnel0)
ISIS-Update: PSNP entry 1600.8906.4022.00-00, seq 10, ht 1196
```

RSVP

Resource Reservation Protocol (RSVP) is an IP service that allows end systems on either side of a routed network to establish a reserved-bandwidth path between them to predetermine and ensure quality of service (QoS) for their data transmission. RSVP allows end systems to request QoS guarantees from the network. Data applications frequently demand relatively lower bandwidth than real-time traffic. The constant high bit-rate demands of a videoconference application and the bursty bit-rate demands of an interactive data application share available network resources. RSVP prevents the demands of high-bandwidth traffic from impairing the bandwidth resources necessary for bursty data traffic. Routers sort and prioritize packets much as a statistical time-division multiplexer would sort and prioritize several signal sources that share a single channel.

RSVP enables real-time traffic to reserve resources necessary for consistent latency. A videoconferencing application can use settings in the router to propagate a request for a path with the required bandwidth and delay across the network to accomplish the application. RSVP can adjust and alter the path between end stations to recover from route changes by repeatedly checking reservations at regular intervals. There are two types of multicast flows:

- **Distinct reservation** This flow originates from exactly one sender.
- **Shared reservation** This flow originates from one or more senders.

How to Configure RSVP

Before you configure RSVP, you must plan carefully to successfully implement RSVP on your network. You must assess the bandwidth needs on router interfaces that RSVP will be implementing. By default, the amount of bandwidth reservable by a single flow can be the entire reservable bandwidth. However, you can limit individual reservations to smaller amounts using the single-flow bandwidth parameter. The reserved bandwidth value may not exceed the interface reservable amount, and no one flow may reserve more than the amount specified. Seventy-five percent of the bandwidth available on an interface is reservable, by default. End-to-end controls for data traffic will assume that all sessions will behave to avoid congestion. Determine the bandwidth to set aside so that bursty traffic will not be deprived as a side effect of the QoS configuration.

After you have planned how to implement an RSVP configuration, you will need to actually sit down and execute the commands to configure RSVP. To configure RSVP, you will need to perform the following tasks.

- **IP rsvp bandwidth** *interface-kbps single-flow-kbps*   This command enables RSVP on an IP interface.

- **IP rsvp sender**   This command enters the senders' names into the RSVP database.

- **IP rsvp reservation**   This command enters the receivers' names into the RSVP database.

- **IP rsvp udp-multicast**   This command enters any multicast address necessary if you use UDP.

- **IP rsvp neighbors**   This command limits which routers may offer reservations based on access lists that are configured.

    Here is the basic configuration for RSVP on a router:

```
hostname Router-1
!
ip subnet-zero
no ip domain-lookup
ip multicast-routing
ip dvmrp route-limit 20000
!
interface Ethernet0
ip address 10.1.1.2.255.0.0.0
no ip directed-broadcast
ip pim dense-mode
ip rsvp bandwidth 10 10
fair-queue 64 256 1000
media-type 10BaseT
!
interface Hssi0
ip address 10.10.10.1 255.255.255.252
no ip directed-broadcast
```

```
ip pim dense-mode
ip rsvp bandwidth 1 1
!
router ospf 100 network 11.0.0.0 0.255.255.255 area 10
network 12.0.0.0 0.255.255.255 area 10
!
ip classless
ip rsvp sender 225.1.1.1 12.1.2.1 UDP 7001 7000 12.1.2.1 Hs0 20 1
!
```

The following commands can help you troubleshoot problems associated with the RSVP process:

- **Show ip rsvp interface**   Displays the RSVP-related interface information.

- **Show ip rsvp installed**   Displays RSVP-related filters and bandwidth information.

- **Show ip rsvp neighbor**   Displays current RSVP neighbors.

- **Show ip rsvp sender**   Displays RSVP sender information.

- **Show ip rsvp request**   Displays RSVP request information.

- **Show ip rsvp reservations**   Displays RSVP receiver information.

- **Debug ip rsvp**   Enables logging of significant RSVP events, such as new senders, subsequent discontinuation of senders, and installation and removal of reservations. The following example shows the output of this command.

```
Router-1#debug ip rsvp

RSVP: PATH message for 10.1.1.1 (ethernet0) from 10.1.1.2
RSVP: send path multicast about 10.1.1.2 on Ethernet0
RSVP: IP to 10.1.1.2 length=52 checksum=720C Ethernet0/0
RSVP: RESV message for 10.1.1.1(Serial0) rom10.10.10.2
RSVP: remove Ethernet0/1 PATH 1.1.1.1(1234)<-10.10.10.2(17:1234)
RSVP: send path teardown multicast about 1.1.1.1 on Ethernet0/2
RSVP: RESV message fro 10.1.1.1(Serial0) from10.10.10.2
RSVP send reservation error to 10.10.10.2 about 10.1.1.1
RSVP: IP to 10.10.10.2 length=40 checksum=1A84 if Serial0
RSVP RESV: no path information for 10.1.1.1
```

CERTIFICATION SUMMARY

As you have learned in this chapter, there is much information about routing protocols to consider when you design a network.

Routing algorithms are defined as conforming to one of two basic algorithms, either distance vector or link state. With distant vector protocols, copies of the routing table are periodically passed from router to router. This step-by-step process occurs in all directions between direct-neighbor routers. This way, the protocol can maintain a database of topology information, but distance vector protocols do not allow a router to know the exact topology of a network. Examples of distance vector routing protocols covered are RIP and IGRP.

Link-state protocols, also known as shortest path first (SPF) algorithms, maintain a complex database of topology information. A link-state routing algorithm maintains full knowledge of distant routers and the ways they interconnect. Link-state routing uses LSPs, a topological database, an SPF algorithm, an SPF tree, and a routing table of paths and ports to each network. Examples of link-state routing protocols covered are NLSP, OSPF, and IS-IS.

There is one more type of protocol that doesn't fall into either category. This is the hybrid protocol. This emerging protocol combines aspects of both distance vector and link state and uses distance vector with more accurate metrics to determine the best paths to destination networks. It differs from most distance vector protocols in that it uses topology changes to trigger routing database updates. An example of a hybrid protocol is EIGRP.

BGP is a protocol you may never encounter in your production network because it is so difficult to configure and maintain that the brunt of this load is handled by ISPs. Remember that if you think that you will need to implement BGP, you should consult the RFCs mentioned in the BGP section to help you make this decision.

NLSP is a Novell link-state routing protocol that runs in an IPX environment. NLSP has the same characteristics of OSPF and functions the same ways. NSLP has several functions that give it functionality that is superior to that of the other IPX routing protocol, IPX RIP. NLSP provides a robust link-state routing protocol that has none of the limitations that IPX RIP encounters, thus making it the protocol of choice on larger IPX networks.

In summary, the topics covered in this chapter have the information to assist you in making the proper decisions when you are working with the protocol in question. The information presented is only an overview of the protocols and technologies. There are more in-depth articles and books that will give you a rock-solid understanding of what you are researching. This chapter does, however, give you the proper tools to make sound decisions about these technologies and lets you know when you should get outside assistance before getting into a project too deep. The following chapters will help you build on the knowledge you have gained from this one, thus creating a sound foundation on which to base decisions.

TWO-MINUTE DRILL

- ❑ RIP is a distance vector routing protocol.
- ❑ RIP uses hop count as its metric to determine path selection.
- ❑ IGRP is a distance vector routing protocol developed by Cisco Systems.
- ❑ IGRP uses a combination of metrics to determine path selection: bandwidth, delay, reliability, load, and MTU size.
- ❑ EIGRP is considered a hybrid routing protocol because it is a combination of distance vector and link-state algorithms. It was developed by Cisco Systems.
- ❑ EIGRP supports automatic route summarization and VLSM addressing.
- ❑ OSPF is a link-state routing protocol.
- ❑ OSPF breaks a network into specific areas to allow for route summarization and to keep routing updates local to the areas that they are assigned.
- ❑ BGP is an exterior routing protocol that is defined in several RFCs.
- ❑ BGP is a policy-based routing protocol you use to connect to ISPs when you have a policy different from that of the ISP you are connecting to.
- ❑ NLSP is an IPX link-state routing protocol that was developed by Novell.
- ❑ IBM routing utilizes several different configurations to run on an IP network.

❑ IBM uses STUN to connect over WAN connections and DLSw to pass SNA and NetBIOS traffic across IP networks.

❑ IP Multicast allows for information to be passed to groups of hosts instead of one host (unicast) or all hosts (broadcast).

❑ DECnet was developed by the Digital Equipment Corporation.

❑ DECnet uses the ISO link-state routing protocol IS-IS.

❑ IS-IS was developed by the International Standards Organization (ISO) so that there would be a routing protocol that mapped directly to the OSI reference model.

❑ IS-IS is a link-state routing protocol that has the same functionality as OSPF.

❑ RSVP allows for dedicated QoS solutions across a network for specific applications, such as video teleconferencing and voice over IP.

SELF TEST

The following questions will help you measure your understanding of the material presented in this chapter. Read all the choices carefully because there may be more than one correct answer. Choose all the correct answers for each question.

1. What metric(s) does RIP use to determine path selections for routing traffic?

    A. Bandwidth

    B. Reliability

    C. Hop count

    D. Delay

2. How often does RIP advertise its routing table to its neighbors?

    A. Every 15 seconds

    B. Every 30 seconds

    C. Every 45 seconds

    D. Every 60 seconds

3. What feature(s) does IGRP incorporate to help prevent routing loops?

    A. Hold-down timers

    B. Flash updates

    C. Poison reverse

    D. Split horizon

    E. All of the above

4. What is the default amount of time that hold-down timers neither advertise nor accept route advertisements?

    A. 90 seconds

    B. 100 seconds

    C. 200 seconds

    D. 280 seconds

5. What routing algorithm does EIGRP use?

    A. Diffusing update algorithm

    B. Dijkstra algorithm

    C. Bellman-Ford algorithm

    D. All of the above

6. The next hop router on an EIGPR primary route is referred to as the _____?

    A. Feasible successor

    B. Successor

    C. Designated router

    D. Backup designated router

7. Who developed OSPF?

    A. Cisco

    B. ISO

    C. IETF

    D. None of the above

8. Where is a list of all the neighbors in an OSPF network located?

    A. Adjacencies database

    B. Link-state database

    C. Neighbors database

    D. Forwarding database

9. What command displays only OSPF route information?

    A. show ip route

    B. show route ospf

    C. show route

    D. show ip route ospf

10. What does BGP use to exchange routing updates between BGP routers?

    A. TCP

    B. UDP

    C. LSP

    D. LSA

11. When is it necessary to use BGP?

    A. When you connect to multiple ISPs

    B. When you connect to a distance vector protocol

    C. When you connect to a link-state protocol

    D. When you have policies different from those of your ISP

12. How do routers learn whether members of a group are on directly attached subnets?

    A. ICMP

    B. IGRP

    C. IGMP

    D. ICQ

13. What command displays the contents of the IP multicast routing table?

    A. show ip route

    B. show ip route multicast

    C. show multicast route

    D. show ip mroute

14. What routing protocol is NLSP based on?

    A. IS-IS

    B. OSPF

    C. EIGRP

    D. RIP

15. How often does NLSP send updates?

    A. Every 60 seconds

    B. Every 2 hours

    C. When the network topology changes

    D. Every hour

16. What command is issued to determine the status of end stations on an IBM network?

    A. SDLC test

    B. STUN test

    C. DLSw test

    D. IBM test

17. What type of routing nodes are there in a DECnet environment?

    A. Level 1
    B. Level 2
    C. Level 3
    D. Level 4

18. What command is issued to display the DECnet routing table?

    A. show ip decnet route
    B. show ip route decnet
    C. show decnet route
    D. show route decnet

19. What command is issued to display the IS-IS link-state database?

    A. show isis adjacencies
    B. show isis database
    C. show database isis
    D. show database adjacencies

20. What are the two types of multicast flows that refer to RSVP?

    A. Distinct reservation
    B. Traffic reservation
    C. Shared reservation
    D. Interface reservation

SELF TEST ANSWERS

1. ☑ **C.** RIP utilizes only one metric, hop count, when determining path selection.
   ☒ **A, B,** and **D** are incorrect because they are metrics used by other routing protocols such as EIGRP and OSPF.

2. ☑ **B.** By default, RIP advertises its routing table every 30 seconds.
   ☒ **A, C,** and **D** are invalid times.

3. ☑ **E.** IGRP uses all of these features to prevent routing loops on a network. These features are improvements from the RIP protocol.

4. ☑ **D.** The answer is three times the update interval (90 seconds) plus 10 seconds, or 280 seconds.
   ☒ **A, B,** and **C** are incorrect because they are invalid times.

5. ☑ **A.** EIGRP was designed to use the (DUAL) diffusing update algorithm.
   ☒ **B** is incorrect because OSPF uses the Dijkstra algorithm. **C** is incorrect because the Bellman-Ford algorithm is used by distance vector routing protocols such as IGRP and RIP.

6. ☑ **B.** The next hop router on the primary route is called the successor.
   ☒ **A** is incorrect because it is a back-up router. **C** is incorrect because it is the primary router in an OSPF network. **D** is incorrect because it is the secondary router in an OSPF network.

7. ☑ **C.** The Internet Engineering Task Force (IETF) developed OSPF in 1988.
   ☒ **A** is incorrect because Cisco developed IGRP and EIGRP. **B** is incorrect because the ISO developed IS-IS.

8. ☑ **A.** A list of all neighbors with which a router has bidirectional communication is located in the adjacencies database.
   ☒ **B** is incorrect because it shows the internetwork topology. **C** is incorrect because there is no neighbors database. **D** is incorrect because it is also known as the routing table.

9. ☑ **D.** The show ip route ospf command displays the routes known to the router through the OSPF process.
   ☒ **A** is incorrect because the show ip route command will show all routes in the routing table, not just OSPF routes. **A** and **B** are incorrect because they have incorrect syntax.

10. ☑ **A.** BGP uses TCP connections to exchange routing updates.
    ☒ **B** is incorrect because BGP needs a connection-oriented protocol to exchange updates;

UDP is connectionless. **C** is incorrect because LSP is used in the OSPF routing process. **D** is incorrect because LSA is also used in the OSPF routing process.

11. ☑ **A and D.** You need to use BGP when you connect to multiple ISPs and when you have policies different from those of your ISP.
☒ **B** and **C** are incorrect because you do not have to use BGP to connect to distance vector protocols or to link-state protocols.

12. ☑ **C.** IGMP is used to determine whether members of a group are present on directly attached subnets.
☒ **A** is incorrect because ICMP is used to ping a device. **B** is incorrect because IGRP is a routing protocol. **D** is incorrect because ICQ is a messaging program used on the Internet.

13. ☑ **D.** The show ip mroute command displays the contents of the IP multicast routing table.
☒ **A** is incorrect because the show ip route command will display the routing table. **B** is incorrect because the show ip route multicast command is an invalid command. **C** is incorrect because the show multicast route command is also an invalid command.

14. ☑ **A.** NLSP is link-state routing protocol that is based on the ISO IS-IS protocol.
☒ **B** is incorrect because OSPF was not developed by the ISO. **C** is incorrect because EIGRP is not a link-state routing protocol. **D** is incorrect because RIP is not a link-state routing protocol.

15. ☑ **B and C.** NLSP sends updates when the network topology changes or at the default setting of every two hours.
☒ **A and D** are incorrect because they are invalid times.

16. ☑ **A.** The SDLC test command is used to determine the status of end stations.
☒ **B, C,** and **D** are incorrect because they have incorrect syntax.

17. ☑ **A and B.** Level-1 routers communicate with end nodes and other level-1 routers; level-2 routers communicate with level-1 routers in the same area and with level-2 routers in different areas.
☒ **C and D** are incorrect because they are invalid routing node levels.

18. ☑ **C.** The show decnet route command is used to display the DECnet routing table.
☒ **A, B,** and **D** are incorrect because they have incorrect syntax.

19. ☑ **B.** The show isis database command displays the IS-IS link-state database.
☒ **A and D** are incorrect because they are invalid commands. **C** is incorrect because it has incorrect syntax.

20.   ☑   **A and C.** Distinct and shared reservation are the two types of multicast flows that allow flows from only one sender or flows from one or more senders.

☒   **B and D** are incorrect because they are invalid terms.

CISCO CERTIFIED DESIGN ASSOCIATE

4

WANs, LANs, and Networking Devices

The purpose of this chapter is to familiarize you with the concepts, applications, and terms frequently used in networking technology. We review the basics of several commonly used layer-1 and layer-2 technologies, discuss relative merits, and look at how this knowledge might be applied in the real world. It is assumed that you are already familiar with the OSI layer model, TCP/IP, and some basic networking concepts (such as the difference between WAN and LAN).

CERTIFICATION OBJECTIVE 4.01

Technologies Required by Networking Devices and Links, and Across the Network

You probably wouldn't be reading this book if you hadn't ever wondered how data gets from one computer to another. You've already read about the OSI layer model and some of the more popular protocol families in use today. This chapter focuses on OSI layers 1 and 2, the physical and data-link layers.

LAN Technologies

Today's local area network usually operates with some form of Ethernet, though FDDI is still in occasional use for servers, and Token Ring is still in use in some smaller networks. This section describes the logical structures and behavior of LAN protocols, as well as the physical characteristics of wiring commonly used in LANs.

Ethernet

Ethernet was invented by Bob Metcalfe at Xerox Palo Alto Research Center (PARC) in 1972, which makes it one of the oldest extant technologies in networking. Students interested in going beyond the coverage in this book are advised to visit Charles Spurgeon's Ethernet Web site at www.host.ots.utexas.edu/ethernet/ethernet-home.html.

Ethernet is a good place to start an overview of networking technology because we will be looking at many important concepts that apply to other networking technologies.

Regular Ethernet

The first Ethernet system ran at 2.94 Mbps and was known as Alto Aloha Network after the Alto workstations it was designed to connect and the Aloha network it was based on. The system was unusual not in its media or speed, but rather in its media access method: Carrier Sense Multiple Access with Collision Detection (CSMA/CD).

An Ethernet network is an electrical shared media system, called a *bus*. (It is also occasionally called a *carrier* in academic or standards literature, hence the first C in CSMA/CD.) Imagine a school bus full of children. The school bus may be thought of as a shared media system for shouting. At any time, any one of the children in the bus may shout out a name and a message, which will be carried across the air in the bus and heard by all other children in the bus. All children listen for their names or "Hey, everybody" as the signal that a message is important. In Ethernet terms, the *carrier* is *sensed* by any station, and *multiple* stations can *access* it at once (in order to shout). All stations hear all messages, but they "listen" only to messages intended for them or to broadcasts (see Figure 4-1).

On the school bus, if any two children happen to shout out at the same time, the two messages will become garbled together, and neither will be understood. In Ethernet, this phenomenon is called a *collision* (see Figure 4-2). When two children shout at the same time, each hears that the messages were lost. In Ethernet, each transmitting station *detects* that the collision occurred because the electrical characteristics of the bus don't match what the station is transmitting. After a collision, each child waits for a random period of time, and then shouts again in the hope of being heard. Ethernet works in a similar way; a collision makes the transmitting stations on the bus stop, wait for a random number of milliseconds, and attempt to transmit again. The concept of collision detection may be clearer if you think of the Ethernet bus in electrical terms. When no stations are transmitting, the bus is in a zero state. When one station transmits, the bus is in a one state. When two stations transmit at the same time, the bus is in a two state, which signals all stations that a collision has occurred.

FIGURE 4-1   Ethernet collision avoidance

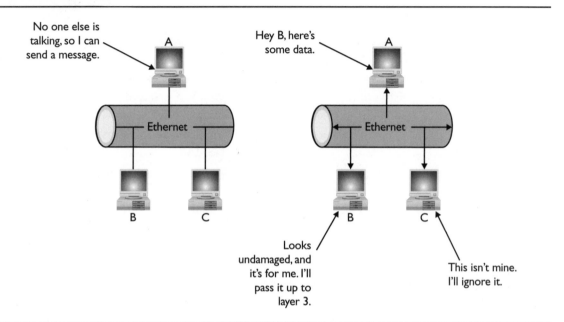

FIGURE 4-2   Ethernet collision

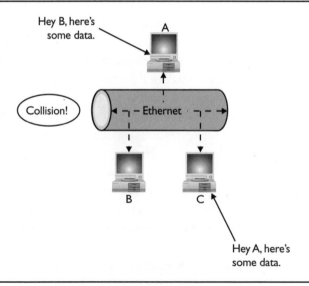

The nature of CSMA/CD gives the network interface card (NIC) two interesting capabilities: chattering and promiscuous mode.

Chattering is a condition caused by a malfunctioning NIC and refers to a NIC that won't be quiet. A chattering NIC does not listen for other traffic, pays no attention to the collisions that it causes, and transmits more or less constantly. This creates a condition known as a "broadcast storm," making network communications nearly impossible to maintain. Broadcast storms may also be caused by misconfigured software, but the effect is the same.

Promiscuous mode, a setting that most NICs have, allows the NIC to eavesdrop. By putting the NIC in promiscuous mode, the computer may listen to all communications occurring on the same Ethernet bus. This is a very useful tool for the network administrator and may be found in administration tools such as UNIX tcpdump and Microsoft Network Monitor. This is also a very useful tool for the network cracker and may be found in a variety of "black hat" toolkits.

Formal specifications for Ethernet were published in 1980 as the DEC-Intel-Xerox (DIX) standard. Ethernet technology was then adopted for standardization by the Institute of Electrical and Electronics Engineers (IEEE, pronounced "I-Triple-E"), which published "IEEE 802.3 Carrier Sense Multiple Access with Collision Detection (CSMA/CD) Access Method and Physical Layer Specifications" in 1983. Ethernet's physical format was what we now call *thicknet*, or 10Base5. That means 10MB of data on a baseband electrical circuit up to 500 meters in length. In an older building, you may still see yellow plastic-coated cable as thick as your thumb, with hand-sized medium attachment units (MAUs, aka vampire taps) dangling from it. If you follow the cable to one end, you'll find a 50-ohm terminator. Both ends of any coaxial Ethernet must be terminated to prevent transmissions from echoing. In addition, one end of the system should be grounded. Another legacy of 10Base5 is the *attachment unit interface (AUI)*, a female 15-pin connector with a sliding latch. This interface is also called DB15 and may be found on old NICs and many Cisco routers, such as the 2501.

Something to keep in mind when you design Ethernet networks is the concept of efficiency. The CSMA/CD standard is widely implemented because it is inexpensive and simple, not because it's efficient. Collisions become exponentially more frequent with every station added to an Ethernet bus, which means that the stations spend more and more time waiting for collision states to clear. To some degree, this is dependent on the NICs used, but a two-station Ethernet bus is not likely to achieve more than 40 percent utilization under optimum conditions. The Ethernet standard also calls for a 1,500-byte frame, which becomes a limitation in faster Ethernet implementations such as Fast Ethernet and Gigabit Ethernet.

on the
Job

Working with 10Base2 can be a good way to remember that networking is based on electricity—in the right conditions, an ungrounded live network cable will give you a nasty buzz. Consider it yet another reason to migrate to a twisted-pair network!

Thicknet proved to be very useful for long-range and backbone connections, but the inflexibility of the cable and expense of MAUs and AUIs led to the development of *thinnet*, or 10Base2. 10Base2 is shorthand for 10MB of data on a baseband electrical circuit up to 185 meters in length (not 200 as the name would lead you to believe). A segment may have up to 30 stations, and up to four segments may be connected in sequence by up to three repeaters. Thinnet's two most important features are its thinner cable (RG-58/U, which is similar to the cable used by television systems) and its network node connections. On a thinnet system, MAU and AUI functionality is embedded into the NIC. The card presents a tubular British Naval Connector (BNC) stub interface to the network, which presents a T-shaped BNC plug to the card. T-adapters connect to the NIC at the base of the T shape and present BNC stub interfaces on the arms of the T shape. This allows network administrators to build thinnet cabling to exact-length specifications and crimp BNC plugs on where necessary. However, T-adapters also present a source of failure because the bus is jointed in several locations. Because thinnet is based on coaxial cable, it must be terminated at both ends and grounded at one. But if one of the T-adapters comes loose from either cable segment that it's attached to, the entire Ethernet bus loses termination and quits working. This was not an uncommon occurrence when thinnet ruled the LAN; rearranging a single user's desk could shut down the entire floor's network! Luckily, if the T-adapter comes loose from the NIC, only that workstation loses connectivity. Thinnet is now rarely used for large production networks, but it is still a popular option for small offices because of its inexpensive components and ease of setup.

The next evolution in Ethernet is 10BaseT, or 10MB of data on a baseband electrical circuit on twisted-pair wire. The 10BaseT specification was published in 1990, and it is currently the most commonly used medium for desktop connections. The 10BaseT system operates over two pairs of wires: one pair (RX) is used for receiving signals, and the other pair (TX) is used for transmitting signals. The two wires in each pair must be twisted together for the entire length of the segment, which is a standard technique used to minimize crosstalk and maximize transmission distance.

Now, let's talk about cabling for a minute. There are currently two accepted sources of specifications for twisted-pair cabling: the Telecommunications Industry Association branch of the Electronic Industries Association (TIA/EIA) and IBM. The EIA is responsible for the "category" (CAT) cable standards and may also be referred to as ANSI/EIA/TIA or EIA/TIA. Note that there also used to be a "level" standard promulgated by the Underwriter's Laboratories, but that standard has been absorbed under EIA/TIA. However, the terms "category" and "level" are still sometimes used interchangeably. IBM is responsible for the "type" cable standards, such as IBM Type 1 and Type 2. As is said in the comp.dcom.lans.* newsgroup hierarchy, the great thing about standards is that there are so many to choose from! Table 4-1 presents some of the common cabling standards that you might encounter.

Strictly speaking, the cable specification does not include the connector used to terminate the cable; however, both the EIA and IBM define specific connectors for use with twisted-pair cable. For CAT 3, CAT 4, and CAT 5,

TABLE 4-1	TIA/EIA and IBM Cable Specifications	
LAN Cable Specifications	**Category**	**Description and Primary Use**
	CAT 1	Two-pair wire used for voice.
	Type 1	Two-pair shielded twisted-pair (STP) wire used for data (4- or 16-Mbps Token Ring).
	CAT 2	ISDN BRI or PRI and T1/E1, can transmit up to 4 Mbps.
	Type 2	Type 1 cable and CAT 3 cable bound together in one shield, used for voice and data (4- or 16-Mbps Token Ring, 10BaseT at 10 Mbps, 100BaseT4 at 100 Mbps).

TABLE 4-1	**TIA/EIA and IBM Cable Specifications**	
LAN Cable Specifications *(continued)*	**Category**	**Description and Primary Use**
	CAT 3	Four-pair wire used for voice and data up to 16 MHz (10BaseT at 10 Mbps, 100BaseT4 at 100 Mbps).
	Type 3	Two-pair unshielded twisted-pair (UTP), similar to CAT 1 (4 or 16-Mbps Token Ring).
	CAT 4	Four-pair wire used for voice and data up to 20 MHz (Token Ring at 16 Mbps, 100BaseT4 at 100 Mbps).
	CAT 5	Four-pair wire used for voice and data up to 100 MHz (100BaseTX).
	Type 5	One strand of multimode fiber, used for data (FDDI).
	CAT 5 enhanced	Four-pair wire used for voice and data up to 125MHz (Gigabit Ethernet, 1,000BaseT). All four pairs are used. Most existing CAT 5 installations meet the requirements of CAT 5E, but this cable is specified for new installations that will utilize Gigabit Ethernet.
	CAT 6	Four-pair wire used for Gigabit Ethernet, up to 250 MHz (all four pairs are used).
	Type 6	Two-pair UTP, patch cables.
	Type 9	Two-pair STP, patch cables.

this standard is EIA-568, which specifies an RJ-45 connector. RJ-45 is the connector that looks like a fat phone line connector. (For your information, the phone line connector is called RJ-11.) For Type 1 cable, the specified connector is a DB9 plug, just like that used in serial communications (modems, palm pilots, console ports, etc.).

You'll note that these standards all support voice and data on the same wire segment, which is a factor that led to the adoption of 10BaseT over 10Base2. New building construction is easier with 10BaseT because a single segment of wire can support one or more cubicles. Table 4-2 shows how this works.

Because each pair is used for sending data in one direction, the pairs must *cross over* in a wire segment for communication to happen. In other words, host A's TX pair must connect to host B's RX pair, and vice versa. However, this crossover function is usually handled in a hub or switch. With the advent

TABLE 4-2	Data	Voice	Voice
Voice and Data on One Cable	Pairs 1 and 2	Pair 3	Pair 4

of 10BaseT, the typical Ethernet installation changed from a bus topology (several stations on a long cable) to a star topology (short cables between stations and a central point). Star topology requires the use of a hub or switch in the middle of the star, which is illustrated in Figure 4-3. Ethernet networks have always had repeaters, hubs, and bridges (an early form of switch), but 10BaseT was the first type of Ethernet to require their use. This is done because star topology eliminates the risk that a single user could break the network. A cable cut will affect only the user whose cable was cut; all other segments are still properly terminated and grounded because the hub or switch is still operational. 10BaseT allows for a 100-meter segment length and up to three repeaters, for a maximum network diameter of 300 meters. We look more closely at hubs (repeaters), switches, and bridges later in the chapter.

The last "classic" 10MB Ethernet specification is 10BaseF, which stands for 10MB of data on a baseband electrical circuit relayed across optical

FIGURE 4-3	An Ethernet hub

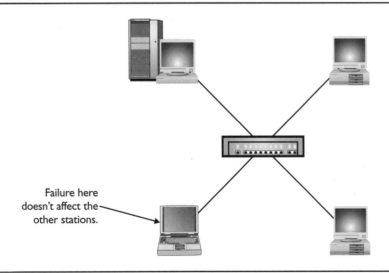

Failure here doesn't affect the other stations.

fiber. This specification was written as part of an industry effort to extend fiber to the desktop; however, the effort was soon abandoned because of the expense and difficult installation of optical fiber. Fiber does offer significant advantages, such as a lack of electrical crosstalk, security, and a 2-kilometer range without the use of repeaters. Additionally, the maximum speed for data transmission over fiber is currently at 2.6 Tbps and may increase. However, fiber is slightly more expensive than copper wire, and fiber equipment is significantly more expensive. Repair of broken fiber is a tricky proposition as well, requiring tools and techniques beyond the reach of your typical networked company. These factors combine to make fiber a poor choice for desktop connectivity. Fiber is occasionally used for Fast Ethernet and is recommended for Gigabit Ethernet, so we'll get further into its characteristics in those sections.

Fast Ethernet   Fast Ethernet refers to a family of technologies that utilize CSMA/CD but transmit and receive data at 100 Mbps. However, because CSMA/CD requires that all stations have a reasonable amount of time to "hear" if a collision has occurred before transmitting fresh data, the higher speed requires a shorter distance. Fast Ethernet will support only a single repeater between two segments of 100 meters in length. The most common implementation of Fast Ethernet is 100BaseTX, or 100 Mbps on a baseband circuit on twisted-pair wire. 100BaseTX requires Category 5 wiring to operate, but it still only uses two pairs and, therefore, can coexist with voice.

The majority of Fast Ethernet equipment produced in the last three or four years implements 10BaseT and 100BaseTX in the same gear, with an autosense function. This type of gear is referred to as 10/100BaseTX. The autosensing function is part of the Fast Ethernet standard and operates by transmission of small frames called *Fast Link Pulses*. Detection of a 10BaseT node on any of its ports will cause a hub to operate solely in 10BaseT mode. There are devices labeled as "smart hubs" which incorporate an internal bridging function to allow one or more ports to operate at a different speed than the others, but these are not strictly hubs and you shouldn't expect that capability from a normal autosensing 10/100BaseTX hub.

The requirement for Category 5 wiring presents a prohibitive expense for a company with a large installed base of Category 3, so the 100BaseT4 standard was produced. 100BaseT4 allows transmission of 100MB of data on a baseband circuit over Category 3 wire, but it requires the use of all four pairs and cannot coexist with voice. A 100BaseT4 segment can be up to 100 meters in length, though Category 5 patch cables and panels are recommended.

100BaseFL refers to Fast Ethernet over fiber. The standard's name is once again shorthand for 100MB on a baseband circuit transmitted over fiber. 100BaseFL is used for relatively long distance connections between buildings or floors, connections where fiber is already installed but copper would have to be pulled, and connections that need to be secured. A copper wire radiates electromagnetic frequencies (EMFs), which can be sensed and used to reconstruct the signal. Figure 4-4 shows the risk. Fiber connections, on the other hand, are very difficult to eavesdrop on. They do not radiate EMF and cannot be tapped without severely reducing signal strength.

Gigabit Ethernet   Gigabit Ethernet has come about at an interesting time in networking, when the functions performed by routers and switches are beginning to merge into single boxes. One side effect of this merge is

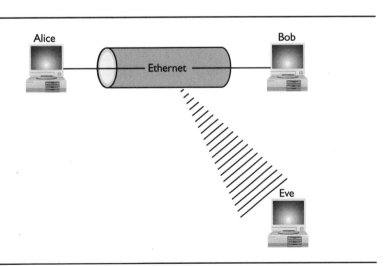

FIGURE 4-4

Eavesdropping on Ethernet

that Gigabit Ethernet is used as a campus network technology nearly as often as it's used in LANs! Gigabit Ethernet requires fiber as a transport media, though there are efforts under way to make it work on CAT 6 and possibly even CAT 5 twisted-pair copper.

1,000BaseSX is the multimode fiber variant of Gigabit Ethernet. It refers to a 1,000MB data transfer on a baseband circuit transmitted over short-range fiber (up to 800 meters). Multimode fiber refers to a type of fiber that allows refraction and reflection of the light beam within its core. This results in several copies of the signal that bounce around independently and slightly out of sync until the receiver gets them and averages to find the message. Attenuation and loss of phase are problems with this technology, enforcing the short distance requirements. However, because the signal does not need to travel as far, relatively inexpensive light-emitting diodes (LEDs) instead of lasers may be used as fiber drivers.

1,000BaseLX/LH is the single-mode fiber variant of Gigabit Ethernet. It refers to a 1,000MB data transfer on a baseband circuit transmitted over long-range (or long-haul) fiber (up to 3.6 kilometers). Single-mode fiber refers to a high-quality type of fiber that maintains a laser signal's integrity throughout its length. Single mode is more expensive and will not work well with LED fiber drivers, but when used with lasers, it provides superior speed and distance.

1,000BaseCX is the code reserved for Gigabit Ethernet on twisted-pair wire. It signifies a 1,000MB data transfer on a baseband circuit transmitted over copper.

Full-duplex Ethernet implementation is the last aspect in Ethernet to review. Do you remember that twisted-pair implementations require the pairs to cross over so that transmit and receive will match up? With that wiring scenario, full-duplex transmission can be enabled, preventing collisions from happening at all. Full duplex requires the NIC to be capable of receiving and transmitting 10 or 100MB at the same time and requires the hub or switch to be capable of buffering data at every port. Full duplex does not "double" the bandwidth because 10 or 100MB per direction was always available, and bandwidth from one direction cannot be "borrowed" for the other. However, full duplex does allow transmission in both directions at the same time and can prevent collisions, radically increasing the efficiency of Ethernet. Figure 4-5 shows how this works.

FIGURE 4-5

Full- and half-duplex
Ethernet

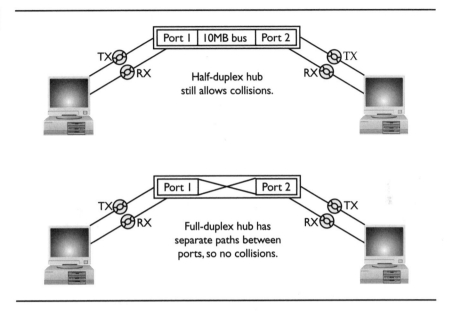

Token Ring

When Ethernet was a struggling new technology, IBM saw an opportunity to address some of its weaknesses. The Token Ring protocol was the company's response. Let's look back to the school bus full of children. The nature of electricity and wire means that we will be working with the same sort of environment, but let's imagine that the school bus driver has told the children to be quiet. Luckily, each child has pencil, paper, and a toy balloon. The child who wants to say something writes it on a paper, marks the recipient's name on the paper, and ties the message to the toy balloon—which is passed around the school bus from child to child in a specified order. Only one balloon may move around the bus at any time, so all other children who have something to say write it on a piece of paper, mark the recipient's name on the paper, and wait. When the balloon comes to them, the children check the message. If it is for them and they are able to read it, they copy the message into their own notebook and mark the original piece of paper "read." That paper is put back on the balloon and passed back to the sender, who takes the balloon out of circulation so that other children may send messages. Broadcast messages are enabled when a message is labeled "everybody" instead of with a specific child's name. Children who receive the balloon read the "everybody" message, put it back, and pass it on.

That is how Token Ring operates, in a nutshell. The balloon is a token, a special frame that message frames are appended to. Frames may be up to 4,096 bytes in length and are labeled with the sending station's layer-2 address and the recipient's layer-2 address. Any number of frames may be appended to the token, so a Token Ring network may be quite large without a noticeable drop in efficiency. Finally, a receiving station actually toggles two switches in the frame header when receiving a message: the address recognized indicator (ARI) and the frame copied indicator (FCI). Using ARI is equivalent to marking the message "seen" and only means that the station knows a message was intended for it. Using FCI is equivalent to marking the message "read and understood" and means that the station copied the message into its buffer and will pass it on to the higher OSI layers.

Token Ring was originally implemented in a 4-Mbps version that used IBM Type 1 cabling and multistation access units (MSAUs or MAUs). In the late 1980s, a 16-Mbps version was produced, which required Type 3 cabling. By that time, Ethernet had already become a clear leader in the local area networks of America, so Token Ring development slowed. A 100-Mbps version was also developed in 1998 but is largely unused; details on it and efforts to develop a 1-Gbps version are available at www.hstra.com.

It may seem counterintuitive, but the MSAU is required in Token Ring networks—you can't just connect a ring of machines with cross-over cables. Therefore, Token Ring is always implemented in a hub-and-spoke fashion. Each port of the MSAU at the hub receives the TX pair and redirects it to the RX of the port to the right, as in Figure 4-6. The rightmost port redirects

FIGURE 4-6

A Token Ring MSAU

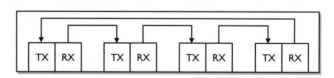

the TX pair to the RX pair of the leftmost port, but this redirection may be broken so that another hub can be stacked into the ring. It does this by attaching a cross-over cable (called a *ring-in/ring-out,* or *RI/RO* cable) between the rightmost and leftmost ports of two MSAUs. Increasing the size of the ring is the only way to grow a network by stacking MSAUs. You can also connect two rings, but that requires a router, bridge, or specialized cascading devices called *controlled access units* and *lobe access managers.* However, connecting two rings is rare; because Token Ring is very efficient and rather slow, increasing the ring size introduces little performance penalty. Token Ring also allows 300 meters between station and MSAU when STP wiring is used and 150 meters when UTP is used. The maximum number of workstations per ring is 75 on UTP wiring, 250 on STP.

The fact that Token Ring is a computer technology instead of a child's game introduces some interesting behavior requirements, though: How will the computers respond to errors or a cable break?

The answer to the error question lies in the fact that computers don't simply pass messages on; they must copy them into storage space, evaluate them, and retransmit—even messages not intended for that computer at all! As long as the message is in memory and being evaluated, every computer in a Token Ring will check the message's cyclical redundancy check (CRC). (Note that this is sometimes called *frame check sequence,* or *FCS.* Properly, FCS refers to OSI layer 2, and CRC refers to layers 3 and 4, but they are used interchangeably.) The CRC is the result of a simple mathematical hash function appended to the end of datagrams and frames at several different layers of the OSI model. For instance, a frame might be evaluated at a binary level for the number of 1's it contains. If there is an even number of 1's, our hypothetical CRC would be 1, while an odd number of 1's would give a CRC of 0. The CRC allows a computer to quickly see if a message has changed from the form in which it was sent, without evaluating what or where the change might be. If the message fails the CRC error check, the station toggles an error detection bit in the token frame before sending the message on. All other stations ignore the message until it returns to the sender, which will have to retransmit.

Cable breaks are more difficult to diagnose from the network's point of view, however. In Ethernet, it's fairly obvious that the cable broke because electrical continuity is lost. That's a major issue on a coaxial network but not a big deal on a hub-and-spoke network, and it's easy to diagnose because you can see which station isn't working. But in Token Ring, any broken cable could mean a failure in communication because the token can't be passed through the ring. Self-diagnosis is a very useful feature for a Token Ring network.

In order to self-diagnose and diagnose each other, the Token Ring NICs spend a fair amount of time sending each other messages that have nothing to do with the applications running in the computers they inhabit. These messages are the networking equivalent of "Hi, I'm still here, and everything's OK." These messages allow the NICs to attach and detach themselves from the ring, establish which NIC is "in charge" of the ring, and establish who the *nearest upstream neighbor (NAUN)* is—in other words, the computer that the NIC should receive a token from. If the NIC does not receive a token from its NAUN in a reasonable amount of time, the NIC will transmit *beacon* frames into the ring, warning all other NICs that there may be a problem. The NIC then detaches itself from the ring and waits to see what happens. When these frames reach the NAUN, it will alert the beaconing NIC that things are okay, if possible, and the ring returns to normal. If that is not possible—for example, because the cable is slightly loose—the NAUN will detach itself from the ring as well. Finally, if the beacon frame returns to the beaconing NIC, the ring's MSAU will force detachment of the NAUN. When a NIC is detached from the ring, its MSAU port is bypassed and ring integrity is complete. After a beacon-initiated detach, both the beaconing NIC and its NAUN will attempt to reattach themselves to the ring, which, of course, will fail for any NIC that is using a broken cable. Figure 4-7 illustrates the beaconing process.

The 16MB variant of Token Ring offers a couple of performance enhancements to be aware of: full duplex, called *direct token ring (DTR)*, and *early token release (ETR)*. DTR is a nonstandard enhancement to Token Ring, which is implemented in some switches. ETR relies on the fact that the token is less important after delivering its message; it only needs to traverse the ring

FIGURE 4-7	Token Ring beaconing

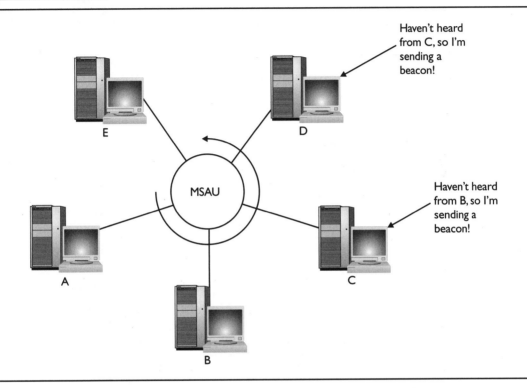

further so that the sending station can receive confirmation of a successful transmission. ETR enables the ring to accept a second token while the first is still in transit if the first has already left its intended recipient. A 16MB Token Ring also increases the frame size to 17KB.

Token Bus

Token Bus is a specialized LAN technology in which bus topology (coaxial cable or nonringed hub and spoke) is used with token passing as the access method. It combines the simpler wiring of bus topology and the guaranteed access time of token passing and is used primarily for industrial control systems.

WAN Technologies

WAN technologies and LAN technologies differ greatly, and most of their differences stem from the physical characteristics of systems designed for transporting traffic hundreds of miles rather than hundreds of meters. In this section, we review some of the WAN technologies available.

Dedicated

Usually when people think of a wide area network, they're thinking of dedicated connections. A dedicated connection is always up and has a fixed cost per month, making it far easier for companies to handle from a software configuration perspective, as well as an accounting perspective.

Dedicated connection services vary widely, but the most variance is in OSI layer 2 rather than layer 1. In fact, you may have noticed that your carrier bills you separately for service (e.g., Frame Relay connectivity at layer 2) and transport (e.g., a layer-1 DS-1 between your site and the nearest Frame Relay–equipped central office). The recent advent of broadband technologies is changing this landscape to some degree, and we cover those changes in the later section "Broadband."

In North America, leased lines frequently come in the speeds listed in Table 4-3.

| **TABLE 4-3** | Typical High-Capacity WAN Links (United States and Canada) |

Transport Name	**Speed**	**Media**
DS-0	56 or 64 Kbps (regionally dependent)	4-wire copper (RJ-48)
DS-1 (aka T1)	1.544 Mbps	4-wire copper (RJ-48)
DS-3 (aka T3)	45 Mbps	2 strands of coaxial copper (RG-59/U, BNC connectors)
OC-3	155 Mbps	2 strands of single-mode or multimode fiber, usually SC connectors
OC-12	622 Mbps	2 strands of single-mode or multimode fiber, usually SC connectors

Higher speeds such as OC-48 (2.4 Gbps) and OC-192 (10 Gbps) are available in some areas. Optical Carrier (OC, also known as STS) standards are used in much of the world, while the Digital Signal (DS) standard is used only in the Americas and Asia. If you would like to dig further into these standards and many more, the IBM Red Books series of technical manuals are invaluable (www.redbooks.ibm.com).

Regardless of the transport type, all high-speed circuits (including LAN media) suffer to some degree from signal interference and attenuation. What enters the circuit on one end as a clean digital signal will lose strength as it travels, lose definition as it passes through repeaters, and be altered by "crosstalk" from other circuits in the same bundle. It emerges on the other end as a large wave in a sea of noise (see Figure 4-8). Optical fiber–based transports do not suffer from crosstalk, but they still lose signal strength and binary definition.

Furthermore, transports using DS standards use time-division multiplexing (TDM) to channelize larger circuits into smaller circuits. A DS-1 can be thought of as 24 DS-0's, and a DS-3 can be thought of as 28 DS-1's. TDM is a useful technology for separating two uses of one circuit, such as voice and data. TDM is more frequently used for limiting or fractioning the use of a circuit (and thereby the cost). For instance, a company may purchase a DS-1 to the Internet but use only 128 Kbps (two DS-0's) of the circuit. This allows the company to minimize costs until requirements for Internet access go up, at which time the number of active DS-0's can be rapidly expanded.

Two devices are used to handle the connectivity and management issues with leased lines: channel service units (CSUs) and data service units (DSUs). CSUs transmit and receive signals to the WAN interface. They also block electrical interference from other network equipment, sense error

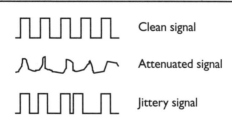

Clean signal

Attenuated signal

Jittery signal

conditions, drop malformed frames, and generate or echo a variety of loopback codes for troubleshooting transport problems. DSUs are used to perform conversion between WAN protocol frames and data frame standards. The DSUs also provide clock if necessary, check timing, retransmit frames if necessary, and provide a DTE interface for routers and hosts to communicate with.

CSUs and DSUs are available separately, largely because phone systems do not require the DSU functionality. However, most data networking implementations use combined devices called *CSU/DSUs* or *DSU/CSUs*. The terms are interchangeable and do not denote a difference in functionality. Additionally, many Cisco router interfaces include the DSU/CSU functionality directly in the interface card. Some consider CSU/DSUs that integrate into the router better because they are less complicated, require fewer power outlets, and won't forget their configuration after a power outage as do certain "bargain-basement" external units. On the other hand, an external unit provides a lot more diagnostic information and allows a troubleshooting engineer to isolate problems more quickly.

Now that we've reviewed some of the basic transport issues, let's look at some of the options that you might be presented with.

Private Facilities If your company is in a campus environment, chances are your buildings have already been connected with copper or fiber. Even if they haven't, installing new cable between the buildings will be less expensive in the long run than paying monthly fees to your carrier. You cannot install cable across a public right of way, but in some areas the local telephone company may be willing to rent so-called dark fiber to you if the distance is short. This is a pair of fiber strands installed between your buildings by and belonging to the telephone company, but it passes through no telephone company switches at all. Another way to get data across public rights of way, rivers, and canyons is to use wireless radio or microwave devices. However, wireless links are not recommended for nontechnical customers because the devices need frequent adjustment. Earthquakes too small to feel, vibration from construction sites and freeways, and high wind can all push the devices slightly out of line in a matter of weeks.

For private facilities, one of the two DSUs on each circuit must be configured to *provide clock*. Long distance networking is extremely timing sensitive, and every circuit has a "heartbeat" that is provided by one of the two devices attached to its endpoints. When you purchase a transport service from a carrier, it will provide clock, but when there is no carrier, you must provide clock yourself. You should also clearly mark which DSU is clock and which is not! It may save time down the road when the circuit doesn't function properly. Your DSUs must also agree on the data-link framing that they will use, but because this is your transport, you can choose the framing that will be used.

Leased Line　WAN links frequently need to travel great distances, over which private transports are not feasible. To handle this situation, you might lease a line from a local telephone company or long distance carrier. A leased line will have the bare minimum of carrier services added to it; it does pass through the carrier's switches, but they do little more than amplify the signal where necessary. A leased line is still a layer-1 solution, so you are still responsible for providing clock and choosing framing. To differentiate them from dark fiber, leased lines are sometimes called "lit fiber."

Billing for leased lines is based on their length and bandwidth, which makes them quite expensive compared with more flexible technologies such as Frame Relay. However, they are still widely used in short distance networks, government networks (because of special tariffs), and latency-sensitive applications.

on the
Job

Frame Relay connections also introduce the element of outside management into your network—the carrier you lease your circuit from will operate a network operations center (NOC) where network health is monitored. This is important to remember when you are scheduling installation of a new circuit before gear is available, because your circuit will show an alarm condition without gear attached. Sometimes the NOC personnel will put the circuit into loopback or disable it to make the alarm go away, which can be a nasty surprise when the equipment finally arrives!

Frame Relay   Frame Relay is the first switched cloud solution we will discuss. Frame has become extremely popular over the last decade because of its low cost, flexibility, and scalability. Much of Frame Relay's flexibility comes from the concept of the *virtual circuit*. The Frame Relay network may be thought of as a cloud—traffic goes in one side and comes out the other, but its path between switches inside the network is indeterminate (see Figure 4-9). Instead, a virtual circuit is established between the two endpoints at OSI layer 2. This circuit consists of an agreement by all the switches in the cloud that a certain amount of bandwidth will always be available between the two endpoints. This bandwidth is referred to as *committed information rate (CIR)*. An endpoint may *burst* above the CIR up to the limit imposed by the layer-1 transport (port speed) which that endpoint is connected to; but there's no guarantee that the additional traffic will get through. If the Frame Relay network is too busy to handle the burst traffic or the receiving endpoint doesn't have enough bandwidth, burst packets are dropped.

There are two types of virtual circuit, *permanent virtual circuits (PVCs)* and *switched virtual circuits (SVCs)*. As you'd expect, a PVC is permanently "nailed up," barring equipment failure or backhoe intervention. An SVC,

FIGURE 4-9	Frame Relay virtual circuit

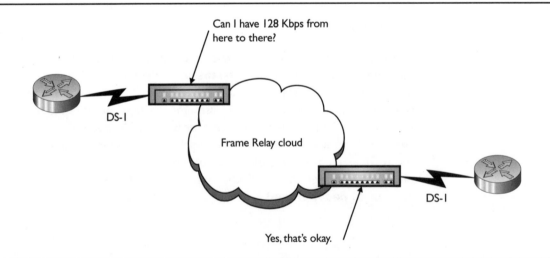

on the other hand, is more like a dial-on-demand analog connection. One endpoint "dials" into the Frame Relay network in order to request a VC. The advantage to this is that one endpoint could establish a circuit to multiple other endpoints; the disadvantage is that the SVC may not be able to connect if the Frame Relay network is busy. Most Frame implementations use PVCs.

Another important factor to consider in all virtual circuit or switched networks is oversubscription. Let's look at an example: DitGlurb2 Enterprises has nine sites in a Frame Relay network. Eight sites have 384-Kbps Frame Relay, and the ninth has a single DS-1 at 1.544 Mbps.

```
8 * 384 = 3,072 Kbps
```

According to this simple calculation, the host site should have two full DS-1's, not one! However, this calculation overlooks the fact that a CIR of 384 Kbps represents potential bandwidth usage, not actual bandwidth usage. Actual usage is dependent on the work being performed at each remote site, not on the circuit that connects the site to the network. Suppose that the various remote DitGlurb2 offices need only 384 Kbps to transmit to headquarters occasionally, and that these high-bandwidth periods are scheduled to rarely overlap. Any four offices can use their full 384 Kbps, or close to it, at the same time, but the host network purchases only one DS-1 to provide the bandwidth. This brings us to a very simple advantage that virtual circuit networks such as Frame Relay offer over leased lines: the ability to oversubscribe host bandwidth.

Imagine a redesign of the DitGlurb2 network to use leased lines. At the remote sites, we can use a DS-1 and limit the channels available at the DSU to 6 ($6 \times 64 = 384$). But in a leased-line network, every DS-0 must correspond to another DS-0 at the other end. Forty-eight DS-0's will be required at the host site, supplying 3,072 Kbps of bandwidth, which means two DS-1's must be installed. Now all eight DitGlurb2 remote offices can transmit at 384 Kbps to headquarters at any time or at the same time. That's fine if they have a need to, and some networks do, but the majority of small networks would not require that kind of bandwidth.

By contrast, in Frame Relay, there is no requirement to match DS-0 to DS-0 within your network. If you purchase a fractional DS-1, you must agree with your carrier on which channels are active, but you do not have to provide a matching number of DS-0's at your host site. This flexibility allows networks like DitGlurb2's to operate every day. Note that some carriers will not allow Frame Relay oversubscription past some multiple of the CIRs dependent on the circuit being oversubscribed. For instance, a two-to-one rule, which is frequently suggested, would look like this if applied to DitGlurb2's network:

```
384 * 8 = 3,072
1,544 * 2 = 3,088
3,088 < 3,072      HOST BANDWIDTH OK
```

But another two remote sites will break the two-to-one rule:

```
384 * 10 = 3,840
1,544 * 2 = 3,088
3,088 < 3,840      MORE HOST BANDWIDTH REQUIRED
```

This is sensible for high-traffic remote sites but can be a problem for the network designer who wants to provide infrequent but fast connectivity to low-traffic sites. The most commonly used way around this requirement is a low CIR, perhaps even as low as 0. Unfortunately, this solution does not work when transport problems or heavy traffic cause burst traffic (over the CIR) to be dropped in the network. Designers may also rely on dial-on-demand routing (DDR) backup circuits in addition to CIR 0 Frame Relay; DDR circuits are more complex to set up and increase the initial financial outlay significantly, but they do provide guaranteed bandwidth.

Low CIR is probably fine for data, but not a good idea for multimedia. After all, data traffic is not very sensitive to latency or jitter, relatively speaking. If some data arrives late (for instance, the banner ad on a Web page), the computer will generally wait for it or do something else until the banner ad finishes downloading. By contrast, a video or voice stream is extremely latency sensitive because of the real-time nature of playback. If one or two video frames arrive late, they will garble the image or confuse the playback software. It's better for them not to arrive at all! This sensitivity to latency and jitter makes Frame Relay a relatively weak transport for multimedia because there is no way to guarantee that information won't be dropped.

ATM   *Asynchronous transfer mode (ATM)* was designed to be a next-generation platform for video and voice traffic, in addition to data. You might think of it as a way to oversubscribe with leased lines, but its primary claim to fame is the ability to guarantee bandwidth for a variety of services (voice, video, and data) across a switched network. Like Frame Relay or the phone network, ATM networks are connection oriented. Before two stations can communicate, a connection must be established between them. Unlike with circuit-switched networks, the connection between two stations does not consume a fixed amount of bandwidth. This is true of Frame Relay as well, but ATM does it one better. Instead of simply allocating bandwidth to the user who requests it first, it allocates bandwidth statistically, so a large number of connections can share the bandwidth of individual links in the network. Because these connections are not dedicated bandwidth channels, they are referred to as *virtual channel connections (VCCs)*. VCCs may also be bundled together into virtual paths for ease of configuration.

The section "Frame Relay" described a PVC's CIR as an agreement between switches in the network that a certain amount of bandwidth would be made available. But what happens if an endpoint with a CIR of 128 Kbps bursts several frames in a row that are all 1.544MB in size? There's no way for the Frame Relay network to know if it's all right to send this burst traffic through before it does so—a switch or router must experience congestion before it can warn its neighbors that they need to discard burst traffic. In the meantime, more and more traffic enters the network in big frames that must be forwarded or discarded. If they are discarded, the transmitting device will send them again until they eventually arrive (however late) at their destinations. Furthermore, a single switch experiencing congestion does not automatically cause the switches around it to discard frames that would normally go through the congested switch. First, the switches may attempt to route around the congested switch, and possibly through slower, longer links.

The time delay created by indirect routing or retransmits is called *latency*. If the large frames are forwarded instead of discarded, they run the risk of disrupting other data streams and introducing latency for those streams. Worst of all is the situation in which a few frames are forwarded through the normal link, a few are forwarded through a lower-bandwidth secondary link, a few are dropped, and so on, for minutes at a time. This situation can cause frames to arrive out of order, dramatically increasing the processor and memory load on the receiving router as it attempts to reorder the frames and extract layer-3 packets. An additional risk with changing routes in a cloud is called *jitter,* which means fluctuations in the rate of data arrival. This means little to a pure data network, but voice and video rely on a constant stream of frames arriving at a constant rate. Pauses in the data flow cause pauses in the playback, and data that arrives faster than the playback speed must be buffered, which is a problem when the application is a two-way Internet phone! For interactive voice and video to work well, the network should provide voice and video data just in time.

ATM proposes to solve the problems of latency and jitter while still providing an excellent data transfer mechanism on the same circuit by radically shrinking the link-layer frame. In ATM, the layer-2 frame is actually called a *cell,* a 53-byte bucket with 5 bytes of header and 48 bytes of payload. This means that 20 percent of bandwidth is spent on overhead. There is a good reason for this: The use of cells allows an ATM switch to respond to changes in network conditions much more quickly than a Frame Relay switch would. ATM switches are also able to rely heavily on application-specific integrated circuits (ASICs) because the cells are small enough to process entirely in hardware. This makes ATM networks fast and provides for unprecedented bandwidth, as well as advanced features like quality of service (QoS). However, ATM comes with a cost: The high ratio of header information to payload wastes an intolerable percentage of bandwidth on circuits slower than fractional DS-3, and the protocol family is decidedly not easy to configure. For details, look at the Web site cell-relay.indiana.edu/cell-relay/FAQ/ATM-FAQ/FAQ.html.

QoS is like the CIR 'contract' used in Frame Relay, only more configurable. There are four QoS levels to be aware of: constant bit rate (CBR), variable bit rate in real-time and non-real-time flavors (VBRrt and VBRnrt), unspecified bit rate (UBR), and available bit rate (ABR). Each of these levels uses a variety of parameters, which should be familiar in concept after you review Frame Relay. These include minimum cell rate (MCR), sustained cell rate (SCR), and peak cell rate (PCR). Table 4-4 shows the relationship of the QoS levels and their possible parameters.

| TABLE 4-4 | ATM Quality of Service Levels |

QoS Level	Usage	MCR	SCR	PCR
CBR	Circuit Emulation Service	Yes	No	No
VBRrt	Voice and video	Yes	No	No
VBRnrt	Latency sensitive data	No	Yes	Yes
UBR	Latency insensitive data	No	No	Yes
ABR	Latency insensitive data (with flow control)	No	Yes	Yes

ATM also supports a variety of data-link layer protocols with different traffic characteristics and system requirements, which are called *ATM adaptation layers (AALs)*. AALs are responsible for moderating the conversion of frame or packet data into cell data and back. These functions are handled by a convergence sublayer (CS) and a segmentation and reassembly (SAR) sublayer. The transmitting CS manages interactions with the layer-3 protocol, and the transmitting SAR chops data up into 48-byte chunks that are fed into the ATM layer to generate 53-byte cells. The receiving SAR strips off ATM layer information and reassembles higher-layer frames and packets. These functions are almost always implemented in hardware for reasons of speed, but they still introduce significant overhead into the data transmission process. Five types of AAL were originally recommended, but two of them have since been merged into one. The four types are as follows:

■ **AAL1**   Supports connection-oriented services that require constant bit rates and have specific timing and delay requirements. An example would be circuit emulation services (CES), which can provide DS1 or DS3 transport over a larger ATM pipe. This is also used for CBR.

■ **AAL2**   Supports connection-oriented services that do not require constant bit rates—in other words, variable bit rate applications like some video schemes. AAL2 has not been widely implemented yet, but is the specified AAL for VBRrt (also not widely implemented).

■ **AAL3/4**   Intended for both connectionless and connection-oriented variable bit rate services. Originally two distinct adaptation layers, AAL3 and AAL4 were merged into a single AAL called AAL3/4 for historical reasons. Used for VBRnrt, this AAL also has native support for *Switched Multimegabit Data Service (SMDS),* a short-lived WAN technology promulgated by the phone companies.

■ **AAL5**   Supports connection-oriented variable bit rate data services. It is a substantially thinner AAL than AAL3/4 because it has no error recovery or built-in retransmission. This tradeoff provides a smaller bandwidth overhead, simpler processing requirements, and reduced implementation complexity. AAL5 is the AAL most frequently used in data networking because TCP can provide the error-recovery and retransmission services that it lacks. This design decision introduces the problem of *beatdown.*

Beatdown is an interesting concept that applies to any network in which a layer with large chunks rides on top of a layer that uses smaller chunks (or *protocol data units,* in the industry jargon). When problems occur in the lower layer, it is generally up to the higher layer to detect these problems and retransmit. For instance, assuming an IP network with hosts A and B, host A may send IP packets to host B. If host B doesn't respond in a suitable period of time or a router along the path responds that the packets were damaged in transit, host A's IP stack will retransmit the same packets.

One of the most common ways for a layer-3 packet to become damaged in transit is for congestion to occur in the cloud. An ATM network is the perfect example because the layer-2 cell is so much smaller than the layer-3 packet or the layer-2.5 AAL frame, and discard decisions are made on a per-cell basis. If a packet is segmented into 20 cells by the ATM network but only 19 make it to host B, host A will retransmit all 20 cells. Beatdown occurs when the retransmission of information becomes an additional source of congestion, preventing new traffic from using the circuit at all and needlessly increasing load on the retransmitting machines. Edge routers can slow this condition by using a protocol called *Weighted Random Early Discard (WRED)* to randomly discard traffic that is not flagged as important before it enters the network. The latest ATM switch software includes better congestion notification that will reduce the number of discarded packets, as well. Frame Relay also implements congestion notification, but the larger frame size makes beatdown rare in Frame Relay networks.

Dial-Up   With the recent development of residential broadband technologies, dial-up seems to have lost a little luster. However, analog and digital dial-up remain extremely flexible and inexpensive methods for connecting two networks on a temporary or permanent basis.

Analog   Modems (modulators-demodulators) have been available since the late 1960s and figure prominently in American culture's depiction of computers. The Internet was popularized on modems, and they will probably be with us for many years to come. Modem technology has come a long way, however. Recent high-speed modem developments have pushed technology to the brink of Shannon's Law and past the FCC's law, and chipsets that have been developed merge the functionality of modems, fax machines, and telephones onto a single card. Table 4-5 presents an overview of modem growth over the years.

There are some things to keep in mind when you are purchasing modems to use with a Cisco router.

TABLE 4-5	Modem Technology Milestones

Year	Speed	Notes
Late 1960s	300 baud	*Baud* is an analog communications term meaning beats per second. If compression is not used, this may be equivalent to bits per second, but compression usually improves modem throughput dramatically.
Early 1970s	2,400 baud	
Late 1970s	9,600 bps	Wide area networking blossomed on this sort of connection in the 1980s.

TABLE 4-5	Modem Technology Milestones *(continued)*	
Year	**Speed**	**Notes**
Late 1980s	1,400 bps	Fax functionality began to appear, and ISA internal modems began to appear, many of them based on the Rockwell RPI chipset (the first software modem).
Early 1990s	2,800 bps	Speakerphone functionality began to appear.
1995	33.6 Kbps	"Winmodem" software modems became popular with manufacturers.
1997	56 Kbps	PCI internal modems began to appear. The 56 Kbps speed requires a perfectly clean copper pair going to a digital circuit and modem bank; this technology is also capped in America to 53 Kbps by FCC regulations.

First, don't necessarily buy the latest and greatest speed demon of a modem. You can use a modem for dial-in or dial-out via asynchronous ports and remote management via the console port. The asynchronous ports can transmit up to 115 Kbps, but the modems dialing in will connect at only 33.6 Kbps (because they are calling into an analog line, not a digital one). The most useful thing you can do with a modem is remote management, but the console port is unable to operate faster than 9,600 bps.

Second, look for modems that can be configured with physical jumpers. This is probably less important with modems used for dial-in and dial-out, but the capability is crucial for a remote management modem. One of the times you'll be most reliant on a modem connected to a router is after a power outage, so a modem that loses its settings after a power outage is not your friend. It's also a good idea to leave remote management modems turned off when they're not needed, for security reasons.

Third, make sure the modem you buy is a real, hardware modem. Winmodems are usually internal models, but the occasional USB-port external model is beginning to turn up. A winmodem requires a Windows PC and will not work with a router. See www.o2.net/~gromitkc/winmodem.html for all the details.

ISDN   Integrated Services Digital Network (ISDN) represents an international effort to re-create the telephone network to provide digital transmission and native support for data and video as well as voice. Two ISDN standards were put forth by the International Telecommunication Union (ITU): *Narrowband ISDN (N-ISDN)* and *Broadband ISDN (B-ISDN).*

N-ISDN is the standard we all think of when designing networks or reading trade magazines; it is widely implemented in most areas of the world. The N-ISDN standard may be delivered over two physical interfaces, plain old telephone system (POTS) or DS-1. In North America, the POTS interface is called "U" style, and it is delivered over two wires. Furthermore, the layer-1 termination device (called an *NT-1*) is integrated into the ISDN terminal adapter (TA) equipment. In the rest of the world, NT-1's are external, wall-mounted devices that connect to the TA via a four-wire S/T interface. N-ISDN service on a POTS line is called basic rate interface (BRI) and appears at the data-link layer as two 64-Kbps B channels and a 16-Kbps D channel. The B channels may be used for voice or PPP-based data calls and can be bonded into a single data channel with Multilink PPP. The D channel is used to transmit signaling requests and protocol information. N-ISDN also defines a DS-1 based mode called primary rate interface (PRI), which is intended as an aggregation facility. PRI appears as 23 B channels and a D channel, all at 64 Kbps. B channels may be used for inbound or outbound calls at random, bonded into data calls, and used for voice calls.

B-ISDN provides the backbone telephone network with the same sort of upgrade that N-ISDN provides to the local copper loop. B-ISDN utilizes SONET rings as the physical layer, at speeds ranging from OC-3 to OC-12. B-ISDN shares D channel signaling protocols with N-ISDN but uses ATM instead of Point to Point Protocol (PPP) as its data-link layer. B-ISDN connections are not rigidly channelized, but rather rely on ATM VCCs to provide traffic management.

Broadband

Recently, so-called broadband home access has been taking the industry by storm by providing Internet access to home users at speeds better than many businesses can afford to purchase. Not surprisingly, businesses are beginning to re-evaluate the price-performance ratio of their existing Internet connections. It won't be long before broadband technologies intended for home use cause significant erosion in the ISDN market and the low end of the Frame Relay market.

xDSL   There are many variants of Digital Subscriber Line, and interested readers are encouraged to see the Paradyne DSL Sourcebook at www.paradyne.com/sourcebook_offer/sb_html.html. The most common versions are covered in this section, but all versions utilize the existing copper loop between a home and the local telephone company's central office (CO). Doing so allows them to be deployed rapidly and inexpensively. However, all DSL variants suffer from attenuation, and speeds drop as the loop length increases. ADSL and SDSL may be deployed only within 17,500 feet of a CO, and IDSL will work only up to 30,500 feet. All DSL variants use ATM as the data-link layer. Following are the DSL variants:

- **ADSL**   Asymmetrical DSL, as its name implies, provides a higher downstream speed than upstream speed. Because aggregate throughput is lower than that for a symmetrical transmission of the same speed, ADSL produces less crosstalk and is easier for telephone companies to implement. ADSL also allows the telephone company to continue providing POTS on the same circuit by providing a splitter box at the customer premise. ADSL can operate at up to 8 Mbps downstream, but performance is typically guaranteed at one speed and capped at another, higher speed. Upstream speeds are typically capped at one-third of the downstream speed.

- **SDSL**   Symmetrical DSL offers the same speed ranges and distance limitations as ADSL, but POTS cannot be provided with the circuit. However, SDSL is the best choice for sites that will transmit a lot of information. Be sure to check your provider's acceptable-use policy before assuming that SDSL is the best choice for your Web server farm, though! Many providers consider *x*DSL a consumer product and do not encourage or support applications that will greatly increase the need for upstream bandwidth.

- **IDSL** ISDN emulation over DSL is a B-ISDN implementation, using N–ISDN signaling protocols and an ATM PVC. IDSL is still an ATM data-link layer, but it provides ISDN-like signal divisions of two B channels and a D channel. All three channels are used for data transmission and are bonded together with multilink PPP; all that is required is an N-ISDN TA with the ability to use "leased-line mode."

Any DSL variant will provide you with an ATM PVC, which may be directed to the Internet or to any location with an ATM transport. This allows use of DSL as a telecommuting technology, with or without the use of encryption software to make a virtual private network.

Cable Another broadband technology worth noting is digital cable. Basically a form of Ethernet, digital cable allows up to 30 Mbps with no distance limitation. Unfortunately, current cable systems are shared media covering huge territories, and performance tends to drop significantly during peak usage periods. Digital cable systems could someday be modified to minimize or eliminate this problem, but doing so would make delivery of television programming more difficult and expensive. Many cable systems prohibit the use of servers and VPN clients within their networks.

EXERCISE 4-1

Technologies Required by Networking Devices and Links, and Across the Network

Professional Orange Widgets, Inc., is a typical small company in growth mode. It has three sites in the area: headquarters, sales, and manufacturing. It also supports telecommuting and must provide access for an internationally roving mobile sales force. It currently has a contract with BigISP.net for roving dial-in, and traffic is redirected from BigISP.net's POPs to a 384-Kbps fractional DS-1 in the sales office. POWI also has leased lines from headquarters to sales, from headquarters to manufacturing, and from headquarters to LittleISP.com at full DS-1 speed. Headquarters is a four-story building with about 20 seats on each floor, plus the company's

Internet firewall, e-mail, FTP, HTTP, Web, and database servers. Manufacturing is a 500-meter–long building with an office at one end and a shipping desk at the other; 10 computers are evenly split between the two sides of the building. Sales is a two-story building with about 50 seats per floor and one application server.

Without getting concerned about brands and models, design and diagram a complete working network for POWI. Discuss your recommendations for cabling.

Bonus Points: Add a fourth site with a leased DS-1 line.

Hint: Take each building separately, and then connect them to each other and the outside world.

Basic Network Environments Using Routers, Switches, and Hubs/Bridges

Networking is a little like playing with Legos—you have a few basic shapes (the two-dot brick, the rectangular brick, and the green ground sheet), some special shapes that add features like wheels or humanoid figures, and some common design requirements (connections may be made only on the vertical surfaces). However, from these simple toys, almost anything can be built. Networks are dynamic, growing entities that are shaped by the people who build them and the requirements and budgets that they must meet. No two are completely alike. Following are some of the basic network devices and design elements that are available to you.

Routers

A router is a device that connects two layer-3 networks. That may make it seem a little out of place in a chapter that has dealt with so much layer-2 technology, but routers are frequently used to connect separate layer-2 networks as well (for instance, the Ethernet LAN and the DS-1 WAN in a typical small office). A router's strongest feature is that it blocks traffic that wasn't intended to go through to the other side. For instance, a typical Ethernet LAN produces a lot of broadcast traffic. Stations ARP for Ethernet MAC addresses constantly, stations broadcast their names and shared resources every few minutes, and stations send each other huge amounts of legitimate traffic. The router's Ethernet interface can hear all this traffic, but it doesn't listen to or accept any of it. The only thing that the router will forward is information intended for a specific destination on another layer-3 network.

Bridges

One of Ethernet's limitations is the *collision domain*. Remember our school bus full of children? The larger the bus and the more children in it, the more likely it is that two children will shout at the same time and cause a collision. Collisions rob the network of efficiency. And when you consider all the ARP and broadcast traffic that computers generate just by being turned on, it doesn't take much of a network to force an Ethernet's throughput down to 10 or 20 percent. Bridges are devices that improve efficiency by splitting the network up into two smaller collision domains. The bridge then watches its interfaces and takes note of which MAC addresses can be found on which network. A frame arriving at the bridge is matched to the MAC table. If the MAC table says that the station the frame was intended for is on the same interface, the bridge assumes that the station has received the frame already. The frame is not forwarded to the other network. But if the frame is a broadcast frame—for instance, an ARP request—the bridge is forced to forward it to the other interface. This means that a bridge will do nothing to prevent a broadcast storm.

Bridges may also be used to translate layer-2 frames between two network topologies. They were commonly used in the early 1990s by companies transitioning from Token Ring to Ethernet. A bridge used in this fashion can introduce latency problems because of the speed and architecture differences between the topologies.

Switches

A switch may be thought of as a multiport bridge; the idea is that you can't have a small enough collision domain. Switches are available for LAN and WAN applications. Modern workgroup Ethernet switches have brought the price per port so low that there is little reason not to provide a single port per Ethernet station, especially because switches are inherently full duplex! Keep in mind that a broadcast will still be resent from all interfaces; however, a switched network is not the cure for a broadcast storm or chattering NIC. Switches and routers are beginning to merge functionality sets, with the use of virtual LANs (VLANs) and router-on-a-card implementations for Cisco Catalyst switches. This is an exciting development but can make it tough for people entering the field to tell one device from another. Don't make assumptions about what the box is or what it's doing! Switches may rely on the concept of oversubscription as well, providing backplane speeds that are typically half of the maximum possible aggregate speed of all ports.

Switches may be *stacked* to increase capacity. This refers to connecting the backplanes of two or more switches with a cable (usually proprietary), which effectively merges the backplanes into a single fabric. Stacking will always increase port density but will not increase backplane speed. That is, attaching two 16-port 1.3-Gbps backplane switches with a cable does not produce a single 2.6-Gbps backplane; it produces a 32-port 1.3-Gbps backplane switch.

Switches may also be *cascaded,* which means uplinking to a larger switch. For instance, imagine a company with four offices on different floors in a large office building. Each floor may have a 24-port 10/100BaseTX workgroup switch, and each switch may have a 1,000BaseSX uplink port. In the main office, the company can install a larger core switch with at least four 1,000BaseSX ports, plus ports for attaching the company's application, database, and e-mail servers. This configuration is useful for isolating the effects of hardware failure and produces a smaller collision domain than a purely stacked-switch design.

Layer-3 switching is the term used to refer to bringing routing functionality into the switch fabric. Switches operate at layer 2, making their decisions by reviewing MAC addresses and building a table of switch decisions (similar to a routing table). Layer-3 switching allows the switch to "be aware" of layer-3 addressing, which makes cross-subnet traffic significantly faster (because all packets do not need to pass through a relatively slow router. Layer-3 switching requires VLAN support and a router, which may be placed in the switch itself or upstream of the switch. VLAN support is too complex to get into here, but in short, it allows a switch to have multiple virtual Ethernet buses attached. Interestingly, an upstream router used for layer-3 switching is one of the only router configurations that does not require two physical interfaces. The networks being routed can be assigned to virtual interfaces on the single interface, as in Figure 4-10. This configuration is called "router on a stick." The addresses of the virtual interfaces are the default gateways of the virtual Ethernet buses. When routing decisions are required (i.e., to send traffic from one bus to another), the traffic is sent up to the router. However, the switch watches where the router sends the traffic and takes note. The rest of the traffic in that session (from the one layer-3 address to the other and back) will be switched at layer 2, without crossing the router's physical interface at all.

Hubs

Hubs, also known as repeaters, are very simple devices that sense electrical signals on one port, amplify them, and repeat them on many other ports.

| FIGURE 4-10 | Layer-3 switching |

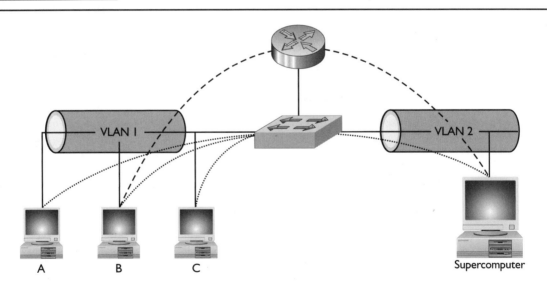

From A to C: Same VLAN, so no routing required. Traffic passes through switch.

From B to supercomputer: Traffic decision is made at router. Further traffic passes through switch without touching router.

The hub makes no attempt to filter or understand the traffic that it is passing, though most hubs will sense collisions or framing errors. Hubs can come with anything from 2 to 100 ports, but buying more than 16 ports may be a waste of money when switches are so inexpensive.

All hubs may be *daisy-chained* (cascaded) by being connected via any two ports with a crossover cable; in fact, most hubs come with a MDI/MDI-X button that causes the crossover to happen internally on one port and allows you to use a straight-through cable instead. However, the IEEE specifications do not allow for more than three daisy-chained repeaters.

Higher-end hubs will also allow stacking, which refers to use of a proprietary port and cable to make the hubs act as one, larger hub. Just as with stacking with workgroup switches, proprietary interfaces are frequently used. A stack of hubs counts as only one hub in daisy-chaining, and the stack will usually survive failure of a single hub within the stack.

Protocols in Use in the Network

Thanks to the explosion in Internet usage, the Internet Protocol (IP) family of protocols is probably the most commonly used technology at layers 3 and 4. It's a rare network today that doesn't offer some TCP/IP service, perhaps alongside another protocol. Many legacy protocols are also in use in networks, and the most common of these are Novell NetWare's IPX/SPX and IBM's SNA. Both Novell and IBM have quit issuing new products with their proprietary protocols enabled by default, using IP as the default instead. Nevertheless, tens of thousands of networks were built with IPX/SPX and/or SNA, and thousands today have not yet had the inclination, technical savvy, or capital to migrate away from those two protocols. Other protocols to be aware of are DECnet and AppleTalk. The production networks that still use these two probably number in the high hundreds or low thousands today, but they are still popular in network education circles. DECnet is preferred because of its strict adherence to OSI layers, and AppleTalk because of its unusual media access algorithm, Carrier Sense Multiple Access/Collision Avoidance (CSMA/CA). CSMA/CA is covered in depth in Chapter 2 (see "AppleTalk and Its Basic Operation"), but its salient difference from Ethernet is that each station must obtain the other's permission to transmit a message.

Reasoning for Those Protocols

The dominance of a protocol can be attributed to a variety of factors, but the most important are relatively open technical standards and the size of the installed base. Of these two, the open standards is more important. It may be hard to remember from looking at today's landscape of TCP/IP networks on Ethernet LANs, but the networking industry is extremely competitive and fast moving. A protocol that loses its technical edge will rapidly lose installed base as well, becoming more irrelevant by the month.

exam
ⓦatch

If you haven't yet read a Request for Comments (RFC), it is a very worthwhile endeavor. I strongly recommend at least skimming the RFC of a protocol that you are trying to understand. Sometimes the writing is dense, but the information is always the most accurate you can find. The RFCs are mirrored widely across the Internet, or they can always be found on the IETF's server at ftp://ftp.isi.edu/. You can also find a great deal of information about the RFC process at www.rfc-editor.org.

Open-standard protocols succeed because they lower the bar of entry and thereby broaden the field of competition. Vendors may implement the standard freely instead of paying its developer for rights to a proprietary application programming interface (API). Educational institutions may train from the standard freely, producing programmers who are already familiar with the standard before they begin to write the commercial implementation. The TCP/IP family is a prime example; like any other protocol ratified by the Internet Engineering Task Force (IETF), TCP/IP may be implemented by any vendor capable of reading and understanding the RFC documents that it is based on.

Installed base size may be achieved through other means, such as being first to a market or bundling the protocol with a system that is valuable for its other attributes. For instance, SNA is a prime example of the first-to-market method—IBM's networking implementations date back to the late 1960s. To put the latest 800MHz workstation in perspective, at least one network with an IBM System/370 and terminal controllers purchased in 1975 is still in use. Similarly, IPX/SPX had an 80 percent market share five years ago not because of its technical merits, but because it was the protocol used by the relatively inexpensive and stable NetWare operating system. NetWare was the "killer app" that enabled small- and medium-sized businesses to transition away from leasing time on mainframe services hundreds of miles away. With NetWare, you could use off-the-shelf PCs on every desktop and a slightly bigger one as your mainframe data store and application space. Offering a killer app is the fastest way to achieve market dominance.

CERTIFICATION OBJECTIVE 4.02

Services Required from the Network

We've covered many technologies from a highly theoretical level; now let's look at a practical application of them. In this section, we review some of the more common services provided to end users and review the network technologies used to implement them.

Common Services

Some of the common services required from the network are authentication, authorization, and access (AAA); groupware (e-mail, folders); Internet access; and proprietary applications or data (databases, electronic forms, and tools).

Authentication, Authorization, and Access

The first thing users need to do on the corporate LAN is authenticate, or tell the system who they are. This function is generally handled by the network operating system (NOS; examples include NT, NetWare, and UNIX) or a specialized server that allows use of special methods (SecurID, RADIUS, or TACACS+). Whatever the box, its response to authenticated users will be a grant of authorization, with which users will have access to the resources they require. These functions may also be handled by external boxes with specialized functions, but usually this sort of box is implementing policy decisions that are made from the NOS standpoint.

Groupware

Frequently, the second thing users do upon logging in is check their e-mail. This may mean a proprietary application such as Lotus Notes or Microsoft Exchange, or it may mean a standards-based usage of POP3 or IMAP4. In either case, authentication will be required if it hasn't already been provided.

Internet

Internet access is as important as telephone access to the modern employee, and most people spend a significant portion of their work time in front of a computer with a Web browser open. New applications are frequently being designed to work inside Web browsers to take advantage of pre-existing layout engines and user interface elements.

Applications and Data

Corporations amass a large quantity of data in the form of sensitive research documentation, account histories, and vendor relationships. A great deal of money and time also go into buying, building, or customizing applications to manipulate this data with, including anything from a desktop office suite to an Oracle database.

How Do Network Technologies Provide Services?

All the services that we've discussed are in OSI layers 5, 6, and 7; in other words, they aren't directly affected by the network that you build to support them. However, it seems to be a rule that programmers always write network-enabled software as if there were no such thing as bandwidth constraints. They key to supporting applications is to build a fast, redundant network that is transparent to the applications and users that use it to communicate.

However, all that changes when you begin to consider security. Security tools such as firewalls, packet filters on routers, and intrusion-detection systems all work by analyzing the layer-3 address and layer-4 port numbers and protocol types of the source and destination machines. This means that to implement an effective policy—for example, users who are not in marketing do not get to use the color laser linotype—you as the network designer need to know the IP addresses of the marketing subnet and the fancy printer as well as the protocols and ports used by the department's printing applications. If you're interested in learning more, see the book *Building Internet Firewalls,* by D. Brent Chapman and Elizabeth D. Zwicky; followed by *Network Intrusion Detection: An Analysis Handbook,* by Stephen Northcutt.

Performance

Network performance can be highly subjective and influenced by more factors than any one network administrator could control or even track. Real-world performance will always seem to be less than the optimum promised by the vendor. There are several design issues to consider to improve performance of the network, even if they don't provide 100 percent or greater utilization.

Bottlenecks

Measure bandwidth as it aggregates through your design—what would happen if some number of these workstations needed to burst traffic to a server? The points where it would be held up may be crippling your network with latency-causing buffers and retransmissions caused by full buffers. Remember to consider the throughput of devices and circuits, too. Your LAN switch may be able to handle a steady 10 Mbps, but your dual Ethernet router may not be made to take that kind of beating without buffering the information. Its hardware may be perfectly capable (it usually is), but its software is designed to make correct decisions about routing, which is inherently a slow process. Most of the data will get through, but packets will be buffered while routing decisions are being made, and buffering introduces latency—potentially, a lot of it.

You can solve bottlenecks in hardware units relatively easily by upgrading hardware, but bottlenecks in WAN circuits are very expensive to fix.

Upgrading circuits is to be avoided if possible because the monthly recurring charge of a circuit is a budget killer. However, sometimes that is the only thing to do. With Internet circuits especially, companies typically have little control over how the Internet circuit is configured or used because customers may visit at any time, internal users may visit any site, and compression is not an option (unless your ISP supports it). But before looking at a circuit upgrade, you might look into filtering out unnecessary traffic, compression, and caching engines. These technologies are not guaranteed fixes by any means, but they can certainly help, especially on a private WAN link.

Traffic Flows

Who's talking to whom, where, and when? How much bandwidth do the conversations take and for how long? These questions can help you solve problems before they become problems by providing EtherChannel to two servers or switching an engineering workgroup into a smaller switched VLAN. These questions can quickly flow into questions of acceptable use if you are on the administrative side. Are your marketing users accessing an accounting server? Why? If they are not supposed to, they can be blocked with an access list; but make sure you're not making the decisions of what's acceptable use. Policy decisions are for management to be making.

QUESTIONS AND ANSWERS

Can Ethernet achieve 100 percent utilization?	Half-duplex Ethernet cannot. Because Ethernet has no "planning authority" managing access to the media, there will always be collisions. Collisions increase with the number of stations and the length of the bus. However, full-duplex Ethernet can achieve 100 percent utilization because there are no collisions.
Can Token Ring achieve 100 percent utilization?	No. Cisco states that the key number for Token Ring saturation is 70 percent.

CERTIFICATION SUMMARY

In this chapter, we covered the physical characteristics, logical structures, and terminology used in the most popular local area and wide area network technology today. The concentrate is on real-world, current technologies, except in cases where review of the technology sheds light on the way computers and networks generally work (as in the case of Token Ring). Becoming an expert in SNA at the expense of a thorough TCP/IP knowledge is a career mistake.

Ethernet in its various forms is generally accepted as king of the LAN, for now. The use of full-duplex transmission in a fully switched network minimizes many of Ethernet's design limitations, such as inefficient collision avoidance and relatively short cable lengths. However, things change quickly in the information technology arena; it can be instructive to review trade magazine archives to see how quickly.

On the WAN, a genteel standards warfare is a distinct possibility. Frame Relay is an extremely popular way to build a network, and most companies have at least one Frame Relay link in their networks. But Frame Relay is not well suited to real-time communications, such as bidirectional voice and video. The big telephone companies and carriers are heavily invested in ATM and B-ISDN as the upgrade path of choice, and that will probably be the way that things go for long distance links that must cross carrier networks. But on the smaller networks, so-called campus area networks or municipal area networks, routed Gigabit Ethernet is becoming a very popular way to connect networks. Look for the carriers to offer Gigabit Ethernet WAN links or perhaps a cheap "fiber emulation service" on their switch clouds in the next two to three years.

✓ TWO-MINUTE DRILL

- ❑ Today's local area network usually operates with some form of Ethernet, though FDDI is still in occasional use for servers, and Token Ring is still in use in some smaller networks.

- ❑ Ethernet was invented by Bob Metcalfe at Xerox Palo Alto Research Center (PARC) in 1972, which makes it one of the oldest extant technologies in networking. Students interested in going beyond the coverage in this book are advised to visit Charles Spurgeon's Ethernet Web site at www.host.ots.utexas.edu/ethernet/ethernet-home.html.

❑ An Ethernet network is an electrical shared media system, called a *bus*. (It is also occasionally called a *carrier* in academic or standards literature, hence the first C in CSMA/CD.)

❑ There are currently two accepted sources of specifications for twisted-pair cabling: the Telecommunications Industry Association branch of the Electronic Industries Association (TIA/EIA) and IBM.

❑ Fast Ethernet refers to a family of technologies that utilize CSMA/CD but transmit and receive data at 100 Mbps.

❑ Token Ring is always implemented in a hub-and-spoke fashion.

❑ Token Ring is very efficient and rather slow, so increasing the ring size introduces little performance penalty. Token Ring also allows 300 meters between station and MSAU when STP wiring is used, and 150 meters when UTP is used.

❑ Token Bus is a specialized LAN technology in which bus topology (coaxial cable or nonringed hub and spoke) is used with token passing as the access method.

❑ WAN and LAN technologies differ greatly, and most of their differences stem from the physical characteristics of systems designed for transporting traffic hundreds of miles, rather than hundreds of meters.

❑ A router is a device that connects two layer-3 networks.

❑ Bridges are devices that improve efficiency by splitting the network up into two smaller collision domains. The bridge then watches its interfaces and takes note of which MAC addresses can be found on which network.

❑ A switch may be thought of as a multiport bridge; the idea is that you can't have a small enough collision domain. Switches are available for LAN and WAN applications.

❑ Hubs, also known as *repeaters,* are very simple devices that sense electrical signals on one port, amplify them, and repeat them on many other ports.

❑ The Internet Protocol (IP) family of protocols is probably the most commonly used technology at layers 3 and 4.

❑ Some of the common services required from the network are authentication, authorization, and access (AAA); groupware (e-mail, folders); Internet access; and proprietary applications or data (databases, electronic forms, and tools).

SELF TEST

The following Self Test questions will help you measure your understanding of the material presented in this chapter. Read all the choices carefully because there may be more than one correct answer. Choose all correct answers for each question.

1. When hubs are stacked, which of the following statements are true?

    A. They logically act like a single hub.

    B. Failure in one does not affect the others.

    C. Maximum segment distance is not affected.

    D. All of the above.

2. You work for a small bank with 110 branches across the state, and the vice president of finance has just asked you to look into providing network redundancy for the branch offices. The branches are currently connected by 128-Kbps or 384-Kbps fractional DS-1 Frame Relay, with a full DS-3 at the host. Luckily, you had specified ISDN-capable routers for the branches when the networks were installed. But now you'll need something for them to dial into. Which of the following circuits should be installed at your headquarters?

    A. One ISDN PRI

    B. A second DS-3

    C. 110 ISDN BRIs

3. While monitoring traffic on your switched LAN, you notice that someone in engineering is probing the accounting subnet with a vulnerability mapping tool. What should you do?

    A. Go to management.

    B. Use a router access list to deny this person's IP address access to the accounting subnet.

    C. Confront the suspicious user and offer her/him a job.

    D. Keep an eye on the suspicious user, document further suspicious activity, but do nothing yet.

4. Is *x*DSL a drop-in replacement for Frame Relay?

    A. Yes, there are some problems, but VPNs will make it all irrelevant anyway.

    B. Yes, but it's cheaper and faster!

    C. No, carriers will not provide business class support.

    D. No, it's technically impossible to route business traffic over an *x*DSL circuit.

5. Which statement is true of bridges?

    A. Microsoft Network Neighborhood browsing, which relies on broadcasts, will not work across a bridge.

    B. Chattering NIC's broadcasts will not be forwarded by the bridge.

    C. The same IP subnetwork may be used on both sides of the bridge.

6. Which statement is true of routers?

    A. A chattering NIC will be heard on both sides of a router.

    B. Microsoft Network Neighborhood browsing, which relies on broadcasts, will not work across a router.

    C. The same IP subnetwork may be used on both sides of the router.

7. Why is TCP/IP more popular than some of the other protocol suites?

    A. It has open specifications, a "killer app," and a large installed base.

    B. Microsoft, Cisco, and Intel formed a coalition to promote its use.

    C. It's technologically superior to anything else.

    D. The U. S. government encourages its use.

8. After analyzing your network, you've found that there is a bottleneck at your DS-1 Internet connection. The circuit is 50 percent utilized on average, and your Web server logs imply that the majority of the traffic is end users of your product FTPing updated drivers. What is the best solution?

    A. Put in another DS-1.

    B. Put in a DS-3.

    C. Move the FTP server to a Web hosting company with an OC-3 to the Internet.

    D. Filter out all the visitors from the largest home ISP.

9. Three workstations are attached to an Ethernet hub, and the first sends a frame to the second. What happens at the third?

   A. The frame is completely ignored.

   B. The frame is copied into the NIC's buffer, and its destination MAC address is checked. Because the destination MAC is not workstation three's, the frame is thrown away.

   C. The frame is copied into the NIC's buffer, and its cyclical redundancy check is verified. The Ethernet header and CRC are stripped off, and the remaining data is passed up the stack to layer 3.

10. Which of these statements is accurate about CSU/DSUs?

    A. A CSU/DSU is required on every Token Ring network.

    B. External CSU/DSUs can be configured to block Telnet access.

    C. CSU/DSUs are like modems for high-speed lines.

    D. CSUs handle IPX/SPX traffic, and DSUs handle TCP/IP traffic.

11. Many custom applications are being redesigned to use Web browsers as their user interface for manipulating and displaying information. How will that affect the network?

    A. Not at all.

    B. Network utilization will go up.

    C. Network utilization will go down.

12. Which of these statements accurately describes layer-3 switching?

    A. Every switch port is assigned a layer-3 network address.

    B. After the routing decision has been made, two entries are added to the switch's layer-2 switching table, forwarding traffic from client to server and back.

    C. Every switch in the cloud checks the layer-3 destination address of a data packet and pings that machine. If it responds to pings, the switch forwards the packet to the next switch, and so forth. Otherwise, the packet is stored until the destination becomes active again.

13. What happens on a Token Ring network when you unplug a workstation?

    A. The ring breaks.

    B. Most MSAUs (or MAUs) will segment and disable a failed or disconnected port.

    C. The ring controller can't ping the missing workstation and removes its MAC from the ring table.

14. In Frame Relay, what happens when one node sends burst traffic to another node?

    A. Traffic within the CIR is still given guaranteed delivery, but traffic that is being burst is given best-effort delivery and might be discarded if the network is congested.

    B. The first node requests a burst port to be opened at the second node; the two nodes negotiate a size, speed, and duration; and the traffic is burst through.

    C. The CIR is temporarily adjusted to the full port speed, and traffic is sent at the CIR speed. After an idle time out, the CIR goes back down to its default value.

15. Your client is moving its warehouse to a new building just on the other side of the freeway from its current location. The company wants to ensure at least 512 Kbps of data throughput between the sites for the most reasonable cost but does not have technically apt people on site full time. What is the best solution to recommend?

    A. Wireless bridges

    B. A Frame Relay Fractional DS-1

    C. A DS-1 leased line

    D. Two Internet connections and a VPN

16. You agree to audit a customer's network and discover that an old 486 used as a print server has its network card in promiscuous mode. What have you likely found?

    A. Network management node

    B. Security breach

    C. Misconfiguration

    D. Something to investigate

17. What's the fastest speed Token Ring can operate at?

    A. 4 Mbps

    B. 16 Mbps

    C. 100 Mbps

    D. 1,000 Mbps

18. 10Base2 is shorthand for

    A. 10MB on a baseband circuit on two-pair UTP

    B. 10MB on a baseband circuit for 185 meters

    C. 10MB on a baseband circuit for 200 meters

19. Identify the transports that are vulnerable to electromagnetic eavesdropping.

    A. Ethernet on Category 5

    B. DS-1 from the local phone company

    C. Token Ring on Type 3

    D. All of the above

SELF TEST ANSWERS

1. ☑ **D.** Stacked hubs are logically like a single hub with however-many power supplies. Stacked hubs can act as a single hub, and failure in one does not affect the others. Note that this is assuming *stacked* hubs with a separate backplane, not *cascaded* hubs. Any hubs cascading from the failed hub's Ethernet ports will be disconnected.

2. ☑ **A.** The PRI gets you 23 branches concurrently dialing in at 64 Kbps or 11 branches concurrently at 128 Kbps. If you have Frame Relay failures at that many branches, you're looking at a backbone failure suffered by your carrier. Those are certainly not impossible, but they don't happen enough to justify the cost of five PRIs!
   ☒ **B** is incorrect because a second DS-3 wouldn't be able to handle the ISDN signaling. **C** is incorrect because 110 BRIs in one site would be very expensive and a logistical nightmare.

3. ☑ **D.** The user hasn't done anything wrong yet (unless scanning is expressly precluded in your published security policy). The user may be trying to learn networking, may not know what the tool does, or may be sitting at a compromised workstation, with no idea that it is scanning. The best thing to do is to watch and log the user's activity, then go to management if you find something more dangerous later.
   ☒ **A** is incorrect because you should never go to management without being 100 percent certain that you're viewing illegal activity. It's a bad idea to get people fired, and the administrator who cries wolf gets ignored quickly. **B** is the next best option, but it's still incorrect if you're not certain that the user is consciously trying to attack the network. **C** is close to correct, but again you don't want to "jump the gun." Try to figure out what the goal of the probes is before you talk to the user. If this user's workstation has been compromised and initiated a situation that you don't fully understand, you may spread panic or disrespect among your user population.

4. ☑ **C.** Prompt, external, and competent technical support is vital for business-class service. Even if you can do a lot by yourself, you can't know everything, and a business is in trouble if a single person controls any system.
   ☒ **A** is incorrect because installing and supporting a properly secured VPN can be more expensive than maintaining the existing Frame Relay network. Using the Internet and a VPN can be very effective and secure, but there are expenses related to doing it right. **B** is incorrect because DSL's ATM transport and higher bandwidth require upgrades and replacement of equipment that was purchased for Frame Relay networks, even if the Internet is used as intermediate transport. **D** is incorrect because there's no technical reason not to replace Frame Relay with DSL where DSL is available; the only reasons are financial and management.

5. ☑ **C.** Bridges are layer-2 devices and do not affect the distribution of layer-3 addresses.
☒ **A** and **B** are incorrect because bridges always forward broadcasts. They must forward broadcasts because they are designed to be nonintrusive, and discarding broadcasts would break many services taken for granted on an Ethernet, such as ARP and DHCP.

6. ☑ **B.** Broadcasts are always dropped by routers. This can be made to work if a Microsoft WINS server is used or certain broadcasts are forwarded to certain "helper" IP addresses.
☒ **A** is incorrect because a chattering NIC's broadcasts are dropped like any other broadcast. It is extremely unlikely that a NIC will mistakenly send traffic that matches the "helper" address forwarding rule, but if that ever happened, the broadcasts would be forwarded. **C** is incorrect because routers must have a different IP subnetwork on every interface. Otherwise, there is no routing to be done, and no way to route between the interfaces. A router is a doorway, and you can't have a doorway in the center of a room.

7. ☑ **A.** The success of TCP/IP comes from its usage on the Internet, preinstallation in various important operating systems, and open specifications.
☒ **B** is incorrect because Microsoft, Intel, and Cisco never formally coalesced to promote TCP/IP (though all three companies have made enormous fortunes by selling TCP/IP products). Coalitions come and go and sometimes have an effect, but their effect is the slow, evolutionary kind (witness the ATM Forum). **C** is incorrect because although many think TCP/IP is a superior protocol family, its weaknesses are glaring and have been fixed in other, unused protocols such as IP, version 6. **D** is also incorrect, although the government's funding of ARPANet was instrumental in TCP/IP's early development.

8. ☑ **C.** If your products become popular, load on your site will only increase. You might be able to keep up with the demand by increasing bandwidth at your site, but doing so makes you responsible for issues like power outages and natural disasters. A hosting service in a hardened building with a huge Internet connection can be a wise investment.
☒ **A** and **B** are acceptable options for short-term fixes, but the long-term solution is to outsource the FTP service. **D** is extremely incorrect: Filtering out the users of large ISPs (called shunning) is a drastic measure and not very wise. Though it is technically feasible and will reduce your traffic significantly, it is the networking equivalent of the A-bomb. A few large players shunning each other will mean the end of the Internet as we know it.

9. ☑ **B.** In order to know that there is something there at all, the third workstation must read the frame off the wire and process its Ethernet header. But because the destination MAC is wrong, nothing is passed to layer 3.

    ☒ **A** is wrong because the workstation cannot ignore the frame without reading it off the wire. Reading it and discarding it could be thought of as "ignoring" the frame, but the frame must be read into the NIC's buffer before the NIC even knows that it exists. **C** delineates the process for accepting a frame that was intended for this workstation, so it is correct for the second workstation but not the third.

10. ☑ **C.** The CSU/DSU transmits, receives, error-checks, and provides conversion from layer-1 and layer-2 WAN standards to router hardware. A modem performs a similar function between analog phone lines and serial ports.

    ☒ **B** is incorrect because the CSU/DSU is a layer-1 and -2 device and cannot block Telnet access (a layer-3 function). **A** is incorrect because a CSU/DSU function has no place on any LAN standard (Ethernet or Token Ring). A CSU/DSU can be attached to or included in a router or bridge with a LAN interface, but the CSU/DSU is not connected directly to or required by the LAN at all. **D** is incorrect because CSU/DSUs are ignorant of all protocol families higher than layer 2, such as TCP/IP and IPX/SPX.

11. ☑ **B.** Though large file transfers may decrease (because the data is stored centrally and manipulated via browser), Web interfaces require a great deal of small, fast transfers. Web interfaces to programs also frequently require that the browser's internal cache-to-disk function be turned off, which will affect all HTTP requests done with that browser. Graphics such as buttons, decorations, and banners will be downloaded with every page refresh. Also, Web interfaces preclude offline usage of data. Instead of downloading a spreadsheet and looking up the information later, users must be connected to the network and participating in data transfer to look up information. Network utilization rises with the use of Web interfaces.

    ☒ **A** is incorrect because any change in architecture will necessarily cause some sort of change in usage. **C** is incorrect because the old architecture of downloading one large file once, modifying it repeatedly, and uploading it back to the server was a more efficient use of network resources. However, it was a less efficient use of employee time and a riskier business model. A machine or application that crashed while editing a downloaded file could corrupt the data or lose all changes since the last download.

12. ☑ **B.** After the routing decision is made at layer 3, the switch's layer-2 tables are modified so that further traffic will be handled at layer 2.

☒ **A** is incorrect because it describes a router with multiple interfaces, not a switch. **C** is incorrect because that level of intelligence has not been programmed into switching or routing gear, and won't be any time soon because it would slow things down considerably without improving anything. Layer 3 is not a good place for this strategy, though a similar technique is used for certain layer-7 applications, such as SMTP mail.

13. ☑ **A.** The ring breaks briefly, and the next workstation begins beaconing that its NAUN is gone, which causes the MSAU to bypass the missing workstation's port.

☒ **B** is incorrect because the MSAU can bypass a port, but it cannot do so by itself. **C** is incorrect because there is no ring table to remove MAC addresses from.

14. ☑ **A.** The CIR cannot be changed on the fly.

☒ **B** and **C** are are examples of applying lessons from other technologies to the technology at hand. They are valid techniques for TCP but not for Frame Relay.

15. ☑ **C.** It is the most economically reasonable solution.

☒ **A** is incorrect because of its technical requirements. Wireless is the most economical solution because there is no recurring lease cost, but wireless links require technical people to keep them adjusted. **B** is incorrect because it will not be as economical as a leased line. Frame Relay links would incur the extra mileage of a link from each site to the nearest central office, and it wouldn't be unusual at all if the two sites are served from different COs! **D** is also incorrect because the same mileage issue applies to a pair of Internet connections. The Internet connections are also priced high because the ISP is providing a lot of extra services that the warehouse can get from its host location (e-mail, Web browsing, etc.). Finally, answer **D** will require software and equipment to provide the VPN encryption and authentication, which introduces additional expense and again requires technical people, possibly on site.

16. ☑ **D.** It doesn't pay to leap to conclusions, but you've certainly found something that needs further investigation.

☒ **A** is fairly unlikely. There are valid reasons for using promiscuous mode, such as for intrusion-detection systems, but it's not likely that an IDS is running on a 486 print server. **B** is at least 50 percent likely, because this might be a sniffer, but it's not instantly the right answer. **C** is also 50 percent likely, because this might be the last administrator's attempt to learn more about BSD networking, but it might also be a sniffer. One suggestion is to disconnect the box and replace it with another type of print server. Leave the box disconnected from the network and examine it with tools that you bring from another box with a write-protected floppy.

17. ☑ **C.** It can operate at up to 100 Mbps.
    ☒ **D,** 1,000 Mbps, has been standardized, but there is no equipment available. Most Token Ring networks running at 16 Mbps are in the process of being replaced with Ethernet.

18. ☑ **B.** The actual specification is 185 meters, which was rounded up because 10Base1.85 seemed unwieldy.
    ☒ **A** is incorrect because 10Base2 doesn't work on UTP, and **C** is incorrect because the standard does not allow for 200 meters of cable.

19. ☑ **D.** Any copper wire will emit electromagnetic "echoes" of the digital pulses traveling on it, which can be captured and reconstructed. Optical fiber is not vulnerable to this attack. Companies with a lot to hide are careful to encrypt traffic that will be passing across publicly accessible areas on copper wire, no matter who provides the wire or what transport is running on it.

5

Performance and Network Design

Part of developing a network to meet the customer's needs is gathering information from the current network and using the data to migrate the existing network to the new network. This information may include data from applications, types of protocols, and addressing schemes. This chapter will develop a framework for analyzing the customer's network problems; determining the customer's requirements for performance, security, capacity, and scalability; and creating a network structure matching the customer's requirements. As part of a future design tool, examples and charts will be shown as a learning aid and an illustration of actual network results.

CERTIFICATION OBJECTIVE 5.01

Framework for Analysis of the Customer's Network Problems

For a baseline study of the customer's existing network, a framework for analysis must be completed. The baseline is used to describe the various network problems that currently occur in the customer's organization. These problems may include latency or congested network traffic to end stations.

The size of the network, number of current problems, and timeline of completion determine the amount of analysis required for developing a framework. If the network is small and well understood, less time can be spent on gathering statistics. However, if the network is large and complex, more time may be spent on observing information flow and data traveling on each segment. The first step in developing a framework is diagramming the logical layout of the existing network. The logical diagram should contain the names and addresses of any existing equipment. Link speeds, network protocols, and network addressing should also be labeled. If there is an existing method for assigning network device names and addresses, it should be adhered to for future growth and development.

The next step in developing a framework is to determine the types of data flow on the network. The flow of data is determined by user application software, network operating systems, and locations of demand nodes (workstations) and data stores (servers). Network traffic can be local (source and destination on the same network) or remote (source on one network, destination on another).

Type of Data Sent Across the Network

In most networks, server farms house application resources and data. As the network grows, so does the number of end nodes and applications. The end nodes, such as servers and user workgroups, advertise broadcast messages to show their existence and roles within the network. Most of the broadcasting is dependent upon the type of protocol used in the network. Some protocols, such as IPX/SPX and AppleTalk, produce a large number of advertisements throughout a network. Be sure to label each application and protocol on the network. Also, it is important to label the network traffic each segment uses and the location of the application in respect to the network. For example, if a server houses an application that is used by remote offices, be sure to document the source and destination. Table 5-1 will help determine the role specific applications fulfill in a network. For future design plans, feel free to copy the blank chart and use it at the customer's site.

- For "Name of Application," list the name of the application, such as Microsoft Word, Lotus, and so on.

- For "Protocol," list the type of protocol, such as TCP/IP, IPX/SPX, and so on.

- For "Source and Destination Local," "Source Local, Destination Not Local," "Source Not Local, Destination Local," and "Source Not Local, Destination Not Local," enter the respective percentage amount that each traffic uses on the particular segment.

TABLE 5-1 List of Functions of Network Applications

	Name of Application	Protocol	Source and Destination Local	Source Local, Destination Not Local	Source Not Local, Destination Local	Source Not Local, Destination Not Local
Segment 1						
Segment 2						
Segment 3						
Segment 4						
Segment 5						

EXERCISE 5-1

Framework for Analysis of the Customer's Network Problems

Ms. Dana Johnson, a network administrator for RDJ Enterprises, is planning to implement a new network. She has provided some basic information.

RDJ Enterprises is a local manufacturing plant that produces ergonomic furniture for homes and offices. There are several small remote facilities located geographically around the main facilities. These facilities provide services, spare parts, and retail sales. A high-level topology of the current network is shown in Figure 5-1.

Figure 5-1 depicts network traffic related to the organization. Server RDJ1 is the central server where all data storage takes place. This server is on segment 1. The server currently has Visio Professional and Microsoft Office, and uses Novell NetWare's GroupWise as e-mailing software. The network operating system is Novell NetWare 3.12. The backbone also contains an Ethernet segment that holds a storage database for updates nightly from other remote sites. Workstations also share the same Ethernet segment.

Each remote site is connected to the central site using T1s. These sites include servers Remote1 (segment 2), Remote2 (segment 3), and Remote3 (segment 4). These servers use the same applications as the main facility, as well as providing local services to shared Ethernet LAN segments. These services include GroupWise and local applications. For example, server Remote3 contains an application called Jet Bizforms, which is used to create invoice slips and expense reports.

FIGURE 5-1 High-level topology of the current network

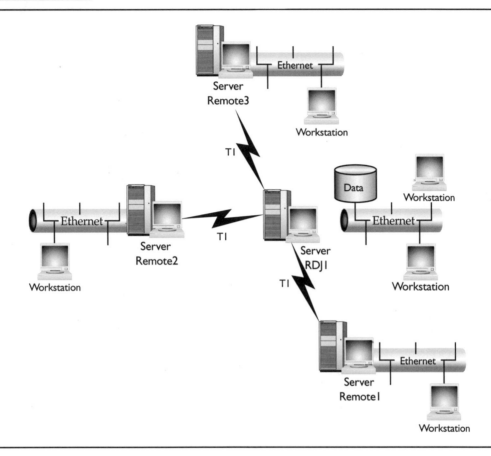

From the information given, answer the following questions; then review the correct answers.

1. Judging from the information given, what modifications would help improve performance on segment 1 (main facility)?

2. What protocol is used in this network?

3. What applications are on each segment on the network?

Answers to Exercise 5-1

1. On the basis of the high-level topology of the network, a good recommendation would be to separate the database storage from the end nodes.

2. Protocol used in the network is IPX/SPX.

3. Applications on each segment of the network are as follows:

   Segment 1: GroupWise, Visio Professional, Microsoft Office

   Segment 2: GroupWise, Visio Professional, Microsoft Office

   Segment 3: GroupWise, Visio Professional, Microsoft Office

   Segment 4: GroupWise, Visio Professional, Microsoft Office, Jet Bizforms

You should now understand how to develop a framework for an analysis of the customer's current network. The next section defines additional design requirements needed for characterizing the customer's existing network.

Capacity

Capacity is defined as the data-carrying capability of a circuit or network, measured in bits per second. The data that passes through the circuit consumes some percentage of the network. When the data is classified in respect to the circuit line, capacity and utilization share common characteristics. An example is an FDDI network with 50 percent utilization. This means that the FDDI network is using 50 percent of its capacity. Several network tools and analyzers may be used for surveying the customer's network to capture network capacity or utilization. The following list suggests media, topology types, and the maximum utilization allowed for a healthy network.

- No shared Ethernet LAN segments are saturated at more than 40 percent utilization.

- No shared Token Ring segments are saturated at more than 70 percent utilization.

- No WAN links are saturated at more than 70 percent utilization.

■ The Cisco router's five-minute CPU utilization rate is no more than 75 percent.

A healthy network should meet all of these criteria.

Security

Most recommendations for network design suggest using a firewall to protect a network from the "outside world." In general, a firewall is hardware/software or a combination of both, used to block or permit network traffic. Firewalls are typically placed in a network by implementing the three-part firewall system. The three-part firewall system has three specialized layers:

■ An isolation LAN that is a buffer between the corporate internetwork and the outside world. The isolation LAN is also called the *demilitarized zone (DMZ)*.

■ A router that acts as an inside packet filter between the corporate internetwork and the isolation LAN.

■ Another router that acts as an outside packet filter between the isolation LAN and the outside internetwork.

exam
ⓦatch

Be sure to understand all parts of the three-part firewall system.

Inside the isolation LAN, services are allowed, such as Domain Name Server (DNS), Telnet, and FTP server. The isolation LAN contains a unique network number that is different from the corporate network number. Also, the isolation LAN is the only area that is allowed to be visible to the outside world and should be advertised through the outside filter.

It is very important to keep firewall routers simple. They should be used only to filter packets. Also, unnecessary services should not be enabled on the router. In order to avoid this,

■ Use static routing.

■ Enable password encryption.

■ Do not allow virtual terminal access.

■ Do not allow IP redirects or caching.

Scalability

Internetworks today are experiencing continuous growth, so they must be scalable to meet the flexible and expanding demands of the organization. A scalable network follows a hierarchical model. This model simplifies the management without overlooking network requirements. Figure 5-2 illustrates a three-layer hierarchical model made up of the core, distributive, and access layers.

- **Core** The core is the central location for the entire enterprise and includes LAN and WAN backbones. The main purpose of the core is to provide an optimized and reliable transport composition.

- **Distribution** The distribution layer represents the campus backbone. The primary function of the distributive layer is to provide access to various parts of the internetwork, as well as access to services.

- **Access** The access layer provides access to corporate resources for a workgroup on a local segment.

exam
ⓦatch *Be sure to understand all three layers and characteristics of a scalable internetwork.*

In order for networks to be scalable, internetworks need to be the following:

- **Reliable and available** The network should be available 24 hours a day, 7 days a week.

- **Responsive** A network's QoS should be monitored without affecting users at the desktop.

- **Efficient** Efficient networks should optimize available resources and control broadcast activity.

- **Adaptable** Disparate and clustered networks should be able to join the main internetwork.

- **Accessible but secure** Dialed-in connections should be enabled, and network integrity should be maintained.

If these characterizations of a scalable network are implemented, a healthy network environment should be the result. Remember that routers

FIGURE 5-2

Diagram of a scalable internetwork

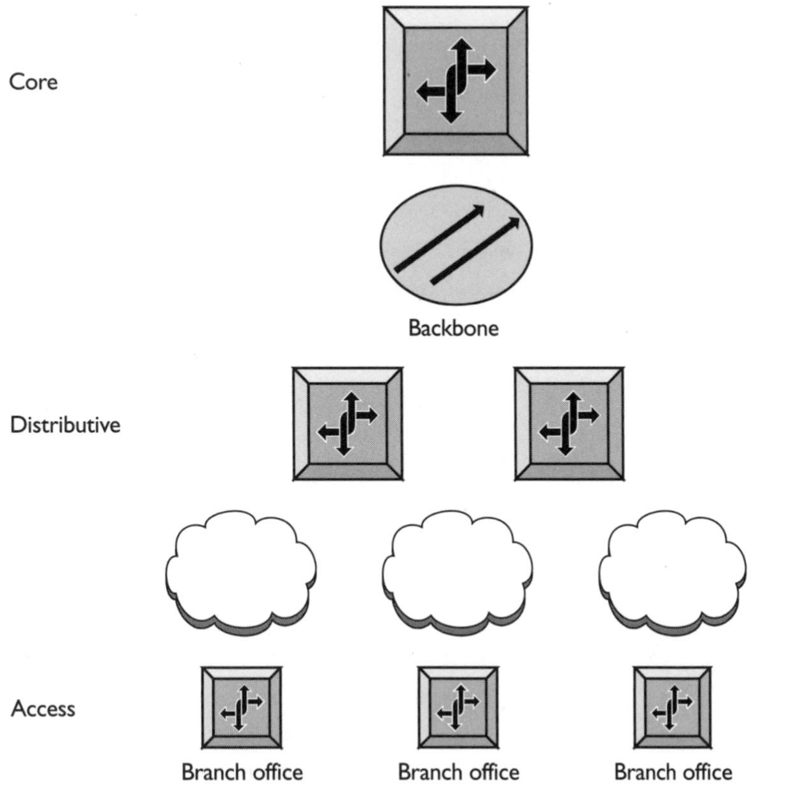

Core

Backbone

Distributive

Access

Branch office   Branch office   Branch office

should be configured on the basis of the key functions that they need to perform at a given layer of the hierarchy.

CERTIFICATION OBJECTIVE 5.02

Customer's Requirements for Performance, Security, Capacity, and Scalability

A customer's network should be designed for optimization in performance, security, capacity, and scalability. Performance requirements include fast and reliable delivery of information across the organization's LAN or WAN.

For some businesses, performance is an issue of great importance. Fast and reliable responses from servers provide speedy service to customers. For example, a loan institute that provides quick loan application processing would require optimum performance for customer satisfaction.

For businesses that require highly secure networks, such as banks or financial institutions, security is very important. These networks pass along information such as account numbers, credit card numbers, and balances. In today's society, numerous hackers continuously try to break into bank accounts and find personal financial information. This information must be encrypted or contained to protect the privacy of the customer.

As the number of end nodes increases on a network segment, the capacity of the line decreases. Segmentation of the network allows the network administrator to measure the capacity of the media. If certain segments of the network become congested, new types of media may be introduced into the network, or the end node may be moved to a new segment to relieve network congestion.

As many businesses forecast anticipated growth, so, too, must the network. A scalable network will allow these growths to take place without affecting end-user performance. Also, troubleshooting of the network is narrowed down to three segments of the internetworking model: core, distributive, and access layers. A baseline analysis of the network should involve the hierarchical model as a guideline for future network development.

Determining the Type of Traffic Being Sent

Traffic in a network may be of many types. Applications provide support for several flow types, including terminal/host, client/server, peer-to-peer, server/server, and distributed computing traffic flow. These types of traffic are characterized by the network's flow of symmetry and direction. Also, flow types determine success of completion, operation, and/or reliability of the application.

Protocol Analyzers and Their Use

Part of designing the customer's network is documenting the number and types of protocols that make up the current network. Along with the many types of operating systems that make up networks today, it is important to consider the different types of protocols and services that these protocols advertise. It is important for the network designer to study and understand how to document the various types of protocols and services. A network designer may achieve the best results in capturing and displaying protocol advertisements on a network by using a *protocol analyzer*. Protocol analyzers are special hardware or software devices that offer various network troubleshooting features, including protocol-specific packet decoding, specific troubleshooting tests, and traffic generation. Part of documenting protocol behavior is also calculating the number of CRCs (cyclical redundancy checks) done on received frames for specific periods of time. As a measure of good network health, a network should not have more than one bad frame per megabyte of data. A popular network analyzer is Network Associates' Sniffer Pro. In Figure 5-3, a PC loaded with Sniffer Pro has captured information on a network.

FIGURE 5-3

Network Associates'
Sniffer Pro

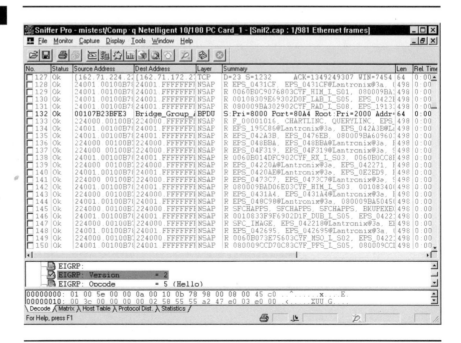

Figure 5-3 displays several characteristics of a common Novell NetWare network. From the decoded information shown, notice the updates or SAPs (Service Advertising Protocols) that each server is broadcasting. For example, SFC_NW0x represents file servers, and EPS_xxxxxx represents print servers. There is also information on BPDUs (Bridge Protocol Data Units). After the information has been captured, the bottom tabs may be used to show matrix, host table, protocol distribution, and statistics.

Types of Security Managers

Most organizations require information within their facility to be secure. Creating security goals as part of network design is a very important step in delivering the desired result to the customer. A number of security managers can safeguard the network from unauthorized entry. Some of these managers are packet filters, firewalls, access control lists, TACACS+, RADIUS, Kerberos, SecureID, and data encryption. Some other managers may include auditing and authentication. Another method for encryption is the public key/private key encryption. This method is known as an asymmetric key system. With public key/private key systems, each secure station on a network has a public key that is openly published or easily determined. All of the devices are allowed to use a station's public key to encrypt the data to send to the station.

PIX

The Cisco PIX Firewall series of products is the highest performance, enterprise-class set of firewalls that delivers high security and fast performance for corporate networks. The PIX Firewall allows users to thoroughly protect their internal networks from the outside world by providing full firewall security policy and protection. Unlike CPU-intensive proxy servers that perform processing on each data packet, the PIX Firewall uses a secure, real-time, embedded system. Cisco's adaptive security algorithm (ASA), used to ensure the maximum in security; and cut-through proxy, used for authentication and authorization; allow the PIX to deliver outstanding performance to more than 16,000 simultaneous connections. The Cisco PIX Firewall also provides failover/hot standby for network reliability, as well as alert notifications via e-mail or pager. The PIX Firewall is capable of supporting multiple interfaces such as inbound, outbound, DMZ (demilitarized zone) 1, DMZ2, and so on. The number of interfaces that a PIX supports is dependent upon the model type. Here is an example of a show configuration command taken by a Cisco PIX Firewall. Notice some of the unique command lines such as "conduit," "global," and "outbound" statements.

```
pixfirewall# sh config
: Saved
:
PIX Version 4.0.7
enable password 8Ry2YjIyt7RRXU24 encrypted
passwd kIQggKv8.UiICW/r encrypted
hostname pixfirewall
failover
names
syslog output 20.3
syslog console
interface Ethernet outside auto
interface Ethernet inside auto
ip address inside 172.71.248.12 255.255.255.128
ip address outside 10.0.80.16 255.255.255.252
arp timeout 14400
global 1 10.0.80.1-10.0.80.1
static 172.71.30.225 172.71.227.172
conduit 172.71.30.246 20 tcp 205.137.243.0 255.255.255.0
conduit 172.71.30.246 21 tcp 202.130.243.0 255.255.255.0
conduit 172.71.30.225 20 udp 202.130.243.0 255.255.255.0
conduit 172.71.30.225 21 udp 202.130.243.0 255.255.255.0
outbound    5 deny 0.0.0.0 0.0.0.0
outbound    5 permit 172.41.176.0 255.255.255.0 9179
outbound    5 permit 172.41.176.0 255.255.255.0 7
outbound    5 permit 172.41.176.128 255.255.255.0 9179
outbound    5 permit 172.41.176.128 255.255.255.0 7
apply 5 outgoing_src
age 10
no rip outside passive
no rip outside default
no rip inside passive
no rip inside default
route outside 0.0.0.0 0.0.0.0 10.0.80.34 1
route inside 0.0.0.0 0.0.0.0 172.41.212.1 1
```

```
timeout xlate 24:00:00 conn 12:00:00 udp 0:02:00
timeout rpc 0:10:00 h323 0:05:00 uauth 0:05:00
no snmp-server location
no snmp-server contact
telnet 172.41.254.16 255.255.255.0
mtu outside 1500
mtu inside 1500
```

ACLs in the Routers

Cisco routers running the IOS (Internetwork Operating System) are capable of placing access control lists on either the outbound or inbound interfaces of a router. ACLs (access control lists) control whether certain traffic is forwarded or blocked at a interface. ACLs are placed on a router's interface to meet criteria such as the packet's upper-layer protocol and source/destination address. An implicit *deny-all* is understood if none of the allowed criteria are met. ACLs should be designed with special provisions. The network designer should always study network traffic flow in order to obtain maximum network performance. A rule of thumb in administering access lists is to place the most general statements at the top and the most specific statements at the bottom. The last statement should be the explicit *deny-all* statement. Standard and Extended are two types of access lists. Standard access lists permit or deny packets based only on the source IP address of the packet. Extended access lists provide a higher degree of control by enabling filtering based on the session-layer protocol, destination address, and application port number. Table 5-2 lists protocols and their respective standard and extended access list numbers.

Many access lists are possible for a protocol. For each new access list, select a different number from the protocol range. In order for an access list to be enforced, it must be first defined, then placed on the particular interface. In the following example, a standard access list is placed on the inbound Ethernet interface of the router.

```
hostname Router
!
!
!
interface Ethernet0
 ip address 172.31.234.55 255.255.255.0
```

```
    ip access-group 1 in
    shutdown
   !
   interface Serial0
    no ip address
    shutdown
   !
   no ip classless
   access-list 1 permit 172.231.0.0 0.0.255.255
   !
   line con 0
   line vty 0 4
    login
   !
   end
```

TACACS+ and Radius

TACACS+ (Terminal Access Control Access Controller Plus) and RADIUS (Remote Authentication Dial-In User Service) are two protocols designed to

TABLE 5-2	Access List	Access List Range
	IP standard	1–99
Standard/Extended Access Lists for IOS 12.0	IP extended	100–199
	Bridge type code	200–299
	DECnet standard/extended	300–399
	XNS standard	400–499
	XNS extended	500–599
	AppleTalk zone	600–699
	Bridge MAC	700–799
	IPX standard	800–899
	IPX extended	900–999
	IPX SAP	1,000–1,099
	Bridge extended	1,100–1,199
	IP extended	1,300–2,699

authenticate users and handle accounting. TACACS+ is a proprietary system developed by Cisco for handling authentication, access, and accounting. RADIUS is an Internet standard, supported by many vendors.

In a network in which only Cisco products are deployed, TACACS+ has some added benefits. In addition to specifying whether somebody has access to a device, it can also specify the level of access and maintain records of activity. This can be useful to know who last modified a configuration, or that support staff can use show commands but cannot get a configuration listing.

RADIUS allows for interoperability with other hardware. This can be useful in a mixed-vendor environment where other vendors do not support TACACS. Maintaining two databases can increase the complexity and support cost of a network.

Other Security Managers (Secure ID, Kerberos)

In high-security environments, usernames and passwords are not reliable for authenticating a user. With many users writing their passwords on Post-it notes and placing them on their monitors, usernames and passwords are not reliably safe. In addition, many people use the same password for all accounts. Many protocols send both usernames and passwords in clear text (FTP, Telnet, POP3, and so on). This allows a user on the network to place a network analyzer on the network and record the username and password, then successfully log in as that particular user.

Kerberos guards against this vulnerability by using tickets (temporary electronic credentials) to authenticate. Tickets have a limited life span and can be used in place of usernames and passwords (if the software supports this). Kerberos encrypts the password into the ticket. It uses a trusted server called the Key Distribution Center (KDC) to handle authentication requests.

Secure ID combines the ownership of a card and the knowledge of a password. In addition to having a name and password, you also are required to have a security card. Someone else who has your username and password, but not the card, can't authenticate. This extra precaution helps ensure that the stated user truly is the user.

Determining Capacity Issues

A common rule for network engineers is the 80/20 rule. This rule states that 80 percent of network traffic should remain local on a LAN and 20 percent of the traffic may be routed to a different network segment or external network. In some cases, server farms and corporate Web servers do not always have to abide by the 80/20 rule. Nevertheless, with many large businesses and corporations moving toward the Internet and Extranet, capacity issues become of great concern.

Planning for Growth and Scalability

When a network is being designed to meet the customer's needs, the company's goals and future plans must be taken into consideration. This projection should be for a one- to two-year period. Some questions to ask the customer are

- Approximately how many more users will access the corporate internetwork during the next two years?

- Approximately how many more sites will be added to the existing network during the next two years?

- Approximately how many more servers will be added to the existing network during the next two years?

CERTIFICATION OBJECTIVE 5.03

Network Structure Matching the Customer's Requirements

A carefully planned and successful network design requires a network structure that has been defined to meet the customer's specific needs. This structure should meet all the criteria for performance, security, capacity, and scalability. This structure should meet the customer's anticipated growth by allowing multiple growth alternatives.

Considering Specified Topology and Internetworking Constraints

Several types of topologies are used in the design of networks in order to meet scalability requirements. The topologies may be flat or meshed.
A flat topology, which is used mainly for small networks, is generally not recommended for networks with many sites and is used when low cost and reasonably good availability are desired. A meshed network may be either full mesh or partial mesh. In a full-mesh topology, every router or switch is connected to every other router or switch. In a partial-mesh topology, there are fewer connections.

Network Design Meeting All the Requirements and Concerns

Finally, after the specified topology that meets the customer's needs has been determined, a design that meets the customer's requirements and concerns should be developed. During the initial development stage, research on the current network should have been done to determine the current problems and to develop solutions. After extensive research and study, the design that has been created should have an overall approval from all levels of staff. Any issues of concern should be addressed and answered. To ensure the satisfaction of the customer, the development staff should issue a checklist.

Reasoning for the Network Created

After the network has been created, a detailed list should be given to the support staff. This list should include modifications done to the existing network, readdressing, or media changes. All areas of concern should be addressed so that all levels of staff have a thorough understanding of the development of the new network.

The following questions are likely to show up on the exam, so familiarize yourself with them.

QUESTIONS AND ANSWERS

What is the maximum allowed utilization percentage on a shared Ethernet LAN segment?	40 percent
What is the TCP/IP standard access list range?	1–99
What Cisco device is used to protect private networks from the public?	Cisco PIX Firewall
What part of a scalable network provides access to corporate resources for a workgroup on a local segment?	Access layer
What feature is used on routers to permit or deny network traffic?	ACLs (access control lists)

CERTIFICATION SUMMARY

This chapter discusses the importance of developing a network to meet the customer's needs by gathering information from the current network and using the data to migrate the existing network to the new network. In determining a baseline study of the customer's existing network, a framework for analysis must be completed. This study may include current problems such as latency or congestion. To assist in the baseline study and to understand data flow, a logical diagram of the customer's network should be drawn. As networks grow, LAN and WAN segments become congested. As a result, transmission of data takes longer periods of time. On shared Ethernet LANs, no segment should reach above 40 percent utilization; on Token Ring segments, no segment should reach above 70 percent utilization; and no WAN link should reach utilization over 70 percent.

Security is a very important issue for most businesses. Firewalls are used to protect a network from the "outside world." They are typically placed in a network by implementing the three-part firewall system, and no special services should be run on them. The Cisco PIX Firewall series of products is the highest performance enterprise-class set of firewalls that delivers high security and fast performance for corporate networks. Security for a network can also be provided through the use of access control lists (ACLs). ACLs are placed on a router's interface to meet such criteria as the packet's upper-layer protocol and source/destination address. Certain guidelines meet protocol-specific access lists. Each protocol has a specified range in which to use either standard or extended access lists. Other security methods include TACACS+, RADIUS, Kerberos, and SecureID. TACACS+ and RADIUS are two protocols designed to authenticate users and handle accounting. TACACS+ is a proprietary system developed by Cisco for handling authentication, access, and accounting. RADIUS is an Internet standard supported by many vendors. Kerberos uses the Key Distribution Center to handle authentication. SecureID is a security card used to authenticate to a server. A password is also required. In order to connect, both the card and password must be present.

As networks continue to grow and organizations expand their networks, they need a model to follow. The three-layer hierarchical model assists the network designer in troubleshooting, as well as in planning for future growth. The three-layer model consists of the core, distributive, and access layers. The core layer provides an optimized and reliable transport composition; the distributive layer provides access to various parts of the internetwork, as well as access to services; and the access layer provides access to corporate resources for a workgroup on a local segment. In order for a network to be scalable, internetworks need to be reliable and available, responsive, efficient, adaptable, and accessible but secure. Traffic in a network may be of many types. Applications provide support for several flow types. These types may include terminal/host, client/server, peer-to-peer, server/server, and distributed computing traffic flow.

As studies of the existing network are being done, protocols and services need to be captured and studied. Protocol analyzers are special hardware or software devices that offer various network troubleshooting features, including protocol-specific packet decoding, special troubleshooting tests, and traffic generation. A popular protocol analyzer is Network Associates' Sniffer Pro.

✓ TWO-MINUTE DRILL

❑ In determining a baseline study of the customer's existing network, a framework for analysis must be completed.

❑ On shared Ethernet LANs, no segment should reach above 40 percent utilization.

❑ On Token Ring segments, no segment should reach above 70 percent utilization.

❑ No WAN links should reach above 70 percent utilization.

❑ Firewalls are used to protect a network from the "outside world."

❑ The Cisco PIX Firewall series of products is the highest performance enterprise-class set of firewalls that delivers high security and fast performance for corporate networks.

❑ Access lists may be placed on a router's interface to block or permit traffic.

❑ There are two types of access lists: standard and extended.

❑ TACACS+ is a proprietary system developed by Cisco for handling authentication, access, and accounting.

❑ RADIUS is an Internet standard supported by many vendors.

❑ Kerberos uses the Key Distribution Center to handle authentication.

❑ SecureID is a security card used to authenticate to a server.

❑ The three-layer hierarchical model assists the network designer in troubleshooting and is used to plan for future growth.

❑ The core layer provides an optimized and reliable transport composition.

❑ The distribution layer provides access to various parts of the internetwork, as well as access to services.

❑ The access layer provides access to corporate resources for a workgroup on a local segment.

❑ Traffic in a network may be of many types. Applications provide support for several flow types, including terminal/host, client/server, peer-to-peer, server/server, and distributed computing.

❑ In order for a network to be scalable, internetworks need to be reliable and available, responsive, efficient, adaptable, and accessible but secure.

❑ Protocol analyzers are special hardware or software devices that offer various network troubleshooting features.

SELF TEST

The following Self Test questions will help you measure your understanding of the material presented in this chapter. Read all the choices carefully because there may be more than one correct answer. Choose all correct answers for each question.

1. What is the first step in developing a framework for analysis for the customer's existing network?

    A. Describe to the customer how a new network will benefit the organization.

    B. Offer solutions that will temporary resolve network latency.

    C. Diagram the logical layout of the existing network.

    D. Diagram the physical layout of the existing network.

2. In completing the network assessment chart, which of the following is (are) an example(s) of a protocol?

    A. MS Word

    B. TCP/IP

    C. IPX/SPX

    D. Peer-to-peer

    E. Client/server

3. The term _____ is defined as the data-carrying capability of a circuit or network, measured in bits per second.

    A. Media

    B. Medium

    C. Capacity

    D. Utilization

4. Which layer of the hierarchical model provides access to various parts of the internetwork, as well as access to services?

    A. Core

    B. Distribution

    C. Access

    D. None of the above

5. ABC Patented Services is a nationwide organization dedicated to providing services for individuals who develop ideas or inventions. Clients submit their ideas or inventions to the nearest location. These ideas are submitted across a 128KB Frame Relay line to the corporate headquarters located in Boston, Massachusetts.

   The design and ideas are then sent by packet to the remote offices for clients to review, change if needed, and submit for recognition and possibly prosperity. What network design requirement would this situation be most concerned with?

   A. Performance

   B. Capacity

   C. Security

   D. Scalability

6. What special hardware or software device is used to offer various network troubleshooting features, including protocol-specific packet decoding, specific troubleshooting tests, and traffic generation?

   A. Router

   B. Protocol analyzer

   C. TACACS+

   D. PIX

7. What layer of the hierarchical model provides access to corporate resources for a workgroup on a local segment?

   A. Core

   B. Distribution

   C. Access

   D. None of the above

8. _____ networks should optimize available resources and control broadcast activity.

   A. Reliable and available

   B. Responsive

   C. Efficient

   D. Adaptable

   E. Accessible

9. A _____ is a hardware device used to protect a network from the "outside world."

    A. Bridge

    B. Analyzer

    C. DNS

    D. Firewall

10. Which statement is true for the three-part firewall system?

    A. It is a router that acts as an outside packet filter between the corporate internetwork and the isolation LAN.

    B. It is a router that is a buffer between the corporate internetwork and the outside world.

    C. It is a router that acts as an outside packet filter between the corporate internetwork and the isolation LAN.

    D. It is a router that acts as an inside packet filter between the corporate internetwork and the isolation LAN.

11. What Cisco proprietary hardware allows users to thoroughly protect their networks from the outside world by providing full firewall security policy and protection?

    A. SPX

    B. PIX

    C. PIT

    D. RADIUS

12. On shared Ethernet LANs, no segment should reach above ___ percent utilization.

    A. 65

    B. 55

    C. 40

    D. 70

13. Which number range is specific to an extended IPX/SPX access control list?

    A. 1–99

    B. 500–599

    C. 100–199

    D. 900–999

    E. 800–899

14. What is the rule that states what percentage of traffic should remain local on a LAN and what percentage of the traffic may be routed to a different network segment or external network?

    A. 70/30

    B. 80/20

    C. 60/40

    D. 50/50

15. What security method provides the ownership of a card, as well as knowing a password?

    A. SecureID

    B. Kerberos

    C. RADIUS

    D. TACACS+

16. Which of the following is (are) suggestions of what not to enable on firewalls?

    A. Password encryption

    B. Dynamic routing

    C. Virtual terminal access

    D. No IP redirects

17. A _____ network's quality of service should be monitored without affecting users at the desktop.

    A. Reliable and available

    B. Responsive

    C. Efficient

    D. Adaptable

    E. Accessible but secure

18. Which of the following are traffic flow types?

    A. Peer-to-peer

    B. Terminal/server

    C. Server/server

    D. Terminal/terminal

SELF TEST ANSWERS

1. ☑ **C.** The first step in developing a framework is to diagram the logical layout of the existing network.

   ☒ **A, B,** and **D** are incorrect because these steps do not exist as a framework for analysis.

2. ☑ **B and C.** In a network assessment chart, TCP/IP and IPX/SPX are examples of protocol types. Other examples are AppleTalk and SNA.

   ☒ **A** is incorrect because MS Word is the name of an application. **D** and **E** are incorrect because peer-to-peer and client/server are examples of traffic flow types.

3. ☑ **C.** Capacity is defined as the data-carrying capability of a circuit or network, measured in bits per second.

   ☒ **A** is incorrect because a medium is defined as the physical environment through which transmission signals pass. **B** is incorrect because "media" is simply the plural of "medium." **C** is incorrect because utilization is the percentage of total available capacity in use on a network or circuit.

4. ☑ **B.** The distribution layer's primary function is to provide access to various parts of the internetwork, as well as access to services.

   ☒ **A** and **C** are incorrect because the core and access layers of the hierarchical model provide different functions and services.

5. ☑ **C.** If credit card information and inventions are being sent across a WAN, security is of utmost importance.

   ☒ **A, B,** and **D** are incorrect because, although these other requirements are also important, they should be second to security in this situation.

6. ☑ **B.** A protocol analyzer is a special hardware or software device used to offer various network troubleshooting features, including protocol-specific packet decoding, specific troubleshooting tests, and traffic generation.

   ☒ **A** is incorrect because a router is a layer-3 device used to route packets based on either source or destination address. **C** is incorrect because TACAS+ is a protocol used to allow authentication. **D** is incorrect because PIX is a Cisco proprietary firewall used to block or permit network traffic.

7. ☑ **C.** The access layer of the hierarchical model provides access to corporate resources for a workgroup on a local segment.

   ☒ **A** and **B** are incorrect because the core and distribution layers of the hierarchical model provide different services.

8. ☑ **C.** Efficient networks should optimize available resources and control broadcast activity.
   ☒ **A, B, D,** and **E** are incorrect because reliable and available, responsive, adaptable, and accessible networks are defined differently.

9. ☑ **D.** A firewall is a hardware device used to protect a network from the "outside world."
   ☒ **A, B,** and **C** are incorrect because a bridge, an analyzer, and a DNS play different roles in a network.

10. ☑ **D.** A specialized layer in the three-part firewall system is a router that acts as an inside packet filter between the corporate internetwork and the isolation LAN.
    ☒ **A, B,** and **C** are incorrect because they do not play any role in the three-part firewall system.

11. ☑ **B.** The Cisco PIX Firewall allows users to thoroughly protect their networks from the outside world, providing full firewall security policy and protection.
    ☒ **A** and **C** are incorrect because SPX and PIT are made-up abbreviations. **D** is incorrect because RADIUS is an Internet standard, supported by vendors to authenticate users.

12. ☑ **C.** On shared Ethernet LANs, no segment should reach above 40 percent utilization.

13. ☑ **D.** The range 900–999 belongs to the IPX/SPX extended access control list.
    ☒ **A, B, C,** and **E** are incorrect because these number ranges belong to different protocols.

14. ☑ **B.** The 80/20 rule states that 80 percent of the traffic should remain local on a LAN and 20 percent of the traffic may be routed to a different network segment or external network.
    ☒ **A, C,** and **D** are incorrect because these numbers have no significance.

15. ☑ **A.** SecureID is a security method in which both the ownership of a card and a password, are needed for authentication.
    ☒ **B, C,** and **D** are incorrect because Kerberos, RADIUS, and TACACS+ are security methods that are defined differently.

16. ☑ **B and C.** Static routing should be used instead of dynamic routing, and virtual terminal access should be disabled on a firewall.

17. ☑ **B.** A responsive network's quality of service should be monitored without affecting users at the desktop.
    ☒ **A, C, D,** and **E** are incorrect because reliable and available, efficient, adaptable, and accessible-but-secure networks are defined differently.

18. ☑ **A and C.** Peer-to-peer and server/server are examples of traffic flow types.
    ☒ **B** and **D** are incorrect because terminal/server and terminal/terminal do not represent types of traffic flow.

CISCO CERTIFIED DESIGN ASSOCIATE

6

Defining the Problems in the Existing Network

CERTIFICATION OBJECTIVE

6.01   Data Required to Characterize the
        Customer's Existing Network

Characterizing the customer's network, by obtaining data, is a fundamental step in developing a network design. Both business and technical data must be collected and studied, and a significant amount of that information is available to help determine the right network design to meet the customer's needs.

In the following sections, we cover the data that is needed to characterize the customer's existing network. After reading each type of data, be sure to note the differences between business and technical data. Figures of worksheets and diagrams are shown throughout the chapter to aid you in understanding and developing your customer's network design.

CERTIFICATION OBJECTIVE 6.01

Data Required to Characterize the Customer's Existing Network

The first steps in planning a proactive network management strategy are to collect statistics and watch trends. In characterizing a customer's existing network, it is important to recognize the data that traverses the network. Business and technical data are two types that are to be observed, recorded, and analyzed. Embodied within this data are the customer's requirements for availability, scalability, affordability, security, and manageability. To characterize a customer's network, determine if the projected growth will cause future problems, understand the current legacy systems that must be brought into the design, identify any bottlenecks, and recognize any business constraints that will be part of the new design.

An important consideration in working on your new design is to understand your customer's business constraints. These constraints include the client's market, products, services, and suppliers. Along with constraints, administrative data will aid you in determining the company's business goals, corporate and geographical structure, current and future staffing, and policies and politics. Examples of business data include software applications such as Accounting Pro Software, Lotus Spreadsheets, and AutoCAD.

During an initial visit with the customer, an explained drawing of the organizational structure of the company should be compiled. This drawing should include departments at all levels because understanding the organization will help you characterize major traffic patterns in the business. After the organization chart has been completed and discussed, ask the customer to explain what success patterns should be implemented to save money, increase revenue, and build competitive relations. Understanding the company's structure and its business goals will help you forecast and determine the scalability of the new internetwork.

In developing a new design for your network, consider the many different marketing techniques used by competitors. These techniques include Web-based and CAD/CAM applications to promote corporate communication and expand into worldwide markets.

Another important factor in determining the criteria for success is the possibility of convergence between two companies. Scalable networks will allow independent entities, such as resellers or wholesalers, to join each other without interruption or downtime. In a WAN environment, many different applications, such as Systems Network Architecture (SNA)–based applications, are migrating to an IP-based network. Also, time-division multiplexing (TDM)–based WAN networks are moving toward high-speed data and voice networks such as Frame Relay routed and ATM switched networks.

Analyzing business factors such as budget and staffing constraints, politics and policies, and scheduling is critical for the design of the new network. These aspects determine whether the organization will receive support from all levels of staff.

Your network design must be able to fit the customer's budget. The budget should include all expenses such as current equipment upgrade, new equipment, software licenses, support (long and short term), training, and labor costs. The budget should also show how the implementation of routing protocols, such as Cisco's proprietary routing protocol Enhanced Interior Gateway Routing Protocol (EIGRP), would reduce the need for complex internetworking skills. After these costs have been determined, develop a plan that will show a return on investment. These projections are critical in convincing upper-level management to continue their support for the project. Also, explain the criticality of training. Training will allow the current staff to understand the new network, perform routine maintenance, and troubleshoot in case of an emergency.

In designing a network to meet the customer's needs, a very important step is characterizing and analyzing the data that is part of the existing network. Listed next are steps in determining the current data network requirements for the customer. Following these requirements will ensure the development of a successful network:

1. Identify security requirements:

   ■ Determine the level of security that will be needed for each network segment.

   ■ Identify all remote traffic from outside routers, mobile users, and telecommuters.

   ■ Determine the placement for firewalls, if necessary.

2. Identify manageability requirements by isolating any need for fault, accounting, configuration, performance, and security requirements.

3. Identify business constraints:

   ■ Develop time-line charts for the project.

   ■ Identify budgetary allowances.

4. Characterize new network traffic:

   ■ Determine features such as error-recovery mechanisms, windowing and flow control, frame sizing, and broadcast/multicast behavior.

   ■ Use tools such as CiscoWorks and protocol analyzers to study protocol behavior.

5. Extract application requirements:

   ■ Document the names and types of applications and protocols.

   ■ Determine the number of users who will use each application.

   ■ Diagram the flow of information from existing and new applications.

6. Identify performance requirements such as

   - Response time

   - Accuracy

   - Availability

   - Efficiency

   - Throughput

   - Maximum network utilization

   - Latency

7. Identify staffing requirements, and diagram a working schedule that will involve all employees. Job descriptions may change, but try to include all members so that full support of the project will take place.

8. Characterize new traffic:

   - Determine if any new applications will be part of the new network and label these applications.

   - Document the number of users who will access the network, the type of protocol, and the criticality of the application.

9. Create a customer needs specification:

   - After documenting and designing the network, determine the need for additional hardware, software, training, and other components.

   - Be sure the customer needs specification contains projected time lines and estimated costs.

Policies and Politics

Understanding policies regarding approved protocols and vendors is very important in any network design. Protocols (routed or routing) are major factors in determining the network architectural topology. Be aware of the various routed protocols such as IP and Internetwork Packet Exchange (IPX). The traffic produced by these protocols should be monitored carefully. Also, determine if an approved or existing routing protocol such as Open

Shortest Path First (OSPF) or Interior Gateway Routing Protocol (IGRP) has been selected as the routing protocol of choice. These routing protocols are important when you are implementing or modifying new networks. For example, IGRP is a distance vector routing protocol, and OSPF is a link-state routing protocol. Not understanding how these routing protocols operate according to change could result in major network downtime.

Network engineers and designers must unfortunately deal with politics, a subject many of them try to avoid, in order to understand how past designs might have failed or group relations were formed. The topics that may be brought up, as part of the design, may have full or no support from upper-level management or network engineers. Pay close attention to those who show support for the issues that are discussed. There will even be some cases in which people will have a negative reaction toward the presentation. If this happens, depict whether these people may fear their jobs will be eliminated because of the new design.

Customer's Current Applications, Protocols, Topology, and Number of Users

An important consideration in designing the customer's future network, especially one that will be scalable, is to understand the existing network. Assessing the existing network will allow you to understand the current applications, protocols, topology, and users. The information that is gathered will help you make decisions about whether to upgrade the current network or start from scratch. In fact, a skilled network designer can take the existing network and make adjustments to it to meet the customer's requirement for improved performance and scalability. Identifying performance problems from the start develops a baseline analysis for future network designs.

This section is intended to assist you in starting a baseline analysis of the customer's network. The figures demonstrate how to analyze a customer's existing network. Next time you go to a customer's site, make a copy of the blank spreadsheets and take them with you. Doing so will help you, as a network designer, to characterize the customer's existing network.

Current Applications

As mentioned earlier, an important step in characterizing a customer's network is to understand the current applications that are operating. These applications can be of many flow types, which can be any of the following:

- Client/server
- Terminal/host
- Peer-to-peer
- Server/server

When documenting the customer's applications, be sure to include every application that is being accessed on the network. Also, make note of the type of traffic flow type that each application uses and also the criticality of each application as it pertains to the organization. Applications should be rated 1 = mission critical, 2 = somewhat critical, and 3 = noncritcal. Special attention should also be given to the number of users who access the particular application and names of servers that the application resides on. Also, write down any concerns you or the customer may have about scalability or plans of corporate migration to an application. Use Table 6-1 to characterize the customer's applications.

TABLE 6-1   Characterizing Network Applications

Name of Application	Traffic Flow Type	Number of Users	Server	Criticality	Comments

Protocol Documentation

As part of analyzing the current network, give special consideration to documenting the customer's current protocols. In Table 6-2, document all protocols and other information that is part of the network.

In the "Name of Protocol" field, list all protocols associated with the network. The protocols can be any of the following:

- TCP/IP
- IPX/SPX
- AppleTalk
- NetBEUI
- SNA

In the "Type of Protocol" field, list any information that may be useful in identifying the protocol. For example, terminal/host, client/server, or session-layer.

In the "Number of Users" field, list the number of users that access the particular protocol.

In the "Name of Server(s)" field, list the name of the servers that the protocol resides on.

In the "Comments" field, list any comments or concerns that are part of the network design.

TABLE 6-2   Documenting the Customer's Current Protocols

Name of Protocol	Type of Protocol	Number of Users	Name of Server(s)	Comments

Network Topology

The customer's network topology is important in determining existing as well as future network development. Understanding the topology of the network will help the designer make educated decisions about issues such as LAN segmentation. The topology of the network can be of many types. These types can include any of the following:

- **Ring topology**   A ring topology connects all workstations in a closed loop, and messages pass to each node or station in turn. The ring connects all stations by using a cable in a ring or circular pattern. Figure 6-1 is an example of a ring network.

- **Bus topology**   A bus topology connects all stations to a cable running the length of the network. The bus physically connects all nodes by means of cables that run between devices, but cables do not pass through a central controller mechanism. The advantage of this network topology is the use of Carrier Sense Multiple Access

FIGURE 6-1

Ring topology

with Collision Detection (CSMA/CD). Figure 6-2 shows an example of a bus topology:

■ **Star topology**   A star topology, the most common topology, connects all workstations to one central station, routing traffic to the appropriate place. An advantage of the star topology is that the failure in one device does not disable the entire network. Figure 6-3 illustrates star topology.

■ **Hybrid topology**   A hybrid topology is a combination of two or more topologies. These topologies are fairly complex and require documentation for troubleshooting. For example, if an end node is experiencing problems reaching the server for an application, understanding where the node is on the network is useful in determining where the problem lies. Figure 6-4 is an example of a hybrid topology.

FIGURE 6-2　　　　Bus topology

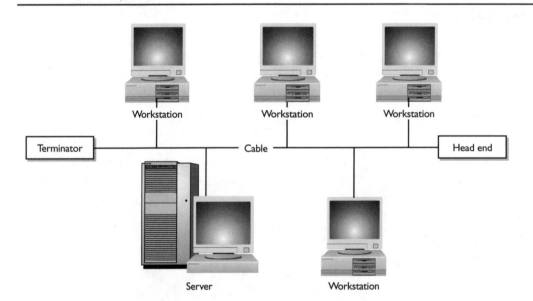

| FIGURE 6-3 | Star topology |

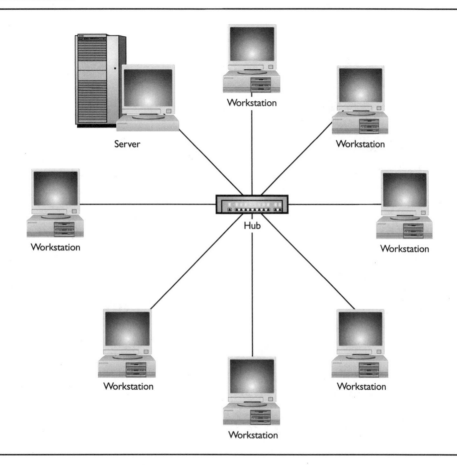

Again, understanding the customer's network by documenting current applications, protocols, and topology are key steps in preparing for the design of the new network. To enforce what was previously mentioned, an example scenario from an organization is included in the following section. Use the preceding figures and tables to document the customer's network. Remember to document every segment of the network.

FIGURE 6-4   Hybrid topology

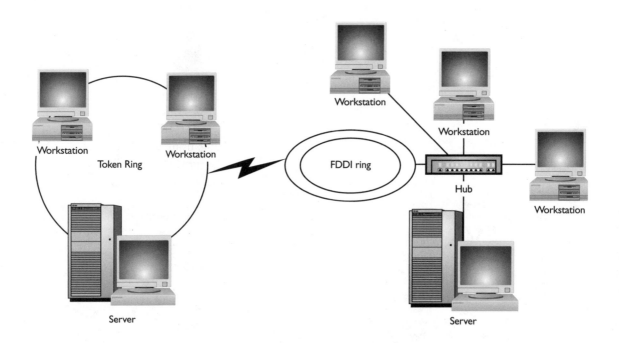

EXERCISE 6-1

Data Required to Characterize the Customer's Existing Network

BPL Engineering is a mechanical engineering firm that designs and produces internal combustion engines. It is located outside a rural area of a metropolitan city. The decision has been made to design a new network that will meet the growing needs of the company. Mr. Goynes and Mr. Winchester, chief engineers at BPL Engineering, have agreed to conduct a network analysis of the firm. Both men believe that the overall network design should provide quick and reliable access to drawings and information the firm provides.

The engineering firm employs 47 users who are separated into two categories: engineering and clerical. The engineering staff, which consists of 25 users, is responsible for designing and consulting. The clerical staff is responsible for general accounting, filing, and customer service–related issues.

Currently, two servers are located in an enclosed room. The servers have different network operating systems running on them. The network operating systems include Microsoft Windows NT, called "ENG1," and Novell NetWare 4.11, called "ENG2."

All employees currently use GroupWise for e-mail purposes and generate reports, graphs, and presentations using Microsoft Office. The engineers are in the only group that uses AutoCAD as the designing application for the firm.

In answer to a question about whether one of the servers has ever failed, Mr. Winchester stated that the Novell NetWare server failed because of a bad NIC, but the firm was able to continue business as usual. Microsoft Office and AutoCAD were still accessible. AutoCAD and Microsoft Office are critical applications that must be available at all times.

Now that you have read the description of the network at BPL Engineering, perform the following exercise.

1. Fill out the following tables to draw a high-level topology of the customer's current network.

Name of Application	Traffic Flow Type	Number of Users	Server	Criticality	Comments

Name of Protocol	Type of Protocol	Number of Users	Name of Server(s)	Comments

2. Draw a high-level topology of BPL Engineering's network.

Answers to Exercise 6-1

1. A high-level topology of the customer's current network looks like this:

Name of Application	Traffic Flow Type	Number of Users	Server	Criticality	Comments
Microsoft Office	Client/server	47	ENG1	1	
AutoCAD	Client/server	25	ENG1	1	
GroupWise	Client/server	47	ENG2	2	

Name of Protocol	Type of Protocol	Number of Users	Name of Server(s)	Comments
IPX	Client/server	47	ENG2	

2. A high-level topology of BPL Engineering's network looks like this:

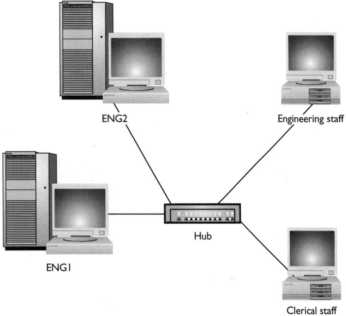

Ways to Identify All the Data

Many devices on the market today allow organizations to capture packets and study them. Protocol analyzers such as Network Associate's Sniffer network analyzer capture and display network statistics. Doing so aids in capturing and identifying data that is part of a network. There are also upgrades that allow the software to perform network enhancement.

Other possible ways of identifying traffic and data that is part of a network is by using the various show commands on the Cisco router. These commands will display traffic information such as protocol and interface usage, drops, and addresses.

During a network assessment, characterizing the availability of all network traffic is also important in developing a successful network. The baseline study of the customer's existing network should focus on the business as well as the technical goals of the organization. Testing and documenting various network characteristics allow a successful implementation of a healthy and scalable network. There are several Cisco commands that check the health of a router. Following are examples of a sample router and the displays of each of the following commands. Note the characteristics of each.

■ **show interfaces** Displays the number of interface resets, number and characteristics of serial/Ethernet interfaces.

```
Router#sh interfaces
Ethernet0/0 is up, line protocol is up
  Hardware is AmdP2, address is 00e0.1e65.a0e1 (bia 00e0.1e65.a0e1)
  Description: MSO Ethernet
  Internet address is 162.71.32.97/27
  MTU 1500 bytes, BW 10000 Kbit, DLY 1000 usec,
     reliability 255/255, txload 4/255, rxload 1/255
  Encapsulation ARPA, loopback not set, keepalive set (10 sec)
  ARP type: ARPA, ARP Timeout 04:00:00
  Last input 00:00:16, output 00:00:00, output hang never
  Last clearing of "show interface" counters never
  Queueing strategy: fifo
  Output queue 0/40, 0 drops; input queue 0/75, 0 drops
  5 minute input rate 32000 bits/sec, 28 packets/sec
  5 minute output rate 185000 bits/sec, 39 packets/sec
     1312977 packets input, 134375093 bytes, 0 no buffer
     Received 16408 broadcasts, 0 runts, 0 giants, 0 throttles
     0 input errors, 0 CRC, 0 frame, 0 overrun, 0 ignored, 0 abort
     0 input packets with dribble condition detected
     1629113 packets output, 664978888 bytes, 0 underruns
     0 output errors, 2375 collisions, 1 interface resets
     0 babbles, 0 late collision, 9207 deferred
     0 lost carrier, 0 no carrier
     0 output buffer failures, 0 output buffers swapped out
Serial0/0 is up, line protocol is up
  Hardware is QUICC Serial
  Description: T1 to MacArthur
  Internet address is 162.71.32.14/30
  MTU 1500 bytes, BW 1544 Kbit, DLY 20000 usec,
     reliability 255/255, txload 4/255, rxload 29/255
  Encapsulation HDLC, loopback not set, keepalive set (10 sec)
  Last input 00:00:00, output 00:00:00, output hang never
  Last clearing of "show interface" counters never
  Input queue: 0/75/0 (size/max/drops); Total output drops: 0
  Queueing strategy: weighted fair
  Output queue: 0/1000/64/0 (size/max total/threshold/drops)
     Conversations  0/5/256 (active/max active/max total)
     Reserved Conversations 0/0 (allocated/max allocated)
```

```
5 minute input rate 181000 bits/sec, 37 packets/sec
5 minute output rate 28000 bits/sec, 29 packets/sec
    1640734 packets input, 649742497 bytes, 0 no buffer
    Received 10174 broadcasts, 0 runts, 0 giants, 0 throttles
    2 input errors, 0 CRC, 2 frame, 0 overrun, 0 ignored, 0 abort
    1342966 packets output, 123549239 bytes, 0 underruns
    0 output errors, 0 collisions, 10 interface resets
    0 output buffer failures, 0 output buffers swapped out
    0 carrier transitions
    DCD=up  DSR=up  DTR=up  RTS=up  CTS=up
```

■ **show processes cpu**   Displays CPU process utilization for the last five seconds, one minute, and five minutes. Shows utilization for routing protocols, buffer management, and interface processes.

```
Router#sh processes cpu
CPU utilization for five seconds: 3%/1%; one minute: 1%; five minutes: 1%
 PID  Runtime(ms)  Invoked  uSecs   5Sec   1Min   5Min TTY Process
   1            4    17424       0  0.00%  0.00%  0.00%   0 Load Meter
   2          108      105    1028  0.32%  0.10%  0.03%  66 Virtual Exec
   3        23856     2904    8214  0.32%  0.03%  0.00%   0 Check heaps
   4            0        1       0  0.00%  0.00%  0.00%   0 Pool Manager
   5            0        2       0  0.00%  0.00%  0.00%   0 Timers
   6            0        2       0  0.00%  0.00%  0.00%   0 Serial Background
   7           16     2904       5  0.00%  0.00%  0.00%   0 /
Environmental monitor
   8          352     1973     178  0.00%  0.00%  0.00%   0 ARP Input
   9            0        3       0  0.00%  0.00%  0.00%   0 DDR Timers
  10            0        1       0  0.00%  0.00%  0.00%   0 SERIAL A'detect
  11        14628    33306     439  0.16%  0.04%  0.01%   0 IP Input
  12         2244    11603     193  0.00%  0.00%  0.00%   0 CDP Protocol
  13            0        1       0  0.00%  0.00%  0.00%   0 Asy FS Helper
  14            0        1       0  0.00%  0.00%  0.00%   0 PERUSER aux
  15            0        1       0  0.00%  0.00%  0.00%   0 PPP IP Add Route
  16            0      147       0  0.00%  0.00%  0.00%   0 MOP Protocols
  17            0        1       0  0.00%  0.00%  0.00%   0 X.25/
Encaps Manage
  18            0       30       0  0.00%  0.00%  0.00%   0 TCP Timer
  19           12        9    1333  0.00%  0.00%  0.00%   0 TCP Protocols
  20            0        1       0  0.00%  0.00%  0.00%   0 Probe Input
  21            0        1       0  0.00%  0.00%  0.00%   0 RARP Input
```

■ **show buffers**   Displays information on the various buffer sizes such as small, medium-sized, large, very large, and huge. Also shows the number of hits and misses on each buffer size.

```
Router#sh buffers
Buffer elements:
     499 in free list (500 max allowed)
     471665 hits, 0 misses, 0 created
Public buffer pools:
Small buffers, 104 bytes (total 50, permanent 50):
     48 in free list (20 min, 150 max allowed)
     109103 hits, 0 misses, 0 trims, 0 created
     0 failures (0 no memory)
Middle buffers, 600 bytes (total 25, permanent 25):
     23 in free list (10 min, 150 max allowed)
     168528 hits, 0 misses, 0 trims, 0 created
     0 failures (0 no memory)
Big buffers, 1524 bytes (total 50, permanent 50):
     50 in free list (5 min, 150 max allowed)
     2966 hits, 0 misses, 0 trims, 0 created
     0 failures (0 no memory)
VeryBig buffers, 4520 bytes (total 10, permanent 10):
     10 in free list (0 min, 100 max allowed)
     1217 hits, 0 misses, 0 trims, 0 created
     0 failures (0 no memory)
Large buffers, 5024 bytes (total 0, permanent 0):
     0 in free list (0 min, 10 max allowed)
     0 hits, 0 misses, 0 trims, 0 created
     0 failures (0 no memory)
Huge buffers, 18024 bytes (total 0, permanent 0):
     0 in free list (0 min, 4 max allowed)
     0 hits, 0 misses, 0 trims, 0 created
     0 failures (0 no memory)
 Interface buffer pools:
CD2430 I/O buffers, 1524 bytes (total 0, permanent 0):
     0 in free list (0 min, 0 max allowed)
     0 hits, 0 fallbacks
 Header pools:
Header buffers, 0 bytes (total 265, permanent 256):
     9 in free list (10 min, 512 max allowed)
     253 hits, 3 misses, 0 trims, 9 created
     0 failures (0 no memory)
     256 max cache size, 256 in cache
 Particle Clones:
```

```
      1024 clones, 0 hits, 0 misses
  Public particle pools:
F/S buffers, 256 bytes (total 384, permanent 384):
      128 in free list (128 min, 1024 max allowed)
      256 hits, 0 misses, 0 trims, 0 created
      0 failures (0 no memory)
      256 max cache size, 256 in cache
Normal buffers, 1548 bytes (total 512, permanent 512):
      384 in free list (128 min, 1024 max allowed)
      167 hits, 0 misses, 0 trims, 0 created
      0 failures (0 no memory)
      128 max cache size, 128 in cache
  Private particle pools:
Ethernet0/0 buffers, 1536 bytes (total 96, permanent 96):
      0 in free list (0 min, 96 max allowed)
      96 hits, 0 fallbacks
      96 max cache size, 64 in cache
Serial0/0 buffers, 1548 bytes (total 14, permanent 14):
      0 in free list (0 min, 14 max allowed)
      14 hits, 0 fallbacks
      14 max cache size, 7 in cache
```

Along with these commands, analyze the following:

- **Network availability**   Document the mean time before failure (MTBF) and mean time before repair (MTBR). Ask engineers and technicians to list the date of the last downtime and describe the cause and duration. Also ask them to list the affected areas.

- **Bandwidth consumed by each protocol**   When a workstation initializes, the network interface card (NIC) in a network passes broadcasts and mulicasts to the CPU of the station. These broadcasts and multicasts are needed to find services and check for names and addresses of remote stations. When investigating the effect of broadcasts on a network, analysts determined that

    - As few as 100 broadcasts or multicasts per second on a Pentium 120MHz CPU used approximately 2 percent of the CPU power with a 3Com Fast Etherlink PCI Ethernet adapter.

    - 1,300 broadcasts per second used 9 percent of the CPU power.

    - 3,000 broadcasts per second used 25 percent of the CPU power.

- **Broadcasts propagated throughout the network** Depending on the number of broadcasts workstations and servers place on a network, flooding the network with traffic congestion is likely. Protocol traffic can include the following:

  - Novell NetWare (IPX/SPX)
  - AppleTalk
  - Transmission Control Protocol/Internet Protocol (TCP/IP)
  - TCP/IP with DHCP
  - NetBEUI
  - NetBIOS with a Windows Internet Name Service (WINS) server
  - Systems Network Architecture (SNA)

  Although broadcast behavior is unavoidable, servers send broadcasts to advertise their services. Table 6-3 is a suggested recommendation for limiting the number of stations that reside on a flat, switched, or single VLAN network.

- **Network accuracy and efficiency** When analyzing the current network, be sure to document the number of CRC errors, input/output dropped queues, and lost or dropped packets that you encounter. To be efficient, a network should be able to support the minimum allowed frame size packet when data is being transferred across a network.

TABLE 6-3	Protocol	Maximum Number of Workstations
Workstation Constraints for a Flat Network	IP	500
	IPX	300
	AppleTalk	200
	NetBIOS	200
	Mixed	200

Time-Sensitive Traffic

Traffic that is required to reach a destination before timing out is called *time-sensitive traffic*. Some methods exist to ensure the delivery of information from source to destination.

Is Remote Access Required?

This section covers the need for remote access for user communities, mobile workers, and telecommuters. Some of the technologies associated with remote access include the following:

- Cable modems
- Integrated Services Digital Network (ISDN)
- Point-to-Point Protocol
- Digital Subscriber Line (DSL)

Many organizations require the costs of remote access links to be inexpensive. However, these services must provide bandwidth as well as quality of service to business. With an increase in video, voice, and data that cross a link, a traffic flow analysis should be conducted.

As the number of telecommuters, remote offices, and mobile workers have increased, the need for network access using remote access has also increased. An analysis of the users and their locations should be evaluated, and the number and type of applications that are accessed across the WAN should be noted.

Remote workers commonly use applications such as e-mail, calendar applications for scheduling, software packages, and Web browsing. These services are bandwidth intensive. Other bandwidth-intensive applications include downloading software patches and transferring files. Those who access the network for a short period of time can sufficiently use an analog line, which uses layer-3 protocols. This is a form of asynchronous routing. The analog modem's highest connection speed today is approximately 56 Kbps. Although latency is typically high on an analog modem, the price for an analog line is relatively low. For workers who require higher speeds, faster connection and transmission, and lower latency, ISDN or DSL modems should replace analog modems.

exam
Watch

Be able to identify typical uses for ISDN. ISDN provides cost-effective remote access to corporate networks for telecommuters and remote offices. It is also used as a support for voice and video and as backup for another type of link.

What Is Mission Critical?

Mission-critical applications are those that allow minimum or no downtime. They are the core applications that keep a business or organization operating. During a network analysis and design, ask the customer the criticality of each application that is currently in operation. Special consideration should be given to these applications. As shown in Table 6-1, earlier in the chapter, list each individual application that is on the customer's network and state the criticality of each.

Is Traffic Routable?

In a network, there can be many different protocols. These protocols, such as IPX or AppleTalk, use broadcasts and multicasts heavily for resource location, address assignment, and routing. Also, routing protocols flood the network every 60 seconds with information. Routing Information Protocol (RIP), for example, will send as many packets as it takes to carry the routing information. On a fairly large network, this could be 10 or more packets.

With this in mind, it is not hard to imagine the number of packets that travel through a network with numerous machines as well as protocols.

A router is an OSI layer-3 device that acts as an intelligent filter by looking at a network-layer address to make its decision and observing the broadcasts and multicast packets. It establishes broadcast domains, which are portions of a network within which a broadcast is seen by all machines. A router does not forward broadcasts unless configured to do so or under specified criteria. If an unknown destination is received, the packet is dropped instead of flooding the network. By not forwarding other broadcasts and multicasts, a router optimizes bandwidth and allows scalability of a network.

The Need for Bridging

Bridges are devices that are used to segment Ethernet LANs. Bridges operate at OSI layer 2 and are typically easy to install because they learn their network topology. The purpose of a bridge is to increase the number of addressable nodes on a network or to link two geographically distant, but similar, networks that use the same protocol. A bridge performs its segmentation by building address tables that associate segment end stations with the segment's port connection. The destination address determines the forwarding decision. If the destination address is both in the routing table and the same network address as the segment, the bridge discards the packet. If the destination address is in the routing table but not on the same network segment, the bridge determines the port associated with the address and forwards the packet to that port. A bridge is useful if the length of the Ethernet cable in a LAN exceeds the maximum distance (100 meters). Also, a single LAN can be divided into two separate LANs with a bridge.

exam
ⓦatch

Along with understanding the differences between routers and bridges, be sure to understand the difference between hubs and repeaters. Hubs are physical-layer devices that connect multiple user stations, each via a dedicated cable. Repeaters are physical-layer devices used to interconnect the media segments of an extended network.

QUESTIONS AND ANSWERS

What command on a Cisco router is used to show the number, type, and addresses of interfaces on a router?	Router#show interfaces
What are two types of data that are to be collected when you are analyzing a network?	Technical and business
A Cisco 1601 router is placed on a fairly large network. What command would check to see if the process utilization is high?	Router#show processes cpu
At what OSI layer does a router operate?	Layer 3

CERTIFICATION SUMMARY

This chapter describes what a network engineer looks for when developing a network to meet the needs of the customer. It explains different types of data such as technical and business, and gives several examples of each. A scalable network is a network that meets the customer's current needs and allows room for future development. When a network is being designed, the engineer must discuss many topics, such as budget, staffing, politics, and policies, with the client. Some of these topics may form a constraint of the development of the network design. Documenting the network and gathering current information about the existing network is a very important step in the development process of creating a new network. A customer's current applications, protocols, topology, and number of users should be labeled. Such applications may include client/server, terminal/host, peer-to-peer, and server/server. When labeling the applications, be sure to include the criticality of each application. Examples of the many different types of protocols are TCP/IP, IPX/SPX, AppleTalk, NetBEUI, and SNA. Each protocol has special characteristics. One example is the suggested number of workstations allowed on a flat network without broadcast issues. Drawing the current network is a fundamental step to determine the scalability of the existing network. When drawing the topology of the network, be sure to understand the characteristics of each type. Ring, bus, star, and hybrid are different types of topologies.

As you can see, a network design must meet many requirements to satisfy the customer. Additional requirements that must be gathered to complete a successful network implementation include security, manageability, application, and performance requirements. Also, you must characterize new network traffic as well as identify business constraints.

Three Cisco commands that are useful to identify current traffic on the network are show interfaces, show processes cpu, and show buffers. From these commands, information may be collected on the addresses and protocols on the serial and Ethernet interfaces of the router. Also, the utilization in different increments of times may also be gathered from the router, and any overflows from large amounts of data may be monitored. Additional devices such as Network Associate's Protocol Analyzers may be used to capture and record protocol utilization on a network.

During a network assessment, information about remote access to applications should be gathered. The several technologies associated with remote access include cable modems, ISDN, PPP, and DSL. The amount of time accessing the applications and costs are some determining factors to determine the appropriate technology to use for remote access.

Applications that allow minimum or no downtime are called mission-critical applications. These applications should be carefully documented and studied prior to network redevelopment. Applications that are part of a network may be routed and/or bridged. Bridges are OSI layer-2 devices used to segment Ethernet LANs. The purpose of a bridge is to increase the number of addressable nodes on a network topology or to link two geographically distant but similar networks that use the same protocol. Routers are OSI layer-3 network devices used to filter network traffic. Broadcast and multicast domains are formed to optimize bandwidth and allow scalable networks.

✓ TWO-MINUTE DRILL

- ❑ The first step in planning a proactive network management strategy is to collect statistics and watch trends.

- ❑ Business and technical are two types of data that are part of a network.

- ❑ Embodied within business and technical data are the customer's requirements for availability, scalability, affordability, security, and manageability.

- ❑ When documenting the customer's existing network, provide documentation/drawings on the current applications, protocols, topology, and number of users that are part of the network.

- ❑ Current applications can be of many types: client/server, terminal/host, peer-to-peer, or server/server.

- ❑ One or more protocols may be part of a network. TCP/IP, IPX/SPX, AppleTalk, NetBEUI, and SNA are examples of common protocols that are part of a network.

❑ To understand the current network and to determine whether the network is scalable, a logical and physical drawing of the network should be taken.

❑ The physical topology of the network can be of many different types. Ring, bus, star, and hybrid topologies are examples of physical topologies. Be sure to understand the characteristics of each.

❑ The following are needed for determining the current data requirements: security, manageability, application, and performance requirements. Also identify business constraints and characterize new network traffic.

❑ Three Cisco commands that are useful in characterizing network traffic are show processes cpu, show buffers, and show interfaces commands.

❑ There are limitations on the suggested number of workstations running certain protocols on flat networks or VLANs. Be able to recognize the maximum number of workstations allowed on a network.

❑ Identify any CRC errors, input/output queue drops, and lost packets that are part of the existing network.

❑ Protocol analyzers such as Network Associates' Sniffer Pro should be used to capture and record data that is part of the existing network.

❑ Remote access for mobile workers and telecommuters can be any of the following: cable modems, ISDN, PPP, and DSL. Be able to understand the advantages and disadvantages of each.

❑ Mission-critical applications are those that allow minimum or no downtime.

❑ Routers are OSI layer-3 devices that optimize bandwidth and make networks scalable by acting as intelligent filters.

❑ Bridges are OSI layer-2 devices that segment two geographically distant but similar networks that use the same protocol.

SELF TEST

The following Self Test questions will help you measure your understanding of the material presented in this chapter. Read all the choices carefully because there may be more than one correct answer. Choose all correct answers for each question.

1. Rachal, Inc., is experiencing slow performance on the network. After the layout of the network and number of devices has been discussed, it is determined that a Cisco 1605 router is placed on a network with a fairly large number of devices. What Cisco command would tell the administrator the capability of the Cisco 1605 in regard to handling the amount of traffic that is on the network without causing latency?

   A. show buffers

   B. show interfaces

   C. show processes cpu

   D. None of the above

2. Which of the following is (are) an example(s) of business data?

   A. Accounting Pro software

   B. AutoCAD

   C. Lotus Spreadsheet Standard

   D. None of the above

   E. All of the above

Use the following diagram and paragraph to answer questions 3–5.

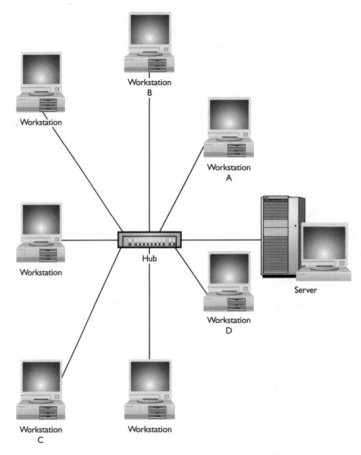

This illustration is a high-level drawing of CJL Enterprise's current network. The organization is on a flat network with a network operating system of Novell 3.1x.

3. The above diagram is an example of a _____ network.

   A. Ring

   B. Hybrid

   C. Star

   D. Bus

   E. None of the above

4. If workstation A was experiencing a bad Network Interface Card or not functioning properly on a network, what other workstations would be affected by the removal of workstation A?

   A. Workstation B

   B. Workstation C

   C. Workstation D

   D. All of the above

   E. None of the above

5. What protocol is this network using?

   A. TCP/IP

   B. SNA

   C. IPX/SPX

   D. AppleTalk

   E. None of the above

6. When a successful network is being developed, what requirement(s) fall(s) under manageability requirements? (Choose all that apply.)

   A. Security

   B. Application

   C. Performance

   D. Staffing

   E. All of the above

7. Which of the following is (are) an application flow type(s)?

   A. Peer-to-peer

   B. Peer-to-network

   C. Server/server

   D. Terminal/host

   E. Server/application

8. What is the maximum suggested number of workstations allowed on a flat network running TCP/IP applications?

   A. 500

   B. 400

   C. 350

   D. 300

   E. 200

9. A _____ is a layer-3 device used as an intelligent filter. It looks at the network-layer addresses to make its decision and observes the broadcast and multicast packets.

   A. Switch

   B. Hub

   C. Router

   D. Repeater

10. What remote access technology primarily is used as a cost-effective backup for another type of link and supports voice and video?

    A. Point-to-Point Protocol

    B. Integrated Services Digital Network

    C. Cable modem

    D. X.25

11. What is the first step in planning a proactive network management strategy?

    A. Determine the customer's needs.

    B. Convince customer about the need for a new network.

    C. Collect statistics and watch trends.

    D. Document current network.

12. What is the name of the type of applications that allow minimum or no downtime?

    A. Mission-critical applications

    B. Business applications

    C. Technical applications

    D. Core applications

13. Which of the following are types of physical networks?

    A. Ring

    B. Hybrid

    C. Square

    D. Pole

    E. Bus

14. _____ are layer-2 devices that segment two geographically distant but similar networks using the same protocol.

    A. Routers

    B. Firewalls

    C. Terminal servers

    D. Bridges

15. Which of the following is a valid input for "Type of Protocol"?

    A. TCP/IP

    B. EIGRP

    C. Peer-to-peer

    D. Information flow

16. Which of the following are tasks necessary to identify performance requirements?

    A. Determine the names and types of applications and protocols

    B. Evaluate accuracy

    C. Determine budget allowances

    D. Estimate response time

The following information has been captured from an organization's router. Use it to answer questions 17 and 18.

```
Ethernet0 is up, line protocol is down
   Hardware is QUICC Ethernet, address is 00e0.1e83.d4a6 (bia 00e0.1e83.d4a6)
   Description: ACS ETHERNET
   Internet address is 154.71.30.67/27
   MTU 1500 bytes, BW 10000 Kbit, DLY 1000 usec, rely 207/255, load 1/255
   Encapsulation ARPA, loopback not set, keepalive set (10 sec)
   ARP type: ARPA, ARP Timeout 04:00:00
   Last input never, output 00:00:01, output hang never
```

```
Last clearing of "show interface" counters never
Queueing strategy: fifo
Output queue 0/40, 0 drops; input queue 0/75, 0 drops
5 minute input rate 0 bits/sec, 0 packets/sec
5 minute output rate 0 bits/sec, 0 packets/sec
   0 packets input, 0 bytes, 0 no buffer
   Received 0 broadcasts, 0 runts, 0 giants, 0 throttles
   0 input errors, 0 CRC, 0 frame, 0 overrun, 0 ignored, 0 abort
   0 input packets with dribble condition detected
   29 packets output, 2006 bytes, 0 underruns
   29 output errors, 0 collisions, 2 interface resets
   0 babbles, 0 late collision, 0 deferred
   29 lost carrier, 0 no carrier
   0 output buffer failures, 0 output buffers swapped out
   0 output buffer failures, 0 output buffers swapped out
Hardware is QUICC Serial
Description: T1 TO Jackson
Internet address is 154.71.27.14/30
MTU 1500 bytes, BW 1544 Kbit, DLY 20000 usec, rely 255/255, load 1/255
Encapsulation HDLC, loopback not set, keepalive set (10 sec)
Last input never, output never, output hang never
Last clearing of "show interface" counters never
Input queue: 0/75/0 (size/max/drops); Total output drops: 0
Queueing strategy: weighted fair
Output queue: 0/64/0 (size/threshold/drops)
   Conversations  0/0 (active/max active)
   Reserved Conversations 0/0 (allocated/max allocated)
5 minute input rate 0 bits/sec, 0 packets/sec
5 minute output rate 0 bits/sec, 0 packets/sec
   0 packets input, 0 bytes, 0 no buffer
   Received 0 broadcasts, 0 runts, 0 giants, 0 throttles
   0 input errors, 0 CRC, 0 frame, 0 overrun, 0 ignored, 0 abort
   0 packets output, 0 bytes, 0 underruns
   0 output errors, 0 collisions, 15 interface resets
   0 output buffer failures, 0 output buffers swapped out
   0 carrier transitions
   DCD=up  DSR=up  DTR=down  RTS=down  CTS=up
```

17. Refer to the preceding listing. This information was obtained with which of the following Cisco commands?

A. show processes cpu

B. show buffers

C. show protocols

D. show interfaces

18. Refer to the preceding listing. Based on the information, approximately how many interface resets have occurred on the Ethernet link?

    A. 2
    B. 15
    C. 17
    D. 6

SELF TEST ANSWERS

1. ☑ **C.** The show processes cpu command displays the amount of router utilization in five-second, one-minute, and five-minute intervals. Observing the results of this command will help determine if the amount of traffic is too much for the router.
   ☒ **A** and **B** are Cisco router configuration commands that observe buffer overflows and types of interfaces, respectively.

2. ☑ **E.** Business data includes all software applications that are essential to an organization.

3. ☑ **C.** The illustration best describes the architectural description of a star network.
   ☒ **A, B,** and **D** have different topological characteristics from those shown in the illustration.

4. ☑ **E.** Because the illustration depicts a star topology, the removal of workstation A will not affect the other workstations. On a star topology, each node is an individual segment of the hub or switch.

5. ☑ **C.** Novell uses IPX/SPX as its protocol in Novell 3.1*x*.

6. ☑ **A and C.** When identifying manageability requirements, isolate the need for fault, accounting, configuration, performance, and security requirements.
   ☒ **B, D,** and **E** are incorrect because application and staffing requirements are steps in determining the current data network requirements for the customer.

7. ☑ **A, C, and D.** Peer-to-peer, server/server, and terminal/host are application flow types.
   ☒ **B** and **E** are incorrect because no such application flow types exist.

8. ☑ **A.** In a flat network, 500 workstations running TCP/IP applications is the maximum suggested number allowed on a network.
   ☒ **B, C, D,** and **E** are incorrect because broadcast behavior caused by workstations and servers puts limitations on protocols such as IPX: 300 workstations; AppleTalk: 200 workstations; NetBIOS: 200 workstations; and mixed protocols: 200 workstations.

9. ☑ **C.** A router is a layer-3 device used as an intelligent filter.
   ☒ **A, B,** and **D** are incorrect because hubs and repeaters are layer-1 devices, and switches are layer-2 devices.

10. ☑ **B.** Integrated Services Digital Network (ISDN) supports voice and video.
    ☒ **A, C,** and **D** are incorrect because these remote access technologies support voice only; however, they may still be used as a backup for another type of link.

11. ☑ **C.** Collecting statistics and watching trends is the first step in planning a proactive network management strategy.

☒ **A, B,** and **D** are also important in planning a proactive network management strategy, but they should be performed after collecting statistics and watching trends.

12. ☑ **A.** Mission-critical applications cause minimum or no downtime.

☒ **B, C,** and **D** are incorrect because they are not those types of applications.

13. ☑ **A, B, and E.** Ring, hybrid, and bus networks are all physical topological types of networks.

☒ **C** and **D** do not exist as a physical topology type.

14. ☑ **D.** Bridges are layer-2 devices that segment two geographically distant but similar networks using the same protocol.

☒ **A, B,** and **C** are also devices used in a network, but they perform other functions. Routers are layer-3 devices used as an intelligent filter for multiple protocols. Firewalls are used to secure networks. Terminal servers are used for non-intelligent devices.

15. ☑ **C.** Peer-to-peer is a valid protocol type.

☒ **A, B,** and **D** are all incorrect. TCP/IP is a routed protocol that belongs in the "Name of Protocol" field; EIGRP is a type of routing protocol; information flow is a directional flow of information in a network.

16. ☑ **B and D.** Performance requirements include evaluating accuracy and estimating response time.

☒ **A** and **C** are incorrect. Determining the names and types of applications and protocols is an example of extracting application requirements. Budget allowances are necessary to identify business constraints.

17. ☑ **D.** The show interfaces command displays the number of interface resets and the number and characteristics of serial/Ethernet interfaces.

☒ **A, B,** and **C** are incorrect because the show processes cpu command displays CPU process utilization, the show buffers command displays information about the various buffer sizes, and the show interfaces command displays information about the protocols.

18. ☑ **A.** Two interface resets have occurred on the Ethernet link.

☒ **B** is incorrect because 15 is the number of interface resets that have occurred on the *serial* link. **C** and **D** are incorrect because 17 and 6 are just random numbers.

CISCO CERTIFIED DESIGN ASSOCIATE

7

Helping the Customer Understand Design Issues

This chapter covers business issues that are relevant to a network design and the health of the existing network. You will learn how to help a customer identify core business issues and use that information to create the network. You will also learn how to determine the health of the network. Finally, you will examine several case studies to test your knowledge with real-world problems.

CERTIFICATION OBJECTIVE 7.01

Customer's Business Issues Relevant to a Network Design Project

As a CCDA, you will be responsible for designing various types of corporate networks. Your customers will expect you to be the expert and will usually accept any recommendations you may offer. This level of responsibility requires you to be knowledgeable about the full scope of the project and the business.

Business Issues

As you will see, business issues have a profound effect on the technical aspects of your project. You should understand the following business issues before starting your network design:

- Budget
- Expansion
- Politics
- Industry
- Communication
- Location
- Training
- Support

- Previous project failure
- Decision-maker
- Success
- Timing
- Other

Budget

The customer's budget for the network design project is by far one of the most important business issues you will have to address. After all, if there is no budget, you have no financial resources with which to purchase equipment and to pay for your services. Of course, you could always donate your time and foot the bill for the necessary equipment. Just kidding!

Budgets are usually expressed in two different ways: The first method sets a budget for the entire project, while the second method sets independent budgets for each section of the project. When the budget is set for the entire project, it is up to you as the consultant to prioritize where the money should be spent to achieve the business goals of the new network. When you prioritize where and how much money should be spent, you are in effect creating separate budgets that will not exceed the total project budget. When you are given independent budgets for different aspects of a project, it means your customer has already prioritized where and how much money should be spent. In both cases, be sure to go over the budgets with your customer and determine whether they realistically meet the project's financial requirements. Remember, it is always better to let the customer know up front what the projected and potential costs of the project could be, rather than go to the customer in the middle of the project asking for more money.

Expansion

The whole idea of business is to make money and grow and make more money. This is why most businesses build additions to buildings, purchase additional buildings, and acquire other companies. Expansion usually means there will be more employees and, potentially, more users on the network. If expansion is not addressed, you could be implementing a million-dollar network that works today but fails tomorrow when branch sites with three or four users grow to a hundred users and need greater access to corporate headquarters. Also, if a new branch site needs to be connected to the corporate headquarters, the network design project should have included provisions for it.

Politics

It would be nice if you could focus solely on the technical aspects of a project without the annoyances of company politics. Unfortunately, in the real world you will encounter your fair share of political webs. Company politics come from the top down and from the bottom up. A poor understanding of company politics can have just as much impact on the network design as an inadequate budget.

It is important to know whether any person or department wants this project to fail. Some internal IT employees might resent the idea of outsourcing the project to an outside consultant and may try to steer you in the wrong direction. The manager who is contracting for your services might have peers who view the possible failure of the project as their opportunity to move up the corporate ladder. You should always go over the political issues with your customer. It will save you a ton of headaches.

Industry

If you truly want to be helpful to your customers, you should understand what industry they are in and how they do business. The idea here is to figure how you can make each customer's business more efficient than that of its competitors. This will require you to do some research on other companies in the industry to determine how your customer can gain a business advantage from a technical standpoint. For example, a large manufacturing company may have a critical ERP (enterprise resource planning) system in place that has poor performance. To make your customer's business more competitive, you might use a product like CiscoAssure to give priority access to ERP traffic, thereby increasing performance. An increase in performance in this area directly affects the productivity of ERP users. When users are more productive, the business is more productive.

Communication

The flow of communication within the business will have a direct effect on the network's design. It is important to understand who needs to communicate with whom and how often this communication occurs. This knowledge will determine how a network will be segmented, how e-mail will be implemented, and whether a direct link is required between two departments or offices. After you understand the business's communication flow, you can use routers, bridges, and VLANs to segment the network properly.

Location

The location of corporate and branch offices will have a direct effect on the cost of communication links. The farther away two sites are from each other, the more expensive communication links will be. Figure 7-1 shows

FIGURE 7-1

Hub-and-spoke topology

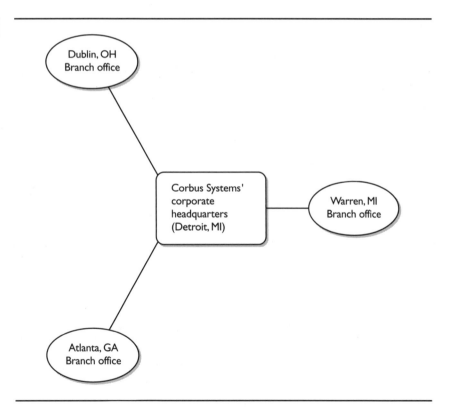

the hub-and-spoke network of Corbus Systems, Inc., has corporate headquarters located in Detroit, Michigan. Its branch offices are located in Warren, Michigan; Dublin, Ohio; and Atlanta, Georgia. Assuming that all branch offices connect to the corporate headquarters via full T1 links, the link between the Atlanta location and corporate headquarters would be the most expensive. Since Warren is closer to Detroit than to Atlanta and Dublin, the link between the Warren location and corporate headquarters would be the least expensive. If full T1 lines are not necessary and a slower connection would suffice, then a virtual private network (VPN) might be the answer. VPNs reduce service costs and long distance/usage fees, lighten infrastructure investments, and simplify WAN operations over time. To determine just how cost-effective a VPN solution could be in connecting remote offices, use the VPN Calculator located on Cisco's Web site at www.cisco.com.

Training

Training is a business issue that is often overlooked. Usually, proper training is replaced with either inadequate training or no training, to save on project costs. It is possible to create a fully functional feature-rich network that nobody knows how to use.

A good training program consists of separate training sessions that are specific to the functions of various user groups. For example, the Research and Development department may need training on using the Internet, while the Information Systems department needs training on network management software. Properly educating your customers will allow them to reap the full benefits of the new network and, you hope, give you the credit and praise you deserve.

Support

When taking on a network design project, you and your customer should establish who will support the new network. If your customer wants you to manage and support the new network after its implementation, make sure a realistic support contract is drafted. If internal employees will be responsible for the new network, it should be tailored to their management needs. For example, if the Information Systems department will be supporting the new network, a centralized management solution should be implemented. If each department will be responsible for its own network segment, then a distributed management solution should be implemented.

Previous Project Failure

A good rule of thumb is this: learn from other people's mistakes. Before immersing yourself in a network design project, you should find out whether the project was previously attempted. If there was a previous attempt, it will be helpful to understand why the project failed. You should consult, if possible, with the person or group that attempted the project. At the very least, you will know what not to do and save yourself a lot of time.

Decision-Maker

The decision-maker is by far the most important person you will come in contact with. This is the person who ultimately decides whether or not there will be a project, outlines the business priorities, lays out the budget, and selects the CCDA who will get the work. Throughout the network design project, there will be many people within the company telling you what features they want and how the project should proceed. Although their requests might be reasonable, you should never deviate from the project plan without consulting the decision-maker.

Success

When you are contracted to implement a new network or upgrade an existing one, you will need to know whether your implementation was successful. It is important to understand that success is not measured by the consultant. Success is measured by the customer. The customer measures success from a business standpoint. This usually means that the project was a success if it makes the business more productive. You can, however, set the customers' expectations and influence their measurements for success. But if you neglect to define a successful implementation, you are sure to come up short. For example, your network implementation might work and provide connectivity to all departments and offices but not be fast enough to satisfy the customer. This would not be considered a successful implementation. Let's face it, some customers are not satisfied with anything. That is why expectations should be set to underscore what a successful implementation will be from both a technical and business standpoint.

Timing

Timing is a business issue that has a direct effect on the flow of the network design project. Timing consists of deadlines for individual project elements and ultimately the entire network design project. Timelines should always be discussed with the customer before you start the project. The goal here is to have a reasonable timeline that both you and the customer are comfortable with. One thing you never want to do is commit to deadlines that you know you cannot meet. Just to be safe, you should always leave room for Murphy's Law: *if anything can go wrong, it will.* In other words, try to pad the timeline as much as possible, leaving some room for error. If your project progresses ahead of schedule, your customer will be pleased. If your project stays behind schedule, your customer will not be pleased. Keep in mind that your customer's expectations are set by the timeline you have agreed upon. The time it takes to complete the project is usually not as important as completing the project on time.

Other Tangibles

Any other business issue that has a direct or indirect impact on the network design project falls into this category. For example, a company may have policies on technology that you must adhere to. This would definitely limit your creative latitude in designing the company's network. So pay close attention to how your customer's business operates. This, along with informative interviews with the customer's key staff members, will empower you with the information you need to put together a successful network design project.

Design Goals

Whenever you take on a network design project, you should always set design goals. Design goals help you gauge your progress and make sure you are covering all bases. Business issues can have a powerful impact on the following design goals:

- Functionality
- Scalability
- Adaptability
- Manageability
- Cost-effectiveness

Functionality

Functionality defines the services the network will provide for its users to meet the business goals of the company. Some business issues such as budget, industry, and timing can have an effect on network functionality. Running over budget, for example, can prevent more expensive network features from being implemented. Industry issues, such as the need to be more competitive, can influence the adoption of new network functions and features. Timing issues, such as deadlines, can make it impossible to add certain network functions and features because the network design project would be thrown off schedule.

Scalability

Scalability is defined as the network's ability to efficiently accommodate continued growth. For example, a five-user network will experience the same performance even if it increases to 50 users on a truly scalable network. Network scalability can be affected by expansion. If, for example, a company opens a branch office to accommodate new business, the corporate network needs to be able to accommodate the new network demands of the branch office.

Adaptability

Adaptability is defined as the ability of a network to support future technologies. Networking standards should be followed whenever possible. Budget is a business issue that can have an impact on a network's ability to adapt to new technologies. For example, you may have chosen to use Category-3 cabling and 10BaseT hubs to save costs. Unfortunately, if you wanted to upgrade that network to 100BaseT, the network would have to be rewired with Category-5 cabling and 100BaseT devices. That would not be a very adaptable network. Even if money were saved on hubs and wiring, the network upgrade would force the initial investment to be wasted. In other words, pay now or pay a lot later.

Manageability

Manageability is defined as the ease with which a network can be proactively monitored, supported, and maintained. For a network to be manageable, it should at least have a robust network management system, a solid network design, and trained technical support personnel. Business issues such as training and support can affect the manageability of a network. If the technical support staff is not educated on the new network, it cannot effectively provide network management and support. Support staff should always be trained on or be knowledgeable of the network management products deployed on the new network. Network management tools such as CiscoWorks2000, HP OpenView, and Network Associates' Sniffer provide you with the manageability enterprise networks need.

Cost-Effectiveness

Cost-effectiveness is defined as the level at which customer requirements are met within a given budget: in other words, getting the most bang for your buck. Your customer may simply require the new network to get data from site A to site B successfully. Let's assume that a Cisco 800 router or a Cisco 2600 router would work and be within budget. Since both routers meet the customer's requirements, we would need to determine which router was more cost-effective. Of course, the Cisco 2600 router is more cost-effective than the Cisco 800 router, because of extra features like modular ports and

100BaseT capability. These added features also make the Cisco 2600 router more scalable and adaptable than the Cisco 800 router.

How to Help a Customer Identify the Core Business Issues

Your customers will usually not know how business issues will affect the network design project. It is up to you to enlighten them about all the gory details. The following case studies are examples that help you identify the business issues along with any other issues that might influence the network design project.

Case Study: Corbus Systems, Inc.

Corbus Systems, Inc., is a computer consulting and training firm with corporate headquarters in Detroit, Michigan. It has branch offices in Trenton, Michigan, and Atlanta, Georgia. It also has training centers in Southfield, Michigan, and Troy, Michigan. Corbus Systems, Inc., plans to add another training facility in Atlanta, Georgia.

Currently, the branch offices maintain their own schedules, customer databases, and consultant databases. Each training center maintains its own schedules, instructor databases, student databases, and computer-based exams. Corporate headquarters wants to consolidate and centralize all databases, schedules, and computer-based exams at its location in Detroit, Michigan. It also wants to be able to meet with all branch office and training center executives without any travel.

Corporate headquarters has two NetWare 3.12 servers and seven Windows 2000 servers. The NetWare servers will be replaced with Windows 2000 in the near future. There are 100 Windows 98 stations and 15 Macintosh stations.

The Trenton branch office has one Windows NT 4.0 server and 20 Windows NT workstations. There are hundreds of customers and consultants in their databases. After the schedules, customer databases, and consultant databases have been moved to corporate headquarters, the Trenton office will need to access this information throughout the day for consultant availability and scheduling. The Trenton office is not enthusiastic about the project. The people at the Trenton office enjoy their autonomy and prefer not to share their resources with the rest of the company.

The Atlanta branch office has one NetWare 3.12 server and five Windows 95 stations. There are not many customers or consultants in their databases. Since business has been slow, they will be accessing corporate headquarters only about twice per day. There is, however, little doubt that business will pick up for the branch office.

Both training centers have five Windows 2000 servers and 20 Windows 2000 workstations. In addition, there are five classrooms with 10 computers each. There are also five testing stations. After the schedules, databases, and computer-based exams have been moved to corporate headquarters, the training centers will need to access this information about two times a day and when computer-based exams need to be downloaded. The new training center being built in Atlanta will be set up identically to the others.

You have been commissioned by the company to provide connectivity between the corporate headquarters and all the branch offices and training centers. Your contact has informed you that although the Information Systems department at corporate headquarters will support the new network, the staff there is not adequately trained for the job.

Figure 7-2 shows Corbus Systems, Inc., before the network design project. Figure 7-3 shows the proposed topology for Corbus Systems, Inc.

What business issues affect the design project, and why?

The first business issue that affects the network design project is location. The branch office in Atlanta is farthest away from the corporate headquarters in Detroit. Therefore, connectivity between the Atlanta branch office and corporate headquarters will potentially be more expensive than connectivity between the other sites and corporate headquarters. The real cost of connectivity will be determined by a combination of location and the connectivity speed desired.

Another business issue that affects this network design project is expansion. The company has plans to add another training center in Atlanta. This means that the network should be scalable enough and with proper provisions to adequately add another site. Also, the Atlanta branch office is not experiencing a lot of business. Since business in Atlanta is

FIGURE 7-2   Corbus Systems, Inc., before the network design project

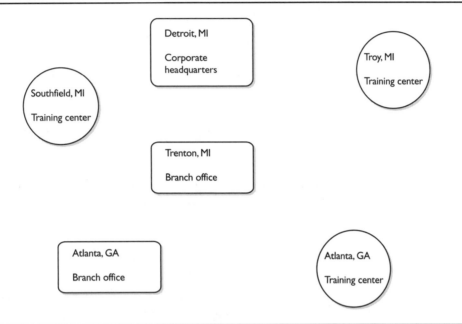

FIGURE 7-3   Proposed topology for Corbus Systems, Inc.

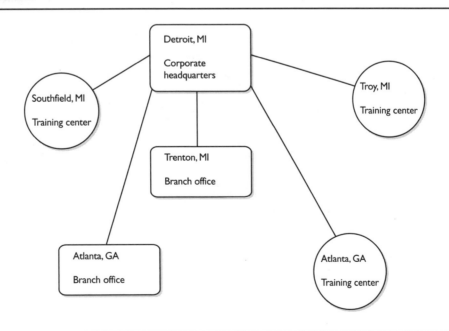

expected to grow and increase the need for communication with corporate headquarters, the network should be scalable and flexible enough to handle the new demands.

Another business issue that affects the network design project is that the customer wants to meet with the executives of all the sites without any travel. Your network should be designed with some way of achieving this goal. For example, videoconferencing might be a solution to explore.

Politics will also affect this network design project. In this case, the Trenton office is not in favor of the project. The people in that office enjoy their autonomy and prefer not to share their resources with the rest of the company. This could make working with them difficult. Knowing this information, do not expect a lot of cooperation from this office at first. Find out from your primary contact who your Trenton contact is. Then explain to the Trenton contact how the new network will benefit everyone at the Trenton office, and try to build rapport. You hope the Trenton office will cooperate and not prevent you from getting your job done. If there is still resistance and noncooperation, then immediately inform your primary contact.

Training and support are issues that will also affect this network design project. Corbus Systems, Inc., has made it clear that the IS department at corporate headquarters will support and manage the new network. This means the network should be designed to support a centralized management solution. Since the IS department is not educated in the technologies and management of the new network, a training program should be implemented. Otherwise, the IS staff will not recognize the real benefits and power of the new network and may criticize what they do not understand.

Case Study: XYZ Manufacturing Corp.

XYZ Manufacturing Corp. is a manufacturing company that produces engine parts for the automotive industry. The company's corporate headquarters are located in Chicago, Illinois, along with three of its manufacturing facilities. It has two other manufacturing facilities in Detroit, Michigan. The company also plans to acquire ABC Industries, another manufacturing company with two facilities in Warren, Michigan.

Corporate headquarters has an AS/400 system, Microsoft SNA Server, Microsoft Exchange Server, 20 terminals, and 10 Windows 98 stations running terminal emulation software. The AS/400 contains the parts databases for the three manufacturing facilities in Chicago. They plan to add the Detroit and Warren facilities' parts databases to the AS/400 as well. The Microsoft SNA Server allows the Windows 98 stations to access the AS/400. The Microsoft Exchange Server is the e-mail server for corporate headquarters and the Chicago manufacturing facilities. They also plan to bring the Detroit and Warren facilities online with the e-mail system. Data entry into the parts databases occurs throughout the day.

Both of the Detroit manufacturing facilities have two Windows NT servers and 10 Windows NT workstations. The Windows NT servers contain parts databases in Microsoft Access format. As is the case at corporate headquarters, data entry into the parts databases occurs throughout the day.

The manufacturing facilities at ABC Industries both have two NetWare 5.1 servers and 25 Windows 95 stations. The parts databases are located on a NetWare 5.1 server running an Oracle database. Data entry of parts information is performed throughout the day.

The CEO has expressed that he wants the company to be more technologically advanced and ultimately more competitive in the manufacturing industry. He has also informed you that they are trying to attain QS-9000 certification and that the new network is crucial to this goal. The QS-9000 audit will occur in six months. If they fail the audit, they will not get certification and will not be eligible to do business with the large automotive suppliers.

You have been commissioned to design a network that provides communication between the corporate headquarters and all of the manufacturing facilities. Although a target budget has been outlined, the CEO has asked for your recommendation on how much a bulletproof network would cost. The CEO has also stated that downtime is not an option, and network speed is mandatory. You have also been asked to put together a support contract that covers the corporate headquarters and manufacturing facilities.

Figure 7-4 shows XYZ Manufacturing Corp. before the network design project. Figure 7-5 shows the proposed topology for XYZ Manufacturing Corp.

What business issues affect the design project, and why?

The first business issue that affects this network design project is location. Since XYZ Manufacturing Corp. has manufacturing facilities outside of Chicago, communication links between corporate headquarters and these facilities may have to be purchased. The cost of the communication links will be determined by the distance between the corporate headquarters and the manufacturing facilities, and by the speed of each link.

Expansion is another business issue that affects the network design project. The inevitable acquisition of ABC Industries makes it necessary to include the Warren manufacturing facilities in the network design project. This means the new network should be scalable enough to accommodate future acquisitions.

Industry is the third business issue that affects the network design project. Since the CEO wants to be more competitive in the automotive manufacturing industry, you should do some research into what competitors are using and how you can give your customer a competitive edge. One example would be the implementation of an enterprise resource planning (ERP) system.

For XYZ Manufacturing Corp., timing is a business issue that is critical for future business. Since the QS-9000 audit occurs in six months, the implied deadline for the network design project is less than six months. Completing the network design project in time for the manufacturing company to prepare for the QS-9000 audit would greatly increase your credibility and potential for future projects.

The budget is the next business issue that affects the network design project. In this case, the customer is willing to spare no expense to get a fast, reliable network in place. To accomplish this goal, you may want to implement redundancy and technologies such as Hot Standby Router Protocol (HSRP).

Support is the final business issue that affects the network design project. The company wants you to support the corporate headquarters and all of

FIGURE 7-4

XYZ Manufacturing Corp. before the network design project

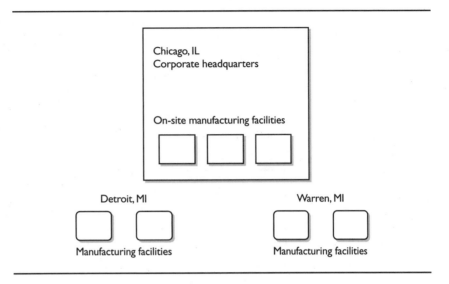

the manufacturing facilities. Be sure to draft a support contract that adequately compensates you for your time. Also, the additional manufacturing facilities that will be acquired from ABC Industries should be addressed in the support contract.

FIGURE 7-5

Proposed topology for XYZ Manufacturing Corp.

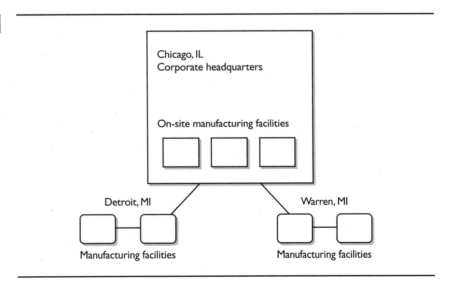

Case Study: Merchant's Books and Mags, Inc.

Merchant's Books and Mags, Inc., sells books and magazines covering various types of subject matter. Their bookstore is located in Boston, Massachusetts, with warehouses in Milwaukee, Wisconsin; Dallas, Texas; and Pontiac, Michigan. The company plans to purchase one more warehouse located in Detroit, Michigan.

Currently, the Boston bookstore has a NetWare 3.12 file server and five Windows 98 workstations. The NetWare server contains the books and magazines inventory databases in B-Trieve format. The five Windows 98 stations are used for data entry for the books and magazines on-site. They plan to replace the NetWare 3.12 server with a Windows 2000 server running SQL Server to manage the books and magazines inventory databases. The warehouse databases will be centralized in the books and magazines inventory databases as well. A Windows 2000 server running Exchange Server will be added to facilitate e-mail for the bookstore and warehouses.

The Milwaukee and Dallas warehouses both have two Windows 95 stations that communicate using peer-to-peer networking. The Windows 98 stations are used primarily for entering inventory data in an MS Access database. Currently, only 10 percent of the titles at both warehouses have been inventoried. After the databases are migrated to the central database at the Boston bookstore, the Milwaukee and Dallas warehouses will require access to the central database about four hours a day.

The Pontiac warehouse is the largest of the company's warehouses, containing more book and magazine titles than the Milwaukee and Dallas warehouses combined. It has a Windows NT 4.0 server running SQL Server 6.5 that stores the warehouse's book and magazine titles. For e-mail, the Pontiac warehouse uses a Windows NT 4.0 server running Microsoft Exchange Server. This warehouse also has 25 Windows 95 stations being used for data entry of warehouse inventory. So far, 15 percent of the titles have been inventoried. After the database is migrated to the central database at the Boston bookstore, the Pontiac warehouse will require access to the central database at least eight hours a day.

The warehouse in Detroit is second in size only to the Pontiac warehouse. It has a Windows NT 3.51 server and five Windows 3.1 stations. The Windows 3.1 stations are primarily used to enter inventory data into a Microsoft Access database residing on the Windows NT 3.51 server. After the Detroit warehouse is purchased by Merchant's Books and Mags, Inc., 15 new employees will be added to its staff. Each of the new employees will be given Windows 2000 stations for e-mail and data entry of inventory. After the Microsoft Access database is migrated to the Microsot SQL Server database at the Boston bookstore, the Detroit warehouse will need access to the central database at least eight hours a day.

The CEO of Merchant's Books and Mags, Inc., has stated that she wants to be more competitive with other bookstores and reach a larger market. She also wants her company to be fully functional before Christmas. Her bookstore has historically done a lot of business during the holiday season.

You have been commissioned to provide point-to-point connectivity between the bookstore and each warehouse. Although the Detroit warehouse has not been purchased, it should be included in the network design project. The budget you have been given is very slim, leaving you little room for unjustifiable expenditures. You have also been instructed to draft a network support contract since the existing support staff is not knowledgeable about the new technologies being implemented.

About six months ago, a consulting firm attempted this network design project and failed. Their proposal to Merchant's Books and Mags, Inc., consisted of full T1 lines to each warehouse from the bookstore and an extensive support contract. The price for T1 lines to each warehouse was too expensive for the CEO's financial taste. Although the support contract covered a lot of key areas, the price was just as unacceptable as the T1 lines. As a result, the network design project never got off the ground.

Figure 7-6 shows the proposed topology for Merchant's Books and Mags, Inc.

What business issues affect the design project, and why?

Location is the first business issue that affects the network design project. Since the Boston bookstore needs to communicate with warehouses in Milwaukee, Dallas, Pontiac, and possibly Detroit, communication costs could potentially be cost prohibitive. The real cost of communication will be determined by the speed of the communication links.

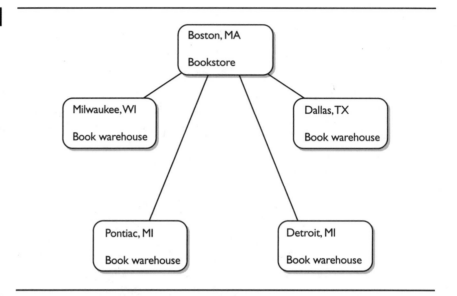

FIGURE 7-6

Proposed topology for Merchant's Books and Mags, Inc.

Expansion is the next business issue that affects the network design project. The inclusion of the Detroit warehouse will make the new network scalable enough to compensate for the additional load on the network. If any more warehouses or new users come online, the network should be prepared.

The third business issue that affects the network design is in the category of industry. Since the CEO of the bookstore wants to be more competitive and reach a larger market, research should be done with those goals in mind. One way to enhance the business is to implement e-commerce to allow customers to purchase books and magazines online. This would surely make the Boston-based bookstore more competitive and able to reach a larger market.

Timing is the next business issue that affects the network design project. Since the bookstore does well during the holiday season, and Christmas is around the corner, the implied project deadline is the month of December. Meeting this deadline would be a fantastic Christmas present for your client. Payment for services rendered would be a nice Christmas present for you.

The budget is another business issue that definitely affects this network design project. Since the budget is very tight, every purchase must be totally justified. Overkill is not an option here. In other words, if it's not needed, it's not wanted. The budget constraints on this network design project make it necessary to fully understand the true needs of the client and to implement the solutions to those needs first and foremost. If there is any money in the budget left over, lower-priority items can be addressed.

Previous project failure is the final business issue we will discuss that affects this network design project. You know that a consulting firm attempted the bookstore project and failed. You also know that there were two major reasons for this failure. The first reason was the total price of T1 lines to every site. This is an area that deserves attention in your network design project. Are T1 lines to every site necessary? Maybe not. The second reason the project failed was that the support contract was too expensive. Since the CEO wants you to draft a support contract, this information is very important. The bottom line is that the price of the entire project was just too expensive for the Boston bookstore. Maybe you could somehow save costs on the communication links to make room for the cost of a good support contract. Another option would be to use expensive T1 links but to replace the support contract with a less expensive training program for the bookstore's existing support staff. A final option would be a combination of the previous options. More specifically, have T1 links only where necessary and low bandwidth links everywhere else. In addition, have an inexpensive support contract along with an adequate training program. If you address the mistakes of those who have come before you, you will be sure to succeed where others have failed.

How to Create a Network Based on the Obtained Information

Now that we have defined the business issues that affect the network design projects in our case studies, we are ready to create the networks with the obtained information.

Case Study: Creating Corbus Systems, Inc.'s New Network

Figure 7-7 shows the network we created from the information we obtained. At the corporate headquarters, we used a Catalyst 5000 switch to accommodate the nine servers and 115 workstations. The Catalyst 5000 switch also provided us with 100BaseT switching and VLANs to segment

FIGURE 7-7   Corbus Systems, Inc.'s new network

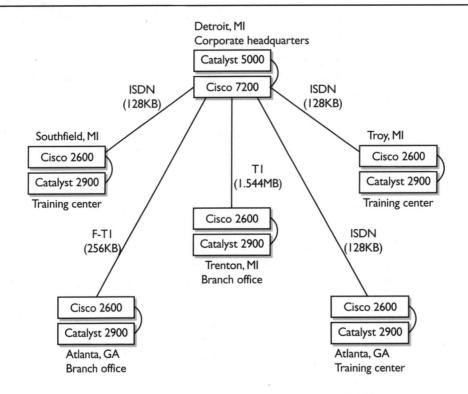

Note: Each of the training centers will also have five Catalyst 1900 switches for the classrooms.

the network. The Cisco 7200 router was used to provide connectivity to the branch offices and training centers. We selected the Cisco 7200 router, because it supports the T1 and ISDN links used on the WAN. CiscoWorks2000 was implemented at corporate headquarters as the network management system for the Information Systems department. Videoconferencing was implemented using Cisco IP/VC to allow corporate headquarters to meet with external company executives.

At the Atlanta branch office, we used a Catalyst 2900 switch to accommodate the server and five workstations. The Catalyst 2900 was selected for its 10/100 autosensing, autoconfiguring switching. The Cisco 2600 router was used to provide fractional T1 access to corporate headquarters. A 256KB fractional T1 was used to accommodate the existing demands the Atlanta branch office puts on the corporate WAN. Since we are using a fractional T1, it is scalable up to 1.544MB, which will accommodate the predicted growth of the Atlanta branch office.

The Trenton branch office used a Catalyst 2900 switch to connect the 20 workstations and server. The Cisco 2600 router was used to provide full T1 access to corporate headquarters. The Cisco 2600 router was selected for its T1 support and modular scalability.

The three training centers each use a Catalyst 2900 to interconnect the 20 workstations and five servers. Each training center also uses a Catalyst 1900 switch for each classroom. Since the training centers need to communicate with the corporate headquarters only twice a day, 128KB ISDN lines were used. A Cisco 2600 router was installed at each training center to support the ISDN connection and have the ability to support higher speeds with additional WAN interface cards if necessary.

Case Study: Creating XYZ Manufacturing Corp.'s New Network

Figure 7-8 shows the network we created from the information we obtained. At corporate headquarters we deployed a Catalyst 2900 switch to interconnect the servers and workstations on the local area network. The Cisco 2900 switch was selected for its 100BaseT switching and modular scalability. A Cisco 7500 router was selected for its scalability and high-speed serial port adapters, making it more than sufficient to accommodate new remote networks.

We deployed Catalyst 2900 switches at the Detroit and Warren facilities to connect the multiple servers and workstations on their networks. Just as with corporate headquarters, the Catalyst 2900 switch was selected for its 100BaseT switching and modular scalability. We connected the two Detroit facilities using Cisco 2600 routers and a T1 line. We then connected one Detroit facility directly to corporate headquarters using the Cisco 2600

FIGURE 7-8

XYZ Manufacturing Corp.'s
new network

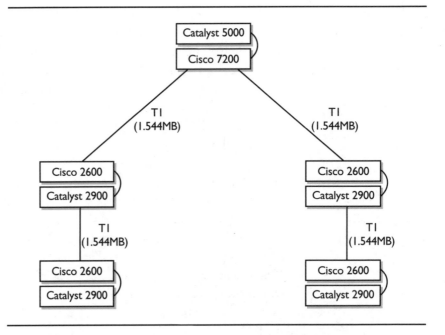

router and another T1 line. We also added an additional Cisco 2600 router
to the Detroit facility to implement HSRP (Hot Standby Router Protocol)
for added network reliability. When one of two routers participating in
HSRP goes down, the second router comes online to take its place. The two
Warren facilities were set up like the Detroit facilities.

Case Study: Creating Merchant's Books and Mags, Inc.'s New Network

Figure 7-9 shows the network we created from the information we obtained.
At the Boston bookstore, we deployed a Catalyst 2900 to connect five
workstations and two servers. The Catalyst 2900 switch was selected for its
100BaseT switching and modular scalability. We used a Cisco 7200 router
to provide WAN connectivity to all four book warehouses. The Cisco 7200
router was selected because of its support for multiple WAN connections,
types, and speeds.

FIGURE 7-9   Merchant's Books and Mags, Inc.'s new network

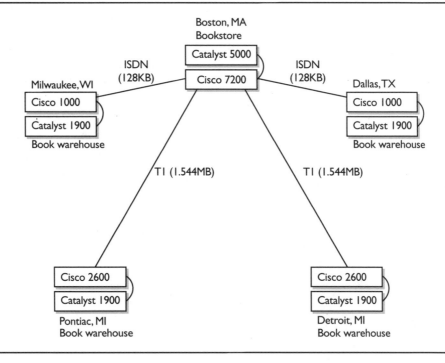

We deployed Catalyst 1900 switches at the Milwaukee and Dallas book warehouses to accommodate their peer-to-peer networks. The Catalyst 1900 switches leave these locations more than enough room for network growth. We used Cisco 1000 routers to provide 128KB ISDN access to the Boston bookstore from the Milwaukee and Dallas warehouses. Speeds faster than 128KB were not necessary due to the light load the small peer-to-peer networks would put on the WAN.

Catalyst 2900 switches were used at the Pontiac and Detroit book warehouses to interconnect the 20 to 30 workstations and servers on those networks. Just as with the Boston bookstore, the Catalyst 2900 switches were selected for their 100BaseT capability and modular scalability. We used Cisco 2600 routers to provide full T1 access to the Boston bookstore from the Pontiac and Detroit warehouses.

Health of the Customer's Existing Network

Wouldn't it be wonderful if you could design every network from the ground up? Unfortunately, this is usually not the case. Many network design projects are upgrades to existing networks. This makes the health of a customer's existing network extremely important. It is always a good practice to document how a network operated before the upgrade. If the existing network had problems, you should know this up front and make the customer aware of them.

How to Determine the Health of the Network

The health of the existing network will directly affect your network design project. How do you determine the health of the existing network? This question is best answered by gathering the following information about the existing network:

- Applications
- Protocols
- Topology
- Bottlenecks
- Business issues
- Availability
- Performance
- Reliability
- Utilization
- Routers
- NMS
- Overall network health

Applications

Information about existing applications should be acquired to get a better understanding of the bandwidth required in the new network. Each application on a network puts a certain load on the network. For example, networks running video, CAD, or animation applications will require more bandwidth than networks used only for e-mail.

Protocols

It is very important that you know which protocols are running on the existing network. This includes routed, routing, and bridged protocols. This information will allow you to make key decisions in terms of both bandwidth and logical addressing. For example, if TCP/IP is running, you may want to come up with an efficient IP addressing scheme to segment the network or decrease the size of your routing tables by using route summarization. As far as bandwidth is concerned, some protocols are noisier than other protocols. Let's say you have a network running both IP and IPX. You should look at ways to eliminate IPX, if possible, from the new network. Unfortunately, applications like B-Trieve require IPX. The new network design should address these issues, and a list of necessary protocols should be created.

Topology

A high-level topology map of the customer's existing network should be created. This map should include all of the major network segments, routers, switches, bridges, and other network devices. The purpose of the topology map is to give you a bird's-eye view of the overall network.

Bottlenecks

A bottleneck is the point at which network traffic slows down to contend for limited bandwidth. You should determine whether there are any potential bottlenecks on the existing network. If there are, they should be addressed in the new network design. A protocol analyzer like Network Associates' Sniffer will help you discover potential bottlenecks.

Business Issues

It is important to know the business issues that affected the original design for the existing network and the business issues that affect the existing network today. Understanding the previous and current business issues will give you insight into why the existing network was implemented with its current design. These business issues should be addressed in the new network design project.

Availability

Availability is the amount of time the network is accessible to its users. You should acquire information about the existing network's downtime, cost of downtime, and average downtime. Downtime occurs when a network is not accessible to its users. The cost of downtime is the cost that the company incurs when its employees and business are not being productive. Assuming that employees are productive all of the time, one downtime cost metric can be defined by the amount of time down multiplied by the wages of employees during that time. The average downtime is the average amount of time between the times that the network goes down. The new network design should address downtime and have better downtime statistics than before.

Performance

Performance is the measurement of response times between network devices. You should know what level of performance your customer is accustomed to. This information should be addressed in the new network design to achieve a faster performing network than before.

Reliability

What good is a network if it is not reliable? Reliability defines a network's ability to get data from one point to another without error. You should gather reliability information about the existing network and address this information in the new network design. A protocol analyzer like Network

Associates' Sniffer will help you in defining a network's level of reliability. On an Ethernet network, some items to look at would be the number of CRC errors, runts, and collisions. The higher these numbers are, the lower the reliability of the network. Whatever you do, make sure the new network design is more reliable than the existing network.

Utilization

Network utilization is defined as the amount of traffic traversing the network versus the available bandwidth. To better understand the utilization of the existing network, use a protocol analyzer. Depending on the results of the protocol analysis, you might decide that more bandwidth is required for the new network.

Routers

The health of the routers on the existing network should be checked for any hardware or software problems that might affect the network. Some statistics to monitor would be CPU utilization, memory utilization, and media errors. You can view this information with the show processes cpu, show processes memory, show memory, and show interface commands.

NMS

An NMS (network management system) is a software application that facilitates the proactive support and monitoring of networked systems. The existing NMS will help you understand the baseline expectations for the new network's NMS. Any data collected previously by the existing NMS would be very helpful in assessing the health of the existing network. Make sure that the NMS for the new network is at least equally as robust as the NMS before it.

Overall Network Health

After the previous information has been gathered about the existing network, you should have a pretty clear picture of the network's overall health. This information will allow you to make informed decisions about the new network design, and it will prevent you from making the same mistakes that were made with the existing network. After the new network is implemented, be sure to assess its overall health and compare it with the previous network. If the new network surpasses the previous network in every area and the customer is thoroughly pleased, you are on your way to becoming a top gun CCDA.

CERTIFICATION SUMMARY

In this chapter, you learned how business issues can affect a network design project. You learned about network design goals and how business issues affect them. After you defined the business issues, you learned how to design a network with the obtained information.

You also learned that the health of the customer's existing network is important to the new network design project. You even learned how to determine a network's health by gathering various pieces of information. Overall, you learned the basics of a CCDA's duties. And that's designing networks!

 # TWO-MINUTE DRILL

- ❑ The following business issues affect the network design project: budget, expansion, politics, industry, communication, location, training, support, previous project failure, decision-maker, success, and timing.

- ❑ Business issues can have a powerful impact on the following design goals: functionality, scalability, adaptability, manageability, and cost- effectiveness.

- ❑ Functionality defines the services the network will provide for its users to meet the business goals of the company.

- ❑ Scalability is defined as the network's ability to efficiently accommodate continued growth.

❑ Adaptability is defined as the ability of a network to support future technologies.

❑ Manageability is defined as the ease in which a network can be proactively monitored, supported, and maintained.

❑ Cost-effectiveness is defined as the level in which customer requirements are met within a given budget.

❑ The following information should be gathered to determine a network's health: applications, protocols, topology, bottlenecks, business issues, availability, performance, reliability, utilization, routers, and NMS.

SELF TEST

The following Self Test questions will help you measure your understanding of the material presented in this chapter. Read all the choices carefully, as there may be more than one correct answer. Choose all correct answers for each question.

1. Your customer wants you to implement a wide area network for his company. Your customer is very concerned with how much the new network will cost. What business issue will affect this network design project?

    A. Budget
    B. Expansion
    C. Politics
    D. Industry

2. Your customer wants you to provide connectivity to all the branch offices. The customer is also in the process of purchasing additional branch offices. What business issue will affect this network design project?

    A. Politics
    B. Expansion
    C. Training
    D. Industry

3. You have been commissioned by the director of Sales and Marketing to design that department's network. You will need to integrate their network with the rest of the corporate network. The Information Systems staff normally does the technical projects and feels uneasy about outsiders modifying their network. What business issue affects this network design project?

    A. Budget
    B. Politics
    C. Expansion
    D. Industry

4. You have been commissioned to implement videoconferencing using Cisco technology. The employees that will be participating in videoconferencing do not know how to use it. What business issue will affect this network design project?

   A. Politics
   B. Expansion
   C. Training
   D. Timing

5. Your customer is in the manufacturing business and wants to be more competitive. What business issue will affect this network design project?

   A. Timing
   B. Expansion
   C. Politics
   D. Industry

6. Your customer wants you to implement a large OSPF network. Your customer informed you that another consulting firm attempted the implementation but was not successful. What business issue affects this network design project?

   A. Previous project failure
   B. Expansion
   C. Timing
   D. Budget

7. Your customer wants you to implement a new network at its new facility. The new facility will be occupied within six weeks. What business issue will affect this network design project?

   A. Budget
   B. Timing
   C. Politics
   D. Industry

8. You are starting a network design project and want your network to have a high level of functionality. What does this mean for the new network?

   A. The new network will provide services for its users to meet the business goals of the company.

   B. The new network will efficiently accommodate continued growth.

   C. The new network will be able to support future technologies with little or no modification.

   D. The new network will be easily monitored, supported, and maintained in a proactive manner.

9. You are starting a network design project and want your network to have a high level of scalability. What does this mean for the new network?

   A. The new network will provide services for its users to meet the business goals of the company.

   B. The new network will efficiently accommodate continued growth.

   C. The new network will be able to support future technologies with little or no modification.

   D. The new network will be easily monitored, supported, and maintained in a proactive manner.

10. You are starting a network design project and want your network to have a high level of adaptability. What does this mean for the new network?

    A. The new network will provide services for its users to meet the business goals of the company.

    B. The new network will efficiently accommodate continued growth.

    C. The new network will be able to support future technologies with little or no modification.

    D. The new network will be easily monitored, supported, and maintained in a proactive manner.

11. You are starting a network design project and want your network to have a high level of manageability. What does this mean for the new network?

    A. The new network will provide services for its users to meet the business goals of the company.

    B. The new network will efficiently accommodate continued growth.

    C. The new network will be able to support future technologies with little or no modification.

    D. The new network will be easily monitored, supported, and maintained in a proactive manner.

12. You are starting a network design project and want your network to have a high level of cost effectiveness. What does this mean for the new network?

    A. The new network will have met the customer's requirements using the best possible equipment affordable.

    B. The new network will provide services for its users to meet the business goals of the company.

    C. The new network will efficiently accommodate continued growth.

    D. The new network will be able to support future technologies with little or no modification.

13. You have been commissioned to reengineer an existing network. What piece of information would give you a better understanding of the bandwidth requirements?

    A. Budget information

    B. Training requirements

    C. Information about existing applications

14. You are upgrading an existing network and want to know whether the existing routers are running properly. What commands could be used to monitor the router's health?

    A. show processes cpu

    B. show memory

    C. show interface

    D. All of the above

15. You have implemented a large wide area network for your customer. Your customer wants its IS department to have the ability to proactively support and monitor networked systems. What should you implement?

    A. Firewall

    B. NMS

    C. Internet e-mail

16. You have been commissioned to upgrade a customer's network. You want to measure the performance of the existing network to compare it to the new one. How would you accomplish this?

    A. Measure the response times between key network devices.

    B. Measure the speed it takes a computer to format its hard drive.

    C. Measure the response time of the keyboard when you type a document.

17. Your customer's network has a bottleneck. You have been commissioned to find it and fix it. What will you be looking for?

    A. The point at which network traffic speeds up

    B. The point at which network utilization is at 2 percent

    C. The point at which network traffic slows down to contend for limited bandwidth

    D. The point at which response times between two network devices happen instantaneously

18. You have just been hired at a large automotive firm. You would like to have an overview of the entire network, including major network segments, routers, switches, bridges, and other network devices. What should you ask for?

    A. Running protocols

    B. Known bottlenecks

    C. Existing applications

    D. Topology map

19. You have been assigned the task of coming up with a new network addressing scheme. What must you know to accomplish this?

    A. Protocols running on the network

    B. Existing applications

    C. Current bottlenecks

SELF TEST ANSWERS

1. ☑ **A.** Budget affects the maximum cost of the network.
   ☒ **B** is incorrect, because it affects a company's growth. **C** is incorrect, because it pertains to negative human interaction. **D** is incorrect, because it pertains to a customer's need to be more competitive.

2. ☑ **B.** Expansion affects a company's growth.
   ☒ **A** is incorrect, because it pertains to negative human interaction. **C** is incorrect, because it pertains to the education of new users on a network. **D** is incorrect, because it pertains to a customer's need to be more competitive.

3. ☑ **B.** Politics affects human interaction.
   ☒ **A** is incorrect, because it determines the maximum cost of the network. **C** is incorrect, because it affects a company's growth. **D** is incorrect, because it pertains to a customer's need to be more competitive.

4. ☑ **C.** Training affects the education of new users on a network.
   ☒ **A** is incorrect, because it pertains to negative human interaction. **B** is incorrect, because it affects a company's growth. **D** is incorrect, because it pertains to a project's deadline.

5. ☑ **D.** Industry affects a customer's need to be more competitive.
   ☒ **A** is incorrect, because it pertains to a project's deadline. **B** is incorrect, because it affects a company's growth. **C** is incorrect, because it pertains to negative human interaction.

6. ☑ **A.** Previous project failure affects a new attempt at the same project.
   ☒ **B** is incorrect, because it affects a company's growth. **C** is incorrect, because it pertains to a project's deadline. **D** is incorrect, because it determines the maximum cost of the network.

7. ☑ **B.** Timing affects a project's deadline.
   ☒ **A** is incorrect, because it determines the maximum cost of the network. **C** is incorrect, because it pertains to negative human interaction. **D** is incorrect, because it pertains to a customer's need to be more competitive.

8. ☑ **A.** It applies to functionality.
   ☒ **B** is incorrect, because it applies to scalability. **C** is incorrect, because it applies to adaptability. **D** is incorrect, because it applies to manageability.

9. ☑ **B.** It applies to scalability.

   ☒ **A** is incorrect, because it applies to functionality. **C** is incorrect, because it applies to adaptability. **D** is incorrect, because it applies to manageability.

10. ☑ **C.** It applies to adaptability.

    ☒ **A** is incorrect, because it applies to functionality. **B** is incorrect, because it applies to scalability. **D** is incorrect, because it applies to manageability.

11. ☑ **D.** It applies to manageability.

    ☒ **A** is incorrect, because it applies to functionality. **B** is incorrect, because it applies to scalability. **C** is incorrect, because it applies to adaptability.

12. ☑ **A.** It defines cost-effectiveness.

    ☒ **B** is incorrect, because it applies to functionality. **C** is incorrect, because it applies to scalability. **D** is incorrect, because it applies to adaptability.

13. ☑ **C.** Different applications put different loads on the network.

    ☒ **A** is incorrect, because it pertains to project deadlines. **B** is incorrect, because it pertains to the education of users on a network.

14. ☑ **D.** Each of the three commands monitors different router health statistics.

    ☒ **A, B,** and **C** monitor various router statistics: show processes cpu monitors processor utilization; show memory monitors memory statistics; and show interface displays media statistics.

15. ☑ **B.** NMS gives support staff the ability to proactively support and monitor networked systems.

    ☒ **A** is incorrect, because it is used to protect an internal network from an external network like the Internet. **C** is incorrect, because receiving e-mail requests is reactive and does not address network management.

16. ☑ **A.** Measuring the response times between key network devices allows performance to be quantified.

    ☒ **B** and **C** are incorrect, because they address performance statistics on the local computer.

17. ☑ **C.** A network bottleneck is the point at which network traffic slows down to contend for limited bandwidth

    ☒ **A, B,** and **D** are all incorrect, because they define characteristics of a network that is performing well.

18. ☑ **D.** A topology map gives you a bird's-eye view of the network.

 ☒ **A** is incorrect, because it is necessary when formulating network addressing. **B** and **C** are incorrect, because they help in determining whether additional bandwidth is necessary.

19. ☑ **A.** The type of protocol being used determines what protocol an addressing scheme will be implemented for.

 ☒ **B** and **C** are incorrect, because they help in determining whether additional bandwidth is necessary.

8

Solutions

T his chapter examines a unique part of the network design and implementation process. This phase resides primarily after implementation and is concerned with selecting and leveraging the tools and strategies necessary for network management.

Selecting and implementing your network design and hardware is typically a one-time process, and with a good plan, your network should remain fairly static throughout its life. Network management is unique because while you will usually select your tools once, the ongoing strategy and processes will likely change frequently, adapting to the changing needs of your network and your management strategy. A network management strategy that fails to adapt to the evolution of your network will soon become useless. Planning for and addressing these changes is necessary to a successful network management strategy.

CERTIFICATION OBJECTIVE 8.01

Network Management

The importance of effective network management grows as network designs become more and more complex and scale to ever-larger internetworks. The ability to monitor and react to network events occurring at distant locations is invaluable to the network administrator as well as to the organization. This ability is often referred to as *proactive network management*. As opposed to reactive management strategies, proactive network management deals with detecting, monitoring, and solving problematic situations before they arise or cause downtime and poor performance.

Certain companies may have a specific functionality set or strategy in mind for evaluating and implementing network management tools. However, most organizations do share a common set of network management goals, aimed at maximizing the availability of their applications and network infrastructures and reducing the overall total cost of ownership. These goals are

■ Connectivity

■ Security

- Cost optimization
- Manageable growth

Cisco has a comprehensive network management strategy available for networks of all sizes. Cisco's goal for its network management products is to provide customers with the best possible, complete, and up-to-date information available for the configurations and performance of its networks. Armed with this quality information, organizations are then able to make informed decisions, further reducing costs and improving performance within the network.

Cisco's network management approach weaves together the use of network management products with availability and access to online diagnostic and analytical information, as well as support and help provided by Cisco's technical support staff and their partners.

For example, the CiscoWorks network management application suite provides automatic data collection and e-mail reporting to Cisco or to a Cisco partner for support. This functionality automates the sometimes lengthy and difficult process of gathering diagnostic information before troubleshooting begins.

A Cisco customer first registers a "profile" with the Cisco Connection Online (CCO) service to provide a quick reference for technical support staff solving problems. The CiscoConnect application within the CiscoWorks software captures information about a customer's routers, including interfaces, controllers, processes, buffer utilization, configuration, protocols, firmware levels, and system software versions. The CiscoConnect application can also notify customers via customized news bulletins of new features and bug fixes relevant to their networks, providing just-in-time information for better network management.

Multiplatform and Standards-Based Solutions

As the worldwide leader in networking, Cisco continues to demonstrate its commitment to standards and to providing wide platform support for its network management tools and strategies.

Cisco network management applications run on standard hardware and operating system platforms, such as UNIX, Microsoft Windows, Hewlett-Packard's OpenView for Windows, and other industry standards. This provides customers with the flexibility to run their network management tools on the platform of their choice. We will look at Cisco's network management applications later in this chapter.

exam
Watch

As of the time of this writing, Cisco has announced that CiscoWorks UNIX is undergoing end of sales and has been replaced by CiscoWorks2000 Resource Manager Essentials. However, for the purposes of this exam, I have left the original references to the UNIX platform as available and supported.

Cisco has also embraced solutions that are based on open standards and are widely accepted within the computer industry. An example of this is the wide support afforded to SNMP (Simple Network Management Protocol) version 2. SNMPv2 is supported on all platforms and devices that run the Cisco Internetwork Operating System (IOS) software.

Let's take a closer look at SNMP and some of the other standards-based options available for network management.

SNMP and the Common Management Options

Cisco fully supports the standards-based SNMP across its entire line of IOS-compatible products. But what exactly is SNMP, and what are the differences between the two versions?

In its simplest terms, the Simple Network Management Protocol is a distributed-management protocol. It is a simple "request-response" application-layer protocol that provides for the exchange of management information between network devices. It belongs within the Transmission Control Protocol/Internet Protocol (TCP/IP) protocol suite family. SNMP enables network administrators to find and solve network problems and to plan for network growth through proactive monitoring and management.

There are currently two versions of SNMP: SNMP version 1 (SNMPv1) and SNMP version 2 (SNMPv2). A third version is currently under review as a proposed standard, but we will focus on SNMPv1 and SNMPv2 for the purposes of this course. Both of these versions share some common features, but SNMPv2 has taken the previous work of SNMPv1 and has built in additional functionality and enhancements.

SNMP Basic Components   Both versions of SNMP share three key elements:

- ■ Managed devices
- ■ Agents
- ■ Network management systems (NMSs)

Managed devices are network nodes that run an SNMP software agent and are located on an SNMP-managed network. They generate and store management-related information and then provide this information to a network management system via SNMP. Sometimes called network elements, these nodes can be routers, access servers, switches, bridges, hubs, computer hosts, application servers, or printers. Essentially, any device that can run an SNMP agent can be a managed device.

Agents are the actual software pieces that are run on the managed devices. They are software modules or applications that understand certain management-related events and occurrences and translate these events into a format compatible with the network management system. They are also responsible for transmitting this information to the NMS.

Network management systems are the core of an SNMP system. An NMS runs a network management application that is responsible for receiving and presenting all of the information collected from the agents to the network administrator. It provides a single centralized point for monitoring and controlling all managed devices, and it supplies the majority of the memory resources and processing power necessary to perform proactive network management. There must be at least one NMS present on each managed network.

SNMP Basic Commands   Four core commands are used by SNMP:

- ■ **read**   This command is used by an NMS to monitor managed devices. The NMS can examine different variables that are maintained by managed devices.

■ **write** This command is used by an NMS to control managed devices. The NMS can change the value of variables stored within managed devices.

■ **trap** This command is used by managed devices to asynchronously report events to the NMS. When certain events occur, a managed device can send a trap to the NMS.

■ **traversal operations** These are used by the NMS to determine which variables a managed device supports and to sequentially gather information in variable tables, such as a routing table.

SNMP uses MIBs to define the variables that are managed. A Management Information Base (MIB) is a collection of hierarchical information, defining the manageable variables as object identifiers. The hierarchy is organized much like the Domain Naming System in use on the Internet, with top-level MIB object IDs controlled by standards organizations and lower-level object IDs delegated to individual organizations. This allows for very fine granularity and permits equipment manufacturers to assign individual MIBs to their equipment. An example MIB would be iso.identified-organization.dod.internet.private.enterprise.cisco.temporary variables. AppleTalk.atInput, represented as 1.3.6.1.4.1.9.3.3.1.

Finally, the Structure of Management Information (SMI) defines the rules for describing management information. The SNMPv1 SMI is defined in Request for Comments (RFC) 1155. Table 8-1 lists the RFCs in relation to SNMPv1 and SNMPv2.

SNMPv1 Protocol Operations As you've already learned, SNMP is a simple request-response protocol. The NMS issues a request and managed devices send back their responses. The NMS and agents use four protocol operations to perform these exchanges:

■ **Get** This is used by the NMS to retrieve the value of an object instance or variable from an agent. If the agent can't give values for all of the instances, it won't provide any at all.

■ **GetNext** This is used by the NMS to retrieve the next object instance in a table or list within an agent.

- **Set** This is used by the NMS to set the values of object instances within an agent.

- **Trap** This is used by agents to asynchronously inform the NMS of a significant event. When an event occurs, the agent will send a trap to the NMS.

SNMPv2 SNMPv2 is a logical evolution and extension of the original SNMPv1 standard. While SNMPv1 is widely used and is accepted as the default network management protocol in the Internet community, SNMPv2 offers a number of improvements to SNMPv1, including additional protocol operations.

The SNMPv2 SMI adds certain SMI-specific data types, such as bit strings, network addresses, and counters. These are in addition to the existing data types defined in the SNMPv1 SMI (see Table 8-2). Bit strings are unique to SNMPv2. Network addresses represent various types of addresses from the protocol families. SNMPv1 supports only 32-bit IP addresses, but SMNPv2 adds support for other addresses. SNMPv1 supports only 32-bit counter sizes, and SNMPv2 supports both 32-bit and 64-bit counters.

TABLE 8-1	**SNMPv1**	**SNMPv2**
RFCs for SNMPv1 and SNMPv2	RFC 1155 defines the mechanisms used for describing and naming objects for the purpose of management. The mechanisms are called the "structure of managed information" or SMI.	RFC 1902 defines the SMI for SNMPv2.
	RFC 1212 defines a more concise SMI description mechanism.	RFC 1905 defines protocol operations for SNMPv2.
	RFC 1157 defines SNMP, the protocol used for network access to managed objects.	
	RFC 1213 defines the Management Information Base II (MIB II), the core set of managed objects for the Internet suite of bnprotocols.	

| TABLE 8-2 | SMI Data Types Comparison for SNMPv1 and SNMPv2 | |

Data Type	SNMPv1	SNMPv2
Integers	Yes	Yes
Octet strings	Yes	Yes
Object IDs	Yes	Yes
Network addresses	32-bit IP only	32-bit IP and others
Counters	32-bit only	32-bit and 64-bit
Gauges	Yes	Yes
Time ticks	Yes	Yes
Opaques	Yes	Yes
Unsigned integers	Yes	Yes
Bit strings	No	Yes

SNMPv2 Protocol Operations   The protocol operations for SNMPv2 are probably where the greatest functional differences reside. The Get, GetNext, and Set operations used in SNMPv1 are exactly the same as those used in SNMPv2. However, SNMPv2 adds and enhances some protocol operations. For example, the SNMPv2 Trap operation performs the same function as it does in SNMPv1. But it uses a different message format and is designed to replace the SNMPv1 Trap.

SNMPv2 also adds two new protocol operations:

- **GetBulk**   This is used by the NMS to efficiently retrieve large blocks of data, such as multiple rows in a table. GetBulk fills a response message with as much of the requested data as will possibly fit. In SNMPv2, if the agent responding to GetBulk operations can't give values for all the variables in a list, it will provide partial results (contrast this with the lack of any values returned with Get).

- **Inform**   This allows one NMS to send trap information to another NMS and receive a response, essentially permitting multiple NMSs to communicate with each other.

The two key areas of incompatibility between SNMPv1 and SNMPv2 are the different message formats and the additional protocol operations found within SNMPv2. For reference, Tables 8-3 and 8-4 detail these differences even further.

| **TABLE 8-3** | SNMPv1 Message Header and Protocol Data Unit (PDU) Field Comparison |

Message Header Fields	Get, GetNext, Response, and Set PDU Fields	Trap PDU Fields
Version Number. Specifies the version of SNMP used.	**PDU Type.** Specifies the type of PDU transmitted (Get, GetNext, Response, and Set).	**Enterprise.** Identifies the type of managed object generating the trap.
Community Name. Defines an access environment (administrative domain) for a group of NMSs. Necessary for inclusion in SNMP operations.	**Request ID.** Associates SNMP requests with responses.	**Agent Address.** Provides the address of the managed object generating the trap.
	Error Status. Indicates one of a number of errors and error types. Only the response operation sets this field. Other operations set this field to zero.	**Generic Trap Type.** Indicates one of a number of generic trap types.
	Error Index. Associates an error with a particular object instance. Only the response operation sets this field. Other operations set this field to zero.	**Specific Trap Code.** Indicates one of a number of specific trap codes.
	Variable Bindings. Serves as the data field of the SNMPv1 PDU. Each variable binding associates a particular object instance with its current value (with the exception of Get and GetNext requests, for which the value is ignored).	**Time Stamp.** Provides the amount of time that has elapsed between the last network reinitialization and generation of the trap.
		Variable Bindings. The data field of the SNMPv1 Trap PDU. Each variable binding associates a particular object instance with its current value.

TABLE 8-4	SNMPv2 Message Header and Protocol Data Unit (PDU) Field Comparison	
Message Header Fields	**Get, GetNext, Inform, Response, Set, and Trap PDU Fields**	**GetBulk PDU Fields**
Version Number. Specifies the version of SNMP used.	**PDU Type.** Specifies the type of PDU transmitted (Get, GetNext, Inform, Response, Set or Trap).	**PDU Type.** Identifies the PDU as a GetBulk operation.
Community Name. Defines an access environment (administrative domain) for a group of NMSs. Necessary for inclusion in SNMP operations.	**Request ID.** Associates SNMP requests with responses.	**Request ID.** Associates SNMP requests with responses.
	Error Status. Indicates one of a number of errors and error types. Only the response operation sets this field. Other operations set this field to zero.	**Nonrepeaters.** Specifies the number of object instances in the Variable Bindings field that should be retrieved no more than once from the beginning of the request. This field is used when some of the instances are scalar objects with only one variable.
	Error Index. Associates an error with a particular object instance. Only the response operation sets this field. Other operations set this field to zero.	**Max Repetitions.** Defines the maximum number of times that other variables beyond those specified by the nonrepeaters field should be retrieved.
	Variable Bindings. Serves as the data field of the SNMPv2 PDU. Each variable binding associates a particular object instance with its current value (with the exception of Get and GetNext requests, for which the value is ignored).	**Variable Bindings.** Serves as the data field of the SNMPv2 PDU. Each variable binding associates a particular object instance with its current value (with the exception of Get and GetNext requests, for which the value is ignored).

SNMP RMON Standard   The SNMP Remote Monitoring (RMON) standard is a standard monitoring specification for monitoring packet and traffic patterns on LAN segments. It is defined as a portion of the MIB II network management database. RFC 1757 defines the objects and RMON groups for managing remote network monitoring devices, and RFC 1513 defines extensions to the RMON MIB for managing 802.5 Token Ring networks.

The RMON specification defines a set of statistics and functions that are exchanged between RMON-compliant consoles or NMSs and configured probe stations. RMON enables network administrators to track the number of packets, packet sizes, broadcasts, network utilization, and errors and conditions such as Ethernet collisions. It can also track host statistics, including errors, level of activity, and traffic patterns between hosts. RMON also supports the capture of historical data, threshold alarming, and packet captures—all based on user-definable parameters. The flexibility that RMON provides enables network administrators to accurately specify and receive comprehensive network-fault diagnosis, planning, and performance-tuning information to proactively manage their internetworks.

The RMON specification defines nine RMON groups of information. Each of these groups provides a specific set of data, allowing for most common networking management requirements. Vendor support for each of the nine RMON groups varies, and it is common for lower-end devices to support only the first four groups (Statistics, Alarms, Traffic Matrix, and Filters). Table 8-5 details each RMON group, its function, and the various elements or variables of the group.

TABLE 8-5	Functions and Elements of the Nine RMON Groups	
RMON Group	**Function**	**Elements**
Statistics	Measures probe statistics for each monitored interface on the device.	Packets dropped, packets sent, bytes sent (octets), broadcast packets, multicast packets, CRC errors, runts, giants, fragments, jabbers, collisions, and counters for packets in these ranges: 64–128, 128–256, 256–512, 512–1,024, and 1,024–1,518 bytes

TABLE 8-5   Functions and Elements of the Nine RMON Groups *(continued)*

RMON Group	Function	Elements
Alarms	Monitors and compares variables in the probe to user-configurable thresholds. If the monitored variable crosses a threshold, an event is generated.	Alarm table, Alarm type, interval, starting threshold, stop threshold (requires the event RMON group to operate)
Traffic Matrix	Gathers statistics for conversations between sets of two addresses, adding table entries for each new conversation.	Source and destination address pairs and packets, bytes, and errors for each pair
Filters	If packets match a user-configurable filter, they might be captured or might generate events.	Bit-filter type (mask or not mask), filter expression (bit level), conditional expression (and, or, not) to other filters
History	Records statistics and stores them for later retrieval.	Sample period, number of samples, item(s) sampled
Hosts	Contains statistics for network hosts.	Host address, packets, and bytes received and transmitted, broadcast, multicast, and error packets
Top Hosts N	Prepares tables of rate-based statistics over a user-configurable interval.	Statistics, host(s), sample start and stop periods, rate base, duration
Packet Capture	Performs packet capture.	Size of buffer for captured packets, full status (alarm), number of captured packets
Events	Generation and notification of events from the device.	Event type, description, last time event sent

Cisco has its own set of RMON-based network management tools: TrafficDirector, an RMON console application, and SwitchProbe stand-alone RMON probes. We will look at these and other network management tools later in this chapter.

CERTIFICATION OBJECTIVE 8.02

Network Management Processes

We've looked at the common goals of network management and have also examined the main technologies (SNMP and RMON) available to provide us with the critical information needed for this management. But what is the process involved in determining the specific goals and the tasks required to meet those goals?

Understanding all of the potential tasks necessary to meet your network management goals can be difficult. According to Cisco Enterprise Network Management marketing material, network management tasks can be divided into three main areas, each of which has its own set of objectives:

- Implementation and change
    - Installation
    - Configuration
    - Address management
    - Adds, moves, and changes
    - Security management
    - Accounting and billing
    - Assets and inventory management
    - User management
    - Data management
- Monitoring and diagnosing
    - Defining thresholds
    - Monitoring exceptions
    - Isolating problems
    - Validating problems

- Troubleshooting problems
- Bypassing and resolving problems
- Design and optimization
  - Data collection definition
  - Baseline creation
  - Trend analysis
  - Response time analysis
  - Capacity planning
  - Procurement
  - Topology design

I'll bet there are a few items in this list that may not have occurred to you, at least not initially. This illustrates the complexity of the network management process: determining the appropriate factors involved without overlooking important (but sometimes hidden) tasks. A solid understanding of these items will allow you to better work with your organizations or clients in specifying and recommending particular network management products and solutions.

Proactive Versus Reactive Network Management

You've probably noticed that I've used the term "proactive" a number of times already in this chapter in discussions of network management and strategies. Although it is becoming an overused buzzword in today's corporate environments, proactive behavior definitely has a firm place in network management.

I'd venture a guess that most of you reading this book have held positions at organizations where all you seem to do is fight the fires as they pop up unexpectedly. This is more common that we'd like to believe, and it occurs at companies of all sizes. The reasons for this are many, but can include the following.

- Lack of staff or qualified personnel
- Lack of training and preparation

- Abundance of new projects and solutions to implement
- Multitude of current problems crying out for attention
- Lack of appropriate tools

What we're discussing is essentially considered reactive network management, and it can also stem from a lack of planning and preparation on behalf of the networking team and their management. As companies have begun to recognize the strategic importance of their internetworks to their core business models, they have focused more attention on network operations and infrastructure reliability than ever before.

Given the explosive growth of the Internet and electronic commerce over just the last year or two, most companies recognize that their networks aren't simply cost centers anymore; they represent the organization's gateway to the customer . . . and to success. A clearly defined and executable network management strategy has become central to most organizations that are serious about their businesses.

Being proactive about network management means monitoring and addressing situations before they become problems. By not waiting until an error has taken a critical firewall router or e-commerce server offline, you can proactively plan and prepare to implement solutions. Cisco has identified a number of other common items that are part of proactive network management. These are

- Collect statistics
- Watch trends
- Conduct routine tests (that is, response time measurements)
- Allocate time at least once a month to compile statistics and write a baseline report that describes the current status of the network
- Define service goals for the network:
  - Acceptable downtime
  - Response time
  - Throughput
  - Ease of use
  - Scalability

■ Write and publish reports on the quality of service that has been delivered in the last month

You should also ensure that you are working with adequate resources to perform quality network management. This should include everything from software and tools to staff and time available.

Every organization has different needs and expects different things of its network management efforts. For example, I currently work for a Fortune 100 company with a large distributed WAN infrastructure that extends across North America. We also interconnect with thousands of other associated companies and sites through our network. Appropriately, at our headquarters location we have a large network operations center, outfitted with a marvelous array of comprehensive monitoring, reporting, and management consoles and applications. This center is staffed 24 hours a day, 365 days a year, with a talented group of network management specialists. It is their job to always watch and monitor each of the thousands of pieces of equipment that comprise our internetwork. When they see signs of potential trouble, they issue alerts and trouble tickets to convey the relevant information to the appropriate group of engineers for troubleshooting and resolution.

While this strategy has worked very well for us, it might not be the appropriate solution for a small accounting firm or antiques shop. The key is to match the level of network management and service with the needs and requirements of the company. To assist in this, Cisco has prepared a checklist for developing proactive network management strategies for your customers and clients:

1. Determine network service goals.

2. Define metrics for measuring whether goals have been met.

3. Define processes for data collection and reporting.

4. Implement network management systems.

5. Collect performance data and record trends.

6. Analyze results and write reports.

7. Locate network irregularities and bottlenecks.

8. Plan and implement improvements to the network.

9. Review and adjust metrics and processes if necessary.

10. Document changes.

Cisco refers to this list as "Selling Cisco Management Products." Not only is it important material to know for your exam, but it provides an excellent overview of the entire network management strategy life cycle. Let's look now at some of the network management products available from Cisco.

CERTIFICATION OBJECTIVE 8.03

Cisco's Network Management Applications

With Cisco as the leader in the networking arena, changes are rapid. Therefore, the following discussion is focused on information as it was presented at the time of the writing of the exam. For the latest information regarding Cisco's network management products, tools, and solutions, please refer to Cisco Connection Online.

CiscoWorks

CiscoWorks is a comprehensive suite of integrated management tools designed to simplify the administration and maintenance of small-to-medium business networks or workgroups. It is a collection of SNMP-based software applications for performing device status monitoring, configuration maintenance, and troubleshooting. ("CiscoWorks" was originally used to refer to the UNIX version; this product has reached end of sales and been replaced with CiscoWorks2000 Resource Manager Essentials. CiscoWorks for Windows and CiscoWorks Blue are still current products.) The following list details the applications bundled within CiscoWorks:

■ **AutoInstall Manager** Performs remote installations of new routers using a neighboring router.

- **CiscoConnect**   Provides connectivity to Cisco and Cisco partners with debugging information, configurations, and topology information to speed troubleshooting and resolution of network problems.

- **CiscoView**   The standard graphical device-management tool for managing Cisco devices. Provides dynamic status, statistics, troubleshooting, and comprehensive configuration information for switches, routers, access servers, concentrators, and adapters. It is also available as a stand-alone product.

- **Configuration File Management**   Provides an audit trail of changes and unauthorized configurations.

- **Contacts**   A contact database, storing information about the contact person for a specific device including the name, phone number, e-mail address, title, location, and address.

- **Device Management**   A device database that holds an inventory of your network, including hardware, software, release levels, individuals responsible for maintaining devices, and location of devices.

- **Global Command Facility**   Provides a way to create configuration "snap-ins" that can be applied automatically to groups of routers that share configurations.

- **Health Monitor**   A device status information viewer, displaying buffers, CPU load, memory available, and protocols and interfaces being used.

- **Offline Network Analysis**   A historical database used for offline analysis, performance trending, and traffic patterns determination.

- **Path Tool**   A path analyzer to collect utilization and error data between devices.

- **Security Manager**   Provides security for CiscoWorks applications and network devices from unauthorized individuals.

- **Software Manager**   Provides a central distribution point and management for router software versions.

The CiscoWorks suite provides a wide variety of tools for performing network management. It is also the right choice of network management tools for the less-experienced or junior network administrator in a small-to-medium business network or workgroup.

Note that "Cisco Hub/Ring Manager for Windows" is not part of the CiscoWorks application suite. This is also never the correct product choice when selecting the best network management tool for the lower-level network administrator!

CiscoWorks Blue Maps

Now referred to as simply CiscoWorks Blue, CiscoWorks Blue Maps enables the network administrator to address the complex and wide range of requirements in integrated IBM Systems Network Architecture (SNA) and IP environments. It provides the ability to create and view logical, dynamic color-coded network maps of Cisco routers, enabled with certain SNA protocols. It requires Cisco routers running IOS 11.0 or later and configured with either remote source-route bridging (RSRB), data-link switching (DLSw), or Advanced Peer-to-Peer Networking (APPN).

This permits management of the entire network from a single management node, using both CiscoWorks and CiscoWorks Blue Maps. For example, you could view a map of all of your RSRB-enabled routers, view statistics, and display a list of circuits and their details by using the RSRB Map application. CiscoWorks Blue Maps provides a clear management option in these consolidated SNA and IP internetworks.

TrafficDirector

TrafficDirector is a comprehensive network traffic-monitoring and troubleshooting RMON console application that analyzes traffic and enables proactive management of internetworks. It provides a graphical user interface for reporting and analysis of RMON collected traffic data from RMON agents in Cisco's Catalyst switches, Cisco IOS software–embedded RMON agents in routers, Cisco SwitchProbe stand-alone network monitoring probes, or any RMON standards-compliant agent.

TrafficDirector offers real-time analysis of traffic behaviors and network usage information as well as proactive trending data for network planners and managers. It consists of a centralized, SNMP-compatible network management console and data-gathering agents located at various points on a network. Some of TrafficDirector's many functions include the following.

Network traffic monitoring and data-flow measurement

- A protocol analysis tool providing centralized troubleshooting for most protocol-related network problems

- Packet filters to enable users to monitor all seven layers of network traffic, including data-link, network, transport, and application layers

- Full-packet capture and seven-layer protocol decodes for the AppleTalk, DECnet, IP, ISO, Novell, SNA, Sun NFS, Banyan VINES, and XNS protocol suites

- Proactive alarms when thresholds are exceeded

- Display and analysis of raw network data in a useful graphical form

- Policy enforcement and charge-back capabilities

- Real-time updates obtained from all segments of a widely dispersed enterprise network

Table 8-6 provides a more complete summary of Cisco's network management products and supported platforms.

TABLE 8-6	Summary of Cisco's Internetwork Management Applications	
Network Management Application	**Devices Supported/Managed**	**Product Platform(s)**
CiscoWorks	Various Cisco devices	SunNet Manager, HP OpenView on SunOS/Solaris, HP OpenView HP-UX, and IBM NetView for AIX
CiscoWorks Blue Maps	SNA-enabled Cisco routers	AIX on RS/6000, HP-UX on HP, and SunOS on Sun
CiscoWorks Blue SNA View	SNA-enabled Cisco routers and SNA devices managed by mainframe	AIX on RS/6000, HP-UX on HP, and SunOS on Sun; Mainframe VTAM
CiscoWorks Blue Native Service Point	Cisco routers	IBM NetView and Sterling NetMaster
Cisco Hub/Ring Manager for Windows	Cisco 2517, 2518, 2519 routers	PC with Microsoft Windows and HP OpenView Windows

TABLE 8-6	Summary of Cisco's Internetwork Management Applications *(continued)*	
Network Management Application	**Devices Supported/Managed**	**Product Platform(s)**
CiscoWorks Windows	Cisco routers, switches, access servers, concentrators, adapters, and ATM switches	PC with Microsoft Windows NT or Windows 95 running CastleRock SNMPc (bundled with CiscoWorks Windows) or HP OpenView Windows (optional)
CiscoView	Cisco routers, switches, access servers, concentrators, adapters, and ATM switches (LightStream 100 and LightStream 2020)	Stand-alone on UNIX workstations Also bundled with CiscoWorks
NETSYS Connectivity Tools	Cisco routers	SunOS, Solaris, and AIX (used with CiscoWorks 3.0 interface)
NETSYS Performance Tools	Cisco routers	SunOS and Solaris (used with NETSYS Connectivity Tools)
ControlStream StreamView VirtualStream	LightStream 2020	Sun SPARCstation with SunOS and HP OpenView
TrafficDirector	RMON console management	SunNet Manager HP OpenView IBM NetView for AIX PC Stand-alone on UNIX workstations Also compatible with CiscoWorks
Total Control Manager/SNMP	Modem and T1 cards in Cisco 5100 access server	PC with Microsoft Windows
Switched Internetwork Solutions (includes VlanDirector, TrafficDirector, and CiscoView)	Comprehensive support for Cisco Catalyst switches	SunNet Manager on Solaris HP OpenView on Solaris

Now that you have a better idea of network management and the tasks and tools involved, here are some possible scenario questions and their answers.

QUESTIONS AND ANSWERS

Tori needs an RMON-based network management tool for her network. She also wants real-time, color-coded analysis, and trending data for planning purposes.	She should select Cisco's TrafficDirector.
I have a number of devices that are all running SNMP agent software and would be considered "managed devices." Is this a managed network?	Don't forget that every managed network requires at least one network management system to receive information, monitor, and control all managed devices.
As part of her administrative duties, Amy regularly collects and compiles statistics and prepares reports on the overall performance and health of her network. She frequently refers to baseline numbers that have been collected and compares current results to the defined service goals laid out by her team. Would Amy's approach to network management be considered proactive or not?	Absolutely! Everything Amy is doing fits perfectly into the definition of proactive network management. (She's likely a valuable asset to her company because of this.)
We have a mixed environment within our network: Microsoft Windows, Sun Solaris, IBM AIX, and HP Open-View platforms. Can we select a Cisco network management tool and deploy it successfully within this heterogeneous environment?	Yes; Cisco provides support for all of the platforms listed, as well as others.

CERTIFICATION SUMMARY

We've looked at the concepts behind network management, as well as the processes involved and the tools offered by Cisco. We've also examined SNMP and RMON as components of a successful network management implementation. The importance of planning your network management strategy can't be underestimated. By planning for a particular network management strategy during the design phases of your network implementation, you can help ensure that this strategy will grow and expand with your network and allow you to be proactive in your day-to-day processes. Continually monitoring and assessing the health and performance of your network will provide benefits throughout the entire life span of your network. By understanding and acting upon the entire range of network management tasks, you will be better prepared to succeed in your efforts.

TWO-MINUTE DRILL

❑ Most companies share the common network management goals of connectivity, security, cost optimization, and manageable growth.

❑ As companies have begun to realize the strategic importance of their internetworks, they have focused more attention on proactive network management.

❑ Cisco network management applications run on standard hardware and operating system platforms, such as UNIX, Microsoft Windows, Hewlett-Packard's OpenView for Windows, and other industry standards.

❑ SNMPv2 is supported on all platforms and devices that run the Cisco Internetwork Operating System (IOS) software.

❑ SNMP is a simple "request-response" application-layer protocol that provides for the exchange of management information between network devices.

❑ SNMP is part of the TCP/IP protocol family.

❑ There are two versions of SNMP: SNMPv1 and SNMPv2.

❑ SNMP managed devices are network nodes that run an SNMP software agent.

❑ SNMP agents are the software modules or applications that are run on the managed devices.

❑ SNMP network management systems (NMSs) receive, monitor, and control all managed devices.

❑ At least one NMS must be present on each SNMP-managed network.

❑ The four core SNMP commands are read, write, trap, and traversal operations.

❑ A Management Information Base (MIB) is a collection of hierarchical information, defining the manageable variables as object identifiers.

❑ The four core SNMP protocol operations are Get, GetNext, Set, and Trap.

❑ The Structure of Management Information (SMI) defines the rules for describing management information.

❑ The SMI data type, bit strings, is unique to SNMPv2.

❑ SNMPv1 supports only 32-bit IP addresses.

❑ SNMPv2 Trap uses a different message format and is designed to replace the SNMPv1 Trap.

❑ SNMPv2 adds two new protocol operations: GetBulk and Inform.

❑ The SNMP Remote Monitoring (RMON) standard is a standard monitoring specification for monitoring packet and traffic patterns on LAN segments.

❑ RMON enables the tracking of the number of packets, packet sizes, broadcasts, network utilization, errors, and host statistics.

❑ The RMON specification defines nine RMON groups of information.

❑ The nine RMON groups are Statistics, Alarms, Traffic Matrix, Filters, History, Hosts, Top Hosts N, Packet Capture, and Events.

❑ Network management tasks can be divided into three main areas: implementation and change, monitoring and diagnosing, and design and optimization.

❑ Cisco's checklist for proactive network management includes

1. Determine network service goals.

2. Define metrics for measuring whether goals have been met.

3. Define processes for data collection and reporting.

4. Implement network management systems.

5. Collect performance data and record trends.

6. Analyze results and write reports.

7. Locate network irregularities and bottlenecks.

8. Plan and implement improvements to the network.

9. Review and adjust metrics and processes, if necessary.

10. Document changes.

❑ CiscoWorks is an SNMP-based suite of software tools designed to simplify the administration and maintenance of small-to-medium business networks or workgroups.

❑ CiscoWorks for Windows is likely the best network management tool for the junior network administrator with minimal training in network management.

❑ CiscoWorks Blue Maps provides dynamic color-coded network maps in consolidated SNA and IP internetworks.

❑ TrafficDirector is an RMON console application that analyzes traffic and enables proactive management of internetworks.

❑ TrafficDirector offers real-time analysis of traffic behaviors and network usage information, as well as proactive trending data for network planners and managers.

SELF TEST

The following Self Test questions will help you measure your understanding of the material presented in this chapter. Read all the choices carefully, as there may be more than one correct answer. Choose all correct answers for each question.

1. As companies have begun to realize the strategic importance of their internetworks, they have focused more attention on _____ network management.

    A. Reactive

    B. Secure

    C. Proactive

    D. Distributed

2. Of the following choices, which are the common goals that organizations share with regard to network management? (Choose all that apply.)

    A. Connectivity

    B. Scalability

    C. Manageable growth

    D. Security

    E. All of the above

3. Which is the most accurate definition of the roles of the SNMP elements?

    A. SNMP agents are network nodes that provide management information to an NMS.

    B. Agents can be routers, access servers, switches, bridges, hubs, computer hosts, application servers, or printers.

    C. Managed devices run the agents and feed information to the NMS.

    D. Centralized agents receive and present all of the information collected from the NMS.

4. SNMPv2 is supported on which of the following devices? (Choose all that apply.)

    A. Cisco 3640 router

    B. Cisco 2514 router

    C. Cisco 5500 chassis-based switch

    D. Cisco 4000 series router

    E. Cisco 1605 router

5. Which one of the following tools will synchronize names with dynamically assigned IP addresses?

   A. DNS/DHCP Manager

   B. CiscoWorks for Windows

   C. Cisco Hub/Ring Manager for Windows

   D. NETSYS/Enterprise/Solver

Jane is the IS manager for a medium-sized recruitment firm. You have just completed designing and implementing a new network design, introducing Cisco router technology to the company's infrastructure for the first time.

She has asked you to recommend a network management tool for its new network, but she has expressed concern about the level of experience that her network administrators have with routers.

She has planned to send her administrators to training as soon as possible, but she would like you to recommend a product that will let them get "up and running" easily. She also has budgetary limitations looming over her.

6. Refer to the scenario above. Of the following network management tools, which would be the best and most cost-effective recommendation to make?

   A. Cisco Hub/Ring Manager for Windows

   B. CiscoView

   C. NETSYS/Enterprise/Solver

   D. CiscoWorks for Windows

7. Which of the following are valid SNMP commands? (Choose all that apply.)

   A. Read

   B. Trap

   C. Send

   D. Set

8. Which of the following are valid protocol operations for SNMPv1? (Choose all that apply.)

   A. GetNext

   B. GetBulk

   C. Get

   D. Trap

   E. Set

   F. Inform

9. How many groups of RMON exist?

    A. 4

    B. 6

    C. 9

    D. 14

10. You have been asked to make a network management tool recommendation. The single requirement is a graphical RMON-based console management application. Which of the following choices is the best?

    A. CiscoView

    B. TrafficDirector

    C. CiscoWorks for Windows

    D. NETSYS/Enterprise/Solver

11. Andy is the network administrator for a network comprised of a large number of Cisco 2519 Token Ring router/hub devices. Which of the following network management tools would be his best choice?

    A. CiscoWorks for Windows

    B. CiscoView

    C. NETSYS/Enterprise/Solver

    D. Cisco Hub/Ring Manager for Windows

12. Which SNMPv2 operation will retrieve multiple rows from a table and will provide at least partial results?

    A. Trap

    B. GetBulk

    C. GetNext

    D. Inform

13. Which RMON group provides information on packets dropped and sent for the interfaces of an RMON-monitored device?

    A. Alarms

    B. Packet Capture

    C. Filters

    D. Statistics

14. Which SNMPv2 protocol operation allows communication between NMSs?

   A. SendNext

   B. GetNext

   C. Inform

   D. Traversal Operations

15. What are the three main areas of network management tasks, as defined by Cisco Enterprise Network Management marketing material? (Choose three.)

   A. Monitoring and diagnosing

   B. Design and optimization

   C. Trending and baselining

   D. Implementation and change

   E. Accounting and billing

   F. Troubleshooting and resolving

Melissa operates a large internetwork for an application service provider, Big ASP, Inc. The servers are a heterogeneous mix of Windows NT and IBM systems, and the Cisco routers, that interconnect the multiple locations are running both IP and SNA (RSRB) protocols. Her director has recently been talking with her about managing and maintaining the network, focusing on the network management aspects. He wants to make sure that problems with the network are identified quickly and addressed before they cause serious issues. Answer questions 16 and 17 based on the scenario presented.

16. Refer to the scenario above. Melissa identifies with the director's concerns and knows that the best strategy for staying on top of the network's issues is to adopt a proactive network management plan. Which of the following items fit with this strategy? (Choose all that apply.)

   A. Collect performance data and record trends.

   B. Review and adjust metrics and processes if necessary.

   C. Define metrics for measuring whether goals have been met.

   D. Determine network service goals.

   E. Analyze results and write reports.

   F. Document changes.

17. Refer to the previous scenario for Big ASP, Inc. Which network management tool will provide management of Melissa's entire network from a single management node?

   A. TrafficDirector

   B. NETSYS/Enterprise/Solver

    C. CiscoWorks Blue Maps

    D. Cisco Hub/Ring Manager for Windows

18. Which of the following products are included within the CiscoWorks bundled suite of management tools? (Choose all that apply.)

    A. CiscoView

    B. Cisco Hub/Ring Manager for Windows

    C. AutoInstall Manager

    D. Configuration File Management

    E. Offline Network Analysis

You have been tasked with selecting a network management tool for monitoring and managing a number of Cisco Catalyst switches. All of the switches are RMON-enabled and the client wants real-time analysis and usage information, as well as a centralized console management station.

Their network administrators are well skilled and have solid experience with advanced network management. The client would also benefit from the ability to perform full seven-layer packet captures and protocol analysis. Finally, they have discussed the possibility of using this tool for enforcing network policy and implementing a network usage charge-back system to the individual departments within their company.

19. Refer to the scenario above. Of the following network management tools, which would you select for this client?

    A. NETSYS/Enterprise/Solver

    B. CiscoWorks Blue Maps

    C. Cisco Hub/Ring Manager for Windows

    D. TrafficDirector

    E. CiscoView

Ted is the Director of Information Systems for a Pacific Northwest Internet startup. He has hired a handful of good network administrators and an experienced network manager. Ted and the network manager have been discussing different network management tools and are trying to select the best tool for their company's needs.

They feel it is important to keep in close contact with both their Cisco reseller/partner and Cisco. They would like to have a system that provides automated network data collection and reporting capabilities, as they believe their network administrators will benefit greatly from the expert assistance available from their partner and Cisco.

They would also like to receive automated news flashes and bug notifications that apply to their specific network equipment from Cisco. This will give them the ability to stay on top of network management issues as they arise and provide a better opportunity for being proactive.

20. Refer to the scenario above. Given their requirements, which of the following network management tools would be the best choice for Ted and his network manager?

    A. NETSYS/Enterprise/Solver

    B. CiscoWorks

    C. Cisco Hub/Ring Manager for Windows

    D. TrafficDirector

    E. CiscoView

21. _____ is a standard monitoring specification for monitoring packet and traffic patterns on LAN segments.

    A. NMS

    B. SNMP

    C. SMI

    D. MIB

    E. RMON

SELF TEST ANSWERS

1. ☑ **C.** Companies have focused more attention on proactive network management.
   ☒ **A** is incorrect because reactive network management is what we're trying to avoid. **B** and **D** don't apply to the question.

2. ☑ **A, C, and D.** Connectivity, manageable growth, and security are three of the four network management goals. The fourth is cost optimization.
   ☒ **B** is incorrect because scalability is more relevant to the actual network design than to network management, although management should also be able to grow with the network.

3. ☑ **C.** Managed devices run the agents and feed information to the NMS.
   ☒ **A** is incorrect because agents aren't "network nodes." **B** actually lists items that would qualify as managed devices. **D** is reversed; the centralized NMS receives and presents all the information collected from the agents.

4. ☑ **A, B, C, D, and E.** All are correct because these devices support SNMPv2, as each of them runs the Cisco IOS software. The difference of a switch versus a router or a different model number is irrelevant to the question.

5. ☑ **A.** Even though this chapter did not cover the DNS/DHCP Manager product, expect to see this type of mixed question on the CCDA exam.
   ☒ **B, C, and D** are incorrect because they are not valid choices for IP address synchronization.

6. ☑ **D.** CiscoWorks for Windows is the best recommendation for Jane. Remember that her administrators are junior and lack router experience.
   ☒ **A, B, and C** are incorrect because they don't meet the requirements of the scenario.

7. ☑ **A and B.** Read and Trap are valid SNMP commands.
   ☒ **C,** Send, is nonexistent; and **D,** Set, is a protocol operation, not a command. Incidentally, **B,** Trap, is both a command and an operation.

8. ☑ **A, C, D, and E.** GetNext, Get, Trap, and Set are all valid SNMPv1 protocol operations.
   ☒ While GetNext, Get, Trap, and Set are also valid for SNMPv1 and SNMPv2, options **B** and **F,** GetBulk and Inform, are available *only* with SNMPv2.

9. ☑ **C.** Nine groups of RMON exist.

10. ☑ **B.** TrafficDirector is the graphical RMON-based console management application required.

☒ **A, C,** and **D** are incorrect because they are not RMON console applications.

11. ☑ **D.** Remember that Cisco 2517, 2518, and 2519 router/hub devices are best managed using Cisco's Hub/Ring Manager for Windows.

☒ **A, B,** and **C** are not the best choices for managing this equipment.

12. ☑ **B.** GetBulk is the protocol operation that will retrieve partial results and will return as much data as will fit at one time.

☒ **A** is incorrect because Trap is used to asynchronously send notification of an event. **C,** GetNext, returns the next instance in a table or list. **D,** Inform, is used to send trap information from one NMS to another.

13. ☑ **D.** The Statistics group provides information on packets dropped and sent.

☒ **A** is incorrect because alarms monitor and compare variables in the probe to user-configurable thresholds. **B** is incorrect because Packet Capture performs packet captures. **C** is incorrect because filters are used to match against packets to generate alarms or initiate captures.

14. ☑ **C.** Inform is the operation that sends traps between NMSs, allowing communication.

☒ **A** is incorrect because SendNext is not a protocol operation; it is invented and has nothing to do with SNMP. **B** is incorrect because GetNext returns the next instance in a table or list. **D** is incorrect because Traversal Operations are actually SNMP commands, not operations. They sequentially place supported device variables into tables.

15. ☑ **A, B,** and **D.** Monitoring and diagnosing, design and optimization, and implementation and change are the three areas defined by Cisco Enterprise Network Management marketing material.

☒ **C** is incorrect because trending and baselining are separate components of design and optimization. **E** is incorrect because accounting and billing are part of implementation and change. **F** is incorrect because troubleshooting and resolving are components of monitoring and diagnosing.

16. ☑ **A, B, C, D, E,** and **F.** All important components of a proactive network management strategy.

17. ☑ **C.** CiscoWorks Blue Maps is the obvious choice in this scenario.
    ☒ **A, B**, and **D** don't meet the requirements of this network. The key to the question is the integration of both IP and SNA environments, and only CiscoWorks Blue Maps will provide the necessary functionality.

18. ☑ **A, C, D, E, and F.** Are all correct because all are integrated into the CiscoWorks suite.
    ☒ **B** is incorrect because Cisco Hub/Ring Manager for Windows is not part of CiscoWorks.

19. ☑ **D.** TrafficDirector is the only tool listed that meets the stringent requirements of this client. Via RMON and centralized console management, it provides the real-time analysis and usage information required. It performs full, seven-layer packet captures and protocol analysis and provides network policy enforcement and charge-back system capabilities.
    ☒ **A, B, C**, and **E** don't meet these requirements and would be inappropriate selections for this client's needs.

20. ☑ **B.** With the inclusion of CiscoConnect in CiscoWorks, they will meet their requirements by selecting CiscoWorks.
    ☒ **A, C, D**, and **E** don't meet these requirements and would be inappropriate selections for this client's needs.

21. ☑ **E.** RMON (Remote Monitoring) is the standard monitoring specification for monitoring packet and traffic patterns on LAN segments.
    ☒ **A** is incorrect because an NMS (network management system) receives, monitors, and controls all managed devices. **B**, SNMP, provides for the exchange of management information between network devices. **C**, SMI (Structure of Management Information), defines the rules for describing management information. **D**, MIB (Management Information Base), is a collection of hierarchical information, defining the manageable variables as object identifiers.

9

The Network
Structure Design

N etwork design can be an individualistic process—somewhat of an art form for architects. Each network reflects the architect's own personality and style and should also deliver the desired results for the customer. Performance, security, capacity, and scalability are the most common customer requirements, and the real skill lies in weaving each of these requirements into a comprehensive end-to-end solution for your customer.

Architecting the network topology is a critical step in the overall success of the network. Decisions made at this stage will affect the network throughout its lifetime. These decisions can also be difficult (if not impossible) to reverse once the network has been implemented. The functionality, management, security, efficiency, and dependability of each network is impacted by these decisions, and careful planning is required to ensure a quality final product.

CERTIFICATION OBJECTIVE 9.01

Standard Internetworking Topologies

Given the weight of network topology choices early in the design process, good network architects use a handful of structured topology models as a guideline for most design decisions. Using these models allows you to deliver the most important customer network requirements:

- Performance
- Security
- Capacity
- Scalability

The three categories examined in this chapter are the *hierarchical, redundant,* and *secure* models. Each of these network topologies represents many years of network design experience and stands as "best practice" in the field of network architecture.

Hierarchical Models

Hierarchies exist almost everywhere in our lives. Essentially, a hierarchy is something structured in layers. From modern corporations to the United States military, hierarchical structures help organize and give shape to many things.

The Open Systems Interconnection (OSI) reference model is a hierarchical, or layered, structure that lends itself to a simplification of roles. When the layers of the OSI model are used, computer communications need only refer to the separate layers to perform the tasks necessary. This also allows each layer to focus on a particular operation or function. A layered approach, which makes implementing, managing, and scaling this structure much easier, is also directly applicable to network design. Through the use of layers, each component of a network can be fitted specifically to layer functionality.

Using a hierarchical model in network design allows you to build networks using layers, permitting a level of modularity and flexibility not present without the hierarchy. By building networks with a layered approach, you can change the network more easily in the future as requirements change or as the network grows and expands. The modularity of a hierarchical network facilitates change by minimizing the impact of network modifications to a subset of the entire network. When change is limited to a smaller portion of the network, it becomes less expensive and easier to implement. This layered structure also makes the network easier to understand and easier to manage. A well-known and well-managed network is infinitely more predictable and dependable—characteristics of a good network.

Cisco's approach to a hierarchical network is a three-layer design. The layers are identified as

- Core
- Distribution
- Access

These layers should be thought of as logical entities rather than physical structures. Although each layer symbolizes functionality necessary in every network, the layers don't need to be separate physical implementations. A single device may represent all the layers, or each layer can reside separately.

The backplane of a device may represent a particular layer itself or the demarcation point between layers. A layer may even be skipped in a particular implementation, although the hierarchy should be observed for performance and scalability reasons. Figure 9-1 shows the hierarchical model.

Core Layer

The core layer is the high-speed switching backbone of the network. In fact, it is sometimes referred to simply as the backbone. The core layer is critical to the overall performance of the entire network and should be designed with this in mind.

The core layer functions as the heart of the network, pumping packets as quickly as possible to all other areas. Because of the importance of the core layer, it must be as reliable and stable as possible. It should have a fixed and limited diameter to provide predictability and quick problem resolution. Scaling the network to a larger size should occur at the distribution layer to help limit the diameter of the core.

The core layer should also be highly redundant and fault tolerant because a failure in the core can impact the entire network. It is responsible for the

FIGURE 9-1   Hierarchical model for network design

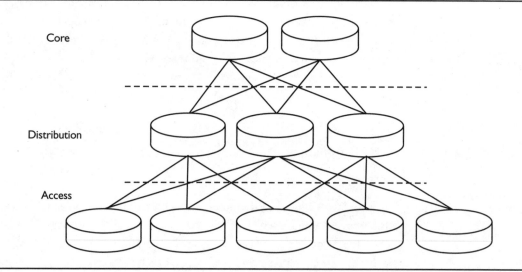

efficient delivery of packets to other locations and thus needs to be easily manageable, rapidly adaptive, and very fast. Any special packet processing or filtering should be strongly avoided at the core because this will contribute to longer latency and slower switching and will negatively impact the remainder of the network.

exam
ⓦatch

On the CCDA exam, you will likely see questions that use basic diagrams and then ask you a question based on the diagrams. A perfect example of this would be an illustration of a network with a Cisco Catalyst 5500 switch in the middle of the diagram with all connections collapsing back into the switch. The question would be, "Which network layer is represented by the Catalyst 5500?" This type of diagram will always indicate the core layer.

Distribution Layer

The distribution layer's primary function is to act as the point for applying policy-based connectivity. It functions as the separation point between the core and access layers and helps to give shape to the core layer by defining and delineating the boundary between the core and itself. This can also be the point at which remote sites access the network. However, it is generally limited to large distributed networks because the access layer is the typical entry point into a network. The distinction between this and the access layer's "access" is simply scale. A large remote site will contain the access layer for the local users, feeding up into the regional location as the distribution layer.

The distribution layer provides a point at which to implement the following functions:

- Aggregation of addresses or areas
- Departmental and workgroup access
- Broadcast/multicast domain definition
- Policy implementations
- Security implementations
- Virtual LAN (VLAN) routing

- Media translations/transition
- Redistribution between routing domains
- Demarcation between static and dynamic routing protocols

A number of Cisco IOS software features are available to help implement policies at the distribution layer, including address filtering, port filtering, and other quality of service (QoS) tools. (These are examined in greater depth in Chapter 14.)

Access Layer

The access layer provides the connection point for users and workgroups to network resources. The layer at which users are allowed into the network, it is characterized by the following features:

- Shared and/or switched bandwidth
- MAC-layer filtering
- Microsegmentation

Microsegmentation uses LAN switches to divide collision domains and provide high bandwidth to individual workgroups. In a small office/home office (SOHO) environment, the access layer provides access to users via wide-area communications such as ISDN, Frame Relay, leased lines, and broadband. Additional features at this layer include dial-on-demand routing (DDR) and static routing. The dynamic routing protocols are more typically found in both the core and the distribution layers.

It is important to note that the access controls, policies, and security implemented at the higher distribution layer often flow down right into the access layer. As a result, you can manage and secure the user all the way throughout the network (as with the current initiatives regarding directory-enabled networking [DEN] and Cisco Networking Services for Active Directory [CNS/AD]).

When thinking of the hierarchical model, remember that all three layers are always *logically* present, even if they are not represented as separate distinct layers. A network can possess all three layers in a single device, or the layers can reside in several different devices and locations throughout the network.

Redundant Models

Certain organizations need very high reliability and minimal downtime in their infrastructure. These needs can range from critical systems to network routes that must be constantly available. Perhaps the best way to address these requirements as a network designer is through the use of redundancy.

The cost of a completely redundant and fault-tolerant internetwork infrastructure usually makes it cost-prohibitive for almost every organization. Therefore, you must be able to accurately determine the right level of redundancy needed in a particular network. You also need to be discriminating in your application of redundancy, applying it where it will provide the greatest benefit to the most critical areas of the network.

The following four categories of redundancy must be considered:

- Workstation-to-router redundancy
- Server redundancy
- Route redundancy
- Media redundancy

Workstation-to-Router Redundancy

Workstations that communicate with devices on different network segments need to interact with the local router. There are many possible methods available for workstations to know about this router:

- **Address Resolution Protocol (ARP)**   IP-based clients use ARP to resolve a MAC address to an IP address. Routers running proxy ARP will respond to the client's ARP query with the router's MAC address. Cisco routers run proxy ARP by default.

- **Static or explicit configuration**   Many IP-based clients will be configured with the static address of their default router. This is also referred to as the default gateway.

- **ICMP Router Discovery Protocol (IRDP)**   It is also possible for a workstation to use RDP over the Internet Control Messaging Protocol (ICMP) to receive hello multicasts and discover the correct router.

- **Routing protocols**   IP-based workstations can also run routing protocols, such as RIP and OSPF, to learn about routers. However, workstations should not operate these routing protocols in active mode.

- **IPX**   IPX-based workstations broadcast queries to locate servers and other network segments. Cisco routers can dynamically respond to these queries to facilitate this communication.

- **AppleTalk**   AppleTalk-based clients save the address of the router that sent the latest Routing Table Maintenance Protocol (RTMP) packet. The client will use this address for communication with other segments.

The most common of the preceding examples is the static configuration of a default gateway in an IP-based environment. However, this is also one of the least dynamic of the examples because most IP implementations don't support multiple default gateway addresses. If the configured default gateway router becomes unavailable, communications can be cut off. Of course, Cisco has addressed this issue by developing the *Hot Standby Router Protocol (HSRP)*.

HSRP allows you to continue configuring your workstations with a static router address for use as their default gateway. However, this address isn't a real address, represented by a physical router interface. Instead, it is the address of a *phantom router*. It is a single logical MAC and IP address configured by the network administrator as part of the HSRP implementation.

HSRP is very similar to some server clustering implementations. It allows two Cisco routers to present a virtual third router to users, eliminating a single point of failure. The routers use "hello" messages to communicate with each other and to determine which will be the active router and which will be the standby router. You can configure a particular router to have a higher priority than the other eligible routers, effectively selecting a certain router as your default active router.

One of the routers will act as the active router, maintaining both a virtual MAC address and a virtual IP address. The active router performs all the work of the phantom router until it fails or becomes unavailable. When this occurs, the standby router will stop receiving "hello" messages from the down router and take over as the new active router, performing all the tasks for the phantom router.

The real benefit that HSRP provides is the ability to configure client workstations with the single IP address of the HSRP phantom router as their default gateway. This provides excellent redundancy and fault tolerance to a network with an HSRP implementation. Figure 9-2 illustrates the HSRP configuration with a client using the HSRP router's IP address as its default gateway.

HSRP can be implemented with more than the minimum two routers required to provide even more redundancy for network segments. Figure 9-3 shows this type of configuration. HSRP will also continue to reply to ARP requests via proxy ARP. When the active HSRP router receives an ARP request for a device on a remote network, it will send the MAC address of the phantom router back to the requesting client.

FIGURE 9-2　　　HSRP providing a phantom router to LAN clients

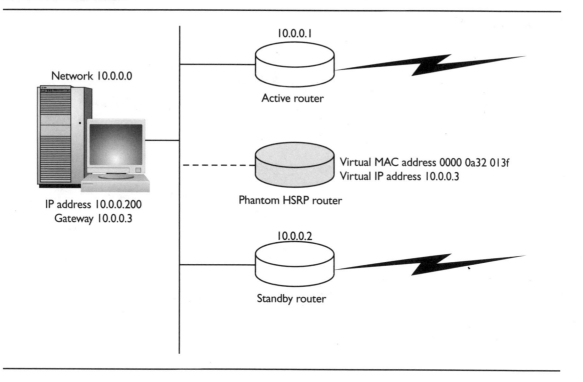

FIGURE 9-3   HSRP implementation with multiple routers

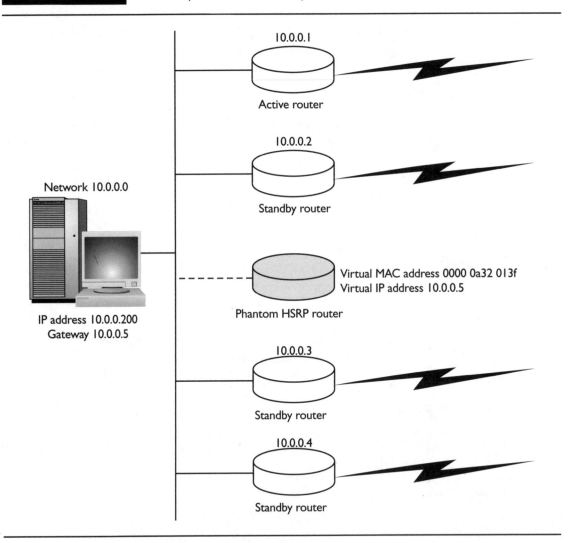

Server Redundancy

A number of different features can be built into or used for LAN servers to make them more redundant and fault tolerant. One of the most elemental is the use of multiple hard drives, which can be configured in a variety of ways to offer better redundancy:

- **Mirroring** This is the exact duplication of data across two drives.

- **Disk duplexing** The same as mirroring but using separate drive controllers, disk duplexing eliminates the chance that a single controller will fail and minimizes the possibility that both will fail at the same time.

- **Redundant array of inexpensive disks (RAID)** Although mirroring and duplexing are forms of RAID, most people think of RAID as involving more than two drives. The most common form of RAID is RAID-5, which is the striping of data across three or more drives, providing fault tolerance if one drive fails.

Servers may have other redundant features, such as redundant power supplies and redundant network interface cards (NICs) or network connections. Of course, it won't do any good if both NICs are connected to the same device and the device fails or loses power. Likewise, your power supplies should be connected to separate, independent sources of power.

Another form of redundancy is the use of server clustering. This typically involves two or more similar servers connected to each other by a private networking link for communications. The servers essentially mirror each other and will function as a single presence to the clients using their services. The servers will also fail services and applications over to each other if one server experiences problems or becomes unavailable.

As with most forms of redundancy, a greater cost is associated with the higher levels of redundancy. You must be able to design the appropriate level of fault tolerance into each situation. A brokerage firm or securities exchange, for which the cost of server downtime can easily reach into the millions of dollars per hour, would be good situations for the highest possible redundancy. A small bakery would likely not need fully redundant clustered servers to run its business.

Route Redundancy

If a remote IP-based client is using a local HSRP configuration and trying to reach the corporate server cluster but the WAN link is down, nothing has been accomplished! There are two strategies for addressing the redundancy of routes:

■ Load balancing

■ Minimizing downtime

Load Balancing Methods for providing load balancing vary with the protocol in use. For example, IPX and AppleTalk support only a single route to a remote location. They don't support any load balancing natively. However, you can "tweak" this on your Cisco routers for the IPX protocol with the command ipx maximum-paths.

IP routing protocols offer more functionality. Generally, you can use up to six parallel links with equivalent cost. The key to implementing redundant routes for load-balancing purposes is to keep bandwidth identical at each layer of the hierarchical model. This effectively keeps all paths to the same location at equal cost, making it straightforward to perform basic load balancing.

Hop-based routing protocols such as RIP will perform load balancing over links with dissimilar bandwidth costs. As traffic flows to the two links, it is balanced equally across both of them. The problem with this configuration is illustrated when the amount of traffic exceeds the slower of the two links. The "fatter" pipe is unable to pick up the additional traffic, so both links are limited to the throughput of the slower link. This is called *pinhole congestion*.

Pinhole congestion occurs when links of different capacities are used—for example, a T1 link and a 56KB link. As both links fill with traffic, the load is balanced across both links; but when the 56KB link becomes saturated, the T1 link will continue to carry only 56KB worth of traffic. The issue is that hop-based routing protocols don't have the ability to "sense" that the T1 link is vastly underutilized and can't send more traffic to this pipe. See Figure 9-4 for an illustration of pinhole congestion.

Two methods exist for eliminating pinhole congestion. The simpler method is to make sure that you design your networks using links of equal bandwidth at each layer of the hierarchical model. The other method is to

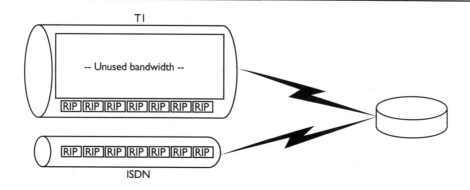

FIGURE 9-4   RIP routing protocol over different capacity links, causing pinhole congestion

employ routing protocols with the intelligence to dynamically adjust for varying bandwidth links. Cisco's proprietary EIGRP routing protocol can perform this type of load balancing across links with different bandwidths or metrics. Cisco calls this feature *variance*. IGRP can also load balance paths with different metrics, but Cisco designed EIGRP to improve on both IGRP and RIP.

IP load balancing also varies with the switching method used by the router. *Process switching* performs load balancing with each individual packet. The other switching methods (optimum, silicon, fast, distributed, autonomous and Cisco's NetFlow switching) perform their load balancing based on destination.

Minimizing Downtime   The second reason for implementing redundant routes is to minimize the downtime across internetworks. An additional reason for maintaining equal bandwidth within each layer of the hierarchical model is to improve the speed of network routing protocols' *convergence*. Convergence is the state achieved when all routers contain the same understanding of the network's topology in their routing tables after a change occurs. Convergence times can be minimized significantly if multiple equal-cost paths to the same location are used.

Convergence is related to the concept of *meshed* network topologies. There are two types of meshed networks: full mesh and partial mesh. A full-mesh network has a separate, individual link to every other router on the internetwork (see Figure 9-5). This design provides total redundancy and excellent performance because each router is only a single hop count away. However, the problem with deploying fully meshed internetworks is the large expense involved with all the links.

The formula for calculating the number of links needed to implement a full-mesh infrastructure is n(n-1)/2 where n is the number of routers to be used in the internetwork. This formula determines the number of links necessary to connect each router to every other router one time.

A full-mesh network with six routers would have 15 links, and the addition of a single router would add six more links, totaling 21 links! The expense in maintaining this exponential growth in router circuits may be more than most organizations wish to incur. Another scalability concern when large numbers of routers broadcast routing updates or other traffic to each other is that these router groups may become consumed with simply processing the broadcast traffic and actually have longer convergence times. Cisco recommends limiting broadcast traffic to 20 percent of the bandwidth available on each

FIGURE 9-5   Full-mesh network topology

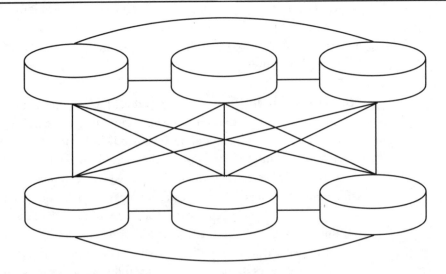

link to provide better control over the number of peer routers exchanging routing updates and service advertisements with each other.

A partial-mesh topology addresses these concerns well. By incorporating elements from both the hierarchical and the redundant models, a partial-mesh topology will help minimize the cost of links and control your routing update scheme. A partial mesh also prevents against total failure when an individual link or router is lost. Figure 9-6 illustrates a typical partial-mesh internetwork topology for a large organization.

Media Redundancy

The importance of redundancy extends to your media as well. The core of a switched hierarchical model is a perfect location for redundant links to each core device. Cisco prevents loops by employing the IEEE 802.1d spanning-tree algorithm. This algorithm ensures that only one path is active at any given time. A redundant link will become active only when the primary path becomes unavailable or gets too congested.

FIGURE 9-6   Classic partial-mesh topology

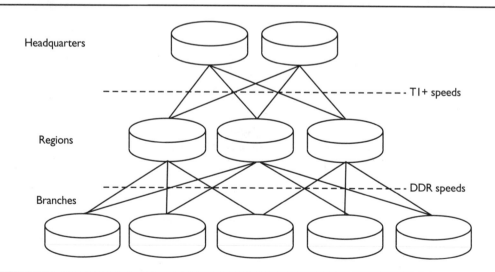

Because of the critical nature of most WAN environments, this is a common location for redundant media. By using backup links, you can help ensure that communications won't be lost with a single circuit failure. This differs from the previously mentioned multiple redundant equal-cost links within a particular layer of the hierarchical model. These backup links are typically not intended for load balancing traffic flow from site to site. They are usually provisioned as standby, fail-over types of circuits, generally providing lower bandwidth, and they will commonly employ a different technology from the primary link.

For example, a dial-up or ISDN line can act as a backup link to a Frame Relay T1 line. By using *floating static routes*, you can assign a higher administrative distance to the backup link. Because the backup DDR line is not normally active, it will be brought up only when the primary route is unavailable. You can thereby avoid the ongoing costs of two identical circuits if they are not needed for load-balancing purposes. Of course, when the primary route fails over to the backup, you likely won't have the same throughput capabilities as the primary link, but you won't lose communication with the other site, and this is the reason for using redundant backup media.

Secure Models

Security is one of the fundamental aspects of any good network design. You always want to protect customer data and systems, but the focus here is on controlling access to networks.

The Cisco IOS software provides a number of security-related features, such as encryption and access lists. We examine these in greater detail in Chapter 14. However, most secure topologies revolve around a firewall system. Firewalls are intended to provide protection for an internal network against unauthorized access from an untrusted network. They do this using two processes: blocking or preventing traffic, and passing or permitting traffic.

Because a firewall primarily filters traffic, you can build firewall systems using Cisco routers and employing packet filtering on the interfaces. Cisco has an IOS add-on called the Cisco IOS Firewall feature set that can make implementing firewall routers much easier. Cisco routers can be used as firewalls in the classic firewalling system—the *three-part firewall*.

FROM THE FIELD

An often-overlooked detail in dealing with backup links from site to site is the physical infrastructure underlying the actual circuits. This physical connectivity is almost always provided through an agreement or contract with a public carrier, such as AT&T, MCI, or Sprint. Because this infrastructure is frequently resold or utilized by the competitive local exchange carriers (CLECs), you often don't really know what carrier is servicing your physical circuits.

The reason this is so important was clearly illustrated to me one day a few years ago. I had designed a small WAN infrastructure for a company, using Cisco routers and Frame Relay circuits from 10 different regional locations. I worked with the CLECs, servicing all the sites to provision and connect the necessary circuits into the Frame Relay cloud. I then configured and installed all the router equipment and brought up all the links.

Things had been running nicely for a few months when I received a phone call from the company's president, asking if I could go to the site to help with a problem. When I arrived, I learned that the primary T1 circuit from the headquarters location was down and that the ISDN backup line had not come up. Because I had personally configured and deployed this equipment, I felt a certain responsibility to figure out the problem.

After spending some time looking over the router settings, I was stumped. Everything seemed to be configured correctly, yet the backup link hadn't come up properly. I decided to investigate the cause of the Frame Relay failure. This course of action proved to be insightful when I discovered that a backhoe had severed a bundle of underground cabling nearby. This cabling carried the company's Frame Relay circuit, but I knew that the ISDN link was laid elsewhere to prevent exactly this sort of situation! This realization prompted a call to the local carrier's offices.

After several minutes of fruitless discussion, I asked for further details regarding the circuits. I then learned what was causing the complete outage for my customer. Unfortunately, both the T1 and the ISDN circuits were provisioned to use the same national carrier. Of course, the cabling that had been cut was not the CLEC's, but one of the national carrier's trunks. So even though I had planned ahead for a Frame Relay outage, I wasn't aware that the backup circuit ran over the same carrier's physical infrastructure.

After some sheepish grins and some apologetic remarks, I explained the reason for the failure. Fortunately, the customer didn't blame me directly for the oversight. The cabling was quickly repaired, and the company was back to business as usual after a few hours. The lesson has stayed with me, and when dealing with WAN links now, I always make sure that my backup circuits will function as intended—over a different carrier's lines.

Three-Part Firewall System

As the name implies, the three-part firewall system uses three parts, or layers:

- An outside filter
- The isolation LAN
- An inside filter

In this scheme, the outside filter provides basic packet filtration, allowing particular traffic types to pass into the isolation LAN. The isolation LAN is also sometimes referred to as the *demilitarized zone,* or *DMZ.* This buffer zone between the external and the internal networks is where you place systems that need to be accessed by external or untrusted users. These systems are called *bastion* hosts. Bastion hosts are secured hosts that external users need to access. They typically provide only a limited number of applications or services. Examples of a bastion host are a Web server, e-mail server, or DNS server. Finally, the inside filter provides the strongest security, controlling access from the isolation LAN to the internal network. Figure 9-7 illustrates the three-part firewall system.

The isolation LAN is treated as a separate subnetwork and should be addressed differently from the internal network. This helps keep the networks separated and makes it easier to advertise routes into just the isolation LAN via the outside filter. Doing so completely hides the internal network, and external users can see only the limited services and applications you have made available in the isolation LAN.

A common configuration would be allowing internal users to have access to the Internet but preventing any inbound access from the outside. The first step is to permit outbound TCP traffic from the internal network. But how do you permit these users to receive the data, such as Web pages, that they have requested? You need to identify the communication exchanges that have originated from within your secured network and permit this return traffic to pass. At the same time, you want to prevent traffic from flowing into the network if it originated from outside the network because

FIGURE 9-7   Three-part firewall system

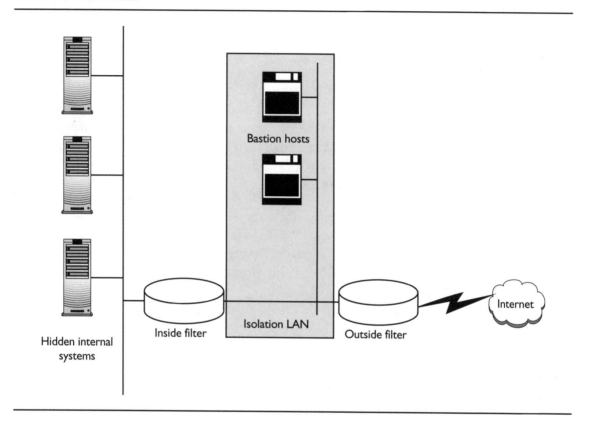

it could indicate an attempt by a cracker or hacker trying to establish a TCP session with an internal host.

The solution to this dilemma is to screen for either ACK or RST bits in the packets. If TCP packets have either the ACK or RST bits set, this indicates that the traffic originated within the network. Cisco uses the *established* keyword to indicate that these bits have been set. All other incoming TCP packets should be blocked because they are not *established* sessions. Again, this can indicate an external threat trying to establish a session with one of the internal hosts.

A summary of this configuration in the three-part firewall system is as follows:

- Allow inbound TCP packets from established sessions on the inside packet filter router.
- Allow inbound TCP packets from established sessions on the outside packet filter router.
- Allow inbound packets from the outside packet filter router to specific TCP and UDP ports on specific bastion hosts. (Don't forget to permit TCP SYN packets here; these are used to establish sessions.)

Don't allow connections to the outside packet filter router. This is a prime target for individuals trying to break into the network. Also, prevent inbound traffic directly from this filter. If it becomes compromised, it should not be permitted to directly access anything else in the internal network.

Keep your bastion hosts and packet filter routers as simple as possible. Introducing unnecessary complexity can provide more opportunities for bugs or problems. By running as few applications and services as possible, you can have better control over the security aspects of these boxes. This is particularly true for bastion hosts providing services to the outside world: fewer applications, fewer potential holes.

Finally, your outside packet filter is your first line of defense. Treat it as such by disabling any unnecessary services on this box. Cisco recommends the following to minimize your outside packet filter's exposure:

- Disable Telnet access.
- Don't define any virtual terminals on the router.
- Use only static routes.
- Don't use the outside packet filter as a TFTP server.
- Disable proxy ARP.

- Disable finger service.
- Disable IP redirection.
- Disable IP route caching.
- Use password encryption.
- Don't use the outside packet filter as a MAC IP server.

Following these suggestions will help ensure a more secure three-part firewall implementation.

CiscoSecure PIX Firewall

Configuring packet-filtering devices for a three-part firewall system can be complex and involved, providing abundant opportunities for misconfiguration and weak spots in this scheme. A better solution exists in true hardware-based firewall devices, such as the CiscoSecure PIX Firewall (formerly known as the Cisco PIX Firewall).

The CiscoSecure PIX Firewall is an integrated hardware/software platform that delivers the highest enterprise-level performance and security. The CiscoSecure PIX Firewall offers several advantages over packet-filtering devices:

- It is far more robust and scalable.
- It is less complex (making it easier to configure a comprehensive security policy).
- It requires no downtime to install.
- No upgrading of routers is required to implement CiscoSecure PIX Firewall.
- No ongoing reconfiguration or daily management is required.

Many organizations today rely on proxy-based firewalls, which have their limitations. Because these systems operate at the application level, they suffer from slower performance; a reliance on expensive, general-purpose platforms; a lack of scalability, redundancy, and fault tolerance; and the security problems inherent in third-party operating systems. The CiscoSecure PIX Firewall includes a number of key features that help position it as the best choice for comprehensive enterprisewide security:

- The CiscoSecure PIX Firewall uses a secure, real-time, non-UNIX, embedded system for operations. This eliminates the security risks that can result from using a general-purpose operating system and helps provide outstanding performance and scalability—up to 256,000 simultaneous connections. Administrators are also provided with detailed auditing and transaction logging, which are crucial to assessing and responding to potential risk situations.

- It provides *stateful inspection* of packets, using the *adaptive security algorithm (ASA)*. ASA provides better performance and scalability than application-level proxy firewalls by creating and maintaining session flows based on source/destination addresses, port numbers, TCP sequence numbers, and other TCP packet flags. This information is stored in a table and is referenced against all inbound and outbound traffic to either permit or deny network access.

- The CiscoSecure PIX Firewall uses a method called *cut-through proxy* to deliver the highest performance and speed possible. By querying a TACACS+ or RADIUS server for user authentication information, the CiscoSecure PIX Firewall can allow verified sessions to flow without further impediment or verification. In contrast, an application-level proxy must continue to examine every packet that traverses its path. By maintaining session-state information, the CiscoSecure PIX Firewall delivers transparent and low overhead access to users.

- The CiscoSecure PIX Firewall also takes advantage of *network address translation (NAT)*. With NAT, you can allow internal users to have access to important external resources while still preventing unauthorized access from the outside world.

- The CiscoSecure PIX Firewall is a very extensible platform, supporting many options, including the Private Link card (supports data encryption between PIX systems across public networks using data encryption standard) and the PIX Firewall IPSec encryption card (allows for virtual private networking, or VPN).

The CiscoSecure PIX Firewall offers many other benefits. It can be deployed in a fail-over/hot-standby configuration with two CiscoSecure PIX Firewalls running in parallel. If one fails, the other will maintain a secured environment. It provides centralized configuration and management through a Java-based GUI tool, the PIX Firewall Manager. It also allows for easier setup and initial configuration with the PIX Firewall Setup Wizard.

Advantages, Disadvantages, Scalability Issues, and Applicability

Each of the models examined so far has its benefits and drawbacks. The following sections look at each model and its characteristics.

Hierarchical Model

The benefits of the hierarchical model are vast. Using a layered approach facilitates change and limits the scope to a subset of the network. Layers also make the network easier to manage and understand. It is easier to troubleshoot and diagnose failures within the network when it is structured as a hierarchy. By maintaining a hierarchical design, you can take advantage of advanced features such as route summarization, which provides increases in network speed and responsiveness. Scalability is inherent to the hierarchical model, and it can be used in networks of all sizes.

Disadvantages are difficult to find in the hierarchical model. A poor design could permit the failure of the entire core layer, thereby bringing down the whole network. However, when designed and implemented skillfully, the hierarchical model is without peer.

Redundant Model

The main benefits of the redundant model are its fault tolerance and resiliency. It provides the ability to design nonstop network infrastructures by minimizing or eliminating single points of failure. There is room for some type of redundancy in networks of all sizes, but the level of redundancy typically increases with the size and importance of a network. Because the different aspects of redundancy are modular in nature, the redundant model can scale very well to fit the needs of even the largest organizations. Of course, redundancy costs money, and the most redundant models, such as a full-mesh internetwork topology, can be oppressively expensive.

Secure Model

The benefits of a secure model are obvious; for instance, it protects against intruders and maintains critical corporate data. When used in conjunction with a solid hierarchical network design, the secure model can be used efficiently as a network grows and expands.

The downsides of security are the additional cost and maintenance involved with security systems, and the fact that *all* security is relative. No system or network is ever totally secured. Nevertheless, security should be applied to virtually every network. Too many small organizations feel that they have little to risk by not protecting their network and internal systems. However, statistics show that the majority of these companies will fail or go out of business shortly after suffering a major attack or loss of corporate data. Not being prepared exposes a company to more risk than it usually acknowledges.

QUESTIONS AND ANSWERS

We currently have a medium-sized network, but we predict explosive growth in the future. What type of network design will provide for this level of scalability?	The hierarchical model will scale to suit this type of network expansion and growth.
I don't want to have any downtime between two particular sites on my WAN, but I can't afford two full-time TI links. What can I do?	Consider implementing a second link as a DDR line, with either a standard telephone line or an ISDN circuit.
I have a Web server that I want to protect while still permitting users to access the Web site. What can I do?	Implement a three-part firewall scheme and place the Web server in the isolation LAN or DMZ.
I need the most effective security solution to protect against Internet hackers. What is my best option?	The CiscoSecure PIX Firewall provides the most secure solution.

CERTIFICATION SUMMARY

This chapter examines the three network topologies: hierarchical, redundant, and secure. Each model offers unique benefits and provides different reasons for its incorporation into design plans. The network design process is critical to the success of the network, and choices based on these models will continue to deliver as promised for many years. Good network design principles can be summarized as follows:

- Always eliminate single points of failure. Redundancy encompasses both load balancing of traffic and backup route availability.

- Keep bandwidth consistent at each layer of the network and ensure the availability of this bandwidth.

- Use the hierarchical model whenever possible. Incorporating layers and modularity results in a scalable, fast network.

- Secure the network. Security is crucial to the ongoing success of a good network design.

The integration of performance, security, capacity, and scalability into your networks is the ultimate goal. By following the models discussed in this chapter, you can have the requirements for a well-designed network covered. In fact, the best networks share one common trait: they include aspects of all three models. By using a combination of the models, these networks will deliver the best performance, fault tolerance, security, capacity, and scalability possible.

 # TWO-MINUTE DRILL

- ❏ Performance, security, capacity, and scalability are the most common customer requirements.
- ❏ The three topologies are the hierarchical, redundant, and secure models.
- ❏ Using a hierarchical model in network design allows you to build networks using layers.

❑ A layered structure makes the network easier to understand, manage, change, and scale.

❑ The three layers in the hierarchical model are core, distribution, and access.

❑ The layers are logical layers rather than physical layers.

❑ The core layer is the high-speed switching backbone of the network and should be highly redundant and fault tolerant.

❑ The core layer provides optimal transport between sites.

❑ Don't perform packet processing or filtering at the core.

❑ The distribution layer provides policy-based connectivity.

❑ Address filtering, port filtering, and media translations/transition occur at the distribution layer.

❑ The access layer provides the connection point to network resources for users and workgroups.

❑ The access layer typically has shared and/or switched bandwidth, MAC-layer filtering, and microsegmentation.

❑ All three layers can reside within a single device.

❑ The four categories of redundancy are workstation to router, server, route, and media.

❑ HSRP uses a phantom router to provide redundancy to IP-based clients.

❑ One router will act as the active HSRP router, maintaining both a virtual MAC address and a virtual IP address.

❑ HSRP will reply to ARP requests via proxy ARP.

❑ Disk mirroring is the exact duplication of data across two drives.

❑ The two strategies for addressing the redundancy of routes are balancing load and minimizing downtime.

❑ IPX and AppleTalk support only a single route to a remote location and don't support any native load balancing.

❑ Keep bandwidth identical at every layer of the hierarchical model for load balancing.

❑ Using hop-based routing protocols to perform load balancing over unequal bandwidth paths can cause pinhole congestion.

❑ Convergence is the state achieved when all routers contain the same understanding of the network's topology in their routing tables after a change occurs.

❑ Convergence times can be minimized significantly through the use of multiple equal-cost paths to the same location.

❑ The two types of meshed networks are full mesh and partial mesh.

❑ Full-mesh networks are usually cost prohibitive to implement and maintain.

❑ Limit broadcast traffic to 20 percent of the bandwidth available on each link.

❑ Partial-mesh networks solve many of the issues of a full-mesh network.

❑ The IEEE 802.1d spanning-tree algorithm ensures that only one path is active at any given time.

❑ Backup links are usually standby, fail-over types of circuits, generally providing lower bandwidth and frequently using a technology different from that of the primary link.

❑ Backup links prevent the loss of communication when the primary circuit becomes unavailable.

❑ Firewalls are intended to provide protection for an internal network against unauthorized access from an untrusted network.

❑ The classic firewall system is called the three-part firewall.

❑ The three-part firewall consists of an outside filter, the isolation LAN, and an inside filter.

❑ The outside filter provides basic packet filtration, allowing particular traffic types to pass into the isolation LAN.

❑ The isolation LAN is a buffer zone between the external and the internal networks and is where bastion hosts are placed.

❑ Web servers, e-mail servers, and DNS servers are examples of bastion hosts and should be in the isolation LAN or DMZ.

❑ The inside filter controls access from the isolation LAN to the internal network.

❑ Ensure that only established sessions are permitted to pass traffic back into the internal network.

❏ Don't allow connections to or traffic directly from the outside packet filter router.

❏ Minimize the applications and services provided by the isolation LAN's bastion hosts.

❏ The outside packet filter should provide few services: no Telnet, no proxy ARP, no TFTP, no dynamic routes, and so on.

❏ The CiscoSecure PIX Firewall is an integrated hardware/software platform that delivers the highest enterprise-level performance and security.

❏ The CiscoSecure PIX Firewall provides stateful inspection of packets, not application-level proxy services.

❏ The CiscoSecure PIX Firewall can take advantage of NAT to hide the addresses of your internal hosts.

SELF TEST

The following Self Test questions will help you measure your understanding of the material presented in this chapter. Read all the choices carefully because there may be more than one correct answer. Choose all correct answers for each question.

1. What are the three network models?

    A. Small, medium, and large

    B. Split horizon, poison reverse, and hold-down timer

    C. Secure, hierarchical, and redundant

    D. Distance vector, link state, and spanning tree

2. Identify the correct statement regarding the hierarchical layers.

    A. The access layer provides policy-based connectivity.

    B. The core layer provides optimal transport between sites.

    C. The distribution layer provides user access to the network.

    D. The access layer is the demarcation point between the core and distribution layers.

3. Where should you expand a network and add a new site?

    A. Core

    B. Distribution

    C. Access

    D. Backbone

4. Complete this statement: The hierarchical model for network design . . .

    A. Provides a guideline for only very large internetworks (typically over 5,000 nodes).

    B. Defines the number of hops permitted in a WAN environment.

    C. Makes implementing changes difficult because the core layer should remain static in size.

    D. Complicates network management procedures and methods.

    E. Allows scalable internetwork design.

5. Which of the following is *not* performed through the hierarchical model's distribution layer?

    A. Workstation connections and updates

    B. Differentiation between static and dynamic routing updates

    C. Application of policies

    D. VLAN routing

6. What variable can RIP use?

   A. Load

   B. Hop count

   C. Link cost

   D. Internetwork delay

7. Which layer is characterized by shared and/or switched bandwidth, MAC-layer filtering, and microsegmentation?

   A. Core

   B. Distribution

   C. Access

   D. Hierarchical

8. Proxy ARP on a Cisco router will assist which of the following remote clients?

   A. An IP client configured with a default gateway

   B. An AppleTalk client running RTMP

   C. An IP client configured to perform broadcasts

   D. An IPX client broadcasting Find Network Number queries

9. Three Cisco routers configured for an HSRP implementation present what to clients? (Choose all that apply.)

   A. One MAC address and one IP address

   B. Three MAC addresses and one IP address

   C. Three MAC addresses and three IP addresses

   D. Two MAC addresses and two IP addresses

   E. One MAC address and three IP addresses

10. Mirroring, duplexing, and clustering refer to what type of redundancy?

    A. Workstation/router redundancy

    B. Load balancing

    C. Media redundancy

    D. Server redundancy

11. Select the appropriate scenario for total server redundancy. (Choose all that apply.)

    A. The NASDAQ stock exchange

    B. A large international bank

    C. North American Aerospace Defense Command (NORAD)

    D. A five-store dry-cleaning chain

    E. All of the above

12. What is the best way to provide WAN load balancing?

    A. Always use a hop-based routing protocol like RIP.

    B. Be sure to use links of varying bandwidth (like ISDN with T1) to prevent pinhole congestion.

    C. Use Cisco's EIGRP to provide the best load-balancing solution.

    D. Ensure that bandwidth remains consistent (equal-cost paths) at each layer of the network.

13. EIGRP was designed to improve which two routing protocols?

    A. OSPF

    B. RIP

    C. NLSP

    D. IGRP

14. Taylor maintains a WAN for the Ohio Department of Education. This internetwork currently connects eight locations in a full-mesh topology using a combination of Cisco 2500 and 4000 series routers and Frame Relay circuits. She has been asked to add two more district locations to the WAN. How many new links must she implement to maintain the existing topology?

    A. 2

    B. 8

    C. 16

    D. 17

    E. 20

    F. 28

The following case study examines a customer network and the specifications of the current design, as well as the planned changes.

FiltraGen is a biomedical research company based in Chicago. It currently uses an IBM ES9000 for all of its research data. This computer is connected to the main corporate LAN, a Token Ring with TN3270 terminals, and PCs. A second location in Miami connects via a point-to-point circuit and supports 40 SNA-based terminals.

Four hundred sixty-five PCs will reside at the Chicago location, distributed across multiple segments. The plan will be to replace all of the 238 existing TN3270 terminals at the Chicago location with PCs and to move the network to an Ethernet architecture. The mainframe will remain in place and continue to serve data via 3270 emulation over TCP/IP as well as SNA for the Miami location. This will allow FiltraGen to eliminate all SNA traffic from its Chicago LAN. The point-to-point circuit will be replaced with a T1 link.

The company's LAN administrator, Gabriel, has implemented three Microsoft Windows NT servers for file and print services and has standardized on Microsoft Exchange for an additional server as the e-mail platform for the company. He would like to add one additional server each for the sales, accounting, and shipping departments for file and print purposes. He would also like to begin providing Internet access to the corporate users across the T1 circuit.

As part of the move to Ethernet, the company has decided to use a Cisco Catalyst 5500 switch to segment the different portions of the network. A Windows NT Workstation will be connected to this switch as a management workstation. The mainframe's front-end processor (FEP) will bypass this switch as well as the router and connect directly into the WAN circuit.

Gabriel's manager, Lian, is concerned about the availability of the WAN link because Miami should not lose access to the data on the corporate mainframe. However, in your discussions with her, you have sensed some financial limitations to the redundancy of this circuit.

FiltraGen has retained you as a network consultant to assist with finalizing plans and to implement the new network architecture. Answer questions 15 to 18 based on the scenario presented.

15. How many NT servers will be in the FiltraGen proposed network design?

    A. 3

    B. 4

    C. 6

    D. 7

    E. 8

16. Refer to the FiltraGen case study. What does the following illustration represent?

   A. A high-level topology of the current network

   B. A high-level topology of the proposed network

   C. A business-process packet flow diagram

   D. An e-mail traffic packet flow diagram

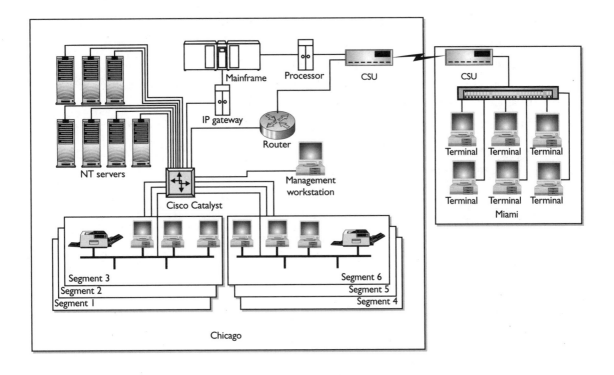

17. Refer to the FiltraGen case study. What does the Cisco Catalyst switch in the preceding illustration represent?

    A. The access layer

    B. The distribution layer

    C. The core layer

    D. The isolation portion of a three-part firewall system

18. Refer to the FiltraGen case study. Given Lian's concerns about the Miami location, what would be the best solution for you to propose?

    A. Implement a second T1 link to provide redundancy.

    B. Implement a second T1 link to provide redundancy and configure for simultaneous load balancing of traffic across both links.

    C. Implement a second router at the Chicago site and configure HSRP to provide redundancy.

    D. Implement a DDR or ISDN link with a floating static route.

19. Cisco recommends limiting broadcast traffic to what percentage of total WAN bandwidth?

    A. 20

    B. 40

    C. 50

    D. 60

20. In the three-part firewall system, where is the appropriate location for a public Web server?

    A. Behind the inside filter.

    B. Inside the isolation LAN.

    C. Outside the outside filter.

    D. You shouldn't use a firewall with a public Web server; you will prevent access by external users.

21. Identify the correct statements regarding the outside packet filter in the three-part firewall system. (Choose all that apply.)

    A. Permit connections to the outside packet filter router.

    B. Deny inbound TCP packets from established sessions.

    C. Disable proxy ARP.

    D. Use static routes only.

    E. Permit TFTP services.

22. Identify the correct features regarding the CiscoSecure PIX Firewall. (Choose all that apply.)

    A. The CiscoSecure PIX Firewall provides NAT functionality to protect internal addressing schemes.

    B. The CiscoSecure PIX Firewall provides stateful packet inspection at the application level by using the adaptive security algorithm (ASA).

    C. The CiscoSecure PIX Firewall is a hardware-only platform that can run a variety of UNIX operating systems.

    D. The CiscoSecure PIX Firewall can take advantage of external user authentication systems to provide a cut-through proxy functionality at the session layer.

    E. All of the above.

SELF TEST ANSWERS

1. ☑ **C.** Secure, hierarchical, and redundant are the three network types.
   ☒ **A** is incorrect because it simply doesn't apply. **B** lists methods of dealing with routing table updates, and **D** lists different routing protocols.

2. ☑ **B.** The core layer provides optimal transport between sites.
   A, **C**, and **D** are incorrect because the access layer provides user and workgroup access, and the distribution layer provides policy-based connectivity. The distribution layer is the demarcation point between the core and the *access* layers.

3. ☑ **B.** Scaling the network should occur at the distribution layer.
   ☒ **A** is incorrect because the core needs to remain at a fixed size, and **C** is incorrect because the access layer is where users and workgroups gain access. **D** is incorrect because the backbone can refer to the core layer or be a part of the core layer.

4. ☑ **E.** The hierarchical model allows scalable internetwork design.
   ☒ **A** is incorrect because the hierarchical model applies to networks of all sizes. **B** is incorrect because this model doesn't relate to the number of hops. **C** and **D** are incorrect because the hierarchical model actually makes changes and management easier, not more difficult or complicated.

5. ☑ **A.** Workstation connections and updates occur at the access layer.
   ☒ **B**, **C**, and **D** are incorrect because all of them are valid distribution layer functions.

6. ☑ **B.** RIP is a hop-based protocol.
   ☒ **A**, **C**, and **D** are incorrect because RIP can't use delay, load, or cost in performing route selections.

7. ☑ **C.** These are characteristics of the access layer.

8. ☑ **C.** An IP client configured to perform broadcasts will receive the Cisco router's MAC address in response to a broadcast ARP query.
   ☒ **A** is incorrect because IP-based clients that use a default gateway don't rely on broadcasts to locate devices on remote segments. **B** and **D** are incorrect because AppleTalk clients and IPX clients don't use Proxy ARP.

9. ☑ **A.** Cisco routers configured for an HSRP implementation present clients with one MAC address and one IP address. Regardless of the number of routers involved, HSRP presents a single MAC and IP address to the clients.

10. ☑ **D.** Server redundancy can employ these features. Mirroring and duplexing refer to physical disk control and operations, and clustering presents duplicate servers as a single logical server to clients.

11. ☑ **A, B, and C.** Total server redundancy is most applicable in critical situations in which downtime cannot be tolerated, whether for reason of cost or other reasons.
    ☒ **D** is incorrect because downtime in such a small business would likely not be critical. **E** is incorrect because D is not appropriate.

12. ☑ **D.** Ensure that bandwidth remains consistent (equal-cost paths) at each layer of the network to provide WAN load balancing.
    ☒ **A** is incorrect because hop-based protocols can't load balance, and **B** is incorrect because links of varying bandwidth are always undesirable. **C** is incorrect because, although EIGRP can definitely balance traffic over links of varying speed, it is not the best solution (even though it is a proprietary Cisco feature).

13. ☑ **B and D.** Both RIP and IGRP are distance vector protocols.
    ☒ **A and C** are incorrect because OSPF NLSP are link-state protocols. EIGRP combines the best features of both distance vector and link-state protocols.

14. ☑ **D.** The correct answer is 17 new links. The formula for a full-mesh topology is $n(n-1)/2$: $8(8-1)/2 = 17$.

15. ☑ **D.** Seven NT servers will be in the FiltraGen proposed network design.

16. ☑ **B.** This high-level topology of the proposed network shows the proposed Catalyst switch as well as the additional servers and the lack of TN3270 terminals.
    ☒ **A and D** are incorrect because, although the case study discussed both the current network and the e-mail system, these are not represented in the diagram. **C** is incorrect because the diagram also doesn't show the business-process packet flow.

17. ☑ **C.** The core layer is represented by the Cisco Catalyst switch in the diagram.
    ☒ **A, B, and D** are incorrect because the switch doesn't function as the access layer or as the distribution layer, and there is no three-part firewall system in the diagram.

18. ☑ **D.** Implementing a DDR or ISDN link with a floating static route to Miami would be the best solution for FiltraGen. This solution addresses her concerns about loss of connectivity as well as the ongoing costs.
    ☒ **A and B** are incorrect because a second T1 link doesn't address Lian's cost concerns and it adds an unneeded feature, load balancing. **C** is incorrect because a second router with HSRP doesn't address the availability of the WAN link.

19. ☑ **A.** Twenty percent is the maximum recommended WAN bandwidth for broadcast traffic.

20. ☑ **B.** Bastion hosts, like Web servers, belong inside the isolation LAN or DMZ.
    ☒ **A, C,** and **D** are incorrect because placing the server behind the inside filter will actually prevent access by external users. Placing it outside the outside filter will not provide any security for the server.

21. ☑ **C and D.** The key is to keep this filter as simple and stripped down as possible.
    ☒ **A** and **E** are incorrect because the opposite statements are true. **B** is incorrect because it indicates denying "established" sessions, but these are the sessions that should be permitted for access to the isolation LAN.

22. ☑ **A and D.** The CiscoSecure PIX Firewall provides both NAT and cut-through proxy functionality.
    ☒ **B** and **C** are incorrect because, although the CiscoSecure PIX Firewall *does* provide stateful packet inspection by using the adaptive security algorithm (ASA), it does this at the session layer, not the application layer. This provides greater speed and efficiency over proxy-type firewalls. The CiscoSecure PIX Firewall is an integrated hardware/software combination that runs a secure, embedded, non-UNIX operating system to help avoid the issues inherent in additionally securing a general-purpose operating system.

CISCO CERTIFIED DESIGN ASSOCIATE

10

Choosing the Best Equipment Based Upon Design Criteria: LANs

CERTIFICATION OBJECTIVES

Through the previous chapters, you have learned how to characterize existing networks, identify and help the customer understand network design issues, and begin the process of envisioning a possible solution. This chapter goes even deeper into the details of LAN architectures and their specifications.

This chapter is very important in the process of trying to gain a better understanding of how to accurately recommend and design particular LAN architectures and technologies for your customers. Without fully realizing the implications of these choices, you could inadvertently paint the customer (and ourselves) into a corner.

CERTIFICATION OBJECTIVE 10.01

Scalability Constraints and Issues for Standard LAN Technologies

Each of the major LAN architectures has its own associated constraints and planning considerations, from the type of media that can be used to the relative performance characteristics. Remember that there are three underlying basic areas in which you can categorize customers' problems:

- **Media** Problems of this type are caused by excessive Ethernet collisions and token latency or delay in Token Ring and FDDI networks. These problems are generally the result of too many active devices on the wire.

- **Protocol** Inefficient protocols that don't scale very well or rely on a great deal of broadcasts are perfect examples of causes of protocol problems.

- **Transport** These issues are related to the need for more bandwidth. Many of today's networks carry demanding traffic, such as video and voice/data integration. These high-bandwidth applications require more than is usually available on your customers' networks.

Media problems are typically addressed with the use of switches to divide a network into individual segments. For protocol problems, it is best to use routers to isolate broadcast domains and perform the translation necessary between different architectures. Finally, the best way to solve transport-related problems is to implement a higher-bandwidth technology like Gigabit Ethernet, switched Fast Ethernet, or FDDI.

CERTIFICATION OBJECTIVE 10.02

Cisco Products and LAN Technologies Meeting Customers' Requirements

It is essential for any good network designer to understand the characteristics and requirements of the underlying networking technologies. We examine the three major technologies in use today so that you can get a better idea of how to best utilize each to its fullest:

- Ethernet
- Token Ring
- FDDI/CDDI

We examine the advantages, disadvantages, and characteristics of each technology; the physical media involved; and the distance and scalability limitations. We also discuss the hardware to use with each standard.

Ethernet

Ethernet is perhaps the most prevalent LAN technology in use today. Ethernet was invented in 1972 by Bob Metcalfe during his work at the Xerox Palo Alto Research Center (PARC) in California. A consortium, comprising Digital Equipment Corporation, Intel, and Xerox (DIX), later standardized Ethernet. Finally, in 1983, the Institute of Electrical and Electronics Engineers (IEEE) ratified Ethernet as a standard, designating it IEEE 802.3, or the IEEE 10Base5 standard.

Types of Ethernet and Their Limitations

Officially, there are five standards for the physical- and Media Access Control (MAC)–layer implementation of 10-Mbps Ethernet. However, we will examine only four of these because the fifth uses broadband transmission technology and is virtually nonexistent in today's networks. Those four are

- 10Base5
- 10Base2
- 10BaseT
- 10BaseF

Additionally, there are a number of standards for 100-Mbps Ethernet at the physical and MAC layer. 100BaseT is also referred to as Fast Ethernet. We will look at the two that are covered by the CCDA exam:

- 100BaseT
- 100BaseFX

Finally, we will examine Gigabit Ethernet.

Ethernet defines two types of devices to be connected to the wire: data terminal equipment (DTE) and repeaters. DTEs are either network interface cards (NICs) or switched port connections—essentially anything that provides an endpoint or electrical termination of the cable. In contrast, repeaters don't terminate the electrical signals on the network cable. Instead, they retransmit or propagate the signals onward.

Scalability Issues

There is a common rule of thumb used in designing Ethernet networks, often referred to as the *5,4,3,2,1 rule* (see Figure 10-1). It states

5. The number of segments allowed

4. The number of repeaters allowed

3. The number of segments populated with nodes

2. The number of segments that shouldn't contain any nodes (These segments would simply be used as interrepeater connections to physically extend the reach of the network.)

1. The single large *collision domain* created

FIGURE 10-1 Illustration of the 5-4-3-2-1 rule

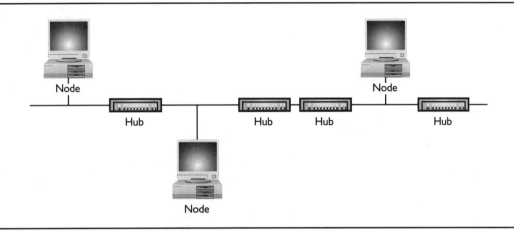

This rule is by no means absolute. Nevertheless, it is very functional, and you should always take it into consideration as a general guideline when designing your networks.

First-Come, First-Served Methodology

Ethernet uses the MAC-layer specification known as *CSMA/CD (Carrier Sense Multiple Access with Collision Detection)*. This is best thought of as a contention-based method wherein each device contends with all other devices for the ability to transmit data on the network. CSMA/CD works as follows:

1. Each device must first listen for other activity on the wire to ensure that the network is available.

2. If the wire is quiet, the device may then initiate its transmission of data.

3. If the device detects other traffic, it will continue to listen for a quiet window to begin its own transmission.

4. A collision may still occur on the wire if two or more devices make the determination to transmit data at the same moment. This will prevent any of the transmissions from succeeding because the frames

would be dropped. Ethernet provides good collision-detection and handling capabilities.

5. If a collision occurs, a jamming signal will be flooded onto the wire. This ensures that all devices are aware of the collision event and won't try to initiate transmissions themselves.

6. The devices involved in the collision are reset with a back-off timer. This algorithm sets a random time frame for each device to wait before attempting retransmission.

A collision domain is sometimes also referred to as a *broadcast domain*. Remember that all nodes in a broadcast or collision domain compete for the network's resources and bandwidth. Ethernet is very good for short, bursty transmissions, but an Ethernet network can reach the level of saturation when it maintains 40 percent utilization over periods of time. At this point, consider using switches to segment the network.

Many protocols commonly in use today rely on broadcast and multicast traffic to locate, use, or advertise resources on the network. These broadcasts and multicasts will still cross hubs, switches, and bridges, allowing continued network functionality without the need for a redesign when these devices are considered.

Broadcast radiation is the term used to describe how broadcast traffic on a network radiates outward from the originator to all other nodes on all parts of a *flat network*. A flat network is a switched or bridged network that isn't divided by routers. Each node in a flat network must examine the traffic passing by on the network to determine if it is intended for itself or another node. In a large flat network, this can cause excessive processing to take place at each node. When broadcast or multicast traffic accounts for more than 20 percent of the network's traffic, the performance of the LAN suffers.

Table 10-1 illustrates some recommendations as to the number of nodes per flat network, listed by protocol.

One leading advantage of switching technology is the ability to eliminate collisions from your network. A switch provides a dedicated point-to-point connection between a switch port and the device connected to it. This serves two purposes: collisions no longer occur because the device is the only entity attempting to transmit and receive on the channel; and bandwidth on each port is dedicated to that device alone.

TABLE 10-1	Protocol	Maximum Number of Nodes
Scalability of Flat Networks by Protocol	IP	500
	IPX	300
	NetBEUI	200
	AppleTalk	200
	Mixed Protocols	200

This provides for an additional benefit of switching, or the ability to run devices in *full-duplex* mode. Normal Ethernet devices operate in *half-duplex* mode. Only one device at any time may transmit while the others must listen and wait. The wire carries traffic in only one direction at a time.

Full-duplex mode permits each device to use one of its two wire pairs to transmit while using the other pair to receive simultaneously. The presence of a switch and full duplex–capable NICs is required to enable full-duplex mode on your devices, but their presence also serves to eliminate the problem of collisions.

Most newer network interface cards support a feature called *auto-negotiation*. Auto-negotiation allows the NIC to automatically detect and negotiate the fastest possible speed, based on the connection at the other end of the cable. If the NIC senses a switched connection, it will attempt to configure itself for a full-duplex connection. If the NIC detects a hub at the other end, it will set itself for a half-duplex connection. The Cisco 2900 series switches support dual-speed connections and will auto-configure each port to the appropriate speed based on the capabilities of the attached device.

Full-duplex mode also allows you to take full advantage of your investment in the cable plant because you can realize virtually 100 percent of the available bandwidth per device. Half-duplex mode usually provides only 60 percent of available bandwidth.

Nondeterministic

Ethernet is a *nondeterministic* architecture. This characteristic is in keeping with the nature of CSMA/CD for which any node at any time may attempt to transmit data onto the network. You can't plan who will be talking at a particular moment in a nondeterministic environment. This architecture also makes it impossible to determine or measure the exact amount of time each node needs between transmissions. The random back-off algorithm used when collisions occur in an Ethernet environment virtually ensures this uncertainty.

Length of Cable to Throughput

As you learned earlier, all segments that are connected by means of repeaters make up a collision domain. Repeaters relay or propagate all electrical signals received, including data transmissions as well as collisions.

This leads to perhaps the most fundamental tenet involved in planning for and designing Ethernet-based networks. Electrical signals take a certain amount of time to travel across the network cabling, and each additional device along the path contributes a specific amount of latency or delay to the signal, known as *propagation delay.*

For Ethernet collision detection to function properly, collisions must be able to be detected before the transmission has finished. Otherwise, the transmitting device would never know that a collision had occurred and wouldn't retransmit the packet. The minimum Ethernet packet size is 512 bits, and this size, 512 bit times, is the basis for determining maximum network diameters and segment lengths.

Let's look at an example: Two nodes are connected via Category-5 cabling to an Ethernet network. The nodes are at opposite ends of the collision domain. Node A has data to transmit, so it listens to the network to determine if it may begin sending. It doesn't sense any other traffic and begins transmitting its packets on the wire. However, Node B also has some data to send, and it was listening to the network at the same time that Node A began transmitting. Node A's traffic hadn't reached Node B quite yet, so Node B didn't hear a "busy" signal and also began sending its own data.

Now comes the fun part: The traffic from the two nodes collides on the network. However, a collision signal must be sent back to Node A from Node B before Node A finishes transmitting its 512-bit packet. The only way this will succeed is if the collision or jam signal is sent before Node A has sent 256 bits, or half of its packet (see Figure 10-2). The collision signal must have up to 256 bit times itself to return across the network to Node A. The result is a *round-trip propagation delay* of 512 bit times or less.

FIGURE 10-2   The process of an Ethernet collision

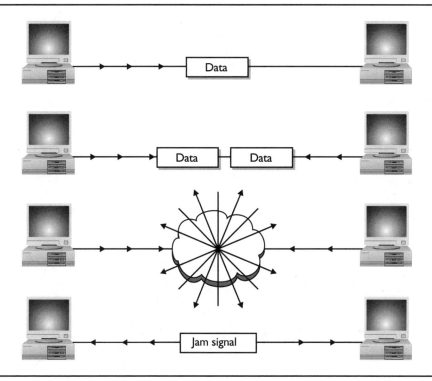

Types of Cable to Use

The following sections describe the various types of cables that are commonly used to create network connections.

10Base5   10Base5 is the original 802.3 specification standardized by the IEEE. It states a maximum collision domain of 2,500 meters with five segments, four repeaters, and three of the segments populated. Each segment may be up to 500 meters long and may have up to 100 attachments (via cable drops) per segment. 10Base5 uses a bus network topology with each device connected along the backbone cable. The naming convention represents the following:

- 10 = the speed in Mbps

- Base = baseband transmission, as opposed to broadband transmission

- 5 = 500 meters: the maximum segment length

This naming convention carries forward roughly throughout the entire Ethernet family.

10Base5 specifies the use of thick coaxial cabling and requires the cable to be electrically terminated with a 50 Ω terminator. This cable type is usually referred to as *thicknet*. Each node is attached to the backbone cable running the length of the network by means of an *attachment unit interface (AUI)* drop cable connected to a *medium attachment unit (MAU)*. The MAU is bolted directly onto the thicknet backbone cable by means of a *vampire* connector or tap. Thicknet is bulky and somewhat difficult to work with. This leads us to *thinnet*.

10Base2   10Base2 is commonly called *thinnet*. This naming refers to the thin coaxial cabling used with 10Base2. The cabling is classified as RG-58, and as the name implies, it is thinner than the original thicknet. Like its cousin, 10Base2 requires the cable to be terminated with a 50 Ω terminator. However, the AUI and MAU functionality from 10Base5 are integrated into 10Base2 NICs. Thinnet is more flexible than thicknet and easier to install and route through designated cable runs. Thinnet is also probably the least expensive of all the cabling options, with thicknet being a bit more expensive because of the additional thickness of the wire used.

10Base2 has a maximum collision domain of 2,500 meters with five segments, four repeaters, and three of the segments populated. Each segment may be up to 185 meters long and may have only 30 attachments per segment. This reduction in the number of attachments per segment from 10Base5 results because of the method of attaching nodes to thinnet. 10Base2 still uses a bus network topology, but each device is connected in sequence directly to the backbone cable through the use of *BNC* connectors.

10BaseT   10BaseT provides for a maximum collision domain of 2,500 meters with five segments, four repeaters, and three of the segments populated. Each one of these segments may be up to 100 meters in length. 10BaseT uses the star network topology and permits two devices attached to each segment (the hub or repeater, and the end node). 10BaseT allows a maximum round-trip propagation delay of 51.2 μs; the bit time is 0.1 μs (microseconds).

10BaseT typically utilizes unshielded twisted-pair (UTP) cabling, composed of four pairs of twisted wires. 10BaseT uses two of these pairs: one for transmission of data and one for receiving. The EIA/TIA 568 standard specifies *categories* of UTP cabling. Category 3 or better cabling must be used for 10BaseT networks. Fortunately, this type of cabling is commonly found in most modern commercial buildings. 10BaseT networks use 8-pin RJ-45 connectors and can take advantage of full-duplex mode in a 10-Mbps switched environment.

Table 10-2 summarizes the constraints of the different copper-based implementations of Ethernet.

10BaseF   10BaseF is a newer specification than either thicknet or thinnet; but in today's environments of 100-Mbps and 1,000-Mbps

TABLE 10-2   Scalability Constraints for Copper-Based Ethernet (IEEE 802.3)

	10Base5	10Base2	10BaseT	100BaseT
Topology	Bus	Bus	Star	Star
Maximum segment length	500 meters	185 meters	100 meters, node to hub	100 meters, node to hub
Maximum number of attachments/segment	100	30	2, node to hub or hub to hub	2, node to hub or hub to hub
Maximum collision domain	2,500 meters (5 segments, 4 repeaters, 3 populated segments)	2,500 meters (5 segments, 4 repeaters, 3 populated segments)	2,500 meters (5 segments, 4 repeaters, 3 populated segments)	See the upcoming section, "100BaseT."

connections, it seems a bit outdated. The original standard for using fiber-optic cabling with Ethernet was the fiber-optic interrepeater link specification or *FOIRL*. 10BaseF is based on this original FOIRL specification and includes 10BaseFP, 10BaseFB, 10BaseFL, and a newer version of the FOIRL standard. When you are designing your networks and choosing to implement a fiber-based cable plant, why run your network at 10 Mbps when you can go much faster?

10BaseF uses dual strands of either 62.5 or 125 μm multimode or single-mode fiber-optic cabling. As for the other 10-Mbps specifications, the maximum collision domain is 2,500 meters, but each variety of 10BaseF has different limitations for segment length as well as the types of connections allowed. Table 10-3 details 10BaseF specifications, and Figure 10-3 gives you a simple illustration of the capabilities of the various media types.

TABLE 10-3	Scalability Constraints for IEEE 802.3 10BaseF Standards				
	10BaseFL (Link)	**10BaseFP (Passive)**	**10BaseFB (Backbone)**	**Original FOIRL**	**New FOIRL**
Application	Mixed/link	Passive star	Backbone or repeater system	Repeater interconnection	Link or star
DTE connections permitted	Yes	Yes	No	No	Yes
Maximum segment length	2,000 meters— 10BaseFL only; 1,000 meters when mixed with FOIRL	500 meters	2,000 meters	1,000 meters	1,000 meters
Cascading of repeaters	Yes/limited	No	Yes	No	Yes
Full duplex capable	Yes	No	No	No	Yes
Maximum collision domain	2,500 meters	2,500 meters	2,500 meters	2,500 meters	2,500 meters

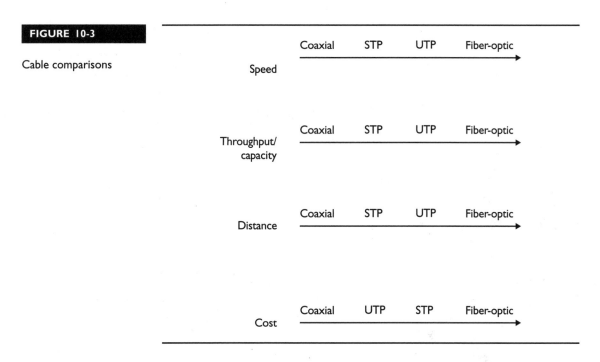

FIGURE 10-3

Cable comparisons

| | Coaxial | STP | UTP | Fiber-optic |

Speed

Throughput/capacity — Coaxial STP UTP Fiber-optic

Distance — Coaxial STP UTP Fiber-optic

Cost — Coaxial UTP STP Fiber-optic

100BaseT 100BaseT has much more restrictive requirements than does 10BaseT. The maximum collision domain allowed here is 205 meters with UTP cabling because of the tenfold increase in the speed of the data transmission. Repeater definitions have also been revised to address the requirements of a 100BaseT environment. This is the result of the work done by a subset of the IEEE 802.3 standards body, which has designated Fast Ethernet as 802.3u.

Repeaters are grouped into two categories, based on the amount of latency each type introduces into the connection:

Class I repeaters have a latency of 0.7 µs or less. 100BaseT networks are also limited to a single Class I repeater hop.

Class II repeaters have a latency of 0.46 µs or less. Two repeater hops are possible when Class II repeaters are used. Class II repeaters are preferred because of the design requirements of 100BaseT networks and the additional distance flexibility they can provide. Figure 10-4 shows the various combinations of media type, repeater class, and segments.

As with 10BaseT, each segment may be up to 100 meters in length. 100BaseT also uses the star network topology and permits two devices attached to each segment (the hub or repeater, and the end node). 100BaseT allows a maximum round-trip propagation delay of 5.12 μs; the bit time is now reduced to 0.01 μs. The Cisco FastHub 400 is a Class II 10/100 dual-speed repeater, ideally positioned for flexible workgroup connectivity.

100BaseT typically utilizes UTP cabling and uses two of these pairs: one for transmission of data and one for receiving. When used in a switched

---

FIGURE 10-4   Fast Ethernet segment lengths

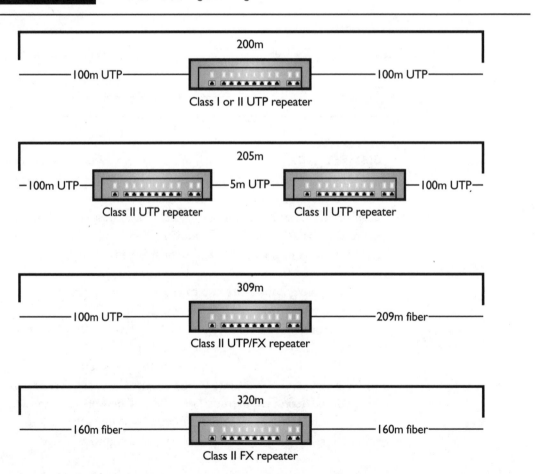

environment, 100BaseT can be operated in full-duplex mode, virtually ensuring full 100-Mbps speeds in each direction. Category 5 or better cabling must be used for 100BaseT networks, and RJ-45 connectors are used to connect the cable to the node and port.

100BaseFX　100BaseFX, the specification that introduces the use of fiber-optic cabling to Fast Ethernet, is based on the 10BaseF standard. The collision domain limitations and segment lengths vary greatly depending on the devices connected, the types of cabling used (multimode or single mode), and whether it is run in full duplex or half duplex.

With multimode fiber, 100BaseFX repeater segment lengths are typically 216 to 320 meters, and switch-to-switch and switch-to-node segments can be up to 412 meters in length. They can be extended up to 2,000 meters when switched connections are run in full-duplex mode. Connections of 10 kilometers or more are feasible when the higher-grade single-mode fiber is used in full-duplex mode.

100BaseFX uses two strands of either 62.5 or 125 μm multimode or single-mode fiber-optic cabling. Table 10-4 summarizes the collision domain distances under certain configurations.

Gigabit Ethernet　Gigabit Ethernet is the latest version of Ethernet to become an IEEE standard, designated as 802.3z. As the name implies, Gigabit operates at 1 Gbps, or ten times the speed of Fast Ethernet. Although not necessarily intended for use at the desktop, Gigabit will

TABLE 10-4	Fast Ethernet Collision Domain Limitations		
	Copper	**Mixed Copper/ Multimode Fiber**	**Multimode Fiber**
Switch to switch or switch to node	100 meters	NA	412 meters/2,000 meters in full-duplex mode
Single Class I repeater	200 meters	261 meters	272 meters
Single Class II repeater	200 meters	309 meters	320 meters
Two Class II repeaters	205 meters	216 meters	228 meters

help to relieve congested network backbone routes as more and more users receive Fast Ethernet connections to their desktops. Three Gigabit specifications have been defined as 1000BaseSX (fiber cable), 1000BaseLX (fiber cable), and 1000BaseCX (short copper cable). A separate IEEE working group has also defined Gigabit Ethernet over UTP as 802.3ab or 1000BaseT (using Category-5 balanced cabling).

Fast Ethernet moved to define two distinct classes of repeaters, but Gigabit does the reverse and specifies only a single repeater type. However, because of the requirements of CSMA/CD at 1 Gbps, only a single repeater may exist in a Gigabit Ethernet collision domain. Unlike 10Base and 100Base Ethernet, this repeater is allowed to run at only 1 Gbps and should not support multiple speeds.

The IEEE 802.3z working group also needed to address the now virtually impossible limitations of the CSMA/CD protocol at Gigabit speeds because it would have limited half-duplex connections to a maximum of 20 meters, which is not very useful for a campus backbone! Therefore, the group increased the minimum frame size to 512 *bytes* in *shared* half-duplex Gigabit environments (see Table 10-5 for scalability constraints) as opposed to the standard 512 bits for 10/100Base. In a full-duplex switched environment, you no longer have the possibility of collisions, so the minimum frame size for switched Gigabit was left unaltered at 512 bits.

TABLE 10-5	Scalability Constraints for Gigabit Ethernet in Half-Duplex Mode		
	1000BaseT (Category-5 Balanced Copper, Uses Four Pairs)	**1000BaseCX (Short Copper Cable)**	**1000BaseSX/ 1000BaseLX (Fiber)**
Max. collision domain: two DTEs/no repeater	100 meters	25 meters	316 meters
Max. segment length: two DTEs/no repeater	100 meters	25 meters	316 meters
Max. collision domain: two DTEs/one repeater	200 meters	50 meters	220 meters
Max. segment length: two DTEs/one repeater	100 meters	25 meters	110 meters

Why Use a Router Instead of a Bridge or Switch?

To make the appropriate choices when recommending equipment and designing networks, you first need to fully understand what role each type of device plays in a network.

Repeaters or hubs simply act as electrical signal regenerators; that is, they work to extend the distance of a network by boosting a signal across the next segment. Traffic is not examined or filtered by repeaters; it is simply forwarded indiscriminately. They are used primarily to compensate for *attenuation*, the weakening or deterioration of an electrical signal as it passes along a length of cabling. Repeaters function at layer 1 of the OSI reference model (see Figure 10-5), also known as the physical layer, or PHY.

Bridges and switches operate at layer 2, examining the MAC address of each data frame as it enters the device. Layer 2 is also referred to as the data-link layer and is actually composed of two sublayers, Logical Link Control (LLC) and Media Access Control (MAC).

A bridge performs a rudimentary form of filtering in which it dynamically learns the MAC addresses from the attached segments. If the frame is on the local segment, the bridge won't forward the frame. However, if the MAC address of the frame is unknown, the bridge will flood the frame out of all

FIGURE 10-5

The OSI model

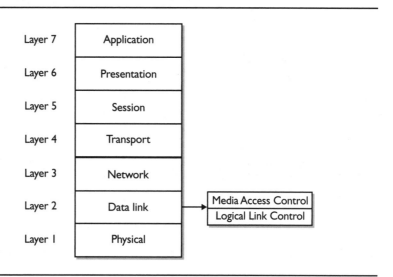

its interfaces except the interface on which the frame arrived. In a large or busy network, this can quickly result in broadcast storms that can choke traffic.

Switches function very similarly to bridges in that they operate at layer 2, learning MAC addresses and passing traffic to the appropriate segment. Switches are critical to the successful deployment of Fast Ethernet because they can enlarge overall network diameter. Switches make excellent choices for performing network segmentation, and the benefits of full-duplex capability shouldn't be underestimated. Figure 10-6 represents a scalable

| FIGURE 10-6 | Example of a 10/100/1000 switched network |

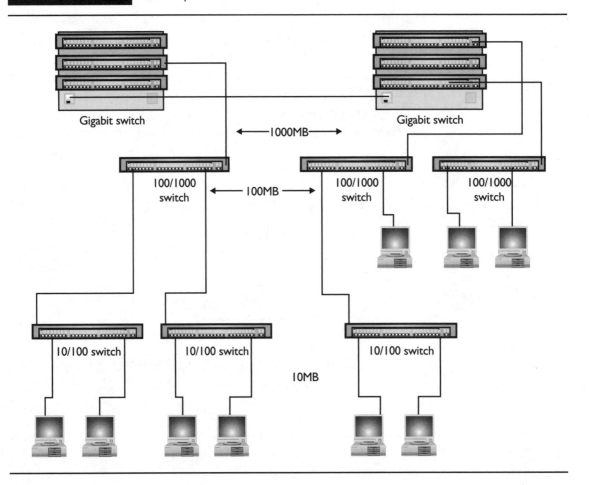

network model, incorporating a full range of switched 10/100/1,000 connections.

A router, on the other hand, performs its magic at layer 3 of the OSI model, also known as the network layer. This is the layer at which common networking protocols such as IP, IPX, and DDP have their fun. One significant advantage that a router has over a switch or repeater is that it can be used to connect two disparate networking technologies (i.e., Token Ring to Ethernet). Also, a router doesn't pass broadcast traffic.

There has been a great deal of talk and information available in the last few years about layer-3 switching; however, there is no such device or technology. A layer-3 switch is a *router,* and layer-3 switching is simply *routing.*

Routers maintain complex tables of network addresses known as *routing tables.* They use the information contained within these tables to make complicated route path selections, based on a number of different criteria established by either the routing protocol itself or the router's human administrator. As a result, you have much more advanced network management capabilities when using routers in your environments.

However, all of this complexity comes at a price: speed. Routers typically perform their functions more slowly than bridges or switches because they need to "touch" much more of the packet as it is passed through the router. Data-link source and destination packet headers are stripped off, recalculated, and then reapplied by the router as it performs its path selections.

Still, routers play a critical role in large complex networks when they are deployed and configured properly. Routers can significantly improve the overall performance of a LAN by filtering and isolating traffic and breaking up broadcast domains into more manageable, better-performing sections. The routers in the Cisco 2500 series are true workhorses in the routing world, with an installed base of over a million routers.

Routers also enable a new level of redundancy within networks. Unlike bridges and switches, which work at layer 2, routers operate at layer 3. This permits routers to make much more intelligent decisions when moving data. You can maintain multiple paths between LAN segments, and routers can choose the best path based on certain criteria, such as bandwidth availability, cost, number of hops, line speed, and current traffic levels.

Routers can also select a different path when network links fail or become unavailable.

Advantages and Disadvantages

Ethernet's wide acceptance and low costs are its primary advantages. It is a very mature technology and has been shown to scale to previously unheard-of speeds (1 Gbps). Ethernet is also very well understood and performs well in most applications. Switching capabilities enhance the attractiveness of Ethernet even further. A wide range of vendors produce products for the Ethernet arena, creating a competitive economic advantage for the consumer.

Because Ethernet is a contention-based architecture, it can realistically scale up to only approximately 40 percent utilization. Beyond that, it reaches a point of saturation at which traffic is simply causing collisions on the wire. There are also no current standards for ensuring any prioritization or quality-of-service on Ethernet. This is a disadvantage in environments that need to provide these features to their LAN users. The solution is typically to throw more bandwidth at the problem and/or implement switched connections.

Nevertheless, Ethernet is the current reigning heavyweight champion of local area network architectures; and it will be difficult, if not impossible, to win its belt away.

Problems with Exceeding the Constraints of the Medium

When Ethernet networks become overcrowded, they bend and then break. The scalability of the CSMA/CD protocol is limited to the size and scale of a network. When too many nodes are attached to the same flat Ethernet network, the resultant traffic drowns itself out in both excessive collisions and severe broadcast storms. This can cripple an Ethernet network, and you should definitely plan to avoid this situation!

There are also the constraints placed on cable segment lengths as well as the type of media to be used. The issues that arise when these stipulations aren't followed can be extremely vexing, and they tend to manifest themselves in odd, erratic patterns. The symptoms of a cable segment that exceeds the guidelines by just a few meters will be almost impossible to reproduce accurately and repeatedly. Instead, sporadic problems will simply appear and disappear without warning. Perseverance is the key to

FROM THE FIELD

Discussing the problems of troubleshooting cable lengths, I recall a particularly relevant chapter in my professional life. I was installing a new network for a luxury hotel in Phoenix, Arizona. When I arrived on site, I was met by the network expert from the parent company of the hotel. He had been working with the network for a few days and had "designed" the new additions. The hotel was getting ready for a new software package installation the following week, and as part of this rollout, we needed to establish a training location. The hotel manager had determined that the best location for this training area was a cabana-type building, situated quite a distance from the main server room. We were planning to deploy the new servers in this training facility initially and link into the rest of the network to access the live data on the existing systems. This had supposedly been "designed" by the hotel's expert. After we spent a few days installing and configuring the servers in the main server room and setting up the facility with the workstations for the users, it was time to move the servers and go live with the training area. Category-5 cable connected the main server room with the cabana and had been put in place by a local cabling company. However, I was having difficulty establishing a connection with the main servers from the training facility.

I discussed this problem with the cabling people, who assured me that the run was 75 meters at most. Nevertheless, the sporadic symptoms definitely pointed to some sort of cabling problems, so I began troubleshooting. Now keep in mind that I am *not* a cabling expert, nor do I fancy myself one. But past problems had already taught me the value of having the appropriate tools, so I pulled out my trusty cable tester and started in on the segment. All of my tests indicated that the run was invalid. So I approached the cabling people for a second round.

After further discussion, I learned that these installers were primarily electricians who simply did some network cabling work on the side. Armed with this knowledge, I insisted that they show me where and how the cabling had been routed. The run snaked under and around most of the hotel buildings and re-emerged from the underground conduit in a wiring closet, midway between the main server room and the training facility.

It re-entered the conduits, twisting and turning until terminating in the cabana. After going over some blueprints of the site, I determined that just this last section of cable was 150 meters or more! When I pointed this out to the hotel's network expert, he seemed unsure of the reason for my consternation. After even more discussion, I learned that both

FROM THE FIELD

the network expert and the cable installers had simply paced out the cable run, walking in a straight line across lawns and counting their steps!

I decided that even though it was well beyond the scope of my responsibilities, I would need to help remedy this fiasco if I ever wanted to finish my part of the job. Unfortunately, the selection of this cabana for the training facility was doomed from the start. There were no other established paths to this building for a valid UTP cable run, and the equipment that the network expert had selected and purchased didn't allow for a fiber connection. Additionally, the installers had demonstrated their lack of ability with simple twisted pair, so I surely wasn't going to ask them to tackle fiber!

This left an ugly solution, to be sure—palm tree–to–palm tree cabling! The only way to get this location connected for the training sessions was to string the cabling from tree to tree, dropping it down through a freshly drilled hole in the wall of the cabana. Of course, this is a terrible solution and should *never* be duplicated. But it did solve the immediate connectivity problem and allow the training sessions to commence the following morning.

A more permanent solution was later implemented under my direction, and the hole in the cabana wall was patched. But I'll never forget looking up into that beautiful Arizona sky and seeing bright green Category-5 cabling strung from the palm trees and gently swaying in the afternoon breeze.

troubleshooting these errors. The old phrase, "an ounce of prevention is worth a pound of cure" is more than relevant for those who are planning and installing Ethernet networks.

Token Ring

Token Ring began its life in the 1970s at IBM. It was originally invented as a proprietary architecture intended for connecting existing mainframe environments with midrange systems and the emerging base of personal computers. The concept was simple: use inexpensive unshielded twisted-pair (UTP) cabling to connect systems across a network to centrally located areas.

Much like for Ethernet, the IEEE created a separate working group to standardize Token Ring and designated it 802.5. The IEEE 802.5 Token Ring specification was finalized in 1985. There is little difference between this specification and the original IBM Token Ring architecture, and today, the IEEE maintains both standards. The term *Token Ring* is now generally used to refer to both specifications.

The primary difference between the two specifications is that while IBM's Token Ring standard specifies both the media to be used and the physical topology of the network, the IEEE 802.5 standard does not.

Token Ring works just as its name implies. A small frame called a *token* is circulated around in a ring pattern on the network. The network is a *logical ring* but is typically structured as a physical star or hub-and-spoke topology.

The token is transmitted onto the network by the first node to come online. This token circles the network, waiting for a node to grab it (see Figure 10-7). As the token circulates, each node is permitted to have the token for only a short time. If the node doesn't have any data to transmit, it passes the token along to the next node. On a Token Ring network, a node must have control of the token to transmit any data across the wire.

Once a node grabs the token, it changes a bit in the frame known as the *start of frame* delimiter to indicate that the token now contains data. The node then adds its data to the frame and sends it back onto the wire. The token continues around the ring until it reaches the destination node.

FIGURE 10-7

Token Ring network with token circulating

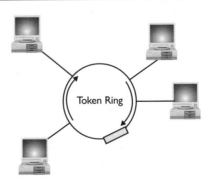

This node removes the token from the network and pulls the data intended for it out of the frame. This node then sets a bit called *frame status*. This is used to indicate that it received the data correctly. It then releases the token back onto the network, destined for the original sending node. Finally, when the source node receives the token, it verifies that the destination node didn't have any trouble by looking at the frame status bit. When everything looks good, the original sending node regenerates a fresh token for the network to use again.

One node within a Token Ring environment is designated as the *active monitor*. This node functions as a central timing source for the ring and performs other ring maintenance activities. The most important of these is the role this node plays when a rogue frame is circulating on the ring. This can happen when a node transmits data on the wire and then goes down unexpectedly. Because each node is ultimately responsible for its own transmissions, this situation can result in an orphaned frame on the wire. The active monitor is responsible for cleaning up after these events by removing the frame and generating a new token onto the network.

A newer feature of Token Ring networks is the *early token release*. If implemented, early token release permits the release of a new token out onto the wire after the initial sender has completed transmitting its frame. This works to increase the capacity and perceived speed of a Token Ring network.

Types of Token Rings and Their Limitations

The term Token Ring encompasses two different specifications: the IEEE's 802.5 and IBM's original Token Ring. These two standards are basically compatible with each other but there are a few differences.

802.5 Members of the IEEE 802.5 working group examined the work done by IBM on Token Ring and determined that they would standardize most of the existing specification as part of their own standard. However, they decided *not* to specify either the physical network topology or the type or class of media (cabling) to use in 802.5 environments. The 802.5 specification has the advantage of being able to adapt more easily to future changes or enhancements to Token Ring in the real world.

IBM   IBM's Token Ring network states that a physical Token Ring topology should be a star or star ring. The wiring radiates out from centrally located hubs. Hubs in a Token Ring network are known by a variety of names:

- Multistation access units (MAUs or MSAUs)
- Smart multistation access units (SMAUs)

We'll refer to all of these devices as MAUs from here. This MAU is not to be confused with the medium attachment unit (MAU) from the original Ethernet 802.3 10Base5 specification.

Where is the ring? It can be difficult when one is looking at the layout of a Token Ring network to visualize the ring because it appears to be laid out very much like any Ethernet network. MAUs contain the logical ring of the network and extend this ring out to each attached node (see Figure 10-8).

FIGURE 10-8   Representation of the ring circulating in a MAU

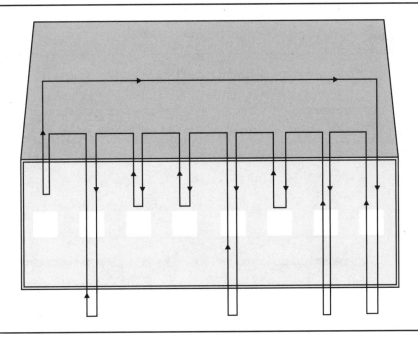

Each MAU has two special ports intended for connecting to other MAUs and to extend the ring further. These ports are *ring in (RI)* and *ring out (RO)* ports. Figure 10-9 illustrates these connection types.

The second major difference in IBM's Token Ring standard is the specification of the medium to be used. IBM Token Ring networks use twisted-pair cabling; a discussion of the IBM cable types will follow.

Table 10-6 summarizes the differences between the IEEE 802.5 specification and the original IBM Token Ring standard.

Types of Cable to Use

IBM has classified its own cabling system, and, of course, the cable types are intended for use with Token Ring networks. However, some of the specifications are similar or identical to other existing cabling standards. The following sections take a closer look at two of the most common of these cable types.

FIGURE 10-9   MAUs connected with ring-in and ring-out ports

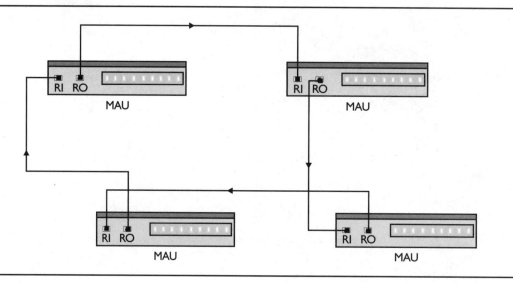

TABLE 10-6	Differences Between IBM Token Ring and IEEE 802.5	
	IBM Token Ring	**IEEE 802.5**
Topology	Star/star ring	Not specified
Media	Twisted pair	Not specified
Maximum stations per segment	260 (STP cable)/72 (UTP cable)	250
Maximum number of segments	33 MAUs	33 MAUs
Access method	Token passing	Token passing
Speed	4 or 16 Mbps	4 or 16 Mbps

Type 3 IBM Type-3 cabling is one of the specifications that is virtually identical to another already existing standard—Category-3 UTP, commonly used in Ethernet 10BaseT networks. You will recall that this cabling consists of four pairs of unshielded twisted wires. Because of the lower speed requirements of Token Ring, a higher grade of cabling like Category 5 (required for 100BaseT) is not necessary.

Type 1 IBM Type-1 cabling is the cable we tend to think of historically associated with Token Ring infrastructures. This thick, stiff, unwieldy cabling once infested office building crawl spaces and ceilings and uses unique IBM connectors. These connectors are considered neither "male" nor "female" because they are rather hermaphroditic in functionality. Two IBM connectors can be reversed and connected directly to each other or simply used individually to connect to wall plates designed for them. Table 10-7 details the IBM cabling types.

Scalability Issues

Token Ring networks possess a fault-tolerance characteristic known as *beaconing*. Because of the dependence on each attached node to perform its job in passing the token, a failed node or MAU could halt all traffic on a token-based network. Beaconing addresses this potential shortcoming by detecting and working to repair these failures. Essentially a Token Ring

TABLE 10-7		IBM Cable Types and Uses	
IBM Cable Type	**Standard Label**	**Uses**	**Cable Description**
Type 1	Shielded twisted-pair (STP)	Nodes and MAUs	Two 22-AWG shielded twisted pairs
Type 2	Voice and data cable	Combined voice/data	Two 22-AWG shielded twisted pairs with four 22 AWG voice-grade twisted pairs
Type 3	Voice-grade cable	Voice or data	Four 22- or 24-AWG unshielded twisted pairs
Type 5	Fiber-optic cable	Nodes and MAUs	Two 62.5/125μm optical fiber cable
Type 6	Data patch cable	Patch cable/nodes and MAUs	Two 26-AWG shielded twisted pairs

algorithm, beaconing works by broadcasting a beacon frame onto the network after detecting a failure at a neighboring node. This frame will continue around the network, initiating an automatic reconfiguration of the network to account for the failed node or MAU. As a result, traffic can return to normal by routing itself around the failed component. Most MAUs can perform this function internally, segmenting off and disabling a failed port.

Applicability

Token Ring networks are commonly found in environments that have had a long history with IBM mainframe systems. They are particularly suited to situations requiring differentiation between groups of client workstations and their levels of priority access to the network. Because of Token Ring's performance characteristics under load, it is also well suited for networks in which network utilization will be high.

Deterministic

Token Ring networks (and token-based systems in general) are considered *deterministic* in nature. This means that when planning or examining a token-based network, you can accurately measure or determine the amount of time each node needs between data transmissions. Deterministic also means that a node can't simply break into the orderly network conversations taking place; who has the token at any given moment determines access.

Advantages and Disadvantages

One of the great aspects of Token Ring is its predictability. As you recall, Ethernet is a first-come, first-served type of architecture that leads to issues of contention. Token Ring is classified as collisionless because a node must possess the token to have permission to transmit any data.

Another advantage of Token Ring networks is the ability to accurately plan networks based on access times and delay requirements. Token Ring supports a sort of reservations and priority-based system if needed. Two fields within Token Ring frames enable this functionality: the *priority* field and the *reservation* field. Individual nodes can be assigned a numeric value associated with their relative priority within an environment. Those stations can then access the token more frequently than their lower-numbered neighbors, ensuring better access for their data. Because of this ability, line-of-business applications and other time-sensitive data can be successfully planned on Token Ring networks.

Finally, Token Ring networks can be pushed much harder than Ethernet. Token Ring can continue to function without errors up to (and sometimes over) 70 percent utilization, which is almost a twofold improvement over Ethernet's performance. It is for this last reason that so many environments with existing Token Ring–based infrastructures are so stubborn about "giving up their 'Ring."

Perhaps the most significant weakness of Token Ring has been its relative speed limitations. The original IBM Token Ring specification was at 4 Mbps and was later increased to 16 Mbps, with the IEEE 802.5 standard following suit each time. These speeds pale in comparison with those of both Fast Ethernet and Gigabit Ethernet. However, recent years have seen work toward a high-speed implementation of Token Ring by the High-Speed Token Ring Alliance (HSTRA). This alliance has been led by IBM, Madge Networks, and Olicom—companies with a sizable interest in the continuation of Token Ring. Wide-scale acceptance of their work in real-world networks remains to be seen.

The other disadvantage of Token Ring networks is that they are typically more expensive than Ethernet to implement.

Scalability Constraints

As with the Ethernet standards, different types of cabling permit different segment lengths for Token Ring networks. In node-to-MAU connections, Type-1 cabling allows a maximum segment length of 101 meters; UTP, or Type 3, permits only 45 meters per segment. The minimum STP or UTP cable length that is usable is 2.5 meters and MAU-to-MAU segments are limited to 150 meters.

Type-6 cable is used to connect nodes to MAUs or to join MAU to MAU, and these patch cables are limited to 45 meters. Repeaters can also be used in Token Ring environments. Using a pair of repeaters, MAUs can be extended up to 365 meters apart with Type-3 cabling or up to 730 meters apart using Type 1 or 2 cable.

Problems with Exceeding the Constraints of the Medium

When Token Ring networks become overpopulated with nodes, problems arise with latency and nodes' not being able to successfully seize the token to transmit their data. This problem can be exacerbated when prioritization on an over-populated ring is used. Lower-priority nodes will essentially be shut out of the ring, unable to catch the token frequently enough to effectively transmit data.

As with Ethernet networks, Token Ring cabling variations will result in the same fate—errors and problems that are difficult at best to diagnose and troubleshoot. The lesson remains the same also: don't violate the numbers that have been included as part of the specification.

FDDI/CDDI

FDDI is an acronym for Fiber Distributed Data Interface. It is also a token-based networking architecture, intended for high speeds and designed originally to use fiber-optic media. It was standardized by the American

National Standards Institute (ANSI) in 1986 as ANSI X3T9.5, and then turned over to the International Organization for Standardization (ISO), which approved ANSI's work and created a compatible FDDI standard.

CDDI is an implementation of FDDI, adapted to permit the use of copper cabling for short runs. CDDI significantly shortens the cable lengths permitted in an FDDI/CDDI environment. Therefore, CDDI's primary use is the attachment of nodes to the larger backbone FDDI rings.

Types of FDDI/CDDI and Their Limitations

Perhaps FDDI's most unusual characteristic is a *counter-rotating ring*. In reality, this ring is two 100-Mbps–capable rings that pass traffic in opposite directions around the network. These rings are classified as the *primary* ring and the *secondary* ring. Only the primary ring is active normally, unless a failure has occurred on the ring. When this happens, the FDDI ring activates its recovery procedures, rerouting traffic back along the secondary ring and wrapping the two counter-rotating rings into a single ring.

Two types of node connections are defined for FDDI networks. They are *dual-attached station (DAS)* and *single-attached station (SAS)*. Figure 10-10 illustrates DAS and SAS nodes. Dual-attached stations are also known as *Class A* stations, and single-attached stations are known as *Class B* stations. As their names imply, a DAS attaches to both rings, and a SAS attaches to only one ring. When a failure occurs on an FDDI network, DAS nodes help reconfigure the rings, but SAS nodes do not (see Figure 10-11).

FIGURE 10-10

FDDI ring with
dual-attached and
single-attached stations

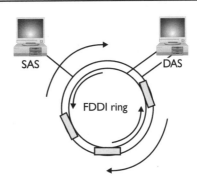

FIGURE 10-11

Wrapped FDDI ring after a failure

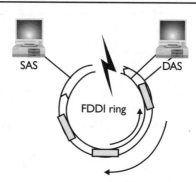

Server farms and critical nodes are usually attached to both rings as Class A stations because this methods provides the most redundancy for these important devices. Essential networking devices (routers, hubs, and bridges) also typically attach to both rings. Cisco routers support a method called *dual homing*. This allows for fault tolerance and redundancy for network paths with two individual connections to each ring. Dual homing prevents against the failure of any one of the router's interfaces.

Individual nodes or personal computers are typically designated as SAS nodes for two reasons:

■ These nodes don't normally require the same level of fault-tolerance as servers and mainframe computers.

■ SAS connections are typically made through the use of hubs to eliminate the problem of insertion or deinsertion into the ring and to isolate failures occurring at the edge of the network.

When a node powers up and attempts to insert itself into the ring, or powers off (removing itself from the ring), it can cause a disruption or failure of the ring if it is directly attached to both rings. These events can cause the rings to initiate redundancy features, wrapping the rings into one ring. However, FDDI hubs or concentrators can negotiate this insertion/ reinsertion on the ring, preventing a ring "failure" situation and maintaining the integrity of the ring. This is an excellent reason to use hubs in designing an FDDI network.

Types of Cable to Use

FDDI and CDDI operate over different media types. The following sections look at the different cabling specifications used in deploying both FDDI and CDDI.

Fiber   FDDI specifies the use of multimode 62.5/125μm fiber-optic cabling. Single-mode fiber is also permitted with the addition of higher-powered lasers to generate and transmit the light down the length of the cable. FDDI is typically implemented as network backbones and long distance campus-based cable runs.

Copper   CDDI is essentially FDDI for copper-based cabling. CDDI has been designed to run for relatively short distances over both IBM Type-1 shielded twisted-pair and Category-5 unshielded twisted-pair copper media. CDDI connections are almost always made between hubs and nodes because a pure CDDI ring would be too short to be useful.

Scalability Issues

Limitations of FDDI and CDDI vary with the type of medium used. The range is vast, from short runs of less than 100 meters with twisted-pair copper to over 60 kilometers with single-mode fiber. Table 10-8 lists these constraints.

TABLE 10-8	FDDI/CDDI Scalability Constraints			
	Multimode Fiber	**Single-Mode Fiber**	**Type-1 STP Copper**	**Category-5 UTP Copper**
Maximum segment length	2 kilometers	40–60+ kilometers	>100 meters	>100 meters
Minimum segment length	None	None	None	None
Maximum number of attached nodes	500	500	500	500

Applicability

FDDI was originally created to address the higher speeds necessary at the core of a network. Large servers and mainframe computers have a significantly greater need for bandwidth than do most individual nodes or personal computers at the network edge. Additionally, networks or network segments that have high-bandwidth demands are likely candidates for FDDI/CDDI connections. Examples of these include engineering departments, graphic arts departments, CAD/CAM users, and users involved with video production or editing.

However, with the advent of Gigabit Ethernet and the promise of High-Speed Token Ring, the real ace in the hole that FDDI has is its resiliency along with fault-tolerance characteristics. Environments that require this redundancy should seriously consider FDDI/CDDI.

Deterministic

Like Token Ring, FDDI is deterministic and provides you with measurable latency and delays. FDDI also supports beaconing much as Token Ring does. However, while Token Ring uses a priority and reservation-based access methodology, FDDI uses a *timed token release* scheme. This permits nodes to transmit multiple frames before releasing the token.

Another difference between 802.5 and FDDI is that only in FDDI is the ring both a logical *and* a physical ring. In fact, FDDI is the only network architecture in which the physical topology is actually a ring.

Talk Only When Token Is in Hand

Access to the token in a FDDI network controls access to transmit. But a node on a FDDI network can transmit as many data frames as it wishes within the preset time limit before releasing the token back onto the network. This timed token release differs significantly from the 802.5 method of one frame at a time. This is also what enables an FDDI network to maintain much higher throughput levels than Token Ring can.

Why Use a Router Instead of a Bridge or Switch?

FDDI uses MAC addresses when framing data for transmission, but it implements a different framing format that creates translation issues when interconnecting FDDI networks with Ethernet or Token Ring. FDDI packages and transmits data with a frame size of 4,500 bytes while Ethernet uses a frame size of 1,500 bytes, requiring the use of either a bridge or router capable of fragmenting and then reassembling the fragments into frames again.

Advantages and Disadvantages

FDDI's advantages are unique and, in the appropriate environment, quite indispensable. The ability of FDDI to transmit a network signal over 60 kilometers is basically unmatched in the LAN arena. The redundant dual rings of an FDDI network provide an added measure of fault tolerance over other architectures.

FDDI uses its available bandwidth more effectively than Token Ring, allowing multiple data frames to be on the ring concurrently. FDDI also supports LAN speeds of up to 100Mbps, providing good network backbone capabilities.

FDDI's disadvantages are also related to the uniqueness of the architecture. First and foremost is the high cost incurred when FDDI networks are implemented. CDDI helps bring this cost down a bit because cheaper copper-based media can be used. But the overall cost is probably the biggest barrier to most organizations that are considering FDDI networks.

An additional consideration is that if an FDDI network experiences multiple failures at different locations (different nodes or ports), you can end up with multiple separate rings. This is obviously undesirable because the network would be divided and traffic wouldn't be able to traverse these separate rings.

Also, keep in mind the overhead and latency associated with having to perform frame translation when you cross different LAN architecture boundaries (Ethernet to FDDI, FDDI to Token Ring, etc.). This requirement can slow down your networks as well as place additional stress on your precious routers and bridges!

Finally, FDDI is a shared LAN implementation, so capacity on an FDDI ring must be divided among all attached nodes. There is also no FDDI switching standard or methodology to address its shared nature or to permit full-duplex functionality.

Problems with Exceeding the Constraints of the Medium

One of the main problems with exceeding the specifications of FDDI is directly related to one of its best features: the dual-ring architecture. The actual maximum number of attached nodes is set at 1,000 for both rings. But because of the purpose of the secondary ring, you should never exceed half of this number. This means that if nodes are limited to 500, either ring will be able to handle the total capacity of the network at any given time. If you were to put 750 nodes across the two rings and you experienced a failure, the resulting fail-over would leave you with 250 more nodes on the wrapped ring than it could handle.

Other considerations include the length of time each node must wait for the token, and thus access to the media. The parameter that controls the timed token release can be manually adjusted; but this should rarely be necessary, even under maximum load. Again, keep in mind that by exceeding either distance or load limitations when designing your networks, you are creating an unstable environment that will be painful to troubleshoot and remedy.

QUESTIONS AND ANSWERS

Colin needs to improve the performance of the Ethernet workstations on his LAN. He is currently running 100BaseT throughout, but he still needs better speed. He also believes that collisions are consuming too much of his bandwidth. What can he do?	Consider deploying switches to replace the 100BaseT hubs currently in use. Switches will eliminate Colin's collision problem and boost the overall performance of his LAN.
Megan is the network designer for MegaSoft, Inc. Recently, she has been discussing possible network architectures with her supervisor, Carol. Carol is concerned about the effect of collisions on network traffic. On which architectures should Megan focus her efforts?	Remember that token-passing networks such as Token Ring (802.5) and FDDI are deterministic and *collisionless* architectures. Access to the network is determined by possession of the token; therefore, collisions won't be a concern for Megan if she deploys Token Ring or FDDI.
ABC Corp. is running a Novell NetWare–based LAN, using IPX and AppleTalk as the protocols. The network administrator, Neil, is responsible for all 250 workstations attached to the single network in the main building. However, these nodes have been having great difficulty locating and attaching to the Novell servers. Why?	The keys to this scenario are the protocols, both IPX and AppleTalk, and the total number of nodes attached to the *single* network. The maximum number of mixed protocol nodes is 200 in a flat network. Neil either needs to reduce the number of nodes (very unlikely in a production network) or consider implementing routers to divide the LAN into multiple *broadcast domains*.
C.J. is the CEO of the large accounting firm, Dewey, Cheatum, and Howe. She needs to ensure that her crack accountants have virtually guaranteed access to both the mainframe and the network servers, particularly during the busy tax season. She is especially interested in fault tolerance. A network design firm is currently making recommendations for a brand-new network. What architecture should she select?	The dead giveaway in this scenario is the requirement C.J. has for reliability and fault tolerance. When the designers present their proposals, she would be wise to select an FDDI-based network. The dual-ring design gives her the redundancy and the resiliency her accountants need.

CERTIFICATION SUMMARY

We have looked at the different networking architectures and their specifications. Keep in mind that certain vendors may implement these architectures somewhat differently from the way they have been presented here because of variations and enhancements within their individual product lines.

Each of the major network architectures has its unique characteristics, and each possesses different benefits and limitations. Ethernet definitely has market share, as well as the widest support from vendors and manufacturers. It also has a wide base of support because most networking people are familiar with Ethernet.

Token Ring brings high network reliability and determinism to environments that benefit from these characteristics. Node prioritization and the ability to push Token Ring network utilization levels up to 70 percent are additional benefits, available for the higher costs of Token Ring.

FDDI extends networks farther than ever before, allowing you to consider connecting nodes in neighboring cities on the same LAN. It also provides high bandwidth and fault-tolerant backbone network segments, enabling new and better-performing network designs. The very high costs of FDDI implementations will limit FDDI's use at the desktop, but the benefits in the core and the back office are unquestionable.

You should now have the understanding necessary to serve your customers well—the ability to measure their needs and problems, identify the type of problem and the classification, and recommend and design the appropriate network architecture and topology to save the day!

 TWO-MINUTE DRILL

❑ Media problems are caused by excessive collisions or latency from too many nodes on the network and are addressed by segmenting with switches.

❑ Protocol problems are typically caused by inefficient protocols causing broadcast storms and are best resolved through the use of routers to split the network.

❑ Transport problems manifest themselves by the demand for greater bandwidth and can be solved through use of higher-bandwidth technology like Gigabit Ethernet, switched Fast Ethernet, or FDDI.

❑ Ethernet was invented by Bob Metcalfe and ratified as a standard by the IEEE as IEEE 802.3, or the IEEE 10Base5 standard.

❑ DTEs terminate the electrical signals on the network cable. Repeaters retransmit or propagate the signals onward.

❑ The 5-4-3-2-1 rule defines the number of segments, repeaters, and populated segments.

❑ Ethernet uses the MAC-layer specification known as CSMA/CD, a contention-based method.

❑ Ethernet networks become saturated at 40 percent utilization and should then be segmented with switches.

❑ A flat network is a switched or bridged network that isn't divided by routers.

❑ Broadcast and multicast traffic shouldn't exceed 20 percent of the network traffic.

❑ Switches provide a dedicated point-to-point connection between each switch port and the device connected to it, eliminating collisions. Switches are also required to perform full-duplex connections.

❑ Ethernet is a nondeterministic architecture in which any node at any time may attempt to transmit data onto the network.

❑ Propagation delay is the measure of the amount of time an electrical signal takes to travel across the cabling segments and through each device along the path. Each item contributes a specific amount of latency or delay to the signal.

❑ Ethernet relies on 512 bit times to calculate maximum network diameters and segment lengths, also known as round-trip propagation delay.

❑ 10Base5 is a bus topology using thicknet coaxial cabling with a maximum segment length of 500 meters and up to 100 nodes attached to the cable via cable drops using AUIs and MAUs.

❑ 10Base2 is a bus topology using thinnet RG-58 coaxial cabling with a maximum segment length of 185 meters and up to 30 nodes directly attached to the cable.

❑ 10BaseT is a star topology using twisted-pair cabling with segments up to 100 meters and only 2 nodes per segment, attached via hubs or repeaters.

❑ 10BaseF is a variety of 10BaseT using fiber-optic cabling.

❑ 100BaseT (Fast Ethernet or 802.3u) is a star topology using twisted-pair cabling with a maximum collision domain of 205 meters with UTP and is limited to two repeater links.

❑ 100BaseFX is the Fast Ethernet specification using fiber-optic cabling and is based on the 10BaseF standard.

❑ Gigabit Ethernet or 802.3z, which operates at 1,000 Mbps, is implemented primarily through the use of fiber-optic cabling and is limited to a single repeater link.

❑ Attenuation is the weakening or deterioration of an electrical signal as it passes along a length of cabling.

❑ Repeaters do not examine traffic, as they function at layer 1 of the OSI reference model, also known as the physical layer.

❑ Bridges and switches operate at layer 2, the data-link layer, examining the MAC address of each data frame as it enters the device.

❑ Bridges and switches dynamically learn MAC addresses and pass traffic to the appropriate segment.

❑ Routers function at layer 3, the network layer. They use routing tables to perform complicated route path selections and can be used to connect different network architectures.

❑ Routers are typically slower than bridges or switches because of the overhead involved, but effectively break up broadcast domains, filter traffic, and provide redundancy between networks.

❑ Token Ring was invented by IBM and standardized as IEEE 802.5.

❑ Token Ring networks circulate a frame called a *token* used to control access to the network. Token Ring usually runs at 4 or 16 Mbps.

❑ Token Ring is a logical ring topology but a physical star topology, using MAUs to attach nodes and typically using STP or UTP twisted-pair cabling.

❑ The active monitor functions as a central timing source and cleans up lost tokens from the ring. Token Ring nodes can transmit one frame at a time on the network.

❑ Token Ring employs beaconing, a fault-tolerant procedure that bypasses failed nodes and maintains the ring's traffic.

❑ Token Ring is a deterministic architecture and can scale up to 70 percent utilization effectively. It supports traffic prioritization and is generally more expensive than Ethernet to implement.

❑ FDDI is a token-based networking architecture standardized by ANSI and ISO, intended for high speeds and designed originally to use fiber-optic media.

❑ CDDI is FDDI using copper cabling.

❑ FDDI uses a dual counter-rotating ring and permits dual-attached stations to initiate a reconfiguration, wrapping the rings into one and routing traffic around a ring failure.

❑ Cisco routers support a method called *dual homing*, allowing for fault tolerance and redundancy for network paths with two individual connections to each ring.

❑ SAS connections are typically made through the use of hubs, negotiating the insertion/reinsertion on the ring, preventing a ring "failure" situation, and maintaining the integrity of the ring.

❑ FDDI uses a physical ring topology and is typically found in the core of a network and used where there are high-bandwidth and fault-tolerance requirements.

❑ FDDI uses timed token release, permitting nodes to transmit multiple frames before releasing the token.

❑ FDDI frames data differently from Ethernet and Token Ring networks, requiring the use of a router to interconnect FDDI to these other architectures.

❑ FDDI is the most expensive architecture available, but it supports great distances.

exam
ⓦatch

The key to answering the CCDA scenario questions is to first read the scenario fully, trying to absorb as many of the pertinent details as possible. Read the first question and then skim through the scenario again to identify any specifications or constraints that may relate to the question. Finally, answer the question based on your understanding of the material, the scenario, and the question.

Also, be judicious with your time during the test. Take enough time to understand the scenarios without spending the entire session reading those wonderful little stories over and over!

SELF TEST

The following Self Test questions will help you measure your understanding of the material presented in this chapter. Read all the choices carefully because there may be more than one correct answer. Choose all correct answers for each question.

1. Ethernet was invented by whom?

   A. Marc Andreessen

   B. Bill Gates

   C. Bob Metcalfe

   D. Steve Jobs

2. Which standards body is responsible for maintaining the 802.X body of specifications?

   A. OSI

   B. IEEE

   C. ISO

   D. ANSI

3. Which Ethernet specification was first?

   A. 1000BaseLX

   B. 10Base2

   C. 100BaseT

   D. 10Base5

4. Which of the following would be considered a DTE? (Choose all that apply.)

   A. Network interface card

   B. Repeater port

   C. Switch port

   D. Router port

   E. All of the above

5. In the 5-4-3-2-1 Ethernet rule, what does the number "3" represent?

   A. The number of unpopulated segments

   B. The number of populated segments

   C. The number of repeaters

   D. The number of total segments

6. When two Ethernet nodes transmit data at the exact same moment, their data frames are both dropped from the network. Why does this happen?

   A. CSMA/CD: The frames collide and are dropped.

   B. Timed Token Release: The token times out and drops the frames.

   C. Ring Insertion: The insertion fails and drops the frames.

   D. Attenuation: The electrical signals grow too strong and drop the frames.

7. What is the maximum number of nodes a flat IP-only network can support?

   A. 1,000

   B. 700

   C. 500

   D. 300

8. Mark is a network architect for a large corporation. He is looking for a way to increase the speed of network access for a group of users. The users all have new PCs and are connected to the network, running 100BaseT and passing into repeaters in the wiring closet. What is the easiest way for him to increase bandwidth and network speed for these users?

   A. Replace the twisted-pair cabling with fiber-optic cabling.

   B. Move the users to Token Ring.

   C. Replace the twisted-pair cabling with thinnet coaxial cabling.

   D. Replace the repeaters with switches.

9. What is the number used to calculate round-trip propagation delay?

   A. 512 token times

   B. 512 bit times

   C. 512 byte times

   D. 512 μm times

Abracadabra Ltd. is a large public relations firm with many well-known international clients. It is planning a move to its new headquarters, situated on a large campus outside town. The members of the network design team are in the middle of their proposal phase for the network, and they are trying to make the correct choices regarding media. They have already selected Ethernet as the network architecture.

Building 1 is the main building with the majority of users located there. This facility is quite large with portions of the building more than 400 meters away from the proposed data center. Building 2 is located 350 meters to the west and has a beautiful view, overlooking Fern Valley. Building 2 is where the accounting, finance, and legal departments will be located.

Building 3 is situated 150 meters to the east, near the river. This is where the maintenance and janitorial facilities will be housed. There are 15 full-time maintenance workers and they have limited needs regarding network access or speed. Building 4 is the next building and will house most of the graphics artists and preproduction employees. Building 4 is located 275 meters to the south of Building 1.

Finally, Building 5 is located 1.7 kilometers to the north of Building 1 and has ample parking to accommodate several hundred visitors. This will be the future home of the marketing and sales departments. Answer questions 10 to 13 based on the scenario presented.

10. Steve has been asked to suggest the medium to be used between the data center in Building 1 and the main wiring closet in Building 2. What are his options?

    A. Two segments of 100BaseFX using a single Class II repeater

    B. One segment of 10BaseT

    C. One segment of switched full-duplex 10Base5

    D. One segment of switched 100BaseFX in half-duplex mode

    E. All of the above

11. Refer to the Abracadabra Ltd. scenario above. Dirk has been tasked with connecting Building 3 to Building 1. What are his options?

    A. One segment of 10Base2

    B. One segment of 100BaseFX

    C. One segment of 10BaseFL

    D. One segment of 10BaseFB

    E. All of the above

12. Refer to the Abracadabra Ltd. scenario above. Tim has been tasked with connecting Building 4 to Building 1. What is his best option?

    A. One segment of switched, full-duplex 100BaseFX

    B. One segment of 10Base5

    C. One segment of 1000BaseSX

    D. One segment of 10BaseFL

    E. All of the above

13. Refer to the Abracadabra Ltd. scenario above. Beth has been tasked with connecting Building 5 to Building 1. What are her options? (Choose all that apply.)

A. One segment of switched, full-duplex 100BaseFX

B. A routed FDDI ring between buildings

C. A series of 10BaseT repeater-based links

D. One segment of 100BaseT, joined to a single Class II UTP/FX repeater, joined again to one segment of 100BaseFX

E. All of the above

14. Which networking device can be used to interconnect a Token Ring network to an Ethernet network?

A. Repeater

B. Switch

C. MAU

D. Router

15. Which device makes path selections based on tables that contain different types of parameters or criteria?

A. MSAU

B. Router

C. Repeater

D. Switch

16. Which term relates to the functions of central timing and rogue token cleanup?

A. Early token release

B. MAU

C. Start of frame delimiter

D. Active monitor

17. Tom and Eric run a small automotive company. A network analyst performs an annual diagnosis of their network and reports that everything is running great. But he is concerned that the average network utilization is over 60 percent. What type of network are Tom and Eric likely using? (Choose all that apply.)

A. 802.5

B. FDDI

C. Token-passing

D. CDDI

E. All of the above

18. Which IEEE specification applies to Token Ring?

    A. 802.3

    B. 802.5

    C. 802.3u

    D. 802.3z

19. Which network technology transmits electrical signals faster over copper?

    A. Ethernet

    B. Gigabit Ethernet

    C. High-speed Token Ring

    D. Fast Ethernet

    E. CDDI

    F. None of the above

20. What does the acronym "MAU" mean? (Choose all that apply.)

    A. Multiple station acceleration unit

    B. Medium-range access unit

    C. Multistation access unit

    D. Multistation attenuation unit

    E. Medium attachment unit

21. Fill in the blank. Token Ring is a _____ ring network.

    A. Theoretical

    B. Logical

    C. Metaphysical

    D. Physical

22. IBM developed a classification system for cabling. What is the term used in these cabling labels?

    A. Category

    B. Class

    C. Token

    D. Type

23. Token Ring and other token-passing architectures are considered to be what?

    A. Deterministic

    B. Nihilistic

    C. Futuristic

    D. Idealistic

    E. Antagonistic

24. What is beaconing?

    A. The method used to set ports to either half or full duplex

    B. The method used to remove orphaned frames from the wire

    C. The method of failure notification; used to reconfigure the network and partition the failure

    D. The method of translating disparate network architectures from one to the other

25. Which types of node connections have been defined in a FDDI architecture? (Choose all that apply.)

    A. DAS

    B. NAS

    C. MSAS

    D. SAS

    E. FAS

26. The term "dual homing" refers to what?

    A. Placing switches in two locations for fault tolerance

    B. Connecting a device using two individual connection points

    C. The dual counter-rotating rings of FDDI/CDDI

    D. Placing routers in two locations for fault tolerance

27. CDDI is certified to run using what media? (Choose all that apply.)

    A. IBM Type-1 STP

    B. IBM Type-3 UTP

    C. Category-3 UTP

    D. Category-5 UTP

    E. 62.5/125μm fiber-optic cable

28. What would be the best description of FDDI's token access methodology?

    A. Varies with the length of the cable segment

    B. One frame per token pass

C. Varies with the number of attached nodes

D. Multiple frames within a certain time frame

Eric and Kyoko own and operate I-PlaceU.com, an Internet-enabled job placement agency. They are considering a brand-new network to support their growing business. They have decided to first concentrate on their cabling choice. Eric, the president of the agency, wants the fastest, most scalable solution possible. However, since Kyoko is the controller and vice president, she wants to implement the cheapest possible cabling solution. Answer questions 29 to 31 based on the scenario presented.

29. If Kyoko wins the argument, what medium will I-PlaceU.com implement?

   A. Shielded twisted-pair

   B. Coaxial

   C. Unshielded twisted-pair

   D. Fiber-optic

30. Refer to the I-PlaceU.com scenario above. If Eric gets things his way, what will his best choice be?

   A. Shielded twisted-pair

   B. Coaxial

   C. Unshielded twisted-pair

   D. Fiber-optic

31. Refer to the I-PlaceU.com scenario above. Since Eric and Kyoko are also married to each other, they decide that the best solution is to compromise. What would be the best compromise involving speed, scalability, and cost?

   A. Shielded twisted-pair

   B. Coaxial

   C. Unshielded twisted-pair

   D. Fiber-optic

32. If an FDDI-based network experiences two simultaneous node failures, what will happen?

   A. Because FDDI is a token-passing network, two failures will cause the token to be dropped, and the network will have to be reinitialized.

   B. The CSMA/CD protocol will handle and correct both failures, and network operations will continue as normal.

   C. DAS nodes will wrap the rings into two separate rings, thereby isolating traffic on separate networks.

   D. Early token release will activate, generating both a Priority token and a Reservation token, compensating for the dual failures.

SELF TEST ANSWERS

1. ☑ **C.** Bob Metcalfe invented Ethernet in 1972 while working at Xerox's Palo Alto Research Center.
   ☒ **A,** Marc Andreessen, **B,** Bill Gates, and **D,** Steve Jobs, are associated with Netscape, Microsoft, and Apple Computer, respectively.

2. ☑ **B.** The Institute of Electrical and Electronics Engineers (IEEE) is the organization that ratifies and maintains the 802.X specifications.
   ☒ **A** is incorrect because OSI is the Open Systems Interconnection model. **C** is incorrect because ISO is the International Standards Organization. **D** is incorrect because ANSI is the American National Standards Institute.

3. ☑ **D.** 10Base5 was the first Ethernet specification, designated IEEE 802.3.
   ☒ **A, B,** and **C** followed this original standard.

4. ☑ **A, C, and D.** Network interface cards (NICs), switch ports, and router ports all provide an electrical termination of the signal.
   ☒ Remember that **B,** a repeater, simply regenerates the signal and passes it along.

5. ☑ **B.** In the 5-4-3-2-1 Ethernet rule, the number "3" represents the number of populated segments.
   ☒ **A,** the number of unpopulated segments, is represented by the number 2 in the 5-4-3-2-1 rule. **C,** the number of repeaters, is represented by the number 4. **D,** the number of total segments, is represented by the number 5.

6. ☑ **A.** CSMA/CD (Carrier-Sense, Multiple-Access with *Collision* Detection) is the correct answer because the frames *collide* and are dropped.
   ☒ Both **B,** Timed Token Release, and **C,** ring insertion, are incorrect because they are related to FDDI/CDDI networks. **D,** attenuation, is actually the gradual weakening and deterioration of an electrical signal as it passes along a cable.

7. ☑ **C.** Remember that this is a limitation of *flat* network designs and that 500 nodes applies to an IP-based network. The number of nodes varies with the type and mix of protocol being used.

8. ☑ **D.** Since the PCs are new, they probably have full duplex–capable NICs. As long as the uplinks to the network backbone have sufficient bandwidth, he can simply drop in the switches and let the users' NICs auto-negotiate full-duplex connections.
   ☒ **A,** Replacing existing copper with fiber is likely not the easiest solution, and moving to Token Ring, **B,** or thinnet, **C,** will actually decrease bandwidth availability.

9. ☑ **B.** This number is based on the minimum Ethernet packet size and is crucial for determining maximum network diameters and total segment lengths. Also remember that this number remains the same for both 10 Mbps and 100 Mbps networks, as well as for switched Gigabit networks.

10. ☑ **D.** You are trying to reach 350 meters out to reach Building 2. Even though the link will run at half duplex, remember that a switch-to-switch 100BaseFX link can extend up to 412 meters.
☒ **A** is incorrect because even though you can use two segments of fiber, each segment is limited to 160 meters for a total of 320 meters—just short of the target. **B** is incorrect because a single segment of 110BaseT is limited to 100 meters; and **C** is incorrect because 10Base5 can't be switched and, therefore, cannot run in full-duplex mode. Technically, a single segment of plain old 10Base5 *would* reach Building 2, but you also don't want to put the people who will pay for your network deployment on a relatively slow 10 Mbps link!

11. ☑ **E.** Each of the listed options has the capability to successfully reach Building 3, 150 meters away.

12. ☑ **C.** The best option for connecting Building 4 to Building 1 is one segment of 1000BaseSX.
☒ This question is tricky. While **A, B,** and **D** will also reach the users at Building 4, keep in mind that the question asked you to choose the "best option." The users in this building are high-bandwidth consumers (remember graphics people?), and the Gigabit link suggested provides these users with the "fat pipe" they will require to do their work.

13. ☑ **A and B.** One segment of switched, full-duplex 100BaseFX or a routed FDDI ring between buildings are the correct options for connecting Building 5 to Building 1. Switched 100BaseFX can extend up to 2 kilometers when run at full duplex, and routers would provide the necessary translation between the Ethernet and FDDI networks.
☒ **C,** 10BaseT, and **D,** 100BaseT, simply can't extend to the distances required by this connection.

14. ☑ **D.** Because routers function at layer 3 of the OSI model, they have the intelligence necessary to translate between two different networking architectures.
☒ **A,** repeaters, **B,** switches, and **C,** MAUs, can't be used to join two different architectures.

15. ☑ **B.** Routers maintain routing tables that contain parameters, such as cost, number of hops, line speed, and traffic levels.
☒ **A,** MSAUs (or MAUs), **C,** repeaters, and **D,** switches, don't use tables to make path selection decisions.

16. ☑ **D.** The active monitor node performs these tasks.

☒ **A**, early token release, can release additional tokens onto the ring; **B**, MAU, is the "repeater" in the Token Ring world; and **C**, start of frame delimiter, indicates to other nodes that the token already contains data.

17. ☑ **E.** The key to the question is not that the analyst is concerned about the 60 percent utilization. What is more important is that the network is "running great" at 60 percent utilization. Excellent performance under heavy utilization is characteristic of token-passing architectures. Finally, the dead giveaway is that each of the listed items is a token-based network. Watch out for this type of question on your exam!

18. ☑ **B.** The IEEE specification that applies to Token Ring is 802.5.

☒ **A**, **C**, and **D** are Ethernet specifications (802.3 = the original Ethernet standard, 802.3u = Fast Ethernet, and 802.3z = Gigabit Ethernet).

19. ☑ **F.** This is a bit of a trick question. However, the reasoning is this: make sure you understand the question when you are looking for the answer. The question asked about *electrical* signals, not data transmission rates. By listing varying network architectures, you tend to think about the data rates, not the laws of physics!

20. ☑ **C and E.** Both of these are correct. A medium attachment unit is used in the Ethernet 10Base5 specification, and a multistation access unit is the name for the repeaters or hubs used in a Token Ring environment.

☒ **A**, **B**, and **D** are imaginary acronyms.

21. ☑ **B.** A Token Ring network is usually a physical star network, while the ring is a logical ring, passing through the MAUs and each attached node.

☒ Some may consider Token Ring to be **C**, metaphysical, but we'd all be in a lot of trouble if it were only **A**, theoretical!

22. ☑ **D.** IBM defined cabling as types, as in Type 1, Type 3, etc.

23. ☑ **A.** You'll recall that this represents the orderly token-based access methodology used, as well as the predictability of Token Ring.

☒ I hope you didn't pick **C**, futuristic, because Token Ring is very real and available now!

24. ☑ **C.** Beaconing is the method of failure notification, used to reconfigure the network and partition the failure. Remember that beaconing sends a beacon frame around the ring to notify other nodes of the failure and to initiate reconfiguration.

☒ **A** refers to auto-negotiation in Ethernet, **B** refers to the active monitor, and **D** refers to a router capability.

25. ☑ **A and D.** Dual-attached stations (DASs) and single-attached stations (SASs) are the two types used with FDDI.
☒ **B, C,** and **E** are not valid options.

26. ☑ **B.** Dual homing refers to connecting a device using two individual connection points. Cisco routers support this method of multiple connections to a network to provide fault tolerance and redundancy for network paths.

27. ☑ **A and D.** CDDI is the copper-based FDDI specification and uses only Type-1 and Category-5 cabling.

28. ☑ **D.** FDDI's token access methodology is best described as multiple frames within a certain time frame. This refers to the timed token release mechanism used by FDDI.
☒ **A** and **C** are incorrect because token access does not depend on the cable length or number of attached nodes. **B** is the method used by 802.5/Token Ring.

29. ☑ **B.** Coaxial cabling has historically been less expensive than the other available media choices.
☒ Because of the extreme popularity of **C**, unshielded twisted-pair media, UTP may actually become cheaper than coaxial cabling; however, presently, UTP is still more expensive. **D**, fiber, is the most expensive of the choices.

30. ☑ **D.** Fiber-optic cabling is far and away the most expensive of all the media types, but it will scale to give Eric the fastest possible speeds—exactly what he wanted.
☒ **A** and **C**, twisted-pair, and **B**, coaxial, typically won't support these same high speeds.

31. ☑ **C.** UTP cabling will give them the speed and scalability they want, as well as a relatively inexpensive media choice.
☒ **B**, coaxial, is inexpensive but slow; and **D**, fiber, is fast but expensive.

32. ☑ **C.** DAS nodes will wrap the rings into two separate rings, thereby isolating traffic on separate networks. You'll remember that dual-attached stations (DASs) will help to reconfigure the rings when a failure occurs. However, when multiple failures occur, the network will be divided into separate rings, isolating the pieces of the network.
☒ **A, B,** and **D** don't apply to node failures on an FDDI network.

11

Choosing the Best Equipment Based on Design Criteria: WANs

There are three main types of wide area network (WAN) connections: point-to-point, cloud-based, and dial-on-demand routing (DDR). All of them are widely used today for network connectivity. As a network architect, you should be closely familiar with all three types of networks and be able to choose the right one, or even a combination of them, for every particular project. Your choice should be based on a series of factors and specifics of a production environment, and it should meet the customer's needs. It is important to keep in mind that every WAN design should provide reliable service, minimize the cost of bandwidth, and optimize bandwidth efficiency.

The main objective of this chapter is to provide you with important information regarding the types of WANs and the specifics of the choice of equipment needed to build networks.

Choosing the equipment may involve making many decisions concerning the devices to use, their cost, their performance, and the type of WAN design to interconnect these devices.

CERTIFICATION OBJECTIVE 11.01

Point-to-Point Connection

A point-to-point link is one of the most widely used and easily configured types of links, and Cisco provides a wide range of routers that support these links. A point-to-point link is used to establish a single communications path between two locations. An important role in this process of connection belongs to a carrier network (a telephone company, for example). A point-to-point link is often referred to as a leased line because the established communications path is constant and reserved permanently for each remote network contacted from the customer premises. Figure 11-1 gives an example of a point-to-point link.

These links support two types of transmissions: datagram transmissions and data-stream transmissions. Datagram transmissions consist of individually addressed frames, and data-stream transmissions represent a stream of data for which the address is checked only once.

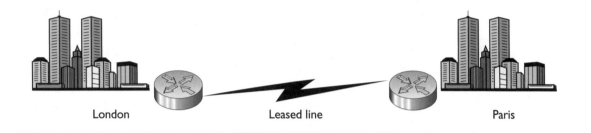

FIGURE 11-1 Point-to-point connection

London   Leased line   Paris

Advantages and Disadvantages

Just like any other solution, point-to-point links have some advantages and some disadvantages. The most important advantages are

- High reliability
- Relatively simple configurations, installation, and troubleshooting of links of this type
- Guaranteed speed on a clear line

The essential disadvantages are

- High lease cost of a carrier network
- Necessity to establish a new equipment on both sides every time you need to connect a new remote network
- Ineffective use of hub router interfaces compared with other types of links

Point-to-Point Encapsulation Types and Their Limitations

To establish communication between two devices, it is necessary to select a suitable encapsulation type. These encapsulation types must be the same on both sides of a point-to-point link. Cisco offers you several different types of encapsulation, and it's your task as a designer to select a proper one.

HDLC (Cisco)

High-level Data Link Control (HDLC) is a group of OSI layer-2 protocols based on IBM's Synchronous Data Link Control (SDLC) protocol. Cisco has its own version of HDLC incompatible with other versions of the protocol. The difference between Cisco's and other versions is in identification of the next-layer protocol.

HDLC is the Cisco default protocol for serial links. Because this protocol is the default, you don't have to configure it manually. But if the protocol has been changed on an interface, you can change it back to HDLC using the following command in the interface configuration mode:

```
Router (config-if)#encapsulation hdlc
```

Because of lower overhead, it is recommended that you use HDLC on clean lines (lines with low numbers of transmit and receive errors) between two Cisco devices.

LAPB

Link Access Protocol (LAP) is a modification of the HDLC protocol for use with X.25 network interfaces. It has lately been modified to make it more compatible with HDLC. The result is Link Access Procedure, Balanced (LAPB). This protocol is standard, so you would probably use it to establish a connection with non-Cisco devices. To enable this protocol on an interface, use the following command in the interface configuration mode:

```
Router (config-if)#encapsulation lapb
```

As distinct from the Cisco HDLC protocol, LAPB has a powerful algorithm for error correction. It can detect missing or out-of-sequence frames and retransmit lost frames without waiting for an upper-level protocol to find the error. These qualities make it irreplaceable on noisy links, but it can slow down your connection on high-quality links compared with HDLC.

PPP

Point-to-Point Protocol (PPP) is a full-duplex, connectionless protocol that supports many different types of links. The advantages of PPP made it the de facto standard for dial-up connections. To enable it on an interface, enter

```
Router (config-if)#encapsulation ppp
```

PPP has a lot of functionality such as error detection, multilink support, and multiple-protocol support.

SDLC

Synchronous Data Link Control (SDLC) can be used with a number of link types. It will implement its functions with point-to-point and multipoint links, half-duplex and full-duplex transmission devices, and circuit-switched and packet-switched networks.

Two types of network nodes are used with SDLC: primary and secondary. Primary nodes control operation of secondary ones. The primary sends a query to the secondary in a certain order, and that station is then able to transmit the outgoing data if it is there. The primary can also manage the link if it is operational and has the right to establish or interrupt links. A secondary node can send information to the primary only after it receives a permission to do that. So, a secondary node is fully controlled by a primary. Use the following command to configure SDLC encapsulation on an interface:

```
Router_Pr (config-if)#encapsulation  sdlc
```

Types of Cable to Use

When you are familiar with the different types of encapsulations that can be used on Cisco routers, you can establish a link between two devices. To do so, you'll need a data terminal equipment/data communications equipment (DTE/DCE) device. A modem is a typical example of a DCE device, and it is usually provided by your carrier network service provider. A DCE device physically connects your equipment to the network, forwards traffic, and gives signals that allow DTE and DCE to synchronize data transmission. A Cisco router can be used as a DCE device to simulate WAN connection without actually using modems. Figure 11-2 shows a typical DCE device usage.

DTE

It is very likely that you will use DTE cables in your everyday work to connect a router to a DCE device. Cisco offers a few different types of

FIGURE 11-2 DCE device

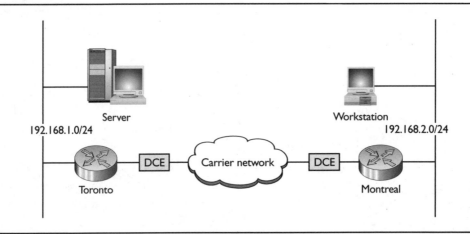

cables. You should select the proper one, proceeding from the requirements of the type of interface you have on your modem and a port type you want to use on your Cisco router. To become familiar with the cables Cisco offers, refer to the Cisco Web site.

DCE

DCE cable is used to simulate a DCE device to interconnect two Cisco routers without using a real DCE device (for example, a modem). You'll probably use it for simulation of a WAN link in a test lab. A Cisco serial interface can provide clocking for a DTE device if it has a DCE cable connected.

DSU/CSU Device

Data service unit/channel service unit (DSU/CSU) is a device that is required when you purchase a high-speed service such as a T1 or a fractional T1. Figure 11-3 illustrates a DSU/CSU device.

The main function of DSU is to provide line control, to convert input/output between a user interface such as V.35 or RS-232 and TDM

Data service unit/channel
service unit

frames on a T1 line. The primary functions of CSU are to receive
and transmit signals from the WAN line, to protect user equipment
from electrical interference with telco equipment, and to respond to
a telco-initiated loopback.

Point-to-Point Connection

Now, that you are familiar with protocols and interfaces, let's create
a sample configuration for routers, as in Figure 11-2. We'll use PPP
encapsulation. The Ethernet interface of Toronto router's IP address is
192.168.1.1, and the Ethernet interface of Montreal router's IP address
is 192.168.2.1.

After completing the configuration, compare it with the one we provide
here. Is it the same? Configuration of the Toronto router in show
running-config format is as follows:

```
version 11.0
service udp-small-service
service tcp-small-service
!
hostname Toronto
!
enable secret 5 $1$55In$2NECj1.v.zBk/0m0KH3sR0
enable password TopSecret
!
interface Ethernet0
   ip address 192.168.1.1 255.255.255.0
!
interface Serial0
   description Leased Line to Montreal
   ip unnumbered Ethernet0
   encapsulation ppp
!
ip route 192.168.2.0 255.255.255.0 Serial0
```

```
!
line con 0
   password console
   login
line aux 0
line vty 0 4
   password telnet
   login
!
end
```

Montreal router's configuration is as follows:

```
version 11.0
service udp-small-service
service tcp-small-service
!
hostname Montreal
!
enable secret 5 $1$55In$2NECj1.v.zBk/0m0KH3sR0
enable password TopSecret
!
interface Ethernet0
   ip address 192.168.2.1 255.255.255.0
!
interface Serial0
   description Leased Line to Toronto
   ip unnumbered Ethernet0
   encapsulation ppp
!
ip route 192.168.1.0 255.255.255.0 Serial0
!
line con 0
   password console
   login
line aux 0
line vty 0 4
   password telnet
   login
!
end
```

Applicability

To establish point-to-point links, you can use a wide spectrum of devices and protocols to connect remote networks. The configuration in this case will be rather simple. These characteristics make Point-to-Point Protocol a good choice for a wide range of uses. Though other types of connections, such as Frame Relay and ATM that are characterized for their lower costs, prevail today, point-to-point connections still can be used for fast connectivity to the ISP or for a backup of other types of links. They are also useful in areas where other types of links, such as ATM or Frame Relay, are not available.

WAN Types in Which to Use Point-to-Point

Today, network carrier providers offer a wide choice of link types to interconnect the networks. In the following sections, we discuss the three most commonly used types.

T1/E1 through T3/E3

The T-carrier system was introduced in the 1960s in the United States by the Bell System. It was the first system that could support the digitized voice transmission successfully. Now the T1 line is widely used for both digitized voice and data transmissions with the original transmission rate of 1.554 Mbps, as is the T3 line, which provides the rate of 44.736 Mbps.

Because American and European communication standards are different, American T1 and T3 lines correspond with European E1 and E3 lines with the transmission rate of 2.048 Mbps for E1 and 34.368 Mbps for E3.

Fractional Links

An original T1 line consists of 24 channels of 64 Kbps each. In addition, a fractional T1 line uses only some of the 24 channels with a data transfer capacity of 64 Kbps each in an original T1 line, leaving the rest of the channels unused. The customer can rent any number of the 24 channels. Renting a fractional T1 line costs less, though the transmission method is not changed. T3 lines are also sometimes leased as a fractional service. Such lines provide up to 672 64-Kbps channels.

High-Speed Serial Interface

The High-Speed Serial Interface (HSSI) is a special kind of DTE/DCE interface developed by Cisco Systems and T3plus Networking to satisfy the need for high-speed communication over WAN links. Though HSSI is not officially standardized yet (it is now in the American National Standards Institute under formal standardization), its specification is available to any company that would like to implement HSSI. The maximum signaling rate for HSSI is 52 Mbps, which allows it to handle most of today's technologies, such as T3, OC-1 (optical carrier with base rate of 51.84 Mbps).

Topology Map

The nature of a connection allows you to implement point-to-point architecture in different topology models. These models were discussed in detail in Chapter 9. For small- and medium-sized offices, you will probably decide to implement hub-and-spoke technology using point-to-point links between the offices. For large networks, you will probably use partial- or full-mesh technologies to provide redundancy. You should remember that as a designer, you can not recommend the use of one or another technology relying on only your preferences or the possible simplicity of configuration. You should analyze many factors, such as customers' needs, availability of different services in your area, cost of channels lease, router performance, and scalability issues.

Meet the Customer's Needs

Point-to-Point Protocol can be recommended to customers when they can lease a public carrier line at a low cost or when a cloud-based connection is not available in the customer's area. Figure 11-4 illustrates that a point-to-point link is a very cost-ineffective solution and should be recommended with caution.

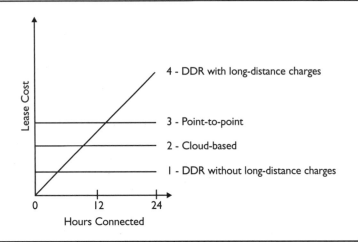

FIGURE 11-4

Lease cost depending on the amount of time connected (This is a typical example; results may vary.)

Bandwidth Limitations

Point-to-point connections give you an opportunity to connect your networks on a wide speed spectrum. The development of HSSI has removed the 2MB limitation on maximum DCE device connection speed.

CERTIFICATION OBJECTIVE 11.02

Cloud-Based Connection

Cloud-based connectivity is a different method of connecting your networks (see Figure 11-5). It appeared quite a while ago when people realized that a point-to-point link was not the cheapest way to interconnect networks. The main idea of these types of connections is that people connect their equipment to a local public carrier network, and the carrier service provider takes care of transmitting the frames among different sites.

The cloud-based network is similar to a television cable. You are not pooling a cable from your house to every TV company that broadcasts your favorite shows. You just connect to your local TV cable provider, and it is no longer your headache to receive the TV channels you want to see.

FIGURE 11-5

Cloud-based network

Advantages and Disadvantages

Cloud-based solutions have the following advantages:

- Lower price than point-to-point solutions
- Capability to use a wide range of speeds
- In many cases, no need to install new equipment when you add new connections

Their disadvantages are

- Possibility that service will not be available in certain areas
- More complicated configuration and diagnostics than with point-to-point solutions
- Because many people use the same cloud, a possibility that the service will be less reliable than with leased lines

Types of Cloud-Based Links and Their Limitations

The modern technology offers you a few different types of cloud-based connections:

- **X.25** The oldest and gradually ousted one. It was born in a world of noisy unreliable lines in 1970s and could provide a very high level of error correction and detection. But with the changes in the world since then, the advantage of high reliability turned into a disadvantage of huge overhead.

- **Frame Relay** A currently popular protocol that provides a wide spectrum of speeds, high reliability, and low cost.

- **Asynchronous transfer mode (ATM)** Developed in the 1980s, when very small fixed-length cells were being transmitted at great speeds across a network. This protocol has the features that allow it to be used for the transfer of multimedia data that is so popular today.

- **Switched Multimegabit Data Service (SMDS)** A new technology that supports very high-speed access across public data networks.

X.25

X.25 is an International Telecommunication Union-Telecommunication Standardization Sector (ITU-T) protocol standard for WAN communications. This is the oldest of the cloud-based protocols, and it is still in use today. This protocol defines how to establish and maintain connections between user devices and network devices.

When X.25 was designed in the 1970s, the networks were quite unreliable, and the circuits were analog and noisy. It has been widely used since then; but some years ago, network designers started to use other protocols, such as Frame Relay and ATM, instead of X.25. It is unlikely that you will have to use X.25 today to build new networks, but you may come across this protocol in the networks you'll have to support and maintain.

X.25 was made to operate effectively with all types of systems connected to the network. The typical example of X.25 use is a packet-switched network (PSN) of a common carrier, such as a telephone company.

X.25 devices are generally placed into three categories:

- **Data terminal equipment (DTE)**   End systems that communicate over an X.25 network (for example, router, host systems, terminals, and PCs) and are located on the individual subscribers' premises

- **Data circuit-terminating equipment (DCE)**   Communications devices (for example, modems and packet switches) that provide an interface between DTE devices and a PSE

- **Packet-switching exchange (PSE)**   Switches that make up the majority of the carrier's network and are tasked with transferring data between DTE devices through the X.25 packet-switched network

It is necessary to establish X.25 sessions when one DTE device contacts another to transfer information. This process can be described as follows:

1. One DTE device requests a communication session from another one.

2. The DTE device that receives the request can accept or refuse the connection.

3. If the second DTE device accepts the request, the two systems begin information transfer.

4. The connection can be terminated by either of the DTE devices.

If the session is terminated, any further communication requires the establishment of a new session.

Virtual circuits are logical connections that are made to provide reliable communications between two network devices. A virtual circuit is a logical, not physical, bidirectional path established from one DTE device to another via an X.25 network. Physically, any number of DCE devices and PSEs can be used for this connection.

There are two types of X.25 virtual circuits: switched and permanent. Switched virtual circuits (SVCs) are used for occasional data transfer. These are temporary connections. Two DTE devices are needed to establish, support, and terminate each communication section of this kind. Permanent virtual circuits (PVCs) are used for frequent and consistent data transfers. The communication session in this case is always active, so DTEs can begin data transfer whenever necessary.

The X.25 protocol suite belongs to the first three levels of the OSI model. The following protocols are used in X.25 implementations: Packet-Layer Protocol (PLP); Link Access Procedure, Balanced (LAPB); and some other physical-layer serial interfaces, such as X.21bis, EIA/TIA-232, EIA/TIA-449, EIA-530 and G.703.

- **X.21bis protocol (or one of those just mentioned under the same category)**   Used on the physical level of the OSI reference model. This protocol defines the electrical procedures for using the physical medium.

- **LAPB**   A data-link layer protocol used for communication and packet framing between DTE and DCE devices. This protocol is discussed in this chapter in the section "Point-to-Point Connection."

- **Packet-Layer Protocol (PLP)**   A protocol on the network layer of the OSI model that manages packet exchanges between DTE devices across virtual circuits. There exist five distinct PLP modes: call setup, data transfer, idle, call clearing, and restarting.

Frame Relay

Frame Relay is a very popular WAN protocol. It operates on the physical and data-link layers of the OSI reference model. Originally, this protocol was designed for use across Integrated Services Digital Network (ISDN) interface, but later it became very popular, and it is now used over many other network interfaces. The main reason for the increased popularity of this protocol is its ability to interconnect a large number of sites in an inexpensive way. Figure 11-6 is an example of Frame Relay connection. Note that, notwithstanding two logical connections of the Berlin router, physically, we have only one connection here.

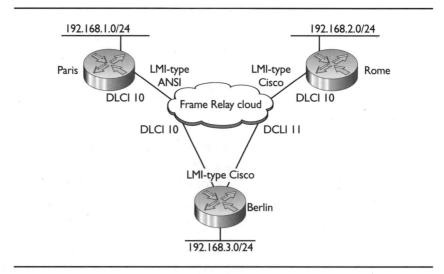

FIGURE 11-6

Typical Frame Relay
connection

Shared bandwidth is a related concept. If you have to connect two remote sites, the ordinary way would be to use a dedicated leased line. This line would belong to you; the bandwidth would be available to you even when you don't need to send any traffic across. Imagine a huge number of clients, each of whom owns a dedicated leased line and uses only a portion of the total bandwidth. Using the Frame Relay technology, all customers share access to the total bandwidth available through the Frame Relay cloud. So the utilization of the pipe becomes more efficient and less expensive at the same time. But what if all the customers decide to transmit data simultaneously over that shared bandwidth?

Statistically, this situation is unlikely to happen, but this possibility still should be kept in mind. There could be a situation when no bandwidth is available. Fortunately, there exists a committed information rate (CIR) that is a certain safety net. If you have installed a 1.5-Mbps Frame Relay access between two sites, you can specify a CIR of 56 Kbps, for example, that would give you a chance to send at least 56 Kbps to your remote site any time. And when the bandwidth is available, you would use all the 1.5 Mbps if you need to. For customers, this model is very attractive because they pay only for what they really need; but at the same time, there is an opportunity to exceed that level when the network bandwidth allows. Some carrier providers would let you purchase a CIR of 0 for a very low price. That would mean that you have no guaranteed bandwidth, but you can still use the cloud to send your frames.

Two general categories of devices attach to a Frame Relay WAN: data terminal equipment (DTE) and data circuit-terminating equipment (DCE), the devices that are discussed in the section "X.25."

Frame Relay provides connection-oriented data-link layer communication. Such connections are associated with a connection identifier. It becomes possible with implementation of a Frame Relay virtual circuit—a logical connection created between two data terminal equipment (DTE) devices across a Frame Relay packet-switched network (PSN).

EXERCISE 11-2

Frame Relay

Let's create the three-router configuration (refer back to Figure 11-6): Paris (IP 192.168.1.1), Rome (192.168.2.1), and Berlin (192.168.3.1). We have already examined full configuration for routers in Exercise 11-1; now we'll pay attention to interface configurations only. The configuration of the interfaces of the Paris router in show running-config format is as follows:

```
interface Ethernet0
   ip address 192.168.1.1 255.255.255.0
!
interface Serial0
   no ip address
   encapsulation frame-relay
   frame-relay lmi-type ansi
!
interface Seial0.10 point-to-point
   description Frame Relay to Berlin
   ip unnumbered Ethernet0
   frame-relay interface-dlci 10 broadcast
!
```

The configuration of the interfaces of the Rome router in show running-config format is as follows:

```
interface Ethernet0
   ip address 192.168.2.1 255.255.255.0
!
interface Serial0
```

```
      no ip address
      encapsulation frame-relay
   !
interface Seial0.10 point-to-point
      description Frame Relay to Berlin
      ip unnumbered Ethernet0
      frame-relay interface-dlci 10 broadcast
   !
```

The Interface configuration of the Berlin router in show running-config format is as follows:

```
interface Ethernet0
      ip address 192.168.3.1 255.255.255.0
   !
interface Serial0
      no ip address
      encapsulation frame-relay
   !
interface Seial0.10 point-to-point
      description Frame Relay to Paris
      ip unnumbered Ethernet0
      frame-relay interface-dlci 10 broadcast
   !
interface Seial0.11 point-to-point
      description Frame Relay to Rome
      ip unnumbered Ethernet0
      frame-relay interface-dlci 11 broadcast
   !
```

Let's take a look at some basic aspects of configuration. We'll start with routers Paris and Rome because their configurations are very similar. We won't pay much attention to the configuration of Ethernet interfaces because they are quite standard. Let's move to the line interface Serial0. Because you are already familiar with the point-to-point configuration of a serial interface, there is nothing new for you here. We don't assign any IP address to the interface and use Frame Relay as an encapsulation type. Note the following line in the Paris router configuration:

```
frame-relay lmi-type ansi
```

You won't find a similar line in the Rome and Berlin router configurations. This means that the telco in Paris provides an ANSI Local Management Interface (LMI), and in Rome and Berlin, the telco provides a Cisco LMI interface. Cisco LMI type is the default for Cisco routers, so you don't have to specify it. If it were changed to another type (ansi or q933a), you could change it back using the Frame Relay lmi-type cisco command.

You can have multiple virtual circuits on one physical interface, so you should separate them somehow, preferably with the help of subinterfaces. So the line

```
interface Seial0.10 point-to-point
```

in the Paris router configuration means that you want to configure logical subinterface 10 on physical interface Serial0 for a point-to-point connection to Berlin. The point-to-point statement shouldn't confuse you. We are not talking about a leased line between Paris and Berlin; we are talking about a logical connection between Paris and Berlin provided through a Frame Relay cloud. The line

```
frame-relay interface-dlci 10 broadcast
```

assigns a data-link identification number (DLCI) provided to you by your telco to the corresponding subinterface and allows broadcast to flow through the subinterface (required for routing protocols such as RIP). Although we use the same number (10) for subinterface and DLCI, it's not a requirement. However, it can be a good practice for complex configurations.

Router Berlin has a configuration similar to that for routers Paris and Rome. The difference is in the two subinterfaces it has. Note that in our configuration, all the traffic between Paris and Rome will flow through the router Berlin. It can be a satisfactory solution if you have a server in Berlin and there is no large traffic flow between Paris and Rome. In the future, if you decide to establish a direct link between Paris and Rome, all you will have to do is order a new virtual circuit from your telco and add a few lines to the configuration of the routers. You'll need no new ports on your routers, no new modems, and no telco employees drilling your walls to install new cables. Isn't that a good reason to use cloud-based solutions?

ATM

ATM is a dedicated connection switching technology that allows you to transmit information for multiple service types, such as video, voice, and data, in small cells of a fixed size. The ATM standard was developed by the Telecommunication Standardization Sector of the International Telecommunications Union (ITU-T) to use as a carrier service. Now ATM has become common in corporate systems because of its fast speeds, ability to carry multiple types of data, and quality-of-service mechanism. Originally, ATM was designed as a high-speed transfer technology for voice, video, and data across public networks. Later, the ATM Forum extended ITU-T's definition of ATM to include such standards as User-Network Interface (UNI), Interim Local Management Interface (ILMI), and LAN emulation (LANE). These changes allowed ATM to be used over both public and private networks.

ATM transfers information in fixed-size units called *cells.* Each cell consists of 53 bytes. The first 5 bytes contain cell-header information, and the rest carry the user information ("payload"). Small cells of a fixed size work well when it comes to transferring voice and video traffic, mainly because such traffic should operate without delays. And such delays usually occur when you have to wait for large data packets to transfer. You may be interested why the cell consists of 53 bytes. U.S. carriers were planning to use ATM for data transmission and recommended 64 bytes for the payload. At the same time, European carriers wanted to use ATM for voice traffic and offered 32 bytes for the payload. The compromise was found—48 bytes for the payload, and after adding a 5-byte header, we have an ATM cell of 53 bytes.

ATM technology combines the advantages of circuit switching (guaranteed capacity and constant transmission delay) with those of packet switching (flexibility and efficiency for intermittent traffic). The asynchronous nature of ATM technology adds to its efficiency of data transfer.

An ATM network consists of an ATM switch and ATM endpoints. The ATM switch is responsible mainly for switching cells to the correct destination. It also gathers statistics and can set up and tear down virtual circuits. ATM endpoints are actually the points of entry into an ATM network.

Two types of interfaces define the communication between the devices: a User-Network Interface (UNI) and a Network-Network or Network-

Node Interface (NNI). The UNI connects ATM endpoints (such as hosts and routers) to an ATM switch. The NNI connects two ATM switches.

The ATM reference model has the following layers:

- **Physical layer**   Similar to the OSI reference model's physical layer. It defines standards that help to transmit data in the medium.

- **ATM layer**   Interacts with the physical layer and adds a 5-byte header to the ATM payload. This layer establishes connections and passes cells through the ATM network.

- **ATM adaptation layer (AAL)**   Adapts information to the ATM 48-byte payload (the portion that follows the header).

- **ATM higher layers**   Accept user data, arrange it into packets, and hand it to the AAL.

As a network designer, you will have to face the question of whether the design should utilize ATM technology. You will probably be charmed by the benefits ATM offers. For example, in the mid-1990s, many network analysts foretold of the day when ATM would be used on an end-to-end basis. But instead, Ethernet's popularity has continued to grow. However, ATM has some benefits worth keeping in mind. The most commonly mentioned ATM advantages include

- **High bandwidth**   Because the cells use fixed-size units of data with simple and predictable header formats, it is fairly easy to create high-speed hardware-based switching equipment.

- **Sophisticated bandwidth sharing**   Cells can be interleaved to allow multiple communication sessions to share a single link through an advanced form of statistical multiplexing.

- **Quality of service (QoS)**   ATM's complex mechanisms allow detailed traffic contracts to be specified and enforced.

- **Long distance transmissions**   ATM technology allows transmitting data across huge distances.

Remember, however, that this technology was developed in the late 1980s when modern technologies, such as Gigabit Ethernet, did not exist.

Keep in mind that the configuration of ATM devices is very complicated. ATM requires expensive equipment, unlike Gigabit Ethernet, which, for example, needs only one relatively inexpensive card for your existing box. New Cisco 1000BaseLX, 1000BaseLH, and 1000BaseZX adapters allow you to have a point-to-point connection at a distance of up to 5km, 10km, and 90km, respectively. This doesn't mean that ATM technology is dead and you shouldn't be familiar with it.

Lack of QoS in Gigabit Ethernet technology still makes ATM technology attractive for some types of application such as video or voice conferences; but in case of data networks, you should be very careful with ATM if you want to recommend it to your customer. The competitors can offer another technical solution that will provide the same or even a higher speed of data transmission, but it will cost much less and will be more supportable.

SMDS

Switched Multimegabit Data Service (SMDS) is a high-speed, packet-switched, datagram-based WAN networking technology that is used to establish communication across public data networks (PDNs). SMDS can use fiber or copper media. It supports speeds of 1.544 Mbps over digital signal level-1 (DS-1) transmission facilities or 44.735 Mbps over digital signal level-3 (DS-3) transmission facilities. SMDS data units are large enough to encapsulate entire IEEE 802.3, IEEE 802.5, and Fiber Distributed Data Interface (FDDI) frames.

The following components allow SMDS networks to provide high-speed data service: customer premises equipment (CPE), carrier equipment, and the subscriber network interface (SNI). CPE includes end devices (terminals and PCs) and intermediate nodes (routers, modems, and multiplexers). Carrier equipment usually includes high-speed WAN switches that should conform to certain network equipment specifications. SNI is the interface between CPE and carrier equipment. Its function is to render the technology and operation of the carrier SMDS network transparent to the customer.

The main distinction of SMDS is the use of larger-size cells that allow it to encapsulate different LAN protocols but may result in delays that make this protocol unsuitable for multimedia traffic. All in all, ATM tends to oust this protocol.

Applicability

Cloud based is one of the most widely used types of connections established among remote sites. It provides high-speed connections at relatively low cost, meeting customers' needs. This type of connection can be used both to link to the Internet provider and to interconnect different sites, though it is not suitable for home offices.

Topology Map

Cloud-based technology can be applied in various topology models. The hub-and-spoke technology can be implemented when offices are connected via cloud-based links. If the network is really large, the mesh topology (full or partial) is worth using. Keep in mind that only after considering such factors as customer needs, availability of services, and cost of carrier networks, are you really ready to offer a cloud-based technology solution to your customer.

Meet the Customer's Needs

Because cloud-based connections include a number of protocols, such as X.25, Frame Relay, and ATM, and provide a wide range of speeds, it will be quite easy to satisfy your customer's needs if you decide to offer the use of cloud-based technology. But you should contact your local carrier provider to make sure the service you want to offer is available in the customer's area.

Bandwidth Limitations

Cloud-based technology includes several different technologies as X.25, Frame Relay, and ATM; therefore, it offers a really wide spectrum of speed. It is possible to declare that the range of speeds available is from 0 Kbps at Frame Relay's CIR = 0 up to 10 Gbps with ATM.

CERTIFICATION OBJECTIVE 11.03

Dial-on-Demand Routing Connection

Dial-on-demand routing (DDR) is a technology that allows you to form WANs using already-existing telephone lines (see Figure 11-7).

DDR over serial lines requires the use of dialing devices that support V.25bis protocol. V.25bis is an ITU-T Standardization Sector standard for in-band signaling to fit synchronous DCE devices. The devices that support V.25bis include analog V.32 modems, ISDN terminal adapters, and inverse multiplexers.

DDR can be used for both primary access and backup access in many ways. Sites can place calls, receive calls, and both place and receive calls. Additionally, the use of dialer rotary groups provides increased flexibility of this service.

FIGURE 11-7   Dial-on-demand connections

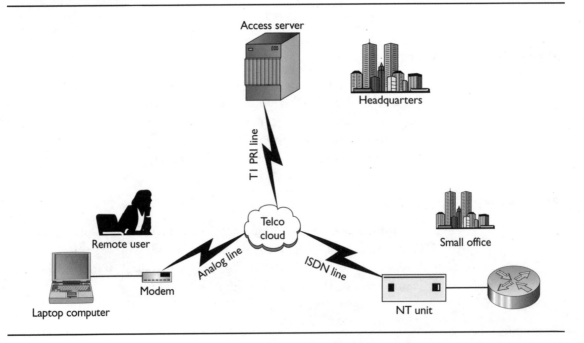

Advantages and Disadvantages

The main advantages of the DDR connection are its wide availability and simplicity. Every office now has phone lines, so you can set up a DDR device practically everywhere. ISDN lines, which provide higher speeds than regular phone lines, are also widely available. The main disadvantage of DDR is its limited speed. Two ISDN B-channels give you only 128 Kbps that may not be enough for large offices or small offices with applications that demand high bandwidth. Another disadvantage of this type of connection is a possible huge phone bill if you have to connect to a remote site making long-distance calls. In this case, a cloud-based or even a point-to-point solution can be more cost-effective.

Types of DDR and Their Limitations

The two types of DDR are ISDN DDR and analog DDR. ISDN DDR has become very popular because of its speed, relatively low cost, availability, and simplicity of installation. Its maximum speed limit is 128 Kbps.

Analog DDR is most often used to connect remote users to the office. This type of connection provides the speed of up to 56 Kbps and is quite convenient because it requires only a telephone line to exist. DDR is also used as a backup link, but in some cases, it can be used as a major data transmission channel (for example, in small offices where the traffic flow is low).

ISDN

ISDN consists of digital telephony and data-transport services offered by regional telephone carriers. ISDN makes possible the digitalization of the telephone network that allows voice, data, video, and other source material to be transmitted over telephone lines.

There are two ISDN user interfaces: basic rate interface (BRI) and primary rate interface (PRI). Each of them includes several 64-Kbps channels referred to as bearer (B) channels and one signaling channel, or D channel. The B channels are used to transfer users' payloads, such as data and voice materials. The D channel is a packet-switched channel linked to a separate packet network shared by all ISDN users. This channel is used for control and signal information.

The PRI consists of 23 64-Kbps B channels and one 64-Kbps D channel in North America and Japan. PRI is also called a 23B+D connection. In other parts of the world, including Europe and Australia, ISDN PRI provides 30 B channels plus one 64-Kbps D channel (a so-called 30B+D connection). PRIs are generally used to connect medium and large PBX routers and mainframes to each other and to a telephone company central office. PRI uses T1/E1 links (discussed in the section "Point-to-Point Connection," earlier in this chapter) as a carrier.

The BRI consists of two 64-Kbps B channels and one separate 16-Kbps D channel. This D channel is meant to carry control and signaling information, although it can support user data transmission under certain circumstances. BRI connections are sometimes called 2B+D connections. They provide transmission of digital information at speeds up to 128 Kbps. B channels can be described as "transparent," circuit-switched data pipes. These channels can establish a connection between any two users on the network wherever they are located if they belong to the ISDN network. D channels can also be used to transmit packet-switched data and to access public packet networks.

BRI connections are used to connect PBXs and individual terminals (desktop computers or workstations, videoconference units, routers, etc.) to a larger PBX or a central office.

The following are the BRI ISDN components: terminals, terminal adapters (TAs), network-termination devices, line-termination equipment, and exchange-termination equipment. There are two types of ISDN terminals: specialized ISDN terminals called *terminal equipment type 1 (TE1)* and non-ISDN terminals, called *terminal equipment type 2 (TE2)*. TE1s connect to the ISDN network using four wires—a twisted-pair, digital link. TE2s connect to the network through a TA. The ISDN TA can be a stand-alone device or can be built in the TE2. Figure 11-8 shows ISDN reference points and components.

The following are definitions of ISDN devices for an ISDN BRI (see Figure 11-8):

- **NT1 unit** This is the component located on the user's side of an ISDN line. It converts the incoming line code from AMI or 2B1Q to bipolar. The NT1 also provides the boundary between customer equipment and the public network. The NT1 device belongs to the customer. Its output is the T interface.

■ **NT2**   This device provides multiple ISDN interfaces on an ISDN line. The NT2 device may be simple, as a bridging device connected to an NT1 unit, or complicated, as a PBX. The interface to this device is the T interface.

■ **TE1**   The terminal equipment 1 is provided with an ISDN interface capability. Its main function is to receive and process bipolar digital signals from the network. This equipment may be a computer with a special built-in card, a fax, or a router. The interface to this device is the S interface. Basically, the S and T interfaces are electrically identical. Certain device interfaces are usually marked as S/T. If the loop length is short enough, the equipment may be served directly from the office, or there may be a U line equipped with an NT1, which thus provides the S/T interface.

■ **TA**   This is the terminal adapter, which adapts non-ISDN equipment to work on an ISDN line. It converts the bipolar signaling from the public network to the unipolar signaling. TA is most frequently used to connect a standard phone or an analog modem to an ISDN line.

FIGURE 11-8	ISDN reference points and components

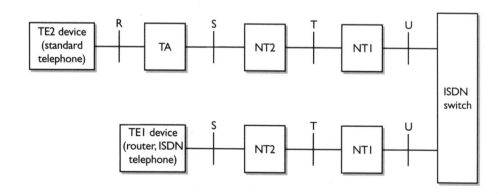

The physical layer of the OSI model defines the physical properties of the ISDN circuit. The physical properties of the ISDN include the connector type, a number of leads in a cable, information about what is on pins 1–8, and what defines a pulse. All these parameters make up the layer-1 specifics of the ISDN line. To specify the electrical standard, agreement was needed on where to measure these requirements. ISDN defines a number of reference points that determine logical interfaces between functional groupings, such as TAs and NT1s. Following are the ISDN reference points (see Figure 11-8):

- **R**   The reference point between non-ISDN pieces of equipment, such as a standard telephone and a TA.

- **S**   The reference point between pieces of user equipment, such as a router and the NT2.

- **T**   The reference point between NT1 and NT2.

- **U**   A reference point specific to the United States and Canada that becomes necessary because average local loop lengths are greater in North America. Where the local loop length exceeds approximately 3,300 feet (1 kilometer) of 22-gauge wire, the strength of the signal must be increased.

Layer 2 provides for procedures established to maintain communication between two network components: the ISDN terminal and the ISDN switch. The terminals constantly communicate with the switch using the Q.921 protocol. Q.921 specifications define the frame structure and the procedures themselves known as link access procedures – D channel (LAPD). The LAPD procedures describe flags, sequence control, flag control, and retransmission.

Layer 3 defines the procedures to establish end-to-end connections on the network (place and terminate calls). Two layer-3 specifications are used for ISDN signaling: ITU-T I.450 (also known as ITU-T Q.930) and ITU-T I.451 (also known as ITU-T Q.931). These protocols support user-to-user, circuit-switched, and packet-switched connections. They specify such messages as call-establishment, call-termination, and information.

To debug an ISDN connection, use the show isdn status command. Following is an example of this command's output on a BRI interface:

```
The current ISDN Switchtype = basic-ni1
ISDN BRI0 interface
Layer 1 Status:
ACTIVE
Layer 2 Status:
TEI = 66, State = MULTIPLE_FRAME_ESTABLISHED
TEI = 67, State = MULTIPLE_FRAME_ESTABLISHED
Layer 3 Status:
2 Active Layer 3 Call(s)
Activated dsl 0 CCBs = 2
CCB:callid=84E2, sapi=0, ces=1, B-chan=1
CCB:callid=856F, sapi=0, ces=2, B-chan=2
Total Allocated ISDN CCBs = 2
```

The status of all three layers is clearly shown. The active status of layer 1 shows that you have a physical connectivity to an ISDN switch. MULTIPLE_FRAME_ESTABLISHED on layer 2 means that you are having the communication with the ISDN switch using the Q.921 protocol. Total Allocated ISDN CCBs = 2 on layer 3 means that both your ISDN B channels are connected to a remote site. If for any reason you cannot place a call or the layer 2 is down, you can use debug isdn q921, debug isdn q931, or debug isdn events commands to trace the problem.

With or Without NT1 Built In (ISDN)?

As mentioned in the previous section, NT1 is a piece of equipment that is located between U and T reference points. Because the U reference point is specific to Canada and the United States, you must always select devices with S/T interfaces outside North America. Would you consider building networks with built-in NT1 in North America? It's up to you. On the one hand, one more piece of equipment can be an additional point of failure you would prefer to avoid; and in some cases, size of NT1 is commensurate with the size of a router. On the other hand, external NT1 gives you a flexibility to move a router you don't need in your headquarters in New York to your branch office in Moscow.

Analog

Use of an analog line is one of the most popular ways of establishing connections between distant sites. Generally speaking, an analog line is an ordinary phone line. All you need to establish the connection is a couple of modems. Personal computers, servers, routers, and many other devices can use modems connected through serial ports to talk to each other. Cisco offers a wide range of devices that support auxiliary modems. Most Cisco devices have an auxiliary port to which the modem can be connected to provide access to the network, although it's not a recommended solution because of the slow speed of such a port and the high level of CPU utilization.

Modern modems support speeds from 300 bps up to 56 Kbps. A variety of modem standards were developed to work via phone lines of varying quality with different speeds. The most popular standards are V.22, V.32, V.34, and V.42 with various modifications. Recently, the new V.90 standard derived from US Robotics' x2 and Rockwell's K56flex was accepted. It allows the downstream speed to increase to 56 Kbps when the upstream speed remains 33 Kbps.

Today, most telephone company offices are interconnected with digital lines that can handle 56-Kbps transmission technologies. Your access server must have a digital connection to your telephone company to implement this technology. In this case, downstream traffic can use a new transmission technique on a regular phone line that avoids the usual digital-to-analog conversion. A V.90 modem doesn't have to demodulate the downstream data, thus allowing you to download data at a speed of 56 Kbps; but the modem still needs digital-to-analog modulation for upstream data.

Dial-on-Demand Encapsulation Types

Remember that it is necessary to select a suitable encapsulation protocol if you want to establish communication between two devices. Dial-up connections use two encapsulation protocols:

- **PPP (Point-to-Point Protocol)** The recommended encapsulation method because it can support multiple protocols. It can be used for synchronous, asynchronous, or ISDN connections. PPP also has some valuable characteristics, such as the ability to perform address negotiation and authentication, and it is interoperable with different vendors.

- **SLIP (Serial Line Internet Protocol)**   More specific than PPP, it works on asynchronous interfaces only and supports only IP. SLIP protocol is used for communication between two devices that are previously configured for communication with each other. SLIP does not provide authentication and is interoperable only with other vendors that use SLIP.

on the **Job**

Keep in mind that you cannot have a 56-Kbps connection speed between two analog modems; you would need a digital access device to acquire this speed. Cisco offers you cost-effective access servers, such as the AS5300 and the AS5800. The good thing about these access servers is that they support both analog and ISDN calls. It means that you can have one phone number for both call types. Visit the Cisco Web site for details.

Applicability

The DDR connection is very cost-effective for such tasks as connecting remote users and small offices and backing up other types of links because of the simplicity of the installation and wide availability of phone and ISDN lines. Unfortunately, such limitations as a low maximum speed (128KB for a BRI interface) can be a limiting factor for large offices.

Topology Map

DDR connections are typically used in hub-and-spoke technology. Your remote users and small offices will dial to your central site to have access to the network. In some rare cases you'll use DDR in mesh design to provide the redundancy.

Meet the Customer's Needs

A DDR connection can be recommended to customers when there is a need to connect remote users and small offices located in the same city, or to back up other types of links. This type of connection should be avoided if you need to connect users and offices located in different cities, because long distance charges will apply and make the connection extremely cost ineffective. In such a case, we recommend the use of other types of connections, such as a cloud-based one or DDR in combination with other technologies, such as virtual private networking (VPN). (Also refer back to Figure 11-4.)

Bandwidth Limitations

Compared with other types of connections, DDR has a very limited spectrum of available speeds. Typical speeds of modern analog modems can be from 2,400 bps if a phone line is extremely noisy, up to 33,600 bps for an analog modem–to–analog modem connection via high-quality phone lines, and up to 56 Kbps for an analog modem–to–digital modem connection. ISDN BRI interfaces provide speeds of 56 Kbps or 64 Kbps for one B channel and of 112 Kbps or 128 Kbps for both B channels connected.

Layer-3 Packet-Switching Modes

Routers are necessary to perform such tasks as running routing protocols to develop a routing topology, but the main job of a router is to switch packets from incoming interfaces to outgoing interfaces. Switching consists of receiving a packet, determining how to forward the packet based on the routing topology and policy requirements, and switching the packet to the right outgoing interface or interfaces. The speed at which a router performs this task is the main factor in determining network performance in a routed network. Cisco supports many switching methods, with varying speeds and behaviors. The following describe some of these switching methods:

■ **Process switching** The slowest of existing switching methods. In process switching, the router examines the incoming packet and looks up the layer-3 destination address in the routing table to choose the exit interface. Then the packet is rewritten with the correct header for that interface and copied to the interface.

Compression and encryption of packets are the examples of processes for which process switching is used.

■ **Fast switching**   Done via asynchronous interrupts that are handled in real time. With this type of switching, an incoming packet matches an entry in the fast-switching cache created when a previous packet to the same destination was processed.

■ **Autonomous switching**   Offers faster packet switching because the ciscoBus controller is allowed to switch packets independently without interrupting the system processor. An incoming packet here matches an entry in the autonomous-switching cache located on the interface processor. This type of switching is available only on Cisco 7000 series routers and in AGS+ systems with high-speed network controller cards.

■ **Silicon switching**   Allows an incoming packet to match an entry in the silicon switching cache located in the Silicon Switching Engine (SSE) of the Silicon Switching Processor (SSP) module, which is available only on some Cisco 7000 series routers.

■ **Optimum switching**   Similar to fast switching but is even faster because it has an enhanced caching algorithm and the special structure of the optimum-switching cache. This process is available only on routers that have a Route/Switch Processor (RSP).

■ **Distributed switching**   Available on Cisco 7500 series routers with an RSP and Versatile Interface Processor (VIP) controllers where it is possible to switch packets received by the VIP with no per-packet intervention on the part of the RSP.

■ **NetFlow switching**   Identifies traffic flows between internetwork hosts and then switches packets in these flows (on a connection-oriented basis) at the same time that it applies relevant services, such as security.

■ **Cisco Express Forwarding (CEF)**   A Cisco-patented technique for very quick packet switching via large networks and the Internet. CEF depends on a forwarding information base (FIB), which allows CEF to be less processor intensive than other layer-3 switching methods, because FIB routing tables contain all the forwarding information for all routes.

■ **Tag switching** Optimizes packet switching through a network of tag switches (routers or switches that support tag switching), whereas other methods enhance the switching of a packet through a single router.

Queuing Mechanisms

Queuing mechanisms are important for any network that may experience congestion, so these methods must be intelligent and reliable. Queuing allows a network device to handle an overflow of traffic as follows:

■ **First in, first out (FIFO) queuing** Provides basic store-and-forward functionality. It stores packets when the network is congested and forwards them when the way is free. The packets leave in the order they arrive. FIFO is a default queuing algorithm, so it requires no configuration. The disadvantage of this method is that it has no mechanism to prioritize traffic.

■ **Priority queuing** Processes the important packets first. High priority is given to a critical application. This mechanism is very useful for time-sensitive protocols, such as Telnet.

■ **Custom queuing** Designed to allow a network to be shared among applications with varying minimum bandwidth or latency requirements. Different protocols are assigned different amounts of queue space.

■ **Weighted fair queuing (WFQ)** A flow-based queuing algorithm that recognizes a flow for an interactive application and schedules that application's traffic to the front of the queue to minimize the response time. WFQ adapts automatically to changing network traffic conditions and requires little or no configuration.

Why Use a Router Instead of a Bridge or Switch?

Routing is very important in scalable network design. However, some network architects believe it is better to build networks using as few routers as possible. This goal was relevant before 1998 when routers were slow. New technologies, such as multilayer switching (MLS), appeared, and these restrictions lost their significance. Large networks almost always benefit from scalability, flexibility, and intelligence of routing. The following are some advantages of routers over switches:

- **Wide range of interfaces**   Unlike switches that support only traditional LAN interfaces such as Token Ring, Ethernet, Fast Ethernet, and FDDI, routers support many other interfaces, such as Serial, PRI, BRI, and HSSL. Therefore, routers can use many various technologies suitable for different situations (Frame Relay, X.25, SMDS, ISDN, etc.).

- **Broadcast filtering**   Unlike switches, routers do not allow broadcasts to go through the interface.

- **Optimal path selection**   Routing protocols offer better path selection capability than layer-2 switches as a result of their complex metrics and path determination algorithm.

- **Priority queuing**   This method allows time-critical applications to process the important packets first.

- **Fast convergence**   Routing protocols pick optimal paths very quickly. Modern layer-3 routing protocols generally takes 5–10 seconds to converge, unlike layer-2 Spanning Tree Protocol's (STP's) 30–50 seconds for convergence.

- **Load balancing**   Routing protocols' load balancing is flexible, easy to configure, and capable of supporting simultaneous paths, unlike layer-2 (switching) balancing techniques that can be extremely bulky and difficult to use.

- **Flexible path selection** Cisco routers offer a variety of tools such as distributed lists, route maps, static routs, and administrative distances that allow managing path selections.

- **Summarized addressing** Layer-2 addresses use a flat address space. MAC addresses do not include components that indicate physical location. As a result, every bridging table in a flat network must contain an address for every node. IP protocol uses subnets that allow layer-3 addresses to be summarized, and this hierarchical approach can allow much larger networks to be built.

- **Security features** Layer-2 switches offer very limited filtering. When supporting address lists, they use MAC addresses, which cannot be regarded as an efficient way to implement policy. Routers can be used to provide complex access lists that function on layer-3 and layer-4 information. This procedure is more useful for policy implementation.

- **Value-added features** A number of technologies, such as DHCP relay, proxy ARP, and network address translation (NAT), can be critical router-based features in network design.

QUESTIONS AND ANSWERS

Your users are complaining that they have a slow response time for a Telnet-based application when they simultaneously download files from an FTP server. How would you resolve this problem?	You should use a queuing mechanism to resolve this issue. We recommend the use of the priority queuing technique because it is specially developed to resolve such types of problems.
Your company is opening a new large branch office. As a network designer, you have to select an appropriate router that will support Inter-VLAN routing and different types of WAN interfaces. Your manager also wants this router to support voice over IP technology for the future needs. What will be the best choice?	Using "Select a Product Tool" on Cisco's Web site, you'll find that Cisco 3640 satisfies all the requested requirements.
You are looking for a new router to place in your regional office in Paris, France. Which interface will you choose for your router: U or S/T interface?	A U reference point is specifically for Canada and the United States only. You must always select devices with S/T interfaces outside North America.

CERTIFICATION SUMMARY

It is important to be familiar with different types of interfaces and connections, but at the same time, it is crucial to realize that interface presence and its quantity are not the only characteristics of a router. Other significant characteristics to keep in mind include

- Router performance (packet-per-second forwarding rate), which is different for different protocols

- Hardware and software features, such as DHCP service, NAT, traffic shaping, and trunking support

We strongly recommend visiting the Cisco Web site, especially its "Compare Products" section, at www.cisco.com/pcgi-bin/front.x/ corona/romeo/compare.pl, and its "Select a Product Tool" section, at www.cisco.com/pcgi-bin/front.x/corona/prodtool/select.pl, and spending some time comparing different products offered by Cisco. Use "Select a Product Tool" to find a product for the environment you are familiar with (your network or networks of your clients). You may be surprised to learn that routers you recommended only a year or two ago are not the best choices today because Cisco already has new products to offer.

 # TWO-MINUTE DRILL

- ❑ There are three main types of wide area network connections: point to point, cloud based, and dial-on-demand routing (DDR).

- ❑ Point-to-point (also referred to as a leased-line) link is used to establish a single communications path between two locations.

- ❑ The most commonly used types of point-to-point encapsulations are now HDLC (Cisco), LAPB, PPP, and SDLC technologies.

- ❑ The following equipment will be necessary to establish point-to-point connection: DSU/CSU devices, DTE/DCE devices.

- ❑ Point-to-point technology usually uses T1/E1, fractional, and T3/E3 links.

❑ Cloud-based connections use a local public carrier network to transmit frames among remote sites. The most important advantage of this type of connection is its low cost as compared with that for point-to-point solutions.

❑ The four most commonly used types of cloud-based connections are X.25, Frame Relay, asynchronous transfer mode (ATM), and Switched Multimegabit Data Service (SMDS).

❑ X.25 was designed a long time ago to operate effectively with all types of systems connected to the network. This protocol is not as popular as it used to be because its main advantage of high reliability turned into a disadvantage of huge overhead.

❑ Frame Relay WAN protocol became very popular because of its ability to interconnect a large number of sites in an inexpensive way. Using this technology, all customers share access to the total bandwidth available through the Frame Relay cloud, and they can request a minimum available bandwidth through committed information rate (CIR).

❑ ATM is a dedicated connection switching technology that allows you to transmit information for multiple service types, such as voice, video, and data, in small cells of a fixed size (53 bytes). ATM technology combines the advantages of circuit switching (guaranteed capacity and constant transmission delay) with those of packet switching (flexibility and efficiency for intermittent traffic).

❑ SMDS is a high-speed, packet-switching, datagram-based WAN networking technology that is used to establish communication across public data networks.

❑ Dial-on-demand routing is a technology that allows you to form WANs over already-existing telephone lines. The main advantages of this type of connection are its wide availability and simplicity, although its limited speed may be a problem. The two types of DDR are Integrated Services Digital Network (ISDN) and analog.

❑ ISDN consists of digital telephony and data transport services offered by regional telephone carriers. ISDN makes possible the digitalization of the telephone network that allows voice, data, video, and other source material to be transmitted over telephone lines.

❑ There are two ISDN user interfaces: the basic rate interface (BRI) and the primary rate interface (PRI). Each of them includes several 64-Kbps channels referred to as B channels and one signaling channel, or D channel. The B channels are used to transfer users' payloads, such as data and voice materials. The D channel is a packet-switched channel linked to a separate packet network shared by all ISDN users. This channel is used for control and signal information.

❑ Routing is very important in scalable network design. The following are the main advantages of routers over switches:

   ❑ Routers support a wide range of interfaces.

   ❑ Routers offer broadcast filtering.

   ❑ Routers offer optimal path selection.

   ❑ Routing protocols' load balancing is flexible, easy to configure, and capable of supporting simultaneous paths.

❑ Several methods for layer-3 packet switching are necessary for fast forwarding of packets among interfaces. Cisco provides different types of switching, beginning with the slow process switching available on any router and finishing with Cisco Express Forwarding available only on high-end Cisco 7500 routers.

❑ Queuing services are mechanisms that allow network devices to handle traffic overflow. These services allow you to prioritize various traffic types to avoid high-volume traffic (such as FTP) to cause delays in delivering time-critical traffic (such as Telnet).

SELF TEST

The following Self Test questions will help you measure your understanding of the material presented in this chapter. Read all the choices carefully because there may be more than one correct answer. Choose all correct answers for each question.

1. What are the main types of wide area network (WAN) connections? (Choose all that apply.)

   A. Cloud based

   B. Remote access

   C. Dial on demand

   D. Point to point

2. What is not an advantage of point-to-point connection?

   A. High reliability

   B. Simple configuration

   C. Low lease cost of a carrier network

3. What is the Cisco default encapsulation type for serial interfaces?

   A. SDLC

   B. PPP

   C. LAPB

   D. HDLC

4. What cable do you use to connect a router's serial interface to a modem?

   A. DCE

   B. DTE

   C. DSU/CSU

5. What speed is provided by T3?

   A. 1.544 Mbps

   B. 2.048 Mbps

   C. 34.268 Mbps

   D. 44.736 Mbps

6. What cloud-based type of connection will you recommend to a customer who requires 256-Kbps connection speed for data transmission?

   A. X.25

   B. Frame Relay

   C. ATM

7. What is the minimum Frame Relay committed information rate (CIR)?

   A. 0

   B. 64

   C. 512

   D. 2048

8. What is the main advantage of X.25 over Frame Relay, ATM, and SMDS?

   A. High connection speed

   B. Low overhead

   C. High reliability in working via noisy analog lines

9. What type of connection requires the least configuration?

   A. Point-to-point

   B. Remote access server

   C. Cloud based

   D. DDR

10. What technology uses small fixed-size cells?

    A. X.25

    B. Frame Relay

    C. ATM

    D. SMDS

11. What queuing mechanism doesn't allow you to prioritize traffic?

    A. Priority queuing

    B. FIFO

    C. Custom queuing

    D. Weighted fair queuing

12. What is not an advantage of dial-on-demand routing?

    A. High speed

    B. Simplicity of installation

    C. Low carrier network lease cost

13. You can establish 56-Kbps connection . . .

    A. Between two analog modems

    B. Between an analog modem and a Cisco 1004 ISDN router

    C. Between an analog modem and a digital access device such as Cisco AS5300

    D. None of the above

14. What is the default encapsulation type for remote users connected through analog modems?

    A. ATM

    B. SLIP

    C. PPP

    D. ISDN

15. What is the role of an ISDN-D channel?

    A. To transfer video images

    B. To transfer a user's data

    C. To transfer control and signal information.

    D. The channel is reserved for future needs

16. What layer is used to place a call in ISDN?

    A. 1

    B. 2

    C. 3

    D. 7

17. What are the advantages of routers compared to switches? (Choose all that apply.)

    A. Fast convergence

    B. Reduction of broadcast traffic

    C. Faster switching of packets between interfaces

     D. Optimal path selection

     E. Access list support

18. What router is most suitable for a home-office ISDN connection?

     A. Cisco 762M

     B. Cisco 2503

     C. Cisco 3660

     D. Cisco 4700-M

19. You are planning to connect a small branch office to the headquarters. You'll be using a point-to-point 512KB connection as the main link with BRI ISDN as a backup. Ethernet equipment is already installed in the office. You also want to connect eight modems to the branch router to let the remote users dial in. What router will you select?

     A. Cisco 1604-R

     B. Cisco 2509

     C. Cisco 2522

20. Which of the following switching methods is the slowest?

     A. Silicon switching

     B. Fast switching

     C. Autonomous switching

     D. Process switching

SELF TEST ANSWERS

1. ☑ **A, C, and D.** The main types of WAN connections are cloud based, dial on demand, and point to point.
   ☒ **B** is not correct because there is no remote access wide area network type of connection.

2. ☑ **C.** The Point-to-Point Protocol usually has a high lease cost compared with that for other types of connections, such as cloud based and DDR.
   ☒ **A** is not correct because point-to-point is one of the most reliable connections. **B** is not correct because a point-to point configuration is simpler than a DDR or cloud-based configuration.

3. ☑ **D.** High-level Data Link Control (HDLC) is the Cisco default encapsulation type for serial interfaces. Cisco uses its own version of HDLC that is incompatible with other versions of this protocol, so you can't use it to connect Cisco equipment to a non-Cisco device.
   ☒ **A, B,** and **C** are not correct because none of them is a default encapsulation type for serial interfaces of Cisco's devices.

4. ☑ **B.** A DTE cable is used to connect a router to a modem.
   ☒ **A** is incorrect because DCE cable can be used to simulate a DCE device if it is interconnecting two routers, but it cannot be used to connect a router to a modem. DSU/CSU device is not a cable; therefore, **C** is incorrect.

5. ☑ **D.** 44.736 Mbps is correct because T3 provides 44.736 Mbps.
   ☒ T1 links, used in America, have **A,** 1.544-Mbps speed. E1 and E3, used in Europe, have speeds of **B,** 2.048 Mbps, and **C,** 34.268 Mbps, respectively.

6. ☑ **B.** Frame Relay is a very cost-effective protocol, offered in many areas.
   ☒ **A** is incorrect because X.25 is not popular as a result of its huge overhead. **C** is incorrect because ATM is an expensive solution more suitable for higher transmission speeds and delay-sensitive traffic such as voice and video.

7. ☑ **A.** CIR = 0 means that you have no guaranteed bandwidth, but you can still use the cloud to send your frames.
   ☒ **B, C,** and **D** are incorrect because the Frame Relay standard allows you to have a CIR = 0.

8. ☑ **C.** X.25 offers fewer speeds than other protocols.
   ☒ **A** is incorrect because Frame Relay, ATM, and SMDS offer higher connection speeds.

B is incorrect because X.25 has a huge overhead due to intensive data transmission error control and correction.

9. ☑ **A.** A point–to–point connection requires much less configuring than cloud-based and DDR connections.

    ☒ **B** is incorrect because remote access server is not a connection type. **C** and **D** are incorrect because cloud-based and DDR connections usually require more complex configurations.

10. ☑ **C.** ATM technology uses small, 53-byte cells to provide high-speed data transmission with guaranteed quality of service.

    ☒ **A, B**, and **D** are incorrect because X.25, Frame Relay, and SMDS allow the transmission of different size packets.

11. ☑ **B.** First in, first out (FIFO) provides only basic store-and-forward functionality. It doesn't make any decisions about traffic priority.

    ☒ **A, C**, and **D** are incorrect because these other queuing methods allow you to specify traffic priorities.

12. ☑ **A.** A dial-on-demand connection has a limitation of 128 Kbps with an ISDN BRI interface and 56 Kbps with an analog modem.

    ☒ **B** is incorrect because the DDR installation requires only a public telephone or an ISDN line that is quite easy to obtain. **C** is incorrect because low carrier network lease cost is one of DDR's advantages.

13. ☑ **C.** You need a special digital access device to use the V.90 protocol, which allows you to have a downstream flow speed of 56 Kbps and an upstream speed of 33.6 Kbps.

    ☒ **A** is incorrect because the maximum connection speed between two analog modems is 33.6 Kbps. **B** is incorrect because you cannot establish a connection between an analog modem and a Cisco 1004 ISDN router.

14. ☑ **C.** PPP is the default encapsulation type for modem connections because it supports many protocols and user authentication.

    ☒ **A** and **D** are incorrect because ATM and ISDN are not encapsulation types. **B** is incorrect because SLIP has many limitations and is not widely used today.

15. ☑ **C.** A D channel is used to transfer control and signal information.

    ☒ **A** and **B** are incorrect because B channels are used to transfer a user's payload, such as video, voice, and data. **D** is incorrect because an ISDN-D channel is used to transmit control and signal information.

16. ☑ **C.** Layer 3 is used to place and terminate calls in ISDN.

    ☒ **A** is incorrect because layer 1 defines the physical properties of the ISDN circuit. **B** is incorrect because layer 2 provides for procedures established to maintain communication between two network components. **D** is incorrect because level 7 is responsible for a user's applications, such as Web, e-mail, and FTP.

17. ☑ **A, B, D, and E.** Routing protocols pick optimal paths more quickly than the relatively slow Switches Spanning Tree Protocols. Routers don't allow broadcast traffic to flow through interfaces and provide a mechanism of optimal path selection. They have a more advanced access list support than the very limited MAC-address filter features of switches.

    ☒ **C** is incorrect because switches usually forward frames faster between interfaces.

18. ☑ **A.** Cisco 762M is the recommended router for a home office because of its low price.

    ☒ **B, C, and D** are incorrect. Although they also support ISDN interfaces, they can't be recommended because of their higher cost and features not required for a home office.

19. ☑ **C.** Only Cisco 2522 offers you the interfaces required for this installation.

    ☒ **A** is incorrect because Cisco 1604-R doesn't allow you to connect eight modems, and **B** is incorrect because Cisco 2509 doesn't have an ISDN interface.

20. ☑ **D.** Process switching interrupts the system processor for the time it takes to copy a packet from an interface buffer to the system memory.

    ☒ All other switching methods are faster; therefore, answers **A, B,** and **C** are incorrect.

12

Customer Network and Routing Protocols with IP

This chapter discusses some specifics for IP addressing, which include address translation, route summarization, private addressing, and variable-length subnet masking (VLSM). These elements are necessary to properly assign an addressing and naming convention for a network design. Network addressing and naming is one of the most important tasks in designing an internetwork. With this information, you should be able to make informed decisions regarding addressing, naming, and routing protocols and the ways they can be used in different situations to provide your customers with an overall design that will meet all of their goals.

When you have completed this chapter, you will have the knowledge to confidently design an internetwork that is secure and redundant and that will address any issues your customer may have. Your logical design will be a useful tool for you and your customer and will ensure that the process of moving from the design stage to physical implementation of equipment moves as smoothly as possible. This chapter also consists of diagrams, tables, and questions to assess your comprehension of the presented information.

CERTIFICATION OBJECTIVE 12.01

Addressing Model for Areas, Networks, Subnetworks, and End Stations

When you begin a network design project, it is very important to incorporate a robust and scalable addressing scheme. One such addressing scheme is a *hierarchical addressing model.* Hierarchical addressing is a model for applying structured addresses so that the leftmost portion of the address refers to blocks of networks. The rightmost portion of the address field refers to individual networks or nodes. When incorporated properly, this addressing model will facilitate *hierarchical routing,* which is used to properly distribute the network topology throughout the network. With this in place, no one router need know the entire network topology, thus reducing the amount of routing traffic across the network.

One of the best-known addressing hierarchies is post office addressing. Suppose, for instance, that you want to mail a letter to your parents. Once your letter hits the post office, it is sorted based on zip code, state, city, and local address. That is what hierarchical addressing is all about, starting out big and working your way down, smaller and smaller, until you get to your destination. This practice is also used in addressing internetworks across the world. You start with a large area and work your way down to the network; subnetwork; and, finally, the end station for completion of the data transfer. There are several benefits to hierarchical routing, such as these:

- **Efficient address allocation**   Using this type of addressing scheme, you can optimize the use of available address space on the network. With random address assignments, you may be unable to use entire blocks of addresses due to addressing conflicts.

- **Reduction in routing table entries**   One of the main goals in a network design is to minimize the size of a routing table by using route summarization. This allows for a single IP to represent a group of networks, thus reducing the number of entries in the router.

Following a solid hierarchical scheme, you will improve a network's performance by optimizing routes, reducing CPU cycles involved with routing calculations, and reducing memory usage and requirements. The following is a list of steps that you can use to help you successfully design a hierarchical addressing scheme.

- **Hierarchical scheme**   A hierarchical scheme should be designed in the following order: autonomous system, area, networks, subnets, and end stations. The exact hierarchy that you use will depend on which routing protocols you decide to use.

- **Route summarization**   Route summarization will reduce the number of routes present in your routing tables. This will also reduce the amount of routing update traffic that will travel across your network.

- **Low-level hierarchy**   When the high-level design is completed, you will need lower-level addressing and naming. For instance, if your customer has offices in different regions or cities, you could use established guidelines for addressing and naming.

- **Map networks to locations**   To aid you in your task of summarization, it is a good idea to associate certain networks with cities, states, or regions. Doing so will allow you to assign blocks of addresses for an area and then summarize those addresses for the rest of the network.

- **Special device addressing**   To assist in troubleshooting, it is suggested that special devices such as routers, servers, switches, and any other high-priority device be given a host address within a certain range. For instance, if you give all of your routers host addresses of .1–.10, switches .11–.20, and servers .21–.30, you will be able to tell what kind of device is not operating properly during troubleshooting just by looking at the IP address. This is an easy standardization that can save you and your customer time trying to figure out what a device is.

- **User station addressing**   To meet scalability requirements, it is suggested that user station addresses be dynamically assigned whenever possible. By using a dynamic addressing product, you will ensure optimization of user station addresses and alleviate configuration changes that will need to be done if a station is moved to another location.

- **Naming scheme**   Names assigned to a device should be meaningful. Just like having a specific address block for routers and other special devices, using a logical naming convention can assist in troubleshooting. For example, if you have devices in different cities, you could use the city name for an abbreviation, like NYC, LA, ATL, or KC. This could be used in conjunction with the device type and even the node address—for instance, ATL7507-01, LA5500-15, or NYCSun-25. By using a naming convention like this, you can know a device's exact location, type, and IP address just by looking at the name.

These steps, when implemented properly, will save you and your customer time, effort, and possibly money in the long run. By adhering to these guidelines, you will ensure that you have properly designed a network in a hierarchical manner that is sure to meet your customer's business and technical goals.

CERTIFICATION OBJECTIVE 12.02

Scalability Requirements

Various pressures put on a network mean that flexibility is an important design goal. Networks must be designed to be scalable and anticipate future demands on a network so that the evolution can take place in a smooth and cost-efficient manner.

When selecting a routing protocol for a customer, you need to consider what the customer wants for scaling the network. Scalability constraints for routing protocols can be summarized as follows:

- Resource requirements
- Convergence
- Metric limitations

Resource requirements include CPU, memory, bandwidth, and the types of networks that are running on the router. These resource requirements depend on many factors, so you should ask the following questions to determine the impact on the network.

- How are static and default routes currently implemented?
- Is route summarization supported, and if so, how?
- How much data is being transmitted during routing updates?
- How often are routing updates occurring?

Convergence occurs when the routers on a network calculate and understand a consistent network topology after a change is detected. This convergence time affects the way that data travels the network and may not provide reliable route information until the convergence is completed. This is a critical design constraint for some time-sensitive applications such as video or voice programs that are operating on the network. The following factors will directly impact the way convergence is reached on a network.

- Network complexity
- Frequency of routing updates
- Routing protocol timers
- The time it takes to detect a link failure
- The time it takes to learn a new route

Metric limitations are inherent in some routing protocols, such as IP/IPX RIP, IGRP, and AppleTalk's RTMP. These limitations, however, are related to distance vector routing protocols only because these protocols use *hop count* as a metric for determining the best route to take when passing traffic. Varying hop count limitations arise with each type of distance vector protocol, as described in Chapter 3. If you are using link-state routing protocols, you do not have anything to worry about because the metric limitations are virtually limitless.

Scalable and Nonscalable Addressing

The capability to extend your internetwork is determined, in part, by the scaling characteristics of the routing protocols used and the quality of the network design.

Network scalability is limited by two types of issues: operational and technical. Typically, operational issues are more significant than technical issues. Operational scaling concerns encourage the use of large areas or protocols that do not require hierarchical structures. When hierarchical protocols are required, technical scaling concerns promote the use of small areas. Finding the right balance is the art of network design.

Distance vector protocols, such as RIP, IGRP, IPX RIP, and RTMP, do not support variable-length subnet masks (VLSMs). This limits their use of a scalable addressing scheme on a network, which hinders the overall performance of the network.

Enhanced IGRP is an advanced distance vector protocol that has some of the properties of link-state protocols (LSPs). EIGRP addresses the limitations of conventional distance vector routing protocols. EIGRP with its support of VLSM will allow for the implementation of a scalable addressing scheme on a network.

Link-state routing protocols, such as OSPF, IS-IS, and NLSP, were designed to address the limitations of distance vector routing protocols. Link-state protocols' support of VLSM will also allow for the implementation of a scalable addressing scheme on a network.

With this in mind, it is important to determine the level of scalability to find the balance between routing protocol functionality and customer needs.

Classful Routing Protocols

A classic classful routing protocol, such as RIP or IGRP, will not transmit any information about a network's prefix length. When routing information is received within the same major network, routers and hosts will assume that the prefix length is the same as that for the interface. This limitation on classful routing protocols, therefore, will not allow different prefix lengths to be used within a major network.

When IP addressing was first being implemented, devices understood only three prefix lengths in association with the different classes: Class A with an 8-bit prefix, Class B with a 16-bit prefix, and Class C with a 24-bit prefix. This became a limitation as networks began to grow, so subnetting was introduced. Classful routing did not transmit any information about the prefix length because it was calculated from the information about the address class that was provided in the first few bits of information.

Classful routing is a severe scalability limitation in network design because it will not allow you to properly utilize valuable address space in a major network. The result is larger routing tables and routing traffic across a network. This limitation may not be as much of a factor if you are designing a small network that would not require all the scalability of a classless routing protocol.

IP addresses use a format called dotted notation, which indicates that a dot (.) separates the octets of an address.

Classless Routing Protocols

Classless routing protocols, such as OSPF, EIGRP, IS-IS, BGP, and RIP version 2, do include prefix-length information in their routing update information. This capability allows classless routing protocols to group networks into one entry, and then use the prefix length to specify what networks are grouped. This means that a router running a classless routing protocol will not have to determine the prefix length for any given network. Different prefix-length information within a major network is allowed and provides greater flexibility in designing a network.

Classless routing gives you the capability to have a different prefix length at different points across a network. VLSM supports more efficient use of address space and reduces routing tables and routing traffic through summarization.

Subnetting

IP addressing is defined by five address classes. Classes A, B, and C are used for public addressing of devices. Class D is used for mulitcast groups, and Class E is reserved for experimental use. Table 12-1 defines how each class is determined by its first octet.

| TABLE 12-1

Public IP Address Classes

Class	Format (n = network field, h = host field)	Address Range
A	n.h.h.h	1.0.0.0 to 126.0.0.0
B	n.n.h.h	128.0.0.0 to 191.255.0.0
C	n.n.n.h	192.0.0.0 to 223.255.255.0
D	Multicast	224.0.0.0 to 239.0.0.0
E	Experimental	240.0.0.0 to 255.0.0.0

IP networks can be divided up into smaller more manageable networks called *subnetworks*, or *subnets*. Subnetting provides you with several benefits, including scalability, address optimization, and network security. It also gives control of all the networks in an organization to the local administration. As a result, anyone outside the network will be hindered from seeing anything other than a single network, and no detailed information concerning an organization's internal network structure will get to the outside.

"Borrowing" bits from the host field and designating them as the network field creates a subnet address. A subnet mask is a 32-bit number associated with an IP address, with each bit in the subnet mask indicating how to interpret a corresponding bit in the IP address. In binary format, a bit of 1 in the subnet mask indicates that the corresponding bit in the IP address is designated as part of the network or subnetwork field. A binary bit of 0 in the subnet mask indicates that the corresponding bit in the IP address is designated as part of the host field.

A default subnet mask for an address depends on its address class, as described in Table 12-1. Class A addresses have one octet (8 bits) for the network and three octets (24 bits) for the host field. This means that the default subnet mask for a Class A network is 255.0.0.0: 8 bits in the network field (binary 1's) and 24 bits in the host field (binary 0's). This leads to Class B and Class C networks, which would have a default subnet mask of 255.255.0.0 and 255.255.255.0, respectively.

Basic Subnetting

When using basic subnetting, you are really addressing without subnets. All the networks that make up your network are treated as the exact same network, as discussed earlier, depending on which address class you are using. For example, you have addresses of 10.56.96.1 and 10.100.50.10 on your network. These addresses can represent two separate subnets in your network, but they are treated as the same network of 10.0.0.0, regardless of the second, third, and fourth octets.

Network addressing with this scheme setup has no way of distinguishing individual subnets in the network. With no segmentation, you are left with one large broadcast domain in which all devices see all the broadcasts on the network. By subnetting, you are able to divide the network into smaller, more manageable subnets, which then are treated as separate networks.

Complex Subnetting

With more advanced subnetting techniques, you can take full advantage of the network address and use it more efficiently. The outside world will see the network the same way, but internally, an organized structure of networks and subnetworks will build on one another. By using subnets, you can efficiently structure your network so that route summarization can be utilized, thus creating a hierarchical network scheme.

A network device uses a subnet mask to determine what part of the IP address is valid for the network, subnet, and host. Given its IP address and subnet mask, a device can determine if an IP packet is destined for any of the following:

- Device on a different network
- Device on a different subnet on the same network
- Device on the same subnet

From the addressing standpoint, subnets are extensions of the network number. When designing a network, you will be tasked with deciding the size of networks based on the organization and growth needs.

exam
Ⓦatch

A subnet mask of 255.255.255.252 also referred to as a serial mask, is useful in addressing WAN links because only two usable addresses can be used for the two router interfaces.

VLSM

Utilizing a classless routing protocol gives you the option of using different sizes of subnets in a major network, or VLSM. VLSM provides prefix-length information with each use of an address across the network. The length of the prefix is calculated at each place that it is used on its journey across the network. This capability gives you flexibility in your network design and provides an efficient use of valuable address space.

VLSMs use a portion of the host address space as a subnet address. This explains the use of the word "variable"; the subnet address field can be of varying lengths. Some of the benefits of VLSMs are

- **IP address optimization**   With the use of VLSMs, you have the flexibility to create networks with varying ranges of hosts' addresses.

- **Route summarization**   VLSMs promote the use of hierarchical addressing plans in a network, allowing for better route summarization and better router performance.

Supernetting

When you design an IP addressing scheme, it is important to design a scheme that will allow you to perform *route aggregation*, also referred to as *route summarization*, or *supernetting*. A key component to network design is determining how routing updates will traverse the network and update the appropriate devices. Supernetting will allow just a few routes, or even one route, to represent many routes. This will significantly reduce the amount of routing information that is passed across the network, thus reducing the amount of route update traffic and the number of routes in the routing tables.

The fact is that reducing route traffic can make a significant impact on traffic, especially low-speed WAN lines. With this in mind, the Internet community standardized supernetting by implementing classless interdomain routing (CIDR). CIDR was developed to help alleviate the problem of IP address usage. The idea of CIDR is that multiple Class C addresses can be aggregated into a larger classless set of IP addresses, which would allow more host addresses. This development has kept the Internet running strong for many years now, and without CIDR, the Internet would have had many difficulties growing as rapidly as it has.

Most systems administrators will haphazardly assign addresses just to get a system up and working. This approach greatly affects the way you design and implement an addressing scheme that will take advantage of the benefits supernetting has to offer. You will also need to evaluate current or planned routing protocols to use on a network because several do not support classless addressing features such as VLSM, or discontiguous subnets.

Configuring Addresses

As discussed earlier in the section "Subnetting," IP addresses use a 32-bit mask, or a subnet mask. This indicates which bits in the address belong to the network/subnetwork portion and which bits belong to the host portion of the address. The following command syntax is used for configuring an interface with an IP address.

- **IP address ip-*address subnet-mask*** This command assigns an address and subnet mask to an interface and initializes IP processing.

This command is all that is needed to configure an address and have the IP process start. Some other commands can be associated with the IP address command on the interface; but for a basic and fully operational setup, this works well.

To verify that you have properly configured the interface, you can issue the show ip interface command. This command displays a summary of an interface's IP information, including IP address and subnet mask.

Flexible Subnet-Addressing Policy with Growth Potential

When designing a network, you want give the customers full optimization of their resources. Subnet addressing is no exception. In developing an addressing plan that is flexible and can adapt to growth, you need to determine a few things first, such as

- What routing protocol to use
- What routers will be used
- How much the network will grow

A good place to start is to determine what kind of routers will be used. (If they are not Cisco, you will not use IGRP or EIGRP because they are proprietary protocols.) Next, determine what routing protocols will be used.

Will you be implementing a routing protocol that supports VLSMs or one that identifies subnets by the address class, such as RIP or IGRP? Finally, find out from your customer how much the network will grow based on where the business is heading in the next few years.

Common Classful Subnetting Rules

Very few rules or guidelines are associated with implementing common classful subnets. With classful routing hosts and routers, calculate the prefix length of a subnet by looking at the first few bits of an address to determine its class. IP hosts and routers in a classful network have a limited capability to understand prefix lengths and subnets. They understand the length for local configurations but not for remote configurations. Classful routing did not transmit any information about the prefix length because the prefix length was calculated from the information about the address class provided in the first few bits.

The suggestion for designing a network that will use a classful routing protocol would be to design it so that it can be easily transferred to a classless routing protocol with minimal configuration and design. By following some of the guidelines in the following sections, you will know how to properly assign network and subnetworks, so that if a classless routing protocol is brought in, these routes can be aggregated and summarized for overall network optimization.

An Addressing Policy for VLSM and CIDR

For route summarization to work correctly, certain requirements must be met:

- Routing protocols must carry the prefix length with 32-bit addresses.

- Routers must base their routing decisions on a 32-bit address and prefix length that can be up to 32 bits.

- Multiple IP addresses that are aggregated must share the same leftmost bit.

Although VLSM and CIDR addressing are somewhat new concepts for IP network designers and administrators, using them is not as complicated as it may seem. By spending some time analyzing network numbers and converting them to binary, you will see the simplicity in how VLSMs and CIDR can work to enhance your network.

By looking at a block of subnets, you can use the following rules to determine if the addresses can be summarized with VLSM or CIDR:

- The number of the subnets to be summarized must be a power of 2 (2, 4, 8, 16, etc.).

- The relevant octet in the first address in the block to be summarized must be a multiple of the number of the subnets.

With these two rules, you will gain the ability to determine if a subnet can be summarized just by looking at the IP addresses. These rules will help you determine the feasibility of implementing a cohesive network that did or did not utilize route summarization. A network that can use route summarization is overall healthier and more stable, and that is the ultimate goal.

CERTIFICATION OBJECTIVE 12.04

Naming Scheme

Names play an important role in meeting a customer's goals for usability. By assigning meaningful names for devices, you enhance user productivity and simplify network management and troubleshooting. A good naming model also strengthens the performance and availability of a network. This section helps you design naming models that will meet your customer's scalability, manageability, availability, and usability goals.

Names can be assigned to many different devices on a network, including routers, servers, printers, and hosts. A good naming model should let a user transparently access a service by name rather than address. Because networking protocols require an address, there are ways to map the address to the device name. This mapping method can be either dynamic or static, but a dynamic method is usually preferred because of the lower administrative maintenance. Among the many questions to be answered before you tackle an in-depth naming scheme are the following:

- What devices need names?
- What naming structure will be used?
- Who will be assigning these names?
- How will address-to-name mapping be accomplished?
- What type of naming system should be used?
- How much redundancy will be allowed between name servers?
- How much traffic will this generate on the network?
- How will the naming system affect network security?

Importance of a Naming Scheme

The importance of a good solid naming scheme cannot be stressed enough. You can design the best logical network and save your customer thousands of dollars, but if the naming scheme is not up to par, that will be the only thing your customer remembers.

The assignment of a good logical naming scheme is so important that this step can make or break a good solid network design. Be sure to convey to your customer and the customer's administrators the importance of maintaining a consistent naming scheme, once the network is in place.

Common Protocols Using Naming Schemes in Their Architecture

In a Novell environment, you assign names to resources, such as print servers, print queues, volumes on a file server, or database servers. There is generally no need to assign names to end systems when using Novell. With NetWare, you can make use of the Novell Directory Services (NDS), which is a global resource-naming system and set of protocols. NDS uses a distributed database approach to naming wherein portions of the database reside on many servers. This approach reduces the possibility that one central server will fail and affect all users, but it also increases the amount of traffic on a network tremendously. When implementing a Novell environment, be sure to carefully study the amount of traffic being generated by these NDS services because they can cause serious problems on an improperly designed network.

on the job

Novell uses Service Advertising Protocol (SAP) broadcasts to inform network clients of available resources and services.

With AppleTalk, you assign names to shared servers, printers, and end systems when file sharing or Web hosting is enabled. In addition to naming servers and printers, you can assign names to AppleTalk Zones. In most cases, it is not necessary to assign more than one zone name to a network segment.

The AppleTalk Name Binding Protocol (NBP) is responsible for mapping names to addresses in this environment. In the AppleTalk environment, an NBP name has the format *object:type@zone*. An example would be Sales:AFPServer@ATL. Macintosh users do not see device names that are not in the *object:type@zone* format. With this in mind, AppleTalk users should be encouraged to use meaningful naming conventions because using creative names actually decreases network productivity and makes network management and troubleshooting more difficult.

Creating an Easy-to-Implement, Logical Naming Scheme

The key to maintaining a good naming scheme is consistency. Once you have made a decision about the naming scheme, stick to it. One of the main factors in being able to continue with a consistent naming scheme for all devices is to design an easy and logical naming scheme. Keep the names short and ensure that they have a meaning. Because the naming scheme will depend on the type of protocols your customer is running, you must be aware of all aspects of the network before starting.

To maximize name usability, make names meaningful, distinct, and short. A user should be able to easily recognize which names go with which devices on the network. A good way of doing this is to include the type of device in the name. For instance, you can suffix names of devices such as router (rtr), server (svr), and user station (pc). You can also be a little bit more specific if you want, and use the actual model number of a device in its name. This will give you even more granularity by showing which router, 7513 or 2501, is in question. By using meaningful suffixes, you will decrease end-user confusion, and it will help extract device names from network management tools. If a network device has more than one interface, such as a router or multi-NIC server, be sure to map all of the addresses to one common name for the device. This way, network management software does not assume that a multipoint device is actually more than one device.

Names can also include a location code to represent a physical or geographical location. Such abbreviations as NYC, LA, ATL, or KC can be used in the name to once again maintain a level of granularity. Examples could be NYCRTR-01, LASVR-29, ATL2501-05, or KC7513-02.

All these methods will produce a consistent naming standard that will be easy for users to understand and will assist in identification and troubleshooting of devices on the network.

Scalability Constraints and Issues

When designing a naming scheme, be aware of the scalability issues that are involved with your customer's network. Make notes on the following scalability features and identify any problems with meeting key attributes for scalability:

- **Accessible but secure**   This can include implementing a naming scheme that is simple but does not compromise the security of the network and its devices.

■ **Adaptable** This means being able to let your naming scheme grow as the network grows so that a naming scheme does not become obsolete within just a few months.

■ **Efficient** Large networks must optimize the use of resources, and device naming is no exception. Do not implement a naming scheme that is confusing and has no meaning to the users. Pick a logical scheme that is short and consistent and has meaning.

■ **Reliable and available** This means having devices dependable and available 24x7. This is important to remember because changing the names on machines can leave some users in the dark about how to access them.

The overall objective is that you can implement a protocol that meets all the goals set forth by your customer and addresses the key points put forth in this chapter. By following the guidelines that have been presented here, you have the tools to design an appropriate naming scheme.

CERTIFICATION OBJECTIVE 12.05

Servers

A server is a network device that can perform many functions and has applications that clients, or users, can gain access to across a network. The following explain a server:

■ A server is a computer that provides services to other computer programs in the same or other computers.

■ The computer that a server program runs in is also frequently referred to as a server (though it may contain a number of server and client programs).

■ In the client/server programming model, a server is a program that awaits and fulfills requests from client programs in the same or other computers. A given application in a computer may function as a *client,* with requests for services from other programs on a *server.*

Many of the programs and applications that can run on servers provide a centralized location of programs so that everyone on the network can have access to these programs. The programs usually take up certain resources, which does not make it feasible to install the application on a user station. As you will see in the following sections, servers have many day-to-day functions that are essential to the proper operation of a network.

Use of a Server

The many uses for servers on a network call for a variety of server types, including the following:

- Domain name servers
- E-mail servers
- File servers
- Print servers
- Web servers

These are just a few of the many servers that are available for use on any network, at any given time. Servers are logically placed in a network design so that all parties can have easy access to the services offered by these servers. By offering a centralized service, servers take the burden off user stations to have specific files or applications loaded and running.

Location of a Server Based on the Network Design

It is important to consider how you want to get the broadcast in a controlled way to the appropriate server. Depending on the location of the server, use one of the following methods:

- **Multiple servers on multiple remote media**   With this method, a secondary DNS server could exist on one subnet and the primary DNS server could reside on another subnet. This meets requirements for redundancy and fault tolerance because client requests need to reach both servers.

■ **Multiple servers on a single remote medium** This method is sometimes referred to as a "server farm" because many servers of different types reside on the same medium. In this case, you would want to direct the broadcast on the server farm so that multiple devices can see it.

■ **Single server on a single remote medium** A medium may be directly connected to the router that blocks the broadcasts, or might be several hops away. The broadcast needs to be handled at the first router it encounters and sent to the server.

Common Naming and Addressing Used for Servers

As stated earlier in the section "Naming Scheme," you can use a couple of different options to determine a naming convention for your servers. A good, solid naming scheme can assist everyone's knowledge of the network design and the basic network functionality. It can also ease the burden on network management personnel and tools by revealing more than just the type of device in question. This equates to monetary savings for your customer, and although it may seem to be time consuming to design and implement, this scheme will also save time in the long run.

An addressing scheme for network devices such as servers should be consistent from one end of the customer's network to the other. If given a network with a consistent addressing scheme and one with an inconsistent addressing scheme, you will see that the latter will cause more problems and hinder troubleshooting more than you can believe. An addressing scheme for devices that are permanent or not using a DHCP server needs to be consistent and should have addresses statically assigned. If you are using a DHCP server, it is wise to designate ranges of address space that are off limits to the DHCP address range. This will keep addresses from changing or creating duplicate addresses on the same network. It is highly recommended that you create these ranges for devices such as routers, servers, switches, and others that will cause network problems if their address changed unexpectedly. Address range allocation can work hand in hand with the naming convention that is utilized with these devices, also.

As with the addressing scheme, it is important to implement a consistent naming scheme. The naming scheme for a server can have levels of granularity that can assist everyone in identification and troubleshooting. One option is for a server to have a svr suffix in a naming scheme and hold the same meaning to facilitate identification or troubleshooting.

To achieve a level of granularity and generate the information you need to create a robust naming scheme that will meet your customer's goals, answer these questions:

- **Where is the device located?** This can be anywhere from another country to a separate floor in an office building.

- **Is the address of the device in the proper range?** Once you have established a consistent address range for network devices, you can answer this question.

- **What is the device model number or manufacturer?** By making this distinction, you will be making positive identification of a server type, not just identifying it as an svr.

You can use the answers to these questions to establish an addressing and naming scheme for all the servers on a network, based on the example in Table 12-2.

You can squeeze the information into a short meaningful name that can answer all your questions about a device for identification or troubleshooting. You have the location, manufacturer, and server type, and you know whether the device falls into the address range that has been designed.

TABLE 12-2   Server Address/Naming Guide

Address Range	Device Type	IP Address	Location	Name
Routers .21 to .30	NT Web Server	10.10.10.25	Atlanta	ATLNTWeb-25
Routers .21 to .30	Sun File Server	10.25.2.30	New York	NYCSunFS-30
Routers .21 to .30	NetWare Print Server	10.1.1.22	Los Angeles	LANWPS-22

CERTIFICATION OBJECTIVE 12.06

Routers

A router is a device that determines the next network point to which a packet should be forwarded toward its destination. The router is connected to at least two networks and decides which way to send each information packet based on its current understanding of the state of the networks in which it is connected. A router is located at any juncture of networks, including each Internet point of presence. A router will create or maintain a table of the available routes and their conditions and use this information along with distance and cost algorithms to determine the best route for a given packet. Typically, a packet may travel through a number of network points with routers before arriving at its destination.

Use of the Router

Routers direct traffic through a network, based on information learned from network protocols. With a network that links hundreds or even thousands of computers, there has to be some agreed-upon way for those devices to address one another and communicate. As a network grows larger, it is not feasible for each computer to keep track of the individual address of every other computer on the network. A scheme needs to be developed to reduce the amount of information each computer has to hold in order to communicate with every other computer.

The scheme used involved splitting a network into many smaller discrete but connected networks. The job of keeping track of all these smaller networks was then given to a specialized computer, called a *router*. Using this method, the network computers keep track of only the computers on their network instead of every network computer.

Routers, by their very nature, seek to route packets from one network to another. This statement has two immediate practical implications:

- The same network number cannot be configured on more than one interface on a router.

- A router does not forward broadcast by default because a broadcast has a destination network number.

Routers are typically used to connect dispersed networks and to make it feasible to connect large groups of computer systems.

Common Naming and Addressing Schemes for Routers

A good solid naming scheme for routers can make clear the network design and basic network functionality. It can also ease the burden on network management personnel and tools, telling you more than just the device type and saving both time and money in the long run.

Each naming scheme, like a network's design, is unique. An addressing scheme for network devices, such as routers, should be consistent from one end of the customer's network to the other. If given a network with a consistent addressing scheme and a network with an inconsistent addressing scheme, you will see that the latter will cause more problems and seriously hinder troubleshooting. An addressing scheme for devices that will be permanently assigned to the network needs addresses to be consistent and should have them statically assigned.

If you are using a DHCP server, it is wise to designate ranges of address space that are off limits to the DHCP address range to keep addresses from changing or creating duplicate addresses on the same network. It is highly recommended that you create these ranges for routers, servers, switches, and other network devices that will cause network problems if their addresses change unexpectedly. Address range allocation can work hand in hand with the naming convention that is utilized with these devices also.

The naming scheme for a router can have levels of granularity that can assist everyone in identification and troubleshooting. A name for a router can have an rtr suffix and hold the same meaning. When rtr is part of the identification of a device, everyone will automatically know what this device is, thus facilitating identification or troubleshooting.

To achieve a level of granularity and gather information into a robust naming scheme that will meet your customer's goals, answer the same questions you addressed for servers:

- **Where is the device located?** This can be anywhere from another country to a separate floor in an office building.

- **Is the address of the device in the proper range?** Once you have established a consistent address range for network devices you can answer this question.

- **What is the device model number or manufacturer?** By making this distinction, you will be making positive identification of an exact router type, not just identifying it as rtr.

You can use the information from the answers to the questions to establish an addressing and naming scheme for all the routers on a network based on the example in Table 12-3.

You can squeeze the information into a short meaningful name that can answer all your questions about a device for identification or troubleshooting. You have the location and model number, and you know whether the device falls into the address range that has been designed. By using a naming and addressing convention like this, you can know exactly where a device is located, what type of device it is, and the IP address of the device just by looking at the name.

TABLE 12-3   Router Address/Naming Guide

Address Range	Device Type	IP Address	Location	Name
Routers .1 to .10	Cisco 2501	10.10.10.1	Atlanta	Atl2501-01
Routers .1 to .10	Cisco 3640	10.25.2.5	New York	NYC3640-05
Routers .1 to .10	Cisco 7507	10.1.1.10	Los Angeles	LA7507-10

Location of Routers Based on the Network Design

In a hierarchical design, network devices can be deployed to do the job they do best. Routers can be added to campus network designs to isolate broadcast traffic. Maximizing overall performance, by modularizing the tasks required of networking devices, is one of the many benefits of a hierarchical design model.

Network designers often recommend a mesh topology to meet availability requirements. In a full-mesh topology, every router is connected to every other router. A full-mesh network provides complete redundancy and offers good performance because there is just a single-link delay between any two sites. A partial-mesh network has few connections, so to reach another router in a partial-mesh network might require traversing intermediate links.

Although mesh networks feature good reliability, they have many disadvantages if they are not designed carefully. Mesh networks have scalability limits for groups of routers that broadcast routing updates or service advertisements. As the number of router adjacencies increases, the amount of bandwidth and CPU resources devoted to processing update increases.

A good rule of thumb is that you should keep broadcast traffic at less than 20 percent of the traffic on each link. This rule limits the number of adjacent routers that can exchange routing tables and service advertisements. This limitation is not a problem if you follow the guidelines for a simple and hierarchical design.

The classic three-layer hierarchical model for network design permits traffic aggregation at three successive routing levels: core, distribution, and access. This makes the three-layer hierarchical model scalable to large international networks. Each layer of the model has a specific role. The core layer provides optimal transport between sites. The distribution layer connects network services to the access layer and implements policies regarding security, traffic loading, and routing. The access layer serves a different function for LAN and WAN designs. For WAN designs, the access layer consists of the routers at the edge of the campus networks. In a LAN, the access layer provides switches or hubs for end-user access.

One last guideline for hierarchical design is that you should design the access layer first; followed by the distribution layer; and then, finally, the core layer. By starting with the access layer, you can more accurately perform capacity planning for the distribution and core layers. You can also recognize the optimization techniques you will need for the distribution and core layers.

User Stations

User stations are devices on a network that directly interface with individuals throughout the network. User stations are more commonly know as *personal computers*, or *PCs*, because they provide users with certain applications, such as e-mail or Web browsing, that can assist in day-to-day duties.

These user stations can run a multitude of varying protocols from TCP/IP, IPX, AppleTalk, and NetBIOS, just to name a few. With a device that is capable of running so many protocols, it is important that you choose the proper devices for a network when making your design. More often than not, the devices running on your customer's user stations will dictate the type of routing protocol you will use, and even the type of overall network design you have.

Use of a User Station

User stations have many uses in today's network environments and can run applications that can utilize a great amount of bandwidth. Applications such as e-mail, Web browsing, and network printing are common everyday applications. However, some other applications are even more intense and utilize even more bandwidth on a network. The following user station applications are network intensive:

- Video teleconferencing
- Streaming video
- Streaming audio
- Graphics file transfer

These applications can directly affect the way the network performs. One user station usually cannot make a big enough difference in network operation; but if everyone on the network has the same attitude, the impact can be tremendous.

Common Naming and Addressing Schemes for User Stations

As for servers and routers, you can use a couple of different options to determine a solid naming convention and addressing scheme for your user stations.

A name for a user station can have a pc suffix in a naming scheme and hold the same meaning, thus facilitating identification or troubleshooting. Be sure to choose the option that will work the best in each situation.

Location of User Stations Based on the Network Design

User stations are almost always located at the edge of a network design. In this case, the term "edge" refers to the access layer that connects you to the distribution layer, which feeds the core layer. User stations do not have any reason to be on the core or even at the distribution layer of a network design. When user stations are at the edge, they will be logically closer to the user, facilitating proper flow of traffic in a hierarchical manner.

By designing a network in a hierarchical manner, you will ensure that all devices from routers to servers to user stations are located in their logical places, and this will help make your design flow between transitions.

IGRP and EIGRP

The Interior Gateway Routing Protocol (IGRP) and Enhanced Interior Gateway Routing Protocol (EIGRP) were developed by Cisco Systems in the mid-1980s and early 1990s, respectively. IGRP, the first routing protocol Cisco developed, was based on the distance vector algorithm. The goals Cisco had in mind when developing IGRP were as follows:

- A stable routing protocol that is optimal for large networks, with no routing loops

- Fast response to changes in network topology

- Ability to handle multiple types of service

- Low processor and bandwidth overhead

- Ability to split traffic among several parallel routes when they are of roughly equal desirability

Even though IGRP is a distance vector protocol like RIP, the key differences were in the metric and poisoning algorithm, and use of a default gateway. There are similarities though. Split horizon, triggered updates, and hold-down timers are implemented much as they are with RIP.

EIGRP uses the same distance vector technology found in IGRP for the underlying metric calculations. The changes were in the route advertising procedures and the calculation of entries into the routing table. These procedures are like those of a link-state routing protocol. The key components of EIGRP are

- Support for VLSMs

- The diffusing update algorithm (DUAL) finite-state machine

- Reliable transport protocol

- Neighbor discovery and recovery

EIGRP's support of VLSMs increases flexibility for the use of subnet masks in network design. The functionality afforded by VLSM is most useful when an organization has a limited address space assigned by the InterNIC and has to optimize these addresses for the entire network.

Neighbor discovery is the process by which a router learns of other routers on directly attached links. EIGRP uses small hello packets for neighbor discovery. The key point is that EIGRP uses partial updates. When the state of the link or router changes, EIGRP sends out only the information necessary to those needing to hear about it instead of sending the entire routing table to all its neighbors. Doing so minimizes the bandwidth used by EIGRP regular update messages compared with those of IGRP.

At the center of EIGRP is DUAL, the decision process for all route computations. DUAL uses distance information to select efficient, loop-free paths and selects the best route for insertion into the routing table as well as a feasible successor. This feasible successor is used if the primary route becomes unavailable, thus avoiding a complete recalculation of the algorithm in the event of a link failure and lowering convergence time.

EIGRP also introduced a Reliable Transport Protocol to ensure guaranteed delivery of routing updates rather than relying on broadcasts. In addition, EIGRP supports IPX and AppleTalk network protocols and routing protocols other than IP. An advantage is that only one routing protocol would have to be configured in a multiprotocol environment.

How Do IGRP and EIGRP Work?

Routers using IGRP broadcast periodic routing table updates to neighbors at 90-second intervals. IGRP provides a number of features to enhance its performance and stability and, at the same time, reduce the possibility of routing loops. These new features include

- Flash updates
- Poison reverse
- Hold-downs
- Split horizon

Flash updates are used by IGRP to speed up convergence on the routing algorithm. A flash update is sent when a network topology change is noticed. Poison reverse updates are sent to remove a route and to place it in hold-down. IGRP poison reverse updates are sent if a route metric has increased by a factor of 1:1 or greater. Hold-downs prevent temporary routing loops while convergence takes place. A newly learned route is used until the hold-down time expires, which is three times the update interval (90 seconds) plus 10 seconds, or 280 seconds. Split horizon prevents a router sending information about a route out of the same interface it learned the route on.

Periodically, each router broadcasts its entire routing table to all adjacent routers. When a router gets this broadcast from another router, it compares the table with its existing table. Any new destinations and paths are added to the routing table. Paths in the broadcast are compared with existing paths; and if the new path is better, it replaces the existing route.

EIGRP discovers neighbors, routes, chooses routes, and maintains routes when there is a change in the network. The main elements of EIGRP are

- Building a neighbor table
- Discovering routes
- Choosing routes
- Maintaining routes

A neighbor table is a table that is maintained by the EIGRP router and that lists adjacent routers. Its purpose is to ensure bidirectional communications between the directly connected neighbors. As with OSPF, EIGRP routers multicast hello packets to discover neighbor routers and to exchange route updates. Each router builds a neighbor table from hello packets that it receives from adjacent EIGRP routers running the same protocol.

exam
ⓦatch

Remember that adjacent routers are the only ones that can exchange routing information.

Hello packets are sent out periodically to verify an EIGRP neighbor's availability. Because EIGRP can run multiple network layer protocols, it maintains a separate neighbors table for each protocol configured.

The neighbor establishment and route discovery process occur at the same time in EIGRP. The following is a step-by-step description of this process:

1. A new router becomes active and sends out a hello packet to all interfaces.

2. Routers receiving the hello packet reply with update packets that contain all the routes that they have in their topology tables. In addition, these update packets have the Init bit set, which indicates this is the initialization process.

3. The new router replies to each neighbor with an acknowledgement packet, indicating that it received the update information.

4. The new router puts all the update information into its topology table.

5. The new router exchanges update packets with each of its neighbors.

6. Upon receiving the update packet, each neighbor sends an acknowledgement packet back.

When all updates are received, the router is ready to choose the primary and backup routes to keep in the topology database.

Route selection is perhaps what distinguishes EIGRP the most from other routing protocols. EIGRP uses the following process to determine which routes to keep in the topology and route tables:

1. DUAL is run on the topology table to determine the best and loop-free primary and backup routes to each destination.

2. The next hop router that is selected as the best path is referred to as the *successor*. Multiple successors can exist if they have the same feasible distance and use different next hop routers. All successors are then added to the route table.

3. The next hop router for the backup path is referred to as the *feasible successor*. If the successor's route is no longer valid and a suitable feasible successor exists, this feasible successor replaces an invalid successor in the routing table without recomputation.

4. The successors and feasible successors are kept in the topology table, along with all other routes, and referred to as *possible successors*. The only routes removed are those that have a metric indicating they are unreachable.

When there is a change in the network, the router that learned about the change advertises it to its neighbors by multicasting an update packet with the change. If the update packets are to notify the neighbors that a router was added to the network, the process for discovering neighbors is accomplished. If the update packet says that a link has a worse metric or is no longer available, the router must find an alternative path.

To obtain an alternative path, the router that lost the link looks for a new feasible successor in its topology table. If a feasible successor exists, it is promoted to successor and added to the routing table and used. The topology table is then recalculated to determine whether there are any new feasible successors, based on the new successor's feasible distance.

If there is no feasible successor available, the following process is performed:

1. Router A flags the failed route as in an "active" state in the topology table. When routes are operating well, they are in a "passive" state.

2. Router A looks for an alternative path by sending out a query packet to all its neighbors to learn whether they have a path to the given destination. The query packet is multicast out every interface, except the interface with the failed route.

3. If a neighbor has a feasible successor that does not use the querying router or has no route at all to the destination, it unicasts a reply packet to the requestor indicating the appropriate information.

4. When the query router receives replies, it reacts based on the answer in the reply.

If one or more routers to which the query is sent do not respond with a reply within the active time of 180 seconds, EIGRP tears down its neighbor relationship with the invalid router and puts routes that used the invalid router into an "active" state. The querying router then generates queries for the router it lost through the invalid router.

Strengths and Limitations

Cisco Systems developed IGRP in the mid-1980s in response to the demand for a more versatile routing protocol. Many customers migrated from RIP to IGRP because IGRP improved on many of the downfalls inherent with RIP. See Chapter 3 for more details.

This routing protocol also provides a simple network that is easy to configure and understand. This will come in handy when you train the administrators who will maintain the network you are designing.

Enhanced IGRP, or EIGRP, is another Cisco proprietary protocol that combines the advantages of a distant vector routing protocol with those of a link-state routing protocol. The combination of these two types of protocols is called a *hybrid protocol*. EIGRP can be easy to configure, but the multitude of associated commands can make it very complex. EIGRP, like IGRP, allows for only one autonomous system per EIGRP routing process. Hence, if you wanted to establish more than one autonomous system, you would need to configure another routing process. This is a handy option to have if you are maintaining a network that is merging with another company's or if you want to isolate traffic from certain areas of your network. You just need to make sure that all the routers in your internetwork have the same autonomous system number.

Why Use IGRP Over EIGRP?

IGRP has several limitations that would keep someone from choosing it as a viable candidate for a network routing protocol, but it also has many functions that can make it the routing protocol of choice in a network. Some of IGRP's key features are as follows:

- IGRP gets its topological data from the data it receives from its neighbors.

- IGRP uses a composite metric of bandwidth, load, reliability, and delay to determine through which paths to route.

- Topology changes come from periodic routing table updates.

Design your network's routing characteristics to meet technical goals. Operational issues such as network simplicity are also important issues to keep in mind. For the chosen routing protocol to properly fit some organizations, it must be easy to set up and manage. It must handle several routed protocols without requiring multiple inconsistent and complex configuration templates. Avoid the risk of unproven technologies because they can be factors in designing routing policies and in sustaining a prosperous career.

Why Migrate to EIGRP?

EIGRP, like IGRP, is a balanced hybrid routing protocol that uses distance vectors, but with more accurate metrics to determine the best path to destination networks. It differs from most distance vector protocols in its use of topology changes to trigger routing database updates across the network. This hybrid routing type converges more quickly than traditional distance vector protocols, much like link-state routing protocols. However, it differs from link-state routing protocols by emphasizing economy in the use of required resources such as bandwidth, memory, and processor overhead, thereby giving users the flexibility of all types rolled into one package.

This new type of protocol brings along with it several new features:

- **Reduced bandwidth usage** EIGRP sends partial updates about a route when either the topology or the metric changes. When the changes are detected, an update about the link only is sent, and it is sent only to the routers that need this updated information.

- **Multiple–network layer support** EIGRP supports the use of multiple protocols like AppleTalk, IP, and Novell NetWare through the use of protocol-dependent modules (PDMs). These PDMs are responsible for network layer–specific protocol information.

■ **Rapid convergence** EIGRP uses DUAL to achieve rapid convergence across a network. A router running EIGRP stores backup or alternate routes. If there is no alternate route existing in the route table, EIGRP will query its neighbors to discover the alternate route. These queries will propagate the network until a feasible alternate route is found. DUAL also guarantees loop-free operation during route computation and allows all routers involved in a route change to synchronize at the same time. All other routers that are not affected by the route change are not involved in recomputations.

Design your network's routing characteristics to meet your customer's technical and operational goals. The EIGRP protocol provides a high-functionality protocol that enables multiple-vendor protocols to communicate using this one routing protocol. You will have to decide if the benefits of EIGRP outweigh the complexity of the configuration and troubleshooting that can be associated with this protocol.

CERTIFICATION OBJECTIVE 12.09

IP RIP and OSPF

Routing Information Protocol (RIP) was one of the first routing protocol standards for TCP/IP that was implemented around the world. RIP is still a very widely used routing protocol today because of its easy configuration and troubleshooting. RIP is still supported across all routing platforms and vendors, making it attractive for interoperability.

OSPF is a link-state routing protocol as opposed to a distance vector or hybrid routing protocol.

See Chapter 3 for more information on RIP and OSPF.

exam
ⓦatch

RIP version 2 supports variable-length subnet masks (VLSMs).

How Do RIP and OSPF Work?

Once RIP is configured on a network, the operation of RIP and its interaction with the routing table is fairly straightforward. By default, every 30 seconds each RIP device sends out a RIP update message, comprised of the following routing information from the routing table:

- Hop count metric
- Destination address or host or network
- IP address of the router sending update

Once a routing device receives an update, it processes the new information, which it compares with that in the existing routing table. If the routing update includes a new destination network, it is added to the routing table. If the router receives a route with a smaller metric to an existing destination, it replaces the existing route. If an entry in the update message has the same destination network and gateway but a different metric, it will use the new metric to update the routing table.

An OSPF network is normally divided into a number of smaller areas that contain hosts and routers. Within the autonomous system, some routers can be configured as an area border router, which means one interface is in one area and another interface can be in a separate area. In this case, the router keeps a topological database for each area it is in. The only way to get from one area to another area is via the backbone, or area 0.

In OSPF, link-state advertisements (LSAs) are sent to all other routers within a given area. By contrast, a distance vector protocol, like RIP, sends all the routing tables in update messages but only to its neighbors. LSAs include data such as the metrics used, interface address, and other variables. A topological database is present in each router and contains the collection of LSA information, giving an overall picture of networks in relation to routers. An OSPF backbone area is used to connect all other areas and is responsible for transferring routing information among areas. There are five types of routing updates in OSPF. These updates are sent only over adjacencies and are in the form of LSAs. Table 12-4 provides a brief description of each type of LSA.

TABLE 12-4   LSA Types

LSA Type	Advertisement Name	Description of Advertisement
1	Router Link	This advertisement describes the collected states of the router's interfaces to an area. This LSA is originated by all routers and is flooded in a single area only.
2	Network Link	This advertisement contains the list of routers connected to a network. This LSA is originated for multiaccess networks by the designated router (DR) and is flooded in a single area only.
3	Summary Link	Each advertisement describes a route to a destination outside the area but inside the AS. Type-3 advertisements describe routes to networks and are originated by the ABRs. They are flooded throughout the advertisement's associated area.
4	Summary Link	Each advertisement describes a route to a destination outside the area but inside the AS. Type-4 advertisements describe routes to AS boundary routers and are originated by the ASBRs. They are flooded throughout the advertisement's associated area.
5	AS External Link	Each AS external link advertisement describes a route to a destination in another AS. Default routes for the AS can also be described by AS external link advertisements. These advertisements are originated by the AS boundary router and flooded throughout the AS.
6	Group-Membership	These advertisements are specific to a particular OSPF area. They are never flooded beyond their area of origination. They advertise directly attached networks that contain members of a particular multicast group.
7	Not-So-Stubby Areas (NSSA)	These advertisements describe routes within the NSSA. They can be summarized and converted into Type-5 LSAs by the ABRs. After conversion they will be distributed to areas that can support Type-5 LSAs. These advertisements are originated by the ABR and flooded throughout the NSSA.
8	Link	These advertisements describe a separate link LSA for each link it is attached to. These LSAs are never flooded beyond the link that they are associated with.
9	Intra-Area-Prefix	These advertisements advertise one or more Ipv6 address prefixes that are associated with a router, attached stub network, or an attached transit network.

Clearly, a network based on OSPF is considerably more complex to design and operate than one based on a distance vector protocol, such as RIP. With a distance vector protocol, the network can be designed, deployed, and troubleshot fairly easily; but in larger networks, problems occur with the size of the routing table updates and speed of convergence. A network based on a link-state routing protocol uses more router processor time and memory but converges very quickly.

Strengths and Limitations

The RIP is limited to networks whose longest path involves 15 hops. The designers believed that the basic protocol design is inappropriate for larger networks. If the system administrator chooses to use larger costs, the upper bound of 15 can easily become a problem. The protocol depends on "counting to infinity" to resolve certain unusual situations. If the system of networks has several hundred networks and a routing loop involving all of them is formed, the resolution of the loop would require either much more time or much more bandwidth. Such a loop would consume a large amount of network bandwidth before the loop would be corrected.

However, in realistic cases, this will not be a problem, except on slow lines. Even then, the problem will be fairly unusual because various precautions are taken that should prevent such problems in most cases. This protocol uses fixed metrics to compare alternative routes. It is not appropriate for situations in which routes need to be chosen based on real-time parameters, such as measured delay, reliability, or load. The obvious extensions to allow metrics of this type are likely to introduce instabilities, of a sort, that the protocol is not designed to handle. See Chapter 3 for more details.

Why Use RIP over OSPF?

RIP, a distance vector routing protocol, is one of the original routing protocols that was developed. Several of RIP's limitations would keep someone from choosing it as a viable candidate for a network routing protocol, but it also has many functions that can make it the routing protocol of choice. Some of the key features that RIP has over OSPF are as follows:

- RIP gets its topological data from the data received from its neighbors.
- RIP uses hop count for its metric feature.
- Topology changes come from periodic routing table updates.

Design your network's routing characteristics to meet technical goals. Operational issues, such as network simplicity, are also important to keep in mind. For the chosen routing protocol to properly fit some organizations, it must be easy to set up and manage. It must handle several routed protocols without requiring multiple inconsistent and complex configuration templates. Avoid the risk of unproven technologies because they can be factors in designing routing policies and in sustaining a prosperous career.

Why Migrate to OSPF?

OSPF was developed in response to a need in the Internet community to introduce a high-functionality nonproprietary Internal Gateway Protocol for the TCP/IP protocol family. OSPF has introduced new concepts such as authentication of routing updates, VLSM, and route summarization.

The rapid growth of today's networks has made RIP a severely limited routing protocol choice. RIP has certain limitations that could cause problems in some of today's larger networks, as follows:

- A 15-hop limit
- Bandwidth usage from periodic updates of entire routing tables
- Slow convergence
- Lack of support for VLSM
- Inability to calculate link delays or costs
- Support for only flat nonhierarchical networks

OSPF, on the other hand, addresses most of the issues presented in the preceding list on the limitations of RIP, including

- No limitation on hop count
- Support for VLSM for IP address optimization
- Use of IP multicast to send link-state updates, which ensures a better use of bandwidth
- Quicker convergence because routing changes are propagated instantly instead of periodically
- Better load balancing, based on the cost of the link
- Support of a hierarchical design, based on areas and route summarization
- Support for routing authentication
- Support for the transfer and tagging of external routes injected into an autonomous system by protocols, such as BGP

The OSPF protocol provides a high-functionality open protocol that enables multiple-vendor networks to communicate using the TCP/IP protocol family. You will have to decide if the benefits of OSPF outweigh the complexity of the configuration and troubleshooting.

CERTIFICATION OBJECTIVE 12.10

Static Routing

Static routing is the use of a manual route programmed into a router to specify where the packets are supposed to go. With static routes, the administrator must manually update this static route entry whenever a network topology change requires an update. Static knowledge can be private, and by default, it is not conveyed to other routers as part of an update process. You can, however, configure your router to redistribute this static information to other routers.

In the case of exterior routing, static routes between autonomous systems offer a number of advantages, including the following:

- No routing protocol traffic traveling across links connecting autonomous systems
- Flexibility over the advertisements of subnets and their routers
- No possibility of one AS routing protocol affecting another

The disadvantages of static routes are obvious because they do not adapt to link failures, and manual configuration can be very complicated and intensive. However, they are popular for connecting networks that do not trust each other, such as an ISP.

How Does Static Routing Work: Interface or Next Hop?

When configuring static routes, you can specify either the next hop address that the packet will take or the packet to route out an interface. Both techniques work properly, offering all the functionality that static routes have to offer, and one does not have any real benefit over the other, but the differences described here can help you make your decision.

Strengths and Limitations

Static routes are useful when you are having trouble getting information from one network to another. They can be used in conjunction with dynamic routing to form a backup. If the dynamic routing process goes down, the static route will take over and route all traffic to its destination. Along with these functions, static routes are useful when network security is an issue. If you are connecting your network to an ISP or any other network that you do not want to be able to see your network topology, just use a static route. This prevents anyone from the outside from being able to see your network's topological layout or networks.

By far the biggest limitation of a static route is that it uses a manually administered route mapping. Any time that a route changes or goes bad, the static route has to be manually changed to reflect the changes. With a dynamic routing protocol, if a route goes bad, the protocol learns a new route, and traffic keeps flowing without any administrative assistance.

Static routes are not the popular choice for designing a large-scale network, but they do have their place, and that is an important aspect to keep in mind when you are designing a network for your customers.

Why Use an Interface?

By specifying a physical interface such as Ethernet 0 or serial 2/2, you are saying that the traffic will go out this interface, no matter what is on the other side. Once it leaves that interface, it is on to its final destination. Now this fixes the problem of next hop addresses changing without your knowing; but if you change the physical interface from, say, Ethernet to Fast Ethernet, you have to change the static route, too. Also, static routes that point to an interface are considered in the routing table to be connected and hence lose their static nature.

Why Use Next Hop?

By specifying a next hop address, you are saying that packets from this network go to this network, or next hop. From there, the next hop router routes them to their final destinations. This choice works very well, but what if you change the address of the next hop? That means that you have to go in and change the static route that you have configured. If you have the next hop designated as an address to an ISP or another network, and it changes address without telling you, that can lead to headaches when you try to figure out the problem. However, if you define a static route with a next hop address that does not fall within one of the networks defined in a network command, no dynamic routing will occur without the redistribute static command.

Why Use Static Routes Over Dynamic Routes?

Static routing has several useful applications when it is utilized properly on a network. The first such application is the implementation of static routes on WAN links. When implementing static routes on WAN links, you can eliminate the need to allow route updates across these low-speed links. Doing so will provide more available bandwidth than with dynamic routing protocols, which may make a significant impact on your customer's network applications. Another useful application of static routes is for security reasons. Dynamic routing tends to reveal everything it knows about an internal network to outside sources. With this in mind, it might not be a bad idea to use static routes when connecting to outside resources so that you can specify what is advertised concerning your network.

Static routing is generally not a sufficient means of maintaining a large or complex network because of the time required to define and maintain the static route table entries. As you can see, the uses for static routes on a network are limited, but these uses can be very handy at times and provide needed functionality.

Routing Protocols

Most routing algorithms can be classified as conforming to one of two basic algorithms: distance vector or link state. The distance vector routing approach determines the direction (vector) and distance to any link in the internetwork. The link-state (also called shortest path) approach learns the exact topology of the entire internetwork, or at least the portion that the router is situated in. A third approach, the balanced hybrid approach, combines aspects of the basic algorithms to take advantage of each one's benefits.

The routing algorithm is fundamental to dynamic routing. Whenever the topology of the network changes because of growth, reconfiguration, or equipment failure, the router's knowledge base of the network must also change. Knowledge of the network needs to be accurate and consistent from router to router. When all routers in a network are operating with the same knowledge, the network is said to have *converged*. Fast convergence is a desirable feature because it reduces the period of time that routers have outdated information for making routing decisions that could be incorrect.

There is no single best routing algorithm for all networks. You must weigh technical and nontechnical aspects of your customer's network to determine the best algorithm. You can configure whatever routing choices best fit the needs of your customer. Distance vector protocols are generally less computationally intensive than link-state methods, but they do not typically scale well to large networks because of several factors, including metric limitations and time to converge.

Common Problems Related to Routing Protocols

Along with making your network more robust and functional, routing protocols can introduce some problems that can affect overall network performance. Routing problems can cause an immense amount of undue traffic and headaches while you are trying to find and fix the problem. By having this information, you are taking a step toward preventing these problems and meeting your customer's goals.

Distance vector routing protocols have a couple of problems that are inherent in the algorithm. These problems are known as routing loops and count to infinity.

Routing loops can occur if the network's slow convergence on a new configuration causes inconsistent routing entries. The count-to-infinity problem occurs when invalid updates about a network continue to loop throughout the network. This process of continually incrementing the hop count will continue indefinitely. However, several solutions are available to alleviate this problem.

Split horizon is one way to eliminate routing loops and speed up convergence across a network. The logic behind split horizon is that it is never useful to send information about a route back in the direction from which the information originally came. Split horizon simply does not allow update information to flow out the same interface it arrived on. Another form of split horizon is called poison reverse.

Poison reverse attempts to eliminate routing loops caused by inconsistent updates. By using this technique, a router that discovers an inaccessible route sets a table entry that keeps the network state consistent while other routers gradually converge correctly on the topology change. Using hold-down timers in correlation with poison reverse is a solution to prevent routing loops on a network.

Hold-down timers prevent regular update messages from inappropriately reinstating a route that may have gone bad. They tell routers to hold any changes that might affect routers for some period of time, which is usually calculated to be just greater than the period of time necessary to update the entire network with the route change. With these solutions in place, you will be sure to alleviate any problems that may be inherent with distance vector routing protocols.

The problems that arise with link-state routing protocols differ from those that are seen in distance vector routing protocols. With link-state routing protocols, there are two primary concerns:

- Bandwidth requirements
- Processor and memory requirements

Running link-state routing protocols, in most situations, requires that routers use more memory and perform more processing. You must ensure that the routers that are selected are capable of providing these resources for routing.

Routers keep track of their neighbors and the networks they reach through other routing nodes. For link-state routing, memory must hold information from various link-state advertisements, the topology tree, and the routing table. The process complexity of computing the shortest path first is proportional to the number of links in the network times and the number of routers in the network.

Another consideration is the amount of bandwidth that is used for initial link-state packet flooding. During the initial discovery process, all routers using link-state routing protocols send LSPs to all other routers. This action floods the network as routers make their peak demand for bandwidth and temporarily reduces the bandwidth available for routed traffic. After this initial flooding stage, link-state protocols generally require network bandwidth only to send infrequent or event triggered LSPs that reflect topology changes.

The only real solution for these problems it to ensure that you have selected a router that has the memory and CPU power to maintain all the routing information and calculations that come with LSPs. Also, if you have low-speed WAN links, it may be a good idea to configure static routes on these interfaces so that the discovery process does not cripple a link.

The last problem with link-state routing protocols is dealing with the link-state updates. The most complex and critical aspect of link-state routing is making sure that all routers get all the LSPs necessary. Routers with different sets of LSPs will calculate routes based on different topological data. Then routes become unreachable as a result of the disagreement among routers about a link. If LSP distribution to all routers is not synchronized correctly, link-state routing can result in invalid routes. Utilizing link-state protocols on a very large network can intensify the problems of faulty LSPs being distributed. With faulty updates, LSPs can multiply as they propagate throughout the network, which will consume more and more bandwidth.

Link-state routing has several mechanisms for preventing or correcting potential problems arising from resource requirements and LSP distribution, as follows:

- Establish a hierarchy made up of different areas. Routers in one area will not need to store and process LSPs from other routers in different areas.

- Reduce the rate of periodic updates.

- LSP updates can go to a multicast group, rather than in a flood to all routers. You can use one or more routers as the depository for LSP transmission. Other routers can use these routers as specialized sources of consistent topology data.

- Link-state implementations can allow for LSP time stamps, sequence numbers, aging schemes, and other related mechanisms to help avoid inaccurate LSP distribution.

With these solutions in place, you will be sure to alleviate any problems that may be inherent in distance vector routing protocols.

Growth of Routing Protocols

When you are making the final selection of your routing protocol, be sure to address the question of how this routing protocol will grow with this network. If it is not answered or is answered incorrectly, it will have one of the biggest impacts on a network. Nobody can see into the future and tell you if a routing protocol will still be operating efficiently in three to five years. For instance, in the early 1980s, who would have thought that the Internet would be as powerful as it is, or that we would be in gigabit traffic, working our way into terabit ranges? However, by gauging your customer's business goals, you can get a good indication of the company's future needs, and you can position it appropriately.

For example, you have a customer that has a network of only 50 or so devices and is running RIP on its routers. You might assume that RIP is good enough and just do some minor upgrading, but did you ask where the company's business is heading in the next few years? If your customer is in the process of merging with another company with offices located throughout the world, you will realize that RIP won't work, and you will opt for a more robust routing protocol.

QUESTIONS AND ANSWERS

If you have several low-speed WAN links that are being saturated with routing protocol updates, what would be a good way of alleviating the unneeded traffic?	Use static routes, which are great for low-speed WAN links because the route mapping is manually entered and does not change; thus, no routing updates are needed.
Why is it important to keep a consistent naming and addressing convention across the entire network?	By keeping these conventions consistent, you won't have any problems identifying devices on your network, no matter where they are located.
What is accomplished by utilizing variable-length subnet masks?	VLSMs allow you to optimize valuable address space on your network. They also allow you to summarize routes, which means that one route represents many other routes on a network. This alleviates unwanted routing updates and keeps your routing table small.

CERTIFICATION SUMMARY

This chapter provides guidelines for creating logical addressing and naming schemes for network devices, such as routers, servers, and end stations. It addresses scalability issues with different routing protocols and discusses the functionality of subnetting and route summarization. This chapter illustrates the importance of using a structure model for addressing and naming to make it easier to understand network topology and network management tools and, most important, to meet the customer's goals.

Structured addresses and names facilitate network optimization and also help you in implementing route summarization, which decreases bandwidth utilization, processing on routers, and overall network instability. Addressing names are essential elements of the logical design phase of any network design process. If designed correctly, all these areas will build on one another until you have a strong network design that will meet all of your customer's technical and operational goals.

TWO-MINUTE DRILL

- ❑ Hierarchical addressing is a model for applying structured addresses.
- ❑ Hierarchical routing ensures efficient address allocation and reduced routing table entries.
- ❑ Scalability constraints for routing protocols include resource requirements, convergence, and metric limitations.
- ❑ Network scalability is limited by two types of issues: technical and operational.
- ❑ Classful routing protocols do not transmit any information about a network's prefix length.
- ❑ Classless routing protocols do transmit information about a network's prefix length.
- ❑ Class A, B, and C address classes are available for public use; Class D is used for multicasting, and Class E is reserved for experimental use.

❑ Variable-length subnet masks (VLSMs) ensure IP address optimization and facilitate route summarization.

❑ Classless interdomain routing (CIDR) was developed to assist in the alleviation of IP address shortage.

❑ A good naming model can strengthen the performance and availability of a network.

❑ Novell NetWare uses Novell Directory Services (NDS), which is distributed among several servers across a network.

❑ AppleTalk Name Binding Protocol (NBP) is responsible for mapping names to addresses in an AppleTalk environment.

❑ You can use a device's location, model number, and IP address in its name for easy identification or troubleshooting.

❑ Servers can be in either a distributed or a centralized model.

❑ Create static address ranges for network devices such as servers, routers, and switches.

❑ End-user stations should adhere to the same logical addressing and naming convention as other devices.

❑ IGRP does not support VLSMs.

❑ IGRP uses a combination of metrics to determine path selection: bandwidth, delay, reliability, load, and MTU size.

❑ EIGRP, developed by Cisco Systems, is considered a hybrid routing protocol because it is a combination of distance vector and link-state algorithms.

❑ EIGRP supports automatic route summarization and VLSM addressing.

❑ RIP does not support VLSMs.

❑ RIP uses hop count as its metric to determine path selection.

❑ OSPF is a link-state routing protocol.

❑ OSPF breaks a network into specific areas to allow for route summarization and to keep routing updates local to the areas to which they are assigned.

❑ Static routes are administratively demanding, requiring manual configuration.

SELF TEST

The following Self Test questions will help you measure your understanding of the material presented in this chapter. Read all the choices carefully because there may be more than one correct answer. Choose all correct answers for each question.

1. What are two of the characteristics of hierarchical routing?

    A. Does not allow route summarization

    B. Optimizes available address space

    C. Can be used only with OSPF

    D. Reduces routing table size

2. Which scalability constraint deals with router processor utilization?

    A. Convergence

    B. Metric limitations

    C. Resource requirements

    D. All of the above

3. Which scalability constraint changes depending on the routing protocol?

    A. Metric limitations

    B. Resource restrictions

    C. Convergence

    D. None of the above

4. Network scalability is limited to what two issues?

    A. Technical

    B. Location

    C. Monetary

    D. Operational

5. What are some limitations to using classful routing? (Choose all that apply.)

    A. Large routing tables

    B. Inability to properly utilize address space

    C. Does not transmit information concerning prefix length

    D. Transmits information concerning prefix length

6. Which group do link-state routing protocols fall into?

   A. Classful

   B. Variable

   C. Classless

   D. Connectionless

7. Which address class has the address range 224.0.0.0 to 239.0.0.0?

   A. Class A

   B. Class B

   C. Class C

   D. Class D

8. Where does a subnet address "borrow" bits from?

   A. Host address

   B. Mask address

   C. Network address

   D. None of the above

9. What does supernetting refer to?

   A. Route aggregation

   B. Route summarization

   C. Classless interdomain routing

   D. All of the above

10. What command will verify that you have properly configured an IP address on a router interface?

   A. show interface ip

   B. show interface

   C. show ip interface

   D. show ip address

11. Which address-to-name mapping method requires more administrative maintenance?

   A. Dynamic

   B. Static

12. When you are naming a device with multiple addresses, such as a router, how many names should be associated with it?

    A. One for every interface

    B. One for every active interface

    C. One name to represent all interfaces

    D. All of the above

13. Which environment uses a directory service that is distributed among several servers?

    A. TCP/IP

    B. Novell NetWare

    C. AppleTalk

    D. NetBIOS

14. In an AppleTalk environment, what items can you assign names to?

    A. Printers

    B. Servers

    C. Zones

    D. All of the above

15. What are some advantages of a good naming scheme? (Choose all that apply.)

    A. Short names

    B. Logical meaning

    C. One name representing a type of equipment

    D. None of the above

16. As a rule of thumb, what should broadcast traffic on a link be limited to?

    A. 50 percent

    B. 10 percent

    C. 40 percent

    D. 20 percent

17. In the classic three-layer hierarchical model, what layer is described as the backbone layer?

    A. Backbone

    B. Core

    C. Distribution

    D. Access

18. What type of server provides dynamically assigned IP addresses from a predetermined range of IP addresses for a network?

    A. DNS

    B. FTP

    C. DHCP

    D. HSRP

19. Which routing protocol(s) gets its (their) topological data from neighbor data? (Choose all that apply.)

    A. OSPF

    B. RIP

    C. EIGRP

    D. IGRP

20. What solutions address the problem of routing loops?

    A. Split horizon

    B. Poison reverse

    C. Hold-down timers

    D. All of the above

SELF TEST ANSWERS

1. ☑ **B and D.** With hierarchical routing, you are able to optimize address space through efficient address allocation; and by utilizing route summarization, you can reduce the number of routing table entries.

   ☒ **A** is incorrect because hierarchical routing does use route summarization. **C** is incorrect because hierarchical routing can be used with many routing protocols.

2. ☑ **C.** Resource requirements are a combination of CPU, memory, bandwidth, and the number of networks that are running on a router.

   ☒ **A** is incorrect because convergence deals with the factors that control how long it takes routers on a network to calculate and understand the network topology after a change. **B** is incorrect because metric limitations deal only with types of routing protocols and not the routers themselves.

3. ☑ **A.** The metric limitation changes, depending on which routing protocol you choose because that hop count is used as a metric. Each distance vector protocol has a different hop count, which gives a different metric for the best route. Link-state routing protocols are not affected by the hop count metric.

   ☒ **B** is incorrect because resource restrictions deal with CPU, memory, bandwidth, and network utilization. **C** is incorrect because convergence deals with the factors that control how long it takes routers on a network to calculate and understand the network topology after a change.

4. ☑ **A and D.** Operational scaling concerns encourage the use of large areas or protocols that do not require a hierarchical structure. Technical scaling concerns promote the use of small areas and protocols for a hierarchical structure.

   ☒ **B** is incorrect because the physical location has no impact. **C** is incorrect because money does not affect scalability.

5. ☑ **A, B, and C.** The limitations with classful routing result because classful routing has a limited understanding of prefix length. This prohibits classful routing from performing subnetting functions, which causes large routing tables and wasted address space.

   ☒ **D** is incorrect because classful routing does not transmit information concerning prefix length; prefix length is calculated from the information about the address class that was provided in the first few bits of information.

6. ☑ C. Classless routing protocols support VLSMs and route summarization.

 ☒ A is incorrect because classful routing protocols do not support route summarization or VLSMs. **B** is incorrect because variable is not a valid routing group. **D** is incorrect because connectionless is associated with a type of service provided by IP.

7. ☑ D. Class D is used for multicast groups that utilize the range 224.0.0.0 to 239.0.0.0.

 ☒ A is incorrect because Class A addresses utilize the address range 1.0.0.0 to 126.0.0.0. **B** is incorrect because Class B addresses utilize the address range 128.0.0.0 to 191.255.0.0. **C** is incorrect because Class C addresses utilize the address range 192.0.0.0 to 233.255.255.255.

8. ☑ A. One creates a subnet address by borrowing bits from the host field and designating them as the network field.

 ☒ B is incorrect because the mask address directly reflects the corresponding bit in the IP address. **C** is incorrect because the borrowed bit is designated as part of the network field.

9. ☑ D. All are correct because each term can be used interchangeably; they perform the same function.

10. ☑ C. This command will display interface information that includes the IP address and subnet mask.

 ☒ A, **B**, and **D** are incorrect because they are invalid commands.

11. ☑ B. Using static mappings each time a new device is added or deleted from a network, you will need to manually update the naming table.

 ☒ A is incorrect because with a dynamic mapping system, whenever a device is added or deleted from a network, the naming table is updated automatically.

12. ☑ C. Having one name to represent the entire device, you prevent identification problems that can arise during troubleshooting.

 ☒ A is incorrect because multiple names would confuse network management tools and personnel. **B** is incorrect because multiple names would confuse network management tools and personnel.

13. ☑ B. NDS (Novell Directory Services) uses a distributed database approach to naming locations where portions of the database reside on many servers. This reduces the possibility that one central server will fail and affect all users.

 ☒ A is incorrect because TCP/IP does not use a distributed directory service. **C** is incorrect because AppleTalk does not use a distributed directory service. **D** is incorrect because NetBIOS does not use a distributed directory service.

14. ☑ **D.** All are correct because with AppleTalk, not only can you name devices like servers and printers, you can name the zones they are on.

15. ☑ **A and B.** A short and logical name for a device can give users just as much information as a long and complex name, but without the confusion.
☒ **C** is incorrect because if all of your routers and servers were named router and server, you would spend countless hours trying to track down a device that is causing problems on your network.

16. ☑ **D.** A limit of broadcast traffic increases network productivity, and anything over 20 percent could be considered a broadcast storm and impair the network.
☒ **A, B,** and **C** are incorrect because they are numbers that are not related to this topic.

17. ☑ **B.** In this model, the core layer is the layer that provides reliable transport and is labeled the backbone.
☒ **A** is incorrect because it is a generic term that describes the core. **C** is incorrect because the distribution layer is the second layer that the core layer feeds. **D** is incorrect because the access layer is the third layer that the distribution layer feeds and is located closest to the user.

18. ☑ **C.** DHCP (Dynamic Host Configuration Protocol) is configured with a range of IP addresses and assigns them to user stations and other devices on a network.
☒ **A** is incorrect because a DNS is a server that performs name resolution for devices on a network. **B** is incorrect because an FTP server is a device that allows people to transfer files from the server to other devices. **D** is incorrect because HSRP is Hot Standby Router Protocol that is used by Cisco for router redundancy.

19. ☑ **B and D.** They are distance vector routing protocols that receive topological data from their neighbors, and this is how they map the network topology.
☒ **A and C** are incorrect because they are link-state routing protocols, and they base the network topology on hierarchical design.

20. ☑ **D.** All these solutions can be used with one another to prevent the problem of routing loops on a network.

CISCO CERTIFIED DESIGN ASSOCIATE

13

Customer Network and Other Protocols

CERTIFICATION OBJECTIVES

I t would be nice if internetworks came in only one flavor, preferably vanilla. Unfortunately, internetworks come in many different flavors. Today's networks consist of Windows NT servers, UNIX Servers, NetWare Servers, Macintosh systems, AS/400s, and other systems that have standard and proprietary protocols running. Currently TCP/IP is the dominant internetwork protocol. What about the other network protocols? They deserve some attention as well.

In this chapter, we will first talk about the IPX protocol, which dominated Novell NetWare networks for many years before TCP/IP gained its popularity. We will then introduce AppleTalk, a protocol suite that most network engineers tend to forget about. We will close the chapter with a discussion on bridging protocols and NetBIOS.

CERTIFICATION OBJECTIVE 13.01

IPX RIP, SAP

IPX is supported by two routing protocols, IPX RIP/SAP and NLSP. IPX RIP is a distance vector protocol that is best used in small WANs. NLSP is a link-state protocol that is best used in larger WANs.

IPX Overview

Back in the '80s, Novell's NetWare product dominated the network market. Novell's primary network protocol was IPX, or Internetwork Packet Exchange protocol. Today, there are still plenty of IPX-based networks for network engineers to manage. These IPX networks either were installed before the growth of IP's popularity, or they required IPX for an application such as B-Trieve. IPX is also easier to administer on a LAN than on TCP/IP. It was not until the release of NetWare 5 that NetWare would begin using pure IP instead of any IPX or IP tunneling.

IPX and the OSI Model

IPX is actually a suite of protocols that work together to transport data from the sender to the receiver reliably. IPX was not originally designed with OSI standards in mind. It does, however, function in layers similar to those in the OSI model.

Figure 13-1 shows the OSI model and the IPX suite of protocols.

It is important to know how the IPX protocols correspond with the OSI model to make troubleshooting easier. For example, without knowing at which layer the IPX component operated, you would not know whether the problem was most likely a software application, router, or hub. Since the IPX component operates at the transport and network layers, focusing your efforts on the router would be a good place to start.

IPX   IPX operates at the network and transport layers of the OSI model. IPX is a routable protocol similar to IP. It is responsible for IPX addressing of individual nodes and internetwork packet delivery. (IPX addressing is covered shortly in the section "IPX addressing.") IPX makes routing decisions based on information from routing protocols like IPX RIP or NLSP. IPX is not a reliable transport by itself. It is a connectionless protocol, similar to UDP/IP, in that it does not expect an acknowledgment that packets were received from a destination node. When IPX needs to communicate with upper-layer protocols, it uses sockets. Sockets are similar to ports used with TCP/IP to communicate with various applications on a single machine.

FIGURE 13-1

IPX suite and the OSI model

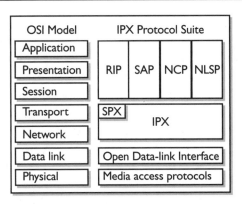

IPX packets contain 30-byte headers with source and destination addresses along with other information, followed by the data area. IPX packets can be anywhere from 30 to 65,535 bytes in length. A 30-byte IPX packet would be one with only header information.

The IPX packet header consists of the following fields:

- **Checksum**   Data integrity checking
- **Packet Length**   Packet length in bytes
- **Transport Control**   Number of routers the packet can cross before being dropped
- **Packet Type**   Service that created the packet
- **Destination Network**   Network address of destination network
- **Destination Node**   MAC address of destination node
- **Destination Socket**   Address of process on destination node
- **Source Network**   Network address of source network
- **Source Node**   MAC address of source node
- **Source Socket**   Address of process on source node

SPX   SPX (Sequence Packet Exchange) operates at the transport layer of the OSI model. It provides reliable transport for IPX communications just as TCP does for IP. SPX creates virtual circuits between nodes to ensure data delivery. Each circuit is assigned a specific ID that is included in the SPX header.

RIP   RIP (Routing Information Protocol) is a distance vector routing protocol used to discover routes to IPX networks. RIP will be discussed in more depth later in the chapter.

SAP   SAP (Service Advertising Protocol) advertises IPX services to network clients. SAP will be discussed in more depth later in the chapter.

NCP   NCP (NetWare Core Protocol) provides clients with file and directory access, printing, synchronization, and security.

NLSP   NLSP (NetWare Link Services Protocol) is Novell's link-state routing protocol for IPX. NLSP was designed by Novell to overcome the limitations inherent in IPX RIP and SAP. NLSP will be discussed in more depth later, in the section "NLSP."

IPX Addressing

In order to be able to communicate on an IPX network, the nodes need to have an IPX address. IPX addressing is very similar to IP addressing. The big difference is that IPX addressing is a lot easier to administer.

IPX addresses are 10 bytes long and are most often written in hexadecimal notation. An IPX address consists of two parts, Network and Node. This is similar to TCP/IP subnets and hosts. The network number is designated by the administrator and must be unique among LANs. This means that two servers communicating with each other across a router must have different network numbers. Devices on each side of the router would have network numbers matching their local server. The important benefit of IPX over TCP/IP is that the node portion of an IPX address requires no administration. IPX automatically uses the machine's MAC address for the node address. Here is an example of an IPX address: 00214E4B.00AE.C004.900D. The first eight hexadecimal digits, 00214E4B, define the network address assigned by the administrator. The next 12 hexadecimal digits, 00AE.C004.900D, define the node address automatically defined by the node's MAC address.

The following steps outline the process of communication using IPX addressing:

1. Source station sends a packet with the destination address to the network.

2. Router grabs packet.

3. Router looks at the network portion of the destination IPX address.

4. Router routes the packet to the appropriate network.

5. Destination station looks at the node portion of the destination IPX address and accepts the packet.

This scenario assumes that the communicating nodes are on different networks. Otherwise, the router would have simply discarded the packet.

How Do They Work?

In order to engineer, manage, and troubleshoot an internetwork, you have to understand how routing protocols actually work. They all have their differences and similarities. Distance vector protocols are usually better suited for small internetworks, while link-state protocols work well in large internetworks. This knowledge will allow you to make informed decisions on your internetwork implementations.

GNS and SAP

When NetWare clients want to access network resources, they rely on NetWare servers to fulfill their requests. Before a NetWare server can start serving a NetWare client, the client must locate the appropriate server. This is accomplished with the GNS (Get Nearest Server) broadcast. GNS allows NetWare clients to query the IPX network for requested services. The first thing a workstation does is transmit a GNS broadcast to locate an available server. All NetWare servers that receive the GNS broadcast check their SAP tables for servers hosting the requested services. If a suitable server is found in the SAP table, the server that found it will respond with a GNS of its own. This GNS will contain the IPX address of the suitable server so that the NetWare client can communicate with it directly. If a suitable server is not found in the SAP table, the GNS broadcast will be ignored.

Knowing how GNS broadcasts and SAP work together is important, especially in routed networks. Routers, by default, do not route broadcasts. This poses an interesting problem. What if you have a NetWare client on Network B that needs to access a NetWare server on Network A? Since routers don't do broadcasts, GNS will most likely fail. Fortunately, a Cisco router can build SAP tables and actually respond to GNS requests just as a NetWare server can. This prevents unnecessary bandwidth utilization across WAN links by keeping local traffic local. This also increases the network's response time to a client's request by returning the IPX address of a remote server from a local router. Otherwise, the client would have to wait for a remote server to respond with the IPX address of the requested remote server.

When NetWare servers process client GNS requests, they have to have a way of keeping track of all the network services. This is where SAP comes in. A NetWare server uses SAP broadcasts to inform other servers of its existence and any other servers it has received SAPs from.

These SAP broadcasts are sent out every 60 seconds. Servers that receive the broadcasts update their SAP tables accordingly. Cisco routers participate in SAP as well, but in a slightly different way from NetWare servers. Cisco routers, by default, do not allow SAP broadcasts to cross. They do, however, track all the SAPs they receive and send out a complete SAP table in 60-second intervals like NetWare servers.

SAP packets are at least 66 bytes in length and can contain information about up to seven servers. They are encapsulated in IPX packets. Table 13-1 shows the field descriptions of a SAP packet.

IPX RIP

As you now know, IPX RIP is a distance vector protocol for routing IPX. It is designed to find the fastest route to a network. IPX RIP is very similar to IP RIP. The main differences are in the default update interval and the routing metrics of hops and ticks.

TABLE 13-1 Field Descriptions of a SAP Packet	Field	Description
	Operation (2 bytes)	The purpose of the packet 01 – general or specific request 02 – general or specific response 03 – Get Nearest Server Request 04 – Get Nearest Server Response
	Service Type (4 bytes)	Type of service device offers 0000 = Unknown, 0003 = Print Queue, 0004 = File Server, 0005 = Job Server, 0007 = Print Server, 0009 = Archive Server, 0024 = Remote Bridge Server, 0047 = Advertising Print Server, above 8000 is reserved
	Server Name (48 bytes)	Name of server
	Network Address (4 bytes)	Network address assigned during installation
	Node Address (6 bytes)	MAC address of server
	Socket Address (2 bytes)	Socket that server will receive requests on
	Hops to Server (2 bytes)	Number of routers to cross to reach destination

An IPX RIP router sends everything it knows to other routers at 60-second intervals. If a change occurs on the network, other routers will have to wait for the scheduled update before being notified. This is fine for small nonvolatile networks, but large, unstable networks could cause a problem.

IPX RIP uses hops and ticks as cost metrics. Hops are the number of routers a packet has to cross before it reaches its destination. If a destination is more than 15 hops away, IPX RIP assumes the destination network is unreachable. Ticks are approximately 1/18th of a second and measure the time it takes a packet to reach its destination.

Table 13-2 compares IPX RIP to IP RIP.

IPX RIP packets are encapsulated in IPX packets and are at least 10 bytes long. The more routes that are to be transmitted, the larger is the packet. Table 13-3 shows the fields in an RIP packet.

To configure IPX RIP, you must complete the following tasks:

1. Enable IPX routing.

2. Configure the IPX network number.

3. Configure the IPX frame type.

4. Configure IPX RIP as the routing protocol.

The following is a sample configuration of IPX RIP:

```
ipx routing
interface ethernet0/0
ipx network 5 encapsulation sap
ipx router rip
```

TABLE 13-2		IP RIP	IPX RIP
Comparison of IPX RIP and IP RIP	Update Interval	30	60
	Cost Metric	hops	hops, ticks
	Routed Protocol	IP	IPX

TABLE 13-3

Fields in a RIP Packet

Fields	Description
Operation (2 bytes)	The purpose of the packet 01 – general or specific request 02 – general or specific response
Network Address (4 bytes)	Network address assigned during installation
Number of Hops (2 bytes)	Ignored in an RIP request packet
Number of Ticks (2 bytes)	The time it takes to reach a destination

The first command, ipx routing, enables IPX routing on the router. The second command, interface ethernet0/0, puts the router in interface configuration mode for Ethernet interface 0/0. The third command, ipx network 5 encapsulation sap, identifies 5 as the router's IPX network segment and the IPX frame type as Ethernet_802.2. If you wanted to use Ethernet_802.3, the default IPX frame type, sap would be replaced with novell-ether. The fourth command, ipx router rip, specifies RIP as the IPX routing protocol.

NLSP

Like OSPF, NLSP is a hierarchical routing protocol. It utilizes objects such as areas and domains. An area is a group of networks that all share the same area address. A domain is a group of areas belonging to the same organization. When a group of domains is linked together, the domains form a global internetwork.

NLSP supports three routing levels. Level-1 routers link networks together within the same area. Level-2 routers link areas together and act as level-1 routers in their area. Level-3 routers link domains together and act as level-2 routers in their domain.

Figure 13-2 shows NLSP routing levels in action. Level-1 routing occurs within Area 1, while level-2 routing occurs between Area 1 and Area 2. Level-3 routing occurs between routing domain A and routing domain B.

NLSP works by storing a complete map of the network and sending updates only when the topology changes. It also sends service information

FIGURE 13-2

NLSP areas, domains, and
routing levels

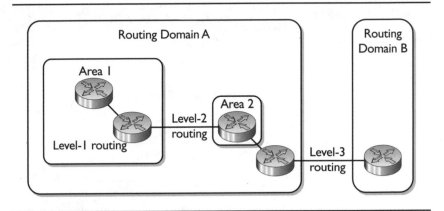

updates only when services change. Before updates can be transmitted,
routers must form adjacencies. In other words, they need to meet their
next-door neighbors. Just as people say "hello" when introducing
themselves, routers send Hello packets out their interfaces. Hello packets
are sent every 20 seconds. A special designated router, elected by Hello
packets, sends Hello packets every 10 seconds. If a router does not receive
at least three Hello packets from a neighbor, it assumes that neighbor is
down. Other adjacent neighbors are then updated. Hello packets are also
sent when the contents of the next Hello to be transmitted are different
from the contents of the previously transmitted Hello packet.

There are two types of NLSP Hello packets: WAN Hello and level-1
LAN Hello packets. WAN Hello packets are for WAN transmissions and
level-1 LAN Hello packets are for LAN transmissions.

WAN Hello Packet Fields

■ **Protocol ID** NLSP routing-layer ID

■ **Length Indicator** Length of fixed portion of header in bytes

■ **Minor Version** Ignored

■ **Reserved** Ignored

■ **Packet Type (5 bits)** Contains 17 possible decimal values

■ **Major Version** Ignored

- **Reserved**   Ignored
- **State (2 bits)**   Router's link state (0 = up, 1 = initializing, 2 = down)
- **Circuit Type (2 bits)**   Any one of the following values:
  - **0**   Ignore entire packet
  - **1**   Level-1 routing
  - **2**   Level-2 routing
  - **3**   Both level-1 and level-2 routing
- **Source ID**   System ID of sending router
- **Holding Time**   In seconds, holding timer used for the sending router
- **Packet Length**   Entire length of packet, in bytes
- **Local WAN Circuit ID**   Unique ID assigned at circuit creation
- **Variable-length Fields**   Optional fields

Level-1 LAN Hello Packet Fields

- **Protocol ID**   NLSP routing-layer ID
- **Length Indicator**   Length of fixed portion of header in bytes
- **Minor Version**   Ignored
- **Reserved**   Ignored
- **Packet Type (5 bits)**   Contains 15 possible decimal values
- **Major Version**   Ignored
- **Reserved**   Ignored
- **No Multicast (1 bit)**   Sender cannot receive traffic addressed to a multicast address
- **Circuit Type (2 bits)**   Any one of the following values:
  - **0**   Ignore entire packet
  - **1**   Level-1 routing

- ■ **2** Level-2 routing
- ■ **3** Both level-1 and level-2 routing
- ■ **Source ID** System ID of sending router
- ■ **Holding Time** In seconds, holding timer used for the sending router
- ■ **Packet Length** Entire length of packet, in bytes
- ■ **R** Ignored
- ■ **Priority (7 bits)** LAN level-1 designated router priority level
- ■ **LAN ID** System ID of LAN level-1 designated router
- ■ **Variable-length Fields** Optional fields

NLSP routers also send link-state packets, LSPs. There are two types of LSPs, nonpseudonode and pseudonode. Nonpseudonode LSPs contain information on all the networks to which the device is connected and any services that reside on the device. A pseudonode LSP, sent by the designated router, lists all the devices that are adjacent to the segment. Cisco routers send LSPs that describe the state of their links. They also maintain a variable indicating whether the link is up, down, or initializing for each adjacency.

NLSP routers use the Hello packets and LSPs to maintain three tables:

- ■ Adjacency
- ■ Link state
- ■ Forwarding

The adjacency table consists of all the router's NLSP neighbors. The link-state table is created from adjacency tables and consists of all the adjacencies and routes in an NLSP area. The forwarding table is created from the link-state table and consists of optimal paths to discovered networks.

When NLSP routers come online and meet all the neighbors in their area, they select a DR (designated router). This would be like you and your neighbors electing a block club leader. Just as the block club leader receives ideas from individual members to pass along to all the other members, the

DR receives topology updates from individual routers and updates all the other routers in the area. The DR sends updates in the form of LSPs that are propagated throughout the entire area until all NLSP routers in the area have been updated. To recap the process, note the following enumerated steps:

1. NLSP routers send Hello packets to each other.
2. NLSP routers elect which one of them will be the DR.
3. NLSP routers communicate only with the DR from now on.
4. DR sends updates with LSPs to all other NLSP routers in the area.

To configure NLSP on a LAN interface, you must complete the following tasks:

1. Enable IPX routing.
2. Define an internal network number.
3. Enable NLSP on the router.
4. Define a set of network numbers that will be part of the NLSP area.
5. Select a LAN interface.
6. Configure the IPX network number of the interface.
7. Configure the IPX frame type.
8. Enable NLSP routing on the interface.

The following is a sample configuration of NLSP on a LAN interface:

```
ipx routing
ipx internal-network CCDA0001
ipx router nlsp
area-address 0 0
interface ethernet0/0
ipx network 10 encapsulation novell-ether
ipx nlsp enable
```

The first command, ipx routing, enables IPX routing on the interface. The second command, ipx internal-network CCDA0001, configures the router with an IPX internal-network number of CCDA0001. The third command, ipx router nlsp, enables NLSP on the router. The fourth command, area-address 0 0, defines all networks as part of the NLSP area. The fifth command, interface ethernet0/0, puts the router in interface configuration mode for Ethernet interface 0/0. The sixth command, ipx network 10 encapsulation novell-ether, defines the IPX network number as 10 and the IPX frame type as Ethernet_802.3. The seventh command, ipx nlsp enable, enables NLSP routing on the Ethernet interface.

To configure NLSP on a WAN interface, you must complete the following tasks:

1. Enable IPX routing.

2. Define an internal network number.

3. Enable NLSP on the router.

4. Define a set of network numbers that will be part of the NLSP area.

5. Select a WAN (serial) interface.

6. Enable IPXWAN on the interface.

7. Enable NLSP routing on the interface.

The following is a sample configuration of NLSP on a LAN interface:

```
ipx routing
ipx internal-network 1234
ipx router nlsp
area-address 0 0
interface serial0/0
no ipx network
encapsulation ppp
ipx ipxwan 1234 10 CCDARTR
ipx nlsp enable
```

The first command, ipx routing, enables IPX routing on the interface. The second command, ipx internal-network 1234, configures the router with an IPX internal-network number of 1234. The third command, ipx router nlsp, enables NLSP on the router. The fourth command, area-address 0 0, defines all networks as part of the NLSP area. The fifth command, interface serial0/0, puts the router in interface configuration mode for serial interface 0/0. The sixth command, no ipx network, disables any previously defined IPX network number. This is required for IPXWAN implementations. The seventh command, encapsulation ppp, enables the Point-to-Point Protocol on the serial interface. The eighth command, ipx ipxwan 1234 10 CCDARTR, selects 1234 as the primary IPX internal-network number, 10 as the IPX network number, and CCDARTR as the local communications server. The ninth command, ipx nlsp enable, enables NLSP routing on the serial interface.

Strengths and Limitations

Throughout your career as an internetworking expert, you will be faced with many decisions. Your customers will expect their network to be fast, reliable and efficient. If the network fails in any of these areas, the entire network fails. At least that's what the customer will think. One way to ensure network success is to choose the most efficient routing protocol. You should always choose a routing protocol that is easy to administer, quick to converge, scalable to client needs, and easy on the bandwidth.

Why Use RIP Over NLSP?

NLSP offers many advantages over RIP, including improved routing, better efficiency, and greater scalability. So why would you use RIP over NLSP? Because RIP is infinitely easier to implement on a small WAN. For example, if you are implementing a WAN consisting of T1 links and fewer than 16 hops across, you would use RIP. RIP is also a lot easier to troubleshoot than NLSP. Using NLSP on a WAN five hops across with fast T1 lines would be overkill. The administrative costs would not justify its implementation.

Why Migrate to NLSP?

If IPX RIP is so easy to administer, why would anyone want to migrate to NLSP? For starters, NLSP has some significant advantages over IPX RIP in larger WANs and is backward compatible with IPX RIP. Let's say you have a WAN over 100 routers across with some fast T1 links and some slow 56KB links. IPX RIP would possibly never converge on a network of this size. Recall that convergence is the time it takes the routers on your WAN to be updated with the same topology information. If a link goes down, an IPX RIP router will send a scheduled update that may never reach all the other routers before that link comes up. Thus, other routers receiving the late update will in turn broadcast that the link is down even though it may already be back online. NLSP, on the other hand, sends updates immediately without having to wait for a scheduled update. IPX RIP would also have scalability problems. Remember, IPX RIP routers assume any network over 15 hops away is unreachable. This limitation makes it impossible to implement IPX RIP as your sole routing protocol on this network. In contrast, NLSP has no hop count limitation. Another problem with IPX RIP on this network is bandwidth usage. IPX RIP and SAP will pull a network of this size to its knees with the 60-second broadcast updates alone. This is especially true across the 56KB links. NLSP routers send updates when changes occur or once every two hours. As far as ease of administration goes, IPX RIP just is not applicable in a network of this size.

Table 13-4 compares IPX RIP to NLSP.

Troubleshooting IPX Routing

In this section, we will examine various IPX-related routing problems. You will be introduced to many IOS commands that will assist you in the troubleshooting process. You will find that both IPX RIP and NLSP share some of the same IOS commands necessary for troubleshooting. We will be covering commands common to both routing protocols and commands that are unique to each one. While a network problem can stem from anywhere on the network, we will focus on routers as the source of problem resolution.

TABLE 13-4		IPX RIP	NLSP
Comparison of IPX RIP and NLSP	Distance vector	Yes	No
	Link state	No	Yes
	Update interval	60 sec.	2 hrs. or topology change
	Hop count limitation	15	127

No Connectivity to Remote LAN

One problem you may encounter in your travels as a CCDA is the inability of clients being able to access a remote server across their Cisco router. This problem can have several possible causes. It also has several solutions.

One possibility is that the router interface to the remote LAN is down. The first thing you should do is check the status of the router's interface. You can do this with the show interface command. This command will show you whether or not the interface and line protocol are down. If the interface is administratively down, you can use the no shutdown command in interface configuration mode to bring the interface back up. If the line protocol is down, it is possible that your router is connected to a hub or switch of a different speed or topology.

A second possibility is that the Ethernet encapsulation methods are mismatched. In other words, servers and routers could be using different IPX frame types. If a router needs to communicate with a network using the Ethernet_802.2 frame type, this must be configured. By default, the Ethernet_802.3 frame type is used when no frame type is specified. The frame type can be verified with the show ipx interface command. If the frame type is different from that of the clients and servers, there is a mismatch. You can change the frame type of the router by using the ipx network command. The following example changes the frame type, or encapsulation, on the router's Ethernet interface to Ethernet_802.2 for IPX network 10:

```
interface ethernet0/0
no ipx network
ipx network 10 encapsulation sap
```

A third possibility is that there is a ring speed specification mismatch in a Token Ring environment. This means that your router might be configured with a ring speed of 4 Mbps while the rest of the Token Ring devices are communicating at 16 Mbps. You can use the show interfaces token command to view the ring speed configured on the router's interface. If the ring speed differs from the rest of the network, you can use the ring-speed command in interface configuration mode to correct the mismatch.

A fourth possibility is that two routers share the same node number. Node numbers should always be unique in an IPX network. There rarely is a conflict since node numbers are usually based on the MAC address of an IPX device, which is always unique. This problem can occur, however, when node numbers are explicitly defined on routers or when a saved configuration of an existing router has been uploaded to a new router. You can use the show running-config command to list the current router configuration. In the list, you will see the command ipx routing *node address*. If the node address does conflict with an existing IPX router, use the following commands to change the node address to be the router's MAC address:

```
no ipx routing
ipx routing
```

You should then use the show running-config command to verify that the node address has been corrected.

A fifth possibility is that there are duplicate network numbers. IPX network numbers should be unique across the IPX internetwork. Otherwise, IPX RIP and NLSP would not be able to route packets properly. To resolve this problem, you would first have to view the output of the following commands: show ipx servers and show ipx route. If a local server shows up as a remote server in the routing table, the router bordering the remote IPX network might be using the same IPX network number. The following commands change the IPX network number to 2:

```
no ipx network
ipx network 2
```

The last possibility we will explore is faulty hardware. Faulty hardware can be the cause of many internetwork problems. The easy problems are those that reveal themselves consistently and can be duplicated. The more difficult problems are the intermittent ones. If you suspect a hardware problem is the cause of lost connectivity, you should check all router ports, interface processors, and other router hardware. You should check and reseat any WAN interface cards (WICs) installed in the router.

No Connectivity Over IPX RIP Router

It is likely that you will come across a problem when IPX clients cannot communicate with IPX servers across IPX RIP routers. There are several potential causes of and solutions to this problem.

One possibility is that IPX routing is not configured on the router. You can use the show running-config command to verify that the ipx routing command was executed. If it was not, enter the ipx routing command in global configuration mode, which will enable IPX RIP on all IPX interfaces with an IPX network number configured.

Another possible cause is that the IPX network number is not configured on the router. Remember that all IPX networks must have a unique network number across the internetwork to communicate. You should use the show ipx interface command to view the state of all the IPX interfaces. If IPX is required and not running on an interface, the command ipx network should be used in interface configuration mode.

A third possibility could be an IPX RIP timer mismatch between routers and servers. If a router is sending updates at 30-second intervals and a server is sending updates at 60-second intervals, new route table updates from the server could be replaced with old route information from the router. You can use the show ipx interfaces command to view the timer's update interval. If the update interval of the router and server are mismatched, use the ipx update-time command in interface configuration mode to put them in sync.

A fourth possibility is that IPX RIP updates are not being sent out the IPX interface. This can be verified by using the debug ipx routing activity command. If updates are not being sent, IPX RIP should be disabled with the no ipx routing command and re-enabled with the ipx routing command. If this does not correct the problem, restart the router.

A fifth possibility is that network filters are not configured correctly. Network filters use access lists that determine which packets get through and which packets stay behind. To view how an access list is configured, use the show access-lists command. Use the show running-config command to discover which access lists are specified in the input- and output-network filters. If the wrong access list was specified for a network filter, disable the network filter with the no ipx input-network-filter or no ipx output-network-filter command in interface configuration mode. Then re-enable the network filter with the ipx input-network-filter or ipx output-network-filter command. If the network filter was using the correct access list, the access list should be re-created with corrections using the access list command.

Router Not Propagating SAP Updates

SAP tables maintain entries of available IPX network services. IPX routers use these tables to fulfill requests from network clients for IPX services. When routers do not send SAP updates correctly to the other IPX routers on the internetwork, it can cause clients to have intermittent or no connectivity to remote servers. This problem has various possible causes and solutions.

A SAP timer mismatch could be one possible cause for this problem. You can view the SAP timer information with the show running-config command. Look for the ipx sap-interval *minutes* command in the output. If the SAP timer is different from the SAP timers of the other routers on your internetwork, there is a mismatch. To change the SAP timer, use the no ipx sap-interval command followed by the ipx sap-interval *minutes* command in interface configuration mode. Make sure you configure the SAP timer with the same interval in minutes as the other IPX routers. If you do not want the router to send SAP updates, set the SAP timer interval to 0 minutes.

Another cause of SAP update problems is a misconfigured SAP filter. In this case, use the show access-lists command to see whether there are any access lists configured. To determine whether SAP filters are being used with access lists, use the show running-config command and look for the ipx input-sap-filter command or the ipx output-sap-filter command. If either of these commands exist, disable them with the no ipx input-sap-filter command or no ipx output-sap-filter command in interface configuration mode. At this point, use the debug ipx sap activity command to verify that SAP traffic is now being forwarded normally. If SAP is operating normally, re-create the disabled SAP filter's access list with the desired SAP traffic access. After the access list has been re-created, use the ipx input-sap-filter command or ipx output-sap-filter command in interface configuration mode to re-enable the SAP filter.

Sometimes a Novell server cannot process SAP updates as quickly as a router is generating them. You can verify this by using the show interface command to check for output drops. If there are excessive output drops, use the show ipx servers command on the router and the display servers command on the Novell server. If the output on the Novell server is only a partial listing of the router's output, this might be an indication of the Novell server not being able to keep up with SAP updates. To configure the delay between packets in a multipacket SAP update, use the ipx output-sap-delay command in interface configuration mode. Novell recommends a delay of about 55 ms.

Intermittent Connectivity

Any problem that is intermittent can always be a difficult one to pinpoint. Intermittent connectivity is no different. The symptom is clients and servers being able to communicate with networks and other servers only some of the time. This has many different causes.

Sometimes, slow serial lines can cause a router to drop SAP packets before they are transmitted. When this happens, intermittent connectivity problems can occur. You should use the show interfaces serial command to examine the output queue drops field. If a large number of packets are being dropped, it might indicate that SAP updates are being lost before making it across the serial link. Use the show ipx servers command on the router and the display servers command on the server. If the Novell server only shows a partial listing, this could indicate SAP updates are being dropped from the router's output queue. If this is the case, unnecessary SAP updates should be filtered with the ipx input-sap-filter, ipx output-sap-filter, or ipx router-sap-filter command in interface configuration mode. You should also use the hold-queue *length* out command in interface configuration mode to increase the output hold queue length and increase performance. If SAP packets are still being dropped, additional bandwidth should be purchased.

The following are other causes that are also responsible for other IPX network problems:

- **IPX RIP timer mismatch**   Also responsible for no connectivity over IPX router.

- **SAP timer mismatch**   Also responsible for routers not propagating SAP updates.

- **SAP delay needs to be set**   Also responsible for routers not propagating SAP updates.

During the troubleshooting process, you might have to use various forms of the debug command. This command uses significant router resources and could affect the performance of your internetwork. You should use the debug command only during off-peak hours when users are the most inactive.

CERTIFICATION OBJECTIVE 13.02

AppleTalk RTMP and AURP

AppleTalk uses two routing protocols: RTMP and AURP. These protocols ensure that data get from one place to another by providing the best possible path. In this section, we will discuss their operation, strengths and limitations, and troubleshooting techniques.

AppleTalk Overview

AppleTalk is a proprietary protocol that was designed by Apple Computer, Inc., in the 1980s. Its purpose was to provide client/server distributed network services for Macintosh users. In other words, users would be able to share files and printers with other users. Apple Computer, Inc., equipped every Macintosh with built-in support for AppleTalk networking. The company's goal was to make engineering an AppleTalk network as easy as using the Macintosh computers it supported.

There are actually two versions of AppleTalk: Phase 1 and Phase 2. The first version, dubbed Phase 1, was the original AppleTalk implementation for local workgroups. Phase 2 was created in response to the severe limitations Phase 1 presented to large corporate area networks. Phase 2 offered enhanced routing capabilities and support for many more AppleTalk nodes than Phase 1. Since its inception, Phase 2 has "phased" out Phase 1 on AppleTalk networks.

AppleTalk uses a concept known as "zones." A zone is a logical network that is independent of the actual physical network. Zones consist of AppleTalk nodes that share a common function or communicate with each other.

Figure 13-3 shows AppleTalk zones in action at Corbus Systems, Inc. Even though the sales department has offices on the first and third floors, all sales offices share the same logical zone. The same is true for the engineering offices on the second and third floors. Administration is the only department whose physical topology matches its logical zone topology.

AppleTalk and the OSI Mode

Just like IPX, AppleTalk is actually an entire suite of protocols that work together to get data from the source to its destination reliably. The AppleTalk suite maps closely to the ISO's OSI model. As you will see, various factors determine which protocol the AppleTalk suite will use at each OSI layer.

FIGURE 13-3   AppleTalk zones

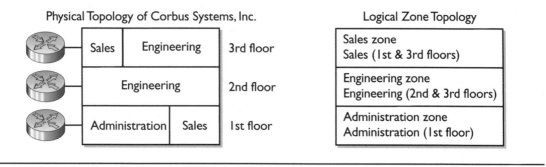

Figure 13-4 shows how the AppleTalk suite of protocols maps to the OSI model.

AFP   AFP (AppleTalk Filing Protocol) operates at both the presentation and application layers of the OSI model. It allows nodes on an AppleTalk network to access files on an AFP file server.

ZIP   ZIP (Zone Information Protocol) operates at the session and transport layers of the OSI model. ZIP maintains mappings of zone names to network numbers on internetwork routers.

ASP   ASP (AppleTalk Session Protocol) operates at the session layer of the OSI model. ASP is used to establish a session between an ASP application on a workstation and an ASP application on a server. Communication is initiated by the workstation only. The server simply responds to the workstation's requests.

ADSP   ADSP (AppleTalk Data Stream Protocol) operates at both the session and transport layers of the OSI model and provides connection-oriented services. ADSP allows two AppleTalk nodes to establish and maintain a connection for data transfer in a continuous stream.

FIGURE 13-4

AppleTalk and the
OSI model

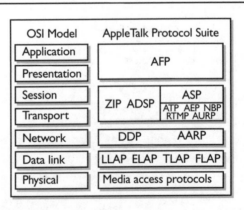

ATP   ATP (AppleTalk Transfer Protocol) operates at the transport layer of the OSI model. ATP provides an efficient mechanism for transferring small amounts of data between nodes without the added overhead that is incurred with ADSP.

AEP   AEP (AppleTalk Echo Protocol) operates at the transport layer of the OSI model. AEP can be used to measure the round-trip packet delivery time from node to node. It can even be used to determine whether a node is online, similar to pinging an IP address.

NBP   NBP (Name-Binding Protocol) operates at the transport layer of the OSI model. NBP maps user-defined names to network addresses and services. NBP for AppleTalk is similar to DNS for TCP/IP.

RTMP   RTMP (Routing Table Maintenance Protocol) operates at the transport layer of the OSI model. RTMP establishes and maintains routing tables of AppleTalk networks. RTMP uses these tables to provide the fastest path to a destination.

AURP   AURP (AppleTalk Update Routing Protocol) operates at the transport layer of the OSI model. AURP provides connectivity between two AppleTalk networks through a foreign network using a protocol such as TCP/IP. This is called tunneling, where AppleTalk hides in TCP/IP packets traversing unknown networks until it reaches its destination AppleTalk network.

DDP   DDP (Datagram Delivery Protocol) operates at the network layer of the OSI model and is a connectionless protocol. DDP provides best-effort delivery and does not verify that packets were received at the destination.

AARP   AARP (AppleTalk Address Resolution Protocol) operates at the network layer of the OSI model. AARP dynamically assigns network layer node addresses and maps those addresses to data-link layer hardware addresses. AARP is similar to TCP/IP's ARP.

LLAP LLAP (LocalTalk Link-Access Protocol) operates at the data-link layer and supports a LocalTalk link.

ELAP ELAP (EtherTalk Link-Access Protocol) operates at the data-link layer and supports an Ethernet link.

TLAP TLAP (TokenTalk Link-Access Protocol) operates at the data-link layer and supports a Token Ring link.

FLAP FLAP (FDDITalk Link-Access Protocol) operates at the data-link layer and supports an FDDI link.

LocalTalk LocalTalk is Apple Computer's proprietary built-in interface for Macintosh computers on an AppleTalk network.

EtherTalk EtherTalk operates at the physical layer of the OSI model. It is responsible for enabling AppleTalk to operate on a standard IEEE 802.3/Ethernet implementation.

TokenTalk TokenTalk operates at the physical layer of the OSI model. It is responsible for enabling AppleTalk to operate on a standard IEEE 802.5/Token Ring implementation.

FDDITalk FDDITalk operates at the physical layer of the OSI model. It is responsible for enabling AppleTalk to operate on a standard ANSI FDDI implementation.

AppleTalk Addressing

Just as IP and IPX clients do, AppleTalk clients require addresses to communicate with one another. Similar to IP and IPX, AppleTalk addresses have a network portion and a node portion. The network portion is 16 bits long and defines the network the AppleTalk client is on. The node portion is 8 bits long and defines the unique node address of the AppleTalk client.

Table 13-5 compares AppleTalk Phase 1 and Phase 2 addressing.

TABLE 13-5		Phase I	Phase 2
Comparison of AppleTalk Phase I and Phase 2 Addressing	Network addresses per segment	I	Unlimited
	Host addresses per network	127	254
	Zones per network	I	255

How Do They Work?

Although both RTMP and AURP route AppleTalk, they have their own individual ways of accomplishing that task. RTMP uses a distance vector approach, and AURP uses more of a link-state approach to routing. To choose the proper AppleTalk routing protocol for a WAN implementation, you have to know how each protocol functions.

RTMP

RTMP is a distance vector protocol used to route AppleTalk on small internetworks. RTMP is most prevalent in situations in which Macintosh computers need to communicate with AppleTalk resources across a small internetwork. These AppleTalk resources are usually AFP file servers and printers.

RTMP routers work by maintaining AppleTalk routing tables. These routing tables contain entries for all network numbers or ranges on the internetwork. The hop count for each network is also maintained. Recall that hop count is the metric used to define the number of routers data must traverse before reaching its final destination. If the hop count value is zero, the destination network is directly connected to the router. If the hop count value exceeds 15, the destination network is unreachable. This is similar to IPX RIP and other distance vector protocols.

In addition to networks and hop counts, the following information is included in RTMP routing tables:

- Network cable range
- Hop count

- Router port to destination network
- Next hop router address
- Condition of routing table (good, suspect, or bad)

When an RTMP router initially comes online, it adds the directly connected networks to its routing table first. Differences in the initialization process depend on whether the router is a seed or nonseed router. Remember, a seed router knows its local zone and local network information. A nonseed router gets this information from other RTMP routers.

Seed routers utilize a very simple initialization routine. After all, they have the advantage of already knowing their network information. When coming online, seed routers simply enter the seeded network information into their routing table with a hop count of zero.

Nonseed routers are forced to do a little more work than seed routers. This is primarily due to nonseed routers not knowing their network information ahead of time. When coming online, nonseed routers ask neighboring RTMP routers for local zone and network information. This request is performed with a ZIP GetNetInfo packet. The seed or nonseed router that receives the GetNetInfo request will then send a response. After receiving this information, the nonseed router adds the appropriate entries for the local networks into its routing table with a hop count of zero.

After RTMP routers initially set up their routing tables, they send RTMP broadcasts every 10 seconds. The RTMP broadcasts contain the router's routing table of networks and hop counts. When other RTMP routers receive the broadcast, they compare their routing table with that of the broadcast routing table. If the RTMP router finds a new route in the broadcast table, it will be added to its routing table with the hop count incremented by 1. Its updated routing table will then be broadcast in the scheduled 10-second intervals and the process will start again. Eventually, all of the RTMP routers on a network will maintain identical RTMP routing tables.

To configure an extended AppleTalk network with RTMP, you must complete the following tasks:

1. Enable AppleTalk routing.

2. Assign the interface an AppleTalk cable range.

3. Assign the interface a zone name.

4. Create an AppleTalk routing process for RTMP.

The following is an example configuration of an extended AppleTalk network:

```
appletalk routing
interface ethernet0/0
appletalk cable-range 10-10 10.128
appletalk zone CCDACITY
appletalk protocol rtmp
```

The first command, appletalk routing, enables AppleTalk routing. The second command, interface ethernet0/0, puts the router in interface configuration mode for Ethernet port 0/0. The third command, appletalk cable-range 10-10 10.128, assigns the interface an AppleTalk cable range of 10-10 and an address of 10.128. The fourth command, appletalk zone CCDACITY, assigns the interface a zone name of CCDACITY. The last command, appletalk protocol rtmp, creates an AppleTalk routing process for RTMP.

To configure a nonextended AppleTalk network with RTMP, you must complete the following tasks:

1. Enable AppleTalk routing.

2. Assign the interface an AppleTalk address.

3. Assign the interface a zone name.

4. Create an AppleTalk routing process for RTMP.

The following is an example configuration of a nonextended AppleTalk network:

```
appletalk routing
interface ethernet0/0
appletalk address 1.128
appletalk zone SYNGRESS
appletalk protocol rtmp
```

The first command, appletalk routing, enables AppleTalk routing. The second command, interface ethernet0/0, puts the router in interface configuration mode for Ethernet port 0/0. The third command, appletalk address 1.128, assigns the interface an AppleTalk address of 1.128. The fourth command, appletalk zone SYNGRESS, assigns the interface a zone name of SYNGRESS. The last command, appletalk protocol rtmp, creates an AppleTalk routing process for RTMP.

AURP

Apple Computer, Inc., designed AURP to provide connectivity between two or more AppleTalk networks across a TCP/IP network. The AURP data is transported through UDP headers. This allows AURP to cross the TCP/IP network transparently. The TCP/IP network does not even know AURP is there. AURP utilizes exterior routers and AURP tunnels to accomplish its routing tasks.

An exterior router is responsible for connecting a local AppleTalk network to an AURP tunnel. It borders an AppleTalk network and a TCP/IP backbone network. The exterior router encapsulates AURP routing data in packets destined for remote AppleTalk networks through a TCP/IP backbone. It de-encapsulates AURP routing data in packets coming from the TCP/IP backbone destined for the local AppleTalk network. To TCP/IP, the AppleTalk exterior router is nothing more than an end node.

An AURP tunnel functions as a virtual link between two or more AppleTalk networks. The tunnel is typically created through a TCP/IP backbone. AURP tunnels come in two flavors: point-to-point and multipoint. Point-to-point tunnels facilitate communication of routes between two AppleTalk exterior routers. Multipoint tunnels, on the other hand, facilitate communication of routes between multiple exterior routers. Figure 13-5 demonstrates a point-to-point AURP tunnel in action.

When exterior routers initially communicate with each other, they exchange route information to establish their routing tables. After the routing tables are created, future updates will occur every 30 seconds and under the following circumstances:

- Network entry is added.

- Network entry is removed.
- Hop count to network is changed.
- Network path is changed from AURP tunnel to local internetwork or vice versa.

The following tasks are required to configure AppleTalk AURP:

1. Enable route redistribution.
2. Configure an interface for tunnel usage.
3. Configure an IP address.
4. Configure a tunnel interface.
5. Create an AppleTalk routing process for AURP.
6. Configure the interface encapsulated packets will be sent out through.
7. Specify the IP address of the AppleTalk exterior router at the end of the AURP tunnel.
8. Enable AURP tunneling.

The following is an example configuration of an AURP tunnel:

```
appletalk route-redistribution
interface serial0/0
ip address 192.168.100.5 255.255.255.0
interface tunnel 0
appletalk protocol aurp
tunnel source serial0/0
tunnel destination 192.168.60.30
tunnel mode aurp
```

FIGURE 13-5

AURP tunnel

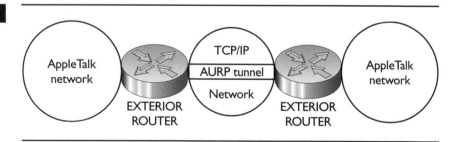

The first command, appletalk route-redistribution, enables route redistribution of AppleTalk. The second command, interface serial0/0, puts the router in interface configuration mode for the serial interface 0/0. The third command, ip address 192.168.100.5 255.255.255.0, sets the IP address of the serial interface to 192.168.100.5 with a subnet mask of 255.255.255.0. The fourth command, interface tunnel 0, puts the router in interface configuration mode for tunnel 0. The fifth command, appletalk protocol aurp, creates an AppleTalk routing process for AURP. The sixth command, tunnel source serial0/0, configures AURP to send encapsulated packets out through serial interface 0/0. The seventh command, tunnel destination 192.168.60.30, specifies that 192.168.60.30 is the IP address of the exterior router at the end of the AURP tunnel. The last command, tunnel mode aurp, enables AURP tunneling.

Strengths and Limitations

Once again, you will have to make a decision. Do I use RTMP? Or do I use AURP? Which routing protocol will provide easy administration, quick convergence, scalability, and low bandwidth usage? This decision will forever be based on the strengths and limitations of each protocol in a particular internetwork implementation.

Why Use RTMP Over AURP?

Remember that RTMP is a distance vector protocol. As a rule, distance vector protocols perform well on small internetworks. An internetwork consisting of E1 links, five routers across, and contiguous AppleTalk internetworks is a good candidate for a distance vector protocol like RTMP. AURP would not be necessary since there are no foreign networks to traverse. In this environment, RTMP would provide easier administration and configuration than AURP. Convergence time would also be sufficient using RTMP on this network. Since this network is no more than five hops across, RTMP would definitely be scalable enough. AURP's enhanced scalability over RTMP is just not necessary in a network of this size. Finally, in regard to bandwidth usage, the fast E1 links make RTMP a sound solution.

Why Migrate to AURP?

As you might guess, AppleTalk networks are not as common as TCP/IP or even IPX networks. You will rarely find an entire WAN running AppleTalk exclusively. With this in mind, you are likely to come across a small AppleTalk LAN in the middle of a large corporate TCP/IP WAN that needs to access services on another small AppleTalk LAN over 20 hops away. RTMP would fail in this environment for a few important reasons. First of all, AppleTalk and RTMP would have to be configured on every router between the two AppleTalk networks. Second, the RTMP broadcasts every 10 seconds would increase router overhead and consume an unacceptable amount of precious bandwidth. Third, RTMP's hop count limitation of 15 makes it impossible for the two AppleTalk networks to communicate 20 hops apart. So what's the solution? Migrate your two AppleTalk networks to AURP. AURP would succeed in this environment for reasons contrary to why RTMP would fail. First, AURP would not need to be configured on every router between the two AppleTalk networks. AURP would need to be configured only on the two routers bordering the AppleTalk networks and the TCP/IP WAN. Second, AURP is not as noisy a protocol as RTMP, which means less router overhead and less bandwidth consumption. Third, there is no hop count limitation imposed by AURP. This means the two AppleTalk networks will be fully accessible to each other across the corporate WAN.

Troubleshooting AppleTalk Routing

In this section, we will examine various AppleTalk-related routing problems. You will be introduced to many IOS commands that will assist you in the troubleshooting process. You will find that both RTMP and AURP share some of the same IOS commands necessary for troubleshooting. We will be covering commands common to both routing protocols and commands that are unique to each one. While a network problem can stem from anywhere on the network, we will focus on routers as the source of problem resolution.

Routing Tables Not Being Updated Through AURP Tunnel

AppleTalk exterior routers are responsible for propagating route information to other exterior routers through AURP tunnels. If route information does not make it successfully through an AURP tunnel, it can cause serious connectivity problems between AppleTalk networks. There are a few causes of and solutions to AURP tunnel failure.

One possible cause of AURP failure is a misconfigured AURP tunnel. First, you should use the show appletalk interfaces command to verify that the AppleTalk interface is up. Then you should execute the show running-config command to view the two commands that configured your AURP tunnel. The first command, tunnel source, should be associated with the IP address of the router's interface. The second command, tunnel destination, should be associated with the IP address of the exterior router on the other side of the tunnel. If either of the commands show incorrect IP addresses, use the tunnel source command or the tunnel destination command in interface configuration mode to make the correction.

An AURP tunnel configuration consists of many router commands. If any one of those commands were omitted, it could cause the AURP tunnel to fail. One such command is the appletalk route-redistribution command. Without this command, changes on the remote AppleTalk network will not be learned through the tunnel. To verify that this command has been executed, use the show running-config command. If you do not see the appletalk route-redistribution command in the router's output, execute it in global configuration mode. If all the other AppleTalk commands are configured properly, your AURP tunnel should succeed.

Sometimes, AURP tunnel failure has nothing to do with AppleTalk routing. It is possible that your AURP tunnel is configured correctly and still fails. Remember, AURP encapsulates route information in foreign protocols like TCP/IP. What if TCP/IP routing is not configured correctly? TCP/IP packets might not make it to their destination, which means AURP packets might not make it to their destination either. The only way to solve this problem is to correct the routing problems of the foreign network.

Bridging Protocols

When designing an internetwork, it is important to make a determination as to whether each protocol should be bridged or routed. In order to make an informed decision, a solid understanding of bridging is necessary.

Bridging Review

Bridging is the process of connecting individual LANs to form one seemingly larger LAN. The process of bridging is provided by devices known as *bridges*. Bridges allow broadcasts from one LAN to cross into a LAN on the other side of the bridge. Bridges operate at the data-link layer of the OSI model. Recall that the data-link layer is responsible for MAC addressing and logical link control processing, creating logical topologies, and controlling media access. Bridges look only at the MAC address of a packet when determining how it should be processed. If a MAC address exists in the bridge's network table, the packet will be sent to the appropriate bridged network. If a MAC address does not exist in the bridge's network table, the packet will be broadcast to all bridged networks.

Transparent Bridging

The operation of transparent bridges is transparent to network clients. When transparent bridges are first initialized, they create a network topology table from the source addresses of incoming frames from all attached networks. The topology table consists of host addresses and network numbers. The purpose of the table is to forward incoming traffic to the appropriate destination. If the destination address of an incoming frame exists in the table, it will be forwarded to the destination network. If the destination address of an incoming frame does not exist in the table, it will be flooded to all attached networks except the source network. Broadcasts and multicasts are also flooded to all attached networks.

Source-Route Bridging

Source-route bridges assume that the source of the incoming frames knows the entire route to its destination. Source-route bridges simply store and forward the frames as indicated by the appropriate frame fields. If a client needs to access a server across a source-route bridged network, it must know the entire route to that server. Otherwise, the source-route bridge could fail to forward the frames to the proper destination network.

Source-Route Transparent Bridging

Source-route transparent (SRT) bridges operate using either source-route bridging or transparent bridging. SRT bridges are typically used on Token Ring networks that contain source-route bridging devices and transparent bridging devices. However, SRT bridges do not perform translation between source-route bridging and transparent bridging. It simply supports both bridging platforms by using the platform designated by incoming traffic.

Source-Route Translational Bridging

Source-route translational (SR/TL) bridging operates using a combination of source-route bridging and transparent bridging. SR/TL bridges are typically implemented on internetworks using Token Ring and Ethernet. Unlike SRT, SR/TL translates between source-route bridging and transparent bridging. This means that devices on Token Ring networks can communicate with devices on Ethernet networks.

Troubleshooting Bridging

As a CCDA, you will be expected to know how to implement various forms of bridging. Your clients will expect nothing less than the best from you. This also means that you will be expected to resolve any problems that may arise from a botched, bridged internetwork. This section will equip you with the knowledge to get you on the right track.

Transparent Bridge: No Connectivity

Although the operation of transparent bridging is the simplest method of bridging, it has its share of problems. One such problem is connectivity failure. This problem has various causes and solutions.

Hardware and media problems must always be looked at as a cause of connectivity problems. Start the troubleshooting process with the show bridge command to view the MAC addresses in the bridging table. If no MAC addresses are in the table, there is definitely a connectivity problem. Next, you should use the show interfaces command to determine whether the interface and line protocol are up. If the interface is down, you may need to replace the interface hardware. If the interface is an add-on card, like a WIC (WAN Interface Card), you can just replace it. Otherwise, if it is a built-in interface, the entire router may need to be replaced. If the interface is up but the line protocol is down, check the cables between the router and the network. If you do not see any cable damage and you don't have a cable tester, you should replace them anyway for good measure.

Another cause of connectivity problems is a poorly configured bridging filter. First, you should determine whether a filter was even configured by using the show running-config command. If so, disable the filter on the interface. If connectivity returns, there is definitely a filter configuration problem. At this point you should modify the filter or applied access lists according to your network's needs.

When input and output queues are full, packets are dropped and connectivity problems occur. This happens when there is excessive multicast and broadcast traffic. To view dropped packets, use the show interfaces command. If you determine that there are excessive drops, a bridging filter may need to be implemented. Another option would be to use other internetworking devices to segment the network. For serial links, increasing the bandwidth, implementing priority queuing, and increasing the hold queue size are all acceptable solutions.

Source-Route Bridge: No Connectivity

Source-route bridging has its share of connectivity problems just like transparent bridging. The difference is that source-route bridging is implemented mainly in Token Ring networks. The problem of no connectivity has many possible causes and solutions.

One possible cause of connectivity problems is a ring number mismatch. When a source-route bridge detects a ring number mismatch, it will not insert itself into that ring. In other words, the SRB will not be able to communicate with other devices on the Token Ring network. To resolve this problem, acquire the correct ring number from another SRB by using the show running-config command. Look for the source-bridge command in the output. If there is a ring mismatch between SRBs or Token Ring nodes, reconfigure the suspect SRB with the source-bridge command. This command allows you to select the source ring number, bridge number, and the target ring number.

When local nodes communicate across a Token Ring WAN, it must insert route information in the RIF of frames destined for remote nodes. If an end node did not support RIF, it would not be able to participate in source-route bridging. You can determine whether an end node supports RIF by using a network analyzer and looking for RIF frames. If you find that no RIF frames are coming from the suspect end node, it may have to be routed or transparently bridged.

Source-route bridges use spanning explorer packets to find remote networks. If routers are not configured to route these explorer packets, connectivity problems can occur. The first command you should execute is show source-bridge. This command allows you to determine whether the spanning explorer count is incrementing. If the spanning explorer count is not incrementing, use the show running-config command to view the router's current configuration. If the source-bridge spanning command is not in the output, the router is not configured to forward spanning explorer packets. To configure the router to forward spanning explorer packets, use the source-bridge spanning command in interface configuration mode. All routers participating in source-route bridging should be configured to forward spanning explorer packets.

Source-Route Bridge: Routing Does Not Function

If routing is not functioning, local nodes will not be able to reach remote nodes on an internetwork. This can be a serious problem if users are dependent on data located on remote networks. There are many causes of and solutions to this problem.

The obvious cause of routing failure is a routing problem. In other words, the routing protocol is configured incorrectly. To resolve this problem, you should gain a thorough understanding of the routing protocol in use and reconfigure it as necessary.

Another cause of routing failure is the omission of the multiring command. The multiring command enables RIF processing on router interfaces. The show running-config command should be executed to display the current router configuration. If the multiring command is not present in the output, add it with the multiring all command.

Source-Route Transparent Bridge: No Connectivity

Many complications can occur when using source-route transparent bridging in a Token Ring/Ethernet environment. When bridging fails, connectivity to remote networks also fails. There are various causes of and solutions to connectivity failure.

One cause of connectivity failure is evident when an attempt is made to bridge frames containing RIFs to an Ethernet network. Recall that RIFs are used in Token Ring frames and not in Ethernet. The solution to this connectivity problem is to implement source-route translational bridging instead of source-route transparent bridging.

Bad media can also be a cause for connectivity failure. If you suspect bad media, use the show interfaces command. If the interface or line protocol is down, bad or incompatible media may be the cause.

Source-Route Translational Bridge: No Connectivity

Recall that source-route translational bridging is used to facilitate communication between Token-Ring and Ethernet networks. Translation of this kind is very fragile and can be a nightmare to troubleshoot. There are various causes of and solutions to translational bridge connectivity problems.

For any connectivity problem, you should verify that bad media is not the cause. You can acquire relevant information with the show interfaces command. If the interface or line protocol is down, bad media is probably the cause.

Another cause of connectivity problems across a translational bridge occurs when Ethernet–to–Token Ring address mapping is not configured correctly. First, you should use the show bridge command to verify the existence of the Ethernet station. Then determine whether the Ethernet port is in forwarding mode by using the show spanning command. Next, use the show rif command to determine whether the target Token Ring station is visible on the internetwork. If both Ethernet and Token Ring stations are visible, configure static MAC addresses for servers on the clients so server advertisements can be heard directly.

NetBIOS and NetBEUI

NetBIOS, Network Basic Input/Output System, operates at the session layer of the OSI model. It operates by exchanging messages between nodes using a name versus a node address. All nodes participating in NetBIOS communication are required to know their name and the names of the other nodes on the network. NetBIOS offers applications a programming interface for sharing services and information across various lower-layer network protocols like IP and IPX. NetBIOS utilizes the following three application services: name service, session service, datagram service. The name service allows an application to do the following:

■ Verify that its NetBIOS name is unique.

■ Delete a NetBIOS name that is no longer required.

■ Use a server's NetBIOS name to discover the server's network address.

The session service allows an application to reliably exchange messages with another application. The datagram service allows applications to communicate without establishing a session.

NetBEUI, NetBIOS Extended User Interface, is a protocol that builds on NetBIOS to provide optimal performance on a single network. Although NetBEUI performs well on a single network, it is not a routable protocol. This means that in order for networks to communicate using NetBEUI, NetBEUI must be bridged. The method you choose to bridge NetBEUI depends on the lower-layer network protocols you choose. NetBEUI can be configured in conjunction with routable protocols such as IP and IPX.

NetBEUI exchanges many broadcasts between client and server stations. This can cause high router overhead. To mitigate this problem, NetBIOS name caching should be used. This allows the router to forward broadcast requests directly across the entire bridged network. To configure NetBIOS name caching, execute the following commands:

```
source-bridge proxy-netbios-only
netbios name-cache timeout minutes
```

```
interface ethernet0/0
netbios enable-name-cache
```

Other Nonroutable Protocols

Along with NetBIOS, there are a few other protocols that cannot be routed. Like NetBIOS, SNA, LAT, and MOP must all be bridged to facilitate end-to-end communication between nodes.

Customer's Requirements

When designing an internetwork, it is extremely important to understand your customer's network requirements and to set their expectations realistically. As a CCDA, you must know which customer requirements are most important. This will greatly affect your internetwork design.

Networks Using Bridged Protocols

Some protocols cannot be routed. The only alternative is to bridge them. If your customer has security requirements that conflict with required protocols, you and the customer must make a decision. For example, SNA is a required protocol when clients need to connect to an SNA server across a router. A security requirement may be to filter SNA traffic by client identification. Since SNA is not routable and must be bridged, access lists cannot be implemented to satisfy the security requirements. One option would be to localize the SNA clients and server to its own network. If localization is not possible, and SNA access security is a low priority, bridging SNA might suffice. Ultimately, it is up to you, the CCDA, to go over the pros and cons of each solution with your customer.

Performance

There are definite performance advantages when using bridges instead of routers. The main performance boost comes from the bridge being a layer-2 device. In other words, data crosses bridges faster than routers because only the MAC address needs to be processed. No packet filtering or upper-layer address routing needs to take place when bridging. This means that router processor overhead is decreased, which, in turn, means that performance is increased.

Strengths and Weaknesses

As with every technology, there are pros and cons to consider when you are choosing bridging versus routing. The biggest strength of bridging is in its ability to forward packets to their destinations quickly. For small internetworks that do not require packet filtering, bridging is the way to go.

Even though bridging provides a fast and efficient way to forward packets on an internetwork, there are occasions when its usage is not appropriate. Bridging might fail on a large internetwork because of broadcast storms. Broadcast storms occur when broadcasts intended for a local network are propagated throughout the entire internetwork. When this occurs, it severely degrades network performance. The alternative would be routing, which does not forward broadcasts by default. Routing is more intelligent than bridging because it operates at layer 3 of the OSI model. Routing is better suited to large internetworks requiring packet filtering because broadcast storms are eliminated and unnecessary network traffic can be filtered from crossing slow WAN links.

As you can see, both bridging and routing have their pros and cons. Ultimately, it is up to you to decide which technology is better suited for your implementation. As a general rule of thumb, bridging should never be an option for slow serial links.

Security Concerns

Security is extremely important to an internetwork implementation. This is especially true on large corporate WANs containing many networks hosting servers with sensitive company data. Security is responsible for keeping unauthorized users out of the network and authorized users in the network.

There are definitely security concerns arising from bridging. The biggest concern is that bridges only filter data-link, or layer-2, addresses. This means that unauthorized users on the other side of the bridge can potentially gain full access to the remote network. If security is not an issue, bridging will suffice. Otherwise, the alternative to bridging is routing. Cisco routers allow network administrators to limit access to networks based on destination address, source address, and other parameters. For security purposes, routing is definitely better than bridging. After all, you cannot apply an access list to a bridge.

Capacity Issues and Ways to Get Around Them

An ideal internetwork consists of fast WAN and LAN links, high-end routers, redundant links, and backup links. Unfortunately, internetworks are not always ideal. When bridging must be used, capacity problems can occur that consume internetwork bandwidth. To alleviate these problems, networks can be segmented into smaller parts. In this manner, only a small portion of the internetwork is affected. Another way to get around capacity problems is to localize the bridged traffic. In other words, put the clients and servers on the same local network. If none of these options are available to you, add more bandwidth (T1s, E1s, FDDI, and so on). Of course, adding more bandwidth costs money.

CERTIFICATION SUMMARY

In this chapter, you learned how various routing protocols operate. You learned that IPX RIP is appropriate for small IPX networks, while NLSP is more suited for large IPX networks consisting of more than 15 routers. You learned that RTMP works well on small contiguous AppleTalk networks, while AURP is best for large noncontiguous AppleTalk networks.

You also learned about bridging protocols. You discovered that NetBIOS, along with SNA, LAT, and MOP, are nonroutable protocols. You learned that bridging may be faster than routing but not as secure. As a CCDA, you will decide when to choose bridging instead of routing.

✓ TWO-MINUTE DRILL

- ❑ IPX operates at the network and transport layers of the OSI model.
- ❑ IPX is supported by two routing protocols: IPX RIP/SAP and NLSP.
- ❑ IPX RIP is a distance vector protocol for routing IPX on small internetworks.
- ❑ Destinations more than 15 hops away are considered unreachable by IPX RIP.
- ❑ The ipx router rip command specifies RIP as the IPX routing protocol.

❏ GNS allows NetWare clients to query the IPX network for requested services.

❏ Cisco routers, by default, do not allow SAP broadcasts to be forwarded.

❏ NLSP is a link-state routing protocol for routing IPX on large internetworks.

❏ NLSP sends routing updates when the topology changes.

❏ NLSP routers maintain three tables: adjacency, link state, and forwarding.

❏ The ipx nlsp enable command enables NLSP routing on the serial interface.

❏ AppleTalk is supported by two routing protocols: RTMP and AURP.

❏ RTMP is a distance vector protocol for routing AppleTalk on small internetworks.

❏ The appletalk protocol rtmp command creates an AppleTalk routing process for RTMP.

❏ AURP provides connectivity between two or more AppleTalk networks across a TCP/IP network.

❏ The tunnel mode aurp command enables AURP tunneling.

❏ Bridges operate at the data-link layer of the OSI model.

❏ The operation of transparent bridges is transparent to network clients.

❏ Source-route bridges assume that the source of the incoming frames knows the entire route to its destination.

❏ Source-route transparent (SRT) bridges operate using either source-route bridging or transparent bridging.

❏ Source-route translational (SR/TL) bridges operate using a combination of source-route bridging and transparent bridging.

❏ NetBIOS, SNA, LAT, and MOP are not routable protocols.

❏ NetBIOS operates at the session layer of the OSI model.

SELF TEST

The following Self Test questions will help you measure your understanding of the material presented in this chapter. Read all the choices carefully, as there may be more than one correct answer. Choose all correct answers for each question.

1. Which is a sample IPX address?

   A. 192.168.0.5

   B. BABECAFE.0040.0534.545A

   C. ZZTOP.0056.2222.53A2

   D. 255.255.0.0

2. By default, how often are SAP updates sent?

   A. Every 10 seconds

   B. Every 30 seconds

   C. Every 60 seconds

   D. Every 2 hours

3. By default, how often are IPX RIP updates sent?

   A. Every 10 seconds

   B. Every 30 seconds

   C. Every 60 seconds

   D. Every 2 hours

4. By default, how often are RTMP updates sent?

   A. Every 10 seconds

   B. Every 30 seconds

   C. Every 60 seconds

   D. Every 2 hours

5. By default, how often are NLSP updates sent?

   A. Every 30 seconds

   B. Every 60 seconds

   C. Every 120 seconds

   D. Every 2 hours

6. An IPX station on network A cannot reach an IPX station on network Z. What could be the problem?

   A. Network Z is running both IP and IPX.

   B. The routing protocol is IPX RIP and network Z is more than 15 hops away.

   C. The routing protocol is NLSP and Network Z is 16 hops away.

   D. Network A is running both IP and IPX.

7. You are configuring a router on an internetwork consisting of six routers, full T1 links, and IPX clients. Which command would you use on the router?

   A. cisco use rip

   B. cisco use nlsp

   C. ipx router rip

   D. ipx router nlsp

8. You are configuring a router on an internetwork consisting of 60 routers, fractional T1 and 56KB links, and IPX clients. Which command would you use on the router?

   A. cisco use rip

   B. cisco use nlsp

   C. ipx router rip

   D. ipx router nlsp

9. You are the administrator of a large corporate WAN. Macintosh stations on the Sales network need to access AppleTalk printers on the Marketing network. There are three AppleTalk networks between the Sales and Marketing networks. What should you do?

   A. Implement IPX RIP

   B. Implement RTMP

   C. Implement NLSP

   D. Implement AURP

10. You are the administrator of a large corporate WAN. Macintosh stations on the Sales network need to access AppleTalk printers on the Marketing network. There are 20 TCP/IP networks between the Sales and Marketing networks. What should you do?

    A. Implement IPX RIP

    B. Implement RTMP

    C. Implement NLSP

    D. Implement AURP

11. You are configuring a router on an internetwork consisting of six routers, full T1 links, and AppleTalk clients. Which command would you use on the router?

    A. appletalk protocol rtmp

    B. appletalk protocol aurp

    C. ipx router rtmp

    D. ipx router aurp

12. You are the administrator of a large corporate WAN. Macintosh stations on the Sales network need to access AppleTalk printers on the Marketing network. There are 20 TCP/IP networks between the Sales and Marketing networks. What command should you execute on the Sales and Marketing routers?

    A. tunnel create rtmp

    B. tunnel create aurp

    C. tunnel mode rtmp

    D. tunnel mode aurp

13. You are in charge of internetwork security at your company. You have decided that bridging puts the company's networks at risk. If you replace bridging with routing, what protocol will *not* be routed?

    A. IP

    B. IPX

    C. NetBIOS

    D. AppleTalk

14. You have implemented NLSP on your internetwork. What function can you expect NLSP level-1 routers to perform?

    A. Link networks together within the same area

    B. Link areas together within the same domain

    C. Link domains together

    D. Convert IPX to AppleTalk

15. You want to improve performance by implementing NetBIOS name caching. What command would you use?

    A. enable netbios name caching

    B. enable netbios-name-caching

    C. netbios enable-name-cache

    D. netbios enable name cache

16. To increase the performance of your internetwork, you want your internetworking devices to process only MAC addresses of incoming frames. How would you implement this?

    A. Implement routing

    B. Implement bridging

    C. Install repeaters

    D. Create IP and IPX access lists

17. You are about to design an AppleTalk Internetwork. What routing protocols should you consider for your design?

    A. IPX RIP and NLSP

    B. RTMP and AURP

    C. IP RIP and OSPF

    D. IGRP and EIGRP

18. You are about to design an IPX Internetwork. What routing protocols should you consider for your design?

    A. IPX RIP and NLSP

    B. RTMP

    C. IP RIP and OSPF

    D. AURP

19. You have a Token Ring network that needs to communicate with an Ethernet network. What should you do to accomplish this?

    A. Implement source-route transparent bridging

    B. Implement source-route translational bridging

    C. Implement IP access lists

    D. Implement IPX access lists

20. You have an internetwork consisting of Token Ring networks and Ethernet networks. The Token Ring networks never need to communicate with the Ethernet networks. What action should you take?

    A. Implement source-route transparent bridging

    B. Implement source-route translational bridging

    C. Implement IP access lists

    D. Implement IPX access lists.

SELF TEST ANSWERS

1. ☑ **B.** It uses only hexadecimal digits and follows the IPX address format.
   ☒ **A** is incorrect because it is a TCP/IP address. **C** is incorrect because ZZTOP does not contain any hexadecimal digits (from 0 to 9 and A to F). **D** is incorrect because it is a subnet mask for a Class B IP address.

2. ☑ **C.** The default update interval is 60 seconds. The update interval can be changed, however.
   ☒ **A** is incorrect and is the default update interval of RTMP. **B** is incorrect and is the default update interval of IP RIP. **D** is incorrect and is the default update interval of NLSP.

3. ☑ **C.** The default update interval is 60 seconds. The update interval can be changed, however.
   ☒ **A** is incorrect and is the default update interval of RTMP. **B** is incorrect and is the default update interval of IP RIP. **D** is incorrect and is the default update interval of NLSP.

4. ☑ **A.** RTMP is the noisiest of all routing protocols.
   ☒ **B** is incorrect and is the default update interval of IP RIP. **C** is incorrect and is the default update interval of IPX RIP. **D** is incorrect and is the default update interval of NLSP.

5. ☑ **D.** NLSP updates are also sent when there is a topology change.
   ☒ **A** is incorrect and is the default update interval of IP RIP. **B** is incorrect and is the default update interval of IPX RIP. **C** is also incorrect.

6. ☑ **B.** Any network more than 15 hops away in an IPX RIP internetwork is considered unreachable.
   ☒ **A** and **D** are incorrect because running both IP and IPX will not cause a conflict.
   C is incorrect because NLSP can reach a network 16 hops away.

7. ☑ **C.** It uses the proper syntax, and IPX RIP is appropriate for an environment this small.
   ☒ **A** and **B** are incorrect because they both use an invalid syntax. **D** is incorrect because it configures the router to use NLSP. NLSP is better suited for larger internetworks.

8. ☑ **D.** It uses the proper syntax, and NLSP is appropriate for an environment this large.
   ☒ **A** and **B** are incorrect because they both use an invalid syntax. **C** is incorrect because it configures the router to use IPX RIP. IPX RIP is better suited for smaller internetworks.

9. ☑ **B.** RTMP is appropriate for contiguous AppleTalk networks of this size.
   ☒ **A** and **C** are incorrect because IPX RIP and NLSP are used in IPX environments.
   D is incorrect because AURP was designed for noncontiguous AppleTalk networks.

10. ☑   D. AURP is appropriate for noncontiguous AppleTalk networks of this size.
    ☒   A and C are incorrect because IPX RIP and NLSP are used in IPX environments.
    B is incorrect because RTMP was designed for small contiguous AppleTalk networks.

11. ☑   A. It uses the proper syntax, and RTMP is appropriate for an environment this small.
    ☒   B is incorrect because AURP is better suited for large noncontiguous AppleTalk networks.
    C and D are incorrect, because they use an invalid syntax.

12. ☑   D. AURP is appropriate for noncontiguous AppleTalk networks of this size.
    ☒   A, B, and C are incorrect because they use an invalid syntax. Furthermore, the tunnel
    mode command is used when implementing AURP and not RTMP.

13. ☑   C. NetBIOS is a nonroutable protocol like SNA, LAT, and MOP.
    ☒   A, B, and D are incorrect because IP, IPX, and AppleTalk are all routable protocols.

14. ☑   A. Level-1 routers link networks.
    ☒   B is incorrect because level-2 routers link areas. C is incorrect because level-3 routers link
    domains. D is incorrect because no NLSP router converts IPX to AppleTalk.

15. ☑   C. It uses the proper syntax and can improve router performance.
    ☒   A, B, and D are incorrect because they use an invalid syntax.

16. ☑   B. Bridging forwards frames based on MAC addresses.
    ☒   A is incorrect because routing is used for logical addresses. C is incorrect because repeaters
    only repeat a signal that would otherwise die on the wire. Repeaters do not process addresses of
    any kind. D is incorrect because IP and IPX access lists apply to logical address and not MAC
    addresses.

17. ☑   B. RTMP and AURP are used to route AppleTalk.
    ☒   A is incorrect because IPX RIP and NLSP are used to route IPX. C and D are incorrect
    because IP RIP, OSPF, IGRP, and EIGRP are mainly used to route IP.

18. ☑   A. IPX RIP and NLSP are used to route IPX.
    ☒   B and D are incorrect because RTMP and AURP are used to route AppleTalk.
    C is incorrect because IP RIP and OSPF are used to route IP.

19. ☑ **B.** Translational bridging allows source-routed and transparently bridged networks to communicate.

☒ **A** is incorrect because source-route transparent bridging allows a router to support both Ethernet and Token Ring networks but not to communicate between them. **C** and **D** are both incorrect because implementing an IP or IPX access list will have no impact on Ethernet–to–Token Ring translation.

20. ☑ **A.** Transparent bridging supports both source-routed and transparently bridged networks.

☒ **B**, translation between Token Ring and Ethernet, is not necessary. **C** and **D** are both incorrect because implementing an IP or IPX access list will have no impact on bridging among the Token Ring and Ethernet networks.

CISCO CERTIFIED DESIGN ASSOCIATE

14

Cisco IOS Software Features

The Cisco Internetwork Operating System (IOS) software is the heart and soul of your routers and of your network. To be able to design a network that meets a customer's requirements for security, performance, scalability, and capacity, you need to have an understanding of the IOS software and some of its features. We will take a closer look at access lists, encryption services, compression services, queuing, and proxy services and the ways to best utilize them.

These IOS features operate in different ways to provide a variety of benefits to an internetwork. You need to be able to have scalability in your large internetworks while maintaining optimal performance. You also need to provide certain levels of security for sensitive data traversing public and private networks. Cost savings and good performance are always attractive to companies of any size, and WAN costs and link efficiency can be enhanced through the use of certain IOS features. Finally, some traffic is more time sensitive, and you need to know how to provide levels of traffic prioritization over your internetworks.

By the time you finish this chapter, you will have this knowledge and will be ready to use these Cisco IOS features effectively in networks of any size.

CERTIFICATION OBJECTIVE 14.01

Access Lists

Cisco routers support a basic form of traffic filtering through the use of *access lists*. Access lists are packet filters that define a set of criteria used by the router when it examines the packets passing through its interfaces. The router uses these lists to determine whether to forward the packet or block it based on the rules defined in the access lists. All routed protocols can be controlled in this way, with separate access lists required for each type of protocol.

Access lists need to be created on a per-protocol basis and then applied to each interface on which you need to control the flow of traffic. Typical access list criteria include packet source address, packet destination address, or upper-layer protocols, although each protocol supports a specific set of criteria that can be defined. Each criterion needs to be defined as a separate statement in the access list. Each of these statements is added sequentially to the end of the existing access list, and the statements can't be edited or deleted once they are entered. You can delete only the entire access list.

This is an important detail because the order of these statements in your access lists is critical to the performance and efficiency of your routers, as is the effectiveness of the lists. When a router is using an access list to examine traffic, the Cisco IOS software begins a process of comparing the packet against each line in the list sequentially. This is known as *top-down processing* because the router starts at the beginning of the access list and moves down through each declaration in the list, looking for a match. As soon as a match is found, the packet is handled according to the access list statement (permit or deny), and the next packet is examined.

Each access list carries with it an implicit "deny all" statement at the end. Even if you haven't added a "deny all" statement to the end of your access list, it will exist and perform as designated. This statement is the key to understanding and developing your own access lists. Additionally, keep in mind that if you start your access list with a "permit all" statement, the packet will not be compared with any other possible exclusion statements you may have included later in the list; the packet will simply be passed without any further scrutiny.

Therefore, you need to create your lists by starting with the most granular statements first, moving through to more and more general statements. A good rule of thumb is to list items in the following order:

- Start with very specific items such as individual IP or IPX addresses.

- List more general items like subnet addresses in the middle.

- Finish the list with broad statements, such as entire network addresses.

Another good tip is to actually create the list offline using a text editor first to work out the details and the order of the statements. Doing so permits you to mentally walk through the list to verify that all traffic is handled properly, ensuring that you don't allow any forbidden traffic or block any permitted traffic. The list can then be uploaded to a TFTP server to copy to your router later. Another good reason for performing this work offline is that the router will implement any new statements immediately, and if you need to delete the list to place new statements at the beginning of the list, the router will function with no access list on that particular interface. Functioning without an access list isn't a very good idea from a security perspective.

on the
①o b

Remember that when you are editing and applying access lists, new entries will be appended to the end of the existing list. As a result, any of your new changes will essentially be canceled out because packets will likely never get to these new statements before being handled. Therefore, it is wise to begin each access list with a "no access-list" statement. This deletes the existing list and guards against the human tendency to forget.

Each router interface can support only a single access list per protocol and supports an access list as either *inbound* or *outbound* (some protocols support applying both an inbound and an outbound access list to a single interface). Therefore, the traffic is analyzed from the perspective of the router, not the network on either side of the router's interfaces. If the access list is inbound, the router examines the incoming packet prior to entering the router. If the packet is permitted, the router allows it in and routes it on its way. If a statement or the lack of an explicit "permit" statement denies the packet, it is blocked and dropped from the wire. If an outbound access list is used, the router will accept the packet and then internally compare the packet with the access list statements. If the packet is permitted, the router passes the packet out the appropriate interface and routes it on its way. If a statement or the lack of an explicit "permit" statement denies the packet, it is dropped or discarded by the router.

on the
①o b

An important detail that is often overlooked is how routing updates are handled. When using an inbound access list, you must include explicit list statements to permit these routing table updates to occur. If you fail to do this, all communication across that particular interface could be lost when the updates get blocked by the implicit "deny all" statement at the end of all access lists.

The two main types of access lists we will discuss are *standard* access control and *extended* access control lists. Cisco also supports reflexive access control lists and dynamic extended access control lists, but these are outside the scope of this course. When you use access lists on your router, each protocol-specific list needs to be identified by either a name or a number. Following are the protocols that can be identified by name:

- Apollo Domain
- IP
- IPX
- ISO CLNS
- NetBIOS IPX

Table 14-1 shows the range of numbers that are valid for each protocol or type of access list. You must strictly adhere to these when numbering your lists.

TABLE 14-1		
Access List Protocols Specified by Number	**Protocol**	**Number Range**
	IP	1–99
	Extended IP	100–199
	Ethernet type code	200–299
	DECnet and extended DECnet	300–399
	XNS	400–499
	Extended XNS	500–599
	AppleTalk	600–699
	Ethernet address	700–799
	IPX	800–899
	Extended IPX	900–999
	IPX SAP	1,000–1,099
	Extended transparent bridging	1,100–1,199
	NLSP route aggregation	1,200–1,299

Standard access lists can be thought of as "quick and dirty"; they are easier to configure and have relatively low router processing overhead. Standard access lists filter traffic based on the source address of the packet. Extended access lists provide you with additional functionality by allowing you to use both source and destination addressing, as well as specifying the protocol and the individual port number. Figure 14-1 illustrates the processing order of an extended access list.

By specifying a particular port number with the protocol, you can apply very granular filtering controls to your networks. See the following example for a list of common port numbers.

```
2500(config)#access-list 133 permit tcp 10.13.32.0 0.0.15.255 eq ?
  <0-65535>  Port number
  bgp        Border Gateway Protocol (179)
  chargen    Character generator (19)
  cmd        Remote commands (rcmd, 514)
  daytime    Daytime (13)
  discard    Discard (9)
  domain     Domain Name Service (53)
  echo       Echo (7)
  exec       Exec (rsh, 512)
  finger     Finger (79)
  ftp        File Transfer Protocol (21)
  ftp-data   FTP data connections (used infrequently, 20)
  gopher     Gopher (70)
  hostname   NIC hostname server (101)
  ident      Ident Protocol (113)
  irc        Internet Relay Chat (194)
  klogin     Kerberos login (543)
  kshell     Kerberos shell (544)
  login      Login (rlogin, 513)
  lpd        Printer service (515)
  nntp       Network News Transport Protocol (119)
  pop2       Post Office Protocol v2 (109)
  pop3       Post Office Protocol v3 (110)
  smtp       Simple Mail Transport Protocol (25)
  sunrpc     Sun Remote Procedure Call (111)
  syslog     Syslog (514)
  tacacs     TAC Access Control System (49)
  talk       Talk (517)
  telnet     Telnet (23)
  time       Time (37)
```

```
uucp       Unix-to-Unix Copy Program (540)
whois      Nicname (43)
www        World Wide Web (HTTP, 80)
```

Lengthy, complicated access lists can place a significant burden on a router. There are two ways to limit this burden:

- Optimize your access lists.
- Use wildcard masking.

Access list optimization involves determining which explicit statements are most frequently used by your routers and moving those statements to

FIGURE 14-1

Extended access list flow chart

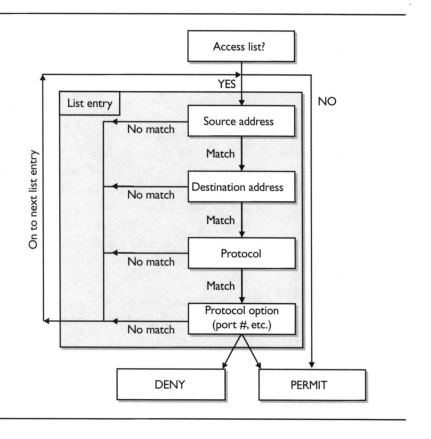

the beginning of the access list. Keep in mind that this process can seriously jeopardize the functionality of your lists if your criteria then appear in an order that affects the packet-filtering process. However, you can reduce the processing necessary to perform filtering if the statements that typically receive more "hits" or matches are nearer to the beginning of the list. In this case, the router can avoid parsing the entire list to find matching criteria for your most common traffic patterns. An excellent method for obtaining these statistics is the IOS command show access-lists. This command displays the number of matches after each statement in parentheses. By examining in-place access lists, you can easily determine if rearranging the statements will help your router's performance. An example list that has already been optimized is shown in the following example:

```
Router# show access-lists 121
Extended IP access list 121
permit tcp host 201.96.38.10 any established (4304 matches)
permit udp host 201.96.38.10 any eq domain (129 matches)
permit icmp host 201.96.38.10 any
permit tcp host 201.96.38.10 host 174.169.23.141 gt 1023
permit tcp host 201.96.38.10 host 174.169.23.135 eq smtp (2 matches)
```

Wildcard masks can also be effectively used to reduce router overhead. A wildcard mask essentially functions as the opposite of an IP subnet mask. In simple terms, a wildcard mask can be used to refer to a range of addresses with a single access list entry. Whereas a subnet mask identifies which part of an IP address is the network and which part is the host, a wildcard mask filters out part of the address and limits what the router must examine before making a permit/deny decision. Let's look at a few examples.

```
10.13.210.0    0.0.0.255
```

This pair indicates that all addresses between 10.13.210.1 and 10.13.210.255 will match the criteria statement.

```
10.13.0.0    0.0.255.255
```

This set shows that any of the addresses between 10.13.0.0 and 10.13.255.255 match the statement. Now let's get tough!

```
10.13.32.0    0.0.15.255
```

Because the subnet mask in use here is 255.255.240.0, this statement actually specifies that the following addresses will match the criteria:

10.13.32.0
10.13.33.0
10.13.34.0
10.13.35.0
10.13.37.0
10.13.38.0
10.13.39.0
10.13.40.0
10.13.41.0
10.13.42.0
10.13.43.0
10.13.44.0
10.13.45.0
10.13.46.0
10.13.47.0

The pattern is easy to see and becomes more apparent as you work with wildcard masks more frequently.

Where Can Access Lists Be Used?

Access lists are quite versatile and can be used in many different ways, including in controlling virtual terminal access, performing traffic flow control, and restricting routing table update contents. However, the only functions supported by Cisco as a valid security measure are filtering and controlling the transmission of packets on a particular interface.

In the absence of access lists, all traffic is essentially allowed to pass across the router and access your network unchecked. As a basic form of security, access lists should be configured for each traffic type you want to control and applied to each interface on which you want to control it. Remember that this is only a basic form of security; if you require much more comprehensive protection, you need to consider the Cisco PIX Firewall, a dedicated hardware/software combination that provides far better security than simple access lists.

Access lists definitely belong on any firewall routers in your infrastructure. These are routers typically positioned between your internal network and an outside, nontrusted network, such as the Internet. This is a perfect situation for an inbound access list, applied to the serial interface through which your Internet access is connected. See Figure 14-2 for an example of this configuration.

Another ideal location for access lists is within each of your *border* routers—routers that are typically located at the edge of your network. They are most efficiently utilized in either the distribution or access layers. Therefore, you can control the flow of traffic from less secure areas of your network to the core or to areas that require more security. Examples include controlling access from branch-office locations and restricting access to a research and development, engineering, or legal department within an organization.

Access lists can also be used effectively in your network to control traffic flow and manipulate the contents of routing tables on specific routers while maintaining a dynamic-update status on the routing tables. Again, you must define and apply an access list for each protocol configured on a specific interface that you wish to control. As you learned in Chapter 9, access lists shouldn't be used at the core layer of the hierarchical model because they can delay the transmission of critical traffic. By placing your access lists in the distribution or access layers, you can also minimize unnecessary traffic and gain better performance.

FIGURE 14-2   Outbound traffic permitted; inbound Internet traffic blocked by access list

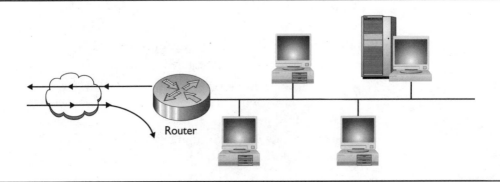

Proxy Services

Although *proxy* can be defined in more than one way, in the context of this discussion, the definition we use is a person authorized to act for another; an agent or substitute. That is exactly what Cisco's proxy services provide through the IOS software. A number of different types of proxy services are available.

Helper Addresses

Routed internetworks are normally configured to block the propagation of broadcast traffic at router interfaces. This is done to prevent the entire network from being overwhelmed with broadcast requests and to keep performance levels high. However, some types of clients require responses to their broadcast cries for help. If they received no reply, their requests would fail.

Cisco IOS software addresses this situation with *helper addresses*. Helper addresses allow you to configure specific server or network addresses that will be able to respond appropriately to these client broadcasts. Cisco provides helper address support for many different protocols, including IP and IPX, and multiple helper addresses can be configured per router interface. This is important in a distributed networking environment where each network segment may not have the requested resource available.

Dynamic Host Configuration Protocol (DHCP, defined in RFC 1531) clients at a remote branch office are perfect examples of Cisco's helper address proxy in action. These clients rely on a DHCP server to respond to their UDP broadcast requests for an IP address assignment. Without an IP helper address configured on their local router, their requests will be dropped and ignored. This means the clients won't receive an IP address lease and won't be able to communicate on the network. When they use an IP helper address, the local Cisco router will know where to forward their DHCP requests and allow the clients to successfully lease an IP address. This practice also prevents you from having to rely on bridging to provide broadcast traffic propagation through your router.

Configuration for DHCP proxy services is simple. When you do not specify a particular UDP port number when configuring the forwarding of these UDP broadcast packets, your router will automatically forward the BOOTP packets, which carry the DHCP information, to the specified address. See Figure 14-3 for an example of helper addresses in a routed environment.

FIGURE 14-3   Effect of Helper addresses on DHCP requests

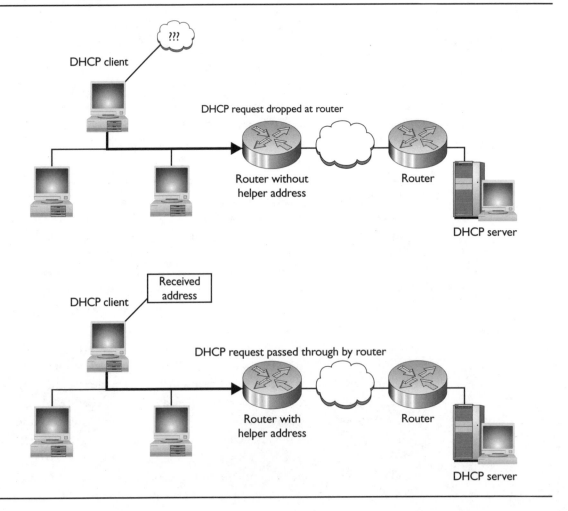

Proxy ARP

An integral part of TCP/IP-based communications is the ability to resolve an IP address to a device's MAC address. You can do this by using Address Resolution Protocol (ARP). However, ARP relies on broadcasts to perform this address mapping. If the local station can't broadcast to the intended destination on a remote subnet, it will fail to establish communications. Proxy ARP functionality, as defined in RFC 1027, provides a solution to this scenario.

When a Cisco router receives an ARP request, it determines if the destination address is located on the same subnet as the interface through which it received the request. If so, the router will ignore the request. If the destination address is located on a remote subnet that is accessible only through another of the router's interfaces, the router will reply to the ARP request with its own MAC address. When it does so, the client receives a "valid" resolution and may begin its communication with the intended device by sending its packets to the router. The router will then route or forward all of this received traffic toward the destination.

Proxy ARP is the most common way for hosts with no routing knowledge or logic to learn of appropriate routes to other subnets and devices. It essentially presents all networks to the clients as local networks, eliminating the need for the clients to understand routing principles. The Cisco IOS software decides whether it has the best route to the destination before replying with the router's data-link address (see Figure 14-4). Proxy ARP is enabled by default on Cisco routers but is often not supported by other types of routers.

IPX Watchdog Packet Spoofing

Novell NetWare environments present some unique challenges in a routed internetwork. For instance, Novell servers that run the NetWare Core Protocol (NCP) need to continually verify their clients' connections. They do this by sending out IPX *watchdog* packets every five minutes to each idle client, and they expect a response. If the server doesn't receive a valid response to its watchdog packet, it assumes the client is no longer available,

FIGURE 14-4

Router replying to client ARP request with router interface address

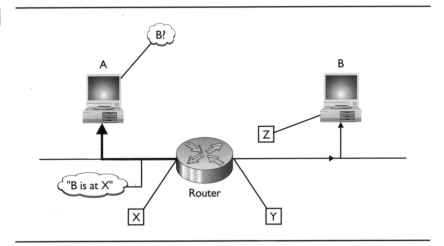

and the server will terminate the connection. This can become a particular concern in a dial-on-demand routing (DDR) configuration or where you have bandwidth constraints.

Because of the frequency of these "keepalive" messages, a DDR link could be forced to call and establish a link every five minutes, even if there are no data packets to transmit from the remote client. A DDR link could even be kept open continuously, depending on its configuration, because of these watchdog packets. You could configure access lists to specifically block this packet traffic, but the Novell server would then terminate communications with the client.

The Cisco IOS software solves this dilemma by providing IPX watchdog packet *spoofing*. The router will answer these watchdog packets locally with spoofed responses as if it were the client. When the server receives a response to the keepalive message, it doesn't know that the response comes from a router. Regardless, this is sufficient to satisfy the server, and it won't terminate the client's connection. Since the watchdog packet is never transmitted to the client, bandwidth is conserved, and in a DDR environment, the dial-up connection is never brought up. See Figure 14-5 for an example of IPX watchdog packet spoofing.

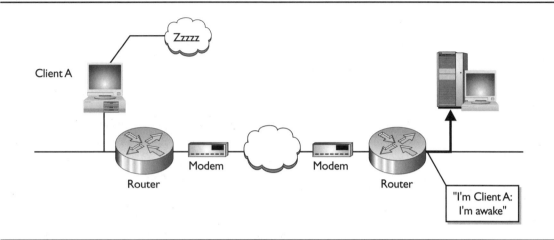

FIGURE 14-5   Process of spoofing IPX watchdog packets

Novell GNS Requests

Novell NetWare clients use a Service Advertising Protocol (SAP) broadcast request known as Get Nearest Server (GNS) to locate and connect to the nearest server providing the services they are requesting. These messages will succeed if there is a local server to process the request. But if the client is located on a remote segment without a server, the request will never make it across the router interfaces to the server subnet.

By default, the Cisco IOS software on your router will respond to these requests when it is appropriate. If the subnet contains a Novell server that can also service the GNS request, the server will process the request. If the client is on a serverless LAN subnet, the router will respond, providing resource discovery capabilities. This functionality allows you to place and service Novell clients in remote locations without needing a local server present.

You can configure SAP filters that allow control over the specific SAP services that the router will accept and advertise, as well as determine what type of GNS responses it will send to requesting clients. You can also configure the delay between the receipt of a GNS client request and the potential response sent by the router. Finally, you can disable the response-generation process entirely.

Where Can Proxy Services Be Used?

A portion of the wide variety of proxy services offered as part of the Cisco IOS software feature set can be put into production use in almost every type of networking situation. Obviously, when remote subnets contain Novell nodes, you no longer need to concern yourself with the local availability of Novell servers to service the clients' GNS requests. The availability of IPX watchdog packet spoofing will also serve to keep these remote clients connected to Novell server services. Remember that watchdog packet spoofing will additionally solve the issue of placing Novell clients in a serverless subnet across a DDR-connected link. This will prevent the dial-up link from coming up just to transmit these responses and will help reduce bandwidth and expenses on your DDR connections.

Proxy ARP services allow your remote TCP/IP clients not to worry about the details of routing, essentially extending the potential reach of your networks by assisting with the address mapping and resolution process. Finally, helper addresses function to control traffic levels and prevent broadcast storms across bridged networks or WAN links. IP helper addresses can be configured so that the router acts as a proxy for the requests, keeping the details hidden from your clients.

CERTIFICATION OBJECTIVE 14.03

Encryption

The need to safeguard sensitive corporate data has greatly increased as businesses and organizations become more involved in e-commerce, business-to-business (B2B), and virtual-private networking over the Internet. Encryption services provided through the Cisco IOS software can help guard against the perils of transmitting unsecured traffic across open, public networks.

Encryption is the orderly scrambling of data according to a predetermined pattern or algorithm to ensure its secure transmission across a network. The Cisco IOS software provides encryption services at the packet level (level 2) and is available only for IP traffic. Other protocols may be *encapsulated* within IP and then encrypted for transmission.

The actual encryption and decryption processes happen at only routers that have been configured specifically to provide encryption with router authentication. These routers are referred to as *peer-encrypting routers* or *peer routers.* The IP header portion and upper-layer protocol headers of each packet are left unencrypted (clear text) so that other routers not participating in the encryption sequence may read them. The remainder of the packet, or the payload, is encrypted so that it can't be read or understood by devices along the way.

on the
!
() o b

To determine the impact of enabling encryption on peer routers, use the IOS command show processes or show process cpu to first establish a baseline of performance on your potential peer routers. Repeat these commands after enabling encryption to assess the added processing. According to Cisco, you don't want to use encryption if your router's processor load is over 40 percent.

Router authentication enables the routers to positively determine the origin of the incoming encrypted data. An encrypted session must be established between peer-encrypting routers prior to the transmission of encrypted data to prevent the interception of sensitive data by an intermediate router or a device that is attempting to "sniff" the traffic on the wire. If the authentication fails, the encrypted session won't be established, and no encrypted traffic will be generated.

In the encryption process, Cisco routers use three standards:

- Digital Signature Standard (DSS)
- Diffie-Hellman (DH) public key algorithm
- Data Encryption Standard (DES)

DSS is used to perform peer router authentication, and DH and DES are used to establish and manage the encrypted sessions between peer routers. DSS uses a two-key system—a public key and a private key—to confirm each router's identity. This method is similar to that used by other public-key systems like Pretty Good Privacy (PGP) but is outside the scope of this course. Both the DH numbers and the DES keys are exchanged during the encrypted session and discarded at the termination of the session.

An important detail to be aware of is that data is encrypted only as it leaves a peer router's outbound interface and travels across the network to the decrypting router. This means that the data is unprotected before it reaches the encrypting router and after it leaves the decrypting router. This may seem obvious, but it's an important factor to consider when you are planning your network's topology. See Figure 14-6 for an example.

Configuring encryption on Cisco routers requires additional processing to be performed and can place a sizable load on your routers. Two methods to alleviate this strain are available on the Cisco 7500 series routers, which offer a slot-based, modular chassis. A module known as an Encryption Service Adapter (ESA) is available for use in the 7200 and 7500 series routers. This adapter offloads the actual encryption processing from the router's central processor and can greatly improve the encryption performance because of the dedicated hardware. Also, the Cisco 7500 series supports the use of the second-generation Versatile Interface Processor (VIP2), allowing the additional VIP2 cryptography engine to handle certain encryption activity.

Where Can Encryption Be Used?

Encryption is very useful when used appropriately in a network. Routers on either side of a public network, carrying sensitive or private data, are obvious candidates for encryption services. For example, routers on the edge of a corporate network connected to branch office locations across the Internet are ideal locations to consider encryption.

FIGURE 14-6 Clear-text transmissions on each network; encrypted across WAN link

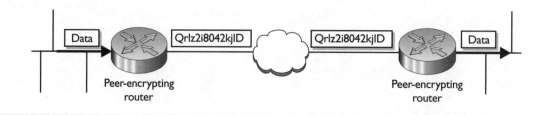

Encryption can also be implemented within an internal network if necessary, although the need to do so may call possible network design issues into question. Other possible uses for peer-encrypting routers are to act as Internet firewall routers or to perform secure routing updates between sets of routers. An overriding concern when encryption is being implemented is an appropriate network topology. In particular, you should always try to keep a direct "line-of-sight" between peer routers; in other words, encrypted traffic should never pass through more than one pair of encrypting routers. Additional transitions between nested levels of encrypting routers will seriously impede the flow of traffic and push the routers' resources to the limit.

Of course, the overhead incurred with enabling encryption on your routers requires serious examination. Encryption should be used only when it is truly necessary and the benefits of a secure data path outweigh the performance penalties. Again, Cisco's recommendation is not to enable encryption if the router CPU load exceeds 40 percent. Pay additional attention when considering combinations of encryption and compression.

CERTIFICATION OBJECTIVE 14.04

Compression

Compression, another feature of the Cisco IOS software, is available over serial connections and can provide a reduction in the size of the packets transmitted across your links. However, there is an underlying principle in dealing with compression: If the data you typically transmit is composed primarily of already-compressed files, you don't want to enable compression on these links. You will simply waste router CPU cycles as you unsuccessfully attempt to further compress this data and you overload your router. Three types of compression services are available in a Cisco infrastructure: header compression, data compression and link compression.

Cisco's header compression method is based on RFC 1144 and uses the Van Jacobson algorithm to perform the necessary calculations. Header compression is particularly effective in low-bandwidth serial link situations.

Essentially, once a connection has been established and packets begin flowing across a link, the header in each packet is somewhat redundant and consumes additional unnecessary bandwidth. Header compression reduces a typical TCP/IP packet's 40-byte datagram header to around 10 bytes for a savings of roughly 75 percent.

on the
Job

In order for Van Jacobson header compression to operate, the compressed packets must arrive at the destination interface in the correct order. This means that no re-ordering of the packets can occur. Priority queuing does change the order of packets as they are transmitted and, therefore, should never be used in conjunction with header compression.

Header compression can be configured in two ways. You can enable it on a particular router interface or specify an *IP Map*, which allows you to use a specific IP address in the compression calculations. Both techniques support *active* and *passive* compression. Active compression will compress every outgoing packet header, and passive compression will recompress the packet headers for transmission only if the packets were originally received by the router in a compressed state.

Data or payload compression is the opposite of header compression in that data compression compacts the data portion of a packet but doesn't compress the header portion. Finally, link compression enables the compression of both the header and the data portions of packets. There are two different types of compression encoding techniques: statistical and dictionary. Statistical encoding uses a fixed or static encoding methodology, which makes it unsuitable for the dynamic and unpredictable nature of internetwork traffic. Dictionary encoding, such as the Lempel-Ziv algorithm, uses a repetitive character identification scheme, replacing these sequences with codes from a dictionary list. This method provides much better response to data variations.

Cisco IOS uses two dictionary-based encoding schemes, the *STAC* and *Predictor* algorithms. STAC is based on the Lempel-Ziv method, but has been further optimized. The result is better compression ratios at the expense of additional CPU time. In comparison, Predictor is more economical with processing but requires more memory. Both compression schemes are used for payload and link compression. A difference is that link compression specifies the use of one set of dictionaries per interface or link, and payload compression uses one set of dictionaries per virtual circuit (VC).

To enable either the STAC or Predictor compression encoding schemes, use the Cisco IOS command:

```
compress stac
```

or

```
compress predictor
```

Point-to-point software compression is available on all LAPB, PPP, and HDLC encapsulations. PPP and LAPB support either the STAC or Predictor method, and HDLC encapsulation supports STAC. As with the functionality available for encryption, certain Cisco routers support compression service adapters (CSAs). These are dedicated modules that can offload the compression tasks from the router's main CPU. Cisco 7200 and 7500 routers with VIP2s and Cisco 7000 routers with the Route Switch Processor (RSP7000) can provide this hardware-based functionality.

Where Can Compression Be Used?

As mentioned earlier, compression allows you to reduce the size of packets and make more efficient use of your bandwidth. There are performance considerations with using compression, but in some situations, compression is beneficial. This is particularly true over slower serial links. The benefit of having compressed data overshadows the additional load placed on the router's CPU.

The IP Map specification is convenient on serial links where there may be many possible paths and you need to enable compression for an individual target connection. If you were to enable compression on an interface basis in this situation, it could lead to undesired results because compression needs to be enabled on *both* sides of a connection; you should never enable compression on connections to a public data network. An example of interface-specific header compression would be both sides of a dedicated point-to-point link or dedicated leased line that connects only two locations.

Again, there are the concerns with the overall performance of your router and the load placed on the router's CPU when you are dealing with compression. To determine a baseline for your router's performance and to establish the impact that compression services may impose, use the IOS command, Show processes, to view the utilization of your router's resources. Cisco also recommends that if you have enabled encryption on your routers, you shouldn't add compression to the mix. This is an important detail, because it means that you will have to carefully plan your topology while being very specific about where either encryption or compression services will be used. Finally, Cisco recommends that compression services should not be performed through the IOS software if your CPU utilization is already above 65 percent consistently. See the following example for the Show process cpu command:

```
2500#show process cpu
CPU utilization for five seconds: 12%/11%; one minute: 11%; five minutes: 11%
  PID  Runtime(ms)  Invoked  uSecs   5Sec    1Min    5Min TTY Process
    1           4      265      15   0.00%   0.00%   0.00%   0 Load Meter
    2        1840      186    9892   0.40%   0.14%   0.29%   0 Exec
    3        2200       45   48888   0.00%   0.11%   0.12%   0 Check heaps
    4           0        1       0   0.00%   0.00%   0.00%   0 Pool Manager
    5           8        2    4000   0.00%   0.00%   0.00%   0 Timers
    6          76       46    1652   0.00%   0.00%   0.00%   0 ARP Input
    7           0        1       0   0.00%   0.00%   0.00%   0 SERIAL A'detect
    8          40       58     689   0.00%   0.01%   0.00%   0 IP Input
    9         492      179    2748   0.00%   0.00%   0.00%   0 CDP Protocol
   11        4928     1363    3615   0.40%   0.31%   0.31%   0 IP Background
   12          32      268     119   0.00%   0.00%   0.00%   0 TCP Timer
   13           0        1       0   0.00%   0.00%   0.00%   0 TCP Protocols
   14           0        1       0   0.00%   0.00%   0.00%   0 Probe Input
   15           4        1    4000   0.00%   0.00%   0.00%   0 RARP Input
   16           0        1       0   0.00%   0.00%   0.00%   0 BOOTP Server
   17           0       23       0   0.00%   0.00%   0.00%   0 IP Cache Ager
   18           0       23       0   0.00%   0.00%   0.00%   0 NBF Input
   19           0        2       0   0.00%   0.00%   0.00%   0 SPX Input
   20           0        1       0   0.00%   0.00%   0.00%   0 Critical Bkgnd
   21          24        9    2666   0.00%   0.00%   0.00%   0 Net Background
   22          12       15     800   0.00%   0.00%   0.00%   0 Logger
   23          92     1315      69   0.00%   0.00%   0.00%   0 TTY Background
```

24	16	1337	11	0.00%	0.00%	0.00%	0	Per-Second Jobs
25	444	1336	332	0.00%	0.01%	0.00%	0	Net Periodic
26	280	572	489	0.00%	0.00%	0.00%	0	Net Input
27	0	266	0	0.00%	0.00%	0.00%	0	Compute load avgs
28	808	23	35130	0.00%	0.06%	0.01%	0	Per-minute Jobs
30	0	2	0	0.00%	0.00%	0.00%	0	IP SNMP
31	76	5	15200	0.00%	0.00%	0.00%	0	SNMP Traps
32	4	26	153	0.00%	0.00%	0.00%	0	IP-RT Background
33	424	19	22315	0.40%	0.03%	0.00%	0	IGRP Router

CERTIFICATION OBJECTIVE 14.05

Queuing

In the battle for network access and bandwidth, queuing services can be a network designer's greatest weapon. Queuing services allow you to assign prioritization levels to the application traffic on your networks. The Cisco IOS software supports a number of varieties of queuing. These include

- First in, first out (FIFO) queuing
- Priority queuing
- Custom queuing
- Weighted fair queuing

Let's look at each one of these methodologies a little closer.

FIFO Queuing

First in, first out (FIFO) queuing is also sometimes referred to as "first come, first served" (FCFS) queuing. Actually, FIFO isn't a "queuing" method at all. It simply acts as a cache, sending out the first packet received or the oldest packet in the queue. It processes the packets sequentially, assigning no priority or weight to the packets. FIFO is the default queuing process when no other queuing strategies have been configured. This method applies to all interfaces, except serial interfaces set to E1 (2.048 Mbps)

FIGURE 14-7

FIFO queuing flow chart

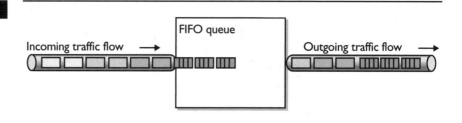

or slower because these serial interfaces use weighted fair queuing by default (see Figure 14-7).

Priority Queuing

Priority queuing is perhaps the most extreme queuing solution available through the Cisco IOS software. However, it is very effective at providing mission-critical applications and time-sensitive protocols like SNA with the highest level of access possible to the available bandwidth. Priority queuing relies on a priority list that has been previously configured by the network administrator. This list specifies packet priority using a number of criteria, including protocol type and port number.

Priority queuing consists of four ranked output queues: high, medium, normal, and low. When a packet enters the router, it is scanned for a match against the priority list. The packet is then sent to the appropriate queue. If the packet doesn't match a list entry, it is assigned to the default queue (by default, the default queue is the normal queue). As packets come in and are assigned to a queue, they will be dropped if the assigned queue is full. IP-based traffic will also receive source quench messages when packets are dropped to indicate that the receiver (the router) can't handle any more packets at the moment.

When the router is ready to transmit traffic, it begins with the most important queue, the high-priority queue, and begins transmitting packets from that queue exclusively. Only when this queue is empty does the router then move on to the medium-priority queue. The router will continue this process, always checking after each packet from the beginning of the queues before moving down to a lower-priority queue. This scheme is very effective for traffic flows that have been assigned high-priority status. Unfortunately, it can also work to the complete exclusion of traffic waiting in the lower-level queues.

Priority queuing can be configured for all router interfaces, but Cisco originally intended this scheme to be used for periodically congested serial WAN links with limited bandwidth. The queue size and undefined packet default handling parameters can be configured as needed by the administrator. Enabling priority queuing requires additional work by the router's CPU, so it should be used sparingly and only where needed (see Figure 14-8).

Custom Queuing

Custom queuing is much more even-handed in its packet handling strategy than priority queuing. Custom queuing uses a predefined packet classification list like priority queuing, but it uses this list to assign traffic to one of 17 different round-robin queues. As with most other items in the world of Cisco, the first queue is designated queue 0. The remaining queues, numbered 1 through 16, are processed sequentially until the

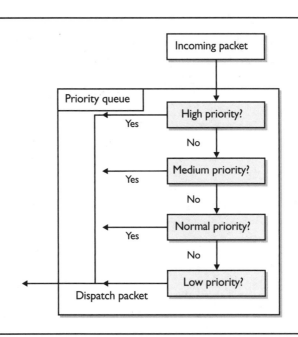

window limit is reached or the queue is empty, with no preference to priority. Each of these queues has a transmission window specified in bytes that determines how many packets the router can send from each queue before moving on to the next queue.

Queues 1–16 can be configured for the packet classification and queue size. Queue 0 is reserved as a system queue and can't be configured as the others. It handles high-priority packets, like keepalive packets, and the router processes all traffic from this queue first. The remaining queues continue in a round-robin fashion.

Essentially, custom queuing allows you to specify the amount of bandwidth each type of protocol can ultimately use. Because you can specify the size of the transmission window, you can control the queuing according to your traffic patterns and needs. For example, you could set your TCP/IP queue window size to be much larger than the transmission window for your IPX/SPX traffic queue. Like priority queuing, custom queuing places additional stress on the router and its processing capabilities and should be used only when you have a justified need for special traffic or protocol processing (see Figure 14-9).

FIGURE 14-9   Custom queuing flow chart

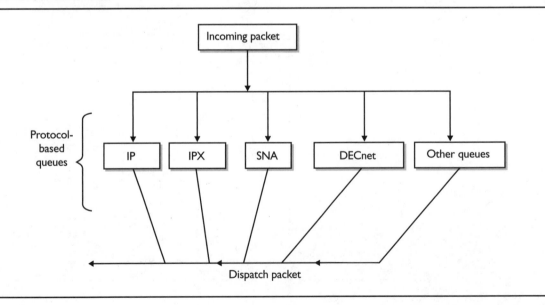

Weighted Fair Queuing

Weighted fair queuing is probably the most common form of queuing used in Cisco environments. It is easier to configure than either custom or priority queuing in that it doesn't require that you first define queue lists. Weighted fair queuing addresses some of the natural shortcomings of the other queuing techniques.

Weighted fair queuing looks at all incoming traffic as two distinct types of data streams: high-bandwidth sessions and low-bandwidth sessions. Contrary to what you might think, the low-bandwidth sessions have priority over the higher-bandwidth streams to prevent the larger sessions from effectively choking out the smaller sessions because of the number of packets being queued. Because the low-bandwidth sessions have fewer packets, they are processed and transmitted with greater "weighting" than the higher-bandwidth sessions. The algorithm that makes this determination looks at the time of the last rather than the first bit received.

Making the determination based on the last bit stops applications with larger packets from monopolizing the outgoing interface's available bandwidth at the expense of traffic with smaller packets. This is an improvement over the default FIFO queuing. With FIFO, for example, FTP traffic that uses larger packets can crowd out the smaller packets of Telnet traffic. Weighted fair queuing makes sure that the smaller packets are fairly represented in the outgoing traffic stream. The high-bandwidth sessions don't have to wait until all the smaller packets have been transmitted—they just have to share the outgoing bandwidth with the other "guys" (see Figure 14-10).

Where Can Queuing Be Used?

When determining where and when to use queuing, remember that you can assign only one type of queuing to each interface. In most situations, weighted fair queuing will be the appropriate queuing choice. It helps ensure that all of your traffic will have a fair chance to traverse your limited-bandwidth WAN links.

Priority queuing and custom queuing both place additional demands on your router's CPU and should be used only when you have a specific protocol or application that needs special attention. If your WAN links have

FIGURE 14-10

Weighted fair queuing flow chart

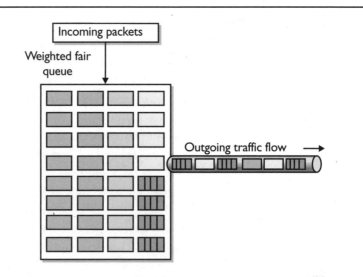

sufficient capacity and you don't experience delays on these links, you don't need priority or custom queuing.

These strategies can be successful in the transmission of high-priority or mission-critical traffic over WAN links that periodically experience congestion. When the links get backed up, priority (and to a lesser extent, custom) queuing will help ensure that your essential traffic reaches its destination in a timely manner. Finally, if you have no bandwidth concerns at all on your WAN links, FIFO may just be the best (non) solution for your network.

FROM THE FIELD

In performing consulting work for clients of all sizes and types across North America, I have experienced many different reactions to the project at hand. I have been received by clients with open arms as the savior of their business/network/project, and I have also been given shoulders colder than the winters in Minnesota!

What I have taken from these experiences is the importance of good communication between you and your customers, whether they are external or internal customers. The

FROM THE FIELD

ability to keep your clients abreast of each step of a project in an informative and concise manner is perhaps one of the most important skills you will ever possess. In step with this skill is the ability to effectively communicate your years of experience and knowledge with the right level of detail to the right audience.

Remember, more often than not, the individuals you need to keep happy and satisfied are not your fellow engineers or peers at the client site. It is the decision-makers who sign your check and invite you back for another day—or not. These people are usually in management or executive management and typically are not involved with the day-to-day operations of their networks. They don't usually come from a technical background and likely will not understand (or care about) the intimate details of "X," "Y," or "Z." Thus, when speaking or writing for this audience, be sure to explain things from a business perspective rather than a technical one. Justification for a decision such as "because it will help secure your e-commerce transactions" will always have a better chance for approval than a technical diatribe on the intricacies of the Diffie-Hellman public-key algorithm.

For example, recently, I was asked to design and implement a network for a client who had purchased a number of Cisco routers for its WAN links. The person responsible for the project had read some marketing material and knew enough to purchase the correct routers for the right spots in the network. However, this person also had gleaned some ideas from the marketing material about what types of features he wanted to deploy in the routers.

The list was quite unbelievable: access lists, network address translation, compression, encryption, queuing, various proxy services . . ., He wanted to turn on all of these features and more because he had "learned" that they all were available to him through the IOS software.

Obviously, I needed to find a way to explain to him why running all of these services on each router was simply not feasible. Rather than trying to go through the details of each IOS feature's requirements and limitations with him, I put it into terms that he could easily and quickly grasp. All that was required was the explanation, "Your routers will blow up," and we were well on our way to a valid compromise! Granted, this is not exactly a business perspective, but it cut to the heart of the matter, and I was able to explain my reasoning further.

When all was said and done, we agreed on a set of features that delivered the appropriate levels of security, scalability, capacity, and performance for his network. Now, I look forward to my next contract with this satisfied customer.

Customer Requirements

Having all the tools in the world available to you and not knowing how or where to use them puts you no further ahead in the network design game. The key to success is possessing the knowledge of where, when, why, and how to use the tools at your disposal through the Cisco IOS software.

Performance

Optimizing and maintaining the performance of an internetwork requires the proper application of your skills and knowledge to the specific configuration presented. Of the services we discussed earlier, the two closest related to performance are compression and queuing.

Compression is best used in situations that require a reduction in transmitted packet size across WAN links. It is ideal for low-bandwidth serial links because it can significantly reduce the amount of traffic flowing through these links. Queuing can optimize traffic patterns for specific types of packets, giving an application or even the overall performance of your router links a boost. The prioritization of traffic flows allows you to customize and improve the way your networks perform.

Remember that from the perspective of your routers' CPUs, compression is not a good playmate with encryption services. Queuing can also be very demanding of router processing cycles. As is the case with most of the services we've discussed, don't employ these features simply because the Cisco IOS makes them available.

Security

Security is definitely one of the biggest concerns for networks of all sizes. If a senior executive from your organization hasn't come back from a trip asking security questions after "reading something about it" in the airline magazine, it would be a surprise! Security issues are omnipresent because security is not an absolute state; it is always relative and changing. However, you need to make the most of the tools at your disposal to ensure the highest appropriate levels of security possible.

Cisco makes this a little easier, of course, with the availability of access lists and encryption services through the IOS software. Access lists can provide a good base level of security on the perimeter of your network by dropping unknown or unwanted packets before they ever reach your internal network. Encryption helps protect sensitive data while it is in transit, ensuring that only those intended to read the data will be able to do so.

Both access lists and encryption services need to be applied in a judicious manner. Neither feature is lightweight in its implementation, and both require justification for use in a production environment.

Capacity

Capacity is always at a premium over (expensive) WAN links. Network administrators are constantly in search of ways to increase capacity without adding cost to their budgets. Queuing is one of the ways to improve this situation. By allowing you to set priorities on your traffic types, you can make the most of a limited capacity.

Priority queuing is a good example of enhancing capacity. Used over periodically congested serial links, priority queuing can help ensure that time-sensitive traffic gets through. However, remember this: If the WAN links are always congested, queuing is insufficient, and compression could be indicated. If the WAN links are never congested, you wouldn't want to use either method.

Scalability

Proxy services allow your network to be expanded without causing you to worry about making certain resources available on each remote subnet. They also allow you to avoid enabling bridging on your routers and WAN links to support these remote clients.

Using access lists can also enhance scalability. By applying access lists on certain router interfaces, you can filter traffic and allow the network to handle many more nodes and conversations. This goes to the bottom line for network scalability and lets you grow your network as appropriate.

QUESTIONS AND ANSWERS

Eric wants to prevent incoming traffic from the Internet from getting to his internal network.	He should implement access lists on the external interface of his router.
I've changed the entries for a few subnets in my existing access lists, but they still are getting through the interface.	Because the existing access list was note deleted, the "changed" entries are actually new entries added to the end of the existing access list, and the previous permit statements are still letting them pass through.
Your IDSN links are "brought up" far more frequently than necessary for the levels of IPX traffic, and it costs your company a great deal of money for these DDR links to be live almost continuously.	Consider implementing IPX watchdog packet spoofing to control the SAP/IPX watchdog packet traffic.
I need to ensure secure communication between two branch offices across the Internet.	Employ encryption services.
I need to make the most of the limited bandwidth on my IDSN serial interfaces.	Compression services could help squeeze more performance from limited bandwidth links.
My enterprise resource planning package is having timeout issues across our WAN links.	This could be a case for priority queuing or possibly for compression services; you probably need more information.

CERTIFICATION SUMMARY

A network is a living, breathing entity that requires care and feeding to grow up big and strong. The Cisco IOS software features that you've examined can provide some of the nutrition your networks require.

Access lists provide a barrier for networks, blocking unwanted traffic and protecting them from harm. Proxy services provide a helping hand to networks, assisting nodes and servers with addressing issues, looking in on them from time to time, and even answering their questions when necessary. Encryption services make certain that your conversations are confidential and that your privacy isn't violated. Encryption also ensures that your essential data isn't compromised and always belongs to you. Compression allows you to accomplish as much as possible while keeping your expenses lower. Finally, queuing helps keep your networks orderly, making sure that you have control over the order and flow of your networks.

Using all of these features appropriately is critical to a healthy, happy network. As with any other living creature, overfeeding of these features and services to your routers will result in a slow, overloaded network. Matching the needs of a particular network with the right feature set is the ultimate goal. Doing so will produce fast, stable, secure, and well-behaved networks that you can be proud of for years to come.

✓ TWO-MINUTE DRILL

- ❑ Access lists are packet filters that define a set of criteria used by the router when it is examining the packets passing through its interfaces.

- ❑ Every access list has an implicit "deny all" statement at the end of the list.

- ❑ A "permit all" statement at the beginning of an access list will automatically pass all packets with no further checking.

- ❑ Create access lists with specific entries first and more general statements at the end.

- ❑ New entries will be appended to the end of an existing access list.

- ❑ Router interfaces support inbound and outbound access lists.

- ❑ Cisco supports standard access control lists (IP 1 to 99) and extended access control lists (IP 100 to 199).

- ❑ Extended access lists allow you to use the individual port numbers of specific protocols.

- ❑ Lengthy, complicated access lists place a significant burden on a router.

- ❑ For access list optimization, move the most frequently used statements to the beginning of the access list.

- ❑ A wildcard mask filters out part of the address and limits what the router must examine before making a permit/deny decision.

❏ Access lists filter and control the transmission of packets on a particular interface.

❏ Good locations for access lists are border routers and firewall routers.

❏ Cisco IOS Proxy services include helper addresses, proxy ARP, watchdog packet spoofing, and GNS requests.

❏ Helper addresses allow you to configure addresses that will respond appropriately to client broadcasts.

❏ ARP relies on broadcasts to perform address mapping.

❏ Proxy ARP responds to clients' ARP broadcasts with the router's MAC address and forwards the client traffic for them.

❏ Proxy ARP is the most common way for hosts to learn of routes to other subnets and devices, and it is enabled by default on Cisco routers.

❏ Novell servers verify client connectivity with watchdog packets.

❏ Cisco routers spoof the watchdog packet reply to minimize dial-up connection times and costs.

❏ Novell clients use a broadcast request known as GNS to locate and connect to the nearest server providing services.

❏ Cisco IOS software will respond to GNS requests when there are no Novell servers on that subnet.

❏ Encryption is the orderly scrambling of data according to a predetermined pattern or algorithm to ensure security.

❏ Cisco peer-encrypting routers provide encryption for only IP-based traffic.

❏ Don't use encryption if your router processor is over 40 percent utilization.

❏ The higher-end Cisco 7500 series routers can provide hardware-based encryption, taking the processing load off the CPU.

❏ Routers on both sides of a public network are good choices for encryption services.

❏ Compression allows you to reduce the size of packets and make more efficient use of your bandwidth.

❑ There are three types of Cisco compression services: header, data, and link.

❑ Cisco IOS uses two compression encoding schemes, the STAC and Predictor algorithms.

❑ Never use encryption and compression on the same router because of the processing strain.

❑ Don't use software-based compression if your CPU utilization is already above 65 percent consistently.

❑ Queuing services allow you to prioritize application traffic on your networks.

❑ Queuing schemes include FIFO, priority, custom, and weighted fair queuing.

❑ FIFO queuing sends out the first packet received and is the default queuing process for nonserial interfaces.

❑ Priority queuing uses priority levels from a priority list to handle time-sensitive traffic.

❑ Custom queuing uses a set of sequential queues and resizable transmission windows.

❑ Weighted fair queuing doesn't use queue lists and makes sure that low-bandwidth streams don't have to wait for larger streams to finish before transmitting.

❑ Priority and custom queuing place additional loads on your router's CPU.

SELF TEST

The following Self Test questions will help you measure your understanding of the material presented in this chapter. Read all the choices carefully; there may be more than one correct answer. Choose all correct answers for each question.

1. Ed has been designing and implementing an e-commerce client/server solution, using Windows NT servers and Oracle databases for his customer. He has been asked by his client to recommend a solution that will provide the best security against the dangers of hackers on the Internet. What would be his best recommendation?

    A. Access lists

    B. Cisco IOS Firewall feature set

    C. PIX Firewall

    D. Cisco Centri Firewall for Windows NT software

2. You've been tasked with designing access list settings for an internetwork router. The router is a Cisco 2513, with one Token Ring interface, one Ethernet interface, and two serial interfaces. All the interfaces are carrying both IP and IPX traffic and need different types of packet filtering. You need to configure access list protection for all interfaces and all protocols. How many access lists will you need to create at a minimum?

    A. 1

    B. 2

    C. 4

    D. 8

    E. 16

3. Which of the following statements is true regarding access lists?

    A. There is an implicit "deny all" statement at the end of each list.

    B. Entries added to an existing list will be placed at the end of the list; the router will process packets until a match is found and will not go further.

    C. If a "permit all" statement is placed at the beginning of an access list, no other statements will block traffic later.

    D. All of the above

4. Place the following access list statement types in order, from beginning to end.

   A. A statement that lists an entire network address

   B. A statement that lists an individual IP address

   C. A statement that says "deny all"

   D. A statement that lists a subnet address

5. Mike is editing an access list in Notepad and then uploading the list to the company's TFTP server. Why would Mike be doing this? (Choose all that apply.)

   A. Mike enjoys working in Notepad and finds it easier than editing from the command line.

   B. Creating the list offline permits Mike to better visualize the effects of the access list.

   C. Mike knows that access lists cannot be created line by line from the Cisco IOS command line.

   D. TFTP servers can handle uploads only in Notepad format.

   E. Mike wants to make sure that he types the statements correctly so that the router doesn't apply a bad statement as soon as he types it.

6. James needs to use an access list to specify that only Web server traffic (HTTP) from one certain Web server will be permitted between his router's Serial0 interface and a remote office's router. What number can he use in creating the list? (Choose all that apply.)

   A. 5

   B. 99

   C. 100

   D. 179

   E. 800

   F. 801

7. Kelly is setting up a new remote site for Shanley Software, Inc. It will be a large location with more than 500 clients, and she needs to cut costs as much as possible. To help save money, she has decided not to place a DHCP server at the remote site. The central office already has a DHCP server. However, she is concerned about how these clients will receive IP addressing. What can she do to best handle this situation?

   A. Assign static IP address manually to each client.

   B. Enable IP helper addresses as part of Proxy Services.

   C. Enable bridging on the Cisco router to allow DHCP traffic to pass from the central office.

   D. Use a PIX Firewall with NAT.

8. Which of the following Cisco IOS Proxy services will allow the mapping of a local data-link address to an IP address to permit communication with a remote device?

   A. Watchdog packet spoofing

   B. Proxy ARP

   C. GNS request proxy

   D. IP helper addresses

Paul maintains a large distributed internetwork with several ISDN connections. The main office network in Denver is a Novell NetWare network, and clients from around the country use this Novell infrastructure for many different types of services. The ISDN links are configured to dial up and connect as needed to transmit packets. The carriers in a number of the states where these ISDN connections are located charge a premium rate per-minute for connection times. Answer questions 9 and 10 based on the scenario presented.

9. Refer to the scenario above. Like any diligent network engineer, Paul is concerned about the costs associated with these links. When looking over the latest monthly reports, Paul is troubled by the amount of time these links are in use and the high costs associated with this level of usage. What can Paul do to best reduce these costs?

   A. Employ IPX watchdog packet spoofing. This will prevent the links from coming up unnecessarily.

   B. Configure an extended IPX access list, specifying both the source and destination address for the servers providing these services. This will allow for better management of the frequency of the ISDN dial-ups.

   C. Configure priority queuing, specifying a higher priority for the IPX traffic and also begin using header compression on the packets.

   D. Use encryption services. Because ISDN is a digital service, it makes better use of bandwidth when it is transmitting encrypted traffic.

10. Refer to the previous scenario. What allows the remote clients that are located on serverless networks to locate and use the services offered by the LAN servers?

   A. Previously applied access lists that help filter the internetworks' traffic

   B. Proxy ARP

   C. Novell GNS request proxy services, previously configured by Paul

   D. IPX Watchdog packet spoofing

   E. Novell GNS request proxy services, enabled by default

Pat is running IPX only on his Cisco 3600 series routers. He wants to enable encryption between two locations, so he plans to configure his local router for IPX encryption. However, when he discusses this plan with his coworker, Gene, a few problems arise. Answer questions 11 and 12 based on the scenario presented.

11. Refer to the scenario above. What are the two problems with Pat's plan?

    A. The required DSS key generation can't be performed over IPX-based links.

    B. IPX can't be encrypted in the Cisco IOS software.

    C. Cisco 3600 series routers don't support the VIP2 or ESA hardware necessary to perform encryption.

    D. Encryption is possible only if both the source and the destination routers have been configured to support it.

12. In the previous scenario, Pat's routers are humming along at a steady 60 percent CPU utilization rate. What is the utilization percentage threshold at which encryption should cease to be an option?

    A. 30 percent

    B. 40 percent

    C. 50 percent

    D. 60 percent

13. What are the three types of compression services available through the Cisco IOS software?

    A. Data, link, header

    B. Header, footer, start-of-address (SOA)

    C. Data, messaging, client/server

    D. Van Jacobsen, Lempel-Ziv, Diffie-Hellman

    E. Van Jacobsen, STAC, Predictor

    F. Link, serial, Frame Relay

14. Terry has a Cisco 4000-series router located in the company's Minneapolis headquarters and has a Frame Relay connection from Serial0 out to his carrier's Frame Relay cloud. There are additional remote offices in Green Bay, Wisconsin; Chicago, Illinois; Detroit, Michigan; and Tampa Bay, Florida, with similar Frame Relay connections into the cloud.

    Terry would like to enable header compression between the Minneapolis location and the offices in Chicago and Tampa Bay. He also wants to make sure that all Minneapolis/Chicago/

Tampa Bay packet headers are subject to this compression, but there should be no compression between Minneapolis and Green Bay or Detroit. Which options will he want to use?

A. IP Map compression/passive compression

B. Serial0 compression/passive compression

C. IP Map compression/active compression

D. Serial0 compression/active compression

15. What is defined by the following: The compression of both the header and data portions of the packet, using either the STAC or Predictor compression algorithms?

A. Payload compression

B. Header compression

C. Active compression

D. Link compression

16. Cisco recommends that software compression not be enabled if your router's CPU utilization is already above _____ consistently. Fill in the blank.

A. 40 percent

B. 60 percent

C. 65 percent

D. 70 percent

17. Weighted fair, priority, FIFO, and custom are all types of what?

A. Proxy services

B. Queuing services

C. Access lists

D. Compression services

Troy is the network administrator for AdLib LLC, an advertising agency based in Seattle. The network is a hub-and-spoke design, with headquarters in Seattle and regional sites in San Francisco, California; Houston, Texas; Kansas City, Missouri; Miami, Florida; Charleston, South Carolina; and Boston, Massachusetts. The main productivity application is based on a traditional IBM mainframe infrastructure, with all regions needing access to the mainframe. Fifteen customer service representatives (CSRs) are based at each regional office, and twice as many are located at the headquarters. Each of these CSRs uses Microsoft Office and a custom call-tracking application, designed specifically for the CSRs. Answer questions 18 to 20 based on the scenario presented.

18. Refer to the scenario above. The mainframe application is time sensitive, and Troy has been asked to help ensure that the traffic from this application gets through the WAN links as quickly as possible. The links are periodically congested. What is Troy's best option?

    A. Increase the WAN bandwidth to all regional offices to make sure this traffic gets through.

    B. Use FIFO queuing to boost the importance of this traffic.

    C. Deploy header compression services to make more bandwidth available for IP-based traffic.

    D. Configure priority queuing and assign SNA traffic to the high-level queue.

19. Refer to the previous scenario. How many CSRs will be using Microsoft Office in Seattle?

    A. 15

    B. 30

    C. 90

    D. 105

    E. 120

20. Refer to the previous scenario. How many users will be using the call-tracking application?

    A. 15

    B. 30

    C. 90

    D. 105

    E. 120

21. Cisco's custom queuing scheme uses a number of round-robin queues that can be configured for certain protocols and queue sizes. What are valid queue numbers for these queues? (Choose all that apply.)

    A. 0

    B. 1

    C. 6

    D. 16

    E. 17

SELF TEST ANSWERS

1. ☑ **C.** The PIX Firewall, with its dedicated security-based combination of hardware and software, is far and away the most secure solution for this demanding situation.

   ☒ **A,** Access lists, are likely insufficient protection in this situation, as are **B,** other firewalling feature sets implemented through the IOS software. **D,** the Cisco Centri Firewall, is a discontinued product and not available.

2. ☑ **D.** You need to have an access list for each type of protocol on each interface. Because each interface needs different types of packet filtering, you can't use the same access list on more than a single interface.

3. ☑ **D.** Each of the statements is valid.

4. ☑ **B, D, A, and C.** The point of the question is to properly order your access list from most granular to least specific. Therefore, begin with **B,** the single IP address; **D,** list the subnet; **A,** list the network; and finish with **C,** "deny all." Remember that the "deny all" statement isn't really necessary because it is implicit in every access list.

5. ☑ **B and E.** Mike knows that as soon as a new statement is entered from the IOS command line, the router will apply it immediately, and he wants to ensure that his statements are properly ordered and will deliver the results he wants.

   ☒ **A** is not a valid answer. **C** is incorrect because access lists *can* be created from the command line, and **D** is also incorrect—you can upload multiple file types via TFTP.

6. ☑ **C and D.** Both 100 and 179 are valid for his access list. He needs to create an extended IP access list to be able to specify both a port number (port 80 for HTTP traffic) and a source/destination addresses. The range for extended IP is 100–199.

   ☒ Both **A** and **B** are standard IP ranges, and **E** and **F** are valid standard IPX ranges.

7. ☑ **B.** Enabling IP helper addresses as part of proxy services will allow DHCP traffic to be forwarded by the router to the DHCP server on behalf of the client.

   ☒ **A,** manually assigning addresses, would be laborious and difficult to manage. **C,** bridging through the router, would allow the DHCP requests to reach the central office's DHCP server but would likely impact performance of the WAN link and the networks. **D,** NAT with a PIX, would allow her to use any set of IP addresses she desires, but it does not perform any address assignments.

8. ☑ **B.** Proxy ARP replies to clients with the MAC address of the local router interface to allow the client to communicate with the remote device.

☒ **A** and **C** both deal with IPX clients, and **D** deals with the forwarding of requests to specific preconfigured addresses.

9. ☑ **A.** The servers in the central office will likely need to send these watchdog or keepalive messages to the remote clients frequently. If there is no other data to transmit, the dial-up link is brought up unnecessarily simply to transmit these watchdog packets. Watchdog spoofing allows the local router to respond to the servers' inquiries directly without having to query the clients across the ISDN links.

☒ **B**, extended IPX access lists, won't help in this situation and doesn't control the frequency of DDR links. **C**, priority queuing, also won't help, although the header compression mentioned would reduce the amount of traffic transmitted—but not the frequency. **D**, encryption, does nothing to make better use of bandwidth.

10. ☑ **E.** Because the clients are on serverless LANs, the routers will, by default, assist in the Get Nearest Server requests on behalf of the clients.

☒ **A, B, C,** and **D** don't provide the functionality desired here.

11. ☑ **B and D.** IPX can't be encrypted in the Cisco IOS software; it needs first to be encapsulated in IP, and then the IP stream is encrypted. Also, both routers need to be configured as peer-encrypting routers; otherwise, the encrypted stream would never be able to be read.

☒ DSS key generation, **A**, is protocol independent because it occurs within the IOS software (the actual DSS key exchange *does* require the IP protocol, but this is well beyond the scope of this course). While it's true that Cisco 3600 series routers, **C**, don't support the VIP2 or ESA encryption hardware, they are not necessary for software-based encryption.

12. ☑ **B.** 40 percent is the threshold at which Cisco recommends no longer implementing encryption services.

13. ☑ **A.** Data, link, and header compression services are available.

☒ You may have chosen options **D** or **E**, but all of these items are algorithms, not actual compression services (Diffie-Hellman is also an encryption algorithm, not used in compression). **B** lists terms dealing with frame fields, **C** simply lists generic information technology terms, and **F** lists terms dealing with interfaces and WAN technologies.

14. ☑ **C.** Using an IP Map allows him to specify the IP addresses of the routers in Chicago and Tampa Bay but exclude Green Bay or Detroit from the compression plans. Active compression will compress all packet headers.

☒ Enabling compression on the Serial0 interface, **B** and **D**, will apply compression to all traffic flowing to and from the Frame Relay cloud. IP Map with passive compression, **A**, won't compress all packet headers as desired—only those previously compressed.

15. ☑ **D.** Link compression is the type of compression being described.

☒ **A**, payload compression, compresses only the data portion; and **B**, header compression, compresses only the header portion of the packet. **C**, active compression, refers to a *method*—not a *type*—of compression.

16. ☑ **C.** Cisco recommends that software compression not be enabled if your router's CPU utilization is consistently above 65 percent.

17. ☑ **B.** Weighted fair, priority, FIFO, and custom are all types of queuing services.

18. ☑ **D.** The best option is to configure priority queuing and assign SNA traffic to the high-level queue.

☒ **A**, increasing WAN links, is usually not the best option because there can be significant costs associated with this. **B**, FIFO queuing, doesn't boost traffic priorities at all—it simply passes packets on a first-come, first-served basis. **C**, header compression, would help reduce some traffic levels, but the traffic in question is SNA based (IBM mainframe), not IP.

19. ☑ **B.** Although this may seem like a ridiculous question, it *is* fair game on the exam. It demonstrates reading comprehension skills and being able to extract specifics from the customer's requirements. Again, expect this type of question, and make sure you reread the scenario carefully.

20. ☑ **E.** Fifteen users from each regional office and 30 from Seattle totals 120.

21. ☑ **B, C, and D.** The queues in question are numbered 1 through 16.

☒ **E**, there are 17 queues, but the first queue, **A**, Queue 0, is reserved as a system queue and cannot be configured as the others.

15

Building a Prototype of the New Network

Once you have completed your network design, it's time to prove that it works and meets all the customer's requirements (or otherwise). You don't want to wait until the network is fully implemented to find out. This is where building a network pilot or prototype is useful to prove to yourself and then the customer that your network design fulfills the requirements.

This chapter discusses the design of pilot and prototype networks and shows how to decide which is suitable for your design. It looks at the steps you need to take to develop a pilot or prototype sufficient to prove your design meets major customer requirement, and then examines the Cisco IOS commands that will help you determine if your design meets your customer's performance and scalability goals. Finally, it covers the actual demonstration to the customer and outlines ways of proving that your design is adequate for the customer's needs.

New Network Design

Once you have completed your network design, it is time to put this design to the test. Somehow you will need to test this design and then prove to the customer that this design meets requirements. You do this by building a demonstration network that will be used to test functionality, scalability, and performance and to illustrate these factors to the customer. The demonstration network must be designed with these requirements in mind and must be capable of adequately illustrating them to the customer.

The Size of the Network Structure Sufficient to Prove Its Adequacy with the Customer's Needs

You must decide how big the demonstration network must be to adequately prove to the customer that your design meets requirements. Identify the factors that are important to the customer and make sure that these can be demonstrated with your network design. Many factors will limit the scale of your demonstration network, but be mindful of the goals of the demonstration and make sure they can be achieved with the network you have built.

Creating a Testable Network with Limited Resources

In an ideal world, you could build the entire network, test it, and then demonstrate it before it was ever used in a production environment. Unfortunately, this will not be possible in most situations. In the real world, most of your resources will be in limited supply. These factors will serve to limit the size of your demonstration network:

- Budget
- Time
- Available skills
- Product availability

Should You Build a Prototype or a Pilot?   Your demonstration network will take the form of either a prototype network or a pilot network.

A prototype is an implementation of a portion of your proposed network sufficient to demonstrate that the network meets requirements. A pilot is used to demonstrate the basic functionality of your design, and can be thought of as a scaled-down prototype.

A prototype is a more comprehensive way of demonstrating your design but will be more expensive than a pilot. The expense might be justifiable in larger network designs but could prove unnecessarily costly for smaller designs. Make sure that the cost of implementing the pilot or prototype is proportionate to the cost of the network design. It is a cost-versus-need decision that you and the customer need to agree on.

For example, if you design a large network, the cost of building a prototype will be relatively small compared with the total cost of the project. In this case, a prototype would be the preferred option. However, if you have proposed a small network, a prototype might be considered expensive relative to the total project budget. In this case, consider a pilot. As a rule of thumb, if your network design is small, a pilot is likely to be suitable; if it is large, a prototype might be the better option.

What Equipment to Use?   As far as possible, use the same equipment in the pilot or prototype network that you will use in the final network. If it is not possible to use new equipment, make sure the equipment you use will have features and performance characteristics similar to those of the equipment you will finally use.

Additional tools should be considered purely for use in the prototype or pilot to make it as realistic as possible. Line simulators can be used in place of expensive WAN links, which might not have yet been purchased. Traffic generators can be used to simulate normal user traffic on the network. Decide which of these tools will be useful in your demonstration to make it as realistic as possible.

What Are You Trying to Prove?   It is important to remember that the ultimate goal of building the pilot or prototype is to validate your design to the customer. To do this, your demonstration network must prove that your network meets the customer's performance and scalability goals.

How to Prove It   The best way to prove your network works is to complete a successful demonstration of your design by running through a number of predefined test scripts on the test network with the customer present. Your demonstration will prove the requirements are met and highlight features that set you apart from the competition.

exam
ⓦatch

You must understand the seven tasks identified by Cisco to build a prototype to demonstrate the functionality of the network design.

Tasks Required to Build a Prototype to Demonstrate the Functionality of the Network Design

Complete the following tasks to build a network prototype that will prove that your design meets customer requirements:

1. Review the customer's requirements.
2. Determine the size of your prototype.

3. Investigate your competition's proposals.

4. Develop a test plan.

5. Purchase and configure the equipment.

6. Practice your demonstration.

7. Test and demonstrate your prototype.

Task 1: Review the Customer's Requirements   Chapter 7 and Chapter 8 discuss how to determine the customer's business and network requirements and how to translate these requirements into a design proposal. Review the results of the work you carried out during those chapters:

- Highlight the customer's major performance, security, scalability, and capacity requirements.

- Decide how you will prove these requirements are met during the demonstration.

- Highlight anything you want to avoid in the demonstration that might portray your design in a bad light.

Task 2: Determine the Size of Your Prototype   Decide how big your prototype needs to be to effectively illustrate that it meets the customer's major requirements. The network prototype needs to incorporate the core network hardware and software features of your network design. You will need to include the following major components of your network design:

- Hardware features
    - Routers
    - LAN and WAN media
    - File servers
    - Clients

■ Software features

　■ Routing protocol

　■ Routed protocol

　■ Cisco IOS features

　■ Applications

Also, consider the tools you might use to help you build the prototype. These may include router configuration tools, simulation tools, or testing software.

Task 3: Investigate Your Competition's Proposals   If you are lucky, you could get information on your competition's design from your account manager. Otherwise, you must make assumptions based on competitors' previous network designs, products they supply, and the customer's requirements. Evaluate their designs and, if necessary, amend your design to include any good ideas and be prepared to justify your design compared with others.

Task 4: Develop a Test Plan   When you develop a test plan, you need to actually design the topology of your test network. Draw a network diagram indicating major hardware components and important configuration parameters.

Draw up a list of all the hardware and software components you will need to build your network. Include items such as routers, switches, LAN media, WAN connections, modems, cables, workstations, servers, WAN simulators, and traffic simulation tools.

Identify any other resources that you might need, such as colleague assistance, documentation, Internet access, and presentation equipment.

List the tests and demonstrations that you will include. Indicate how these tests are important to

■ Prove the design meets customer requirements.

■ Display the strengths of the Cisco equipment you are using.

■ Show the superiority of your design over those of your competitors.

Task 5: Purchase and Configure the Equipment   Purchase and configure all hardware and software to meet customer requirements. The configurations you use should be as close as possible to those to be used on the live network.

Task 6: Practice Your Demonstration   Run through the demonstration with your colleagues before you do it in front of your customer. Ask for constructive criticism and amend your plan as necessary.

Task 7: Test and Demonstrate Your Prototype   Now it's time to test if your design meets your customer's requirements and to demonstrate your findings.

Tasks Required to Build a Pilot to Demonstrate the Functionality of the Network Design

You might decide to build a pilot if your network design is small or the relative cost of building a prototype is deemed to be too high. If you have decided that a pilot is sufficient to demonstrate your network design functionality, include the following steps in your plan:

1. Test your design.
2. Investigate your competition's proposals.
3. Write a test script for the demonstration.
4. Practice your demonstration.
5. Test and demonstrate your pilot.

Task 1: Test Your Design   Make sure that your pilot network is capable of meeting your customer's performance requirement. Ensure that response times are within the agreed-upon limits.

Task 2: Investigate Your Competition's Proposals   Find out what your competitors will be proposing, and use this information to promote your design over theirs.

Task 3: Write a Test Script for the Demonstration   Write a script of the tests and demonstrations that you will carry out. Indicate how these tests are important to

- ■ Prove the design meets customer requirements.
- ■ Display the strengths of the Cisco equipment you are using.
- ■ Show the superiority of your design over those of your competitors.

Task 4: Practice Your Demonstration   Run through the demonstration with your colleagues before you do it in front of your customer. Ask for constructive criticism and amend your plan as necessary.

Task 5: Demonstrate Your Pilot   Present your demonstration to the customer.

<table>
<tr><td>EXERCISE 15-1</td></tr>
</table>

New Network Design

GH Leisure is a large organization that owns five motor-racing circuits throughout the United Kingdom. It is responsible for promoting, organizing, and administering all events held at these circuits. Currently, its central administration center is located in the South of England at Gunner's Hill racing circuit, which is also used as a call center for spectator bookings. It has small local offices at each of the four remaining circuits. The main booking system is held at Gunner's Hill on an IBM mainframe, which uses SNA. Microsoft Windows NT servers used for e-mail and file and print services, along with a small SQL stock control system, are located at each site. A number of Apple Macintoshes are also scattered throughout the sites to be used for promotional design purposes. Each site is connected to the central site with Frame Relay.

In the immediate future, GH Leisure hopes to purchase the Swanlea motor-racing circuit, home to the largest event on the British motor-racing calendar and expecting about 100,000 spectators.

It has been decided that the current network structure is not adequate for the rapidly expanding company. Previously, all network segments and features were added as needed, with no overall network design. As the company grows, it is becoming apparent that wide area links are failing regularly, causing the smaller offices to be cut off from the central site. With the purchase of a much larger circuit imminent, GH Leisure is expecting a large increase in the amount of traffic. It has never had a problem with security in the past but recognizes that with increased media and public interest likely, its computer systems could generate more interest. Any security breach would be considered disastrous because it would be heavily publicized in the racing media.

Purchasing the new circuit and hosting such a high-profile event would depend on the company's ability to prove its business can adequately deal with the workload. The development of the network is seen as a key stage in its ability to do so.

Using the GH Leisure Case Study, carry out the following tasks:

1. Decide if you would consider a prototype or pilot network more suitable for demonstrating the functionality of your network design. Defend your choice.

2. List the customer's major performance, security, scalability, and capacity requirements.

3. You have decided to build a prototype network. Develop a test plan as indicated in task 4 of building a prototype network.

Answers to Exercise 15-1

1. The network design project outlined in the GH Leisure case study is an excellent candidate for a prototype network. The large sums of money likely to be involved, along with the importance placed on the network design project, would justify this method. Such a customer would likely have to be absolutely certain that the network design would meet its goals before considering implementing it. The ability to host the new event seems to be crucial for the company. Therefore, the need for a prototype justifies the cost.

2. The customer's performance goals are not explicitly defined in the case study text. It can be assumed that the performance needs to be comparable with current performance but accommodate the additional workload. It is up to you as the designer to determine the customer's specific performance requirements by talking to the customer. Monitor the current network performance to see what the company is used to. The customer has identified that Frame

Relay links sometimes fail, so you need to address this problem with a backup link (such as ISDN) or a change in the service provider.

Security has not previously been an important issue for the company, but it has stressed that this is no longer the case. You will need to incorporate stringent new security measures because the customer's systems will probably now be a target for attacks. Talk to the customer about where the sensitive information might be held or transmitted.

The obvious, immediate scalability issue is the integration of the new site if the purchase of the new circuit goes ahead. Because GH Leisure seems to regularly acquire new circuits, it is also sound practice to design the network to allow easy integration.

The new network design needs to efficiently deal with its current capacity. But with the purchase of the new site, the expected additional capacity must also be handled. You need to investigate the volume of traffic caused by the current workload and estimate additional traffic requirements by comparing it with the predicted workload.

3. To begin, draw a network diagram of your proposed network structure, indicating major hardware and software components. Identify which portions of this network you wish to include in your prototype, and draw up a list of all the hardware and software you will need. Develop a list of the customer's requirements for the network and identify how you intend to prove these are met during the demonstration. Also, decide how you will prove that your design is superior to the design of a competitor, and make sure to highlight the strengths of the Cisco equipment you are using.

CERTIFICATION OBJECTIVE 15.02

Cisco IOS Software Commands

After you have built the demonstration network, decide how you will test your network and gather performance information. Many of the tools on the market will help with this task; however, the Cisco IOS itself provides a host of useful features.

Commands Necessary to Determine the Network's Adequacy with the Customer's Performance and Scalability Goals

The Cisco IOS will be present on every Cisco router on your network. You can gain anything from simple connectivity tests to detailed traffic flow information from each one of these routers by using a combination of tools, show commands, and debug commands. Many of the commands can be used for a number of different tests. For example, the basic ping command can be used not only for simple connectivity tests but also to prove security and gain basic performance statistics.

The routers will be accessed by Telnet or direct console cable connection, and it is important to choose the most suitable router to run the test on. If you are connecting via a console cable, use a terminal emulation program (such as HyperTerminal) configured at 9,600 baud, 8 data bits, no parity, and one 1-stop bit.

Commands Necessary to Show That the Network Works

The commands listed in this section are the most useful for testing a demonstration network. *Show* commands display the status of certain processes on the router, and *debug* commands give far more detailed information but must be used with care. These are by no means all the show and debug commands available; a full list can be found in the Cisco IOS Command Reference.

Show Interface   The show interface command displays interface configuration and information on layer-2 errors. By using this command you can

- Verify the configuration of the interface.
- Check security by looking at applied access lists.
- Check for unexpected layer-2 problems.

```
bud2504#sh interface s0
Serial0 is up, line protocol is up
  Hardware is HD64570
  Internet address is 10.26.255.253 255.255.255.252
```

```
MTU 1500 bytes, BW 1544 Kbit, DLY 20000 usec, rely 255/255, load 1/255
Encapsulation HDLC, loopback not set, keepalive set (10 sec)
Last input 0:00:04, output 0:00:03, output hang never
Last clearing of "show interface" counters never
Output queue 0/40, 0 drops; input queue 0/75, 0 drops
5 minute input rate 2000 bits/sec, 2 packets/sec
5 minute output rate 2000 bits/sec, 2 packets/sec
   161 packets input, 15053 bytes, 0 no buffer
   Received 46 broadcasts, 0 runts, 0 giants
   0 input errors, 0 CRC, 0 frame, 0 overrun, 0 ignored, 0 abort
   160 packets output, 14811 bytes, 0 underruns
   0 output errors, 0 collisions, 2 interface resets, 0 restarts
   0 output buffer failures, 0 output buffers swapped out
   11 carrier transitions
   DCD=up  DSR=up  DTR=up  RTS=up  CTS=up
bud2504#
```

Show Buffers   The show buffers command displays usage information on each of the router's buffers, along with the number of buffer misses. This is a very useful command for characterizing your network traffic.

The router dynamically allocates buffers to store packets while it waits for the routing table lookup and other processing to complete. There are six buffer types capable of holding packets:

- Small (104-byte buffers)
- Middle (600-byte buffers)
- Big (1,524-byte buffers)
- Very big (4,520-byte buffers)
- Large (5,024-byte buffers)
- Huge (18,024-byte buffers)

Each buffer can hold only a limited number of packets at any one time. If a buffer is full and another packet it submitted to it, the router registers a buffer miss and tries to create a new buffer. This buffer creation process can be CPU intensive with many packets. If a new buffer cannot be created, the router drops the packet and registers a failure.

By using this command you can

■ Examine the number of hits to determine the most common packet size.

■ Determine causes of high CPU utilization by examining buffer creations.

■ Determine the causes of dropped packets through the buffer failures.

In the following example, you can see that the majority of packets hit the small buffer pool; therefore, the most common packet size is under 104 bytes. You can experiment with this command by using an extended ping with different-sized packets and then viewing the effects on the router's buffers.

```
bud2504#show buffers
Buffer elements:
     500 in free list (500 max allowed)
     352 hits, 0 misses, 0 created

Public buffer pools:
Small buffers, 104 bytes (total 50, permanent 50):
     50 in free list (20 min, 150 max allowed)
     164 hits, 0 misses, 0 trims, 0 created
     0 failures (0 no memory)
Middle buffers, 600 bytes (total 25, permanent 25):
     25 in free list (10 min, 150 max allowed)
     33 hits, 0 misses, 0 trims, 0 created
     0 failures (0 no memory)
Big buffers, 1524 bytes (total 50, permanent 50):
     50 in free list (5 min, 150 max allowed)
     9 hits, 0 misses, 0 trims, 0 created
     0 failures (0 no memory)
VeryBig buffers, 4520 bytes (total 10, permanent 10):
     10 in free list (0 min, 100 max allowed)
     1 hits, 0 misses, 0 trims, 0 created
     0 failures (0 no memory)
Large buffers, 5024 bytes (total 0, permanent 0):
     0 in free list (0 min, 10 max allowed)
     0 hits, 0 misses, 0 trims, 0 created
     0 failures (0 no memory)
Huge buffers, 18024 bytes (total 0, permanent 0):
     0 in free list (0 min, 4 max allowed)
     0 hits, 0 misses, 0 trims, 0 created
     0 failures (0 no memory)
```

```
Interface buffer pools:
TokenRing0 buffers, 4516 bytes (total 32, permanent 32):
        32 in free list (0 min, 48 max allowed)
        16 hits, 0 fallbacks
BRI0 buffers, 1524 bytes (total 4, permanent 4):
        3 in free list (0 min, 4 max allowed)
        3 hits, 0 fallbacks
        1 max cache size, 1 in cache
BRI0: B-Channel 1 buffers, 1524 bytes (total 16,
permanent 16):
        12 in free list (0 min, 16 max allowed)
        12 hits, 0 fallbacks
        4 max cache size, 4 in cache
BRI0: B-Channel 2 buffers, 1524 bytes (total 16,
permanent 16):
        12 in free list (0 min, 16 max allowed)
        12 hits, 0 fallbacks
        4 max cache size, 4 in cache
Serial0 buffers, 1524 bytes (total 32, permanent 32):
        15 in free list (0 min, 32 max allowed)
        193 hits, 0 fallbacks
        0 max cache size, 0 in cache
Serial1 buffers, 1524 bytes (total 32, permanent 32):
        15 in free list (0 min, 32 max allowed)
        17 hits, 0 fallbacks
        0 max cache size, 0 in cache
bud2504#
```

Show Processes   The show processes command displays information
about active processes on the router.

```
bud2504#sh processes
CPU utilization for five seconds: 0%/0%; one minute: 4%; five minutes: 3%
 PID QTy       PC Runtime (ms)    Invoked    uSecs    Stacks TTY Process
   1 Mwe  326E946         60          7     8571 2588/3000   0 RIP Router
   2 Lst  30DF80E        120          4    30000 1832/2000   0 Check heaps
   3 Mst  3107962          0          2        0 1764/2000   0 Timers
   4 Lwe  3162360          0          2        0 1760/2000   0 ARP Input
   5 Mwe  317BF86          4          1     4000 1776/2000   0 RARP Input
   6 Hwe  316DC30          0          3        0 3500/4000   0 IP Input
   7 Mwe  319746C          0         24        0 1652/2000   0 TCP Timer
   8 Lwe  3199238          4          1     4000 3752/4000   0 TCP Protocols
   9 Mwe  31E6022         12         17      705 1636/2000   0 CDP Protocol
  10 Mwe  31B0154        428        121     3537 3528/4000   0 IP Background
  11 Lsi  31C89BA          0          2        0 1856/2000   0 IP Cache Ager
  12 Mwe  3178964          4          1     4000 1584/2000   0 BOOTP Server
```

```
13 Cwe  30D4E66        0        1       0 1788/2000    0 Critical Bkgnd
14 Mwe  30D4D02       16        7    2285 1504/2000    0 Net Background
15 Lwe  31014F8        4        7     571 3740/4000    0 Logger
16 Msp  30F9DEC       72      111     648 1640/2000    0 TTY Background
17 Msp  30D4C24        0      113       0 1864/2000    0 Per-Second Jobs
18 Msp  30D4BBA       16      113     141 1508/2000    0 Net Periodic
19 Hwe  30D5094        0       12       0 1760/2000    0 Net Input
20 Msp  30D4C4A       28        2   14000 1868/2000    0 Per-minute Jobs
21 Mwe  326E498        4        2    2000 1552/2000    0 RIP Send
22 ME   31B6F18        4        6     666 1648/2000    0 IP-RT Background
23 M*         0     1088      113    9628 2268/4000    0 Exec
```

As can be seen from the preceding command output, total CPU utilization is presented over five-second, one-minute, and five-minute time periods. Each running process is shown along with the number of times it has been invoked and the length of time it has been using the CPU.

The optional cpu keyword will give detailed CPU utilization statistics on the router, and includes each processes utilization over five-second, one-minute, and five-minute time periods.

The show processes command can be used in a demonstration to prove the health of the router hardware. You can prove that the CPU can easily handle all the tasks required and that the correct processes are running.

Show Processes Memory Like the show processes command, the show processes memory command displays total router memory, memory used, free memory, and memory used by each process. Again, this command is useful to prove the health of your router and its ability to cope with future demands.

The following command output shows that router bud2504 has used only 1,249,348 bytes of a 18,456,284-byte memory.

```
bud2504#show processes memory
Total: 18456284, Used: 1249348, Free: 17206936
 PID  TTY  Allocated     Freed    Holding   Getbufs   Retbufs Process
   0    0      21744       300    1159856         0         0 *Init*
   0    0        156      7392        156         0         0 *Sched*
   0    0     924144    200528          0    567424     75456 *Dead*
   1    0       3452         0      14260         0         0 RIP Router
   2    0          0         0       2676         0         0 Check heaps
   3    0        252       252       2676         0         0 Timers
   4    0         92         0       2768         0         0 ARP Input
   4    0         92         0       2768         0         0 ARP Input
```

6	0	128	0	4804	0	0 IP Input
7	0	0	0	2676	0	0 TCP Timer
8	0	684	0	5360	0	0 TCP Protocols
9	0	2124	1280	3520	0	0 CDP Protocol
10	0	1432	0	6108	0	0 IP Background
11	0	0	0	2676	0	0 IP Cache Ager
12	0	708	0	3384	0	0 BOOTP Server
13	0	128	0	2804	0	0 Critical Bkgnd
14	0	5444	0	2768	0	0 Net Background
15	0	112	0	4788	0	0 Logger
16	0	4928	252	2676	0	0 TTY Background
17	0	0	0	2676	0	0 Per-Second Jobs
18	0	0	0	2676	0	0 Net Periodic
19	0	184	0	2860	0	0 Net Input
20	0	0	0	2676	0	0 Per-minute Jobs
21	0	104	76	2832	0	0 RIP Send
22	0	452	0	3128	0	0 IP-RT Background
23	0	812	0	5488	0	0 Exec

```
                              1249096 Total
bud2504#
```

Ping   The ping command is one of the most useful and commonly used tools of network technicians. It supports all major networking protocols, including IP, IPX, AppleTalk, and DECnet and is an echo reply test to verify that a network node can be reached. A ping request sends a message to a specified destination and requests that it respond with an echo response to indicate it is alive. Ping displays the minimum, maximum, and average round-trip delays, along with the number of successful attempts, as shown here:

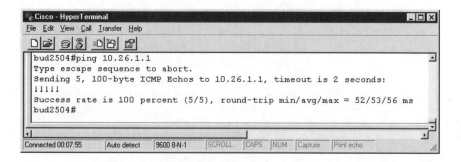

IP ping uses an ICMP echo request packet; that packet is sent to your remote node. If the remote node receives this request, it will return an

ICMP echo reply to your station. By default, five 64-byte echo requests are sent each time the ping command is run; you can alter these settings by using an extended ping, which allows you to modify the packet size, repeat count, and type of service. Another useful trick is to set the repeat count high and the timeout to 0, giving you a very simple packet generator.

Ping can be the most effective tool you can use to demonstrate your pilot or prototype network. It can be used to simply prove station-to-station connectivity and basic response times. It is also a useful tool to prove basic network security by failures caused by access lists.

Trace   Trace is similar to ping in proving network connectivity, but it also gives you other important information. The trace utility displays the route of the packet as it passes through the network to reach its destination, as shown in the following illustration. You can demonstrate an efficient routing system by tracing routes to different addresses on the network with expected results.

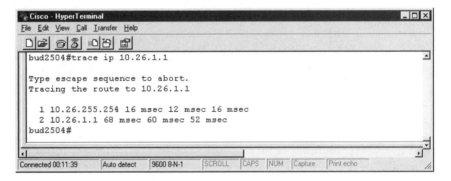

Trace works by repeatedly sending UDP packets to the same destination with its Time To Live (TTL) incremented by one each time it is sent. Each router will respond to the sending host with a "Timeout Exceeded" message when it receives the packet. Therefore, trace gets a response from every router it traverses, giving you a full route to the target system.

Although trace is a widely used and extremely useful utility, it sometimes gives incorrect routing results. Therefore, it should be treated as useful but not entirely accurate.

on the job

The ability of tools such as ping and trace to detect a network node will depend on a number of factors. It is quite possible for neither utility to detect a device that is functioning on the network as expected. The prime candidates for preventing these utilities from working are access lists. An ICMP filter could stop a ping from responding, or an UDP filter could prevent a trace. Therefore, it might be useful to try the other if one does not work. However, if you are satisfied that this is not the case, the lack of response could be due to a number of other possible causes. Assuming the device is functioning correctly with correct IP configuration and is wired to the network, the most likely causes of failures are line failures or routing problems. Remember that a ping is a two-stage process: a packet has to know not only how to get to the destination but also how to return to the sender.

Show *Protocol* Route   Each protocol running on your router has its own routing table. To view these tables use the show *protocol* route command. This will give you a full list of all the networks known to a router, the method it will use to get there, and the way it was learned.

```
cs# show ip route
Codes:  I - IGRP derived, R - RIP derived, O - OSPF derived
        C - connected, S - static, E - EGP derived, B - BGP derived
        * - candidate default route, IA - OSPF inter area route
        E1 - OSPF external type 1 route, E2 - OSPF external type 2 route
Gateway of last resort is 131.119.254.240 to network 129.140.0.0
O E0 150.150.0.0 [160/5] via 131.119.254.6, 0:01:00, Ethernet0
E    192.67.131.0 [200/128] via 131.119.254.244, 0:02:22, Ethernet0
O E0 192.68.132.0 [160/5] via 131.119.254.6, 0:00:59, Ethernet0
O E0 130.130.0.0 [160/5] via 131.119.254.6, 0:00:59, Ethernet0
E    128.128.0.0 [200/128] via 131.119.254.244, 0:02:22, Ethernet0
E    129.129.0.0 [200/129] via 131.119.254.240, 0:02:22, Ethernet0
E    192.65.129.0 [200/128] via 131.119.254.244, 0:02:22, Ethernet0
E    131.131.0.0 [200/128] via 131.119.254.244, 0:02:22, Ethernet0
E    192.75.139.0 [200/129] via 131.119.254.240, 0:02:23, Ethernet0
E    192.16.208.0 [200/128] via 131.119.254.244, 0:02:22, Ethernet0
E    192.84.148.0 [200/129] via 131.119.254.240, 0:02:23, Ethernet0
E    192.31.223.0 [200/128] via 131.119.254.244, 0:02:22, Ethernet0
E    192.44.236.0 [200/129] via 131.119.254.240, 0:02:23, Ethernet0
E    140.141.0.0 [200/129] via 131.119.254.240, 0:02:22, Ethernet0
E    141.140.0.0 [200/129] via 131.119.254.240, 0:02:23, Ethernet0
```

The show *protocol* route command is useful to prove that your routing protocols are working as expected. If you were having problems reaching networks, this would be the first place to investigate the problem.

Show Access-Lists   Access lists act as filters on network traffic, and are used for security and traffic management purposes. The show access-lists command will show all configured access lists on the router, along with details of how they are affecting network packets. The syntax of the command is show access-lists *access-list-number | name.* Simply using show access-lists will display all the configured access lists.

```
Router# show access-lists 103
Extended IP access list 103
    permit tcp host 208.92.32.130 any established (6109 matches)
    permit udp host 208.92.32.130 any eq domain (134 matches)
    permit icmp host 208.92.32.130 any
    permit tcp host 208.92.32.130 host 171.69.2.141 gt 1023
    permit tcp host 208.92.32.130 host 171.69.2.135 eq smtp (2 matches)
    permit tcp host 208.92.32.130 host 198.92.30.32 eq smtp
    permit tcp host 208.92.32.130 host 171.69.108.33 eq smtp
    permit udp host 208.92.32.130 host 171.68.225.190 eq syslog
    permit udp host 208.92.32.130 host 171.68.225.126 eq syslog
    deny    ip 150.136.0.0 0.0.255.255 224.0.0.0 15.255.255.255
    deny    ip 171.68.0.0 0.1.255.255 224.0.0.0 15.255.255.255 (2 matches)
    deny    ip 172.24.24.0 0.0.1.255 224.0.0.0 15.255.255.255
    deny    ip 192.91.152.0 0.0.0.255 224.0.0.0 15.255.255.255
    deny    ip 192.125.173.0 0.0.0.255 224.0.0.0 15.255.255.255
    deny    ip 192.125.174.0 0.0.0.255 224.0.0.0 15.255.255.255
```

In the preceding example, you can see the number of times a packet has been affected by each line of a specific access list by looking at the number of "matches." The access list is processed one line at a time and is exited when a match is found. An implicit deny all statement at the end of the list filters out any packets with no matches.

Show access-lists can be used to prove network security. After attempting to access restricted resources, you can use the show access-lists command to ensure the correct line of the correct access list filters the packet.

Debug   Debug commands give highly detailed information on events occurring on the router. By default, the output from this debug will be sent to the console, but it may be redirected to other destinations such as a syslog server or a monitor.

However, the debug commands place a heavy load on the router because they are assigned a high priority by the CPU. If the router is already struggling, enabling a debug might cause it to fail or cause performance to degrade dramatically.

The following output shows all IP packets passing through the router bud2504.

```
bud2504#debug ip packet
IP packet debugging is on
bud2504#
IP: s=10.26.1.1 (Serial0), d=10.26.255.253 (Serial0), len 50, rcvd 3
IP: s=10.26.255.253 (local), d=10.26.1.1 (Serial0), len 50, sending
IP: s=10.26.1.1 (Serial0), d=10.26.255.253 (Serial0), len 50, rcvd 3
IP: s=10.26.255.253 (local), d=10.26.1.1 (Serial0), len 50, sending
IP: s=10.26.1.1 (Serial0), d=10.26.255.253 (Serial0), len 50, rcvd 3
IP: s=10.26.255.253 (local), d=10.26.1.1 (Serial0), len 50, sending
IP: s=10.26.1.1 (Serial0), d=10.26.255.253 (Serial0), len 50, rcvd 3
IP: s=10.26.255.253 (local), d=10.26.1.1 (Serial0), len 50, sending
IP: s=10.26.1.1 (Serial0), d=10.26.255.253 (Serial0), len 50, rcvd 3
IP: s=10.26.255.253 (local), d=10.26.1.1 (Serial0), len 50, sending
IP: s=10.26.1.1 (Serial0), d=10.26.255.253 (Serial0), len 50, rcvd 3
IP: s=10.26.255.253 (local), d=10.26.1.1 (Serial0), len 50, sending
IP: s=10.26.1.1 (Serial0), d=10.26.255.253 (Serial0), len 50, rcvd 3
IP: s=10.26.255.253 (local), d=10.26.1.1 (Serial0), len 50, sending
```

The debug command can be very useful in a demonstration because it will allow suitably skilled people to see exactly what is happening on the router when sample traffic is sent.

Using Other Tools to Test a Prototype or Pilot

Although the Cisco IOS provides a comprehensive suite of tools for testing your network, you might want to consider some of the many other third-party tools and utilities for a variety of reasons. Many vendors provide more graphical front ends to their utilities, which might be more meaningful to less-technical customers. Some customers might be familiar with certain products and might be keen to see these being used during the demonstration.

Tools such as traffic generators and line simulators will be essential to simulate a realistic production environment. A traffic generator could be used to simulate traffic at different periods during the day. A line simulator can be used to demonstrate performance and reliability of different types of WAN links.

Define the Goals

After you learn what tools are available to test the network, you are in a good position to clearly define the results you will demonstrate. These goals are those previously defined by the customer, along with your own that will be used to determine whether the network "works." The goals can be divided into two categories: business and technical.

As a network designer, you are more likely to have technical goals, which are easier to define. You will be more interested in network throughput, efficient routing updates, and redundancy. The customer, although likely to be interested in such features, will be more interested in general business goals such as "ensuring that the network can be modified to meet future changes" or "guaranteeing availability at peak hours." It is up to you to decide how best to achieve these goals and prove that your design will do so.

You need to list these goals, prioritize them, and indicate the steps you will take to prove they are met. It is likely that some of these goals will be absolutely mandatory for the network to be successful, whereas others might be "nice-to-have" features that will make your design stand out from the competition. It's important to clearly distinguish between these types of goals in your documentation. All the goals you have defined should be clearly understood by everyone involved in the demonstration and must be documented for reference during the demonstration.

Determine Adequacy with the Customer's Goals   Once you have defined the performance, scalability, and security goals, test the network to determine if the goals have been met before you demonstrate to the user. Armed with a list of goals and ways to prove them, run the actual tests and record whether they pass or fail; and if they fail, note why.

Then you can amend your network design to ensure these goals are met before your customer demonstration.

During this predemonstration test, identify which goals are achievable, which are not, and the reasons some cannot be achieved. It might be impossible to meet a goal under the current budget or time scale. If this is the case, let the customer know and give advice on how the goal can be achieved.

CERTIFICATION OBJECTIVE 15.03

Demonstration to the Customer

After putting all the hard work into designing a scalable, secure, and robust network, use the demonstration as an opportunity to show your customers what a good design you have come up with. As outlined earlier, the three key goals of the demonstration are to

- Prove the design meets customer requirements
- Display the strengths of the Cisco equipment you are using
- Show the superiority of your design over those of your competitors

As with any demonstration, it is essential to pitch it at the right level for your target audience. Make the demonstration meaningful for as large a portion of the audience as possible. Avoid both talking down to people and being too technical in your discussion. As a network designer, you might be tempted to show off the clever technical aspects of your design, but this approach could lose or bore less technical people. You will do well to learn ahead of time which members of the audience are the decision-makers and tailor your presentation to them.

Professional presentation techniques are also essential. Regardless of how good your design might be, a poor-quality presentation will undermine your image and the customer's trust in you. Research how a presentation should be carried out, and if possible, get experienced colleagues' advice.

FROM THE FIELD

It is always a temptation to pitch your demonstration to people similar to yourself. After all, if you have spent a long time designing a network with many clever features, you want to let someone know about them. Unfortunately, the decision-makers of a company are often not the technicians or network designers, but the managers or directors. The prime concern of these people is that the network design they will be purchasing will fulfill their business needs. Although they will often listen to the advice of technicians and designers, it is the impression you make on them that counts.

The demonstration is all about meeting the customer's needs. Make sure the demonstration network can prove that you can meet the stated basic needs and mention features that you intend to include but that are not yet implemented.

I have seen many presentations of good products that fail because of a misunderstanding of the target audience or a failure to demonstrate salient points. Poorly designed networks, on the other hand, have been sold by presenters with polished sales techniques and an ability to tell customers what they want to hear.

Proving That the Network Works

As far as the customer is concerned, if the network meets the company's requirements, the network works. By this point, each of the customer's goals will have a related list of tasks to be completed. The customer should be reminded why each goal is important and should understand how the tasks you perform will prove it has been met.

Use practical demonstrations on the network where possible, and use Cisco command output to give more precise information. Actually running an application successfully across the network might prove a customer goal has been met. Backing this demonstration up with more precise statistical information (such as throughput and utilization) will always be beneficial. Not all goals can be proven through practical demonstrations. Some features will need to be explained verbally, particularly because your prototype is not likely to be fully functional. For example, fault tolerance might be tricky to prove if you are demonstrating with limited resources.

Be prepared to justify your decisions when other options are available.

Costs and Risks

Every component of your network design has an associated cost. Your customer is likely to need to know why you are recommending costly features over cheaper alternatives. Also, if your design is significantly more costly than your competitor's, you need to justify the difference. There is no point in trying to force a customer into accepting expensive options when other cheaper options are preferable. Ultimately, the customer will be constrained by a budget.

For example, a Cisco 2500 router might currently be adequate to service a branch office at the moment. However, the customer has indicated that in the future, mission-critical application servers are to be moved to this office. Therefore, you might recommend a Cisco 4000 or Cisco 7200 to service future needs, thus improving network scalability.

In another example, you could recommend ISDN backup on Frame Relay circuits. This solution has a significant cost (line rental, hardware, and configuration), but it also carries an associated risk if it is not implemented.

This is a cost-versus-need decision you must help a customer make.

Assessment of Costs and Risks

As the network designer, you must highlight the costs of each network feature, the benefit it will give, and the associated risk if it is not implemented. Draw up a variety of options for each feature, detailing the benefit each offers over the others, and list the associated costs. This list will give the customer more input into the design of the network and a better understanding of your design.

Some of the costs of your design will be simple one-off costs, such as the purchase of high-end routers, but others will be longer-term costs. Features such as backup ISDN lines or larger WAN links for future development will incur considerable monthly costs. Your customer will need to know the long-term costs of the network implementation, not just the immediate costs.

Eventually, the customer will decide what costs and risks are acceptable. It is your job to clearly explain these costs and risks, along with any viable alternatives.

QUESTIONS AND ANSWERS

A customer has asked me to demonstrate my proposed network design. Where do I start?	Decide if you need to build a prototype network or if a pilot might be sufficient. Your aim is to prove your design meets customer requirements.
Which type of demonstration network do I use? Should I use a prototype or a pilot?	The choice depends mainly on the size, complexity, and budget of the network design project. A pilot will tend to be more suitable for smaller, simpler networks for which cost is an issue. A prototype will be necessary for larger, more complicated networks with larger budgets. It is a cost-versus-need decision, and the cost of the network should be in proportion with the project budget.
What exactly is a prototype?	A prototype is an implementation of a portion of your network design sufficient to demonstrate that it meets customer requirements.
What exactly is a pilot?	A pilot demonstrates the basic functionality of your design. It can be thought of as a scaled-down prototype.
I have decided that a prototype will be more suitable. How do I start building it?	Follow the seven-task model that Cisco recommends to build a prototype that demonstrates the functionality of the network design.
I am in the process of building a prototype network and have used a traffic generator to simulate everyday traffic. I want to ensure that the routers I am using can deal with this traffic load. How can I go about this using Cisco IOS commands?	Show processes will give you information of the load placed on the processor. Show processes memory will give you information on memory utilization.
A router on the prototype network started performing badly after I placed simulated traffic on the network. Should I run debug IP to find the cause of the problem?	No because debug ip will place an even greater burden on your router's resources. If you have significantly increased the network traffic, it could be that your router is not powerful enough to cope. Start diagnosing the problem using show processes and show processes memory.
When testing the demonstration network, I have found that I can ping from node A to node B but not from A to B. What could the problem be?	Access lists might be causing the ping ICMP echo request or ICMP echo reply packet to be filtered on a router interface. Use show ip access-lists to determine if this is the case.

QUESTIONS AND ANSWERS

I cannot ping a device that I know is connected to the network. What could the problem be?	One of the routers you are crossing from the source node to destination node might not be able to find a route to the destination network. You need to look at the routing tables of the routers between the source and the destination. Use show ip route to display the router's routing table. Another problem could arise if an access list is filtering out the echo. Use show ip access-lists on each intermediate router to see if this is the case.
I have a good idea to give an additional security feature to the customer. Should I include these proposals in the network demonstration?	That depends on a number of factors. If your customer has identified a high level of security as a design goal, definitely include it because it would prove your design meets customer requirements. If not, you could include it if it might show that your design is superior to those of the competitors or if it showcases the features of the Cisco equipment you intend to use. In these cases, propose it to the customer as an option, explaining the associated costs and benefits.

CERTIFICATION SUMMARY

Building a demonstration network and presenting it to the customer is probably the most important task of your network design process. After all, the purpose of network design is to have it implemented for a satisfied customer. The demonstration stage is critical to see this happen.

Your demonstration network will take the form of either a prototype or a pilot, and its size will depend on the overall budget of the network design project and your customer's requirements. You will need to prove the adequacy of the network design using Cisco IOS commands and other third-party tools where necessary. It is crucial that your demonstration covers all the major customer requirements and is pitched at the appropriate audience. Let the decision-makers know the options they have as well as the costs and any potential risks associated with these options.

Ultimately, you want the customer to implement your design. Therefore, a professional demonstration is your opportunity to prove that your network meets customer goals and is superior to your competitor's design.

✓ TWO-MINUTE DRILL

❑ Your demonstration network will take the form of either a prototype or a pilot network.

❑ A prototype is an implementation of a portion of your proposed network sufficient to demonstrate that the network meets requirements.

❑ A pilot is used to demonstrate the basic functionality of your design and can be thought of as a scaled-down prototype.

❑ You need to perform seven tasks to build a prototype that demonstrates the functionality of the network design:

1. Review the customer requirements.

2. Determine the size of your prototype.

3. Investigate your competition's proposals.

4. Develop a test plan.

5. Purchase and configure the equipment.

6. Practice your demonstration.

7. Test and demonstrate your prototype.

❑ You need to perform five tasks to build a pilot to demonstrate the functionality of the network design:

1. Test your design.

2. Investigate your competition's proposals.

3. Write a test script for the demonstration.

4. Practice your demonstration.

5. Test and demonstrate your pilot.

❑ Make sure that the cost of implementing the pilot or prototype is proportionate to the cost of the network design.

❑ The ultimate goal of building the pilot or prototype is to validate your design to the customer.

❑ Show interfaces displays interface configuration and information on layer-2 errors.

❑ Show buffers is a very useful command for characterizing your network traffic.

❑ Ping supports all major networking protocols including IP, IPX, AppleTalk, and DECnet and is an echo reply test to verify that a network node can be reached.

❑ Show access-lists can be used to prove network security.

❑ The debug commands place a heavy load on the router.

❑ The show *protocol* route command is useful to prove that your routing protocols are working as expected.

❑ Trace works by repeatedly sending UDP packets to the same destination with its Time To Live (TTL) incremented by one each time it is sent.

❑ The show processes command displays information on active processes on the router.

❑ Show processes memory displays total router memory, memory used, free memory, and memory used by each process.

❑ Tools such as traffic generators and line simulators will be essential to simulate a realistic production environment.

❑ Draw up a variety of options for each feature, detailing the benefit it offers over others and the associated cost.

❑ Be prepared to justify your decisions when other options are available. Make sure you are aware of why you have made these.

❑ It will eventually be the customer who decides what costs and risks are acceptable. It is your job to clearly explain what these are and to offer any viable alternatives.

❑ List customer goals, prioritize them, and indicate the steps you will take to meet them.

SELF TEST

The following Self Test questions will help you measure your understanding of the material presented in this chapter. Read all the choices carefully because there may be more than one correct answer. Choose all correct answers for each question.

1. What is the first task you should perform to build a network prototype to demonstrate the functionality of the network design?

   A. Purchase and configure the equipment.

   B. Develop a test plan.

   C. Review the customer requirements.

   D. Determine the size of your prototype

2. Which of the following are major sections to include in a test script for demonstrating your network? (Choose all that apply.)

   A. Demonstrate end-to-end IP connectivity throughout the network.

   B. Prove that the design meets customer requirements.

   C. Display the strengths of the Cisco equipment you are using.

   D. Show the superiority of your design over those of your competitors.

3. You have designed a small network for a local company, which has asked that you demonstrate the basic functionality of its network, but it does not want to spend more than absolutely necessary. What do you recommend?

   A. Build a prototype network.

   B. Build the new network and test it. When you are satisfied, switch over from the existing network to the new network.

   C. Build a pilot network.

   D. Integrate the new design into the existing network segment by segment.

4. Which one of the following is not a major task you should complete when building a network pilot to demonstrate network functionality?

   A. Review customer requirements

   B. Investigate your competition's proposals

   C. Write a test script for the demonstration.

   D. Practice your demonstration.

5. When you are building a network prototype to demonstrate the functionality of the network design, which task immediately follows "investigate your competition's proposals"?

    A. Develop a test plan.

    B. Test and demonstrate your prototype.

    C. Modify your prototype to improve on the competition's proposals.

    D. Review the customer requirements.

6. Which of the following non-Cisco equipment would be useful to make your demonstration network as realistic as possible? (Choose two.)

    A. A line simulator

    B. Microsoft DHCP server

    C. A proxy server.

    D. A traffic generator

7. Which of the following commands are useful for determining the health of network routers? (Choose two.)

    A. ping

    B. show processes

    C. show route

    D. show processes memory

8. Which command gives the number of packets that have been blocked by the router?

    A. debug ip packet

    B. show access-lists

    C. show security

    D. trace

9. Which command uses the TTL field of UDP packets?

    A. ping

    B. show processes

    C. trace

    D. show processes memory

10. Which command can you use to find out the most common size of packets passing through your router?

   A. extended ping
   B. show packets
   C. show buffers
   D. debug ip

11. You are getting very slow response times across a 2501 router, which was recently upgraded from IOS 10.3 to 12.0. It appears that many IP packets are being dropped. Which is the first command you should use to diagnose the problem?

   A. debug ip
   B. show ip access-list
   C. ping
   D. show processes memory

12. Which of the following statements are true? (Choose all that apply.)

   A. During the demonstration you should make sure you thoroughly demonstrate every feature of your network.
   B. The ultimate reason for your demonstration is to prove that your network design is superior to those of your competitors.
   C. You must tailor your presentation for your expected audience.
   D. Each customer requirement should be addressed during the demonstration.

13. Which of the following must you achieve during your demonstration? (Choose all that apply.)

   A. Display the strengths of the Cisco equipment you are using.
   B. Prove the design meets customer requirements.
   C. Show the superiority of your design over those of your competitors.
   D. Prove the network can integrate with other technologies.

14. Which of the following are possible risks a customer could incur by choosing a Cisco 2500 series router over a Cisco 4000 series? (Choose all that apply.)

   A. Loss of network scalability
   B. Fewer features than a competitor's design
   C. No extended ping feature
   D. Fewer fault-tolerance options

15. Which of the following could be considered business goals? (Choose all that apply.)

    A. Ensure sufficient throughput at peak hours.

    B. Provide an infrastructure to gain an advantage over competitors.

    C. Improve the flow of information throughout the organization.

    D. Ensure sufficient fault tolerance between the central office and branch offices.

16. During your practice demonstration, you find that you cannot ping a device that you know is connected to the network. You try pinging other devices on that segment, and these do not reply either. However, these devices can all access a file server on the same segment. Which of the following would be a possible course of action?

    A. Use an extended ping to locate which router cannot route the packet any further. Then use debug ip rip on that router to determine routing protocol problems.

    B. Use an extended ping to locate which router cannot route the packet any further. Then use show ip route on that router to determine if that router has a route to the destination.

    C. Use a trace to locate which router cannot route the packet any further. Then use debug ip rip on that router to determine routing protocol problems.

    D. Use a trace to locate which router cannot route the packet any further. Then use show ip route on that router to determine if that router has a route to the destination.

17. Which of the following tasks should be completed during the customer review stage of building a prototype network to determine the functionality of the network? (Choose all that apply.)

    A. Highlight the customer's major performance, security, scalability, and capacity requirements.

    B. Decide how you will prove that these requirements are met during the demonstration.

    C. Ensure your proposal is superior to those of your competitors.

    D. Highlight anything you want to avoid in the demonstration that might portray your design in a bad light.

18. What command will give you information on layer-2 errors on a router's interface?

    A. show interface errors

    B. show errors

    C. debug errors

    D. show interface

19. Which of the following statements are true? (Choose all that apply.)

   A. Always use dial on demand ISDN lines as backup to Frame Relay circuits.

   B. Let the customer decide which features to implement based on associated costs and benefits.

   C. Inform the customer of any risks involved in any portion of your network design.

   D. Always choose a Cisco 4000 router over a Cisco 2500 for increased performance.

SELF TEST ANSWERS

1. ☑ **C.** "Review the customer requirements" is defined as the first task to be carried out when you are building a network prototype to demonstrate the functionality of the network design.
   ☒ **A** is incorrect because purchasing and configuring the equipment is the fifth task in the Cisco model. **B** is the fourth task, and **D** is the second task.

2. ☑ **B, C, and D.** The main reason for constructing the demonstration network is to prove that your design meets customer requirements. It is important to justify your decision to use Cisco equipment by highlighting the strengths of the equipment, and at the end of the day, if your competitors' designs also work, you must encourage the customer to favor your design.
   ☒ **A** is incorrect because although demonstrating end-to-end IP connectivity might be a specific customer requirement, it is not a major test goal for every network.

3. ☑ **C.** Building a pilot is a cost-effective method for proving the basic functionality of a network design. For smaller networks with limited budgets, a pilot is often the preferred method.
   ☒ **A** is incorrect because the cost of building a prototype would be high compared with the overall cost of the network design. The company has asked for only basic functionality tests and is concerned about unnecessary costs. **B** is incorrect because this would be a very expensive option. Two networks would be run side by side, allowing no reuse of the existing network infrastructure in the new design. **D** is incorrect because the network segments would not be tested at all before they are installed in the live environment. Also, certain end-to-end connectivity tests could not be conducted until the whole network is complete.

4. ☑ **A.** You would need to consider customer requirements when you carry out the first task, "test your design," but reviewing customer requirements is not identified by Cisco as being a major task when you are building a network pilot.
   ☒ **B** is incorrect because "investigate your competition's proposals" is the second task in the model. **C** is incorrect because "write a test script for the demonstration" is task 3. **D** is incorrect because "practice your demonstration" is task 4.

5. ☑ **A.** Developing a test plan is task 4 of the Cisco model to build a network to demonstrate the functionality of the network design. Investigate your competition's proposals is task 3.
   ☒ **B** is incorrect because "test and demonstrate your prototype" is step 7. **C** is incorrect because modifying your proposal to improve on the competition's proposals is not a step in the Cisco model. **D** is incorrect because "review the customer requirements" is the first task.

6. ☑ **A.** By using a line simulator, you can simulate expensive WAN links before they are implemented. **D** is correct because a traffic generator could be used to simulate normal daily network traffic, thus making the demonstration as realistic as possible.

    ☒ **B** is incorrect because Microsoft DHCP server will allocate only IP settings to clients. **C** is incorrect because a proxy server would be useful only for controlling access to the Internet or an intranet.

7. ☑ **B and D.** The show processes command gives detailed information on processor utilization and the processes it is running. This command can be used to determine whether this is acceptable for this router. In addition, the show processes memory command gives information on the total, used, and free memory of the router.

    ☒ **A** is incorrect because ping is used to determine if a network node is alive and reachable and does not indicate whether a router is healthy. **C** is incorrect because show route will display only the IP routing table of the router.

8. ☑ **B.** The show access-lists command will show all configured access lists on the router, along with details of how they are affecting network.

    ☒ **A** is incorrect because debug ip packet will show current IP packet information but will not show historical information or count packets being blocked. **C** is incorrect because show security is not a Cisco IOS command. **D** is incorrect because trace will trace the route of a packet to a given destination, not give any information on packets being blocked on the router you are using.

9. ☑ **C.** The trace command uses the UDP TTL timer to trace the route to a given network node. The TTL is incremented by one every time a UDP packet is sent, causing the next-hop router to return a "Timeout Exceeded" message.

    ☒ **A** is incorrect because ping uses UDP echo request packets. **B** is incorrect because show processes gives information on processes and processor utilization. **D** is incorrect because show processes memory gives information on router memory.

10. ☑ **C.** The show buffers command will give you information on router buffer utilization. There are several different buffers, each holding different-sized packets. By examining the most highly utilized buffer, you can get a good idea of the most common size of packets passing through the router.

    ☒ **A** is incorrect because an extended ping is a network connectivity test. It allows you to alter the size of the packets you are sending but cannot help you characterize network traffic. **B** is incorrect because show processes gives information on processes and processor utilization. **D** is incorrect because show processes memory gives information on router memory.

11. ☑ **D.** Upgrading an IOS from version 10.3 to 12.0 requires considerable additional memory. The show memory command will let you know if you have enough available memory to carry out routing functions for buffer utilization.

    ☒ **A** is incorrect because the last thing you want to do on a heavily loaded router is run a debug command. Debug commands place a great deal of stress on the router, which, in this case, would cause performance to worsen or the router to fail altogether. **B** is incorrect because although dropped IP packets could be caused by an IP access, in this case, the only thing that has changed on the router is the upgrade of the IOS. If the router was not dropping packets before the upgrade, nothing has changed to indicate it might be an access list problem. **C** is incorrect because ping could be used to prove that packets are actually being dropped but could not indicate why.

12. ☑ **C and D.** You must make sure you pitch your demonstration correctly so that it can be understood by your audience. **D** is correct because the main reason for the demonstration is to prove to the customer that your design meets the stated requirements.

    ☒ **A** is incorrect because your prototype or pilot might not yet support all the intended features. Many technical features might not be of interest to some members of the audience. **B** is incorrect because the ultimate goal of your demonstration is to prove that it meets customer requirements.

13. ☑ **A, B, and C.** You need to justify why you are proposing a Cisco network as opposed to any other brand. Proof that the design meets customer requirements is primarily what your audience will be looking for. Also, your competitors might fulfill the customer's requirements, but you need to show why your design is best.

    ☒ **D** is incorrect because although this might be a customer requirement or an advantage of your design, it will not always be the case.

14. ☑ **A and D.** A Cisco 4000 series router is modular and more powerful than a Cisco 2500 series router. Also, a Cisco 4000 router is modular and potentially has more interfaces than a 2500. Therefore, you have more options to increase fault tolerance if the need arises.

    ☒ **B** is incorrect because if your design has fewer features than a competitor's, the customer is not necessarily at risk. If the design meets requirements with either router, this feature should be recommended as an additional cost option. **C** is incorrect because extended ping is available on all Cisco routers.

15. ☑ **B and C.** It is a goal of the business that requires your network design as an enabling technology. Also, your network design will enable the improvement of information flow and might be part of this process, but this is a goal for the business as a whole.

    ☒ **A** is incorrect because it is a technical goal. You could prove this quite easily during a demonstration by simulating peak usage and measuring user throughput. **D** is incorrect because it also is a technical goal that can be met by purely technical means if you choose to implement a sufficient feature and associated hardware.

16. ☑ **D.** You can determine how far the packet is from the destination using trace. Then if you connect to this router, you can use show ip route to look at its entire routing table. It could be necessary to add a static route or reconfigure the routing protocol.

    ☒ **A** and **B** are incorrect because extended ping will not tell you how far the packet has progressed; it will just give a success or failure because it is a goal of the business that requires your network design as an enabling technology. **C** is incorrect because RIP is not necessarily the routing protocol you are using. Show ip route would be a simpler option even if RIP is used.

17. ☑ **A, B, and D.** You must understand the needs of the customer to be able to design a suitable network and you must be able to demonstrate that your network meets the customer's goals. It is quite possible that you will consider your prototype network not to be up to standard in a number of areas for a variety of reasons, such as limited time scales or budgets. You would obviously want to avoid emphasizing these during the demonstration.

    ☒ **C** is incorrect because you would investigate your competitors' proposals at a later stage (task 3) and then emphasize the superiority of your design during the demonstration (task 7).

18. ☑ **D.** The show interface command will give the configuration of a specified interface, its current status, and any layer-2 errors.

    ☒ **A** is incorrect because show interface errors is not a recognized Cisco IOS command. **B** is incorrect because show errors is not a recognized Cisco IOS command. **C** is incorrect because debug errors is not a recognized Cisco IOS command.

19. ☑ **B and C.** You must help the customer decide which design options are most suitable for the circumstances. This will be a cost-versus-need decision the customer will have to make. Also, if there any risks are involved in your network design, you must explain them and the reasons for them to the customer. Offer alternatives wherever possible.

☒ **A** is incorrect because ISDN backup is commonly used with Frame Relay but will not always be the best option given the customer's circumstances. **D** is incorrect because it would work out to be very costly. Most customers will be constrained by budget and would prefer to use a 2500 series where suitable.

A

About the CD

This CD-ROM contains a browser-based testing product, the *Personal Testing Center*. The *Personal Testing Center* is easy to install on any Windows 95/98/NT computer.

Installing the Personal Testing Center

Double-clicking the Setup.html file on the CD will cycle you through an introductory page on the *Test Yourself* software. On the second page, you will have to read and accept the license agreement. Once you have read the agreement, click the Agree icon and you will be brought to the *Personal Testing Center's* main page.

On the main page, you will find links to the *Personal Testing Center,* to the electronic version of the book, and to other resources you may find helpful. Click the first link to the *Personal Testing Center,* and you will be brought to the Quick Start page. Here you can choose to run the *Personal Testing Center* from the CD or install it to your hard drive.

Installing the *Personal Testing Center* to your hard drive is an easy process. Click the Install to Hard Drive icon, and the procedure will start for you. An instructional box will appear, which will walk you through the remainder of the installation. Installing the *Personal Testing Center* to the hard drive will create a program group for it in the Start Programs folder.

If you wish to run the software from the CD-ROM, follow the steps given above until you reach the point where you would select the Install to Hard Drive icon. Instead, click the Run from CD icon, and the exam will automatically begin.

To uninstall the program from your hard disk, use the Add/Remove Programs feature in your Windows Control Panel. InstallShield will run uninstall.

Using the Personal Testing Center

Whether you choose to install the *Personal Testing Center* to your hard drive or run it from the CD, it functions in the same manner. As described in the following sections, the *Personal Testing Center* runs inside an Internet Explorer 4 or 5 browser window, and offers a variety of options for saving your scores and reviewing your answers.

Managing Windows

The testing application runs inside an Internet Explorer 4 or 5 browser window. You should navigate from screen to screen by using the application's buttons, not the browser's buttons. We recommend that you use the full-screen view to minimize the amount of text scrolling you need to do. However, the application will initiate a second iteration of the browser when you link to an Answer in Depth or a Review Graphic. If you are running in full-screen view, the second iteration of the browser will be covered by the first. You can toggle between the two windows by pressing ALT-TAB, click the Maximize button to maximize the second window, or click the Restore Window button and arrange the two windows so they are both visible on the screen at the same time. The application will not initiate more than two browser windows, so you won't be left with hundreds of open windows for each Answer in Depth or Review Graphic that you view.

Saving Scores as Cookies

Your exam score is stored as a browser cookie. If you've configured your browser to accept cookies, your score will be stored in a cookie named History. If you don't accept cookies, you cannot permanently save your scores. If you delete the History cookie, the scores will be permanently deleted.

JavaScript Errors

If you encounter a JavaScript error, you should be able to proceed within the application. If you can't, shut down your Internet Explorer 4 browser session and relaunch the testing application.

Test Type Choices

With the *Personal Testing Center*, you have three types of tests to choose from: Live, Practice, and Review. Each test type will draw from a pool of over 280 potential questions. Your choice of test type will depend on whether you would like to simulate an actual Cisco Certified Design Associate exam (Live exam), receive instant feedback on your answer choices

(Practice exam), or review concepts using the testing simulator (Review exam). Note that selecting the Full Screen icon on Internet Explorer's standard toolbar gives you the best display of the *Personal Testing Center.*

Live

The Live, timed test type is meant to reflect the actual exam as closely as possible. You will have 120 minutes in which to complete the exam. You will have the option of skipping questions and returning to them later, moving to the previous question, or ending the exam. Once the timer has expired, you will automatically go to the scoring page to review your test results.

Practice

When choosing the Practice exam, you have the option of receiving instant feedback as to whether your selected answer is correct. The questions will be presented to you in numerical order, and you will see every question in the available question pool for each section you chose to be tested on.

The Practice exam gives you the option of seeing the correct answer after you've answered a question by clicking the Answer icon. The number of questions you answered correctly, along with the percentage of correct answers, will be displayed during the post-exam summary report.

You can end the Practice exam at any time, but your post-exam summary screen may reflect an incorrect percentage based on the number of questions you failed to answer. Questions that are skipped are counted as incorrect answers on the post-exam summary screen.

Review

During the Review exam, you will be presented with questions similar to those in both the Live and Practice exams, except that the Answer icon will not be present and every question will have the correct answer posted near the bottom of the screen. However, if you wish, you can choose to answer a question without looking at the correct answer. The Review exam allows you to return to previous questions and skip to subsequent questions, as well as to end the exam by clicking the Stop icon.

The Review exam is recommended when you have already completed the Live exam once or twice, and would now like to find out which questions you answered correctly.

Answers in Depth

For the Practice and Review exam types, you will have the option of clicking a hyperlink titled Answers in Depth, which will present relevant study material aimed at exposing the logic behind the answer in a separate browser window. By having two browsers open (one for the test engine and one for the review information), you can quickly alternate between the two windows while keeping your place in the exam. Additional windows are not generated as you follow hyperlinks throughout the test engine.

Scoring

The *Personal Testing Center* post-exam summary screen, called "Benchmark Yourself," displays the results for each section you chose to be tested on, including a bar graph, similar to the one in the real exam, that displays the percentage of correct answers. You can compare your percentage to the actual passing percentage for each section. (Note, however, that the passing percentage displayed on the post-exam summary screen is not the actual percentage required to pass the exam.) You'll see the number of questions you answered correctly compared to the total number of questions you were tested on. If you choose to skip a question, it will be marked as incorrect. Ending the exam by clicking the End button with questions still unanswered lowers your percentage, as these questions will be marked as incorrect.

Clicking the End button and then the Home button allows you to choose another exam type or test yourself on another section of the exam.

CISCO CERTIFIED DESIGN ASSOCIATE

Glossary

10Base2   Also called *thinnet*. This naming refers to the thin coaxial cabling used with 10Base2. The cabling is classified as RG-58, and as the name implies, it is thinner than the original thicknet. Like its cousin, 10Base2 requires the cable to be terminated with a 50-ohm terminator. However, the AUI and MAU functionality from 10Base5 are integrated into 10Base2 network interface cards (NICs). Thinnet is more flexible than thicknet and easier to install and route through designated cable runs. Thinnet is also probably the least expensive of all the cabling options, with thicknet being a bit more expensive because of the additional thickness of the wire used. *See also* Thin Ethernet.

10Base5   Also called *thicknet*. 10Base5 is the original 802.3 specification standardized by the Institute of Electrical and Electronics Engineers (IEEE). It states a maximum collision domain of 2,500 meters with five segments, four repeaters, and three of the segments populated. Each segment may be up to 500 meters long and may have up to 100 attachments (via cable drops) per segment. 10Base5 uses a bus network topology with each device connected along the backbone cable. *See also* Thick Ethernet.

10BaseF   10BaseF is a newer specification than either thicknet or thinnet, but in today's environments of 100-Mbps and 1000-Mbps connections, it seems a bit outdated. The original standard for using fiber-optic cabling with Ethernet was the Fiber-Optic InterRepeater Link (FOIRL) specification. 10BaseF is based on this original FOIRL specification and includes 10BaseFP, 10BaseFB, 10BaseFL, and a newer version of the FOIRL standard. When you are designing your networks and choosing to implement a fiber-based cable plant, why run your network at 10 Mbps when you can go much faster? 10BaseF uses dual strands of either 62.5 or 125 µm multimode or single-mode fiber-optic cabling.

10BaseT   10BaseT provides for a maximum collision domain of 2,500 meters with five segments, four repeaters, and three of the segments populated. Each one of these segments may be up to 100 meters in length. 10BaseT uses the star network topology and permits two devices attached to each segment (the hub or repeater, and the end node). 10BaseT allows a maximum round-trip propagation delay of 51.2 µs; the bit time is 0.1 µs (microseconds).

100BaseFX   100BaseFX, the specification that introduces the use of fiber-optic cabling to Fast Ethernet, is based on the 10BaseF standard. The collision domain limitations and segment lengths vary greatly depending on the devices connected, the types of cabling used (multimode or single mode), and whether it is run in full duplex or half duplex. With multimode fiber, 100BaseFX repeater segment lengths are typically 216 to 320 meters, and switch-to-switch and switch-to-node segments can be up to 412 meters in length. They can be extended up to 2,000 meters when switched connections are run in full-duplex mode. Connections of 10km or more are feasible when the higher-grade single-mode fiber is used in full-duplex mode.

100BaseT   100BaseT has much more restrictive requirements than does 10BaseT. The maximum collision domain allowed here is 205 meters with unshielded twisted-pair (UTP) cabling because of the tenfold increase in the speed of the data transmission. Repeater definitions have also been revised to address the requirements of a 100BaseT environment. This is the result of the work done by a subset of the Institute of Electrical and Electronics Engineers (IEEE) 802.3 standards body, which has designated Fast Ethernet as 802.3u. 100BaseT typically utilizes UTP cabling and uses two of these pairs: one for transmission of data and one for receiving. When used in a switched environment, 100BaseT can be operated in full-duplex mode, virtually ensuring full 100-Mbps speeds in each direction.

AAL   *See* asynchronous transfer mode adaptation layer.

ABR   *See* available bit rate.

access control list (ACL)   In a network, a database with valid users and an allowed access level for each user.

access layer   The access layer provides a way for users to come into contact with the network. LAN switches at this layer segment the LAN to avoid too many collisions on Ethernet or to reduce the number of nodes requiring the token on Token Ring. This layer may also include banks of modems or ISDN equipment for remote users to dial into. Also, the access layer provides the connection point for users and workgroups to network resources.

access lists   Access lists are packet filters that define a set of criteria used by the router when it examines the packets passing through its interfaces. The router uses these lists to determine whether to forward the packet or block it based on the rules defined in the access lists. All routed protocols can be controlled in this way, with separate access lists required for each type of protocol.

accounting management   This helps define the costs of running various parts and services of the network. It is used to measure the amount of resources consumed and may be used for billing purposes.

acknowledgment (ACK)   The communications protocol, which acknowledges the transmission receipt.

ACL   *See* access control list.

active compression   Active compression will compress every outgoing packet header.

active monitor   One node within a Token Ring environment is designated as the active monitor. This node functions as a central timing source for the ring and performs other ring maintenance activities.

adaptability   Adaptability is defined as the ability of a network to support future technologies. Networking standards should be followed whenever possible. Budget is a business issue that can have an impact on a network's ability to adapt to new technologies.

adaptive security algorithm (ASA)   Cisco's algorithm used to ensure the maximum in security, and cut-through proxy, used for authentication and authorization, allow the PIX to deliver outstanding performance to more than 16,000 simultaneous connections.

Address Resolution Protocol (ARP) An Internet Protocol (IP) that maps Internet addresses dynamically to the actual addresses on a local area network (LAN). Internet Protocol (IP-based) clients use ARP to resolve a Media Access Control (MAC) address to an IP address. Routers running proxy ARP will respond to the client's ARP query with the router's MAC address. Cisco routers run proxy ARP by default.

adjacencies database This database is a list of all the neighbors with which a router has bidirectional communication.

ADSP *See* AppleTalk Data Stream Protocol.

Advanced Peer-to-Peer Networking (APPN) Meant to be a replacement for a Systems Network Architecture (SNA), this type of network architecture permits the creation of dynamic routing across various network topologies.

Advanced Program-to-Program Computing (APPC) This permits internetwork communication by creating the conditions within the Systems Network Architecture (SNA) and involves LU6.2 and its associated protocols without a common host system or terminal emulation.

Advanced Research Projects Agency Network (ARPANet) A wide area network (WAN) supported by the U.S. Defense Advanced Research Projects Agency (DARPA) and intended to support advanced scientific research.

AFP *See* AppleTalk Filing Protocol.

API *See* application programming interface.

APPC *See* Advanced Program-to-Program Computing.

Apple Update-based Routing Protocol (AURP) As the name implies, AURP is a routing protocol that only passes along updates to the routing table. AURP is also a distance vector protocol, but it broadcasts changes only to a routing table, reducing the amount of traffic being processed across the WAN link and thus increasing performance. AURP does not, however, replace Routing Table Maintenance Protocol (RTMP) as the routing protocol of choice in a LAN environment because AURP can be implemented only on "tunnel" interfaces that run across an IP network. The AURP protocol takes all traffic and encapsulates it into an Internet Protocol (IP) packet for transmission across the tunnel. Once it reaches the other end, it is unencapsulated back into its original form.

AppleTalk The AppleTalk protocol suite was developed by Apple Computer for use in its Macintosh line of personal computers. AppleTalk is a local area networking system that was developed by Apple Computer, Inc. AppleTalk networks can run over a variety of networks that include Ethernet, FDDI, and Token Ring, as well as Apple's proprietary media system LocalTalk. Macintosh computers are very popular in the education and art industries, so familiarity with the way they communicate using their native protocol is very useful.

AppleTalk Data Stream Protocol (ADSP) ADSP is used for application-to-application data transfer. It provides a reliable bidirectional transport over DDP.

AppleTalk Filing Protocol (AFP) AFP is used to find and manipulate files on hosts using the AppleShare file sharing software.

application layer This layer (layer seven) contains the actual applications running on the workstations and servers.

application programming interface (API) A means by which an application gains access to system resources, usually for the purpose of communication (sending and receiving data), data retrieval, or other system services. In the specific area of terminal emulation, an API provides for the simulation of keystrokes and for writing into and reading from the presentation of space (device buffer). It may also provide for sending and receiving structured fields.

application-specific integrated circuit (ASIC)   A processing chip designed for multiple functions. Though this chip allows for optimized performance because it was set during manufacturing, it does not use its memory efficiently.

APPN   *See* Advanced Peer-to-Peer Networking.

Area   A group of contiguous networks and attached hosts that are specified to be an area by a network administrator or manager.

ARP   *See* Address Resolution Protocol.

ARPANet   *See* Advanced Research Projects Agency Network.

AS   *See* autonomous system.

ASA   *See* adaptive security algorithm.

ASIC   *See* application-specific integrated circuit.

Asymmetrical Digital Subscriber Line (ADSL)   As its name implies, ADSL provides a higher downstream speed than upstream speed. Because aggregate throughput is lower than that for a symmetrical transmission of the same speed, ADSL produces less crosstalk and is easier for telephone companies to implement. ADSL also allows telephone companies to continue providing the Plain Old Telephone System (POTS) on the same circuit by providing a splitter box at the customer premise. ADSL can operate at up to 8 Mbps downstream, but performance is typically guaranteed at one speed and capped at another, higher speed. Upstream speeds are typically capped at one-third of the downstream speed.

asynchronous transfer mode (ATM)   A transmission protocol that segments user traffic into small, fixed-size cells. Cells are transmitted to their destination, where the original traffic is re-assembled. During transmission, cells from different users are intermixed asynchronously to maximize utilization of network resources.

asynchronous transfer mode adaptation layer (AAL)   Layer 3 of the asychronous transfer mode (ATM) architecture. Adapts user traffic into and from ATM 48-byte payloads. Five levels exist: AAL1, AAL2, AAL3, AAL4, and AAL5.

ATM   *See* asynchronous transfer mode.

attachment unit interface (AUI)   Another legacy of 10Base5 is the AUI, a female 15-pin connector with a sliding latch. This interface is also called DB15 and may be found on old network interface cards (NICs) and many Cisco routers, such as the 2501.

AUI   *See* attachment unit interface.

AURP   *See* Apple Update-based Routing Protocol.

auto-negotiation   Auto-negotiation allows the network interface card (NIC) to automatically detect and negotiate the fastest possible speed, based on the connection at the other end of the cable. If the NIC senses a switched connection, it will attempt to configure itself for a full-duplex connection. If the NIC detects a hub at the other end, it will set itself for a half-duplex connection. The Cisco 2900 series switches support dual-speed connections and will auto-configure each port to the appropriate speed based on the capabilities of the attached device.

autonomous switching   Autonomous switching offers faster packet switching because the CiscoBus controller is allowed to switch packets independently without interrupting the system processor. An incoming packet here matches an entry in the autonomous-switching cache located on the interface processor. This type of switching is available only on Cisco 7000 series routers and in AGS+ systems with high-speed network controller cards.

autonomous system (AS)   Part of the Internet layer that routers use to relate to network connectivity and packet addressing. The router checks the network address and only routes on the host address if the source and destination are on the same network.

autonomous system (AS) number   The AS number identifies routers that belong within an internetwork. This number must be the same on all routers across the internetwork in order for the systems to communicate and share routing information.

availability   Availability is the amount of time the network is accessible to its users. You should acquire information about the existing network's downtime, cost of downtime, and average downtime.

available bit rate (ABR)   One of five Asynchronous Transfer Mode (ATM) forum–defined service types. Supports variable bit rate (VBR) data traffic with flow control, a minimum guaranteed data transmission rate, and specified performance parameters.

backbone   In a wide area network (WAN) such as the Internet, a high-speed, high-capacity medium that is designed to transfer data over hundreds or thousands of miles and connect usually shorter, slower circuits. A variety of physical media are used for the backbone services, including microwave relays, satellites, and dedicated telephone lines.

backplane   The backplane of a device may represent a particular layer itself or the demarcation point between layers. A layer may even be skipped in a particular implementation, although the hierarchy should be observed for performance and scalability reasons.

backup designated router (BDR)   The BDR accomplishes the same thing if the designated router (DR) fails.

basic rate interface (BRI)   BRI format (the most common format) is made up of two 64-Kbps B channels, used for data or voice, and one 16-Kbps D channel, used by the carrier for control and signaling. Each B channel can be used to make a second connection, or the channels can be used together. This allows for the user to make a data connection to the Internet or to a corporate local area network (LAN) and use the other channel for voice. When the second channel is not needed for voice, it may be used to double the amount of bandwidth available for data. It is also possible to configure both B channels to connect at all times or only when bandwidth requirements dictate.

bastion host   Bastion hosts are secured hosts that external users need to access. They typically provide only a limited number of applications or services. Examples of a bastion host are a Web server, e-mail server, or Domain Name System (DNS) server.

BDR   *See* backup designated router.

beaconing   Token Ring networks possess a fault-tolerance characteristic known as *beaconing*. Because of the dependence on each attached node to perform its job in passing the token, a failed node or multistation access unit (MSAU) could halt all traffic on a token-based network. Beaconing addresses this potential shortcoming by detecting and working to repair these failures. Essentially a Token Ring algorithm, beaconing works by broadcasting a beacon frame onto the network after detecting a failure at a neighboring node. This frame will continue around the network, initiating an automatic reconfiguration of the network to account for the failed node or MSAU. As a result, traffic can return to normal by routing itself around the failed component. Most MSAUs can perform this function internally, segmenting off and disabling a failed port.

beatdown   Beatdown occurs when the retransmission of information becomes an additional source of congestion, preventing new traffic from using the circuit at all and needlessly increasing load on the retransmitting machines.

B-ISDN   *See* Broadband Integrated Services Digital Network.

BOOTP   *See* Bootstrap Protocol.

Bootstrap Protocol (BOOTP)   A Transmission Control Protocol/Internet Protocol (TCP/IP) network protocol that lets network nodes request configuration information from a BOOTP server node.

Border Gateway Protocol (BGP)   BGP is the primary routing protocol used throughout the Internet by Internet service providers (ISPs) to connect enterprise networks. BGP is known as an interdomain routing protocol that guarantees loop-free operation and exchange of routing information between different autonomous systems. BGP is defined in detail in Request for Comments (RFCs) 1163, 1267, 1654, 1772, and 1930.

border session   *See* External Border Gateway Protocol; Internal Border Gateway Protocol.

bottlenecks   A bottleneck is the point at which network traffic slows down to contend for limited bandwidth. You should determine whether there are any potential bottlenecks on the existing network. If there are, they should be addressed in the new network design. A protocol analyzer like Network Associates' Sniffer will help you discover potential bottlenecks.

BRI   *See* basic rate interface.

bridge   Bridges are devices that improve efficiency by physically splitting the network up into two smaller collision domains. The bridge then watches its interfaces and takes note of which MAC addresses can be found on which networks. A frame arriving at the bridge is matched to the MAC table. Bridges operate on layer 2 of the Open Systems Interconnection (OSI) model, which is the data-link layer. When a bridge first activates and receives a frame, it floods it out all its physical interfaces except the interface the frame came through. In addition, the bridge will take note of the transmitting node, and from that point on, whenever a frame comes through the bridge, it will know which interface to send it out to reach its destination.

Broadband Integrated Services Digital Network (B-ISDN)
B-ISDN provides the backbone telephone network with the same sort of upgrade that N-ISDN provides to the local copper loop. B-ISDN utilizes Synchronous Optical NETwork (SONET) rings as the physical layer, at speeds ranging from OC-3 to OC-12. B-ISDN shares D channel signaling protocols with N-ISDN but uses ATM instead of Point-to-Point Protocol (PPP) as its data-link layer. B-ISDN connections are not rigidly channelized, but rather rely on ATM VCCs to provide traffic management.

broadcast radiation   Broadcast radiation is the term used to describe how broadcast traffic on a network radiates outward from the originator to all other nodes on all parts of a flat network.

broadcast storm   A chattering network interface card (NIC) does not listen for other traffic, pays no attention to the collisions that it causes, and transmits more or less constantly. This creates a condition known as a broadcast storm, making network communications nearly impossible to maintain. Broadcast storms may also be caused by misconfigured software, but the effect is the same.

budgets   Budgets are usually expressed in two different ways: The first method sets a budget for the entire project, while the second method sets independent budgets for each section of the project. When the budget is set for the entire project, it is up to you as the consultant to prioritize where the money should be spent to achieve the business goals of the new network.

bus topology   A bus topology connects all stations to a cable running the length of the network. The bus physically connects all nodes by means of cables that run between devices, but cables do not pass through a central controller mechanism. The advantage of this network topology is the use of Carrier Sense Multiple Access with Collision Detection (CSMA/CD).

Carrier Sense Multiple Access with Collision Detection (CSMA/CD)   In a local area network (LAN), a network transmission method in which the network randomly decides which computer can use the network. This method is employed by small-sized to medium-sized networks. Larger networks use token passing or polling.

CDDI *See* Copper Distributed Data Interface.

CEF *See* Cisco Express Forwarding.

central office (CO) The nearest office to the user's facility telephone switching office that serves private and corporate users to their own loop lines.

channel service unit *See* data service unit/channel service unit.

chattering Chattering is a condition caused by a malfunctioning network interface card (NIC) and refers to a NIC that won't be quiet. A chattering NIC does not listen for other traffic, pays no attention to the collisions that it causes, and transmits more or less constantly.

CIR *See* committed information rate.

Cisco Express Forwarding (CEF) CEF is a Cisco-patented technique for very quick packet switching via large networks and the Internet. CEF depends on a forwarding information base (FIB), which allows CEF to be less processor intensive than other layer-3 switching methods because FIB routing tables contain all the forwarding information for all routes.

CiscoConnect Provides connectivity to Cisco and Cisco partners with debugging information, configurations, and topology information to speed troubleshooting and resolution of network problems.

CiscoView The standard graphical device-management tool for managing Cisco devices. Provides dynamic status, statistics, troubleshooting, and comprehensive configuration information for switches, routers, access servers, concentrators, and adapters. It is also available as a stand-alone product.

CiscoWorks CiscoWorks network management application suite provides automatic data collection and e-mail reporting to Cisco or to a Cisco partner for support. Providing this functionality automates the sometimes lengthy and difficult process of gathering diagnostic information before troubleshooting begins. CiscoWorks is a comprehensive suite of integrated management tools designed to simplify the administration and maintenance of small-to-medium business networks or workgroups.

CiscoWorks Blue Maps   CiscoWorks Blue Maps enables the network administrator to address the complex and wide range of requirements in integrated IBM Systems Network Architecture (SNA) and Internet Protocol (IP) environments. It provides the ability to create and view logical, dynamic color-coded network maps of Cisco routers, enabled with certain SNA protocols. Now referred to as simply CiscoWorks Blue.

cloud-based connectivity   Cloud-based connectivity is a different method of connecting your networks. It appeared quite a while ago when people realized that a point-to-point link was not the cheapest way to interconnect networks. The main idea of these types of connections is that people connect their equipment to a local public carrier network, and the carrier service provider takes care of transmitting the frames among different sites.

CO   *See* central office.

collision   Collisions occur when two or more devices think that no other devices are using the local area network (LAN), so they start to transmit data. It is possible for two nodes to transmit at the same time, which would result in a collision. A collision makes a transmitting station on the bus stop, wait for a random number of milliseconds, and attempt to transmit again. The concept of collision detection may be clearer if you think of the Ethernet bus in electrical terms. When no stations are transmitting, the bus is in a zero state. When one station transmits, the bus is in a one state. When two stations transmit at the same time, the bus is in a two state, which signals all stations that a collision has occurred.

Command Terminal (CTERM)   This is the terminal emulation protocol of DNA. CTERM uses DECnet to provide a command terminal connection between DEC terminals and DEC operating systems such as VMS and RSTS/E.

committed burst size (Bc)   It determines the maximum number of bits on a virtual circuit guaranteed to be transmitted over a certain time period (committed rate measurement interval, or Tc), assuming they are received contiguously by the Frame Relay switch. The sum of the individual Bc values for all virtual circuits on the stream should be less than or equal to the physical link speed. Bc is a configurable parameter and is usually computed as Bc equals the average number of bits per frame multiplied by the average number of frames per transmission.

committed information rate (CIR)   The maximum guaranteed throughput for a Frame Relay line. In other words, if you pay for a 128KB line, you'll get 128KB throughput. Because the same circuit within the cloud may service more than one customer's Frame Relay circuit, there will be times when everyone tries to transmit at the same time, and the physical bandwidth of the medium is exceeded and congestion occurs. Conversely, only one customer may be trying to transmit. At these times, the customer transmitting may be able to "burst" over guaranteed capacity.

compression   The process of reducing a file's size by means of a compression utility. Compression, another feature of the Cisco Internetwork Operating System (IOS) software, is available over serial connections and can provide a reduction in the size of the packets transmitted across your links. However, there is an underlying principle in dealing with compression: If the data you typically transmit are composed primarily of already-compressed files, you don't want to enable compression on these links. You will simply waste router CPU cycles as you unsuccessfully attempt to further compress this data and you overload your router. *See also* active compression; data compression; header compression; link compression; passive compression.

compression service adapter (CSA)   These are dedicated modules that can offload the compression tasks from the router's main CPU. Cisco 7200 and 7500 routers with VIP2s and Cisco 7000 routers with the Route/Switch Processor (RSP7000) can provide this hardware-based functionality.

configuration management   This deals with installing, modifying, and tracking the various configuration parameters of network hardware and software. It also includes boot loading utilizing BOOTP or Dynamic Host Configuration Protocol (DHCP).

convergence   Convergence is the state achieved when all routers contain the same understanding of the network's topology in their routing tables after a change occurs. Convergence times can be minimized significantly if multiple equal-cost paths to the same location are used.

Copper Distributed Data Interface (CDDI)   Its primary difference is that is runs over copper and not fiber. CDDI is not very popular; however, it has been used when companies did not want to replace the copper wiring with fiber but still wanted to gain the speed that CDDI gave them. Functionally, a CDDI is similar to FDDI.

core layer   The core layer is the backbone of the network. This is crucial to the stability of the network and should provide for redundancy and fault tolerance. Because the core is where all the corporate data transfer occurs, the equipment you select should have low latency and good manageability. Access lists and other filters should be avoided in this layer. In addition, the core layer is the high-speed switching backbone of the network. In fact, it is sometimes referred to simply as the backbone. The core layer is critical to the overall performance of the entire network and should be designed with this in mind.

cost-effectiveness   Cost-effectiveness is defined as the level at which customer requirements are met within a given budget: in other words, getting the most bang for your buck. Your customer may simply require the new network to get data from site A to site B successfully.

counter-rotating ring   Perhaps the most unusual characteristic of Fiber Distributed Data Interface (FDDI) is a counter-rotating ring. In reality, this ring is two 100-Mbps–capable rings that pass traffic in opposite directions around the network. These rings are classified as the primary ring and the secondary ring. Only the primary ring is active normally, unless a failure has occurred on the ring.

CPE   *See* customer premises equipment.

CRC   *See* cyclical redundancy check.

CSA   *See* compression service adapter.

CSMA/CD   *See* Carrier Sense Multiple Access with Collision Detection.

CSU   *See* data service unit/channel service unit.

custom queuing   Custom queuing was designed to allow a network to be shared among applications with varying minimum bandwidth or latency requirements. Different protocols are assigned different amounts of queue space.

customer premises equipment (CPE)   A term for telephones, computers, Private Branch eXchanges (PBXs), and other hardware located on the end user's side of the network boundary, established by the United States Federal Communications Commission (FCC).

cyclical redundancy check (CRC)   An automatic error-checking method used by MS-DOS when writing data to a hard or floppy disk in its drive mechanism. Later, upon reading, the same error-check is conducted and the results of the two checks are compared to make sure the data have not been altered. Also called *cyclic redundancy check* or *frame check sequence* (FCS refers to OSI layer 2, and CRC refers to layers 3 and 4, but they are used interchangeably).

DAP   *See* Data Access Protocol.

Data Access Protocol (DAP)   This provides remote file access to systems supporting the Digital Network Architecture (DNA).

data communications equipment (DCE)   In the RS232 specification, a communications device such as a modem (analog) or a data service unit (DSU) that resides between a computer, terminal, printer, bridge, or router, and a communications circuit. DCE cable is used to simulate a DCE device to interconnect two Cisco routers without using a real DCE device (for example, a modem). You'll probably use it for simulation of a wide area network (WAN) link in a test lab. A Cisco serial interface can provide clocking for a data terminal equipment (DTE) device if it has a DCE cable connected.

data compression   Data compression is the opposite of header compression in that data compression compacts the data portion of a packet but doesn't compress the header portion. Also called *Payload compression.*

Data Encryption Standard (DES)   This is used to establish and manage the encrypted sessions between peer routers. The DES keys are exchanged during the encrypted session and discarded at the termination of the session.

data-link connection identifier (DLCI)   The addresses used by Frame Relays, in combination with time-division multiplexing (TDM), to keep different data separate, regardless of its simultaneous transmission. DLCIs are logical entities, existing within a multiplexer to properly divide the bandwidth of a single physical circuit so that it can service several virtual circuits. Also, DLCIs are significant only locally.

data-link layer   This layer (layer 2) concerns the framing of data and Media Access Control (MAC) addressing in which two end nodes agree on how they will signify the beginning and end of a frame.

data-link switching (DLSw)   DLSw was designed to allow Systems Network Architecture (SNA) and Network Basic Input/Output System (NetBIOS) traffic to travel across an Internet Protocol (IP) network. DLSw was implemented to overcome some of the problems inherent in source route bridging in large networks. Keep in mind that DLSw is not a layer-3 protocol. When implemented, it is totally layer 2 between the routers that are configured.

data service unit/channel service unit (DSU/CSU)   A device, very much like a modem in function, designed to connect an organization's communications equipment directly to a digital communication line like a T1. As a device designed for higher-grade digital equipment, it is less concerned with analog-to-digital conversion than it is with shaping, multiplexing, and regenerating the digital data stream.

data terminal equipment (DTE)   The part of a computer, terminal, printer, bridge, or router that serves as a data source and/or data sink. DTEs are either network interface cards (NICs) or switched port connections, essentially anything that provides an endpoint or electrical termination of the cable. It is very likely that you will use DTE cables in your everyday work to connect a router to a DCE device. Cisco offers a few different types of cables. You should select the proper one, proceeding from the requirements of the type of interface you have on your modem and a port type you want to use on your Cisco router.

Datagram Delivery Protocol (DDP)   DDP provides a connectionless datagram service for AppleTalk networks. DDP allows AppleTalk to be routed rather than bridged.

datagram transmission   Datagram transmissions consist of individually addressed frames.

data-stream transmission   Data-stream transmissions represent a stream of data for which the address is checked only once.

DCE   *See* data communications equipment.

DDP   *See* Datagram Delivery Protocol.

DDR   *See* dial-on-demand routing.

debug   Debug commands give highly detailed information on events occurring on the router. By default, the output from debug will be sent to the console; but it may be redirected to other destinations, such as a syslog server or a monitor.

demilitarized zone (DMZ)   An isolation local area network (LAN) that is a buffer between the corporate internetwork and the outside world. This buffer zone between the external and the internal networks is where you place systems that need to be accessed by external or untrusted users.

DES   *See* Data Encryption Standard.

designated router (DR)   The DR is the elected router that represents all the routers on the network. *See also* backup designated router.

deterministic network   Token Ring networks (and token-based systems in general) are considered deterministic in nature. This means that when planning or examining a token-based network, we can accurately measure or determine the amount of time each node needs between data transmissions. Deterministic also means that a node can't simply break into the orderly network conversations taking place; who has the token at any given moment determines access.

DH   *See* Diffie-Hellman (DH) public key algorithm.

DHCP   *See* Dynamic Host Configuration Protocol.

dial-on-demand routing (DDR)   DDR allows you to form WANs using already existing telephone lines. DDR over serial lines requires the use of dialing devices that support V.25bis protocol. V.25bis is an International Telecommunication Union-Telecommunication Standardization Sector (ITU-TSS) standard for in-band signaling to fit synchronous DCE devices. The devices that support V.25bis include analog V.32 modems, Integrated Services Digital Network (ISDN) terminal adapters (TAs), and inverse multiplexers.

dictionary encoding   Dictionary encoding, such as the Lempel-Ziv algorithm, uses a repetitive character identification scheme, replacing these sequences with codes from a dictionary list. This method provides much better response to data variations.

Diffie-Hellman (DH) public-key algorithm   This algorithm is used to establish and manage the encrypted sessions between peer routers. DH numbers are exchanged during the encrypted session and discarded at the termination of the session.

diffusing update algorithm (DUAL)   An algorithm that achieves rapid convergence across a network.

digital cable   Basically a form of Ethernet, digital cable allows up to 30 Mbps with no distance limitation. Unfortunately, current cable systems are shared media covering huge territories, and performance tends to drop significantly during peak usage periods. Digital cable systems could someday be modified to minimize or eliminate this problem, but doing so would make delivery of television programming more difficult and expensive. Many cable systems prohibit the use of servers and virtual private network (VPN) clients within their networks.

Digital Signature Standard (DSS)   This is used to perform peer router authentication. DSS uses a two-key system—a public key and a private key—to confirm each router's identity. This method is similar to that used by other public-key systems like Pretty Good Privacy (PGP) but is outside the scope of this course.

Digital Subscriber Line (DSL)   There are many variants of Digital Subscriber Line (*x*DSL). All versions utilize the existing copper loop between a home and the local telephone company's central office (CO). Doing so allows them to be deployed rapidly and inexpensively. However, all DSL variants suffer from attenuation, and speeds drop as the loop length increases. Asymmetrical DSL (ADSL) and Symmetrical DSL (SDSL) may be deployed only within 17,500 feet of a CO, and Integrated Services Digital Network emulation over DSL (IDSL) will work only up to 30,500 feet. All DSL variants use ATM as the data-link layer. *See also* Asymmetrical Digital Subscriber Line; Integrated Services Digital Network over Digital Subscriber Line; Symmetrical Digital Subscriber Line.

discard eligible (DE)   This marking notifies downstream network devices that, if they experience congestion, these frames should be discarded. Some frames may also be preferentially marked DE when congestion is high, allowing mission-critical data to pass through the network and dropping less important data. Traffic-shaping filters often use this marking when voice (or video) and data are carried over the same medium. Since voice is delay sensitive and data are not, the data frames may be marked DE during periods of congestion to ensure the voice frames pass through with as little delay as possible.

disk duplexing   Disk duplexing eliminates the chance that a single controller will fail and minimizes the possibility that both will fail at the same time.

distance vector protocols   Distance vector protocols, of which Routing Information Protocol (RIP) is the most common, count the number of hops (how many routers the packet must cross) to make routing decisions.

distinct reservation   This flow originates from exactly one sender.

distributed switching   Distributed switching is available on Cisco 7500 series routers with a Route/Switch Processor (RSP) and Versatile Interface Processor (VIP) controllers where it is possible to switch packets received by the VIP with no per-packet intervention on the part of the RSP.

distribution layer   The distribution layer separates the access layer from the core layer. This layer has the job of implementing policy, security, defining areas, and workgroups and routing between them and media translation (for example, Ethernet to Token Ring). This is where most access lists and quality of service implementations should be made. Additionally, the distribution layer's primary function is to act as the point for applying policy-based connectivity. It is generally limited to large distributed networks because the access layer is the typical entry point into a network.

DLCI   *See* data-link connection identifier.

DLSw   *See* data-link switching.

DMZ   *See* demilitarized zone.

DNS   *See* Domain Name System.

domain   A collection of connected areas. Routing domains provide full connectivity to all end systems within them.

Domain Name System (DNS)   Because the actual unique Internet Protocol (IP) address of a Web server is in the form of a number difficult for humans to work with, text labels separated by dots (domain names) are used instead. DNS is responsible for mapping these domain names to the actual IP numbers in a process called *resolution*. Sometimes called a *Domain Name Server*.

downtime   Downtime occurs when a network is not accessible to its users. The cost of downtime is the cost that the company incurs when its employees and business are not being productive. Assuming that employees are productive all of the time, one downtime cost metric can be defined by the amount of time down multiplied by the wages of employees during that time. The average downtime is the average amount of time between the times that the network goes down.

DR   *See* designated router.

DSL   *See* Digital Subscriber Line.

DSS   *See* Digital Signature Standard.

DSU   *See* data service unit/channel service unit.

DTE   *See* data terminal equipment.

DUAL   *See* diffusing update algorithm.

Dynamic Host Configuration Protocol (DHCP)   A software utility that is designed to assign Internet Protocol (IP) addresses to clients and their stations logging onto a Transmission Control Protocol/Internet Protocol (TCP/IP), and eliminate manual IP address assignments.

EBANYAN   This is almost identical to IBANYAN, except it uses Banyan's network interface card (NIC) drivers instead of packet drivers or drivers specific to File Transfer Protocol (FTP) cards. EBANYAN works only with Ethernet clients, not with VINES PC-Dialin or Token Ring.

EBGP   *See* External Border Gateway Protocol.

Echo protocol   The Echo protocol causes a host to echo the packet it receives and is often used to test the accessibility of another site on the Internet. If no user application is attached to the echo port, the kernel automatically responds to the echo request from another host.

EGP   *See* Exterior Gateway Protocol.

EIGRP   *See* Enhanced Interior Gateway Routing Protocol.

electromagnetic interference (EMI)   Interference that occurs when sufficient power from signals escapes equipment enclosures or transmission data. These signals are found in the radio frequency portion of the electromagnetic spectrum.

EMI   *See* electromagnetic interference.

encryption   A system of rules for changing computer data into unintelligible symbols so that it is not deciphered by others unless they have the password. Encryption is very useful when used appropriately in a network. Routers on either side of a public network, carrying sensitive or private data, are obvious candidates for encryption services. For example, routers on the edge of a corporate network connected to branch office locations across the Internet are ideal locations to consider encryption. Encryption can also be implemented within an internal network if necessary, although the need to do so may call possible network design issues into question.

Enhanced Interior Gateway Routing Protocol (EIGRP)   Cisco later improved on IGRP by releasing EIGRP, which combines the advantages of a distant vector routing protocol with that of a link-state routing protocol to determine the best path and allow for the passing of subnet mask information. The combination of these two types of protocols is called a *hybrid* protocol, and it gives users the flexibility of both types all rolled up into one package.

error index   This associates an error with a particular object instance. Only the response operation sets this field. Other operations set this field to zero.

error protocol   The Error protocol, which reports errors, is used as a diagnostic tool, as well as a means of improving performance, and is not normally accessed by users.

error status   This indicates one of a number of errors and error types. Only the response operation sets this field. Other operations set this field to zero.

Ethernet   Ethernet is a broadcast medium invented by Bob Metcalfe at Xerox Palo Alto Research Center (PARC) in 1972, which makes it one of the oldest extant technologies in networking. It operates at 10 megabits per second (Mbps) using Carrier Sense Multiple Access with Collision Detection (CSMA/CD).

expansion   Expansion usually means there will be more employees and, potentially, more users on the network. If expansion is not addressed, you could be implementing a million-dollar network that works today but fails tomorrow when branch sites with three or four users grow to a hundred users and need greater access to corporate headquarters.

Exterior Gateway Protocol (EGP)   One of many categories of routing protocols for spanning different autonomous systems.

External Border Gateway Protocol (EBGP) session   This allows routers from two different autonomous systems to exchange information. These routers are usually adjacent to each other and share the same medium and subnet.

Fast Ethernet   Fast Ethernet refers to a family of technologies that utilize Carrier Sense Multiple Access with Collision Detection (CSMA/CD) but transmit and receive data at 100 Mbps. However, because CSMA/CD requires that all stations have a reasonable amount of time to "hear" if a collision has occurred before transmitting fresh data, the higher speed requires a shorter distance. Fast Ethernet will support only a single repeater between two segments of 100 meters in length. The most common implementation of Fast Ethernet is 100BaseTX, or 100 Mbps on a baseband circuit on twisted-pair wire. 100BaseTX requires Category-5 wiring to operate, but it still uses only two pairs and, therefore, can coexist with voice.

fast switching   Fast switching is done via asynchronous interrupts that are handled in real time. With this type of switching, an incoming packet matches an entry in the fast-switching cache created when a previous packet to the same destination was processed.

fault management   When a network grows beyond just a few nodes, fault management software becomes invaluable in troubleshooting and the timely repair of faults. This is used to isolate areas where the trouble lies and generally sounds an audible alarm to alert administrative personnel to the existence of a fault. In the case of a wide area network circuit, it may alert both client-side and carrier-side personnel to the fault.

FCFS   *See* first come, first served queuing.

FCS   *See* cyclical redundancy check.

FDDI   *See* Fiber Distributed Data Interface.

feasible successor   The backup next hop router.

FECN   *See* forward explicit congestion notification.

Fiber Distributed Data Interface (FDDI)   A 100-Mbps fiber-optic (not copper wire) network, also characterized by its counter-rotating ring-style topology, which works as built-in redundancy in case of a break in the main ring. FDDI is often used as a backbone network because of its speed and reliability. It generally connects file servers and other high-traffic nodes.

Fiber-Optic InterRepeater Link (FOIRL)   A fiber-optic signaling method based on the Institute of Electrical and Electronics Engineers (IEEE) 802.3 standard governing fiber optics and its technology. This link allows up to 1,000 meters of multimode duplex fiber-optic cable, especially in a point-to-point link.

FIFO queuing   *See* first in, first out queuing.

File Transfer Protocol (FTP)   An Internet allowing the exchange of files. A program enables the user to contact another computer on the Internet and exchange files.

first come, first served (FCFS) queuing   *See* first in, first out queuing.

first in, first out (FIFO) queuing   FIFO queuing provides basic store-and-forward functionality. It stores packets when the network is congested and forwards them when the way is free. The packets leave in the order they arrive. FIFO is a default queuing algorithm, so it requires no configuration. The disadvantage of this method is that it has no mechanism to prioritize traffic. Also called *first come, first served (FCFS) queuing.*

flash updates   A flash update is sent asynchronously when a network topology change has been detected. It works in correlation with Interior Gateway Routing Protocol (IGRP) periodic routing updates.

flat network   A flat network is a switched or bridged network that isn't divided by routers. Flat networks are important specifically because each node in a flat network must examine the traffic passing by on the network to determine if it is intended for itself or another node. In a large flat network, this can cause excessive processing to take place at each node. When broadcast or multicast traffic accounts for more than 20 percent of the network's traffic, the performance of the local area network (LAN) suffers.

FOIRL   *See* Fiber-Optic InterRepeater Link.

forward explicit congestion notification (FECN)   The Frame Relay message designed to detect a congestion problem and then let the receiving device know of the impending congestion.

forwarding database   *See* routing table.

fractional link   An original T1 line consists of 24 channels of 64 Kbps each. In addition, a fractional T1 line uses only some of the 24 channels with a data transfer capacity of 64 Kbps each in an original T1 line, leaving the rest of the channels unused. The customer can rent any number of the 24 channels. Renting a fractional T1 line costs less, though the transmission method is not changed. T3 lines are also sometimes leased as a fractional service. Such lines provide up to 672 64-Kbps channels.

frame   A generic term used to specify a single unit of data, which is most often a fragment of a larger unit. Much like a picture frame that defines the edges of the picture, a Frame Relay frame defines the beginning and end of a single unit of data, wherein the payload may be up to 4,096 bytes (4,096 × 8 bits per byte = 32,768 bits).

frame check sequence (FCS)   *See* cyclical redundancy check.

Frame Relay   A connection-oriented, packet-switched technology that can run from 16 Kbps to over 2 Mbps, with the most common instances being multiples of 64 Kbps. This was originally designed to run over Integrated Services Digital Network (ISDN) interfaces and is considered the successor to X.25. Much of Frame Relay's flexibility comes from the concept of the virtual circuit. The Frame Relay network may be thought of as a cloud—traffic goes in one side and comes out the other, but its path between switches inside the network is indeterminate.

FTP   *See* File Transfer Protocol.

Get Nearest Server (GNS)   Novell NetWare clients use a Service Advertising Protocol (SAP) broadcast request known as GNS to locate and connect to the nearest server providing the services they are requesting. These messages will succeed if there is a local server to process the request. But if the client is located on a remote segment without a server, the request will never make it across the router interfaces to the server subnet.

GIF   *See* Graphics Interchange Format.

Gigabit Ethernet   Gigabit Ethernet is the latest version of Ethernet to become an Institute of Electrical and Electronics Engineers (IEEE) standard, designated as 802.3z. As the name implies, Gigabit Ethernet operates at 1 Gbps, or ten times the speed of Fast Ethernet. Although not necessarily intended for use at the desktop, Gigabit Ethernet will help to relieve congested network backbone routes as more and more users receive Fast Ethernet connections to their desktops.

GNS   *See* Get Nearest Server.

Graphics Interchange Format (GIF)   A bitmapped graphics file format. GIF is often employed for graphics exchange on networks and uses a high-resolution graphics compression technique.

groupware   Application programs able to increase the joint productivity of groups of coworkers.

HDLC   *See* High-level Data Link Control.

header compression   Header compression can be configured in two ways. You can enable it on a particular router interface or specify an IP Map, which allows you to use a specific Internet Protocol (IP) address in the compression calculations. Both techniques support active and passive compression.

helper address   Helper addresses allow you to configure specific server or network addresses that will be able to respond appropriately to these client broadcasts. Cisco provides helper address support for many different protocols, including Internet Protocol (IP) and Internetwork Packet Exchange (IPX), and multiple helper addresses can be configured per router interface. This is important in a distributed networking environment, where each network segment may not have the requested resource available.

hierarchical model   The benefits of the hierarchical model are vast. Using a layered approach facilitates change and limits the scope to a subset of the network. Layers also make the network easier to manage and understand. It is easier to troubleshoot and diagnose failures within the network when it is structured as a hierarchy.

High-level Data Link Control (HDLC)   A standard bit-oriented communication line protocol developed by the International Organization for Standardization (ISO). It is also considered a bit-oriented link-layer protocol. HDLC is a group of OSI layer-2 protocols based on IBM's Synchronous Data Link Control (SDLC) protocol. Cisco has its own version of HDLC incompatible with other versions of the protocol. The difference between Cisco's and other versions is in identification of the next-layer protocol.

High-Speed Serial Interface (HSSI)   The HSSI is a special kind of DTE/DCE interface developed by Cisco Systems and T3plus Networking to satisfy the needs for high-speed communication over wide area network (WAN) links. Though HSSI is not officially standardized yet (it is now in the American National Standards Institute (ANSI) under the formal standardization), its specification is available to any company that would like to implement HSSI. The maximum signaling rate for HSSI is 52 Mbps, which allows it to handle most of today's technologies, such as T3, OC-1 (optical carrier with base rate of 51.84 Mbps).

hold-down timers   Hold-down timers are used to prevent routing loops during network convergence. They neither advertise nor accept advertisements about a route for a specific length of time. This time is three times the update interval (90 seconds) plus 10 seconds, or 280 seconds by default.

Hot Standby Router Protocol (HSRP)   HSRP allows you to continue configuring your workstations with a static router address for use as their default gateway. However, this address is not a real address, represented by a physical router interface. Instead, it is the address of a phantom router. It is a single logical Media Access Control (MAC) and Internet Protocol (IP) address configured by the network administrator as part of the HSRP implementation.

HSRP   *See* Hot Standby Router Protocol.

HSSI   *See* High-Speed Serial Interface.

HTML   *See* Hypertext Markup Language.

hubs   Hubs, also known as *repeaters*, are very simple devices that sense electrical signals on one port, amplify them, and repeat them on many other ports. The hub makes no attempt to filter or understand the traffic that it is passing, though most hubs will sense collisions or framing errors. Hubs can come with anything from 2 to 100 ports, but buying more than 16 ports may be a waste of money when switches are so inexpensive.

hybrid topology   A hybrid topology is a combination of two or more topologies. These topologies are fairly complex and require documentation for troubleshooting. For example, if an end node is experiencing problems reaching the server for an application, understanding where the node is on the network is useful in determining where the problem lies.

Hypertext Markup Language (HTML)   A language for creating documents to be displayed on the World Wide Web with graphics, text, and connections (hyperlinks) to other documents. HTML instructs how a page should be displayed with various tags.

IANA   *See* Internet Assigned Numbers Authority.

IBANYAN   Software for Banyan. It works with all Banyan clients, including Ethernet, Token Ring, and PC-Dialin (Banyan's dial-up solution). When using IBANYAN, the client PC encapsulates its TCP/IP traffic in VINES packets.

ICMP   *See* Internet Control Message Protocol.

ICP   *See* Internet Control Protocol; Interprocess Communications Protocol.

IDP   *See* Internet Datagram Protocol.

IDSL   *See* Integrated Services Digital Network emulation over Digital Subscriber Line.

IEEE   *See* Institute of Electrical and Electronics Engineers.

IETF   *See* Internet Engineering Task Force.

IGP   *See* Interior Gateway Protocol.

IGRP   *See* Interior Gateway Routing Protocol.

Institute of Electrical and Electronics Engineers (IEEE)   A U.S. professional organization active in creating, promoting, and supporting communication specifications and standards.

Integrated Services Digital Network (ISDN)   Integrated Services indicates the provider offers voice and data services over the same medium. Digital Network is a reminder that ISDN was born out of the digital nature of the intercarrier and intracarrier networks. ISDN runs across the same copper wiring that carries regular telephone service. Before attenuation and noise cause the signal to be unintelligible, an ISDN circuit can run a maximum of 18,000 feet. A repeater doubles this distance to 36,000 feet.

Integrated Services Digital Network emulation over Digital Subscriber Line (IDSL)   IDSL is a Broadband Integrated Services Digital Network (B-ISDN) implementation, using Narrowband Integrated Services Digital Network (N-ISDN) signaling protocols and an asynchronous transfer mode permanent virtual circuit (ATM PVC). IDSL is still an ATM data-link layer, but it provides ISDN-like signal divisions of two B channels and a D channel. All three channels are used for data transmission and are bonded together with multilink Point-to-Point Protocol (PPP); all that is required is an N-ISDN terminal adapter (TA) with the ability to use leased-line mode.

Interior Gateway Protocol (IGP)   One of many routing protocol categories supporting one confined geographic area, e.g., a local area network (LAN).

Interior Gateway Routing Protocol (IGRP)   A Cisco proprietary distance vector routing protocol. Like Routing Information Protocol (RIP) version 1, IGRP does not allow for passing subnet mask information in routing updates. IGRP was developed by Cisco Systems in the mid-1980s in response to the demand for a more versatile routing protocol. Many customers migrated from RIP to IGRP because IGRP improved on many of the downfalls inherent with RIP.

Intermediate System to Intermediate System (IS-IS) This is another link-state protocol, designed by International Organization for Standardization (ISO). It is based on DECnet Phase V routing but was later modified to include support for other protocols, including TCP/IP. ISO is the same group that brought us the seven-layer model. IS-IS is designed to work in conjunction with End System to Intermediate System (ES-IS) and connectionless network service (CLNS), also developed by ISO. Although IS-IS was created to route in Connectionless Network Protocol (CLNP) networks, a version has since been created to support both CLNP and IP networks. This variety of IS-IS is usually referred to as *integrated IS-IS* and has also been called *dual IS-IS*.

Internal Border Gateway Protocol (IBGP) session This allows routers in the same autonomous system to exchange information. It is used to synchronize and coordinate routing policy throughout the autonomous system. These routers can be located anywhere within the autonomous system.

Internet Assigned Numbers Authority (IANA) The predecessor organization to the Internet Corporation for Assigned Names and Numbers (ICANN).

Internet Control Message Protocol (ICMP) A protocol for sending error/control messages. ICMP employs Transmission Control Protocol/Internet Protocol (TCP/IP).

Internet Control Protocol (ICP) This protocol is used to notify the user of an error and to advertise changes in network topology.

Internet Datagram Protocol (IDP) This protocol is a connectionless datagram protocol that forms the basis for XNS addressing. IDP packets are limited to a maximum size of 576 bytes, excluding the data-link header.

Internet Engineering Task Force (IETF)   The organization providing standard coordination and specification development for Transmission Control Protocol/Internet Protocol (TCP/IP) networking

Internetwork Packet Exchange (IPX)   Novell NetWare's built-in networking protocol for local area network (LAN) communication derived from the Xerox Network System protocol. IPX moves data between a server and/or workstation programs from different network nodes. Sometimes called an *Internetnetwork Packet Exchange.*

Internet Protocol (IP)   Originally developed by the U.S. Department of Defense (DoD) for internetworking dissimilar computers across a single network. This connectionless protocol aids in providing a best-effort delivery of datagrams across a network.

Internet service provider (ISP)   The organization allowing users to connect to its computers and then to the Internet. ISPs provide the software to connect and sometimes a portal site and/or internal browsing capability.

Internetwork Operating System (IOS)   A Cisco operating system used in its routers as a primary control program.

Interprocess Communications Protocol (ICP)   This protocol provides both datagram and reliable message delivery service.

IOS   *See* Internetwork Operating System.

IP   *See* Internet Protocol.

IPX   *See* Internetwork Packet Exchange.

ISDN   *See* Integrated Services Digital Network.

IS-IS   *See* Intermediate System to Intermediate System.

ISP   *See* Internet service provider.

Joint Photographic Experts Group (JPEG)   The committee, under the auspices of the International Organization for Standardization (ISO) and the Consultative Committee for International Telephony and Telegraphy (CCITT), that developed the JPEG graphics standard defining how to compress still pictures. JPEG can achieve compression ratios of 10:1 or 20:1, superior to Graphics Interchange Format (GIF) ratios, without noticeable picture-quality degradation.

JPEG   *See* Joint Photographic Experts Group.

Kerberos   Kerberos guards against this username and password safety vulnerability by using tickets (temporary electronic credentials) to authenticate. Tickets have a limited life span and can be used in place of usernames and passwords (if the software supports this). Kerberos encrypts the password into the ticket. It uses a trusted server called the *Key Distribution Center (KDC)* to handle authentication requests.

LAN   *See* local area network.

LANE   *See* local area network emulation.

LAP   *See* Link Access Protocol.

LAPB   *See* Link Access Procedure, Balanced.

LAT   *See* local area transport.

LAVC   *See* local area VAX cluster.

leased lines   Wide area network (WAN) links frequently need to travel great distances, over which private transports are not feasible. To handle this situation, you might lease a line from a local telephone company or long distance carrier. A leased line will have the bare minimum of carrier services added to it; it does pass through the carrier's switches, but they do little more than amplify the signal where necessary. A leased line is still a layer-1 solution, so you are still responsible for providing clock and choosing framing. To differentiate them from dark fiber, leased lines are sometimes called "lit" fiber.

level-1 routing   Routing within an area.

level-2 routing   Routing between areas.

Link Access Protocol (LAP)   LAP is a modification of High-level Data Link Control (HDLC) protocol for use with X.25 network interfaces. It has lately been modified to make it more compatible with HDLC.

Link Access Procedure, Balanced (LAPB)   Link Access Protocol (LAP) is a modification of High-level Data Link Control (HDLC) protocol for use with X.25 network interfaces. It has lately been modified to make it more compatible with HDLC. The result is Link Access Procedure, Balanced (LAPB). This protocol is standard, so you would probably use it to establish a connection with non-Cisco devices.

link compression   Link compression enables the compression of both the header and the data portions of packets.

link-state advertisement (LSA)   This advertisement is forwarded to all routers on the network, so all routers on the network receive first-hand updates. Compare this to distance vector protocols in which the update is received only by a neighbor, then put into that neighbor's routing table.

link-state database   It shows the internetwork topology information about all routers in the network. This is also called the *topological database.*

link-state protocol   Link-state protocols take into account the entire cost of the route, which includes the speed of the link as well as the distance, by learning the entire topology of the network.

lit fiber   *See* leased lines.

LLC   *See* Logical Link Control.

LMI   *See* Local Management Interface.

load balancing   The fine-tuning process of a system (computer, network, etc.) to allow the data to be distributed more efficiently and evenly.

local area network (LAN)   A system using high-speed connections at 2 to 200 megabytes per second (MBps) over high-performance cables to communicate among computers within a few miles of each other, allowing users to share peripherals and a massive secondary storage unit, the file server. *See also* virtual local area network.

local area network emulation (LANE)   The services and protocols that allow asynchronous transfer modes (ATMs) to be connected with local area networks (LANs).

local area transport (LAT)   This is designed to handle multiplexed terminal traffic to and from time-sharing hosts.

local area VAX cluster (LAVC)   This communicates between VAX computers in a cluster.

Local Management Interface (LMI)   Not really an interface, an LMI is actually a protocol that periodically (usually about every 10 seconds) requests status information from the Frame Relay cloud. There are three flavors of LMI: one is referred to as "the gang of four," or Cisco LMI; another is ANSI Annex D; and the third is ITU Q933a. All three function in similar ways.

Logical Link Control (LLC)   Provides a common point for the interface of the Media Access Control (MAC) layers.

logical unit (LU)   In Systems Network Architecture (SNA), the LU is one end of a communication session.

loop   A loop occurs in a network when multiple paths exist between two segments.

LSA   *See* link-state advertisement.

LU   *See* logical unit.

MAC   *See* Media Access Control.

Maintenance Operation Protocol (MOP)   MOP is used for utility services such as uploading and downloading system software, remote testing, and diagnostics.

MAN   *See* metropolitan area network.

manageability   Manageability is defined as the ease with which a network can be proactively monitored, supported, and maintained. For a network to be manageable, it should at least have a robust network management system, a solid network design, and trained technical support personnel.

MAU   *See* multistation access unit.

mean time between failure (MTBF)   The average length of time from the point when a component is created until its first failure, mechanical or electronic; because MTBF is calculated from laboratory tests performed under extreme conditions, the figure is not particularly useful for comparison shopping.

mean time to repair (MTTR)   Average time it takes to correct failures in hardware, etc.

Media Access Control (MAC)   A sublayer in the Open Systems Interconnection (OSI) data-link layer that controls access, control, procedures, and format for a local area network (LAN), for example, Institute of Electrical and Electronics Engineers (IEEE) 802.3, 802.4, and 802.5 standards.

mesh network   A configuration presenting at least two paths between any two nodes.

metropolitan area network (MAN)   A public speed network operating at 100 megabits per second (Mbps) or more that can transmit voice and data messages within a 50-mile range.

microsegmentation   Microsegmentation uses local area network (LAN) switches to divide collision domains and provide high bandwidth to individual workgroups. In a small office/home office (SOHO) environment, the access layer provides access to users via wide-area communications such as Integrated Services Digital Network (ISDN), Frame Relay, leased lines, and broadband.

mirroring   This is the exact duplication of data across two drives.

mixed-media bridging   Mixed-media bridging (also called *encapsulated bridging*) involves transporting frames between one media type (Ethernet) and another (e.g., Token Ring or Fiber Distributed Data Interface). Because of the differences in framing among these protocols, certain issues must be resolved before they can be successfully bridged. In particular, Ethernet does not allow for the inclusion of the Routing Information Field (RIF) that Source Route Bridging (SRB) requires, nor does Token Ring allow for a variable payload size.

MOP   *See* Maintenance Operation Protocol.

MSAU   *See* multistation access unit.

MTBF   *See* mean time between failure.

MTTR   *See* mean time to repair.

multistation access unit (MSAU/MAU)   The name IBM uses for Token Ring wiring concentrator.

NAK   *See* negative acknowledgment.

Name Binding Protocol (NBP)   NBP keeps track of the names associated with resources' addresses in AppleTalk that are assigned for ease of recognition by the end user. NBP's function is similar to that of DNS in the Transmission Control Protocol/Internet Protocol (TCP/IP) world.

Narrowband Integrated Services Digital Network (N-ISDN)
N-ISDN is the standard we all think of when designing networks or reading trade magazines; it is widely implemented in most areas of the world. The N-ISDN standard may be delivered over two physical interfaces, Plain Old Telephone System (POTS) or Digital Signal 1 (DS-1).

NAT   *See* network address translation.

NAU   *See* network address unit.

NBP   *See* Name Binding Protocol.

NCP   *See* NetWare Core Protocol.

negative acknowledgment (NAK)   A code letting a sender know that a character or block of data was not properly received.

neighbor table The purpose of a neighbor table is to ensure communication between the directly connected neighbors. Enhanced Interior Gateway Routing Protocol (EIGRP) multicasts hello packets to discover neighbor routers and exchange route updates. Each router builds a neighbor table from the hello packets that it receives from neighbor EIGRP routers running the same network-layer protocol.

NetBIOS *See* Network Basic Input/Output System.

NetFlow switching NetFlow switching identifies traffic flows between internetwork hosts and then switches packets in these flows (on a connection-oriented basis) at the same time that it applies relevant services, such as security.

NetRemote Procedure Call (NetRPC) This procedure call is used to access VINES applications such as StreetTalk and VINES Mail. A program number and version identify all VINES applications. Calls to VINES applications must specify the program number, program version, and specific procedure within the program.

NetRPC *See* NetRemote Procedure Call.

NetWare Core Protocol (NCP) This protocol is used by clients in a NetWare network to access NetWare servers' services and to manage those connections, as well as to access shared files and printers.

NetWare Link Services Protocol (NLSP) This protocol is a link-state routing protocol that provides fast convergence and reduced routing and service update traffic in an IPX environment. NLSP is based on the International Organization for Standardization (ISO) Intermediate System–to–Intermediate System (IS-IS) protocol. NLSP was created to improve scalability, reduce overhead, manage demands more effectively, and increase efficiency and effectiveness of routing in an IPX network.

network address translation (NAT)   With NAT, you can allow internal users to have access to important external resources while still preventing unauthorized access from the outside world.

network address unit (NAU)   In Systems Network Architecture (SNA), the origin or destination of information transmitted by the path control network; it may be a logical or physical unit or a systems service control point. Sometimes called a *network addressable unit.*

Network Basic Input/Output System (NetBIOS)   A program in Microsoft's operating systems that links personal computers to local area networks (LANs).

network command   The network command associates an IP address with a network that is connected to the router.

network interface card (NIC)   A board with encoding and decoding circuitry and a receptacle for a network cable connection that, bypassing the serial ports and operating through the internal bus, allows computers to be connected at higher speeds to media for communications between stations.

network layer   This layer (layer 3) is concerned with routing. The purpose of routing is to get a packet from its source to a remote destination for which it knows the address but not how to get there.

network management   Network management is a combination of software, hardware, and operational procedures designed specifically to keep a network operational and at maximum efficiency. Network management is achieved through the placement of one or more monitors (computers running monitoring software) on the network. *See also* proactive network management.

network management system (NMS)   An NMS is a software application that facilitates the proactive support and monitoring of networked systems. The existing NMS will help you understand the baseline expectations for the new network's NMS. Any data collected previously by the existing NMS would be very helpful in assessing the health of the existing network. Make sure that the NMS for the new network is at least equally as robust as the NMS before it.

network operations center (NOC)   A centrol location for network management.

network service access point (NSAP)   These addresses are the interface between layer 3 and layer 4.

Network Service Protocol (NSP)   This provides reliable virtual connection services with flow control to the network layer Routing Protocol.

network termination (NT) device   Intermediate equipment specified by Integrated Services Digital Network (ISDN). NTs connect the four-wire subscriber wiring to two-wire local loops. There are three supported NT types.

network utilization   Network utilization is defined as the amount of traffic traversing the network versus the available bandwidth. To better understand the utilization of the existing network, use a protocol analyzer. Depending on the results of the protocol analysis, you might decide that more bandwidth is required for the new network.

networks   Networks are dynamic, growing entities that are shaped by the people who build them and the requirements and budgets that they must meet.

Network-Network Interface (NNI)   In Asynchronous Transfer Mode (ATM) networking, the interface between two ATM devices. Also called *Network-Node Interface.*

NIC   *See* network interface card.

N-ISDN   *See* Narrowband Integrated Services Digital Network.

NLSP   *See* NetWare Link Services Protocol.

NMS   *See* network management system.

NNI   *See* Network-Network Interface.

NOC   *See* network operations center.

Novell Routing Information Protocol (RIP)   Novell RIP is a distance vector routing protocol like IP RIP, but with a major difference. IPX RIP uses two metrics in making routing decisions on a network: ticks to measure time and hop count. RIP will first check the tick metric for alternative paths, and if two or more paths are equal, it moves on to hop count. It makes the decision based on the age of the entry and the most recent entry wins. Sometimes known as *IPX RIP.*

NSAP   *See* network service access point.

NSP   *See* Network Service Protocol.

NT device   *See* network termination device.

OC   *See* Synchronous Transport Signal.

Open Shortest Path First (OSPF) routing protocol   OSPF is a link-state routing protocol written for large and rapidly growing networks. It allows you to break down a large network into smaller, more manageable areas. OSPF is an open standard, developed by the Internet Engineering Task Force (IETF) and supports only IP routing. It is a good solution choice for large heterogeneous networks because most router vendors support it.

Open Systems Interconnection (OSI)   The model for internetworking is a seven-layer model. Although nothing in the real world maps exactly to the OSI model, it provides networkers with a common frame of reference to aid them in design and troubleshooting. The Open Systems Interconnection (OSI) reference model is a hierarchical, or layered, structure that lends itself to a simplification of roles.

optical carrier (OC)   *See* Synchronous Transport Signal.

optimum switching   Optimum switching is similar to fast switching but is even faster because it has an enhanced caching algorithm and the special structure of the optimum-switching cache. This process is available only on routers that have a Route/Switch Processor (RSP).

OSI   *See* Open Systems Interconnection.

OSPF   *See* Open Shortest Path First.

packet assembler/disassembler (PAD)   A hardware and software device in some PCs that allows users to access an X.25 network; installation is governed by the International Telecommunications Union (ITU) Recommendations X.3, X.28, and X.29.

Packet Exchange Protocol (PEP)   This protocol provides a more reliable datagram delivery service than IDP. A unique number is used to identify responses as belonging to a particular request. The sending host sets the packet ID field to a fixed value, and then looks for PEP responses containing the same packet ID value.

packet internetwork groper (ping)   A troubleshooting tool for sending an Internet Control Message Protocol (ICMP) echo request message to a target message. Network speed is shown by the amount of time needed for a message to return.

Packet-Layer Protocol (PLP)   PLP is a protocol on the Network layer of the Open Systems Interconnection (OSI) model that manages packet exchanges between data terminal equipment (DTE) devices across virtual circuits. There exist five distinct PLP modes: call setup, data transfer, idle, call clearing, and restarting.

packet-switching exchange (PSE)   Switches that make up the majority of the carrier's network and are tasked with transferring data between DTE devices through the X.25 packet-switched network.

PAD   *See* packet assembler/disassembler.

passive compression   Passive compression will recompress the packet headers for transmission only if the packets were originally received by the router in a compressed state.

payload compression   *See* data compression.

PDM   *See* protocol-dependent module.

PDN   *See* public data network.

peer routers   Routers that have established a TCP connection using the DLSw+ standard to transport SNA or NetBIOS traffic. Also called *peer-encrypting routers.*

PEP   *See* Packet Exchange Protocol.

performance   Performance is the measurement of response times between network devices. You should know what level of performance your customer is accustomed to. This information should be addressed in the new network design to achieve a faster performing network than before.

performance management   Its tools allow network administrators to monitor the number of packets, frames, or bytes passing through a given segment within the network. This data may also include the number of collisions, retransmissions, and errors incurred. On wide area network (WAN) segments, this helps management know whether carriers are adhering to negotiated service-level agreements (SLAs). It also defines which servers are being accessed the most and how many users are logged on at a given time.

permanent virtual circuit (PVC)   A predefined pathway through the public telephone network set up during the provisioning period and never torn down. Multiple PVCs may reside on a single physical circuit. This allows a company to purchase a single T1 at its headquarters and, for example, split it into one 384-Kbps circuit to remote location A; one 256-Kbps circuit to location B; and, one 128-Kbps circuit to location C, with 768-Kbps access to the Internet.

physical layer   This layer (layer 1) covers the actual, physical, and electrical components on a network.

physical unit (PU)   A terminal, printer, or similar device connected to the controller in a Systems Network Architecture (SNA) network.

PIM   *See* Protocol-Independent Multicast.

ping   *See* packet internetwork groper.

pinhole congestion   Pinhole congestion occurs when links of different capacities are used, for example, a T1 link and a 56KB link. As both links fill with traffic, the load is balanced across both links; but when the 56KB link becomes saturated, the T1 link will continue to carry only 56KB worth of traffic.

PIX   The Cisco PIX Firewall series of products is the highest performance enterprise-class set of firewalls that delivers high security and fast performance for corporate networks. The PIX Firewall allows users to thoroughly protect their internal networks from the outside world by providing full firewall security policy and protection. Unlike CPU-intensive proxy servers that perform processing on each data packet, the PIX Firewall uses a secure, real-time, embedded system.

Plain Old Telephone System (POTS)   Voice-only, dial-up telephone service. The analog communications system good for voice and slow data communication but lacking the bandwidth for high-speed digital communications.

PLP   *See* Packet-Layer Protocol.

point-to-point circuit   A private circuit with only two endpoints.

point-to-point connection   A connection in which point A connects to point B with no side trips. A point-to-point link is one of the most widely used and easily configured types of links, and Cisco provides a wide range of routers that support these links. A point-to-point link is used to establish a single communications path between two locations. An important role in this process of connection belongs to a carrier network (a telephone company, for example). A point-to-point link is often referred to as a leased line because the established communications path is constant and reserved permanently for each remote network contacted from the customer premises.

Point-to-Point Protocol (PPP)   A serial communication protocol most commonly used to connect a personal computer to an Internet service provider (ISP). PPP is the successor to Serial Line Internet Protocol (SLIP) and may be used over both synchronous and asynchronous circuits. Also, PPP is a full-duplex, connectionless protocol that supports many different types of links. The advantages of PPP made it the de facto standard for dial-up connections.

poison reverse   This is another form of split horizon. Instead of marking a network as unreachable, poison reverse does not include it in routing updates as split horizon does. Also, instead of sending an update out the interface from which a route was originally learned, it sends the update with a metric of infinity (in the case of Routing Information Protocol, infinity is 16) so that the route will never be used.

POTS   *See* Plain Old Telephone System.

PPP   *See* Point-to-Point Protocol.

Predictor algorithm   The Predictor algorithm is more economical with processing than the STAC algorithm but requires more memory. *See also* STAC algorithm.

presentation layer   This layer (layer 6) deals with formatting data sent across the network. Because data is useful to a computer only if it can be understood, a common formatting must be agreed upon. Common media formats available on the Web include HTML, Java, JPEG, and GIF graphics, and various types of streaming audio and video.

PRI   *See* primary rate interface.

primary rate interface (PRI)   The PRI is made up of up to 23 64-Kbps B channels (30 B channels in Europe) and one 64-Kbps D channel, for a total bandwidth of 1.544 Mbps (2.048 Mbps in Europe), with all but 64 Kbps (the D channel) available for data. Just as with the BRI, every channel may make a separate call, multiple channels may be combined for greater bandwidth, or all channels may be used at once as a single link.

priority queuing   Priority queuing processes the important packets first. High priority is given to a critical application. This mechanism is very useful for time-sensitive protocols, such as Telnet. Priority queuing is perhaps the most extreme queuing solution available through the Cisco Internetwork Operating System (IOS) software. However, it is very effective at providing mission-critical applications and time-sensitive protocols like Systems Network Architecture (SNA) with the highest level of access possible to the available bandwidth. Priority queuing relies on a priority list that has been previously configured by the network administrator.

proactive network management   The ability to monitor and react to network events occurring at distant locations is invaluable to the network administrator, as well as to the organization.

process switching   Process switching is the slowest of existing switching methods. In process switching, the router examines the incoming packet and looks up the layer-3 destination address in the routing table to choose the exit interface. Then the packet is rewritten with the correct header for that interface and copied to the interface. Compression and encryption of packets are the examples of processes for which process switching is used.

propagation delay   Electrical signals take a certain amount of time to travel across the network cabling, and each additional device along the path contributes a specific amount of latency or delay to the signal, known as propagation delay.

protocol   A protocol is simply a set of rules governing a level of communication. Two computers cannot communicate unless they first agree on how to communicate. The first agreement two devices must make is over what medium they will communicate: copper wire, optical cable, radio waves, and so on. That is one protocol. From there, they agree on how to frame their messages, meaning where they begin and end. This is yet another protocol.

protocol-dependent module (PDM)   A PDM is responsible for network layer–specific protocol information.

Protocol-Independent Multicast (PIM)   An IETF-endorsed multicast routing protocol.

PSE   *See* packet-switching exchange.

PSTN   *See* public switched telephone network.

PU   *See* physical unit.

public data network (PDN)   A wide area network (WAN) through which organizations and individuals access long distance data communications services, in the United States based usually on the X.25 and Transmission Control Protocol/Internet Protocol (TCP/IP) protocols.

public switched telephone network (PSTN)   With a total of 300 million connections, probably the largest network using circuit switching.

PVC   *See* permanent virtual circuit.

Quality of Service (QoS)   A measure of network effectiveness based on a number of factors, including transit delay; cost; and the likelihood of packets being lost, duplicated, or damaged.

queuing   *See* custom queuing; first in, first out queuing; priority queuing; weighted fair queuing.

queuing service   Queuing services allow us to assign prioritization levels to the application traffic on our networks.

R reference point   The R reference point defines the reference point between non-ISDN equipment and a terminal adapter (TA).

RADIUS   *See* Remote Authentication Dial-In User Service.

RAID   *See* redundant array of inexpensive disks.

redundant array of inexpensive disks (RAID)   Although mirroring and duplexing are forms of RAID, most people think of RAID as involving more than two drives. The most common form of RAID is RAID-5, which is the striping of data across three or more drives, providing fault tolerance if one drive fails.

redundant model   The main benefits of the redundant model are its fault tolerance and resiliency. It provides the ability to design nonstop network infrastructures by minimizing or eliminating single points of failure. There is room for some type of redundancy in networks of all sizes, but the level of redundancy typically increases with the size and importance of a network. Because the different aspects of redundancy are modular in nature, the redundant model can scale very well to fit the needs of even the largest organizations.

reliability   Reliability defines a network's ability to get data from one point to another without error. You should gather reliability information about the existing network and address this information in the new network design. A protocol analyzer like Network Associates' Sniffer will help you in defining a network's level of reliability. On an Ethernet network, some items to look at would be the number of cyclical redundancy check (CRC) errors, runts, and collisions. The higher these numbers are, the lower the reliability of the network.

Remote Authentication Dial-In User Service (RADIUS)   This is one of two protocols designed to authenticate users and handle accounting. RADIUS is an Internet standard, supported by many vendors. RADIUS allows for interoperability with other hardware. This can be useful in a mixed-vendor environment where other vendors do not support Terminal Access Control Access Controller Plus (TACACS+). Maintaining two databases can increase the complexity and support cost of a network.

Remote Monitoring (RMON)   This is a standard monitoring specification for monitoring packet and traffic patterns on local area network (LAN) segments. It is defined as a portion of the MIB II network management database. Request for Comment (RFC) 1757 defines the objects and RMON groups for managing remote network monitoring devices and RFC 1513 defines extensions to the RMON MIB for managing 802.5 Token Ring networks.

Resource Reservation Protocol (RSVP)   RSVP is an Internet Protocol (IP) service that allows end systems on either side of a routed network to establish a reserved-bandwidth path between them to predetermine and ensure Quality of Service (QoS) for their data transmission. RSVP allows end systems to request QoS guarantees from the network. Data applications frequently demand relatively lower bandwidth than real-time traffic. The constant high bit-rate demands of a videoconference application and the bursty bit-rate demands of an interactive data application share available network resources. RSVP prevents the demands of high-bandwidth traffic from impairing the bandwidth resources necessary for bursty data traffic.

RID   *See* router identifier.

ring topology   A ring topology connects all workstations in a closed loop, and messages pass to each node or station in turn. The ring connects all stations by using a cable in a ring or circular pattern.

ring-in/ring-out (RI/RO) ports   Each multistation access unit (MSAU) has two special ports intended for connecting to other MSAUs and to extend the ring further. These ports are ring-in (RI) and ring-out (RO) ports.

RIP   *See* Routing Information Protocol.

RI/RO ports   *See* ring-in/ring-out ports.

RMON   *See* Remote Monitoring.

Route/Switch Processor (RSP)   A processor available on Cisco 7500 series routers and on Cisco 7000 series routers with the 7000 series Route/Switch Processor (RSP7000) and 7000 series Chassis Interface (RSP7000CI) that flow-switches IP packets as opposed to process-switching them by default.

router   A router is a device that connects two layer-3 networks of the Open Systems Interconnection (OSI) model, the network layer. Routers are the usual method for connecting different media, such as Ethernet to Token Ring or Frame Relay to asynchronous transfer mode (ATM). Routers keep track of all the networks they hear about through the use of a routing table. They also advertise their own existence and their entire routing table with their neighbors. In this way, routers learn enough of the topology of the network to determine the optimal route for packet forwarding. Routers are frequently used to connect separate layer-2 networks as well, for instance, the Ethernet local area network (LAN) and the DS-1 WAN in a typical small office. A router's strongest feature is that it blocks traffic that wasn't intended to go through to the other side.

router identifier (RID)   The DECnet address of a router.

router rip command   The router rip command specifies that you are using the RIP routing process.

Routing Information Protocol (RIP)   RIP is a routing protocol that advertises its routing table to the rest of the IPX routers on the network every 30 seconds. It is also used by IPX clients to find paths to other networks and to measure the distance to other routers. In addition to hop count, IPX RIP utilizes tick count. One tick equals 1/18 second. RIP is used by XNS to maintain a database of network hosts and exchange information about the topology of the network. Routing Information Protocol (RIP) was one of the first routing protocol standards for Transmission Control Protocol/ Internet Protocol (TCP/IP) that was widely implemented around the world. RIP is still supported across all routing platforms and vendors, which is also an attractive feature for interoperability. *See also* Novell Routing Information Protocol.

Routing Protocol (RP)   This distributes routing information among DECnet hosts. It divides routing classes into two levels: level 1, which handles intra-area routing; and level 2, which handles interarea routing.

routing table   The routing table is generated when an algorithm is run on the database. Each router has a unique routing table. This is also called the *forwarding database*.

Routing Table Maintenance Protocol (RTMP)   RTMP is Apple's distance vector routing protocol, which, by default, broadcasts its routing table to its neighbors every 10 seconds. RTMP is responsible for establishing and maintaining the routing table in all routers that are running AppleTalk. RTMP falls into the category of distance vector routing protocols such as Routing Information Protocol (RIP) and Interior Gateway Routing Protocol (IGRP).

routing update   A router maintains this information in its routing table and periodically shares information from that table to other routers on the network. This sharing is called a *routing update*.

Routing Update Protocol (RUP)   This protocol is used to distribute network topology.

RP   *See* Routing Protocol.

RSP   *See* Route/Switch Processor.

RSVP   *See* Resource Reservation Protocol.

RTMP   *See* Routing Table Maintenance Protocol.

RUP   *See* Routing Update Protocol.

S reference point   The S reference point defines the reference point between user terminals and a network terminal device type 2 (NT2).

SAP   *See* Service Advertising Protocol.

scalability   Scalability is defined as the network's ability to efficiently accommodate continued growth. For example, a five-user network will experience the same performance even if it increases to 50 users on a truly scalable network. Network scalability can be affected by expansion. If, for example, a company opens a branch office to accommodate new business, the corporate network needs to be able to accommodate the new network demands of the branch office.

SCP   *See* Session Control Protocol.

SDLC   *See* Synchronous Data Link Control.

SDSL   *See* Symmetrical Digital Subscriber Line.

secure model   The benefits of a secure model are obvious; for instance, it protects against intruders and maintains critical corporate data. When used in conjunction with a solid hierarchical network design, the secure model can be used efficiently as a network grows and expands.

SecureID   SecureID combines the ownership of a card and the knowledge of a password. In addition to having a name and password, you also are required to have a security card. Someone else who has your username and password, but not the card, can't authenticate. This extra precaution helps ensure that the stated user truly is the user.

security management   This type allows administrative personnel to restrict access to certain areas of the network. Security may include a hardware or software firewall system, password authentication, and levels of access.

Sequenced Packet Exchange (SPX)   This maps to layer 4 of the OSI model, the Transport layer. SPX is used to add reliability to the connectionless nature of the IPX datagram. It adds fields to the IPX header, allowing for guaranteed packet delivery.

Sequenced Packet Protocol (SPP)   This protocol provides a reliable virtual connection service for private connections. This protocol provides reliable transport delivery with flow control and establishes connection IDs at the time of connection to distinguish between multiple transport connections. Each packet transmitted is assigned a sequence number, and the destination host acknowledges receipt.

Serial Date Link Control   *See* Synchronous Data Link Control.

Serial Line Internet Protocol (SLIP)   The standard (one of two) for how a workstation or PC can dial up a link to the Internet that defines the transport of data packets through an asynchronous telephone line, allowing computers not part of a local area network (LAN) to be fully connected to the Internet. SLIP is preferable to shell access (a dial-up, text-only account on a UNIX computer) because users, no matter what Internet tools they have chosen, can run more than one Internet application at a time and download data directly.

Service Advertising Protocol (SAP)   This is used by NetWare servers and routers to advertise their available services. Other routers and servers on the network keep track of the services being provided and the servers that are providing them in an internal database, much like keeping a routing table. NetWare clients send SAP Get Nearest Server (GNS) requests to locate the nearest server that provides a given service.

service-level agreement (SLA)   Performance objectives between which the user and the provider of a service have reached consensus.

service profile identifier (SPID)   The telephone company assigns a number to an ISDN device to let it know which line it can access.

Session Control Protocol (SCP)   This manages logical links for DECnet connections.

session layer   This layer (layer 5) keeps track of multiple data streams as users access the Internet. If a company has a single T1 circuit but 30 users all vying for use of the Internet at the same time, this layer ensures all users receive their data.

shared bandwidth   Shared bandwidth is a related concept. If you have to connect two remote sites, the ordinary way would be to use a dedicated leased line. This line would belong to you; the bandwidth would be available to you even when you don't need to send any traffic across. Imagine a huge number of clients, each of whom owns a dedicated leased line and uses only a portion of the total bandwidth.

shared reservation   This flow originates from one or more senders.

show access lists   This command displays the number of matches after each statement in parentheses. By examining in-place access lists, you can easily determine if rearranging the statements will help your router's performance.

show buffers   The show buffers command displays usage information on each of the router's buffers, along with the number of buffer misses. This is a very useful command for characterizing your network traffic.

show processes memory   The show processes memory command displays total router memory, memory used, free memory, and memory used by each process. Again, this command is useful to prove the health of your router and its ability to cope with future demands.

show protocol route   Each protocol running on your router has its own routing table. To view these tables, use the show protocol route command. This will give you a full list of all the networks known to a router, the method it will use to get there, and the way it was learned.

silicon switching   Silicon switching allows an incoming packet to match an entry in the silicon switching cache located in the Silicon Switching Engine (SSE) of the Silicon Switching Processor (SSP) module, which is available only on some Cisco 7000 series routers.

Simple Network Management Protocol (SNMP)   A standard for managing hardware devices connected to a network, approved for UNIX use, that lets administrators know, for example, when a printer has a paper jam or is low on toner. In other words, the Simple Network Management Protocol is a distributed-management protocol. It is a simple request-response application-layer protocol that provides for the exchange of management information between network devices.

SLA   *See* service-level agreement.

SLIP   *See* Serial Line Internet Protocol.

smart hubs   There are devices labeled as "smart hubs" that incorporate an internal bridging function to allow one or more ports to operate at a different speed than the others; but these are not strictly hubs, and you shouldn't expect that capability from a normal auto-sensing 10/100BaseTX hub.

SMDS   *See* Switched Multimegabit Data Service.

SMI   *See* Structure of Management Information.

SNA   *See* Systems Network Architecture.

SNI   *See* subscriber network interface.

SNMP   *See* Simple Network Management Protocol.

SNPA   *See* subnetwork point of attachment.

source route bridging (SRB)   Source route bridging was invented by IBM and is applicable only to Token Ring networks. Token Ring provides for an optional field in the frame header called the *routing information field (RIF)*. The RIF is made up of 12 bits for the ring identifier and 4 bits for the bridge identifier.

source route/translational bridging (SR/TLB)   SR/TLB was introduced to allow SRB and transparent bridging domains to communicate. SR/TLB employs an intermediate bridge that translates between the two bridging protocols. There is no set standard for how this is accomplished.

source route/transparent (SR/T) bridging   SR/T was introduced by IBM to address some of the weaknesses of SR/TLB. SR/T devices include both SRB and transparent bridging protocols and don't translate between the two. Instead, to accomplish SR/T bridging, any node that wants to transmit out of its own domain must include a new field in the frame header. That new field is 1 bit long and known as the Routing Information Indicator (RII). When an SR/T bridge receives a frame, it first checks to see whether the RII bit is set. If the RII is set, the bridge performs SRB. If the RII is not set, the bridge performs transparent bridging.

Spanning Tree Protocol (STP)   STP prevents the formation of logical looping in the network.

SPID   *See* service profile identifier.

split horizon   One way that some routing protocols, including RIP, prevent loops is the split horizon. The split horizon causes the router to send updates out every interface except the one from which it first heard about a given network. This solution is similar to the operation of a layer-2 bridge. Split horizon is a routing technique in which route information is prevented from exiting the router interface through the information that was received.

spoofing   Gaining access to a network or its service by pretending to be a legitimate user.

SPP   *See* Sequenced Packet Protocol.

SPX   *See* Sequenced Packet Exchange.

SRB   *See* source route bridging.

SR/T bridging   *See* source route/transparent bridging.

SR/TLB   *See* source route/translational bridging.

SSCP   *See* system services control point.

STAC algorithm   The STAC algorithm is based on the Lempel-Ziv method, but has been further optimized. The result is better compression ratios at the expense of additional CPU time.

star topology   A star topology, the most common topology, connects all workstations to one central station, routing traffic to the appropriate place. An advantage of the star topology is that the failure in one device does not disable the entire network.

statistical encoding   Statistical encoding uses a fixed or static encoding methodology, which makes it unsuitable for the dynamic and unpredictable nature of internetwork traffic.

STP *See* Spanning Tree Protocol.

StreetTalk This maintains a distributed directory of the names of network resources. In VINES, names are global across the Internet and independent of the network topology.

Structure of Management Information (SMI) The SMI defines the rules for describing management information.

STS *See* Synchronous Transport Signal.

subnetwork point of attachment (SNPA) This is the point at which an ES or IS is physically attached to a subnetwork. The SNPA address uniquely identifies each system attached to the subnetwork. In an Ethernet network, the SNPA is the 48-bit MAC address.

subscriber network interface (SNI) The interface point between the customer premises equipment (CPE) and a communication service.

successor The next hop router on the primary route. *See also* feasible successor.

SVC *See* switched virtual circuit.

switch Switches are basically bridges with higher throughput capability. There are differences, of course. One important difference is the ability of a switch to support full-duplex operation. That is, a switch can receive and transmit at full bandwidth at the same time, whereas a bridge can do only one or the other. Switches determine the route to a destination based on the Media Access Control (MAC) address contained in the frame. A switch may be thought of as a multiport bridge; the idea is that you can't have a small enough collision domain. Switches are available for local area network (LAN) and wide area network (WAN) applications. Modern workgroup Ethernet switches have brought the price per port so low that there is little reason not to provide a single port per Ethernet station, especially because switches are inherently full duplex.

Switched Multimegabit Data Service (SMDS) SMDS is a new technology that supports very high-speed access across public data networks. SMDS is a high-speed, packet-switched, datagram-based wide area network (WAN) networking technology that is used to establish communication across public data networks (PDNs). SMDS can use fiber or copper media. It supports speeds of 1.544 Mbps over digital signal level-1 (DS-1) transmission facilities or 44.735 Mbps over digital signal level-3 (DS-3) transmission facilities. SMDS data units are large enough to encapsulate entire Institute of Electrical and Electronics Engineers (IEEE) 802.3, IEEE 802.5, and Fiber Distributed Data Interface (FDDI) frames.

switched virtual circuit (SVC) The wide area networking equivalent of a telephone call. That is, a connection is established when it is required and torn down when it is not. SVCs are used extensively in X.25 networks and also in Frame Relays, though not to as great an extent. In some cases, SVCs are used as load balancers or congestion relievers; that is, a second pathway is created during periods of heavy traffic.

Symmetrical Digital Subscriber Line (SDSL) Symmetrical DSL offers the same speed ranges and distance limitations as Asymmetrical DSL (ADSL), but the Plain Old Telephone System (POTS) cannot be provided with the circuit. However, SDSL is the best choice for sites that will transmit a lot of information. Be sure to check your provider's acceptable-use policy before assuming that SDSL is the best choice for your Web server farm, though! Many providers consider *x*DSL a consumer product and do not encourage or support applications that will greatly increase the need for upstream bandwidth.

Synchronous Data Link Control (SDLC) The IBM code-independent link-control protocol that is transparent to the bit pattern being handled; a single format is used for both data and control information. SDLC can be used with a number of link types. It will implement its functions with point-to-point and multipoint links, half-duplex and full-duplex transmission devices, and circuit-switched and packet-switched networks. Sometimes called *Serial Data Link Control.*

Synchronous Transport Signal (STS)   The Synchronous Optical NETwork (SONET) standard for Optical Character One (OC-1) optical fiber transmissions, 51.84 MBps. The number may change according to the number of frames multiplexed; when the information fields are treated as a single concatenated payload, a "c" is added.

system services control point (SSCP)   One of the controlling points in the Systems Network Architecture (SNA).

Systems Network Architecture (SNA)   Systems Network Architecture (SNA) was developed by IBM in the mainframe computer era (1974, to be precise) as a way of getting its various products to communicate with each other for distributed processing. SNA is a line of products designed to make other products cooperate. In your career of designing network solutions, you should expect to run into SNA from time to time because many of the bigger companies (i.e., banks, healthcare institutions, and government offices) bought IBM equipment and will be reluctant to part with their investment. SNA is a proprietary protocol that runs over SDLC exclusively, although it may be transported within other protocols, such as X.25 and Token Ring. It is designed as a hierarchy and consists of a collection of machines called *nodes*.

T reference point   The T reference point defines the reference point between network terminal (NT1) and (NT2) devices.

TA   *See* terminal adapter.

TACACS+   *See* Terminal Access Control Access Controller Plus.

tag switching   Tag switching optimizes packet switching through a network of tag switches (routers or switches that support tag switching), whereas other methods enhance the switching of a packet through a single router.

T-carrier system   The T-carrier system was introduced in the 1960s in the United States by the Bell System. It was the first system that could support the digitized voice transmission successfully. Now the T1 line is widely used for both digitized voice and data transmissions with the original transmission rate of 1.554 Mbps, as is the T3 line, which provides the rate of 44.736 Mbps.

TCP/IP   *See* Transmission Control Protocol/Internet Protocol.

TDM   *See* time-division multiplexing.

TEI   *See* terminal equipment type 1.

Terminal Access Control Access Controller Plus (TACACS+)
This is one of two protocols designed to authenticate users and handle accounting. TACACS+ is a proprietary system developed by Cisco for handling authentication, access, and accounting. In a network in which only Cisco products are deployed, TACACS+ has some added benefits. In addition to specifying whether somebody has access to a device, it can also specify the level of access and maintain records of activity. This can be useful to know who last modified a configuration, or that support staff can use show commands but cannot get a configuration listing.

terminal adapter (TA)   A device used to connect equipment that does not have an Integrated Services Digital Network (ISDN) interface to the digital network, functionally equivalent to a modem and usually plugging into the expansion bus.

terminal equipment type 1 (TE1)   A TE1 is a specialized Integrated Services Digital Network (ISDN) terminal used to connect to ISDN through a four-wire, twisted-pair digital link.

terminal equipment type 2 (TE2)   A TE2 is a non-ISDN terminal that predates the ISDN standards. It connects to an ISDN link through a terminal adapter (TA), which may be either a stand-alone device or a board inside the TE2.

TFTP   *See* Trivial File Transfer Protocol.

Thick Ethernet (thicknet)   A cabling system in which transceivers are connected to each other by stiff large-diameter cable and to nodes through flexible multiwire cable. *See also* 10Base5.

Thin Ethernet (thinnet)   A cabling system using thin, flexible coaxial cable to connect each node to the next. Thicknet proved to be very useful for long-range and backbone connections, but the inflexibility of the cable and expense of multistation access units (MSAUs) and attachment unit interfaces (AUIs) led to the development of thinnet, or 10Base2. 10Base2 is shorthand for 10MB of data on a baseband electrical circuit up to 185 meters in length (not 200 as the name would lead you to believe). Thinnet's two most important features are its thinner cable (RG-58/U, which is similar to the cable used by television systems) and its network node connections. *See also* 10Base2.

time-division multiplexing (TDM)   A technique that divides the capacity of a local area network (LAN) circuit into time slots, some as small as a microsecond, each used by a different signal. TDM is a useful technology for separating two uses of one circuit, such as voice and data. TDM is more frequently used for limiting or fractioning the use of a circuit (and thereby the cost).

time-sensitive traffic   Traffic that is required to reach a destination before timing out.

Token Bus   This is a physical bus topology and broadcast medium, like Ethernet, with a single controller that broadcasts a token, specifying a recipient. When a node is designated as the recipient of the token, it may transmit on the network. This can be thought of as a Token Ring over Ethernet.

Token Ring   A local area network (LAN) specification that was developed by IBM in the 1980s for PC-based networks and classified by the (Institute of Electrical and Electronics Engineers) IEEE as 802.5. It specifies a star topology physically and a ring topology logically. It runs at either 4 Mbps or 16 Mbps, but all nodes on the ring must run at the same speed.

top-down processing When a router is using an access list to examine traffic, the Cisco Internetwork Operating System (IOS) software begins a process of comparing the packet against each line in the list sequentially. This is known as top-down processing because the router starts at the beginning of the access list and moves down through each declaration in the list, looking for a match. As soon as a match is found, the packet is handled according to the access list statement (permit or deny), and the next packet is examined.

topological database *See* link-state database.

topology *See* bus topology; hybrid topology; ring topology; star topology.

trace Trace is similar to ping in proving network connectivity, but it also gives you other important information. The trace utility displays the route of the packet as it passes through the network to reach its destination. You can demonstrate an efficient routing system by tracing routes to different addresses on the network with expected results.

TrafficDirector TrafficDirector is a comprehensive network traffic monitoring and troubleshooting Remote Monitoring (RMON) console application that analyzes traffic and enables proactive management of internetworks. It provides a graphical user interface for reporting and analysis of RMON collected traffic data from RMON agents in Cisco's Catalyst switches, Cisco IOS software embedded RMON agents in routers, Cisco SwitchProbe stand-alone network monitoring probes, or any RMON standards-compliant agent.

Transmission Control Protocol/Internet Protocol (TCP/IP)
A set of communications standards created by the U.S. Department of Defense (DoD) in the 1970s that has now become an accepted way to connect different types of computers in networks because the standards now support so many programs. TCP/IP is the standard protocol suite of the Internet and is the most widely used protocol in the world today. Currently, TCP/IP is mostly thought of in terms of version 4, which is the version in use on the Internet. Version 6 is in development and expected to replace version 4 in the near future.

transparent bridging　Transparent bridging is used primarily in Ethernet networks but may also be found in Token Ring and Fiber Distributed Data Interface (FDDI). It is so named because the bridge's existence is transparent to the rest of the network. Remember that bridges learn Media Access Control (MAC) addresses as nodes transmit through the bridge; then they forward, filter, or flood, depending on whether they know where the destination node lies.

transport layer　This layer (layer 4) takes care of keeping track of the frames that are sent across the network. If a frame arrives at its destination with errors, the transport layer drops it and requests a retransmission.

Trivial File Transfer Protocol (TFTP)　TFTP is a less robust version of FTP and is very often used in the networking world for upgrading images on routing and switching equipment.

U reference point　The U reference point defines the reference point between network terminal (NT1) devices and line-termination equipment in a carrier network. (This is only in North America, where the NT1 function is not provided by the carrier network.)

UBR　*See* unspecified bit rate.

UDP　*See* User Datagram Protocol.

UNI　*See* User-Network Interface.

unspecified bit rate (UBR)　An Asynchronous Transfer Mode (ATM) service level unable to guarantee bandwidth availability.

User Datagram Protocol (UDP)　A Transmission Control Protocol/Internet Protocol (TCP/IP) normally bundled with an Internet Protocol (IP) layered software that describes how messages received reach application programs within the destination computer. UDP is connectionless. That means that instead of taking the time to set up a connection from one point to another, UDP simply passes a datagram to the IP layer where it is passed on to the network for delivery.

User-Network Interface (UNI) The asynchronous transfer mode (ATM) forum standard for connecting users with a local switch.

utilization *See* network utilization.

variable bit rate (VBR) a service category defined by the asynchronous transfer mode (ATM) form that supports variable traffic with average and peak parameters.

VARP *See* VINES Address Resolution Protocol.

VCC *See* virtual channel connection.

Versatile Interface Processor (VIP) An interface processor that is used with both the Cisco 7000 series and Cisco 7500 series routers. It is installed in the interface processor slots of the Cisco 7000 series and 7500 series routers. It utilizes a single motherboard with up to two port adapters.

VINES Address Resolution Protocol (VARP) VARP is used to find node Data Link Control (DLC) addresses from the node Internet Protocol (IP) address.

VINES Internet Protocol (VIP) This protocol moves datagrams throughout the network.

VIP *See* Versatile Interface Processor.

virtual channel connection (VCC) The unidirectional virtual channel links between two endpoints in an asynchronous transfer mode (ATM) network.

virtual local area network (VLAN) Workstations connected to a device that can define membership in a local area network (LAN).

virtual private networking (VPN) VPNs reduce service costs and long distance/usage fees, lighten infrastructure investments, and simplify WAN operations over time. To determine just how cost-effective a VPN solution could be in connecting remote offices, use the VPN Calculator located on Cisco's Web site at www.cisco.com.

VLAN   *See* virtual local area network.

VPN   *See* virtual private networking.

WAN   *See* wide area network.

weighted fair queuing (WFQ)   WFQ is a flow-based queuing algorithm that recognizes a flow for an interactive application and schedules that application's traffic to the front of the queue to minimize the response time. WFQ adapts automatically to changing network traffic conditions and requires little or no configuration.

WFQ   *See* weighted fair queuing.

wide area network (WAN)   A network using high-speed long-distance common-carrier circuits or satellites to cover a large geographic area.

wildcard mask   Wildcard masks can also be effectively used to reduce router overhead. A wildcard mask essentially functions as the opposite of an Internet Protocol (IP) subnet mask. In simple terms, a wildcard mask can be used to refer to a range of addresses with a single access list entry. Whereas a subnet mask identifies which part of an IP address is the network and which part is the host, a wildcard mask filters out part of the address and limits what the router must examine before making a permit/deny decision.

X.25   X.25 is an International Telecommunication Union-Telecommunication (ITU-T) Standardization Sector standard and is one of the first successful attempts at a standard for data communication across a wide area network (WAN). This is the oldest of the cloud-based protocols, and it is still in use today. This protocol defines how to establish and maintain connections between user devices and network devices.

***x*DSL**   *See* Digital Subscriber Line.

Xerox Network System (XNS)   A multilayer protocol system and distributed-file system LAN architecture that Xerox developed in the 1970s. XNS, adopted at least in part by other vendors, allows one workstation on a network to use files and peripherals of another as if they were local. XNS is similar to the Transmission Control Protocol/Internet Protocol (TCP/IP) suite, but it is a five-layer model and was the basis for the OSI seven-layer model. XNS was adopted in part by Novell.

XNS   *See* Xerox Network System.

Zone Information Protocol (ZIP)   ZIP keeps track of AppleTalk workgroups, known as *zones*, and restricts queries for network services to the local workgroup rather than propagating them across the entire network.

INDEX

A

AAL (ATM adaptation layer), 469

AAL1, 189

AAL2, 189

AAL3/4, 190

AAL5, 190

AARP (AppleTalk Address Resolution Protocol), 575

Access layer (in hierarchical model), 36, 226–227, 360, 362, 519–520

Access list flow chart, 608

Access list protocols by name, 607

Access list protocols by number, 607

Access lists, 232–233, 604–612

    as a basic form of security, 611

    burden of on routers, 609–610

    to control traffic flow, 612

    creating using a text editor, 605

    in distribution or access layer, 612

    editing and applying, 606

    on firewall routers, 612

    inbound or outbound, 606

    for IOS 12.0, 233

    optimizing, 609–610

    order, 605

    scalability, 633

    security and, 633

    types of, 232, 607

    uses for, 611–612

Access servers (AS5300 and AS5800), 479

Accounting management (network), 34

Acknowledgement (ACK) packet, 3, 70, 123

ACLs (access control lists). *See* Access lists

Active compression, 622

Active monitor (Token Ring), 418

Adaptive security algorithm (ASA), 230, 378

Address recognized indicator (ARI), 176

Address Resolution Protocol (ARP), 61, 363, 615, 618

Addressing schemes
    for routers, 517–518
    for servers, 514–515
    for user stations, 521

Adjacencies database, OSPF, 127

Adjacency table, NLSP, 562

ADSL (Asymmetrical DSL), 194

ADSP (AppleTalk Data Stream Protocol), 574

Advanced Peer-to-Peer Networking (APPN), 141, 341

Advanced Program-to-Program Computing (APPC), 141

T

U

LICENSE AGREEMENT

THIS PRODUCT (THE "PRODUCT") CONTAINS PROPRIETARY SOFTWARE, DATA AND INFORMATION (INCLUDING DOCUMENTATION) OWNED BY THE McGRAW-HILL COMPANIES, INC. ("McGRAW-HILL") AND ITS LICENSORS. YOUR RIGHT TO USE THE PRODUCT IS GOVERNED BY THE TERMS AND CONDITIONS OF THIS AGREEMENT.

LICENSE: Throughout this License Agreement, "you" shall mean either the individual or the entity whose agent opens this package. You are granted a non-exclusive and non-transferable license to use the Product subject to the following terms:

(i) If you have licensed a single user version of the Product, the Product may only be used on a single computer (i.e., a single CPU). If you licensed and paid the fee applicable to a local area network or wide area network version of the Product, you are subject to the terms of the following subparagraph (ii).

(ii) If you have licensed a local area network version, you may use the Product on unlimited workstations located in one single building selected by you that is served by such local area network. If you have licensed a wide area network version, you may use the Product on unlimited workstations located in multiple buildings on the same site selected by you that is served by such wide area network; provided, however, that any building will not be considered located in the same site if it is more than five (5) miles away from any building included in such site. In addition, you may only use a local area or wide area network version of the Product on one single server. If you wish to use the Product on more than one server, you must obtain written authorization from McGraw-Hill and pay additional fees.

(iii) You may make one copy of the Product for back-up purposes only and you must maintain an accurate record as to the location of the back-up at all times.

COPYRIGHT; RESTRICTIONS ON USE AND TRANSFER: All rights (including copyright) in and to the Product are owned by McGraw-Hill and its licensors. You are the owner of the enclosed disc on which the Product is recorded. You may not use, copy, decompile, disassemble, reverse engineer, modify, reproduce, create derivative works, transmit, distribute, sublicense, store in a database or retrieval system of any kind, rent or transfer the Product or any portion thereof, in any form or by any means (including electronically or otherwise) except as expressly provided for in this License Agreement. You must reproduce the copyright notices, trademark notices, legends and logos of McGraw-Hill and its licensors that appear on the Product on the back-up copy of the Product which you are permitted to make hereunder. All rights in the Product not expressly granted herein are reserved by McGraw-Hill and its licensors.

TERM: This License Agreement is effective until terminated. It will terminate if you fail to comply with any term or condition of this License Agreement. Upon termination, you are obligated to return to McGraw-Hill the Product together with all copies thereof and to purge all copies of the Product included in any and all servers and computer facilities.

DISCLAIMER OF WARRANTY: THE PRODUCT AND THE BACK-UP COPY OF THE PRODUCT ARE LICENSED "AS IS." McGRAW-HILL, ITS LICENSORS AND THE AUTHORS MAKE NO WARRANTIES, EXPRESS OR IMPLIED, AS TO RESULTS TO BE OBTAINED BY ANY PERSON OR ENTITY FROM USE OF THE PRODUCT AND/OR ANY INFORMATION OR DATA INCLUDED THEREIN. McGRAW-HILL, ITS LICENSORS, AND THE AUTHORS MAKE NO GUARANTEE THAT YOU WILL PASS ANY CERTIFICATION EXAM BY USING THIS PRODUCT. McGRAW-HILL, ITS LICENSORS AND THE AUTHORS MAKE NO EXPRESS OR IMPLIED WARRANTIES OF MERCHANTABILITY OR FITNESS FOR A PARTICULAR PURPOSE OR USE WITH RESPECT TO THE PRODUCT. NEITHER McGRAW-HILL, ANY OF ITS LICENSORS, NOR THE AUTHORS WARRANT THAT THE FUNCTIONS CONTAINED IN THE PRODUCT WILL MEET YOUR REQUIREMENTS OR THAT THE OPERATION OF THE PRODUCT WILL BE UNINTERRUPTED OR ERROR FREE. YOU ASSUME THE ENTIRE RISK WITH RESPECT TO THE QUALITY AND PERFORMANCE OF THE PRODUCT.

LIMITED WARRANTY FOR DISC: To the original licensee only, McGraw-Hill warrants that the enclosed disc on which the Product is recorded is free from defects in materials and workmanship under normal use and service for a period of ninety (90) days from the date of purchase. In the event of a defect in the disc covered by the foregoing warranty, McGraw-Hill will replace the disc.

LIMITATION OF LIABILITY: NEITHER McGRAW-HILL, ITS LICENSORS NOR THE AUTHORS SHALL BE LIABLE FOR ANY INDIRECT, SPECIAL OR CONSEQUENTIAL DAMAGES, SUCH AS BUT NOT LIMITED TO, LOSS OF ANTICIPATED PROFITS OR BENEFITS, RESULTING FROM THE USE OR INABILITY TO USE THE PRODUCT EVEN IF ANY OF THEM HAS BEEN ADVISED OF THE POSSIBILITY OF SUCH DAMAGES. THIS LIMITATION OF LIABILITY SHALL APPLY TO ANY CLAIM OR CAUSE WHATSOEVER WHETHER SUCH CLAIM OR CAUSE ARISES IN CONTRACT, TORT, OR OTHERWISE. Some states do not allow the exclusion or limitation of indirect, special or consequential damages, so the above limitation may not apply to you.

U.S. GOVERNMENT RESTRICTED RIGHTS: Any software included in the Product is provided with restricted rights subject to subparagraphs (c), (1) and (2) of the Commercial Computer Software-Restricted Rights clause at 48 C.F.R. 52.227-19. The terms of this Agreement applicable to the use of the data in the Product are those under which the data are generally made available to the general public by McGraw-Hill. Except as provided herein, no reproduction, use, or disclosure rights are granted with respect to the data included in the Product and no right to modify or create derivative works from any such data is hereby granted.

GENERAL: This License Agreement constitutes the entire agreement between the parties relating to the Product. The terms of any Purchase Order shall have no effect on the terms of this License Agreement. Failure of McGraw-Hill to insist at any time on strict compliance with this License Agreement shall not constitute a waiver of any rights under this License Agreement. This License Agreement shall be construed and governed in accordance with the laws of the State of New York. If any provision of this License Agreement is held to be contrary to law, that provision will be enforced to the maximum extent permissible and the remaining provisions will remain in full force and effect.

Get Certified with Help from the

THIS CCDA® STUDY GUIDE FEATURES:

■ **TWO-MINUTE DRILLS AT THE END OF EVERY CHAPTER QUICKLY REINFORCE YOUR KNOWLEDGE AND ENSURE BETTER RETENTION:**

There are limitations on the suggested number of workstations running certain protocols on flat networks or VLANs. Be able to recognize the maximum number of workstations allowed on a network.

■ **SPECIAL WARNINGS THAT PREPARE YOU FOR TRICKY EXAM TOPICS:**

If you haven't yet read a Request for Comments (RFC), it is a very worthwhile endeavor. I strongly recommend at least skimming the RFC of a protocol that you are trying to understand. Sometimes the writing is dense, but the information is always the most accurate you can find. The RFCs are mirrored widely across the Internet, or they can always be found on the IETF's server at: ftp://ftp.isi.edu/. You can also find a great deal of information about the RFC process at www.rfc-editor.org.

A STUDY GUIDE YOU'LL USE EVEN *AFTER* THE TEST!

■ **"ON THE JOB" NOTES PRESENT IMPORTANT LESSONS THAT HELP YOU WORK SMARTER:**

Frame Relay connections also introduce the element of outside management into your network—the carrier you lease your circuit from will operate a network operations center (NOC) where network health is monitored. This is important to remember when you are scheduling installation of a new circuit before gear is available because your circuit will show an alarm condition without gear attached. Sometimes the NOC personnel will put the circuit into loopback or disable it to make the alarm go away, which can be a nasty surprise when the equipment finally arrives!

■ **Q & A SECTIONS LAY OUT PROBLEMS AND SOLUTIONS IN A QUICK-READ FORMAT. FOR EXAMPLE:**

 A Cisco 1601 router is placed on a fairly large network.
What command would check to see if the process utilization is high?

 Router#show processes cpu

■ **MORE THAN 450 REALISTIC PRACTICE QUESTIONS WITH ANSWERS THAT HELP PREPARE YOU FOR THE REAL TEST**

Question: *Rachal Inc. is experiencing slow performance on the network. After the layout of the network and number of devices has been discussed, it is determined that a Cisco 1605 router is placed on a network with a fairly large number of devices. What Cisco command would tell the administrator the capability of the Cisco 1605 in regard to handling the amount of traffic that is on the network without causing latency?*

    A. *Show buffers*   **C.** *Show processes cpu*
    B. *Show interfaces*   **D.** *None of the above*

Answer: C. *The show processes cpu command displays the amount of router utilization in five-second, one-minute, and five-minute intervals. Observing the results of this command will help determine if the amount of traffic is too much for the router. A and B are Cisco router configuration commands that observe buffer overflows and types of interfaces respectively.*